BRITISH POETRY MAGAZINES
1914–2000

*A History and Bibliography
of 'Little Magazines'*

BRITISH POETRY MAGAZINES
1914–2000

A History and Bibliography
of 'Little Magazines'

Compiled by
David Miller and Richard Price

THE BRITISH LIBRARY

AND

OAK KNOLL PRESS

© 2006 David Miller and Richard Price

First published in 2006 by
The British Library
96 Euston Road
London NW1 2DB
and
Oak Knoll Press
310 Delaware Street
New Castle
DE 19720

ISBN 1-58456-197-1 (Oak Knoll)
ISBN 0-7123-4941-3 (BL)

Cataloguing in Publication Data
A CIP record for this book is available from both
The British Library and the Library of Congress

Designed and typeset in Quadraat by Geoff Green Book Design, Cambridge
Printed in England by Biddles Ltd., King's Lynn

Contents

Acknowledgements

D AVID MILLER WOULD like to acknowledge his debt to R. J. Ellis, Geoffrey Soar, and Wolfgang Görtschacher for the invaluable help they have given over the years with this research into the history of UK little magazines. I would also like to thank the various poets, editors, scholars, and librarians who have given me advice or information, including Paul Buck, Anthony Rudolf, Keith Jebb, Maurice Scully, John Welch, Peter Philpott, Glyn Pursglove, Lee Harwood, Robert Sheppard, Stuart Mills, Nate Dorward, James Ferguson, Andreas Schachermayr, and Chris McCabe. Thanks also to my colleagues in the School of Arts, Communication and Culture at Nottingham Trent University, especially Lynne Hapgood, David Worrall, John Lucas, and Stan Smith, for their much appreciated support.

Richard Price would like to thank the following at the British Library for helping in the making of this book: James Egles (formerly, Overseas English Collections), David White (Collection Development Support Unit), Duncan Heyes, Candida Ridler, and Andy Simons (Modern British Collections), Kristian Jensen (British and Early Printed Collections), Arthur Cunningham and Cynthia McKinley (formerly, Publishing), and all the library assistants who have patiently helped me retrieve thousands of little magazines over the years. I am especially grateful to the British Library for awarding me a three-month sabbatical, and to David Way (Publishing) for keeping faith with the book over so many years. I am also indebted to the following, either for information on their own involvement in little magazines, or for their knowledge of the little magazine world: Elizabeth James (Victoria and Albert Museum), Prof. A. T. Tolley, cris cheek, Gerry Loose, Ronald Senator, Peter Riley, Edwin Morgan, Simon Smith, Ulli Freer, and William Allen.

Introduction

1. DEFINITIONS

THE LITTLE MAGAZINE is not difficult to define: it is an anthology of work by strangers; an anthology of work by friends; an exhibition catalogue without the existence of the exhibition; a series of manifestos; a series of anti-manifestos... It's printed by photo-litho; or typed onto a mimeograph stencil... It's a twenty-year sequence; or it turns out to be a one-off.

Its history is as unproblematic. Certainly it is associated with artistic movements such as the Pre-Raphaelites, whose *The Germ* flourished briefly in the middle of the nineteenth century, or the Vorticists, whose *Blast*, first published in 1914, inaugurates the period of this book. But the chapbooks of songs, ballads, and tales sold in earlier centuries may claim ancestor status, as might manuscript copies of poems distributed among a select few. Though the little magazine is probably called "little" because of the comparatively low numbers made of any given issue, larger circulation literary journals published commercially have influenced the little magazine (and vice versa), and it can be difficult to say where a little magazine stops and a more commercial literary journal starts. It is also not easy to ascertain the circulation figures for either kind of publication.

Faced with these definitional complexities, the compilers of an annotated bibliography and union catalogue of little magazines might best describe the little magazine in terms of individual characteristics, some of which need to be present in any given magazine to qualify for its inclusion, and some of which, if not necessary to the definition, give a better sense of the rarer, "classic", little magazine.

For the purposes of this book, with its specific focus on poetry, the little magazine can be very broadly defined as a publication that contains or concerns itself with poetry (which may mean an absence of poetry itself, if the prose or artwork has a strong connection to poetry)

and
is intended to last more than one issue (although many little magazines are not successful in that ambition, and we have included some deliberate one-offs)

and
is published on a non-commercial basis (although we have included some magazines that aspired to commercial success and even some which appear to have achieved it)

and
has the explicit or implicit intention to assert its contents' difference, be it formally, regionally, ethnically or otherwise, from a poetry 'norm', 'centre', or 'establishment' (although we have also included magazines whose distance from a notional norm is difficult to measure).

This last element elides identity politics with poetics; it is in poetics that the "classic" element of the little magazine is encountered. A classic little magazine, in the view of the present authors, publishes the work of a group of artists or writers who assert themselves as a group (e.g. the Surrealist Group of England's publication of *The International Surrealist Bulletin* in the mid Thirties)

and/or
work that is singular and independent of any specific group or movement

and/or
work that explicitly or implicitly asks to be measured in relation to the originality of its forms, either by offering the work as innovative, for example *Kingdom Come's* championing of the New Apocalyptic poets during the Second World War, or, on the contrary, by taking issue with the work of the formally novel and asserting traditional forms instead (a stance taken by *The Dark Horse*, a magazine begun in 1995 and still extant)

and/or
work within notionally hybrid genres, such as *And*'s visual poetry, *Kroklok*'s sound poetry, or the prose poem

and/or
work deriving from and/or circulating to a small number of artists and writers (e.g. Robert Sheppard's *Pages*, published between 1987–1998, though later published on the Web), serving to

maintain a kind of magazine-enabled community, keeping the individuals abreast of each other's work and providing other forms of friendly interchange, such as wider literary information

and/or
work that suggests a self-conscious sense of the physical and graphic design of the magazine as being in tune with the content, be it the futurist-like cover to Irish modernist *The Klaxon* (1923) or the pre-Punk do-it-yourself attitude of "bag mags", where different pages made by different authors are simply arranged in a bag (the last issue, in 1970, of *The Black Country Meat Chronicle* was in this form)

and/or
strong assertions – artistic, literary and political views – perhaps even to the point of exaggeration, unfairness, and even vitu-peration (*Blast* is perhaps the best example of this)

and/or
work that displays an engaged awareness of literary and artistic movements abroad, whether that be the American avant-garde in Peter Manson and Robin Purves's *Object Permanence* (1994–1997), or the translation of European authors in Lee Harwood's *Soho* (1964)

and/or
work that, simply, as time has gone by, has proven to be influential.

2. LITTLE MAGAZINES AS A RESOURCE FOR LITERARY HISTORY

A detailed history of the modern British little magazine has yet to be written, but it is hoped that this book and the key texts mentioned in the *How To Use This Book* chapter, cited throughout, form the building blocks with which to begin to construct such a history.

But why are little magazines worthy of such treatment at all?

One answer to this question is that work published in the little magazine is often that much closer to the original creative process than the version of the work that is later, in the process of being collected for a volume of poems, a novel, or book of essays, afforded more time for reflection and revision. Of course, it may not be collected in a later publication at all.

Little magazines are the first place of publication for many authors later felt to be significant. As documented here, Norman McCaig's first poems appeared in the 1930s and 40s, but his wider reputation would only be formed a decade or so later, by which time he had repudiated his earliest work. One of Basil Bunting's earliest appearances was as a reviewer of Conrad in the 1924 magazine *The Transatlantic Review*, but his rediscovery, and the publication of *Briggflatts*, took place in the 1960s (in part associated with the rise of a flourishing little magazine scene).

Perhaps because of the language-saturated qualities of poetry, and the dominance of poetry within little magazines, authors who begin their early careers with poems may go onto find a quite different literary form more suited to them. The playwright Harold Pinter and the novelist Ian Rankin, for example, each tried poetry before they had successes in the genre for which they would find renown.

Little magazines are also a marker of milieu. For instance, a survey of literary taste for any particular period can be made by analysing who was or was not published where, a process which tests under the pressure of evidence later assertions and remembrances of movements and schools. If there was an Auden Generation, did the poets concerned tend to be published in particular places? If they did, were there poets who specifically weren't published in those magazines? Were there particular magazines for that grouping? And so on.

Other literary trends can be looked at empirically via the little magazine, too. Translation, for instance. Translations which might never find book publication nevertheless may educate and inspire the little magazine readership (which is likely to contain a high proportion of writers, thus making a real impact on homegrown literatures). In looking at publication patterns the measure of engagement with a specific literary culture from overseas can be gauged, for instance the rise of East European translation in the latter half of the century. As our survey shows, the modern British little magazine has been both a landbridge and a landing strip for creative work from Europe and the Americas.

These reasons, and no doubt many others of the kind, make the little magazine, as a key node in any literary infrastructure, worthy of collection and study. A library that houses and develops a little magazines collection is an immense resource for biographer and literary historian, allowing the exploration of not just the early thoughts, experiments, and impetuosities of particular authors but of broader literary trends and debate as well.

The little magazine is not only of interest, however, as a seed nursery for emerging authors before they are transplanted into celebrity. Major writers, for instance, have found actually editing a little magazine to be fundamental to their artistic practice for a significant part of their creative life, a pattern than can be seen in Wyndham Lewis, Hugh MacDiarmid, Laura Riding, Lee Harwood and Ian Hamilton Finlay. The literary magazine is, we would argue, a kind of artistic form in itself. The art of the editor is always a collaborative, commissioning but coercive art, like the art of a film director; like the exhibition curator, the editor has to decide what works will be presented, and what context will be provided in that presentation; the physical appearance of a magazine means that it has its own visual rules to play within or to subvert.

Perhaps the central importance of little magazines, however, is that they represent the ongoing, contemporary presentation and dissemination of the most innovative and exploratory writing of the day. Indeed, many significant writers continue to contribute to magazines long after they have become famous, finding this form of publication sympathetic to the experimental spirit of their art. James Joyce's continued publication in little magazines is one such case, with his final work, *Finnegans Wake*, appearing serially in *transition*. Readers and literary historians can also recover work that has been hitherto neglected but which, with the passage of time, emerges with renewed significance. Of course, very few little magazines achieve the greatness of the form at its best, but we hope that this book will be a first guide to the British little magazines that have tried.

How to Use This Book

1. Contemporary Poetry as the Focus

This is an annotated bibliography of poetry magazines published in the United Kingdom and the Republic of Ireland from 1914 to 2000.

Although the commentary and annotations are most concerned with the little magazines of our title, quite simply a magazine's publication of contemporary poetry, of whatever persuasion, is the prime criterion for inclusion.

Like any major artistic genre, poetry contains complexities across and within its own sub-genres and the mode of publication inevitably reflects that. There is a blurring between what is, say, a cultural review, a general literary magazine, a region- or country-based arts magazine, and a poetry magazine, even before the shades of difference between the publications within the "poetry magazine" category are considered. All may contain significant numbers of poems; all may influence the poetry climate of the day.

What is, classically, a little magazine, is discussed in our Introduction, but the complexity of the poetry infrastructure has lead us not to offer a select listing of such titles (though this is an enterprise that is surely worth going on to do). Rather we have adopted a much broader selection where blurring within and outside the "poetry magazine" category is accepted as in the nature of poetry and its championing. Because our first interest lies in surveying the broad poetry landscape the overall bibliography is also broad. Because our second and greater interest is in magazines which published work that was either experimental or new to the British Isles, our annotations concern themselves most with the world of the classic little magazine.

2. British and Irish Magazines

This book's main focus is on magazines produced in England, Scotland and Wales. Magazines from Northern Ireland and the

Republic of Ireland are also listed with annotated entries. Tom Clyde's *Irish Literary Magazines: an Outline and Descriptive Bibliography* (Irish Academy Press, 2003) is the key work in this field and, to avoid unnecessary duplication and in deference to Clyde's expert knowledge, we have generally not annotated entries for Irish magazines to the same degree.

Very occasionally we have included magazines from overseas which have important British content or appear to have been under British editorial control.

3. 1914–2000

The bibliography begins in the emblematically important year of 1914 – important as the start of the First World War, and as the year in which the first issue of *Blast* was produced – and finishes in the first year of the new millennium. The fleeting nature of poetry magazines and, in many cases, their only retrospective capture in research libraries means that the later period is likely to be less comprehensively documented than earlier years.

The book is divided by periods which seem to us meaningful in terms of the history of the little magazine and which allow the dedicated poetry reader a reasonable chunk of time through which to browse. These are: 1914–39; 1940–49; 1950–59; 1960–75; 1976–2000. The magazines are arranged alphabetically by title within these chapters, with each chapter being prefaced by our commentary on the trends of the period.

We recognise the artificiality of any periodisation, however, and so the Timeline provides a way through some of the highlights of the whole period, and the Geographical, Name, Subject and Title indexes should facilitate searches of various kinds across our designated periods.

B. THE ANNOTATED ENTRIES

1. Basic Details and Indexes

Each entry records, where possible, the basic details of title, editor, place of publication, publisher, issue numbering and dates of publication.

Titles are also found in the Title Index, editors in the Name Index, and place of publication is used in the Geographical Index. These indexes can be used not just to locate specifics but, by analysing them, to build up a picture of poetry magazine publication as a whole. The latter approach informs some of the comments in the introductory sections to each chapter.

The Subject Index provides access by poetry sub-genres, e.g. Sound Poetry, but also by literary movements, e.g. Surrealism, and social, political and other subjects which have been identified as a significant aspect of a magazine.

2. Further Details

This book also records a number of other kinds of relevant information, including: a "Note" (for title changes and other bibliographic information); "Index" (the details of any publication that indexes the magazine); the details of any "Anthology" of the writers associated with the magazine; the details of a relevant "Interview" with an editor; any "Study" of the magazine; any associated "Website"; and any "Reprint".

Of particular interest is the "Related Imprint" information, in which an associated press and examples of that press's publications are noted. Poetry magazines often work within a broader publishing infrastructure and we have tried to show this here.

Many of the entries have an additional commentary in which we have attempted to draw out some of the character of the magazine (with particular topics indexed in the Subject Index), or at least mention key, interesting, and characteristic contributors. Contributors are in turn indexed in the Name Index which can be used to build up a sense of a particular author's range of publication. As noted above, our emphasis in the annotations has been on the quintessential little magazine, so that more conventional (and well-known) magazines do not generally receive as much critical attention even though we have sought to include them.

This book is intended to be a starting point for further study of particular magazines, as well as surveying the wider magazine infrastructure. To this end, each entry refers the reader to any identified existing commentary about a publication, such as those found in earlier directories or books on the subject. Where a magazine has been described in some detail in another reference work, this is recorded in the "Profiled in" information. In the "Index" and "Profiled in" fields certain key texts, which we regard as essential tools for researchers of poetry's contexts and the little magazine, are abbreviated as set out in the Abbreviations section below.

3. Holdings in Libraries

This book is not only an annotated bibliography but a union catalogue of holdings as well. For each entry, we have consulted the catalogues of the British Library, Cambridge University Library, the National Library of Scotland, Trinity College Dublin and University College London's Little Magazines and Small Press Collection.

The Poetry Library, although not so strong in its holdings for the first half of the century, is an extremely rich resource for later magazines: in many cases, equal to or better than the national and academic libraries. Its holdings are placed beneath the list of libraries with a century-long breadth.

Each of these libraries has an abbreviation, set out in the Abbreviations section below. Where any of these libraries is not listed in the entry it means that we have not been able to locate holdings in that library for the particular magazine.

Where appropriate, the shelfmark of the particular library's holdings is also given. Where there is a shelfmark on its own, without a holdings statement, it can be assumed that the Library has the whole run. In the case of University College London and the Poetry Library, whose alphabetical-by-title shelfmarks are not used in this book, we have indicated that the Library has the complete run of the magazine by simply using the Library's abbreviation on its own.

Where a magazine is not well-represented by our core libraries the holdings of a further library that does have the magazine are noted. Such libraries are not given an abbreviation but spelt out in full.

Some magazines are known to have existed but have not been located. These are nevertheless recorded here.

4. Abbreviations

The following abbreviations are used for key libraries and key reference works:

BL	British Library
Bloomfield	B. C. Bloomfield, *An Author Index to Selected British 'Little Magazines' 1930–1939*.(London: Mansell, 1976)
CUL	Cambridge University Library
Görtschacher 1	Wolfgang Görtschacher, *Little Magazine Profiles: The Little Magazines in Great Britain, 1939–1993*. (Salzburg: University of Salzburg, 1993)
Görtschacher 2	Wolfgang Görtschacher, *Contemporary Views on the Little Magazine Scene*. (Salzburg: Poetry Salzburg, 2000)
Hayes	Richard J. Hayes (ed.) *Sources for the history of Irish civilisation. Articles in Irish periodicals*. (Boston: G. K. Hall, 1970)
Hoffman, Allen and Ulrich	Frederick J. Hoffman, Charles Allen and Carolyn F. Ulrich, *The Little Magazine: A History and a Bibliography*. 2nd ed. (Princeton: Princeton University Press, 1947)
NLS	National Library of Scotland
Sader	Marion Sader (ed.), *Comprehensive Index to English Language Little Magazines, 1890–1970*. Series 1 (Millwood, N.Y.: Kraus-Thomson, 1976)
Stanton	Michael N. Stanton, *English Literary Journals, 1900–1950: A Guide to Information Sources*. (Detroit: Gale Research, 1982)
Sullivan 1914-1984	Alvin Sullivan (ed.), *British Literary Magazines: The Modern Age, 1914–1984*. (London: Greenwood, 1986)
TCD	Trinity College Dublin
Tolley 1930s	A. T. Tolley, *The Poetry of the Thirties*. (London: Gollancz, 1975)
Tolley 1940s	A. T. Tolley, *The Poetry of the Forties*. (Manchester: Manchester University Press, 1985)
UCL	University College London Little Magazines, Alternative Press and Poetry Store
UK Little Magazines Project	The Little Magazines Project, Nottingham Trent University. Research team: David Miller, David Worrall, John Lucas, and Stan Smith (and formerly R. J. Ellis). Web: www2.ntu.ac.uk/littlemagazines/

Chapter A: 1914–1939

From *Blast* to *Kingdom Come*

THE FIRST ISSUE of Wyndham Lewis's *Blast*, a large pink slab of sans serif shrieks and shouts, was published in June 1914, two months before the start of the First World War. Its second issue, which did not appear for another year, was its last. The excitement of mechanised violence on an industrial scale that had characterised the 1914 issue had by then given way to a more subdued and ambiguous tone. The English Vorticist artists associated with the magazine differed from their Italian Futurist counterparts in coming to express doubt rather than exhilaration in their approach to the dehumanisation of the modern world.

Although *Blast*'s appearance in 1914 in a sense inaugurates the chosen period of this volume and chapter, its example should not be seen in isolation. The recent lineage of classic British little magazines can be traced back through various magazines to the *The Germ* (1850), disseminator of Pre-Raphaelite ideas. More significantly, *Blast* had been immediately pre-dated by a number of magazines which reviewed, contextualised and speculated on new movements in literature and art. These included John Middleton Murry's *Rhythm* (1911-1913) and longer-running magazines which would continue beyond *Blast*'s short life, such as A. R. Orage's *The New Age* and Ford Madox Hueffer's *The English Review*. The *Times Literary Supplement*, no little magazine and to be much vilified by various avant-gardes over the coming century, had only recently been founded and was reviewing books, however its detractors might object, across a large subject range. The *Poetry Review* under Harold Monro from 1912 to 1913 had only recently been a publisher of modern and modernist verse, too.

Blast is therefore a beginning in the history of the modern little magazine but only one beginning.

Understandably, less confrontational magazines lasted longer. In the 1920s T. S. Eliot's *The Criterion* built on their example, further encouraging receptivity to modernist modes. Closer to the agit-prop tactics of *Blast*, however, was the first of the Imagist anthologies *Des Imagistes*. These collections are included as a kind of little magazine on the grounds of their frequency, their presentation of a named group (including the poets Richard Aldington, H. D., Amy Lowell, John Gould Fletcher, Pound himself and others), and the campaigning nature of the Imagist 'project'. The Imagists were not the only grouping of the day, however. The Georgian poets, such as Rupert Brooke and John Drinkwater, were represented in Lascelle Abercrombie's *New Numbers* which lasted for four issues in 1914, building on Vivian Locke Ellis's magazine *Open Window* (1910–11), Middleton Murry's *Rhythm* and James Guthrie's *Root and Branch* (1912–1919). Despite being pilloried later for their weak prosody, their ruralism and general stylistic backwardness the Georgians had begun, tentatively, to modernise the diction of English poetry while building a substantial readership. Even Edward Thomas's poems, written in the last two years of his life and published largely posthumously following his death on the Front, found some little magazine publication before he died (in Austin O. Spare's *Form*, where "Lob" was first published in 1916). His poems can also be seen within the context of the infrastructure serving the Georgian poetry whose qualities they rapidly exceeded.

The Imagists, with a considerable American contingent, were championed by the irrepressible Ezra Pound who followed the Georgians in compiling successive group anthologies to spread the word. Magazines with Pound as a regular contributor such as *The New Age* and *The Egoist*, edited by Dora Marsden and Harriet Shaw Weaver, supported the Imagists, too. Indeed, in the same way that *Blast* can be said to have adopted some of the rhetorical tactics of the badges, fliers and posters of the Suffrage movement without the focussed political direction, it may be that Pound's involvement in *The Egoist*, once a feminist magazine, *The New Freewoman*, was a literary (and male) occupation of what had been, until his intervention, a more clearly radical feminist journal. Harold Monro at the Poetry Bookshop, publisher of *Poetry and Drama* and *The Monthly Chapbook*, was typically even-handed and published both movements, albeit issuing the Georgian anthologies under the Poetry Bookshop imprint.

Perhaps *Blast*'s aesthetic and rhetorical aggression when compared with the real bloodbath of the First World War damaged the example of creative possibilities there are within the little magazine when taken as an artform in itself. Over the century very few British magazines concerned with art or literature would combine *all* that made *Blast* a classic little magazine, from its proselytising of a small group of avant-garde writers and artists to the matching of its typography and graphic design with its editorial perspective. Understandably, Wilfred Owen, recovering in 1917 from shell shock in the Craiglockhart War Hospital on the outskirts of Edinburgh, would use his editorship of the hospital magazine *The Hydra* for his mental recuperation and the development of his own poetry rather than for any artistic 'explosion'. The stakes were privately and nationally higher now, a tragic state of affairs underlined by another literary magazine, Edith Sitwell's *Wheels*, which published Owen's posthumous poetry just two years later.

The First World War's effect on poetry in England can be seen in Owen's angry example (and in the artful plain-speaking of Edward Thomas) but in Scotland and, especially, in Ireland, the effects were more directly political. Ireland's little magazine heyday was arguably at the turn of the century with W. B. Yeats's drama-focused magazines *Beltaine* (1899-1900), *Samhain* (1901-1908) and *The Arrow* (1906), and the anonymously edited *Dana* (1904–1905).

The War's catalytic effect on Ireland meant that several of the contributors to the otherwise unassuming *The Irish Review* would later lose their lives in the Easter Rising and its vicious aftermath. That *The Irish Review* published the manifesto of the Irish Volunteers in June 1914, the same month that *Blast* was first issued, again contrasts political urgency with artistic rhetoric. Once unshackled from Britain, to a degree, Ireland in the 1920s and 30s when seen through the lens of the literary magazine is a country where immense (if sometimes emigrant) creative forces are faced and faced off by a sensitive and censoring emergent state. Successive titles, *The Irish Statesman*, *The Klaxon*, *To-morrow*, and *Ireland To-day* were closed as moral and religious sensibilities were offended again and again by explicit modernist experiments.

In Scotland, C. M. Grieve ("Hugh MacDiarmid"), a young war veteran and contributor to *The New Age*, used his various little magazines as well as his analytical contributions to the *Scottish Educational Journal* (out of scope for this volume) to urge a radical-isation of Scottish culture and politics and to assemble and encourage the writers of "the Scottish Renaissance". The work of his many but shortlived 1920s publications, *Northern Numbers*, *The Scottish Chapbook*, *The Northern Review* and *The Scottish Nation*, pub-lishing and discussing authors such as Lewis Grassic Gibbon, Neil Gunn, Edwin and Willa Muir and William Soutar with an interna-tionalist sensibility, was consolidated by James H. Whyte's *The Modern Scot* from 1930. Other journals such as *The Free Man*, *Outlook*, *The New Alliance* and the popular *Scots Magazine* (again, out of scope for this bibliography) began to re-establish a distinct literary culture within Scotland. Wales's literary revival, Dylan Thomas notwithstanding, would be more associated with the coming of the Second World War rather than the aftermath of the First, kick-started by Kiedrych Rhys's *Wales* (First Series, 1937–1940) and Gwyn Jones's *The Welsh Review* (1939–1948).

By the 1930s the broadly left political complexion of the literary journals contrasted with the right-wing and centrist politics of the successive Governments actually in power. Orage's enthusiasm for the Social Credit ideas of C. H. Douglas, particularly when seen as a blueprint for postwar rejuvenation, was articulated in *The New Age* and then in Orage's later journal, *The New English Weekly* (1932-1949). The latter may be better known for being the first publisher of three of Eliot's *Four Quartets* but Eliot and the other authors being published there, including Dylan Thomas, Hugh MacDiarmid, William Carlos Williams, David Gascoyne and Basil Bunting, were appearing in a publication primarily devoted to rather theoretical political ideas. *Purpose* (1929–1940) was another Social Credit magazine with a literary dimension, publishing poetry by Dylan Thomas and Lawrence Durrell and literary essays by Henry Miller, W. H. Auden and, again, T. S. Eliot. Douglas's own magazine *The Fig Tree*, subtitled "a Douglas Social Credit quarterly review" (First series, 1936–1939) published Eric Gill, Stella Gibbons, Ruth Pitter, and, almost inevitably, the prolific interjector Ezra Pound.

Little magazines of a more socialist sympathy were also part of the literary scene. Almost all were London-based though *Cambridge Left* (First Series, 1933–1934) suggests that university life could have an influence on political preference. This suggestion is confirmed by those later identified as communist spies, such as Anthony Blunt and Donald Maclean, who appeared in several of the magazines of the day. Though their own work may be closer to the preoccupations of the private school than the aspirations of the public library, the Oxbridge poets of the "Auden generation" – Auden, Stephen Spender, Cecil Day Lewis and Louis MacNeice – also identified themselves with leftist causes. Their poetry was published in many magazines but is especially associated with Geoffrey Grigson's broadly left-leaning *New Verse* (1933–1939). Sylvia Pankhurst's *Germinal* (1923)–[1924] was a literary offshoot of her *The Workers' Dreadnought* newspaper, published in the East End by the Workers's Suffrage Federation. The appearance of Soviet authors Aleksandr Blok and Anna Akmatova is likely to have been a political as well as a literary decision, although that is not to say they would have been the natural choice of the Soviet authorities of the day. The *Bermondsey Book* (1923–1930) edited from Ethel Gutman's bookshop was similarly internationalist with Luigi Pirandello and Edna St. Vincent Millay, for example, among its contributors.

Bookshops were clearly important cultural nodes for publication and events, not just for bookselling. The Poetry Bookshop in central London was an outstanding example of this, not only publishing *The Monthly Chapbook*, other little magazines and volumes of poetry but organising regular readings and even offering accommodation for visiting poets. *The Modern Scot* was similarly attempting to build and sell through a cultural infrastructure its editor, the American James H. Whyte, was also trying to build: the magazine was published in conjunction with his art gallery and bookshop. In England, *The Left Review* was published at Collett's Bookshop and the 'virtual' bookshop of the Left Book Club produced its own poetry serial *Poetry and the People*. As mentioned above, *The Bermondsey Book* relied on its bookshop association, too.

One of the most interesting magazines of the period, Jon Randell Evans's *The Twentieth Century* (1931–33) was the voice of The Promethean Society, a group that believed in scientific responses to social issues. Anti-monarchy, pro birth control, liberal towards homosexuality and libertarian in its outlook on censorship, the Society would have found no favour within any of the political orthodoxies of the day, and few now. It attracted Auden, Lewis Grassic Gibbon (writing under his real name, J. Leslie Mitchell), Naomi Mitchison and George Barker to its pages. In 1933 it published the supplement "Twentieth Century Verse" with an essay by Henry Porteus recognising, early in his career, the quality of Auden's poetry.

Britain viewed through its literary magazines was far from the parochial backwater it is sometimes misremembered as being. The openness of British literary magazines to American modernist authors and indeed the editorial control by U. S. editors has already been demonstrated in the discussion above, to which the presence of Ford Madox Ford's intercontinental *The Transatlantic Review* (1924) can be added. Russian and European modernism was actively encouraged in Sidney Hunt's *Ray* (1927) where visual and sound poetry and the visual arts in general were particularly strong. *Ray* published no less than Hans Arp, I. K. Bonset (i.e. Theo van Doesburg), Giorgio de Chirico, Otto Dix, Wassily Kandinsky, El Lissitzky, Kasimir Malevich, Laszlo Moholy-Nagy, Ben Nicholson, Kurt Schwitters and Mies van der Rohe. Edwin

Muir and Janko Lavrin published many translations of central and eastern European authors in their *The European Quarterly* (1934–1935).

Reluctance to enjoy all things French may be an English stereotype but the evidence suggests the contrary. Surrealism in particular was encouraged by journals such as Roger Roughton's *Contemporary Poetry and Prose* (1936–1937) which published texts by René Char, André Breton and Paul Eluard as well as René Magritte, Luis Bunuel and Salvador Dali. E. L. T. Mesens's *London Gallery Bulletin* published the Surrealists, too; a complete set of the *Bulletin* was owned by Breton himself. Another myth regarding the English character, its determination to avoid discussing politics, was punctured by the English Surrealists. In 1936 the Surrealist Group of England published no. 4 of *The International Surrealist Bulletin* and issued their *Declaration on Spain* demanding that the British Government stopped supporting the anti-democratic nationalists in Spain. The leftist tenor of several poetry magazines in the 1930s also suggests that the English are not necessarily the apolitical people they have been characterised as.

In a similar way there were a number of groups of artists and writers who allowed themselves to be seen as a movement of a kind and asserted themselves as such through the little magazine. History may not recall the Promethean Society, the Emotionists or the Islanders particularly well but that there were these groups alongside the better known Vorticists suggests that intellectualised, self-conscious movements are not as foreign to Britain as may at first be thought. One group, the New Apocalypse poets, were promulgated through *Seven* (1938–1947) and *Kingdom Come* (1939–1943). Taking their bearings to some extent from Dylan Thomas and from Surrealism, this grouping was composed of poets such as W. S. Graham, Norman MacCaig, Tom Scott, Nicholas Moore, Vernon Watkins, Robert Greacen, and Henry Treece whose work would find greater exposure during the Second World War, to the extent that the group tends to be seen as a 1940s school.

Organisations devoted to the appreciation of both writing and reading poetry were part of the period between the wars and are glimpsed through the magazines they published. Perhaps some operated rather like the workshops of later years. At a local level these included the Belfast Writers' Club, The Bristol Poets' Fellowship, The Calder Valley Poets' Society, The Glasgow Literary Club and the Oxford English Club. The Poetry Society emerged from an actually very busy field of aspirationally national organisations including The Academy of Poetry, The British Association of Literary Amateurs, The Empire Poetry League, The International Institute of British Poetry, The National Poetry Circle, and The Verse Speaking Fellowship.

This variety of voices should not, however, be taken to indicate an even spread of publication across the country. One stereotype about British publishing is borne out by the magazines in this period: the publication of literary magazines in Britian and Ireland was dominated by London. 117 titles published in London are recorded in our survey, about a half of all magazines. Dublin was next with 17 titles, appearing to have produced slightly more than either sleepy Oxford or Cambridge in this period (fourteen titles each) but, calculated on number of new titles, all three publishing centres were operating at less than 15% of the output of the English capital. Edinburgh, arguably a publishing giant in the nineteenth century, could not muster 10% of London's output in the 1914–1939 period. In fact, the most culturally significant Scottish magazines were issued from towns in the regions, Montrose for *The Scottish Chapbook* and *The Scottish Nation*, Dundee for *The Modern Scot* or not in Scotland at all, such as Edwin Muir's London-published *The European Quarterly*.

Northern Ireland appears to have punched above its demographic weight with six new titles from Belfast in this period, while Wales almost failed to muster a punch at all: we found that more new titles were published in Belfast than in the whole of Wales. Qualitatively, though, perhaps only *The Northman* (1926–50) from Queen's University had high literary ambitions and these only during the 1940s when John Gallen and Robert Greacen were editors. It is also the case that literary magazines are not the only measure of cultural change: the founding of the Gregynog Press in 1923, the birth of Plaid Cymru in 1925, the nationalist arson at the British Bombing School at Penyberth in 1936, and of course Dylan Thomas's British success, suggest that Wales was in fact very much changing at both a cultural and a political level during this period. The literary magazines which began towards the end of the 1930s, *Wales* and *The Welsh Review*, can therefore be seen as emerging from a culture which had already begun to reconfigure itself in relation to its neighbour but which may have required these magazines to begin the process of Wales addressing itself.

1 The Abinger Chronicle / [edited by Sylvia Sprigge]. Abinger Common: [The Abinger Chronicle], Vol. 1 no. 1 (Christmas 1939)–vol. 5 no. 1 (Sept. 1944)

Index: Bloomfield (Vol. 1 no. 1 (Christmas 1939) only)
Profiled in: Hoffman, Allen & Ulrich, Sullivan 1914–1984

Abs: A magazine publishing a core of work from residents living in or near the Surrey village of Abinger Common. Poets included R. C. Trevelyan, Nicholas Moore, John Griffin, E. M. Skipper, Denton Welch, Ida Procter, Stuart Piggott, Sylvia Sprigge, E. D. Idle, Peggy Whitehouse, Nicolai Gumilev, Clare Cameron, Ursula Wood, Sylvia Lynd, Geoffrey Eley, and others. More well-known contributors – of prose – included E. M. Forster, Ralph Vaughan Williams and Max Beerbohm. A 'Supplement to the *Abinger Chronicle*' was published as *The Abinger Garland: Poems [by] Nicolai Gumilev*, translated by Yakov Hornstein (Dorking: A. A. Tanner & Son, 1945) BL: PP.6036.dd.(2.)

BL: P.P.6036.dd

2 The Adelphi / edited by John Middleton Murry; Max Plowman; Richard Rees; Henry Williamson; George Godwin; B. Ifor Evans. London: [The Adelphi], 1923–1955

Note: Imprint and editors vary. Vol. 1 (June 1923)–vol. 4 (June 1927) were published as *The Adelphi*. Vol. 1. no. 1 (Sept 1927)–vol. 3. no. 4. (Aug 1930) were published as *The New Adelphi*. A new series, Vol. 1. no. 1 (Oct 1930)–vol. 31. no. 4. (Third Quarter 1955) reverted to the original title.
Index: Each volume carries its own index.
Profiled in: Hoffman, Allen & Ulrich; Stanton; Sullivan 1914–1984; Jason Harding, "The Adelphi: the reaction against Romanticism", in *The Criterion: cultural politics and periodical networks in inter-war Britain* (Oxford: Oxford University Press, 2002), pp.25–43, BL: YC.2002.a.7159
Related Work: John Gregory (ed.), *Words on the West Wind: selected essays from The Adelphi, 1924–1950*, [Longstanton]: [Henry Williamson Society], [2000]

A general literary review but with a particular interest, in the first decade or so, in the writings of D. H. Lawrence and Katherine Mansfield. It published many of the poets of 'the Auden Generation', but favoured literature which was plain speaking and was generally against the experimental and modernist.

BL: P.P.5939.beb.
CUL: Q900.C.214
NLS: Y.188
TCD: Vol.1 no.1–vol. 1 no. 4 (1923). (PER 80–852). New series, Vol. 4 no. 2 (May 1932) only. (OLS L–7–246 no.3); Vol. 26 no. 4 (1950)–vol. 29 no. 4 (1953). (E.Attic.V.)
UCL: Vol. 23 no. 3 (1947). (L Housman Coll)

3 The Adelphi Magazine / edited by Henry Danielson. London: [The Adelphi Magazine], No. 1 (June 1922)

Profiled in: Hoffman, Allen & Ulrich
Fiction, with just a few poems. Not related to the magazine of similar title.

BL: P.P.5939.bgd.
CUL: L727.B.31
NLS: 5.380
TCD: 166.n.33.no.6

4 Aengus: an all poetry journal / edited by H. O. White, then Francis Stuart. Dublin: Wood Printing Works [Printer], Midsummer 1919–July 1920

Index: Rudi Holzapfel, *Author Index 3* (Blackrock: Carraig Books, 1985)
Profiled in: Hoffman, Allen & Ulrich; Tom Clyde, *Irish Literary Magazines: an outline and descriptive bibliography* (Dublin: Irish Academic Press, 2003), BL: 2725.g.3414

A poetry-only magazine in which it was intended that eight writers each produced in turn one issue of the journal. The eight were: Richard Rowley, Anna G. Keown, H. [i.e. Francis] Stuart, E. R. Dodds, C. O'Leary, H. O. White, D. L. Kelleher, and F. R. Higgins.

TCD: 99.d.207
National Library of Ireland: IR 8205 A 1
Alba Nuadh See The Free Man A77

5 Albannach: a little anthology of 1938 Scots poetry / edited by C. J. Russell and J. F. Hendry. Dingwall: C. J. Russell, 1938

Index: A list of contributors is given in the entry for *Albannach* in the Scottish Poetry Library catalogue, www.spl.org.uk.

Contibutors include writers of the Scottish Renaissance, such as Hugh MacDiarmid, Norman MacCaig, William Soutar, Robert Garioch and others.

BL: 11455.l.30.
CUL: 1991.8.148
NLS: HP2.80.3945; Second copy: 1939.17
TCD: OLS L–6–994 no.18 Copy B; Second copy: PAM POEMS 44.14
Scottish Poetry Library

6 The Anglo-Norman Review / edited by A. C. Voisin. Jersey: British Association of Literary Amateurs and the Anglo-Norman Literary Circle, April 1929. New Series, No. 1 (Oct. 1929)–3 (Dec. 1929)

The local articles, short fiction and very occasional poems of this magazine did not live up to the promise of the sub-title of the first typewritten issue, "The Most Interesting Magazine Ever Published in the Channel Islands". The tone is generally jovial and without ambition. Membership of the Anglo-Norman Literary Circle was bundled with a subscription to this magazine and to the British Association of Literary Amateurs' *The Literary Amateur*.

BL: P.P.6072

7 The Apple – of Beauty and Discord / edited by Herbert Furst. London: Colour Publishing Company, Vol. 1 no. 1 (1920)–[vol. 3 no. 1] (1922)

Profiled in: Hoffman, Allen & Ulrich; Stanton
Reprint: Nendeln, Liechtenstein: Kraus Reprint, 1973

Concerned with literature and art. Contributors included John Rodker, Robert Graves, and Osbert Sitwell. Critical contributions by Ezra Pound, T. Sturge Moore, and others.
BL: Vol. 1 no. 1 (First Quarter, 1920) – vol. 2 no. 2 (Second Quarter, 1922) (P.P.1931.qab.)

CUL: Vol. 1 no. 1 (First Quarter, 1920) – vol. 2 no. 2 (Second

Quarter, 1922) (T727.A.6)
NLS: Vol. 1 no. 1 (First Quarter, 1920) – vol. 2 no. 2 (Second Quarter, 1922) (Q.92.)
TCD: Vol. 1 only. (24.dd.8)
UCL

8 Arena / edited by Martin Turnell. London: Sands & Co, Vol. 1 no. 1 (April 1937)–no. 4 (1938)

Index: Bloomfield

In the first issue this describes its intention to be a '[Roman] Catholic general quarterly review'. It published almost no poems, though four by J. Uhl appear in the last issue. It did, however, have some articles on poetry: "A Note on Alfred Noyes" by D. A. Traversi in vol. 1 no. 2 (July 1937); "Marxism and English Poetry" by D. A. Traversi, and "Surrealism" by Martin Turnell, both appeared in Vol 1 no. 3 (Oct–Dec 1937).
BL: P.P.5939.cal.
CUL: Q900.C.205
NLS: U.448
TCD: 96.o.141

9 Art and Letters / edited by Frank Rutter, Charles Ginner, and H. Gilman. London: Art and Letters, Vol. 1 no. 1 (July 1917)–vol. 3 no. 2 (Winter 1920)

Profiled in: Hoffman, Allen & Ulrich; Stanton; Sullivan 1914–1984
Reprint: London: Frank Cass, 1970. 2 vols. BL: P.901/687

Eliot contributed essays on drama. Poetry included work by Wilfred Owen, Siegfried Sassoon, and Isaac Rosenberg, as well as Edith Sitwell, Richard Aldington, Herbert Read, and T. S. Eliot. Ezra Pound was also a contributor.

BL: P.P.1931.lg.
CUL: L727.B.28
NLS: U.391
TCD: 73.ee.52

10 Artwork: an illustrated quarterly of arts & crafts / edited by Herbert Wauthier. London: The Artwork Publishing Company, Vol. 1 no. 1 (1924)–vol. 7 no. 28 (1931)

Note: Sometimes cited as *Art Work*.

Though dedicated to modern arts and crafts, Artwork very occasionally included some art theory by those also associated with literature, notably Wyndham Lewis on "The politics of artistic expression" (vol. 1 no. 4, May–Aug. 1925). Contributors included the artists Eric Gill and William McCance.

BL: P.P.1711.dbb.
CUL: L400.B.16
NLS: Y.185

The Autumn Anthology *See* The Mitre Anthology of Poetry A124

11 Axis: a quarterly review of contemporary 'abstract' painting and sculpture / edited by Myfanwy Evans.
London: [Axis], 1 (1937)–8 (1937)

Index: Bloomfield
Profiled in: Hoffman, Allen & Ulrich
Reprint: New York: Arno, 1968

A handsome showcase for modern European art, with essays from contributors such as Herbert Read, Jean Hélion, John Piper, S. John Woods, and Geoffrey Grigson. Illustrations were usually in black and white, but there are some colour lithographs. Although about art, this can be seen as a complementary journal to some of the little magazines interested in surrealist writing, such as *Contemporary Poetry and Prose*.

BL: PP.1931.pdb
CUL: L400.B.45
NLS: 5.890
TCD: 99.c.113
UCL: 3 only

12 Banba / [edited by Eamon O'Duibhir?]
Dublin: Gael Co-operative Society, Vol. 1 no. 1(May 1921)–vol. 3 no. 3 (Aug. 1922)

Note: Mostly in English, but includes some work in Irish
Index: Index to Vol. 1 only, issued with last issue of that volume
Profiled in: Tom Clyde, *Irish Literary Magazines: an outline and descriptive bibliography* (Dublin: Irish Academic Press, 2003), BL: 2725.g.3414

Short stories and articles about Irish culture and history. Increasingly less poetry as the magazine goes on. The poems tend to owe something to Yeats in his 'Innisfree' period. Contributors include F. R. Higgins and Daniel Corkery.

BL: P.P.6158.gb
TCD: 35.bb.45, 46
National Library of Ireland: IR 05 b 1

Queen's University Belfast: hAP73.B3

13 The Bermondsey Book: a quarterly review of life & literature. London: Cecil Palmer, then Heinemann, Vol. 1 no. 1 (Dec 1923)–vol. 7 no. 2. (March/May 1930)

Index: Bloomfield (Vol 7 no 2 (March/April/May 1930) only)
Profiled in: Hoffman, Allen & Ulrich, Stanton, Sullivan 1914–1984
Anthology: Sidney Gutman (compiler), *Seven Years' Harvest. An anthology of the Bermondsey Book, 1923–1930* (London: William Heinemann, 1934), BL: 12356.r.1.

A general review of the Left, with its editorial office at Ethel Gutman's Bermondsey Bookshop. A very eclectic magazine, with contributors including Luigi Pirandello, George Bernard Shaw, Edna St. Vincent Millay, Thomas Hardy, Aldous Huxley and Walter de la Mare.

BL: P.P.5938.bam.
CUL: L727.C.1
NLS: Q.110
TCD: PER 91–200

14 The Black Hat: An Unusual Review / edited by D. Thompson and H. Kelly. London: [The Black Hat], Vol. 1 no. 1 (Sept. 1930)–no. 8 (Oct. 1932)

BL: Newspaper Collections

15 Blast: review of the great English vortex / edited by Wyndham Lewis. London: John Lane, The Bodley Head, 1 (June 20 1914)–2 (July 1915)

Index: Sader
Profiled in: Stanton; Sullivan 1914–1984
Study: Paul Edwards (ed.), *Blast: Vorticism 1914–1918* (Aldershot: Ashgate, 2000), BL: YC.2000.b.1882
Related Work: Seamus Cooney (ed.), *Blast 3* (Santa Barbara, CA: Black Sparrow Press, 1984). A compendium in honour of Wyndham Lewis. BL: CDM.1997.b.664
Reprint: *Blast: review of the great English vortex*. Foreword by Bradford Morrow (Santa Barbara: Black Sparrow Press, 1981)

Blast published "Vorticist" poetry, prose, manifestos, and art. Heavily influenced by Italian Futurism, it was typographically innovative, using sans serif styles of differing sizes for its Marinetti-poster-like "blasts" and "blesses", which are poems of a kind. Its bright pink covers must also have been calculated to raise an eyebrow.

Contributors include Ezra Pound, T. S. Eliot and others.

BL: Cup.410.g.186
CUL: Q727.B.6
NLS: Q.55
TCD: OLS X–2–126 no.1, 2

16 Bolero: a magazine of poetry.

Oxford: Andrew Murray, No. 1 (Summer 1938)–3 (Spring 1939)

Note: Absorbed by *Kingdom Come* in Spring 1940
Index: Bloomfield
Profiled in: Hoffman, Allen & Ulrich

Little magazine associated with the Mass Observation movement.

BL: P.P.5126.bm.
CUL: L727.C.103
NLS: 1942.23
TCD: No. 2–3. (133.n.111.no.1,2)

17 A... Book of Poems by the Poet's Fellowship. Bristol: [First Book, 1920]-Third Book (1922)

BL: First Book: 011604.ff.15.; Second Book: 011604.ff.17.; Third Book: 11644.d.61.
NLS: Second and Third Book only: 1963.100

18 The Booster: a monthly in French and English / edited by Alfred Perlès. Paris: [The Booster], Vol. 2 no. 7 (Sept. 1937)–nos.10–11 (Dec. 1937–Jan. 1938)

Note: Continued by: *Delta*
Profiled in: Hoffman, Allen & Ulrich
Related Imprint: Editions du Booster
Reprint: New York: Johnson Reprint, 1968. This reprints Vol. 2 no. 7–nos.10–11, and also includes *Delta*.

Despite being founded by the American Country Club of France, this became an avant-garde magazine when Perlès became editor with vol. 2 no. 7. Contributors included Henry Miller, Anaïs Nin, Gerald Durrell, Lawrence Durrell, Patrick Evans, Oswell Blakeston, William Saroyan. Mostly prose, but includes some poems and prose poetry.

BL: Vol. 2 no. 7–no. 8 (Oct. 1937) (P.P.4291.ddc.). Johnson Reprint (Durrell 85)
CUL: Vol. 2 no. 7–nos.10–11. (T700.C.31)

19 An Branar. Baile Atha Cliath (Dublin): Muinntir an Bhranair, Iml. 1 uimh. 1 [Vol. 1 no. 1] (Abrán 1919)–iml. 2 uimh. 1 [vol. 2 no. 1] (Lughnasa 1920)

Short stories, articles, and a little poetry, e.g. from L. S. Gogan, 'Torna', and Séamus Ó hAodha. Solely Irish language.

BL: P.P.6180.ibc
TCD: PER 80–824

20 Bristol Poets Fellowship Quarterly. Bristol: [Bristol Poets Fellowship Quarterly], No. 1 (Sept.1925)–4 (June 1926)

BL: 1. (Cup.500.c.16.)
TCD: 123.c.122

21 Broadsheet. Edinburgh: Porpoise Press, No. 1 (1922)–12 (1924). Then, as *The Porpoise Press Broadsheets*. Second series no. 1 (1925)–Fourth series no. 6 (1928)

Study: Alistair McCleery, *The Porpoise Press, 1922–39* (Edinburgh: Merchiston, 1988), BL: 2708.e.1387
Related Imprint: The Porpoise Press published fiction, poetry, drama and some non-fiction. It was taken over by Faber in 1930 and abandoned as an imprint in 1939

Poets included Hugh MacDiarmid, Eric Linklater, Heinrich Heine (in translation), Walter de la Mare, William Jeffrey, Lewis Spence, and Margaret Sackville.

BL: First series: WP.8083/1–12. Later Series: W.P.8083/13, etc.
CUL: S718:01.C.4
NLS: All, but some items are held at different shelfmarks from the main shelfmark, 6.1339
Scottish Poetry Library: No. 6, 11; Second series, no. 1, 3–6; Third series, no. 3; Fourth series, no. 2, 6.

22 A Broadside / edited by W. B. Yeats, E. C. Yeats and S. M. Yeats. [With illustrations by Jack B. Yeats.]. Dundrum, Co. Dublin: Dun Emer Press, Vol. 1 no. 1 (June 1908)–vol. 7 no. 12 (May 1915). New series, *Broadsides: a collection of old and new songs*, edited by W. B. Yeats and F. R. Higgins. Dublin: Cuala Press, No. 1 (Jan. 1935)–12 (Dec. 1935). New series, *Broadsides: a collection of old and new songs*, edited by Dorothy

Wellesley and W. B. Yeats. Dublin: Cuala Press, No. 1 (Jan. 1937)–12 (Dec. 1937)

Profiled in: Tom Clyde, *Irish Literary Magazines: an outline history and descriptive bibliography* (Dublin: Irish Academic Press, 2003), BL: 2725.g.3414

Related Imprint: Dun Emer Press, a key press of the Irish Revival, published a number of works by W. B. Yeats, and other Irish writers, in the early years of the century; Cuala Press built on this success, publishing works by Yeats, but not exclusively so.
Related Work: Liam Miller, *The Dun Emer Press, later the Cuala Press* (Dublin: Dolmen Press, 1973), BL: X.0900/318.(7.)
Reprint: *Broadsides: a collection of old and new songs, 1935* (Irish University Press, 1971)

These little four-page publications, beautifully made, contained illustrations that were often hand coloured. The poems were song-like, either reprinting traditional ballads, cowboy ballads, or publishing new work. Contributors included John Masefield, James Stephens, Lady Gregory, Seamus O'Sullivan, and others in the first series, and F. R. Higgins, Lynn Doyle, Frank O'Connor, and others in the later two series. Tom Clyde notes a further continuation, *Broadsides: a collection of new Irish and English songs* but no locations are known.

BL: Lacking No. 2 (July 1908). C.191.b.22.
CUL: 879.b.55
NLS: S.295.d
TCD: *A Broadside*. (Press A, Cuala A.c.1a–84a). New Series, 1935 and 1937. (Press A, Cuala A.55)

23 The Burning Bush. Eton: [Burning Bush], No. 1 (4 June 1928)–6 (1930)

A general student magazine. Most of the poetry is anonymous, jokey, or parodic.

BL: P.P.6145.bfb.

24 The Calendar of Modern Letters: a quarterly review / edited by Edgell Rickword, Douglas Garman and Bertram Higgins. London: Lawrence Wishart, Vol. 1 no. 1 (Mar. 1925)–vol. 4 no. 2 (July 1927)

Note: After the February 1926 issue it became simply *The Calendar*
Index: Sader
Profiled in: Hoffman, Allen & Ulrich; Stanton; Sullivan 1914–1984; Jason Harding, "*The Calendar*: standards of criticism", in *The Criterion: cultural politics and periodical networks in inter-war Britain* (Oxford: Oxford University Press, 2002), pp.44–63, BL: YC.2002.a.7159
Anthology: F. R Leavis (ed.) *Towards Standards of Criticism. Selections from "The Calendar of Modern Letters" 1925–7* (London: Wishart & Co, 1933), BL: 20017.a.26
Reprint: *The Calendar of Modern Letters: March 1925–July 1927 ... New impression with a review in retrospect by Malcolm Bradbury*. London: Cass, 1966. 3 vol. BL: X.909/6954.

BL: P.P.5939.bec.
CUL: Q727.C.24
NLS: U.392. Reprint: NG.1570.c.9
TCD: 78.uu.58
UCL

25 Cambridge Left. Cambridge: Vol. 1 no. 1 (Summer 1933)–vol. 2 no. 1 (Autumn 1934). [New Series] No. 1 (Lent 1954)–[1957]. [Further Series] 1960

Index: Bloomfield (1933–1934 only)
Profiled in: Hoffman, Allen & Ulrich

Contributors to the first series include: W. H. Auden, Naomi Mitchison, John Cornford, John Drummond, Donald Maclean, J. D. Bernal, Gavin Ewart, Charles Madge, and Richard Goodman. Geoffrey Strickland and Fred Grubb were among those who contributed to the new series.

BL: Vol. 1. no. 1–vol. 1 no. 2; [New Series], No. 1 only. (P.P.5938.bcl)
CUL: Vol. 1 no. 1–vol. 2 no. 1; [New Series] 1954–1957; [Further Series] 1960. (CA.C.41.5)
NLS: Vol. 1 no. 1–vol. 2 no. 1. (U.444. PER)

26 Cambridge Poetry / edited by Christopher Saltmarshe, John Davenport and Basil Wright; then John Davenport, Hugh Sykes, and Michael Redgrave. London: Leonard and Virginia Woolf, 1929, 1930

Note: Published as Hogarth Living Poets no. 8 and no. 13 respectively
Profiled in: Tolley 1930s

Contributors included Richard Eberhart, William Empson, Ronald Bottrall, Julian Bell, John Lehmann, J. [i.e. Jacob] Bronowski, Michael Redgrave, and Kathleen Raine. Hogarth Press also published an anthology edited by Margaret Thomas, *An Anthology of Cambridge Women's Verse* (1931; Hogarth Living Poets, no. 20), BL: 11613.f.1/20. Later, a volume of *Poets of Tomorrow* bore the subtitle *Cambridge Poetry 1940*, the anonymous introduction making direct reference to the earlier *Cambridge Poetry*.

BL: 11613.f.1/8., 11613.f.1/13.
CUL: CAM.D.31.33
NLS: T.28.f

27 The Candle / edited by Oliver W. F. Lodge. Holmbury St. Mary: Vol. 1 no. 1 (Jan. 1938)–no. 4 (June 1940)

Note: Vol. 1 no. 4 is a six-page pamphlet consisting entirely of the poetry of William Foster, which was published by the College of William and Mary, Virginia.
Index: Bloomfield (No.1–3 only)
Profiled in: Hoffman, Allen & Ulrich

BL: Vol. 1 no. 1 only. (P.P.5126.bl)

28 Caravel / edited by Sydney Salt and Jean Rivers. Majorca, 1 (1934)–5 (1936)

Index: Bloomfield
Profiled in: Hoffman, Allen & Ulrich
Related Imprint: Caravel Press, which published e.g. Sidney Salt, *Contemporary Legends* [prose] (1935), BL: X.958/3118; and Charles Henri Ford, *A Pamphlet of Sonnets*, with a drawing by Pavel Tchelitchew (1936), BL: Cup.407.g.3.

Includes contributions by William Carlos Williams, Dylan Thomas, and Edith Sitwell.

Poetry Collection, Lockwood Memorial Library, State University of New York at Buffalo

29 Carmina: a review devoted to poetry / edited by Maurice Leahy. London, then Westcliff-on-Sea: Catholic Poetry Society, No. 1 (Aug. 1930)–12 (1932)

Index: Bloomfield
Profiled in: Hoffman, Allen & Ulrich, Stanton

BL: Destroyed in the Second World War. (P.P.5126.bbb)
CUL: L727.C.8
NLS: Y.230 PER
TCD: Lacking no. 6. (22.zz.74, nos.21–31)

30 Causerie: the intimate magazine / edited by Horace Shipp. No. 1 (Nov. 1939)–4 (Feb. 1940)

'CAUSERIE first of all sets out to please, to entertain. There will appear in each issue a short story. There will be poetry, anecdote, quotation: "all for your delight." The younger generation will, we hope, indulge us if we imagine that in these days the element of romance and beauty is more to be desired than that of realism.' – editorial in first issue. Only a few poems were ever published.

BL: P.P.5939.bgo.
CUL: Vol. 1 no. 1. (CA/U68)
NLS: 6.266

31 Change: the beginning of a chapter in twelve volumes / edited by John Hilton and Joseph Thorpe. London: [Change], Vol. 1 (Jan. 1919)–2 (Feb. 1919)

A small format magazine devoted to general cultural issues. In fact it only ran to two volumes. Notable for its attractive use of arts-and-crafts-like typography and woodcuts. Designed, in the words of its first editorial, for 'Those who, without subscribing to the creed of any Ism, have dreamed of a world in which service rather than profit might be the background of life and work...' The poems, anonymous or identified only by initials, are song-like.

BL: P.P.5938.bai.
CUL: T718.D.23

The Chapbook (ed. Harold Monro) *See* The Monthly Chapbook A128

32 The Chapbook: the magazine of the Glasgow Literary Club / [edited by Ida Kelsall]. Glasgow: [The Glasgow Literary Club] Vol. 1 no. 1 [1933]–no.4 (Dec. 1935)

Edited anonymously, but the inference is that the editor is Ida Kelsall. The first issue contains messages of goodwill from R. B. Cunninghame Graham, Hilaire Belloc, and James Bridie, among others. Short articles, short fiction, news (Marion Angus gave a talk and reading at the Club in 1934) and occasional poems.

BL: P.P.6203.la.
CUL: L727.C.35

33 The Chelsea Review. London: [The Chelsea Review], No. 1 (Mar. 1928)–2 (Apr. 1928)

BL: Newspaper Collections

34 Cinema Quarterly /edited by Norman Wilson. Edinburgh: [Cinema Quarterly], Vol. 1 no. 1 (Autumn 1932)–vol. 3 no. 4 (Summer 1935)

Note: Incorporated by *World Film News*
Profiled in: Hoffman, Allen & Ulrich

Wholly about film, but includes articles by Herbert Read, "Towards a Film Aesthetic" and Hugh MacDiarmid on "The Poet and The Film".

BL: Lacking Vol. 2. no. 4. (P.P.1912.fge.)
CUL: L415:6.C.55
NLS: NG.727
TCD: Vol.1 no.4 (Summer 1933); vol.2 no.4 (Summer 1934); vol.3 no1. (1934)–no. 4(1935). (26.bb.229,Nos.1–6)

35 The Civil Service Author. [No. 1, 1920s?]– . ISSN: 0959–0064

Note: Details of editors and places of publication are based on holdings dating from No. 94 (1990). Title changed to *The SCPSW Writer* with No. 155 (2001).

From the 1990s, from when holdings are known, editors involved included Iain R. McIntyre, John Ward, Joyce Thornton and Adrian Danson. In this period the places of publication included London, Stockport, Beauly, Ardgay and Bromley.

BL: 91– . (ZC.9.a.2441)
Poetry Library: 90–121, 123–131, 133–

36 The Cocoon / edited by V. W. W. S. Purcell. Cambridge: V. W. W. S. Purcell, No. 1 (Mar. 1920)–4 (Feb. 1921)

"The keynote of our paper is youth, the producers are young, the contributors will be young, it will make public the work of youthful poets, essayists and critics, and it will present the views of the younger generation of politicians and economists." – Victor Purcell's editorial in the first issue. Contributions included an essay on Gabriele D'Annunzio by Alec Macdonald and an essay by Edward L. Davison, defending modern poetry, by which was meant Thomas Hardy, Walter de la Mare and others. Poets included Rosamond Lehmann, Edgell Rickword, Davison and others.

BL: P.P.6058.hc.
CUL: CAM.B.31.33
NLS: No. 2 (May 1920)–4. (5.491)
TCD: No. 2 (May 1920)–4. (106.a.83, nos.4–6)

37 The Colosseum / edited by Bernard Wall. London: [The Colosseum], Vol. 1 no. 1 (Mar. 1934)–vol. 5 no. 22 (July/Sept. 1939)

Note: Subtitle varies
Profiled in: Hoffman, Allen & Ulrich

A general literary review, publishing very little poetry but reviewing some and occasionally containing articles on aspects of poetry. It saw itself as "Not a Polite Review". Contributions included articles by Paul Claudel and Paul Valéry.

BL: P.P.5939.beg
CUL: Q900.C.212
NLS: Y.186
TCD: E.Attic.o.101–103

38 Comment / edited by Sheila MacLeod and Victor Neuburg. London: [Comment], Vol. 1 no. 1 (7 Dec. 1935)–vol. 3 no. 58 (30 Jan. 1937)

Profiled in: Stanton
Contributors included Dylan Thomas, Ruthven Todd, D. S. Savage, G. S. Fraser, and Julian Symons.

BL: P.P.5264.rc

Contemporaries *See* Contemporaries and Makers A39

39 Contemporaries and Makers / edited by John Kaestlin. Cambridge: John Kaestlin, [Vol. 1 no. 1] (Summer 1933)–vol. 2 no. 1 (Summer 1935)

Note: Became just *Contemporaries* from vol. 1 no. 2 onwards
Index: Bloomfield; Vol. 2 no. 1 carries a list of contents for all preceding issues
Profiled in: Hoffman, Allen & Ulrich

Contributors included Charles Madge, Joseph Gordon Macleod, Gavin Ewart, and Donald Maclean (later known as a spy). An appreciative account by John Drummond of Pound's *A Draft of XXX Cantos*, with extensive quotation, appears in the first issue, and Pound responds in the second issue with a letter concerning the alleged censorship of London publishing houses. Vol. 1 no. 4 includes the editor's article, "What have they done since Dunbar? – A survey of American Negro poetry".

BL: ZA.9.a.10985
CUL: CAM.B.31.37
NLS: NJ.309
TCD: 122.a.157

40 Contemporary Poetry: a monthly
publication devoted to the younger
poets of the English language / edited
by G. Edmund Lobo. Dublin: William Calton,
No. 1 (Mar. 1925)–no. 8 (Spring 1927)

Note: From Spring 1926 known as *Contemporary Poetry and
Song*, at which point a parallel numbering is adopted, no. 1
(Spring 1926)–no. 5 (Spring 1927)
Index: Rudi Holzapfel, *Author Index 3* (Blackrock: Carraig
Books, 1985)

Profiled in: Hoffman, Allen & Ulrich; Tom Clyde, *Irish
Literary Magazines: an outline and descriptive bibliography*
(Dublin: Irish Academic Press, 2003), BL: 2725.g.3414
Despite its subtitle, an aesthetically conservative magazine.

BL: P.P.5126.k.
NLS: Vol. 1, no. 1 (Mar. 1925)–vol. 1, no. 3 (May 1925).
(T.9.a)
TCD: 1925–1926. (98.d.112.)
National Library of Ireland: Ir 82189 c 83

41 Contemporary Poetry and Prose /
edited by Roger Roughton. London: [Roger
Roughton], No. 1 (May 1936)–10 (Autumn
1937)

Index: Bloomfield, Sader; Index to issues 1–8 published in
No. 8
Profiled in: Stanton; Sullivan 1914–1984; Adrian Caesar,
Dividing Lines: poetry, class and ideology in the 1930s
(Manchester University Press, 1991), BL: YC.1991.a.765
Related Imprint: Contemporary Poetry and Prose Editions.
Books from this imprint included Benjamin Péret, *A Bunch
of Carrots*, selected & translated by Humphrey Jennings and
David Gascoyne, 1936 (BL: W.P.8986/1) and its second
edition, published as *Remove Your Hat*, also 1936 (BL:
W.P.8986/1a.), as well as 1/20 by E. E. Cummings, [1937]
(BL: W.P.8986/2).
Reprint: London: Frank Cass, 1968. (English little
magazines, no. 4). BL: X.909/14649

Published from the Arts Café, No. 1 Parton St, London, this
was one of the magazines responsible for widening the
knowledge of surrealist literature in Britain in the 1930s.
Contributions included texts (not illustrations) by Luis
Buñuel, René Char, Salvador Dali, René Magritte, André
Breton and Paul Eluard; Roger Roughton, Kenneth Allott,
David Gascoyne, George Barker, and Dylan Thomas; Gavin
Ewart, Francis Scarfe, Ruthven Todd, Roy Fuller, Edgar
Foxall, Wallace Stevens, Jack Lindsay and others. No. 2
(June 1936) was a special Surrealist issue. The no. 4/5
double issue (Aug–Sept. 1936) carried six prose poems by

Picasso, and an article on Picasso's art by Dali. The
Declaration on Spain issued by the Surrealist Group in
England, accompanied no. 7 (Nov. 1936).

BL: P.P.5126.gbf
CUL: L727.C.37
NLS: Lacking no. 10. (U.412)
TCD: 121.p.323, Nos.5–12

Contemporary Poetry and Song *See*
Contemporary Poetry: a monthly publication
devoted to the younger poets of the English
language A40

42 Coterie / edited by Chaman Lall then
Russell Green. London: Hendersons, No. 1
(May 1919)–6/7 (1920/21). Then, as *New Coterie*,
No. 1 (Nov. 1925)–6 (Summer/Autumn 1927)

Note: *New Coterie* was published by E. Archer
Index: Sader
Profiled in: Hoffman, Allen & Ulrich; Stanton; Sullivan
1914–1984
Reprint: Millwood, N. Y.: Kraus Reprint, 1967

Outside their anthologies, an important outlet for the work
of the Imagist poets. Contributors, including those outside
Imagism, included: T. S. Eliot, Richard Aldington, E. C.
[i.e. Edmund] Blunden, Wilfred Owen (posthumously),
H.D., Amy Lowell, and Harold Monro. Chaman Lall edited
no.1–5; Russell Green appears to have edited 6/7 and the
entire run of *New Coterie*.

BL: *Coterie* (P.P.5126.beg). *New Coterie* (P.P.5938.ddc)
CUL: T727.B.26
NLS: *Coterie* (P.61). *New Coterie* (5.2809)
TCD: *New Coterie* (66.n.176)
UCL: *Coterie*: 1–5. *New Coterie*: 1–5.

43 The Country Heart / edited by Maude
E. King. London: Allen & Unwin for the
Vineyard Press. No. 1 (Jan./Mar. 1921)–8
(Oct./Dec. 1922).

Note: Continues: *Vineyard Magazine*.

A general literary review, with a rural slant. Poems included
those by Katharine Tynan, Margaret M. Radford, and Isabel
Derby.

BL: P.P.5938.bae
TCD: 93.e.18

44 Cranks / compiled by Obert, Sebert, and Ethelberta Standstill. London: A. H. Stockwell, 1921

A parody of the Sitwells' *Wheels*.

BL: 011648.g.48
NLS: 1922.5

45 The Criterion / edited by T. S. Eliot. London: Cobden Sanderson, then Faber, Vol. 1 no. 1 (Oct 1922)–vol. 18 no. 71 (Jan. 1939)

Note: Vol. 1 no. 1 (Oct 1922)–vol. 3 no. 12 (July 1925) were published as *The Criterion*. Vol. 4. no. 1 (Jan 1926)–vol. 5. no. 1. (Jan. 1927) were published as *The New Criterion*. Vol. 5. no. 2 (may 1927)–vol. 7. no. 4. (June 1928) were published as *The Monthly Criterion*. Vol. 8. no. 30 (Sept 1928)–vol. 18. no. 71 (Jan. 1939) reverted to the original title. Imprints varied: Cobden Sanderson, 1922–25; Faber and Gwyer, 1926–29; Faber and Faber, 1929–1939
Index: Each volume has its own index. A subject and author index is contained within *The Criterion*, 1922–1939, ed. T. S. Eliot, London: Faber, 1967
Profiled in: Stanton; Sullivan 1914–1984
Related Imprint: Faber
Study: Jason Harding, *The Criterion: cultural politics and periodical networks in inter-war Britain* (Oxford: Oxford University Press, 2002), BL: YC.2002.a.7159; Wilfried Böhler, *Der Literat als Vermittler ökonomischer Theorie: T.S. Eliot im "Criterion," 1922–1939 = Literary man on economics*, T.S. Eliot in the "Criterion," 1922–1939. Frankfurt am Main: P. Lang, 1985. In German, but includes abstracts in English. BL: YA.1989.a.18100; Ian Hamilton, 'The Straight and Narrow', in Hamilton, *The Little Magazines: A Study of Six Editors* (London: Weidenfeld and Nicolson), 1976, BL: X.989/50900
Reprint: *The Criterion*, 1922–1939, ed. T. S. Eliot, London: Faber, 1967

A general literary review, published 'commercially', though more likely cross-subsidised, e.g. by funds raised from Faber's *Nursing Times*. Perhaps one of the most influential critical reviews of its day.

BL: P.P.5939.bea.
CUL: Q700.C.46
NLS: Y.186
TCD: Microfilm: PER 80–822
UCL: Vol. 3 no. 12. (Joyce Pers)

The Critic (1928) *see* The Free Critic: literature, art, music, drama A76

46 David: an international review of politics and literature / edited by A. J. Henderson, Allan H. Taylor, and Erik Warman. London: Holborn Publishing, No. 1 (Mar. 1932)–3 (May 1932)

Index: Bloomfield
Profiled in: Hoffman, Allen & Ulrich

A short-lived general literary review, publishing very little poetry, namely poems by Alexander MacKendrick and A. N. Taylor.

BL: P.P.5938.ddf.
CUL: L206.B.1
NLS: 5.521
TCD: 95.e.45

47 The Day / [edited by Thomas Dennehy?]. Cork: [The Twenty Club], No. 1 (17th Mar. 1916)–9 (21st Dec. 1918)

Note: Title also in Irish: *An Lá*
Profiled in: Tom Clyde, *Irish Literary Magazines: an outline and descriptive bibliography* (Dublin: Irish Academic Press, 2003), BL: 2725.g.3414

Focusing on writing from the Cork area, and reviews of work by Cork writers. The Twenty Club was set up in November 1915 as a group with a mission to envigorate the arts in the local area.

BL: An unnumbered, undated issue for St. Patrick's Day, [1918?]. (10390.h.28)
TCD: 7–9. (120.gg.34)
National Library of Ireland: Ir 8208 d 1.

48 The Decachord: a magazine for students and lovers of poetry / edited by Charles John Arnell then Phillipa Hole. Torquay: Poetry Publishing Company, Vol. 1 no. 1 (March/April 1924)–vol. 23 no. 113 (Sept./Oct. 1946)

Note: Publishers varied. Publication suspended Aug. 1926–Jan. 1927, Mar.–June 1931
Index: Bloomfield (Vol. 7 no. 26–vol. 11 no. 48 only; and not the book reviews)
Profiled in: Hoffman, Allen & Ulrich; Stanton; Sullivan 1914–1984
Related Works: *A West Country New Anthology of Contemporary Poets*, ed. C. J. Arnell. 2 vols (Exeter: Poetry Publishing Co. [1930–33]), BL: W.P.10525.

A magazine that championed traditional forms in poetry, rather than modernist ones. It had a West Country bias, especially in the first decade, but not exclusively so. Published many now long-forgotten poets, though also Hugh MacDiarmid and Edmund Blunden. Charles John Arnell was editor, 1924–31; Phillipa Hole, 1931–46.

BL: P.P.5126.bc.
CUL: Vol. 1–vol. 4. (L727.C.90.)
NLS: Vol. 1–vol. 4. (U.392)
TCD: Vol. 1–vol. 4. (38.a.137,Nos.1–15)

49 **Delta** / Edited by Alfred Perlès. Paris: John Goodland, Année no. 2 no. 2 (Apr. 1938)-année no. 3 no. 1 (Easter 1939)

Note: Continues: *The Booster*
Profiled in: Hoffman, Allen & Ulrich
Reprint: *Delta* is included in the Johnson Reprint (New York, 1968) of *The Booster*

More emphasis here on poetry than its prose-focused predecessor. Although some texts are in French, most are in English. Contributors included Kay Boyle, Antonia White, Dylan Thomas, David Gascoyne, Lawrence Durrell, Artur Lundkvist, Nicholas Moore, Oswell Blakeston, Roger Burford, Patrick Evans, John Gawsworth, Karel Capek, Anaïs Nin, Henry Miller, Anne Ridler, Ronald Bottrall, Tambimuttu, Elizabeth Smart, the editor, and others.

BL: Johnson Reprint. (Durrell 85)
CUL: T700.C.31

50 **The Dial Monthly** / London: Robert Scott, Specimen Number, then Vol. 1 no. 1 (Jan. 1913)-vol. 2 no. 19 (July 1914)

Not to be confused with the American magazine *The Dial*. A liberal Christian magazine "for Church Women and others" which looked at social questions, culture, and the arts. Contributors included G. K. Chesterton, Maude Goldring, Annie Matheson, Katharine Tynan, with essays including one devoted to Rabindranath Tagore by William Scott Palmer, and an account by Dorothy Wright of "Women and Girls in the Middle Ages". A particularly startling issue was that of May 1914, in which paintings by David Bomberg and A. E. Wadsworth are reproduced (in black and white) and John Rodker's essay "The 'New' Movement in Art" is published, dealing with Wyndham Lewis and the art associated with *Blast*. This is described as Futurist, Vorticism apparently not yet a word in currency. The anonymous editor adds a note: "We hold no brief for any style in art, but is seems to us that the movement is important, and therefore worthy of the attention of all thinking people, although it may appear to some people to be vergingon the insane."

BL: Vol. 1 no. 1–vol. 2 no. 19. (P.P.357.bcg)

51 **Dope: twentieth century broadsheet** / edited by Bernard Causton. London: [Dope], No. 1 (New Year 1932)–2 (Summer 1932)

Index: Bloomfield
Profiled in: Hoffman, Allen & Ulrich

A magazine with a satirical tone, *Dope* includes amusing and what it sees as silly excerpts from the press. Contributors include W. H. Auden and Oswell Blakeston.

BL: Newspaper Collections

52 **Down West: being the year book of the West Country Essay Club.** London: J. B. Shears & Sons, 1923–24

Includes three poems, all pseudonymous.

BL: P.P.5938.bba.
TCD: PAM K.21 no.33

53 **The Dublin Magazine: a quarterly review of literature, science and art** / edited by Seamus O'Sullivan [a.k.a. James Sullivan Starkey]. Dublin: Dublin Magazine, Vol. 1 no. 1 (Aug 1923)–vol. 3 no. 1 (Aug 1925); New series: Vol. 1 no. 1 (Jan. 1926)–vol. 33 no. 2 (Jan. 1958)

Index: Hayes; Sader. Each volume from 1923–1925 has its own index. Rudi Holzapfel, *An Index of contributors to the Dublin Magazine* (Dublin: Museum Bookshop, 1966), BL: 2713.m.2. There is also a typescript index compiled by Starkey for the years 1923–1953, which is held by TCD at OL 052.09415 DUB 1
Profiled in: Hoffman, Allen & Ulrich; Princess Grace Irish Library Electronic Irish Records Dataset, www.pgil-eirdata.org; Sullivan 1914–1984; Tom Clyde, *Irish Literary Magazines: an outline and descriptive bibliography* (Dublin: Irish Academic Press, 2003), BL: 2725.g.3414; Gerry Smyth, *Decolonisation and Criticism: the construction of Irish literature* (London: Pluto Press, 1998), pp.133–136, BL: YC.2001.a.4091
Anthology: Seamus O'Sullivan (ed.) *Editor's choice: a little anthology of poems selected from the Dublin Magazine* (Dublin: Orwell Press, 1944), BL: 11605.b.35.
Related Imprint: Dublin Magazine published Gordon Bottomley's *Maid of Athens* (1945) in a limited ed. of fifty

copies, for private circulation, BL: YL.1989.b.89.
Related Work: Patricia Coughlan and Alex Davis (eds.),
Modernism and Ireland: The Poetry of the 1930s (Cork: Cork
University Press, 1995), BL: YC.1997.a.299.
Reprint: Vol. 1 (1923)-New Series Vol. 1 (1926) is reprinted
by: Millwood, New York: Kraus Reprint, 1967

A conservative stalwart of the Irish literary scene. Much
later, in 1961, *The Dublin Magazine* was the self-conscious
model for *The Dubliner*.

BL: Lacking vol. 2 no. 9–vol. 3 no. 1. (P.P.6180.ibd.)
CUL: L900.B.77
NLS: U.409 PER
TCD: Per 81–832

54 Edwardian Poetry [edited by T. I. F. Armstrong, a.k.a. John Gawsworth] London: Richards, [Book 1], 1936/1937

Free verse was banned from this attempt to assert the
qualities of the shorter lyric. Contributors included
Gawsworth, Hugh MacDiarmid, E. H. W. Meyerstein, Ruth
Pitter, A. S. J. Tessimond, E. H. Visiak, Anna Wickham, Roy
Campbell and others. Like Gawsworth's other similar
attempt, *Neo-Georgian Poetry*, only one issue was ever
published.

BL: 11605.c.6.
CUL: L727.C.31
NLS: T.28.b

55 The Egoist: an individualist review / edited by Dora Marsden, then Harriet Shaw Weaver. London: [The Egoist], Vol. 1 no. 1 (1914)–vol. 6 no. 5 (1919)

Note: Imprints varied. Continues: *The New Freewoman*
Index: Sader
Profiled in: Sullivan 1914–1984
Related Imprint: The Egoist Press published books by
Richard Aldington, Jean Cocteau, H.D., T. S. Eliot,
Marianne Moore, and Ezra Pound, as well as Joyce's *Portrait
of an Artist As a Young Man*
Reprint: Millwood, New York: Kraus Reprint, 1967.
Microfilm: New York: Datamics, [undated]
Study: Jayne E. Marek, *Women Editing Modernism: "little"
magazines & literary history* (Lexington: University Press of
Kentucky, 1995), BL: YA.1997.a.13656; Mark Morrison,
"Marketing British Modernism: *The Egoist* and Counter-
Public Spheres", in *Twentieth Century Literature*, Vol. 43 no. 4
(Winter 1997), pp.439–467; BL: 9076.850000 Website:
www.nonserviam.com/egoistarchive/marsden/index.html

This magazine encouraged, interspersed within cultural

and broadly political and philosophical articles, the
publication of Imagist poetry, the American modernists H.
D., William Carlos Williams, T. S. Eliot, and Marianne
Moore, as well as D. H. Lawrence, May Sinclair, Dorothy
Richardson, and James Joyce. Ezra Pound contributed
reviews. Richard Aldington was initially literary editor, H.
D. taking over for 1916, and T. S. Eliot becoming so in
1917, remaining until the end in 1919. His essay 'Tradition
and the Individual Talent' was published in the concluding
issue. *The Egoist* was much more of a literary magazine than
its predecessors *The New Freewoman* and *The Freewoman*,
outside the scope of this bibliography. These magazines,
although feminist, were periodicals that were more radical
than the conventional suffrage weeklies of the day, and
their broadening of feminist ideas beyond the question of
the vote laid the foundation for the considerable literary
(largely male) content of *The Egoist*. See Lucy Delap, "The
Freewoman, Periodical Communities, and the Feminist
Reading Public" in *Princeton University Library Chronicle*, Vol.
LXI no. 2 (Winter 2000), pp.233–276. See also [*The Imagist
Anthologies*].

BL: C.116.h.7.
CUL: Q900.B.56
UCL: Kraus Reprint

56 Emotionism / [edited by R. O. Dunlop]. London: The Emotionist Group at the Hurricane Lamp Gallery, Vol. 1 no. 1 (Feb. 1928)

Poetry, music, fiction and art were all part of the Emotionist
Group's activity. Peggy Ashcroft and Philip Henderson
were to become perhaps the best known of the group. R. O.
Dunlop supplies a definition of Emotionism in four short
paragraphs, and the magazine is illustrated by the artists
from the group.

BL: P.P.5938.dia.
CUL: T727.B.41
TCD: 38.a.137, no.28

57 The Enemy: a review of art and literature / edited by Wyndham Lewis. London: The Arthur Press, Vol. 1 no. 1 (Jan. 1927)–no. 3 (Jan. 1929)

Note: Suspended publication Oct 1927–Dec 1928
Index: Sader
Profiled in: Hoffman, Allen & Ulrich; Sullivan 1914–1984
Reprints: New York : Kraus Reprint Corporation, 1967;
London: Frank Cass & Co, 1968. (English little magazines,
no.2). BL: P.901/284.; Santa Rosa: Black Sparrow, 1994. BL:
ZC.9.b.6091

Largely the writings of Lewis himself, notable for Lewis's criticism of D. H. Lawrence, James Joyce, and Gertrude Stein.

BL: Cup.410.g.185.
CUL: L700.B.131
NLS: Kraus Reprint. (NG.1569.b.10)
UCL

58 The English Digest. London (printed in Dublin): Vol 1 no.1 (Oct. 1938)–vol. 78 (Dec. 1965)

BL: P.P.5938.bbi. Microfilm: Mic.C.12685
NLS: Vol. 9 no. 1 (Mar. 1942)–v. 24 no. 4 (June 1947). Lacking Vol. 10 no. 1 (1943). (P.39)

59 The English Review / edited by Ford Madox Hueffer; then Austin Harrison; then Ernest Remnant; then Douglas Jerrold; then Wilfrid Hindle; then Derek Walker-Smith. London: Duckworth, then others. Vol. 1 no. 1 (Dec. 1908)–vol. 64 no. 7 (July 1937)

Note: Ceased publication when merged with *The National Review*, out of scope for this bibliography
Profiled in: Sullivan 1837–1913: Hoffman, Allen and Ulrich; Douglas Goldring, South Lodge: Reminiscences of Violet Hunt, Ford Madox Ford and the *English Review* circle (London: Constable, 1930), BL: 10860.aaa.11; Malcolm Bradbury, "The English Review" in London Magazine No. 5 (Aug. 1958): 46–57, BL: P.P.5939.cbg; Eric Homberger, "Ford's English Review: Englishness and its Discontents,"*Agenda* Vol. 27 no. 4– vol. 28 no. 1 (Winter 1989/Spring 1990): 61–66., BL: PP.5109.AAC; Mark Morrison, "The Myth of the Whole: Ford's *English Review*, the *Mercure de France*, and Early British Modernism" in ELH Vol. 63 no. 2 (1996 Summer) pp.513–33, BL: DSC3730.650000 (also available electronically)

Ford Madox Hueffer (later known as Ford Madox Ford) is said to have started the magazine in response to Thomas Hardy's failure to find a periodical to publish one of his more adult poems. Editor for little more than the first year, in that time Hueffer published many of the best writers of the day, including early work by the then little known Norman Douglas, Ezra Pound, Wyndham Lewis and D. H. Lawrence. Austin Harrison edited between 1910 and 1923 and continued what had also been a strong internationalist element by publishing such writers as Chekhov, Maeterlinck, Katherine Mansfield, Nabokov, Yone Noguchi, and Turgenev, as well as Aldous Huxley, Harold Monro, and other new English writers. Remnant gave the

review an explicitly Conservative point of view. Jerrold's editorship from 1931 to 1935 rescued the magazine as a serious reviewing journal of literary modernism, but, after Wilfrid Hindle's six month stint, Derek Walker-Smith reverted to right-wing politics and the magazine ended its days largely devoid of literary interest.

BL: P.P.5939.bo
CUL: Q900.c.142
NLS: U.451
TCD: Yeats PER 9; E.Attic B.1.64
UCL: Vol.1 no. 1–2; vol. 2 no. 1–4; vol. 4 no. 4; vol. 11 no. 2; vol. 12 no. 4; vol. 13; vol. 15; vol. 17 no. 2–4; vol. 18 no. 4; vol. 20 no. 1. (Little Magazines Collection) Also, Vol. 6 no. 4; Vol. 36 no. 6 (Laurence Housman Collection)

60 Epilogue: a critical summary / edited by Laura Riding. Deya, Majorca and London: Seizin Press and Constable, Vol. 1 (1935)–4 (1938)

Note: Vol. 4 was a single work, *The World and Ourselves*, edited by Laura Riding and published by Chatto and Windus
Index: Bloomfield (No. 1–3 only)
Profiled in: Hoffman, Allen & Ulrich
Related Imprint: Seizin Press

Robert Graves was listed as the Assistant Editor. Both Riding and Graves contributed poems to this general cultural review. "… we are not 'literary' except in that we regard words as the most authoritative indexes of value, since they are at once the most specific and the most sensitive instruments of thought; we have no professional prejudice in favour of words as an aesthetic medium." – Laura Riding, from the first issue's editorial. Other contributors included Norman Cameron, William Archer, Sally Graves, Honor Wyatt and others. The last volume published questions posed by writers, including Graves, Naomi Mitchison and Willa Muir, concerning the pre-war world crisis, with possible answers by members of various professions.

BL: Vol. 1–3 (PP.5939.beh.), Vol. 4 (12358.e.23)
CUL: Q900.C.210
NLS: Y.191
TCD: Vol. 1–3 (112.p.172–174)

61 **The Eton Candle** / edited by Brian Howard. Eton: [Eton Candle], Vol. 1 (Mar. 1922).

Note: Only one number was published. With a supplement.

The supplement includes work by Osbert and Sacheverell Sitwell and Aldous Huxley.

BL: PP.6145.bfa
CUL: T980.B.1

62 **The European Quarterly** / edited by Edwin Muir and Janko Lavrin. London: Stanley Nott, Vol. 1 no. 1 (May 1934)–no. 4 (Feb. 1935)

Index: Bloomfield
Profiled in: Hoffman, Allen & Ulrich, Sullivan 1914–1984
Reprint: Nendeln, Liechtenstien: Kraus Reprint, 1973.

This eclectic cultural review, edited by the poet and critic Edwin Muir and the Russian academic Janko Lavrin, published early translations of work by Otokar Březina, Lorca, Kafka, Blok, Tadeusz Micinski, and Kierkegaard. George Barker, David Gascoyne and C. M. Grieve (i.e. 'Hugh MacDiarmid') also appeared, as did various essays on the politics and culture of Europe.

BL: PP.5939.bgi
CUL: L700.C.24
NLS: U.445
TCD: 93.s.29

63 **The Exile** / edited by Ezra Pound. Dijon; Chicago: M. Darantiere, No. 1 (Spring 1927)–4 (Autumn 1928)

Index: Sader
Profiled in: Hoffman, Allen & Ulrich
Reprint: New York: Johnson Reprints, 1967
BL: No. 1 (Spring 1927) and 2 (Autumn 1927) only. (PP.6264.lc.)
CUL: Q718.D.8
TCD: No. 2 (Autumn 1927) (122.u.214)
UCL: Johnson Reprints facsimile

64 **Experiment** / edited by William Empson; Jacob Bronowski, Hugh Sykes, and Humphrey Jennings. Cambridge: [Trinity College], No. 1 (Nov. 1928)–7 (Spring 1931)

Note: Editors and imprints varied over the period of the magazine
Index: Bloomfield (no.5–7 only). Each issue had its own index.

Profiled in: Hoffman, Allen & Ulrich, Sullivan 1914–1984, Tolley 1930s; Jason Harding, "Experiment in Cambridge: 'A Manifesto of Young England'"in *Cambridge Quarterly* 27 (1998), 287–309, BL: P.901/34; Kate Price, "Finite but unbounded: *Experiment* magazine, Cambridge, England, 1928–1931"in *Jacket* 20 (Dec. 2002), www.jacketmagazine.com/20/price-expe.html
Related Work: Samuel Putnam, Maida Castelhun Darnton, George Reavey and J. Bronowski (eds.) *The European Caravan: an anthology of the new spirit in European literature. Part I. France, Spain, England and Ireland* (New York: Brewer, Warren & Putnam, 1931). No more published. BL: X.989/30707.
Microfilm: La Cross, Wis.: Brookhaven Press, [undated]

As well as his poetry, chapters from Empson's *Seven Types of Ambiguity*, first appeared in *Experiment*. The other editors also contributed their own poetry; other poets included T. H. White, Kathleen Raine, George Reavey, J. M. Reeves, and Conrad Aiken.

BL: P.P.6119.crb.
CUL: CAM.C.31.56
NLS: Lacking no. 7. (Q.110)
UCL: 1–5

65 **The Eye.** London: Martin Lawrence Gazette, No.1 (Sept.1935)–[9] (Spring 1938)

Index: Bloomfield (No.1–9 only)
BL: Newspaper Collections

66 **Fanfare: a musical causerie** / edited by Leigh Henry. London: [Fanfare], Vol. 1 no. 1 (Oct. 1921)–7 (Jan. 1922)

Note: Absorbed by *Musical Mirror*
Profiled in: Hoffman, Allen & Ulrich

Although dedicated to understanding and advocating new music, included poems by Richard Aldington, John Gould Fletcher, Jean Cocteau, John Rodker and others.

BL: P.P.1947.ibb.
CUL: L409.B.20
TCD: 106.a.83, nos.19–25

67 **Fanfreluche: a miscellany.** Cambridge: Loft Press, No. 1 (1924)–2 (1925)

CUL: CAM.C.31.45
NLS: No. 2 only. (1925.11)

68 Farrago / edited by Peter Burra. Oxford: Simon Nowell Smith, [Vol. 1] no. 1 (Feb. 1930)–vol. 1 no. 6 (June 1931)

Index: With Vol. 1. Also, Bloomfield
Profiled in: Hoffman, Allen & Ulrich

General literary review. Includes poems by Goronwy Rees, Randall Swingler, Evelyn Waugh, and Cecil Day Lewis. Other contributors include John Sparrow and R. H. S. Crossman.

BL: P.P.6117.in.
CUL: No. 1–2. (T727.C.41)
NLS: Q.126
TCD: No. 1–2. (78.dd.109)
UCL

69 The Fig Tree: a Douglas Social Credit quarterly review / edited by C. H. Douglas. London: Social Credit Secretariat Ltd, No. 1 (1936)–12 (1939); New Series, Belfast: K.R. P. Publications Ltd, Vol. 1 no. 1 (June 1954)–no. 4 (Mar. 1955)

Contributors to the first series included Eric Gill, Stella Gibbons, Ruth Pitter, and Ezra Pound. The new series, which was edited anonymously (and not by the late C. H. Douglas), was barely literary at all.

BL: P.P.3611.abs.
CUL: L223.C.82
NLS: First series. (Y.186.). New Series (1961.10.)
TCD: First series. (99.p.25, 26)
UCL: First series, no. 5–8.

70 The Flying Horse / edited by T. W. H. Crosland; then W. Sorley Brown. London: W. T. Searle at the First Edition Bookshop, No. 1 (Oct 1923)–4 (July 1924); New series: Vol. 1 no. 1 (Mar. 1927)– [Vol. 4], no. 17 (Feb. 1931)

Part little magazine, part bookseller's catalogue, with poems, aphorisms, comment on contemporary poetry and, for some reason, anti-Scottish polemic. Walter de la Mare contributes one poem. The first series was edited by Crosland; the new series, following Crosland's death in 1925, was edited by W. Sorley Brown from a Galashiels address and devoted to Crosland's life and works. The National Library of Scotland's catalogue suggests the new series ran to 1931, but no locations have been found for the later issues.

BL: No. 1 (Oct 1923)–no. 4 (July 1924); New series: Vol. 1 no. 1 (Mar. 1927)–no. 2 (Apr. 1927). (P.P.5938.bda.)
CUL: No. 1 (Oct 1923)–no. 3 (Mar. 1924). (L727.B.4.)
NLS: No. 1 (Oct 1923)–no. 4 (July 1924); New series: Vol. 1 no. 1 (Mar. 1927)–no. 2 (Apr. 1927). (Q.83.)
TCD: No. 1 (Oct 1923)–no. 3 (Mar. 1924); New series: Vol. 1 no. 2 (Apr.1927). (106.a.82, nos.14–17)

71 Focus / [edited by Robert Graves and Laura Riding]. [Majorca]: [Robert Graves and Laura Riding], No. 1 (January 1935)–4 (Summer 1935).

Note: No imprint or editor details are given.

Mostly journal-like pieces by various writers living on Majorca. Includes contributions by Robert Graves and Laura Riding, including one long collaborative poem, 'Majorcan Letter, 1935' (No. 4).

BL: Cup.503.k.23

72 Fords & Bridges: an Oxford and Cambridge magazine. Oxford: [Fords & Bridges], Vol. 1. no.1 (Feb. 1936)–vol. 5 no. 2. (May 1939)

Note: Vol. 2 and vol. 4 each consists of only one number
Index: Bloomfield

BL: P.P.6118.hi.
CUL: CAM.B.41.20
NLS: U.399

73 Form / edited by Austin O. Spare; W. H. Davies. London: John Lane, Vol. 1 no. 1 (Apr. 1916)–no 2 (Apr. 1917). New series: Vol. 1 no. 1 (Oct. 1921)–no. 3 (Jan. 1922)

Note: Subtitle and imprint varies. First series: 'a quarterly of the arts'. New series, published by Morland Press, 'a monthly magazine containing poetry, sketches, essays of literary and critical interest' and 'a monthly magazine of the arts'.
Index: Sader
Profiled in: Hoffman, Allen & Ulrich
Reprint: New York: Kraus, [undated].

Austin O. Spare edited the first series, but was joined by W. H. Davies for the new series. A large format magazine with many bold illustrations. Contributors included Yeats, Laurence Housman, Edward Eastaway (i.e. Thomas), Frank Brangwyn, and others.

BL: First series (1899.r.6.). New series (PP.5938.dh)
CUL: T727.A.11
NLS: First series only. (7.11.)

74 **The Forum** / edited by C. F. Holland and W. R. Marshall. London: W. R. Marshall, No. 1 (Nov. 1921)–9/10 (Aug. 1922)

BL: PP.5841.db
TCD: PER 81–129

75 **Forum.** Walthamstow: Academy of Poetry, Nov.–Dec. 1938

BL: Destroyed in the Second World War. (P.P.5126.gbi.)

76 **The Free Critic: literature, art, music, drama.** London: Vol. 1 no. 1 (Mar. 1928)–vol. 2 no. 2 (Apr. 1929)

Note: Variant title: *The Critic*

CUL: L727.B.13
TCD: Vol.1 no.1–vol.2 no.1 (Mar. 1929). (38.a.138, nos. 4–16)

77 **The Free Man** / Robin Black. Edinburgh: Scots Free Press, Vol. 1 no. 1 (6th Feb. 1932)–vol. 3 no. 14 (5th May 1934). Then, as *New Scotland (Alba Nuadh)*, Vol. 1 no. 1 (12th Oct. 1935)–nos. 29/30 (June/July 1936). Then, as *The Free Man*, 1936–1947

Related Imprint: Free Man Pamphlet

Contributors to this weekly included several modern Scottish Renaissance writers including Hugh MacDiarmid (under his real name, C. M. Grieve), Robert Garioch, and William Soutar, as well as the novelists Neil M. Gunn and Lewis Grassic Gibbon. Catherine Kerrigan states in Sullivan 1914–1984 that the last series of *The Free Man* ran from 1936 to 1937, but no location has yet been found for this.

NLS: First series. (Q.48.) *New Scotland* (7.110)

The Freewoman *See* The Egoist A55

Gathered Leaves *see* Poesy: a magazine for the lover of the Muses A168

78 **Germinal** / edited by E[stelle] S[ylvia] P[ankhurst]. London: [Estelle Sylvia Pankhurst], Vol. 1 no. 1 (July 1923)–no. 2 [1924]

Profiled in: Hoffman, Allen & Ulrich
Related Imprint: Advertised in and allied to Pankhurst's newspaper *The Dreadnought*

Fiction, poems, and reviews. Included a number of translations from Russian authors, including Alexander Blok and Anna Akmatova. The editor is not identified, except by the initials E.S.P.; Sylvia Pankhurst also contributes her own poems. Illustrated, including portraits of George Bernard Shaw, Upton Sinclair and Rabindranath Tagore.

BL: P.P.6018.oac
NLS: 5.491
TCD: 38.a.138, nos.23, 24

79 **The Golden Bowl: a magazine of life, art, and thought** / edited by E. A. Hay and J. Selwyn Dunn. Guildford: Golden Bowl Hand Press, [No. 1, Sept. 1927]–7 (Winter 1932–3)

A conservative and even anti-modernist magazine which used an Arts & Crafts aesthetic invoking rural values. Woodcuts reinforce the effect. John Drinkwater contributes a poem in the third issue.

BL: PP.6036.dc.
CUL: 2–7. (L727.B.7)
NLS: 5–7 (5.526)
TCD: 5–7 (PER 90–565)

80 **The Golden Hind: quarterly magazine of art and literature** / edited by Clifford Bax and Austin O. Spare. London: Chapman and Hall, Vol. 1 no. 1 (Oct. 1922)–vol. 2 no. 8 (July 1924)

Profiled in: Hoffman, Allen & Ulrich; Stanton; Sullivan 1914–1984
Reprint: Nendeln, Liechtenstein: Kraus Reprint, [undated]; Delmar, N.Y.: Scholars' Facsimiles, [undated].

Attractively illustrated review. Includes poems by F. S. Flint, W. H. Davies, and Laurence Housman. Ford Madox Ford contributes "A Third Rate Poet".

BL: L.R.300.bb.23
CUL: T727.A.16
NLS: X.210.a
TCD: Vol. 1. (24.cc.14). Vol. 2 (98.b.20)

81 Good Cheer / edited by Stan A. Andrews and William F. Gibbons. London: Stan A. Andrews and William F. Gibbons; printed by L. Warner (Hinckley), Vol. 1 no. 1 (Apr. 1938)

General review, with poems, non-fiction (a profile of Albert Schweitzer), jokes, and fiction. The tone is good-humoured and rather genteel. All contributors are anonymous.

BL: P.P.5938.bbh

82 Good Speech: quarterly bulletin of the Verse Speaking Fellowship. London: No. 11 (Apr. 1931)–49 (July/Aug. 1940)

Note: Continued: *The Speaking of Poetry*. Subsequently incorporated in *Speech News*, out of scope for this bibliography

BL: P.P.5126.eb

83 The Granta. Cambridge, then London: Vol. 1 no. 1 (18th Jan. 1889)–[vol. 78, 1973?]. New series, vol. 1 no. 1 (Spring 1979)– . ISSN: 0017-3231

Note: Most issues in the old series were also given an individual issue number.
Profiled in: Sullivan 1837–1913
Related Imprint: Granta

A magazine which began as a student magazine in a light, humorous vein, with a more literary character largely emerging only after the Second World War. The relaunch as simply *Granta* in 1980 seems to have been followed by capitalisation of the brand by Penguin. Although *Granta* had published Cambridge students such as Ted Hughes in the post-war years especially, under Penguin the Granta imprint became a publisher of novels and non-fiction as well as a magazine of relatively high production values focused on prose.

BL: Vol. 1 no. 1–vol. 75 no.5. Lacking no. 1206. (PP.6058.I). New series. Lacking no. 44 and 46/48. (P.901/3462)
CUL: CAM.B.41.16
NLS: Vol. 1 no. 1–[vol. 78, 1973?]. Lacking 1235–1242 and Apr. 1957. (Q.34 SER). New Series: 1–13, 15– . (HJ2.200 SER)
TCD: Vol. 36 no.807 (1927)–Nov. (1973). New Series. (PER 82–209)
UCL: New Series: 1–28.

84 Group Theatre Paper. London: No.1 (1936)–7 (1937)

Index: Bloomfield

CUL: No. 1. (L999.C.3.622)

85 The Gypsy. London: Pomegranate Press then the Gypsy Press, No. 1 (May 1915)–no. 2 (May 1916)

Profiled in: Hoffman, Allen & Ulrich

General literary review, which included poems by Walter de la Mare, Herbert Shaw, Henry Savage, Arthur Symons and others. No editor stated. Impressively illustrated throughout by Allan Odle.

BL: P.P.5938.dg.
CUL: T727.B.1
NLS: Vol. 1, no. 1 (3rd ed.) (May 1915). (S.297.c.)
TCD: 106.a.83, nos. 2, 3

86 The Hamyarde / edited by Anthony Praga. London: The Ham Bone Club, Vol. 1 no. 1 (Oct 1922)– vol. 1 no. 2 (Nov. 1922)

Humorous and satirical, with short articles, poems and aphorisms.

BL: P.P.5793.bl

87 The Heaton Review. Bradford: Percy Lund Humphries, Vol. 1. (1927)–7 (1934)

Index: Bloomfield (Vol.4–7 only)

A general illustrated review with high production values, with a focus on Heaton, Bradford and Yorkshire, but not exclusively so. Poems appear only occasionally. Contributors include J. B. Priestley, C. Lovat Fraser, Laurence Binyon, John Galsworthy, Herbert Read, and others.

BL: P.P.6080.ff.
CUL: L900.B.136
TCD: 38.a.136, Nos.1–7

88 Hillmn / edited by Ernest Collings and Vera Mellor. London: [Ernest Collings], No. 1 (July 1920)–5 (July 1921)

Note: The pagination is continued across the whole run; the whole totalling 39 numbered pages

Collings and Mellor were the sole contributors to this small, slim little magazine, characterised by black and white line drawings by Collings in an Art Nouveau style. Both contributed prose pieces and poems. "Material for a bibliography of modern foreign art" was serialised across the five issues. The meaning of the title is not explained, but it is not a misprint.

BL: P.P.5938.bal.
CUL: L727.D.21
TCD: 37.rr.200, Nos.21–25

89 The Hydra: journal of the Craiglockhart War Hospital / [edited by Wilfred Owen and others]. Edinburgh: Craiglockhart War Hospital, No. 1 (28 April 1917)–12 (29 Sept. 1917). Then, New Series, edited by J. B. Salmond. No. 1 (Nov. 1917)–9 (July 1918)

Website: http://www.hcu.ox.ac.uk/jtap/hydra/

The magazine of military patients convalescing at Craiglockhart. Owen edited six issues from August 1917, publishing two poems of his own (the first poems he ever published), as well as work by his mentor Siegfried Sassoon. J. B. Salmond would go on to edit the popular *Scots Magazine* between the wars, perhaps its most creative period (out of scope for this bibliography). *The Hydra* is extremely rare: the Owen Collection at the English Faculty Library, Oxford University, is the only known location in Britain. Columbia University Libraries have two issues, namely no. 10 (Sept. 1, 1917) and no. 11 (Sept 15, 1917), which were Sassoon's own copies. No. 10 includes Owen's first printed poem, "Song of songs", published anonymously.

Oxford University, English Faculty Library: First Series. Lacking New Series Feb-April 1918

Imagist Anthology See [The Imagist Anthologies] A90

90 [The Imagist Anthologies]

Ezra Pound, (ed.), *Des Imagistes: an anthology* (London: Poetry Bookshop; New York: Albert & Charles Boni, 1914), BL: Cup.503.a.12.; *Some Imagist Poets. An annual anthology* (London: Constable, 1915, 1916), BL: 12200.d.10/5.; *Some Imagist Poets* (Boston: Houghton Mifflin, 1917); BL: RF.2001.a.42; *Imagist Anthology* (London: Chatto & Windus, 1930), BL: 011644.g.148.
Anthology: Peter Jones (ed.) *Imagist Poetry* (Harmondsworth: Penguin, 1972), BL: X.907/12006; *La Parola e l'immagine. Antologia dei poeti imagisti da Ezra Pound a Amy Lowell.* [With parallel texts of the poems in English and

Italian.] (Milano: Mursia, 1968), BL: X.909/16552.
Bibliography: J. Howard Woolmer, *A Catalogue of the Imagist Poets.* With essays e.g. by Wallace Martin (New York: J. Howard Woolmer, 1966), BL: X.900/11386.
Exhibition Catalogue: *The Glenn Hughes Drama and Imagist Poetry Collection.* [Austin: University of Texas at Austin, Humanities Research Center] 1959. BL: X.900/10318.

Study: Ruggero Bianchi, *La Poetica dell'Imagismo* (Milano: Mursia, 1965), BL: X.908/14397

S. K. Coffman, *Imagism: a chapter for the history of modern poetry* (Norman: University of Oklahoma Press, [1951]), BL: 11870.e.25

John T. Gage, *In the Arresting Eye: the rhetoric of Imagism* (Baton Rouge: Louisiana State University Press, 1981), BL: X.520/25447

Jean Gould, *Amy: the world of Amy Lowell and the Imagist movement* (New York: Dodd, Mead, 1975), BL: X.950/6856

J. B. Harmer, *Victory in Limbo: Imagism, 1908–1917* (London: Secker and Warburg, 1975), BL: X.981/9972

Guiyou Huang, *Whitmanism, Imagism, and modernism in China and America* (Selingsgrove [Pa.]: Susquehanna University Press, 1997), BL: 98/07048

Glenn Hughes, *Imagism and the Imagists. A study in modern poetry* (London: Oxford University Press, 1931), BL: 11822.r.9

Tracey Elaine Jackson, *Imagist Poetry: a survey and reassessment.* Doctoral Thesis. (University of Ulster, 1997), BL: DX209343

William Pratt (ed.), *The Imagist Poem: modern poetry in miniature* (New York: Dutton, [1963]), BL: X.908/16041

William Pratt and Robert Richardson (eds.), *Homage to Imagism* (New York: AMS Press, 1992), BL: YC.1993.b.6984

A. D. Robinson, *The Transition from Symbolism to Imagism 1885–1914, with particular reference to the perceptual relationship between poet and external world.* Doctoral thesis. (University of Oxford, 1982), BL: D69219/86

Andrew John Thacker, *Language and Reification in Imagist Poetics 1909–1930.* Doctoral thesis. University of Southampton, 1990. BL: DX172132

Daniel Tiffany, *Radio Corpse: Imagism and the cryptaesthetic of Ezra Pound* (Cambridge, MA: Harvard University Press, 1995), BL: YC.1996.b.4006

Ming Xie, *Ezra Pound and the Appropriation of Chinese Poetry: Cathay, translation, and Imagism* (New York: Garland, 1999), BL: YC.1999.a.1323

The Imagists' work emphasised the factual, the visual, the spoken and a search for new rhythms. Their poetry was supported in Britain in magazines such as *Coterie* and *The*

Egoist, Poetry and Drama and its successor *The Monthly Chapbook*; in America, Harriet Monroe's *Poetry* (Chicago) published many of the poems that would go into the first anthology, and Amy Lowell and H.D. were key to the wider audience Imagism would soon have. Imagism asserted itself through a number of anthologies which in a way operated as an occasional magazine. *Des Imagistes* contained work by Richard Aldington, H. D., F. S. Flint, Skipwith Cannell, Amy Lowell, William Carlos Williams, James Joyce, Ezra Pound, Ford Madox Hueffer, Allen Upward, and John Cournos. *Some Imagist Poets* had six contributors: Richard Aldington, H. D., John Gould Fletcher, F. S. Flint, D. H. Lawrence, and Amy Lowell. The last volume, *Imagist Anthology* (1930), contains work by Aldington, Cournos, H. D., Fletcher, Flint, Madox Ford, Joyce, Lawrence and Williams. The Imagists formed one of the key movements in English language modernism.

BL: *Des Imagistes*, 1914 (Cup.503.a.12.); *Some Imagist Poets*, 1915, 1916 (12200.d.10/5.) *Some Imagist Poets*, 1917 (RF.2001.a.42); *Imagist Anthology*, 1930 (011644.g.148.)
CUL: *Some Imagist Poets*, 1916, 1917 (Q718.d.) *Imagist Anthology*, 1930 (9720.d.372)
NLS: *Des Imagistes*, 1914 (T.17.a.); *Some Imagist Poets*, 1915, 1916 (T.19.b.), *Imagist Anthology*, 1930 (T.27.d.). Lacking *Some Imagist Poets*, 1917.
TCD: *Imagist Anthology*, 1930 (125.g.115)
UCL: *Some Imagist Poets*, 1916

Des Imagistes *See* [The Imagist Anthologies] A90

91 Inisfáil: published to maintain a sympathetic contact between Irishmen living abroad. Dublin: Hibernian Bank Chambers, [1] (Mar. 1933)

Profiled in: Tom Clyde, *Irish Literary Magazines: an outline and descriptive bibliography* (Dublin: Irish Academic Press, 2003), BL: 2725.g.3414

Linen Hall Library, Belfast

92 Inisfáil: a quarterly magazine / edited by Mary Kavanagh [i.e. Margaret Spain]. Dublin: Inisfáil, [Vol.1] no. 1 (Dec./Jan./Feb. 1930/31)–vol. 1 no. 2 (Mar./Apr./May 1931)

Profiled in: Tom Clyde, *Irish Literary Magazines: an outline and descriptive bibliography* (Dublin: Irish Academic Press, 2003), BL: 2725.g.3414

Appears to be all work by the Spain sisters, sometimes

under pseudonyms: poems, drama, short stories, travelogue, essays, and translations of Heinrich Heine.

National Library of Ireland: IR 05 i 24

93 International Surrealist Bulletin. (Bulletin internationale du surréalisme) Prague, then London: No.1 (Avril 1935)–?

Note: No. 4 (Sept. 1936) was issued by the Surrealist Group in England

Related Works: *The International Surrealist Exhibition*. London: New Burlington Galleries, 1936. Catalogue to accompany the International Surrealist Exhibition of 1936. BL: YA.1995.b.6003; Hugh Sykes Davies... [et al.] *Declaration on Spain*. [London]: [The Surrealist Group in England], [1936], BL: HS.74.1056/70. Issued with no. 4, with *Contemporary Poetry and Prose* (no. 7, Nov. 1936), and probably in its own right. The declaration exhorts the British Government to stop supporting, by default, the fascists in Spain.

BL: [1]; 4 (P.423/60)
UCL: 4

94 Ireland To-day / [edited by Michael O'Donovan, i.e. Frank O'Connor]. Dublin: Ireland Today, Vol. 1 no. 1 (June 1936)–vol. 3 no. 3 (Mar. 1938)

Index: An index of Vol. 1 and 2 accompanied vol. 2; Hayes
Profiled in: Princess Grace Irish Library Electronic Irish Records Dataset, www.pgil-eirdata.org; Tom Clyde, *Irish Literary Magazines: an outline and descriptive bibliography* (Dublin: Irish Academic Press, 2003), BL: 2725.g.3414; Brian P. Kennedy, "Ireland To-Day: a brave Irish periodical" in *Linen Hall Review*, Vol. 5 no. 4 (Winter 1988), pp.18–19, BL: P.803/1502
Reprint: New York: Kraus Reprint, 1971

Describing itself on its sub-title banner as "social, national, economic, cultural" this was a well-produced physically and intellectually substantial magazine that tried to continue the forum for different voices and points of view that *The Irish Statesman* had attempted. It was edited anonymously. The reference to "The Editors", was to the named editors of the different sections – Art, Music, Theatre, Film, and Books – but the overall editor appears to have been Frank O'Connor alone. Contributors included Brian Coffey, Daniel Corkery, Denis Devlin, C. Ewart Milne, Sean O'Faolain, Liam O'Flaherty, Patrick Kavanagh, Maud Gonne MacBride and others. Vol. 1 no. 4 (Sept. 1936) contained a symposium on Spain, and the Spanish Civil

War was often in the magazine's pages. The correspondence could be weighty, e.g. Father Victor White and Eric Gill debate the nature of modernity and industrialisation in the letter pages of 1937, and Gill takes up the theme in his essay in the last issue, "Is there a Papal social programme?" The magazine was compelled to close following right-wing Catholic objections to, for example, its coverage of the Spanish Civil War.

BL: Lacking the index. (PP.6189.E)
CUL: Q488.C.3
NLS: P.211
TCD: 92.p.71–74
Linen Hall Library, Belfast
Queen's University Belfast

95 The Irish Commonwealth: a monthly review of social affairs, politics and literature / edited by A. de Blácam. Dublin: Irish-Ireland Publishing Company, Vol. 1. no. 1 (Mar. 1919)–no. 3 (May 1919)

Index: Hayes
Profiled in: Tom Clyde, *Irish Literary Magazines: an outline and descriptive bibliography* (Dublin: Irish Academic Press, 2003), BL: 2725.g.3414

A general cultural review, which also published some poems, some in Irish. Contributors included F. R. Higgins, and Daniel Corkery on 'The Despised Aisling'.

BL: P.P.6158.dc
National Library of Ireland: Ir 8205 i 1

96 The Irish Review: a monthly magazine of Irish literature, art & science / edited by David Houston; then Padraic Colum; then Joseph Plunkett. Dublin: Irish Review Publishing Company), Vol. 1 no. 1 (Mar. 1911)–vol. 4 no. 41 (Nov.1914)

Index: M. Griffin, *Index to The Irish Review* (Dublin: Fellowship of the Library Association, n.d.); Hayes; Rudi Holzapfel, *Author Index 3* (Blackrock: Carraig Books, 1985)
Profiled in: Tom Clyde, *Irish Literary Magazines: an outline and descriptive bibliography* (Dublin: Irish Academic Press, 2003), BL: 2725.g.3414

Wide-ranging articles, reproductions of work by John B. Yeats and Jack B. Yeats, short stories by George Moore and James Stephens, and poems by Emily Lawless, Daniel Corkery, Patrick Pearse, Thomas MacDonagh, A.E., and W. B. Yeats, and many others besides. A manifesto for the Irish

Volunteers appeared in the June 1914 issue. Several contributors to the generally stolid cultural nationalism of *The Irish Review* were soon to risk and lose their lives as participants in the Easter Rising in Dublin in 1916.

BL: PP.6158.ea
CUL: Q900.C.79
NLS: U.459
TCD: OLS 186.n.52–55

97 The Irish Statesman / edited by G. W. Russell. Dublin: Irish Statesman Publishing Company, Vol. 1 (1919)–vol. 2 (19th June 1920). Then New Series, Vol. 1 no. 1 (15th Sept. 1923)–vol. 14 no. 6 (12th Apr.1930)

Note: Second series absorbed *Irish Homestead*, out of scope for this bibliography
Index: Edward Doyle Smith, *A Survey and Index of the 'Irish Statesman' (1923–1930)* (Ann Arbor, Mich.: University Microfilms International, 1966). A Ph.D thesis from the University of Washington D.C.
Profiled in: Tom Clyde, *Irish Literary Magazines: an outline and descriptive bibliography* (Dublin: Irish Academic Press, 2003), BL: 2725.g.3414; Princess Grace Irish Library Electronic Irish Records Dataset, www.pgil-eirdata.org
Microfilm: [Dublin]: Irish Microforms Ltd., [undated]

With Co-Operative links, this newspaper had a professional editorial team and some financial security: it was more literary than little, and in fact more broadly cultural than literary; it was determined to represent a wide range of views concerning Ireland and other topics of concern. Its contributors included George Bernard Shaw, James Stephens, and Sean O'Faolain, as well as George Russell himself ("A.E."), who contributed many of the articles, often under any of several pseudonyms. Other items of interest include a very early poem by Patrick Kavanagh. Closed following an inconclusive but expensive libel action.

BL: First Series, 28th June 1919–19th June 1920. New Series. (Newspaper Collections)
NLS: New Series, Vol. 7 no. 18 (8th Jan. 1927); vol. 8 no. 1 (12th Mar. 1927). (6.1822)
TCD: PER 80–410

98 The Irish Tribune: a weekly review of affairs. Cork: Vol. 1 no. 1 (March 1926)–vol. 2 no. 43 (Dec. 1926)

Note: Vol. 1 no. 1–no. 4 were published as *The Tribune*

Noted in Princess Grace Irish Library Electronic Irish Records Dataset, www.pgil-eirdata.org. Important forum for Daniel Corkery and his literary and historical ideas concerning Irish culture.

TCD: 138.a.31

99 The Island / edited by Josef Bard. London: Favil Press, Vol. 1 no. 1 (June 1931)–no. 4 (Dec. 1931)

Index: Bloomfield
Profiled in: Hoffman, Allen & Ulrich

Illustrated journal of "The Islanders", a group of artists and authors, according to the editorial in the first issue, "united from the outset in a strong desire to stand together and to offer a joint resistance to commercialised art." Contributors include Leon Underwood, Laurence Josephs, Henry Moore, Blair Hughes-Stanton, Thelma Spear, Grace E. Rogers, Eileen Agar, Catherine Carswell, Gertrude Hermes, Muriel Stuart, Naomi Mitchison, John Gould Fletcher, C. R. W. Nevinson, and Mahatma Gandhi.

BL: P.P.5938.dk.
CUL: L727.B.6
NLS: 6.164

100 Janus / edited by Reginald Hutchings and John Royston Morley; then John Mair and John Royston Morley. London: [John Mair and John Royston Morley], distributed by Holborn Publishing and Distribution, No. 1 (Jan. 1936)–[2] (May 1936)

Poems, short stories, drawings, articles and reviews. Contributors included Oswell Blakeston, A. E. Coppard, John Pudney, David Gascoyne, Ezra Pound (an extract of a letter to the magazine), James Hanley, Dylan Thomas, W. H. Auden (on poetry and film), Gertrude Stein, and the editors.

BL: P.P.5939.bei
NLS: 5.889
UCL: [2] (May 1936) only

101 The Jongleur: a quarterly sheaf of verses / edited by Alberta Vickridge. Frizinghall, Bradford: [Alberta Vickridge], No. 1 (Spring 1927)–Autumn/Winter 1955

Note: The numbering jumps in 1937 from no.42 to no.63, because of a mistake in the roman numerals. It is later discontinued altogether. The last issue, Autumn/Winter 1955, appeared in February 1956
Index: Bloomfield (No.13 (1930)–71 (1939) only)

Profiled in: Hoffman, Allen & Ulrich; Stanton
Related Imprint: Jongleur Press

Contributors included Wilfred Childe and Dorothy Una Ratcliffe.

BL: No. 2 (Summer 1927)–Autumn/Winter 1955. (P.P.5126.bba.)
CUL: L727.C.88
NLS: Y.148.
TCD: No.1–Autumn/Winter 1954 (E.Attic V.550–555)

102 Kingdom Come: the magazine of war-time Oxford / edited by John Waller and Kenneth Harris, and, subsequently, Miles Vaughan Williams, Mildred Clinkard, Alan Rook, Stefan Schimanski, and Henry Treece. Oxford: Vol. 1 no. 1 (Autumn 1939)–vol. 3 no.12 (Autumn 1943)

Note: Subtitle varies. Editors and imprints varied. Absorbed *Bolero* in Spring 1940 and *Light and Dark* in Summer 1940
Index: Bloomfield (Vol. 1 no. 1 only)
Profiled in: Hoffman, Allen & Ulrich, Sullivan 1914–1984, Tolley 1940s
Anthology: Stefan Schimanski and Henry Treece (eds.) *War Time Harvest: An Anthology of Poetry and Prose from the Magazine 'Kingdom Come'* (London: Bale & Staples, 1943), BL: 012208.dd.2/7

Poets included Keith Douglas, Anne Ridler, Norman Nicholson, Herbert Read, Edmund Blunden, Lawrence Durrell, Roy Fuller, David Gascoyne, Norman MacCaig, Ruth Pitter, Hugh MacDiarmid, and – in G. S. Fraser's translation – André Breton, Paul Eluard and Giorgio de Chiroco. When Alan Rook, Stefan Schimanski, and Henry Treece became the new co-editors in Autumn 1941, they championed poets associated with 'New Apocalyptic' poetry, such as J. F. Hendry.

BL: P.P.6118.hk.
CUL: L900.B.171
NLS: Y.147
TCD: Vol.1 no.1–vol.2 no.4. (26.bb.229, Nos.11–18). Vol.3 nos.9–12. (133.n.114)

103 The Klaxon / edited by Lawrence K. Emery [i.e. A. J. Leventhal]. Dublin: [The Klaxon], Winter 1923/4

Profiled in: Princess Grace Irish Library Electronic Irish Records Dataset, www.pgil-eirdata.org; Tom Clyde, *Irish Literary Magazines: an outline and descriptive bibliography*

(Dublin: Irish Academic Press, 2003), BL: 2725.g.3414
Related Work: Patricia Coughlan and Alex Davis (eds.),
Modernism and Ireland: The Poetry of the 1930s (Cork: Cork
University Press, 1995), BL: YC.1997.a.299.

The Futurist, noisy title suggests an engagement with
modernity, and *Blast* seems to have influenced it a great
deal. There is a sympathetic article on *Ulysses* by Laurence
K. Emery [i.e. A. J. Leventhal], an article by Thomas
McGreevy on "Picasso, Mamie [i.e. Mainie] Jellett and
Dublin criticism", and a prose poem by John W. Blaine, but
the other poetry seems to look back not forward, e.g. work
by F. R. Higgins and a translation of Brian Merriman with a
number of archaisms. Advertisements for products such as
Gibsol, The Supreme Skin Ointment, and the fact that
printers had refused to publish the issue of *The Dublin
Magazine* which was originally to carry Leventhal's review of
Joyce, suggest that squaring artistic ambition with
commercial requirements and the wider cultural
environment in Ireland was not going to be easy. Only one
number was issued.

BL: P.P.4881.tc.
CUL: T727.b.81
TCD: OLS JOH 138 no.13

104 Laughing Horse: a magazine of satire from the Pacific slope / edited by Roy E. Chanslor and James T. Van Rensselaer Jr., then also with Willard Johnson. Berkeley, California: [No. 1, Apr. 1922]–no.21 (Dec. 1939)

Note: Later published from other locations, including
Santa Fe, New Mexico
Profiled in: Hoffman, Allen & Ulrich

Includes contributions by and about D. H. Lawrence. April
1926 was a special Lawrence issue.

CUL: L999.C.3.901

105 Leaves – 'Billeoga': Irish-Ireland monthly. Dublin: Leaves, Vol. 1 no. 1 (Jan. 1938)–no. 3 (Michaelmas 1938)

Profiled in: Tom Clyde, *Irish Literary Magazines: an outline and
descriptive bibliography* (Dublin: Irish Academic Press, 2003),
BL: 2725.g.3414

Republican political magazine, edited anonymously.

BL: P.P.6189.f.
National Library of Ireland: Vol. 1 no. 2 (Feb. 1938)

106 The Left Review / edited by Montagu Slater, Amabel Williams-Ellis, and T. H. Wintringham; joined by Alick West; then Edgell Rickword only; then Randall Swingler only. London: c/o Collett's Bookshop, Vol. 1 no. 1 (Oct. 1934)–vol. 3 no. 16. (May 1938)

Note: Continues *Viewpoint*
Index: Bloomfield
Profiled in: Hoffman, Allen & Ulrich; Stanton; Sullivan
1914–1984; Tolley 1930s
Reprint: London: Frank Cass, 1968. BL: P.701/196.

For a cultural review, this published a surprisingly high
number of poets, including Auden, Spender, C. Day Lewis,
Lorca, Neruda, and Mayakovsky. Vol. 2 no. 10 contained a
special supplement on Surrealist art. Vol. 2 no. 14 was a
special Scottish issue.

BL: P.P.5938.baw
CUL: Q231.C.15
UCL

107 Life and Letters. London and Manchester: Percy Brothers, Vol. 1 no. 1 (Nov. 1923)–vol. 2 no. 10 (Aug. 1924)

Note: Absorbed *To Day*

A general literary review, with only a few poems per issue.
Contributors included: Cecil Day Lewis, William K.
Seymour, W. H. Davies, Arthur Symons, and Ford Madox
Ford (the latter, a long letter of advice on writing). Not to
be confused with the long-running journal that began in
1928.

BL: P.P.5939.bge
CUL: L727.C.11
TCD: 96.b.27

108 Life and Letters / edited by Desmond McCarthy, then Hamish Miles, R. Ellis Roberts, Robert Herring and Petrie Townshend. London: Vol. 1 no. 1 (June 1928)–vol. 65 no. 154 (June 1950)

Note: Imprints varied. Suspended publication from May to
August 1935. Vols. 1–12 were also numbered 1–64; vols.
13–65 were also numbered 1–154. Absorbed *The London
Mercury* in May 1939. Title variants: *Life and Letters Today*
(Sept. 1935–June 1945), and *Life and Letters and the London
Mercury and Bookman* (July 1945–Jan. 1946)
Index: Sader
Profiled in: Hoffman, Allen & Ulrich; Stanton; Sullivan

1914–1984; Tolley 1930s; Tolley 1940s
Related Work: *The Days of Mars: a memoir, 1940–1946* by Bryher (i.e. Annie Winifred Ellerman), London: Calder and Boyars, 1977 (BL: X.808/8275) recounts some of Ellerman's experiences as a backer of *Life and Letters*

Not a true little magazine, in that it was published on a commercial footing, but a significant literary journal, particularly strong in the early years on Bloomsbury authors, and then, in the 1930s, on the poets of 'the Auden generation'; Vernon Watkins was also published here. The editors served in the following periods: Desmond McCarthy, 1928–34; Hamish Miles, 1934; R Ellis Roberts, 1934–35; Robert Herring and Petrie Townshend, 1935–36; and Robert Herring alone, 1937–50.

BL: PP.5939.bgf
CUL: Q727.C.23
NLS: Y.177
TCD: 100.u.67–112
UCL

109 Light and Dark: for Oxford and Cambridge. Buckingham: Light and Dark, Vol. 1 no. 1 (1937)–vol. 2 no. 3 (1938)

Note: Absorbed by *Kingdom Come* in Summer 1940
CUL: CAM.B.31.62
NLS: 6.243
TCD: 121.p.323, nos.18–24

110 The Literary Review. Bedford: E. D. Martell, Vol. 1 no. 1 (1928))–no. 3 (1929)

CUL: L718.C.41
TCD: 97.c.67

111 The Literary Review. London: Vol. 1 no. 1 (Mar.1936)–11 (1937)

Index: Bloomfield (But not nos. 6, 7 or 9)
Profiled in: Stanton

A general review interspersed with a little poetry.

BL: Vol. 1 no. 1–5, no. 8, no. 10 only. (P.P.5939.cak.)

Little Wings *See* Wings: the official organ of the Flight Pen Club A232

112 The Little Review: literature, drama, music, art / edited by Margaret Anderson and Jane Heap. Chicago, then New York, Vol. 1 no. 1 (Mar. 1914)–vol. 12 no. 2 (May 1929)

Note: From Vol 3. no. 9 (Mar. 1917), published in New York
Index: Sader
Study: Jayne E. Marek, *Women Editing Modernism: "little" magazines & literary history* (Lexington: University Press of Kentucky, 1995), BL: YA.1997.a.13656
Anthology: Margaret Anderson (ed.), *The Little Review Anthology* (New York: Hermitage House, 1953), BL: 12300.cc.26
Related Work: Ezra Pound, *Pound/The Little Review: the letters of Ezra Pound to Margaret Anderson: The Little Review correspondence*, edited by Thomas L. Scott, Melvin J. Friedman, with the assistance of Jackson R.Bryer (New York: New Directions, 1988), BL: YA.1992.b.5867.
Reprint: Vols 1–12. New York: Kraus Reprint Corporation.

A key little magazine of the period, which published British and Irish authors as well as American. An archive of the magazine is held by University of Wisconsin, Milwaukee.

BL: Vols 1–12: Kraus Reprint. (Cup.503.ee.1)
CUL: T700.C.6
UCL: Vols1–12: Kraus Reprint. (Joyce Pers)

113 The Little Revue / edited by William Little. Edinburgh: [L. Warner (Hinckley) for William Little], Vol. 1 no. 1 (Feb. 1939)–no. 3 (Apr. 1939)

Light short stories, diary pieces, and poems, almost all anonymous.
BL: P.P.6028.dbd

114 The Liverpool Chapbook / [edited by John Pride]. Liverpool: [Liverpool Chapbook], No. 1 (Winter (Nov.) 1920)

"It is high time that the tradition that only London can produce and support a publication devoted to serious art should be exploded." – Foreword from the first and probably only issue, a sixteen page miscellany of poetry (Lascelles Abercrombie, Giovanni Orgoglio, William T. Platt) and drawings. Edited anonymously, but Liverpool University Library identifies the editor as John Pride.

BL: P.P.6064.cbc.(2.)
Liverpool University Library: SPEC SF/PR (P.C.3)

115 London Aphrodite / edited by Jack Lindsay and P. R. Stephensen. London: Fanfrolico Press, No. 1 (Aug 1928)–6 (June 1929)

Index: Sader
Profiled in: Hoffman, Allen & Ulrich; Sullivan 1914–1984
Related Imprint: Fanfrolico Press
Related Work: Jack Lindsay, *Fanfrolico and After* (London: Bodley Head, 1962), BL: 011879.w.5.; Harry F. Chaplin, *The Fanfrolico Press: a survey*, with a preface by Jack Lindsay (Sydney: Wentworth Press, 1976), BL: 2771.lb.1/23
Reprint: New York: Johnson Reprint, 1968

A vigorously Nietzschean magazine which deplored the work of Gertrude Stein, T. S. Eliot, Ezra Pound, Laura Riding, D. H. Lawrence, and James Joyce. Except for Jack Lindsay's own poetry, it published very few poems that are remembered today, though two sonnets by Aldous Huxley are of curiosity value. Other contributors included Liam O'Flaherty, T. F. Powys, Rhys Davies and Laurence Powys. The magazine's financial failure is said to have caused the demise of the Fanfrolico Press.

BL: P.P.5938.ban
CUL: T727.C.36
NLS: Q.126
TCD: 122.c.41
UCL

London Bulletin *see* London Gallery Bulletin A116

116 London Gallery Bulletin / edited by E. L. T. Mesens. London, No. 1. (April 1938)–18/20 (June 1940)

Note: From No. 2 (May 1938), published as *London Bulletin*.
Index: Bloomfield (nos. 1–17 only). Nos. 1–9 were indexed in nos. 10 and 11. Cumulative index in reprint noted below
Profiled in: Hoffman, Allen & Ulrich; Sullivan 1914–1984
Reprint: New York: Arno Press, 1970
Microfilm: New York: New York Public Library, 1965

A significant Surrealist periodical, with contributors who include Paul Eluard, André Breton, Herbert Read, and others such as Samuel Beckett. Constructivist and abstract art was also featured. A bookseller's catalogue (Sims Reed, [April, 2004]) shows that Breton was an owner of the complete set of this magazine.

BL: No. 1–16. (P.P.1931.pbc.) No. 17 (Tambi.102)
NLS: Microfilm of complete set. (Mf.103(3).)
UCL: No. 13 (April 1939). (Coop Depos H.32/4)
National Art Library, Victoria and Albert Museum

117 The London Mercury / edited by J. C. Squire; then R. A. Scott-James. London: The Field Press, Vol. 1 no. 1 (Nov. 1919)–vol. 39 no. 234 (Apr. 1939)

Note: Incorporated by: *Life and Letters*
Index: Each volume had its own index. An index for 1919–1929 was also published
Anthology: H. C. M. [i.e. H. Cotton Minchin] (ed.) *The Mercury Book: being selections from the London Mercury* (London: Williams & Norgate, 1926; and Second Series, 1927), BL: W.P.8749.; *The Mercury Book of Verse. Being a selection of poems published in The London Mercury 1919–1930* (London: Macmillan & Co., 1931), BL: 11601.l.12
Profiled in: Stanton; Sullivan 1914–1984
Reprint: Millwood, N.Y.: Kraus Reprint.

With circulation figures of 10,000 in its first year, rising to 20,000 later on, this was no little magazine. Its early editorial stance was conservative and hostile to ostentatious experiment, though some of the poets it published contradicted that stance. Poems under the first editor included those by Hardy, Rupert Brooke, W. H. Davies, Walter de la Mare, Robert Frost, W. B. Yeats, Edmund Blunden, John Betjeman, Graham Greene and D. H. Lawrence. When R. A. Scott-James took over in 1934, he included work by Auden, Spender, C. Day Lewis, Louis MacNeice, George Barker, Christopher Fry, Jack Lindsay and Edwin Muir (who also contributed criticism).

BL: P.P.5939.bp.
CUL: Q718.C.7
NLS: Y.217
TCD: 48.cc.1–39
UCL: Lacking vols.34–36. (Coop Depos B.II273/5–7, B.II274/1)

118 Loquela Mirabilis. Langford: The Latin Press, Vol. 1 no. 1 (Nov. 1936)–vol. 2 no. 1 (May 1937)

Index: Bloomfield

Small, pocket size magazine (c.15cm high, 12cm across), printed by Guido Morris at his Latin Press near Bristol. The emphasis is on art, but poetry includes the Latin of Peter Abelard with a translation by Helen Waddell, and a song by Edmund Waller. Eric Gill and Guido Morris contribute articles. The editor is anonymous.

BL: Cup.510.acd.1.
CUL: L999.C.1.1
NLS: 5.883
TCD: 121.p.323, Nos.1–4

119 Lysistrata. Oxford: Basil Blackwell, Vol.
1 no. 1 (Feb. 1934)–vol. 2 no. 1 (1935)

Index: Bloomfield

BL: Vol.1 no.1 only (ZA.9.a.3229)
CUL: L980.C.61
BL: U.412.
TCD: PER 80–824

**120 The Magazine of Today: an
illustrated review of modern life and
literature.** London: [Magazine of Today],
Vol. 1 no. 1 (May 1930)–no. 5 (Sept. 1930)

Note: Afterwards incorporated in the commercial *Today and
Tomorrow*

BL: P.P.6018.fak.
CUL: L.900.B.49

121 The Masquerade. Windsor: [The
Masquerade], Vol. 1 no. 1 (June 1933)

Index: Bloomfield

A magazine of contributors from Eton. Includes poems by
Noël Coward and others, and items by James Barrie, M. R.
James, Henry Newbolt, Harold Nicolson, and John Buchan

BL: P.P.5985.bca

122 The Melody. Cambridge: National
Poetry Circle, Vol. 1 no. 1 (1931)–vol. 2 no. 2
(1933)

Note: Subsequently incorporated with *Rejection*.
Related Imprint: The National Poetry Circle also published
The N. P. C. Fortnightly and, from 1962, *The New Melody*.

BL: Destroyed in the Second World War. (P.P.5126.bf.)

123 The Microcosm / edited by Dorothy
Una Ratcliffe. Leeds: [Dorothy Una Ratcliffe],
[Vol. 1 no. 1, 1914?]–vol. 9 no. 4 (Winter 1925)

Anthology: Dorothy Una Ratcliffe (ed.) *The Book of The
Microcosm* (Leeds: Microcosm Office [1926.]) BL: 12270.i.8.;
Ratcliffe (ed.) *The Sea-Microcosm* (Leeds: Microcosm Office,
[1929]), BL: 12298.ee.7.; Ratcliffe (ed.), *Listen! The Children's
Microcosm: a collection of new poems, plays, prose, and drawings
for or about children* (Leeds: Microcosm Office, 1931), BL:
12812.e.22.

Articles, reviews, short stories, drawings, and poems, many
with an interest in Yorkshire, including the publication of

poems in Yorkshire dialects. Poets include Wilfred
Rowland Childe, Lascelles Abercrombie, Herbert Read,
Lord Dunsany, Alice Meynell, J. R. R. Tolkien (a poem
entitled "The City of the Gods"), Laurence Binyon, G. K.
Chesterton, Harold Monro and others. There was also an
article by the editor of *Poetry* (Chicago), Harriet Monroe, on
'Science and Art Again' (Winter 1922). Each issue's profits
were given to different charities, with expenses
underwritten by Sir Edward Allen Brotherton. The first five
volumes were apparently for private circulation only. At
least two supplements were issued after *The Microcosm's*
closure: Ratcliffe's *To the Blue Canadian Hills. A week's log in a
Northern Quebec camp* (Leeds, [1928]), BL: 10480.e.38., and
Ratcliffe (ed.) *Hoops of Steel. An anthology of dedicatory poems.
Being a farewell supplement to :The Microcosm* (Glasgow, 1935),
BL: 011653.0.53. Ratcliffe would later edit *The Northern
Broadsheet* in the 1950s, which shared the Yorkshire interest
and some of the contributors to *The Microcosm*.

BL: Vol. 6 no. 2, vol. 6. no. 4–vol. 9 no. 4. (P.P.6030.e.)
CUL: Vol. 5 no. 2, vol. 5 no. 4–vol. 9 no. 4. (L900.B.80)
NLS: Vol. 6 no. 1–vol. 9 no. 4. (U.391)
TCD: Vol.5 no.2; vol. 5 no. 4;vol.6 no.1–4;vol.7
no.1–4;vol.8 no.1–4; vol.9 no.1–4. (67.dd.121, Nos.1–18)
Poetry Library: Vol. 8 no. 3–vol. 9 no. 4

124 The Mitre Anthology of Poetry.
London: Mitre Press, 1929. Then as *The Spring
Anthology*, 1930–1945; 1960–1973

Note: Two single volumes, *The Autumn Anthology* (1930) and
The Winter Anthology (1931) were also issued
Related Imprint: Mitre Press published many other
volumes of poetry, single collections as well as anthologies.

Well-meaning but unambitious verse. Despite a break of
fifteen years after the War, *The Spring Anthology* lasted until
1973.

BL: W.P.9695.
CUL: L727.D.11
NLS: T.31.a.
TCD: 1931–1945. (110.t.193–201 1931–1945); 1960–1964.
(33.uu.250– 1960–1964); 1965. (OLS B–6–434 1965); 1967
(SP–67 13 1967); 1968. (SP–68 22 1968); 1970 (v81–1 307
1970); 1971. (33.uu.261 1971); 1972. (33.uu.262 1972);
1973. (33.uu.263 1973)

125 The Modern Quarterly / edited by
John Lewis. London: Lawrence and Wishart,
Vol. 1 no. 1 (Jan. 1938)–vol. 2 no. 3 (July 1939).
Then, New Series, Vol. 1 no. 1 (Dec. 1945)–vol.
8 no. 4 (Autumn 1953)

Note: Continued by: *The Marxist Quarterly*

Anthology: John Lewis (ed.), *The Modern Quarterly Miscellany* (London: Lawrence and Wishart, [1947]), BL: 5939.bes.

Essays, including Jack Lindsay on Ossian. A general cultural review, with a special interest in philosophy. No poems as such, but some articles on poetry.

BL: Lacking Vol. 4 no. 2 (P.P.5939.ben)
CUL: Q900.C.208
NLS: Y.188
TCD: E.Attic K.141-147

126 The Modern Scot: the organ of the Scottish Renaissance / edited by James H. Whyte. Dundee: Vol. 1 no. 1 (Spring 1930)-vol. 6 no. 4 (Winter 1936)

Note: Amalgamated with *The Scottish Standard* to form *Outlook*
Index: Bloomfield; Each volume contains its own index
Anthology: J . H. Whyte (ed.) *Towards a New Scotland. Being a selection from 'The Modern Scot'* (London: A. Maclehose, 1935), BL: 010369.h.36
Profiled in: Hoffman, Allen & Ulrich; David Finkelstein, Margery Palmer McCulloch and Duncan Glen, *Scottish Literary Periodicals: Three Essays* (Edinburgh: Merchiston Publishing, 1998)
Study: Tom Normand, *The Modern Scot: modernism and nationalism in Scottish art, 1928-1955* (Aldershot: Ashgate, 2000). BL: YC.2002.a.9419

A key literary review in Scotland in the 1930s. Includes critical essays by Catherine Carswell, Herbert Read, Séan O'Fáolin, Edwin Muir and C. M. Grieve ('Hugh MacDiarmid'); short stories by Willa Muir; translations of Kafka, Thomas Mann and Paul Eluard. Adam Kennedy's novella, *Orra Boughs*, was published as vol. 1 no. 3.

BL: P.P.6197.ff.
CUL: L900.B.55
NLS: U.424
TCD: PER 90-798
UCL: Vol. 2 no. 2 (1931)

127 The Monologue / edited by Lyn Irvine. London: Lyn Irvine, Vol. 1 no. 1 (1 Feb 1934)-no. 24 (1 Feb. 1935).

No poems, but discussion of poetry. It is what it says it is: almost entirely the monologue of the editor, on general issues from T. S. Eliot and the critics to Mae West and 'the love interest'. A blog of its day. Includes a long open letter to C. Day Lewis, and accounts of fascist Austria. According to the published list of subscribers, Walter de la Mare subscribed to it, as did Rebecca West, Clive Bell, Graham

Greene and the Scottish novelist Nan Shepherd. Produced on a Gestetner machine. Issue no. 23 (Jan 15th 1935) reproduces the text of a postcard Ezra Pound sent, saying why he would not subscribe - (basically, because Clive Bell did).

BL: P.P.5939.bef.
CUL: L900.B.125

128 The Monthly Chapbook / edited by Harold Monro. London: The Poetry Bookshop, No.1 (July 1919)–6 (Dec. 1919). Then as *The Chapbook, no. 7 (Jan. 1920)–40 (1925)

Note: Continues: *Poetry and Drama*
Profiled in: Hoffman, Allen & Ulrich; Stanton; Sullivan 1837–1913
Bibliography: J. Howard Woolmer, *The Poetry Bookshop 1912–1935: A Bibliography* (Revere, Penn.: Woolmer/Brotherston Ltd, 1988), BL: 2725.e.802
Study: Joy Grant, *Harold Monro and the Poetry Bookshop* (London: Routledge and Kegan Paul, 1967), BL: 2713.ct.14; Dominic Hibberd, *Harold Monro: poet of the New Age* (Basingstoke: Palgrave, 2001), BL: YC.2001.a.4084
Related Imprint: The Poetry Bookshop published many individual collections, for example by Charlotte Mew, and various single sheet series and the *Georgian Poetry* anthologies
Reprint: *Poetry and Drama*, New York: Kraus Reprint, 1967. *The Monthly Chapbook*, New York: Kraus Reprint, 1976

Open to different strands of modern and modernist poetry, *The Monthly Chapbook* and its pre-war predecessor *Poetry and Drama* (1913–14; BL: P.P.5193.bd) were strong supporters of the much reviled but in fact quietly modern "Georgian" poets and the more obviously modernist Imagists (see [*The Imagist Anthologies*]). In *The Monthly Chapbook* there were essays on poetry by Eliot, F. S. Flint, Richard Aldington and others, and poems by E. E. Cummings, Robert Frost, Marianne Moore, Wallace Stevens and many more. In the first issue of *Poetry and Drama* Monro sets out why he resigned the editorship of *The Poetry Review*, citing the need for independence from commercial and private interference. The British Library has the main archive of the magazine's publisher, The Poetry Bookshop, within its Department of Manuscripts (BL: Add MSS 57756–68). This bookshop in central London was not only a specialist retailer and publisher, it held many readings and even had accommodation for visiting poets, such as Wilfred Owen, helping to create a more open reception for new poetry in England.

BL: Cup.400.b.2.
CUL: T727.C.21
NLS: T.25.b

TCD: No.40 [1925] only. (OLS L–6–678 No.40 (1925)
UCL

More Songs from the Ship and Castle *See*
Songs from the Ship and Castle A201

129 **Motley**. Eton: The Motley, No. 1. (1 Nov.
1930).

Appears to be a student magazine, with occasional poems.
Compton Mackenzie contributes an essay on 'My first
literary efforts'.

BL: P.P.6145.bfg

130 **Motley** / edited by Mary Manning.
Dublin: [Dublin Gate Theatre], [Vol. 1. no. 1]
(Mar. 1932)–vol. 3 no. 4 (May 1934)

Profiled in: Hoffman, Allen & Ulrich; Tom Clyde, *Irish
Literary Magazines: an outline and descriptive bibliography*
(Dublin: Irish Academic Press, 2003), BL: 2725.g.3414
Related Work: Patricia Coughlan and Alex Davis (eds.),
Modernism and Ireland: The Poetry of the 1930s (Cork: Cork
University Press, 1995), BL: YC.1997.a.299.

The house journal of the Dublin Gate Theatre, so with a
focus on drama, but includes poems by Michael Sayers,
Padraic Colum, John Betjeman, and others, as well as a
piece by the Cubism-influenced Mainie Jellett, "Modern Art
and the Dual Ideal of Form Through the Ages".

BL: P.P.5196.i
TCD: 79.a.121

131 **My Queen Magazine.** London: [My
Queen Magazine], No. 1 (21 July 1914)–12 (17
Nov. 1914)

BL: Destroyed in the Second World War. (P.P.6004.tb)

132 **Neo-Georgian Poetry** / [edited by T.
I. F. Armstrong, a.k.a. John Gawsworth],
London: Richards, 1936–1937

An attempt to assert the qualities of the shorter lyric, with a
nod to the Georgian anthologies of twenty years previous.
Contributors included Gawsworth, Stella Gibbons, Hugh
MacDiarmid, E. H. W. Meyerstein, Seamus O'Sullivan, Ruth
Pitter, A. S. J. Tessimond, E. H. Visiak, Anna Wickham and
others. Like Gawsworth's other similar attempt, *Edwardian
Poetry*, only one issue was ever published.

BL: 11654.c.64.

CUL: L727.c.32
NLS: T.31.c

The New Adelphi *See* The Adelphi A2

133 **The New Age** / edited by Frederic A.
Atkins; A. E. Fletcher; Arthur Compton-
Rickett; Joseph Clayton; Holbrook Jackson and
A. R. Orage; then Orage solely; then Arthur
Moore; then Arthur Brenton. London, Vol. 1
no. 1 (4th Oct. 1894)–vol. 19 no. 659 (25th
April 1907); New Series, Vol. 1 no. 1 (2nd May
1907)–New Series, vol. 62 no. 22 (7th April
1938)

Note: Incorporated by *The New English Weekly*
Index: The Modernist Journals Project indexes issues under
Orage's editorship (see Website below)
Profiled in: Sullivan 1837–1913; The Modernist Journals
Project (see Website below)
Study: Paul Selver, *Orage and the New Age Circle: Reminiscences
and reflections* (London: Allen & Unwin, 1959), BL:
010608.h.17; Wallace Martin, *The New Age under Orage:
Chapters in English Cultural History* (Manchester: Manchester
University Press, [1967]), BL: X.909/11825; Gary Taylor,
Orage and the New Age (Sheffield: Sheffield Hallam University
Press, 2000), BL: YC.2001.a.9057
Related Imprint: New Age Press
Reprint: The Modernist Journals Project has digitised
issues under Orage's editorship (see Website below)
Website: Modernist Journals Project, Brown University,
www.modjourn.brown.edu/ MJP_Home.htm

Although beginning as a cultural review for liberal and
centre left voices, including Ramsay MacDonald, it was
when A. R. Orage became involved in 1907, with funding
from George Bernard Shaw and the Theosophist financier
Lewis Alexander Wallace, that this weekly started to
become one of the most influential magazines of its day.
Orage was co-editor with Jackson for less than a year, and
then held sway as sole editor from January 1908 until
September 1922. While he published essays by Chesterton,
Wells, and Bernard Shaw which debated the good and ills
of socialism, Orage's encouragement of writers of a
younger generation brought excellent critics to his pages
and made it a magazine read by many authors who would
write their mature work in the 1920s and 30s. Arnold
Bennett reviewed fiction, but also introduced the work of
little-known continental writers, helping to create the
context for the enthusiastic reception, among writers at
least, of Chekhov and Dostoyevski. T. E. Hulme, Edwin
Muir, and Ezra Pound were regular contributors of

comment, and, for instance, the ideas behind Imagism were described early on in *The New Age*. MacDiarmid contributed and one of the first Suffragettes to be sent to prison, Teresa Billington-Greig contributed, too. After the War, Orage began to disseminate the ideas of C. H. Douglas's Social Credit ideas for rejuvenating the national economy, but also became more introspective under the influence of G. I. Gurdjieff's mystical teachings. The magazine declined following Orage's departure.

BL: Newspaper Collections
CUL: Microfilm P483
NLS: Lacking a number of pages and issues from the New Series, namely: Vol. 13, pp.129–30; vol. 13 no. 25; vol. 15–18; vol. 19 no. 7; vol. 20–21; vol. 23 no. 5; vol. 24; vol. 34 no. 25; vol. 35 no. 1, 3, 5–9, 11, 13–15, 18–19, 21; vol. 35 no. 26. (U.403)
UCL: New Series. Vol. 1–8. (Co-op Deposit)

134 The New Alliance. Edinburgh: The New Alliance, vol. 1 no. 1 (Autumn 1939). Then New Series, Vol. 1 no. 1 (Mar. 1940)–vol. 6 no. 6 (Dec.1945/Jan. 1946). Then as *The New Alliance & Scots Review*, Vol. 7 no. 1 (Apr. 1946)–vol. 13 no. 5 (Sept./Oct. 1951)

Index: Bloomfield (Vol. 1 no. 1 (1939) only)
Profiled in: Hoffman, Allen & Ulrich

"A quarterly printing chiefly the work of Scottish and Irish writers and artists." Contributors included Edwin Muir, Hugh MacDiarmid, F. R. Higgins and others. Robert Kemp's celebrated Edinburgh Festival version of Sir David Lindsay's *The Satire of the Three Estates* was published as vol. 9 no. 5.

BL: Lacking New Series, Vol. 8 no. 1–9, vol. 8 no. 12; vol. 9. no. 1–4, 6–12; vol. 10 no. 10–vol. 12 no. 1. (P.P.6203.acc.)
CUL: Vol. 1 no. 1. (L999.C.3.1487)
NLS: First series, 6.276. New series, Y.197. *The New Alliance & Scots Review*, Y.197

135 The New Broadside. London: The Poetry Bookshop, no. 1 [1923]–23 [1931]

Note: Continues: *Rhyme Sheet*.
Bibliography: J. Howard Woolmer, *The Poetry Bookshop 1912–1935: A Bibliography* (Revere, Penn.: Woolmer/Brotherston Ltd, 1988), BL: 2725.e.802
Related Work: Joy Grant, *Harold Monro and the Poetry Bookshop* (London: Routledge and Kegan Paul, 1967), BL: 2713.ct.14; Dominic Hibberd, *Harold Monro: poet of the New Age* (Basingstoke: Palgrave, 2001), BL: YC.2001.a.4084
Related Imprint: The Poetry Bookshop published various

individual collections and *The Monthly Chapbook*

A single ballad- or nursery-rhyme-like poem featured on these single sheets, topped and tailed by an illustration by a contemporary artist. Some had contemporary poetry, others much older work. The British Library has the main archive of the Poetry Bookshop within its Department of Manuscripts (BL: Add MSS 57756–68).

BL: Cup.1247.h.13

The New Coterie *See* The Coterie A42

136 New Days: the journal of new conditions / edited by Louis Vincent. London: [New Days], Vol. 1 no. 1 (18 Sept. 1915)–vol. 2 no. 3 (Apr. 1916)

BL: Newspaper Collections

137 The New English Weekly / edited by A. R. Orage; then Philip Mairet. London, 21 Apr. 1932–22 Sept. 1949

Note: From 5th Jan 1939, published as *The New English Weekly and the New Age*.
Index: Vol. 1–16; each of these volumes has its own index.
Profiled in: Stanton; Sullivan 1914–1984
Anthology: Montgomery Butchart (ed.), *Political and Economic Writings. From the New English Weekly, 1932–1934, with a preliminary section from the New Age, 1912* (London: Stanley Nott, 1936), BL: 8234.a.36
Related Works: John Carswell, *Lives and letters: A.R. Orage, Beatrice Hastings, Katherine Mansfield, John Middleton Murry, S.S. Koteliansky, 1906–1957* (London: Faber, 1978), BL: X.989/52259; Philip Mairet, *A. R. Orage. A memoir* (London: Dent, 1936), BL: 010822.g.29.
Reprint: Microform: New York: Datamics, [undated].

A magazine devoted to the discussion of Major C. H. Douglas's economic theory Social Credit. It also published poetry, and contributors included Dylan Thomas (very early – in 1933), Hugh MacDiarmid, Ezra Pound (poems, correspondence and argument by him), William Carlos Williams, David Gascoyne, Edwin Muir, Eric Gill, Ronald Duncan, George Barker, Sean O'Faolain, Lawrence Durrell, Llewelyn Powys, Janko Lavrin, Franz Kafka, Basil Bunting and three of *The Four Quartets* by Eliot. These – 'East Coker', 'The Dry Salvages', and 'Little Gidding' – were also issued as individual 'supplements' in their own right. Pound contributed some poems under the pseudonym Alfie Venison. A. R. Orage served as editor from 1932 to 1934, Mairet from 1934 to 1949. Philip Mairet, 1934–1949. Social Credit captured the imagination of a number of authors in the interwar years. Some copies with William Carlos Williams's handwritten notes are held at Yale University Library.

BL: Newspaper Collections
CUL: Q900.A.12
NLS: U.403.
TCD: New Store

The New Freewoman *See* The Egoist A55

138 The New Keepsake. London: Cobden-Sanderson, 1931.

Short fiction, autobiography and poems. Contributors included Edmund Blunden, W. B. Yeats, Vita Sackville–West, Hilaire Belloc, Siegfried Sassoon, Rose Macaulay, Dorothy Wellesley, and J. C. Squire. With decorations by Rex Whistler.

BL: P.P.6670.aa
NLS: T.184.a
TCD: 88.r.125

139 The New Keepsake for the year (Le Nouveau Keepsake pour l'année) / edited by X. M. Boulestin. London, Paris: Chelsea Book Club, 1921

Note: Includes contributions in French. The issue was published in 1920 but for the year 1921

Includes work by Harold Monro, D. H. Lawrence, André Salmon, Osbert Sitwell, John J. Adams, and Richard Aldington. Interspersed with black and white illustrations by various artists.

BL: P.P.6708.
CUL: T727.D.5
NLS: T.159.c

140 New Numbers. Dymock: [Lascelles Abercrombie], Vol. 1 no. 1 (Feb.1914)–no. 4 (Dec. 1914)

Profiled in: Hoffman, Allen & Ulrich

This published solely the poetry of Rupert Brooke, John Drinkwater, Wilfrid Wilson Gibson, and Lascelles Abercrombie; as such, a key early periodical of Georgian poetry, and in so being consolidating one strand in the more ambitious work of Vivian Locke Ellis's pre-war magazine *Open Window* (1910–1911; BL: P.P.5938.bah). The fourth issue of *New Numbers* contains the first printing of Brooke's war sonnets. The editor is not identified.

BL: Cup.401.h.8.
CUL: T727.B.2
NLS: Q.119
TCD: 90.n.54
UCL

141 The New Oxford Outlook / Richard Crossman and Gilbert Highet, and others. Oxford: Basil Blackwell, Vol. 1 no. 1 (1933)–vol. 2 no. 3 (1935)

Note: Continues: *The Oxford Outlook*.
Index: Bloomfield
Profiled in: Hoffman, Allen & Ulrich

BL: P.P.6117.ibb.
CUL: L985.C.11
NLS: Y.181

New Oxford Poetry *See* Oxford Poetry A160

142 The New Review: an international notebook for the arts / edited by Samuel Putnam. Paris: Brewer, Warren and Putnam Inc., Vol. 1 no. 1 (Jan./Feb. 1931)–no. 5 (Apr. 1932)

Related Work: Samuel Putnam, *Paris was our Mistress: Memoirs of a Lost & Found Generation* (New York: Viking, 1947), BL: 10175.bb.28; Patricia Coughlan and Alex Davis (eds.), *Modernism and Ireland: The Poetry of the 1930s* (Cork: Cork University Press, 1995), BL: YC.1997.a.299
Reprint: Microfilm: New York: New York Public Library, [undated]

Contributors included Thomas McGreevey and Ford Madox Ford. No holdings known in the United Kingdom, but Yale University Library have a complete set. Princeton University has a significant archive of Putnam's correspondence concerning *The New Review*.

New Scotland *see* The Free Man A77

143 New Verse / edited by Geoffrey Grigson. London: No. 1 (Jan 1933)–32 (Autumn 1938); New series, Vol. 1 no. 1–no. 2 (Jan 1939)

Index: Bloomfield; Sader
Profiled in: Hoffman, Allen & Ulrich; Stanton; Sullivan 1914–1984; Tolley 1930s; Tolley 1940s; Adrian Caesar, *Dividing Lines: poetry, class and ideology in the 1930s* (Manchester University Press, 1991), BL: YC.1991.a.765;

Jason Harding, "*New Verse*: an Oxford Clique", in *The Criterion: cultural politics and periodical networks in inter-war Britain* (Oxford: Oxford University Press, 2002), pp.88–106, BL: YC.2002.a.7159
Study: Ian Hamilton, 'The Billhook', in Hamilton, *The Little Magazines: a study of six editors* (London: Weidenfeld and Nicolson), 1976, BL: X.989/50900
Anthology: Geoffrey Grigson (ed.), *New Verse. An anthology* (London: Faber, 1939), BL: 2292.b.30.
Reprint: Kraus Reprint, 1966

'The object of NEW VERSE needs expansion in no complex or tiring manifesto. Poets in this country and during this period of the victory of the masses, aristocratic and bourgeois as much as proletarian, which have captured the instruments of access to the public and use them to convey their own once timid and silent vulgarity, vulgarising all the arts, are allowed no longer periodical means of communicating their poems. [...]' – front page, no. 1. Often associated with 'the Auden generation', but in fact it published more broadly. Contributors included Grigson, Auden, MacNeice, Bernard Spencer, Kenneth Allott, Norman Cameron, Kathleen Raine, David Gascoyne, Philip O'Connor, Gavin Ewart, Naomi Mitchison, Joseph Gordon Macleod, Charles Madge, William Empson, Allen Tate, George Barker, Dylan Thomas and others. No. 26–27 (Nov. 1937) was a double issue devoted to Auden, with contributions from Isherwood, MacNeice, Spender, Edwin Muir, Dylan Thomas (e.g. 'I sometimes think of Mr Auden's poetry as a hygiene...'), Ezra Pound ('I might be inclined to answer yr note IF I cd. discover why your little lot neglects to import cummings, W.C.W. and one or two other items of interest'...) and others. The very last issue has a short and not altogether favourable piece by Wyndham Lewis on the recently deceased W. B. Yeats (e.g. "Yeats... comes back to us as the memory of a limp hand.")

BL: P.P.5126.bh.
CUL: Q727.C.31
NLS: All, but New Series is reported missing. (Y.172)
TCD: 2–7, 9–11, 14, 17, 23–32. New Series, 1–2. (133.n.115)
UCL
Poetry Library: Reprint of complete set. Also: 22, 26/27

144 New Vision: a quarterly review.
West Wickham, 1938

BL: P.P.5938.bbk

145 The New Weekly / edited by R. A.
Scott-James. London: [The New Weekly], no.1 (21 Mar. 1914)–23 (22 Aug.1914)
Profiled in: Stanton

BL: Newspaper Collections
CUL: L900.B.143
NLS: Q.48

146 New Writing / edited by John
Lehmann. London: The Bodley Head, No. 1 (Spring 1936)–5 (Spring 1938); New series, No.1 (Autumn 1938)–3 (Christmas 1939)

Note: Imprint varies: The Bodley Head, then Lawrence and Wishart, then The Hogarth Press. Continued by: *Folios of New Writing*
Index: Sader; Bloomfield
Profiled in: Hoffman, Allen & Ulrich; Stanton; Sullivan 1914–1984; Tolley 1930s; Tolley 1940s
Anthology: John Lehmann (ed.), *Poems from New Writing, 1936–1946* (London: John Lehmann, 1946), BL: 11606.b.13.; John Lehmann (ed.), *Pleasures of New Writing: an anthology of poems, stories and other prose pieces from the pages of New Writing* (London: John Lehmann, 1952), BL: 12299.ee.27.
Reprint: New York: Johnson Reprint, [undated]

Mostly a publisher of prose, but poetry included work by Auden, Spender, Lorca, Dylan Thomas, David Gascoyne, Louis MacNeice, and Odysseus Elytis.

BL: PP.5938.bbd
CUL: L727.C.23
NLS: Y.190
TCD: 33.aa.71–89
UCL

147 Night and Day / edited by John Marks
and Graham Greene. London: Chatto and Windus, Vol. 1 no. 1 (1st July 1927)–no. 26 (23rd Dec. 1937)

Index: Bloomfield
Profiled in: Stanton

BL: LB.31.b.8050
NLS: Birk.248(13)

148 Northern Lights / edited by Alan
Hadfield. Harrogate: [Northern Lights Press], No. 1 (Spring 1939)–2 (1939)

Note: Subtitle: *The new North Country quarterly of literature and art.*
Related Imprint: Northern Lights Press Pamphlets published *Nutshell Notes on Penal Reform ... With Prison Poems: the Maidstone Muses*, by R. A. Wing, Joe Bedeker, F. de

Montaigne, and Alan Hadfield, 1944 (BL: W.P.4009/1), and 2nd ed., also 1944 (BL: W.P.4009/2)

First issue included a foreword by Laurence Housman, short fiction (including a piece by J. F. Hendry), an appreciation of Yeats, and various poems, including one in an unidentified dialect by Q. Nicholas. A reprint of a Walter de la Mare poem also appears.

BL: No. 1 only. (P.P.6081.bal.)
UCL
Bodleian Library, Oxford: Per. 2705 e.985

149 Northern Numbers: being representative selections from certain living Scottish poets / compiled by C. M. Grieve. Edinburgh: T. N. Foulis, Series 1 (1920)–Series 3 (1922)

An attempt, as stated in the first editorial, by Grieve (i.e. Hugh MacDiarmid) to package contemporary Scottish poetry in the same way that the Georgian anthologies offered largely English poetry. Contributors included: John Buchan, Violet Jacob, Neil Munro, T. S. Cairncross, Roderick Watson Kerr, Charles Murray, Lewis Spence, Lauchlan MacLean Watt, Marion Angus, Helen Cruickshank, William Jeffrey, William Soutar, and others.

BL: 11605.bbb.4
CUL: 9700.d.2580–
NLS: T.9.e.
UCL: Series 1

150 The Northern Review: a progressive monthly of life and letters / edited by Hugh MacDiarmid. Edinburgh: C. M. Grieve, Vol. 1 no. 1 (May 1924)–no. 4 (Sept. 1924)

Note: Imprint varied. After the first issue, published by Wells Gardner, Darton & Co in London
Profiled in: Sullivan 1914–1984

The editor and the initial publisher were one and the same, 'Hugh MacDiarmid' being the pseudonym for C. M. Grieve. This was a general cultural review, publishing essays, short fiction, reviews and poems, and attempting to link Scotland to artistic movements in Europe. MacDiarmid's own poetry was the most important it published; Edwin Muir in conversation with the composer F. G. Scott, and Muir on German poetry, are also of interest.

BL: P.P.6203.bid
NLS: U.413

151 The Northman / edited anonymously and later by John Gallen and Robert Greacen and others. Belfast: Queen's University, Vol. 1 (1926)–vol. 3 no. 6 (1932). Then, as The New Northman. Vol. 1 no. 1 (Winter 1932)–vol. 9 no. 2 (Summer 1941). Then, as The Northman, Vol. 9 no. 3 (Autumn 1941); Vol. 11 no. 1 (Winter 1941/42)–vol. 17 no. 1 (Spring 1950)

Profiled in: Tom Clyde, Irish Literary Magazines: an outline and descriptive bibliography (Dublin: Irish Academic Press, 2003), BL: 2725.g.3414

A university magazine which began with a mix of news about student clubs with short stories, squibs, poems, and reviews. Many items are signed just by initials. Although work by John Hewitt had already appeared, with the Winter 1940–41 issue a more outward-looking remit was announced, debated over several issues, then the anonymity of the editorship was suspended and John Gallen and Robert Greacen emerged as editors with the Autumn 1941 issue (at which point the title reverted to The Northman). Contributors in the early 1940s included rather a lot of work by the editors themselves, as well as work by Alex Comfort, Roy McFadden and Nicholas Moore, and Henry Treece's essay "Some notes on the Apocalyptic Movement". The magazine had reverted to a more university-based magazine by the mid-1940s.

BL: P.P.6180.ch
TCD: Vol.11 no.1. (126.n.91)
UCL: The New Northman: Vol. 7 no.3 (1939)–vol. 11 no. 1 (1941/2)
Queen's University Belfast: Lacking some issues in 1941–50 period. (qLH5.N8)

152 The N. P. C. Fortnightly: news and information (news and notes) for the members of the National Poetry Circle. Cambridge: National Poetry Circle, no. 3 (16 Nov. 1931)–193?

Related Imprint: The National Poetry Circle also published Melody

BL: Destroyed in the Second World War. (P.P.5126.bbc)

153 On the Boiler / edited by W. B. Yeats. Dublin: Cuala Press, October 1938

Index: Bloomfield; Stephen H. Goode, Index to Commonwealth Little Magazines (New York: Johnson Reprint, 1966), BL: HUR011.3409171

Profiled in: Hoffman, Allen & Ulrich; Tom Clyde, *Irish Literary Magazines: an outline and descriptive bibliography* (Dublin: Irish Academic Press, 2003), BL: 2725.g.3414 Reprint: Shannon: Irish University Press, 1971

Yeats was the sole contributor to this magazine which ran for only one issue.

BL: Cup.407.a.4
NLS: 6.242
TCD: Press A Cuala A.b.5

154 The Orpheus / edited by Godfrey C. Wengenwroth. Paisley: The Orpheus, No. 1 (May 1923)–Fourth Year no. 6 (Mar–Apr. 1927)

Note: Incorporated into *The Outside Contributor*, out of scope for this bibliography
Anthology: Orpheus Publications published: *First Flights: an anthology of poems* (1925), BL: 011604.e.15.; *Golden Thoughts: an anthology of verse* [1926], BL: 011604.g.41.; and *Blossoms: an anthology of poems* [1927], BL: 11603.dd.8.

Sub-titled "the magazine of distinction". Short stories, non-fiction sketches, poems, and reviews. A commercial operation which published unambitious and anodyne work but tried to encourage new writing. It had a free poetry criticism service to subscribers. It was absorbed into the more freelance journalism orientated *The Outside Contributor*, BL: P.P.5264.ta., which itself only lasted for the month of April 1927 following the takeover.

BL: P.P.6197.lg

155 Outlook / edited by David MacEwen, with literary editor J. H. Whyte. Edinburgh: The Scottish Standard Ltd, Vol. 1 no. 1 (Apr. 1936)–no. 10 (Jan. 1937)

Note: Incorporated *The Modern Scot* and *The Scottish Standard*.

A general cultural review centred on Scottish issues but not exclusively so. With essays, short fiction, and poems. Contributors included many Scottish Renaissance writers such as Neil M. Gunn, Edwin Muir, Compton Mackenzie, George Friel, Hugh MacDiarmid, Catherine Carswell, Edward Scouller, William Soutar, and Agnes Mure Mackenzie, as well as, for example, Rebecca West.

BL: P.P.6203.acb.
CUL: L900.C.170
NLS: U.424

156 The Outpost: a monthly magazine of literature, art & national life / [edited by Charles Polhill?]. London: Charles Polhill, Vol. 1 no. 1 (June 1925)–no. 5 (Dec. 1925)

Related Work: *The Origin of Christmas*, by Charles Polhill, [London: Charles Polhill, 1925], BL: 04504.de.45.

A general cultural review, which had a translation feature, 'Poems from many lands'.

BL: P.P.6018.faf.(1.)
CUL: L900.B.146

The Outside Contributor *See* The Orpheus A154

157 The Owl / edited by Robert Graves; then Robert Graves and William Nicholson. London: Martin Secker, Vol. 1 no. 1 (May 1919)–no. 2 (Oct. 1919); then, as *The Winter Owl*, Vol. 2 no. 3 (Nov. 1923)

Note: Editors and imprints varied. The artist William Nicholson joined Graves for the last issue, which was published by Cecil Palmer rather than Secker
Profiled in: Hoffman, Allen & Ulrich

The Owl published modern rather than overtly modernist poetry: Hardy, John Masefield, Walter de la Mare, Sassoon, John Crowe Ransom, and Graves himself. The large format, wide margins, occasional coloured illustrations and jaunty bird on the cover make this rather a handsome publication.

BL: P.P.6018.oab.
CUL: MEYNELL.14
NLS: *The Owl*, T.451.e. *The Winter Owl*, X.200.a
TCD: Vol. 1 no.1–no. 2. (50.cc.1, 2). Vol. 2 no. 3. (26.bb.163)
UCL: Vol. 1 no.1

158 The Oxford & Cambridge Miscellany / edited by Herbert Baxter, Alan Porter, L. de G. Sieveking, and Alec Macdonald. Oxford: Blackwell, June 1920.

Profiled in: Hoffman, Allen & Ulrich

One issue only. Poetry, short fiction, sheet music, and articles on art. Contributors included Edmund Blunden, Robert Graves, Edgell Rickword, Edith Sitwell, and others.

BL: P.P.6118.hd.

CUL: CAM.B.31.34
NLS: 6.99
TCD: 62.e.27

159 The Oxford Outlook / N. A.
Beechman, Beverley Nichols and others.
Oxford: Vol. 1 no. 1 (May 1919)–vol. 12 no. 58
(May 1932)

Note: No. 9 is omitted in the numbering. The volume
numbers are independent of the issue numbers, i.e. there
are only 58 issues in total. Continued by: *The New Oxford
Outlook*
Index: Bloomfield (Vol. 10 no. 51–vol. 12 no. 58 only)
Profiled in: Hoffman, Allen & Ulrich

Subtitled "a literary and political review", with articles on
poetry, language and politics. Poetry by Stephen Spender,
Edith Sitwell, Robert Graves, Cleanth Brooks, and others.

BL: P.P.6117.iba
CUL: L985.C.11
NLS: P.206
UCL: 5–6, 10–12, 20, 50

160 Oxford Poetry / edited by Gerald H.
Crow, Geoffrey Dennis, Sherard Vines [and
others]. Oxford: Blackwell, then Fantasy Press,
then Magdalen College, 1910–1932, 1936,
1937, 1942, 1943, No. 1 (1946), No. 2 (1946),
1947–1957, 1959, 1960; No. 1 (1970)–3 (1970);
Vol. 1 no. 1 (June 1983)–vol. 11 no. 1 (Winter
2000) ISSN: 1465–6213

Note: The volumes for 1936 and 1937 bore the title *New
Oxford Poetry*
Index: www.gnelson.demon.co.uk/oxpoetry/index/
index.html
Website: www.gnelson.demon.co.uk/oxpoetry/

An annual for most of the century, *Oxford Poetry* for many
years published only the work of Oxford undergraduates or
graduates, a practice discontinued in the early 1980s.
Editors have included W. R. Childe, Aldous Huxley,
Dorothy L. Sayers, Vera Brittain, Robert Graves, David
Cleghorn Thomson, W. H. Auden, C. Day Lewis, Louis
MacNeice, Stephen Spender, John Heath-Stubbs, Kingsley
Amis, Geoffrey Hill, Jonathan Price, Anthony Thwaite,
Adrian Mitchell, John Fuller, Mark Wormald, Mick Imlah,
Peter McDonald, Mark Ford, and others. It began as a Basil
Blackwell publication, but from 1952 to 1959 was
published by the Fantasy Press. It was revived in the 1980s
and published by Magdalen College and is likely to be

revived again. A magazine entitled *The Oxford Poetry
Magazine* appeared for one issue in 1973 but was not related
to *Oxford Poetry*.

BL: 1910–1932 (Cup.410.d.81); 1936 (11655.bbb.2); 1937
(11655.bb.83); 1942–1943, 1947–1957, 1959
(Cup.410.d.81); Vol. 1 no. 1 (June 1983)–vol. 2 no. 2, vol. 3
no. 1–no. 2, vol. 4 no. 1–vol. 5 no. 1 (1990), vol. 5 no. 3
(1990)–vol. 7 no. 1 (1993), vol. 10 no. 1 (Easter 2000)–vol. 11
no. 1 (Winter 2000) (P.901/3428)
CUL: 1910–1957, Imperfect set (P727.d.1); No. 1 (1946)–2
(1946) (L999.c.3.16); Vol. 1 no. 1 (June 1983)–vol. 9 no. 2,
vol. 10 no. 1–vol. 11 no. 1 (Winter 2000) (L727.c.919)
NLS: 1910–1930 (6.1727 (1914)); 1936 (P.sm.1765); No. 1
(1946)–2 (1946) (6.403); Vol. 1 no. 1 (June 1983)–Vol. 11 no.
1 (Winter 2000) (HJ4.1804)
TCD: Vol. 1 no. 1 (June 1983)–vol. 11 no. 1 (Winter 2000)
(PER 93–550)
UCL: 1910–1914, 1917, 1918, 1921–1922, 1929, 1931, 1937,
1942–1943, 1949–1950, 1953; Vol. 1 no. 1 (June 1983)–vol. 2
no. 2, vol. 3 no. 1, vol. 4 no. 1–vol. 5 no. 1.
Poetry Library: Vol. 1 no. 1 (June 1983)–no.2, vol. 3 no.
1–no.3, vol. 4 no. 2, vol. 5 no. 1– vol. 9 no. 2, vol. 10 no. 1

161 The Palatine Review. Oxford:
[Palatine Review], No. 1–4 (Jan.–Oct. 1916)

Profiled in: Hoffman, Allen & Ulrich

Contributors include Clive Bell, Philip Heseltine, and T. W.
Earp on Charles Péguy. Aldous Huxley contributes poems.

BL: P.P.6117.iaa

162 The Panton Magazine: literature,
art, music, drama. London: [Panton Arts
Club], Vol. 1 no. 1 (Jan./Mar. 1927)–no. 4
(Oct./Dec. 1927)

Profiled in: Hoffman, Allen & Ulrich

General literary review, that included some poems.
Presumably published the work of Club members.

BL: P.P.5938.ddd
CUL: L727.B.3
TCD: 95.c.99

163 The Parnassian. Mytholmroyd: The
International Institute of British Poetry and
Calder Valley Poets' Society. Vol. 1 First Quarter
(Mar. 1925)–[?]

Note: Editor varies

The Parnassian published the poems of members of the

Institute and Society, and gave brief reports of their meetings and the poems read there. The Institute and Society appear to have been founded as early as 1915.

BL: Vol. 1 First Quarter (Mar. 1925)–Sept. 1986. (P.P.5126.be.)
UCL: Vol.7 no. 1 (1974)–Sept. 1985
Poetry Library: 6 [Third Quarter, 1971, First Quarter, 1972, First Quarter, 1973], 7 [2nd Quarter, 1973, Third Quarter, 1973]; and two unnumbered issues [May 1976, April 1977]

164 The Patch-Box. London: [The Patch-Box], Vol. 1 no. 1 (May 1914)

Short fiction, an article on Tennyson's early home, an article in part on Futurism and Cubism, an article on the Russian artist Marie Bashkirtseff, reviews, and poems by L. Cranmer-Byng, Henry Baerlein, S. D. Collingwood, and Cicely C. Kenworthy. Edited anonymously.

BL: P.P.5793.bg
NLS: 5.238

165 Penguin Parade / edited by D. K. Roberts, then J. E. Morpurgo. Harmondsworth: Penguin, No. 1 (1937)–11(1945). Second Series, No. 1 (1947)–3 (1948)

Profiled in: Stanton; Sullivan 1914–1984

Commercially produced miscellany of fiction and poetry.

BL: 12208.a.1/120. Second Series: 12208.a.1/120.a.
CUL: L996.D.3
NLS: 5.3064
TCD: 1. (BAN 943)

166 Phoenix. Eastbourne: Eastbourne College, No. 1 (Dec. 1938)–2 (July 1939)

A general literary magazine, intended to raise funds for the "Distressed Areas", presumably Eastbourne itself. Poets included Walter de la Mare (reprinted from an earlier publication) and others.

BL: P.P.6020.fce

167 Phoenix: a magazine for young writers / edited by Cynthia Crawshaw, Norman Hampson, J. A. Shaw, Norman Swallow, Basil Wigoder, and others. [Ayton: 1939–1942?]

Includes short stories and some poems. Contributors

include Edward Lowbury, Mary Miles, Ian Bancroft, and Philip Larkin, who contributes the poem "The Conscript" (vol. 3 no. 1).

BL: Vol. 3 no. 1 (Oct. 1941)–vol. 3 no. 4 (Nov. 1941). (P.P.6028.dg.)

168 Poesy: a magazine for the lover of the Muses / edited by E. F.Herdman. Bishop Auckland: Vol. 1 no. 1 (July 1915)–vol. 2 no. 15 (Nov. 1917)

Note: Vol. 1 was bound as *Gathered Leaves*
Profiled in: Hoffman, Allen & Ulrich

BL: P.P.5126.h

169 The Poet / edited by A. L. Wilson. Balerno, Midlothian: Celandine, Vol. 1 no. 1 (1936)–[vol. 14 no. 6 (Nov./Dec. 1953)?]

Note: A *Supplement* was published from 1939–1948
Profiled in: Hoffman, Allen & Ulrich
Anthology: *The Poet Anthology*, ed. Harry Crouch (Balerno: Celandine, 1937–?)

BL: Vol. 1 no. 1–vol. 13 no. 2/6. (P.P.5126.gbg.) Supplement: P.P.5126.gbg. (2.)
NLS: Supplements are shelved with main sequence. Vol. 1–4. (Y.176). Vol. 5–14. (P.1a.691.)

170 Poetry / edited by C. J. Arnell, then S. Fowler Wright. Ventnor, then London: [Poetry], 1918–1925. Then, as *Poetry and the Play*, Vol. 8 no. 71 (Apr. 1925)–vol. 13 no. 90 (Summer 1931)

Note: Publisher and place of publication varied. Subtitle variants included: "a magazine of new lyrics", "a magazine of verse, comment and criticism"
Anthology: C. J. Arnell (ed.) *An English Lute: a new anthology of English verse*, London: C.W. Daniel, [1922]. BL: 011604.ff.18. S. Fowler Wright (ed.), *Voices on the Wind: an anthology of contemporary verse* (London: Merton Press; First Series, 1922; Second Series, 1924), BL: 011604.g.23. Wright also edited a number of regional anthologies, allied to the magazine and published by the Merton Press, including: *Poets of Merseyside* (1923), BL: 011604.f.63.; *A Somerset Anthology of Modern Verse* (1924), BL: 11604.ee.23; *Some Yorkshire Poets* (1924), BL: 11604.ee.24.
Profiled in: Hoffman, Allen & Ulrich; Stanton

The assessment by Hoffman, Allen & Ulrich of the poems published in the magazine seems right: "serious and competent, but imitative efforts". It also published reviews and articles on poetry and, from 1925, on drama. Allied to *Poetry* was The Empire Poetry League, also known as simply The Poetry League, which had been established by 1922 or earlier. Its aim was to organise meetings, lectures, and generally to develop knowledge of current poetry. Membership of what appears to have been a rival to the Poetry Society meant a free subscription to the magazine. S. Fowler Wright edited from 1921.

BL: P.P.5126.bb
CUL: *Poetry*, 1921–25. *Poetry and the Play*. (L727.c.26)
TCD: *Poetry and the Play*. (65.gg.63–66)

Poetry and Drama *See* The Monthly Chapbook A128

171 Poetry and the People. London: Poetry and the People, No. 1 (1938)–20 (1940)

Note: Continued by: *Our Time*
Index: Bloomfield (Nos.1–15 only)
Profiled in: Hoffman, Allen & Ulrich; Tolley 1930s

Dedicated to the publishing of poetry from the various geographical sections of the Poetry Group of the Left Book Club. Contributors included Jack Lindsay, Nicholas Moore, Idris Davies, and Roger Woddis. Later issues also included short articles.

BL: No. 5 (Nov. 1938), 9 (Mar. 1939), 11 (May 1939)–20 [Aug. 1940]. (P.P.5126.bn.)
CUL: No. 3–12, 16–20. (L727.B.25)
TCD: [No. 3] (Sept.1938); 4 (Oct.,1938); 6 (Dec.1938)–8 (Feb.,1939); 12 (June 1939); 16 (Jan.1940)–20 (Sept.1940). Note: [No. 3] Sept.1938; 18–20 (1940) shelved at 26.bb.222, No.1–4. But No.4 (Oct. 1938)– 6 (Dec.1938)–8 (Feb.,1939); 12 (June 1939); 16 (Jan.1940); 17(Feb. 1940) shelved at 131.d.33, Nos.21–27

Poetry and the Play *See* Poetry A170

172 The Poetry Journal. London, then Ilfracombe: Arthur H. Stockwell, Vol. 1 no.1 (Apr. 1937)–[vol. 4 no. 2 (May/Sept. 1943)]. Then, New Series, Oct. 1948–Feb.1951?

The editor is not identified. The magazine published many unambitious but heartfelt poems from writers who remain unknown today, and short articles on general topics concerning poetry (most of which were unsigned). Many of the poems are concerned with the Second World War, the cause of the publisher's move from London to Dorset in 1941.

BL: Lacking: Vol. 1, no. 2, no. 4, no. 5, no. 9; vol. 2, no. 5, no. 6; vol. 3, no. 3, no. 5. Also lacking: New Series, Feb. 1950–Feb.1951. (P.P.5126.bp.)
CUL: Vol. 3 no. 7–vol. 4 no. 2. New Series, Oct. 1948–Feb. 1951. (L727.D.75.)
TCD: Vol. 3 no. 7–vol. 4 no. 2. New Series, Oct. 1948; Feb. 1949; June 1949; Jan. 1950. (131.d.33,No.2–13)

173 Poetry London / edited by Anthony Dickens and J. M. Tambimuttu, then Tambimuttu only, then Richard March and Nicholas Moore. London: [Vol. 1] no. 1 (Feb. 1939)–vol. 6 no. 23 (Winter 1951)

Note: Imprint varied. The volume number and issue number are independent sequences, i.e. there were only 23 issues in total. Variant titles: *Poetry and Poetry (London)*
Index: Bloomfield (Vol.1 no. 1–2 only)
Profiled in: Hoffman, Allen & Ulrich; Stanton; Sullivan 1914–1984; Tolley 1940s
Related Imprint: Editions Poetry London published scollections by Nicholas Moore, Keith Douglas, G. S. Fraser, W. S. Graham, Kathleen Nott, Kathleen Raine, John Waller and others. It also published a six-volume poetry series called PL Pamphlets, BL: W.P.12672, as well as fiction, anthologies, and literary criticism
Reprint: [Vol. 1] no. 1–no. 6 (May/June 1941) is reprinted in *Poetry London*, London: Frank Cass, 1970

Published at irregular intervals, but an eclectic magazine with international range, regarded as one of the best of the period. Following his move to the United States, Tambimuttu set up *Poetry London-New York*, with Dickins as London editor, which ran for four issues from 1956–1960 (BL: P.P.7615.ma), and then, much later, the short-lived *Poetry London / Apple* magazine, published in London again, which had two issues, appearing in 1979 and 1982 (BL: P.901/3258). Ronald Duncan was also involved editorially. A significant collection of Tambimuttu's correspondence concerning *Poetry London* is held by the British Library's Manuscripts Department, and many of the books owned by him are held within the printed collections, with the shelfmark prefix Tambi.

BL: P.P.5126.bbi
CUL: L727.B.16
NLS: Vol. 1 no. 1 (5.5690); vol. 2 no. 7–vol. 6 no. 23. (Y.132.)
TCD: Vol. 2 no. 7–vol. 6 no. 23. (55.bb.115, Nos.1–16). Another copy of Vol.2 no.10. (137.a.66)
UCL: 2–4, 6, 14, 16, 18
Poetry Library: Vol. 2 no. 7–vol. 5 no. 23 [Reprint]. Also: vol. 3 no. 11

174 **Poetry Past and Present.** London: [Poetry], Vol. 1 no. 1 (1929)

CUL: L727.C.86
UCL

175 **The Poetry Quarterly** / edited by William Kingston Fudge, then George Whybrow. London: Vol. 1 no. 1 (Winter 1933)–no. 6 (Spring 1934)

Profiled in: Hoffman, Allen & Ulrich

Fudge edited from Winter [i.e. Jan.] 1933 to July 1933. Whybrow from Autumn 1933 onwards.

BL: P.P.5126.gbd.
CUL: L727.C.21
NLS: U.461
TCD: 90.n.55

176 **Poetry Quarterly** / edited by Katherine Hunter Coe; then C. Wrey Gardiner. Dawlish then London: Channing Press, then The Grey Walls Press, Vol .1 no. 1(Summer 1939)–vol. 15 no. 1 (Spring/Summer 1953)

Note: Continues: *Poetry Studies*. Vol.15 no.1 was incorrectly numbered vol. 15 no.5
Index: Sader; Bloomfield (vol. 1 no.1–2 only)
Profiled in: Hoffman, Allen & Ulrich; Stanton; Sullivan 1914–1984; Tolley 1940s
Related Imprint: The Grey Walls Press published a number of individual collections
Reprint: Nendeln, Liechtenstein: Kraus Reprint Coe was editor from 1939 until 1940, when Gardiner became sole editor.

BL: Vol. 1 no. 1–vol. 12 no. 4; vol. 13 no. 3. (P.P.5126.gbe.)
CUL: L727.C.34
NLS: Vol. 1–6, Y118; vol. 7–15, U.461.
TCD: 50.cc.71–72
UCL: Vol.1 no. 2–vol. 13 no. 4
Poetry Library: Vol. 7 no. 1–2, 4; vol. 8 no. 2; vol. 9 no. 1–2, 4; vol. 10 no.1–2; vol. 11 no. 1; vol. 12 no. 1–4; vol. 13 no. 2–4; vol. 14 no. 2–3; vol. 15 no. 1

177 **The Poetry Review** / [edited by Harold Monro] and then others, including Stephen Phillips, Galloway Kyle, Muriel Spark, John Gawsworth, Thomas Moult, Derek Parker, Eric Mottram, Edwin Brock, Harry Chambers, Douglas Dunn, Roger Garfitt, Mick Imlah, Andrew Motion, Peter Forbes, David Herd and Robert Potts, and Fiona Sampson. London: The Poetry Society, Vol.1 no. 1 (Jan. 1912)– . ISSN 0032–2156

Note: Continues: *The Poetical Gazette*
Index: Indexed selectively by: *Abstracts of English Studies; Index to Book Reviews in the Humanities; MLA International Bibliography*
Profiled in: Sullivan 1837–1913
Website: www.poetrysociety.org.uk. Selected issues have been digitised and appear at www.poetrymagazines.org.uk
Related Work: Dominic Hibberd, *Harold Monro: poet of the New Age* (Basingstoke: Palgrave, 2001), BL: YC.2001.a.4084

Monro's brief editorship from 1912–13 was outstanding, with essays that engaged with modernist poetry and its precursors. This included articles by Lascelles Abercrombie, Henry Newbolt, John Drinkwater and Harriet Monroe, editor of *Poetry* (Chicago). There were also contributions by Richard Aldington, Pound and William Carlos Williams. The magazine took decades to recover from Monro's departure. After Stephen Phillips's undistinguished three-year editorship, Galloway Kyle took the helm. Very few poets or poems of note were published by him. Muriel Spark was briefly editor from 1947 to 1949. Her attempts to bring better work into the magazine were consolidated and expanded by John Gawsworth (editor from 1949 to 1952). The 1950s and 60s were perhaps more conservative and only in 1972, with the appointment of Eric Mottram, did the magazine begin to engage with the range of British contemporary poetry. Mottram's fascination with American modernist poetry could be said to be a return to Monro's Anglo-American editorial policy, too. Under his editorship *Poetry Review* introduced British readers to new work from across the Atlantic. Editorial pressure from the Poetry Society's conservative funders, The Arts Council of Great Britain, appears eventually to have led to Mottram's departure, in 1978, and several years of editorial instability. Peter Forbes's editorship in the 80s and 90s will be remembered for the magazine's association with "The New Generation" promotion of younger poets. Forbes's magazine was quietly eclectic in the poetry it published but perhaps shy of intellectual engagement with texts, a gap to some extent filled by the joint editorship of David Herd and Robert Potts begun in 2002. This was characterised by a broader eclecticism, a stronger engagement with American and British avant-garde, longer, sometimes more academic essays and articles, and a partnership with the Whitechapel Gallery which involved reproducing art in the magazine and hosting readings at the Gallery. In 2005 the poet Fiona Sampson, with a background in European poetry and translation, took over the helm.

BL: Vol. 1 no. 1– . Lacking: Vol. 2 no. 2, 4, 5; vol. 19 no. 1, 3, 5; vol. 21 no. 1–5. (P.P.5126.gb)
CUL: P727.B.21
NLS: Vol. 1–63. Lacking: Vol. 62 no. 2. (Y.193). Vol. 64– .
Lacking: Vol. 87 no. 4; vol. 88 no. 1 (HJ8.86 SER)
TCD: Vol. 1–64. (130.t.36–90). Vol. 65– . (PER 820)
UCL: Vol.1; vol. 20 no. 2; vol. 31 no. 2; vol. 35 no. 4; vol. 55– . (Little Magazines Collection). Vol. 40 no. 1 (Laurence Housman Collection)
Poetry Library: Vol. 1 no. 3, 8; vol. 22 no. 2; vol. 39 no. 2; vol. 46 no. 3; vol. 58 no. 4–vol. 61 no. 4; vol. 62 no. 3; vol. 63 no. 1–vol. 66 no. 4; vol. 67 no. 3–

178 Poetry Studies. Dawlish: Channing Press, No. 1 (Spring 1933)–22 (Spring 1939)

Note: Continued by: *Poetry Quarterly*

Profiled in: Hoffman, Allen & Ulrich; Stanton

BL: P.P.5126.gbe
CUL: L727.C.33
NLS: Y.188
TCD: 50.cc.70

179 Poets' Guild Quarterly. Buckhurst Hill: Ruth Elliott, Vol. 1 no. 1 (July–August–September 1931)

Related Imprint: Ruth Elliot also self-published *In Silver Ink, and other poems*, (Buckhurst Hill, [1932]; BL: 11640.ee.53.)

BL: Destroyed in the Second World War. (P.P.5126.bg)

180 Poets of Tomorrow / [edited by John Lehmann?] London: Hogarth Press, First Selection (1939)–Third Selection (1942)

Note: The Second Selection bears the subtitle "Cambridge Poetry 1940"
Profiled in: Tolley 1930s; Tolley 1940s

Edited anonymously but almost certainly by John Lehmann, who managed the Hogarth Press from 1938–1946, these three selections were specifically designed to publish young poets. They were: in the First Selection, Peter Hewett, H. B. Mallalieu, Ruthven Todd, and Robert Waller; in the Second Selection, John Bateman, Stephen Coates, Alexander [ie Alex] Comfort, Maurice James Craig, Mark Holloway, Nicholas Moore, Jock Moreton, George Scurfield, Gervase Stewart, E. V. Swart and Terence Tiller; and in the Third Selection, Lawrence Little, David Gascoyne, Laurie Lee, Adam Drinan, and Arthur Harvey.

BL: W.P.12987
CUL: L727.C.100
NLS: T.32.a

The Porpoise Press Broadsheets *See* Broadsheet [of the Porpoise Press] A21

181 The Programme / edited by George Sayer, Veronica Ward, Alan Hodge, Kenneth Allott and others. Oxford: [The Oxford English Club], No.1 (Feb. 1935)–13 (Nov. 1937)

Index: Bloomfield
Profiled in: Hoffman, Allen & Ulrich

Included poetry by William Carlos Williams, F. T. Prince, Oswell Blakeston, Dylan Thomas, Frederic Prokosch, and others.

CUL: L718.C.19
TCD: 133.n.112

182 Purpose / edited by John Marlow; W. T. Symons and Philip Mairet; W. T. Symons. London: C. W. Daniel, Vol. 1 no. 1 (Jan./Mar. 1929)–vol. 12 no. 3/4 (July/Dec. 1940)

Index: An index to vol. 9 only, included with the volume
Profiled in: Hoffman, Allen & Ulrich, Sullivan 1914–1984
Related Work: Desmond Hawkins, *When I Was: a memoir of the years between the wars* (London: Macmillan, 1989), BL: YC.1989.a.10213, gives an account of Hawkins's involvement in the magazine.

A magazine in its early years devoted to discussion of Major C. H. Douglas's economic theory of Social Credit. It also published poetry by, for example, Dylan Thomas and Lawrence Durrell, and essays by T. S. Eliot, Henry Miller, W. H. Auden, and Ezra Pound. The editors served for the following periods: John Marlow, 1929; then W. T. Symons and Philip Mairet, 1930–34; then W. T. Symons, 1935; then W. T. Symons, general editor, and A. Desmond Hawkins literary editor, 1936–40.

BL: P.P.1247.aef.
CUL: L900.C.246
TCD: 36.q.133–138

A Quarterly by the Bristol Poets' Fellowship *See* The Bristol Poets Fellowship Quarterly A20

183 **The Quiet Hour** / edited by William James-Bailey. Birmingham: William James-Bailey, 1937–[1938?]

Includes occasional, anonymous poems. The editor appears to have been a vicar.

BL: No.1, 3, 6–8, 11, 12 only. (P.P.6063.dcd)

184 **The Quorum: a magazine of friendship.** London: [The Quorum, 1920]

This appears to have existed only as a pilot or "specimen" issue. A general literary review, it included poems by E. E. Bradford, Dorothy L. Sayers, and J. G. Nicholson.

BL: PP.5938.dea.(1)
TCD: 106.a.82.No.18

185 **The Ray** / edited by B. J. Brooke and G. D. Bone, and subsequently others. Petersfield, Hampshire: Bedales School, No. 1 (Spring 1925)–9 (Autumn 1927)

Short stories, poems, woodcuts, and articles. A school magazine with high production standards and, despite the in-jokes, a clear and intelligent interest in the world outside the school, be it Catullus or the General Strike. Not, however, to be confused with Sidney Hunt's *Ray*. G. D. Bone is probably Gavin David Bone, who later wrote on Anglo-Saxon poetry.

BL: PP.6150.nak

186 **Ray** / edited by Sidney Hunt. London: Sidney Hunt, [No. 1, 1927]–2 (1927)

Note: The first issue had the subtitle "Miscellany of art"; the second issue had the subtitles "Miscellany of art, poetry and ideas"; "the most beautiful [magazine in the world]"; and "the most expensive magazine in the world"
Index: An index is provided in *Form: a quarterly of the arts*, no. 5 (Sept. 1967), BL: P.421/41, where extracts are also reprinted.

A magazine strongly influenced by Russian art and graphic design. In fact several Russians contribute visual and textual work, including visual poetry. Contributors were, in their entirety: Hans Arp, I. K. Bonset (i.e. Theo van Doesburg), Giorgio de Chirico, Otto Dix, Betty Edwards, Claude Flight, Naum Gabo, Albert Gleizes, Sidney Hunt, Marcel Janco, Matthew Josephson, Wassily Kandinsky, El Lissitzky, Emile Maelspine, Kasimir Malevich, Laszlo Moholy-Nagy, Ben Nicholson, Kurt Schwitters, Michel Seuphor, Gertrude Stein, Josef Peeters, Mies van der Rohe,

and Herwarth Walden. With such a confluence of largely European and Russian modernists represented in its pages, this was a highly unusual magazine to have been published in the British Isles. It is one of the highlights of the interwar little magazine in Britain.

CUL: T400.c.6.
NLS: 5.438
Bodleian Library, Oxford: Per. 3963 d.114 (v.1–2)

187 **The Red Hand Magazine** / edited by W. Forbes Patterson. Belfast: W. Forbes Patterson, Vol. 1 no. 1 (Sept. 1920)–no. 4 (Dec. 1920)

Note: Last issue was published in Glasgow, apparently following a police raid on the Belfast offices
Profiled in: Tom Clyde, *Irish Literary Magazines: an outline and descriptive bibliography* (Dublin: Irish Academic Press, 2003), BL: 2725.g.3414
Reprint: Dublin, Ireland: Irish Microforms Ltd., 1976. (Irish political and radical newspapers of the twentieth century. Republican sectional list 1895–1923)

A republican magazine. Contributions included work by Peadar Pol, Michael Walsh, James M'Carthy, Edmund B. Fitzgerald, Liam P. O Riain, Eamon MacGearailt, Mary Mackay and others.

BL: Microfilm, Newspaper Collections
NLS: Microfilm, HP.2.76.232
TCD: Microfilm, 86.rr.125

188 **Rejected MSS** / edited by N. F. Hidden, H. D. Willcock, and N. R. Cohn. Oxford: No. 1 (June 1934)–2 (Dec. 1934)

Index: Bloomfield

Published poems and short fiction, and a review of the first issues of F. R. Leavis's *Scrutiny* (with Leavis's reply). Poets included Ian Serraillier, Norman Cohn, Rosemary Roberts, Brenda Pool, Alastair W. R. Millar, Penelope Bowers, Eíthne nic Liamóg and others. The idea was that most of the work submitted would already have been rejected by other magazines.

BL: P.P.5938.bbb

189 **Rejection: a magazine of literary and general interest.** London: Vol. 1 (1932)–vol. 2 no. 11 (1934)

Note: Absorbed: *The Melody*
CUL: L900.B.187

190 **Satire and Burlesque** / edited by J. Carveth Wells, then S. M. Telkar. London: Satire Publishing, Vol. 1 no. 1 (Oct. 1934)–vol. 2 no. 5 (July/Aug. 1935)

Mostly prose, but some poetry, including by John Singer, and "Literary Lullabies" by Terence Stanford (vol. 1 no. 2), which includes rhymed verses on Wyndham Lewis, Aldous Huxley, the Powys brothers, Marie Stopes, John Masefield, J. B. Priestley, and others. It appears to have suffered a ban of the first two issues by the London Federation of Wholesale Newsagents, which was lifted by vol. 1 no. 3 (Dec. 1934). S. M. Telkar took over editorship from Wells with vol. 2 no. 2. (Mar. 1935)

BL: P.P.5270.al

191 **The Scottish Bookman** / edited by David Cleghorn Thomson. Edinburgh: Scottish Contacts Service, No. 1 (Sept. 1935)–6 (Feb. 1936)

BL: P.P.6203.aca
CUL: L718.D.2
TCD: 49.t.233

192 **The Scottish Chapbook** / edited by C. M. Grieve. Montrose: C. M. Grieve, Vol. 1 no. 1 (Aug. 1922)–vol. 2 no. 3 (Nov./Dec. 1923)

Profiled in: Hoffman, Allen & Ulrich; Sullivan 1914–1984; David Finkelstein, Margery Palmer McCulloch and Duncan Glen, *Scottish Literary Periodicals: Three Essays* (Edinburgh: Merchiston Publishing, 1998)

One of the most important little magazines of modern Scotland. Edited by C. M. Grieve, the real name of "Hugh MacDiarmid", it published groundbreaking self-penned articles on Scottish literature's history and culture, and MacDiarmid's own lyric poems. Other contributors included several writers of the Modern Scottish Renaissance, including Edwin Muir, Neil M. Gunn, and William Soutar. Its motto was: "Not traditions – precedents."

BL: P.P.6203.l
CUL: L727.B.30
NLS: NJ.708
TCD: Vol.1 no.12–vol.2 no.2. (67.dd.120, Nos.11–13)

193 **The Scottish Nation** / edited by C. M. Grieve. Montrose: C.M. Grieve, Vol. 1 no. 1 (May 8 1923)–vol. 2 no. 8 (Dec 25 1923)

For a time running concurrently with Grieve's *The Scottish Chapbook* this magazine, despite the title, was perhaps more outward-looking, e.g. publishing an early account (for an English-speaking audience) of Friedrich Hölderlin. This internationalism complemented the theme in its sister magazine of re-making Scotland.

BL: Newspaper Collections
NLS: Microfilm of set from The Mitchell Library, Glasgow. (Mf.7.(5.)). Also, two issues in hard copy: Vol. 1 no. 6– no. 7. (8.74)

194 **The Scottish Standard.** Glasgow: [The Scottish Standard], Vol. 1 no. 1 (Feb. 1935)–no. 13 (Feb.1936).

Note: Amalgamated with *The Modern Scot* to form *Outlook*.

BL: P.P.6203.bii
NLS: U.424

195 **Scrutiny** / edited by L. C. Knights and Donald Culver; F. R. Leavis, Denys Thompson, D. W. Harding, W. H. Mellers and H. A. Mason. Cambridge: The Editors; distributed by Deighton, Bell and Co., Vol. 1 no. 1 (May 1932)–vol. 19 no. 4 (Oct. 1953); vol. 20 (1963)

Note: Editors vary.
Index: Vol. 15 contains an index to all preceding volumes, as does vol. 20.
Anthology: Eric Bentley (ed.), *The Importance of Scrutiny. Selections from Scrutiny: a quarterly review, 1932–1948* (New York: New York University Press, 1964), BL: P.P.8007.io.; F. R. Leavis (ed.), *A Selection from Scrutiny* (Cambridge: Cambridge University Press, 1968), BL: X.909/13037.
Profiled in: Hoffman, Allen & Ulrich; Stanton; Sullivan 1914–1984; Tolley 1930s; Tolley 1940s; Jason Harding, "Scrutiny: critics from Cambridge", in *The Criterion: cultural politics and periodical networks in inter-war Britain* (Oxford: Oxford University Press, 2002), pp.64–87, BL: YC.2002.a.7159
Related Work: Ian MacKillop, *F. R. Leavis: a life in criticism*, corrected ed. (London: Penguin, 1997), BL: YC.1998.a.210
Reprint: Cambridge: Cambridge University Press, 1963, BL: P.P.5938.bar/3.
Microform: Millwood, New York: Kraus Microform, [undated]

A general literary review, published commercially, but seen by some as a little magazine. It published literary criticism almost entirely, though very occasionally some poems did appear. Vol. 20 was published by Cambridge University Press with reprints of the previous volumes. This included 'A Retrospect' by the key (but not founding) editor, F. R. Leavis, errata and indexes. Leavis actually joined the editorial board of Knights and Culver only with vol. 1 no. 3

BL: Vol. 1 no. 1 (May 1932)–vol. 19 no. 4 (P.P.5938.bar) Vol. 20 (P.P.5938.bar/4)
CUL: T900.C.21–
NLS: Y.190
TCD: 125.q.41–56a
UCL

196 Seed / edited by Herbert Jones and Oswell Blakeston. London: E. Lahr, [1] (Jan.1933)–[2/3] (April/July 1933)

Index: Bloomfield
Profiled in: Hoffman, Allen & Ulrich

An understated modernist little magazine. Contributions include 'magician' by H. D., prose poems, a calligraphic or visual poem by Sidney Hunt, Herbert Jones's 'layout for a poem' consisting solely of parallel lines, and, perhaps surprisingly, John Betjeman reviewing an Oswell Blakeston collection not entirely unfavourably. Other contributors included Kay Boyle, Rhys Davies, Robert Herring, Mary Butts, and others. Oswell Blakeston was the pseudonym of Henry Joseph Hasslacher.

BL: P.P.5938.bas
CUL: L727.C.16
NLS: 5.526
TCD: [2/3]. (121.p.323, no.16)

197 Seven / edited by John Goodland and Nicholas Moore, then Philip O'Connor and George Cruickshank, then Sydney Tremayne, then Randall Swingler and J. R. St John, then Callander Taylor. Taunton, then Cambridge, then London: Goodland and Moore [and successive publishers], [Vol. 1] no. 1 (Summer 1938)–vol. 7 no. 2 (1947)

Note: Publication suspended Spring 1940–Mar. 1941.
Index: Bloomfield; Sader
Profiled in: Hoffman, Allen & Ulrich; Stanton; Sullivan 1914–1984 (profile of first two years only); Tolley 1930s; Tolley 1940s
Reprint: New York, Kraus-Thomson.

Microfilm: Marvin Sukov Collection, University of Wisconsin, BHP/9. La Crosse, Wis.: Brookhaven Press, [undated]

Short fiction, poems, and cartoons. Published poetry associated with the "New Apocalypse" poets, such as Dorian Cooke, G. S. Fraser, J. F. Hendry, Norman MacCaig, Tom Scott, Henry Treece, and Nicholas Moore himself, but, from the re-launch in March 1941, the general tone of the magazine is comparatively lighter. Also published David Gascoyne, George Barker, Roy Fuller, Keidrych Rhys, Anne Ridler, John Singer, Sydney D. Tremayne, Jack Lindsay, Howard Sergeant, Wallace Stevens, Ronald Bottrall, Elizabeth Smart, George Seferis, Hugh MacDiarmid, as well as those associated with The Booster, such as Lawrence Durrell, Henry Miller, and Anaïs Nin.

BL: P.P.5939.bep
CUL: [Vol. 1] no.1–vol.7 no. 1. (L727.C.77.)
NLS: P.213
UCL: [Vol. 1] no.1– no. 8

198 The Signature / edited by D. H. Lawrence, Katherine Mansfield and John Middleton Murry. London, No. 1 (Oct. 4 1915)–3 (Nov. 1 1915)

Profiled in: Hoffman, Allen & Ulrich

Solely the prose of Lawrence, Middleton Murry, and Katherine Mansfield (using the pseudonym Matilda Berry).

BL: P.P.5938.bb.(2.)
CUL: T718.c.26
NLS: RB.s.1235

199 Soma / edited by K. S. Bhat. London: K. S. Bhat, No. 1 (June 1931)–5 (1934)

Index: Bloomfield

Short fiction, playscripts and poetry. Contributors included Oswell Blakeston, Sonia Rosa Burstein, Paul Selver (who also translates various European poets), Albert Young, B. Sh. Saklatvala, Laurence Powys, T. F. Powys, John Gawsworth, Rhys Davies, Mary Butts and others.

BL: P.P.5938.bap.
CUL: T718.C.2
NLS: 1–5. (X.187.g). Pictorial supplements (6.304)
TCD: 122.c.74–78

Some Imagist Poets See [The Imagist Anthologies] A90

200 **Songs for Sixpence: a series of single new poems by young Cambridge poets** / edited by J. Bronowski and J. M. Reeves. Cambridge: Heffer & Sons, No.1–6, 1929

Contributors included T. H. White and William Empson.

BL: 11605.bb.1
CUL: CAM.D.291.3

201 **Songs from the Ship and Castle.** Bristol: Henry Hill Ltd, [First Year] 1930–[Eleventh Year, 1944]?

Note: The volume for 1931 is entitled *More Songs from the Ship and Castle*

BL: 1 (1930), 5 (1934), 8 (1937), 9 (1938), 10 (1939), 11 (1944). (P.P.5126.bk.)
CUL: 5–11. (Upper Library)
TCD: 5 (1934) (32.rr.113, No.18). 8 (1937), 9 (1938). (132.p.126, Nos.15, 15a)

202 **The Speaking of Poetry: the bulletin of the Verse Speaking Fellowship.** London: Verse Speaking Fellowship, No. 1 (Apr. 1928)–no. 10 (Jan. 1931).

Note: Continued as: *Good Speech*

BL: P.P.5126.eb

The Spring Anthology *See* The Mitre Anthology of Poetry A124

203 **Static** / edited by Richard Kersey and T. J. B. Spencer. No. 1–3? (1933?)

No holdings known

204 **Terence White's Verse-Reel.** London: [Terence White's Verse-Reel], 1939–?.

BL: Destroyed in the Second World War. (P.P.5126.bbg)

205 **This Quarter** / edited by Ethel Moorhead and Ernest Walsh. Paris: [This Quarter], Vol. 1 no. 1 [1925]–vol. 5 no. 2. (1932)

Note: Vol. 1. no. 2 was published in Milan; vol. 1. no. 3, 4 were published in Monte Carlo
Profiled in: *This Quarter* Vol. 1 no. 3
Related Work: Kay Boyle, *The Year Before Last* (London: Faber, 1932), BL: 12717.aaa.18; also, later edition, with an afterword by Doris Grumbach (London: Virago, 1986); BL: YC.1987.a.2236. This novel contains a fictionalised portrait of Ethel Moorhead.

A general literary review founded by Scottish ex-suffragette Ethel Moorhead with funds left to her by fellow activist, Fanny Parker. After the death of the American poet Ernest Walsh, the magazine was edited by Ethel Moorhead alone, i.e. from vol. 1 no. 3 onwards.

BL: Lacking Vol. 2. no. 2 and the Antheil musical supplement to vol. 1 no. 2. (P.P.4291.ddb)
CUL: T727.C.1
TCD: Vol.2 no.2; vol. 2 no. 4. (OLS L–7–250 no.14–no.15). Vol.4 no. 3; vol.5 no.1; vol. 5 no. 2. (OLS L–7–249)
UCL: Vol.3 no. 3; Vol. 5 no. 1

206 **This Unrest** / edited by Donovan Brown. Oxford: Donovan Brown, at Ruskin College, No. [1, 1933]–4 (Feb. 1935)

Index: Bloomfield

A general cultural review, with occasional poems. Contributors include Charles Madge, C. Day Lewis, Naomi Mitchison, André Gide and Ludwig Tureck, Gavin Ewart, and others.

BL: Photocopy of complete run. (X.905/226)

207 **Thoth.** Cambridge: No. 1 (1939)–3 (1939)

Index: Bloomfield

CUL: CAM.B.31.59

208 **To Day** / edited by Holbrook Jackson. London: Vol. 1. no. 1 (Mar.1917)–vol. 10 no. 58 (Dec. 1923)

Note: Absorbed *T.P.'s Weekly*, out of scope for this bibliography. Absorbed by *Life and Letters*. The volume numbering runs parallel to the individual issue numbering, i.e. there are only 58 issues in total. Variant title: *To-Day*
Profiled in: Sullivan 1837–1913
Reprint: Vol. 1 (March–August 1917), New York: Kraus Reprint, 1970

BL: Lacking no. 21, 22. (P.P.5938.bag.)
CUL: L727.C.11

NLS: Vol. 1, Kraus Reprint. (5.5443)
TCD: Vol.2 no.7 (Sept. 1917)–Vol.10 no.58. (27.t.25–29)
UCL: Vol. 3 no. 17 (1918). (L Housman Coll)

209 To-morrow / [edited by H. [i.e. Francis] Stuart and Cecil Salkeld.] Dublin: [Tomorrow], Vol. 1 no. 1 (Aug. 1924)–no. 2 (Sept. 1924)

Profiled in: Hoffman, Allen & Ulrich; Tom Clyde, *Irish Literary Magazines: an outline and descriptive bibliography* (Dublin: Irish Academic Press, 2003), BL: 2725.g.3414

Included work by Yeats (notably "Leda and the Swan"), Joseph Campbell, F.R. Higgins, Liam O'Flaherty, Iseult Stuart, Arthur Symons and others. Lennox Robinson's story "The Madonna of Slieve Dun", in which a girl is raped by a tramp, but then believes she is to be the mother of a new Christ, caused him to be sacked as Librarian to the Plunkett Foundation. The artist Cecil Salkeld ceased to co-edit after the first issue. The Irish printer refused to print the second issue, which was therefore printed in Manchester.

BL: P.P.7611.cac.
CUL: NPR
TCD: 202.u.1 no.1A+1B
UCL: Vol. 1 no. 1

210 Townsman: a quarterly review / edited by Ronald Duncan. London: Ronald Duncan, Vol. 1. no. 1 (Jan. 1938)–vol. 5. no. 20. (Feb. 1944). Then, as *The Scythe*, no. 21 (July 1944)–24 (June 1945).

Note: Title varied. Some issues of no. 16 were also called *The Scythe*, a title used solely for 19 (Summer 1943), then 21 (July 1944) onwards
Index: Bloomfield (Vol. 1 no. 1–vol. 2 no. 8 only)
Profiled in: Hoffman, Allen & Ulrich; Stanton; Sullivan 1914–1984
Reprint: Nendeln, Liechtenstein: Kraus Reprint, 1972

Contributors included Ezra Pound, Joseph Macleod, and others.

BL: P.P.5938.bbg
NLS: Vol. 1 no. 1–vol. 5 no. 17 (Sept. 1942). (5.4884.)
TCD: Vol.1 no. 1–Vol.2 no.6 (Apr. 1939). (26.cc.194 No. 8–12)
UCL: Kraus Reprint

211 The Transatlantic Review / edited by Ford Madox Ford. Paris and London: Transatlantic Review and Duckworth; and New York: Thomas Seltzer, Vol. 1 no. 1 (Jan. 1924)–vol. 2 no. 6 (Dec. 1924)

Note: The American edition was printed last, and can contain additions to the earlier editions.
Index: Sader
Profiled in: Hoffman, Allen & Ulrich; Sullivan 1914–1984
Anthology: *Transatlantic Stories*. With an introduction by Ford Madox Ford (London: Duckworth, 1926), BL: 12710.dd.26.
Study: Bernard J. Poli, *Ford Madox Ford and the Transatlantic Review*. (Syracuse: Syracuse University Press, 1967), BL: X.981/2083
Reprint: New York: Kraus Reprint, 1967

As its title suggests, intended to link American literature with European. Not an especially prolific publisher of poetry, but William Carlos Williams, E. E. Cummings, Paul Valéry, Tristan Tzara, and H. D. did contribute. Mina Loy's long letter on Gertrude Stein in vol. 2 is an early and significant statement on the nature of Modernism. Outside poetry, Joyce, Conrad, Ford, and Hemingway all had contributions. Basil Bunting reviewed Conrad's *The Rover*. Hemingway guest-edited the August 1924 issue. Not to be confused with *The Transatlantic Review* that ran in the 1950s and 60s.

BL: London and Paris edition only (P.P.4291.dg.)
CUL: T700.C.1
UCL: Kraus Reprint

212 Transition / edited by Eugene Jolas and Elliot Paul. Paris, No. 1 (1927)–27(Apr./May 1938). New Series, No. 1 (1948)–6 (1950)

Note: No. 21–24 was published in The Hague; no. 25/26 in New York. A supplement accompanies no. 23, and is described as *Transition Pamphlet no. 1*
Index: Index covering nos. 1–12 included with no.12; "transition bibliography" for nos.1–22 included with no. 22.
Anthology: Eugene Jolas (ed.), *Transition Workshop*, (New York: Vanguard Press, 1949), BL: 11392.a.3
Profiled in: Hoffman, Allen & Ulrich
Study: Dougald McMillan, *"transition": the history of a literary era, 1927–1938* (London: Calder and Boyars, 1975), BL: X.989/50926
Reprint: Reprint of New Series, Nendeln: Kraus, [1967]

A key journal of modernism, best-known for its publication of Joyce's 'Work in Progress', later to be known as *Finnegans*

Wake. Although not published in Britain or Ireland, included here for its importance to British and Irish writers and readers.

BL: Cup. 400.a.30
CUL: T727.C.31
NLS: Reprint of New Series, No. 1 (1948)–6 (1950). (6.2210)
TCD: OLS JOH 123
UCL: No. 1–27. (JOYCE Pers)

The Tribune *See* The Irish Tribune: a weekly review of affairs A98

213 The Twentieth Century / edited by
Jon Randell Evans. London: [The Promethean Society], Vol. 1 no. 1 (Mar. 1931)–vol. 5 no. 27 (1933)

Note: The volume designation was independent of the issue designation, i.e. there were 27 issues in total, collected in five volumes

Related Work: Desmond Hawkins, *When I Was: a memoir of the years between the wars* (London: Macmillan, 1989), BL: YC.1989.a.10213, gives an account of the Society and the magazine.

The Promethean Society was a radical political group which stressed the need for researched, rational responses to domestic and world problems. The ideas of H. G. Wells seem to have been an influence. It was perhaps most controversial for its anti-royalist stance, but had a much broader programme that included birth control, disarmament, a liberal attitude towards homosexuality and an end to censorship. Although mainly containing essays, correspondence, Society reports, short fiction and reviews, the magazine also published poetry. Literary contributors included the novelist J. Leslie Mitchell (better known as Lewis Grassic Gibbon), Auden, Desmond Hawkins, John Galsworthy, Francis Stuart, Naomi Mitchison, George Barker (including an essay on "Poetry and Contemporary Inertia"), Hugh Gordon Porteus (e.g. on Ezra Pound) and Wyndham Lewis (on "The Artist as Crowd"). Vol. 4 no. 24 (Feb. 1933) contains a supplement entitled "Twentieth Century Verse", with an essay on Auden by Porteus, and poems by Auden, Michael Roberts, George Barker, Richard Goodman, Randall Swingler, and A. L. Morton. The magazine is not to be confused with the commercially successful *Twentieth Century*, begun in 1951 as successor to the longstanding *Nineteenth Century*, in turn begun in 1877.

BL: Vol. 1 no. 1–no. 6; vol. 2 no. 8, 9, 11, 12; vol. 3 no. 13, 14, 18–20; vol. 4 no. 24. (P.P.5939.caf)
CUL: L900.B.127
NLS: P.34

214 Twentieth Century Verse / edited by
Julian Symons. London, No. 1 (Jan 1937)–18 (July 1939)

Index: Sader. Issue 15/16 contains an index for nos. 9–16
Profiled in: Hoffman, Allen & Ulrich; Stanton; Sullivan 1914–1984; Tolley 1930s; Tolley 1940s; Adrian Caesar, *Dividing Lines: poetry, class and ideology in the 1930s* (Manchester University Press, 1991), BL: YC.1991.a.765
Reprint: New York: Kraus Reprint, 1966

Contributors included Symons, Ruthven Todd, D. S. Savage, Philip O'Connor, Gavin Ewart, Geoffrey Taylor, George Barker, Dylan Thomas, and others. No. 6–7 is a double issue given over to the work of Wyndham Lewis. The 12–13 double issue is especially strong on American poetry, with poems by Wallace Stevens, Delmore Schwartz, John Berryman, Theodore Roethke and others. A questionaire about American poetry in the same issue had respondents who included William Carlos Williams, Wallace Stevens, and Marianne Moore.

BL: 1–4, 6–13, 15–18. (P.P.5126.bi). 1, 2, 6/7, 9, 14–18. (Tambi.114)
CUL: CA/U68
TCD: 133.n.114
UCL

215 The Tyro: a review of the arts of painting, sculpture, and design / edited by Wyndham Lewis. London: Egoist Press, No. 1 (1921)–no. 2 (1922)

Profiled in: Hoffman, Allen & Ulrich
Reprint: London: Frank Cass, 1970. (English little magazines, no. 5)

Contributors included Lewis, T. S. Eliot, and Herbert Read.

BL: C.127.k.1.
CUL: CA/U59
TCD: Facsimile reprint. (166.n.33, no.7)
UCL

216 The Ulster Book / edited by Ruddick Millar. Belfast: Quota Press, No. 1 (1929)

Profiled in: Tom Clyde, *Irish Literary Magazines: an outline and descriptive bibliography* (Dublin: Irish Academic Press, 2003), BL: 2725.g.3414
Related Imprint: Quota Press published a number of single author poetry collections as well as plays, fiction and work of local interest. It began in the 1920s and seems to have been in business until the early 1950s

"*The Ulster Book* has been compiled to encourage literary

talent in Ulster and to bring Ulster books to the notice of the public." – editorial. Essays (e.g. William Moore on William Boyce, "The Belfast Milton"), short fiction and poems from Ulster writers, including the editor.

BL: P.P.6180.ck

217 The Ulster Free Lance / edited by William Carter. Belfast: Belfast Writers' Club, April 1932.

Profiled in: Hoffman, Allen & Ulrich; Tom Clyde, *Irish Literary Magazines: an outline and descriptive bibliography* (Dublin: Irish Academic Press, 2003), BL: 2725.g.3414

Linen Hall Library, Belfast

218 The Ulster Review: a progressive monthly of individuality / edited by Alfred S. Moore; then J. R. Gregg. Belfast: Ulster Review, Vol. 1 no. 1 (June 1924)–vol. 2 no. 10 (Mar./Apr. 1926)

Profiled in: Tom Clyde, *Irish Literary Magazines: an outline and descriptive bibliography* (Dublin: Irish Academic Press, 2003), BL: 2725.g.3414

National Library of Ireland: Ir 05 u 6

219 Unrest / edited by Jack Conroy and Ralph Cheyney. London: Stockwell, [Vol. 1] (1929)–[Vol. 3] (1931)

Note: Imprint varies

From the Introduction of the first volume: "In the mad scramble of anthologies vomited from the stolid presses by trainloads are poems of every hue except red, every minor tone and every temper except that of revolt. Purple passion is cheek-to-jowl with plaster sanctity; and the compacent chirpings of the ain't-you-glad-you're-living bards knock elbows with the pessimistic adumbrations of the Sad Young Men who wallow in the cynical philosophy of Schopenhauer and chew the bitter cud of futility over double chocolate sundaes, no more brown than their thoughts and much sweeter, in thousands of Midwest Kandy Kitchens." There was an associated organisation, called Rebel Poets, to which each volume was a yearbook. Each volume consisted of a polemical introduction and then broadly leftwing poems of an aesthetically conservative nature.

BL: 1929–1930 (11780.a.78) 1931 (12229.bb.33)
CUL: 1929 (L727.c.1208.1), 1930 (L727.c.1208.2), 1931 (L727.c.1208.3)

NLS: T.29.c.
TCD: 1929–1930. (179.s.104)

220 The Venture / edited by Anthony Blunt, H. Romilly Fedden and Michael Redgrave. Cambridge: [The Venture], No. 1 (Oct. 1928)–6 (June 1930)

Index: Index for Nos. 1–6 contained with no. 6. Bloomfield (Nos.5–6 only)
Profiled in: Hoffman, Allen & Ulrich, Tolley 1930s

General illlustrated review of the arts. Includes poems by Louis MacNeice, John Drinkwater, William Empson, and John Lehmann. Anthony Blunt, later better-known as a spy for the Soviet Union, was co-editor until June 1929 only, but continued to contribute art criticism after that point.

BL: P.P.6119.eb.
CUL: CAM.C.31.57
UCL: 1, 5

221 Verse and Song. London: [Verse and Song], Vol. 1 no. 1 (1928)–no. 6 (1928)

CUL: L727.C.87

Verse-Reel *See* Terence White's Verse-Reel A204

222 Viewpoint: a critical review / edited by D. A. Willis. Croydon: Viewpoint, Vol. 1 no. 1 (April 1934)–no. 2 (Sept. 1934)

Note: Subsequently incorporated in *The Left Review*
Index: Bloomfield
Profiled in: Hoffman, Allen & Ulrich; Tolley 1930s

"A revolutionary review of the arts." A general review. Published only one poem, by Anthony McDean. Dennis Botterill contributed several pro-Pound reviews.

BL: P.P.5938.bav
CUL: Vol. 1 no. 1. (L231.C.26.)

The Vineyard *See* The Country Heart A43

223 Vision: a magazine & review of mysticism and spiritual reconstruction / edited by Dorothy Grenside and Galloway Kyle. London: Erskine Macdonald, Vol. 1 no. 1 (May 1919)–vol. 2 no. 7 (July 1920)

Index: Vol. 1 has its own index

Characterised by an interest in the spiritual, spiritualism, and the mystical, including articles on spiritual aspects of poetry. Contributors included Katharine Tynan, V. Compton-Burnett, and others. Poems were published occasionally.

BL: P.P.636.cih.
CUL: L198.C.17
TCD: 35.gg.59, 60

224 The Voice of Scotland: a quarterly magazine of Scottish arts and affairs / edited by Hugh MacDiarmid. Dunfermline, then Glasgow, then Edinburgh: vol. 1. no. 1 (June 1938)–vol. 9 no. 2 (1958)

Note: Irregular frequency
Index: Scottish Poetry Index Vol. 8 (Edinburgh: Scottish Poetry Library, 1999), BL: ZC.9.b.6227; Bloomfield (Vol. 1 no.1–vol. 2 no. 1 only)
Profiled in: Alan Riach's introduction in Scottish Poetry Index Vol. 8, pp.69–72

Contributors to this general literary review included Norman MacCaig, Sydney Goodsir Smith, Edwin Morgan, and Robert Garioch. A proof copy of the unpublished Vol. 9 no. 3 is held by Edinburgh University Library, and another by the National Library of Scotland.

BL: Vol. 1 no. 1–vol. 2 no. 1; vol. 2 no. 4; vol. 3 no. 3–no.4; vol. 4 no. 1, no. 3; vol. 5 no. 1–no.3; vol. 6 no. 2–vol. 9 no. 2. (P.P.6203.aae.)
NLS: Vol. 1 no. 1–vol. 9 no. 2. (NH.714). Note: Lacking in hardcopy: Vol. 2, no. 4–vol. 3, no. 1 ; vol. 3, no. 3 ; vol. 4, no. 2, all of which can nevertheless be supplied in microfilm (Mf.24(6)). Vol. 9 no. 3 (proof). (RB.s.335)
Poetry Library: Vol. 6 no. 2

225 Voices: in poetry and prose / edited by Thomas Moult. London: Hendersons, Vol. 1 no. 1 (Jan. 1919)–vol. 5 no. 4 (Autumn 1921)

Profiled in: Hoffman, Allen & Ulrich; Stanton; Sullivan 1914–1984
Reprint: Nendeln, Liechtenstein: Kraus Reprint, 1975

Contributors included D. H. Lawrence, John Galsworthy, Robert Graves, May Sinclair, and W. H. Davies.

BL: P.P.5938.bak
NLS: Vol. 1 (Jan.–June 1919) only. (T.33.i.)

226 The Voyager / edited by Stephen W. Smith. Bristol: Partridge and Love, Vol. 1 no. 1 (Mar. 1924)–no. 4 (June 1924)

A general review. Poets include: Francis Andrews, Esther Raworth, Donald Cooper, and the first two issues contain a supplement of poems by members of the Bristol Poets' Fellowship. W. H. Shewring contributes an article on the poetry of Charlotte Mew in no. 3; a jaunty Apollinaire-like bestiary in rhyme, with woodcuts, is contributed by E. A. Smith in the last issue.

BL: P.P.6044.db
NLS: 5.381
TCD: 67.dd.120, Nos.31–34

227 Wales / edited by Keidrych Rhys, and others. Llangadog: Wales, No. 1 (Summer 1937)–11 (Winter 1939–40). Then, New series. Carmarthen: Druid Press, No. 1 (July 1943)–8/9 (Dec. 1945) [corresponding, in old series terms, to No. 12–20/21, after which the series reverts to old series numbering]. No. 22 (June 1946)–47 (Dec. 1959)

Note: Not published between Winter 1940 and July 1943. A single issue Wales: Wartime Broadsheet was issued in 1940. No. 5 in the new series (Autumn 1944) is designated Vol. IV no. 5. A further numbering system is added when Vol. VI no. 2 (June 1946) is given the additional running number no. 22. Variant title: Wales: A National Magazine
Index: Bloomfield (Nos. 1–11 only)
Profiled in: Hoffman, Allen & Ulrich; Sullivan 1914–1984; Tolley 1930s; Tolley 1940s
Related Imprint: Two booklets were published in the late 1940s in the Wales Pamphlet series, BL: 8140.f.18, both broadly political. The publisher, Druid Press, also issued books by Lynette Roberts, R. S. Thomas, John Cowper Powys, and others.
Related Work: Keidrych Rhys (ed.), Modern Welsh poetry (London: Faber, 1944), BL: 11605.b.31
Reprint: No. 1–11, London: Frank Cass, 1969. English little magazines, no. 7.

A largely but not exclusively English-language journal which asserted a common identity for Welsh poets writing in English. Contributors included: Keidrych Rhys, Dylan Thomas, Glyn Jones, John Prichard, Nigel Heseltine, Ken

Etheridge, Idris Davies, Ll. Wyn Griffith, Vernon Watkins, Charles Fisher, Lynette Roberts and Aneirin ap Gwynn, as well as J. F. Hendry, Hugh MacDiarmid, and Julian Symons. Dylan Thomas co-edited the March 1939 issue with Keidrych Rhys. Nigel Heseltine seems to have taken over as a caretaker editor for the period 1939–40, except that Rhys had to step back in the ring when Heseltine joined the Royal Air Force. Though not officially the anthology of *Wales*, many of the poets from the magazine feature in *Modern Welsh Poetry*, edited by Keidrych Rhys (London: Faber, 1944), BL: 11605.b.31.

BL: P.P.6195.m. The *Wartime Broadsheet*. (P.P.6194.lf)
CUL: 1–11, with *Wartime Broadsheet*. (Cass reprint); New series, 1–8. [Reverted to old series numbering]: 24–31, 40–41. (L485.c.22)
UCL: 1–11, with *Wartime Broadsheet*. (Cass reprint); New series no. 4–6. [Reverted to old series numbering]: 36–38, 40, 41, 47.
Poetry Library: New series: 6–8/9. [Reverted to old series numbering:] 22–25, 29–31

228 The Wayfarer / edited by Charles W. Hervey. Birmingham: [Charles W. Hervey], Nov. 1935–[Jan. 1936?]

Various thoughts of the editor, with some unassuming anonymous verse.

BL: P.P.6063.dcc

229 The Welsh Review / edited by Gwyn Jones. Cardiff: [The Welsh Review], Vol. 1 no. 1 (1939)– vol. 7 no. 4 (1948)

Index: Bloomfield (Vol. 1 no.1–vol. 2 no. 1 only)
Profiled in: Hoffman, Allen & Ulrich

A magazine which "...although conducted in English will recognize the unique importance of the Welsh language and the distinctive national culture inseparable from it." –from the editorial of the first issue. A general literary magazine, but poetry contributors included: W. H. Davies, Idris Davies, Wyn Griffith, Alun Lewis, Peter Hellings, Gwyn Williams, Lynette Roberts, Ursula Lavery and Keidrych Rhys, as well as Hugh MacDiarmid. Articles of note include T. S. Eliot on "What is Minor Poetry?" (vol. 3 no. 4, Dec. 1944) and the essays in the Welsh Literary Tradition feature in vol. 6 no. 4 (Winter 1947).

BL: P.P.6194.ld
CUL: Q733.C.6
TCD: 130.d.71–73
UCL
Poetry Library: Vol. 3 no. 3–vol. 4 no. 2, 4; vol. 5 no. 2–3; vol. 6 no. 3–vol. 7 no. 1, 3–4

230 Wheels / edited by Edith Sitwell. Oxford, then London: Blackwell, then Leonard Parsons, then C. W. Daniel, [First] (1916)–Sixth (1921)

Note: First four volumes were published by Blackwell; the fifth by Leonard Parsons; the sixth by C. W. Daniel
Profiled in: Hoffman, Allen & Ulrich; Sullivan 1914–1984

Perhaps most notable for its posthumous publication of seven poems by Wilfred Owen in the fourth volume (1919). Parodied by the one-off magazine *Cranks*.

BL: Cup.403.s.1
NLS: T.20.b
UCL

231 The Window / edited by Eric Partridge and Bertram Ratcliffe. London: Eric Partridge Ltd, Vol. 1 no. 1 (Jan. 1930)–no. 4 (Oct. 1930)

Index: Bloomfield
Profiled in: Hoffman, Allen & Ulrich

Fiction and poetry, including poems by John Drinkwater, Edmund Blunden and Laurence Powys.

BL: P.P.5938.bao
CUL: Q727.C.14
TCD: Vol.1 no.2 (Apr. 1930)–no. 4. (112.p.160–162)
UCL: Vol.1 no.2 (Apr. 1930)

232 Wings: the official organ of the Flight Pen Club / edited by C. Hugh Scott. Sway, Hampshire: C. Hugh Scott (printed by L. Warner, Hinckley), Vol. 1 no. 1 (Dec. 1928)–no. 2 (Mar. 1929). Then, as *Little Wings*, Vol. 1 no. 3 (June 1929)–no. 12 (Mar. 1940)

Poems and stories, apparently by club members.

BL: P.P.5938.bbc

The Winter Anthology *See* The Mitre Anthology of Poetry A124

The Winter Owl *See* The Owl A157

The World and Ourselves *See* Epilogue: a critical summary A60

233 Yellowjacket / edited by Constantine Fitzgibbon. London: Vol. 1 no. 1 (March 1939)–no. 2 (May 1939)

Index: Bloomfield
Profiled in: Hoffman, Allen & Ulrich

A general review. Poems by Gavin Ewart, Robert Waller, Mario Francelli, John Betjeman and Jean Cocteau. Short stories by Dylan Thomas. Wrapped in yellow cellophane that apparently came off too easily, for which they were criticised.

BL: P.P.5938.bbm
CUL: L727.C.94
TCD: 121.p.323,nos.15, 15a

234 Yorkshire Poetry / edited by S. Matthewman, then Denis Botterill. Leeds: Swan Press, Vol. 1 no. 1 (April 1922)–vol. 3 no. 25 (Winter 1924); New Series, No. 1 (Feb. 1925)–4 (Aug. 1925)

Related Imprint: The Swan Press published many single-author collections of poems. They also published the series North-Country Chap-Books, BL: Cup.510.bce.10

"The chief purpose of this magazine is to reprint and thus preserve in a more permanent manner the poems with appear week by week in the *Yorkshire Weekly Post*." - editorial in first issue. However, original poems soon featured. By the time of the new series, edited by Denis Botterill, many of the poems were appearing for the first time. The better-known contributors included Herbert Read, Lascelles Abercrombie, Wilfred Rowland Childe, and Dorothy Una Ratcliffe.

BL: P.P.6030.d
TCD: Vol. 1 no. 1 (April 1922)–vol. 3 no. 25 (Winter 1924). (37.rr.200, Nos.1–20)

235 Youth / edited by William A. Harris, then J. W. F. Hill, then S. D. Colwell, then Rolf Gardiner. Cambridge, then London: First Series, no. 1 (May 1920)–10 (June 1923). New series, no. 11 (Oct. 1923)–no. 15 (Autumn/ Winter 1924)

Note: The subtitle "An expression of progressive university thought" was superseded by "An international quarterly of young enterprise" with the new series. At the same time the imprint changed from Youth to The International League of Youth (British Section)

Contributors to this cultural review included Major C. H. Douglas, Marie Stopes, and A. S. Neill on social and political topics, Arnim T. Wegner on "The Social Poetry of Young Germany", and Rabindranath Tagore on "The Renaissance of Asian Culture". The review also published occasional poems. A supplement, *German Youth: A Symposium* was published by the International League of Youth in 1923 (BL: P.P.6058.hca.(2)).

BL: P.P.6058.hca
CUL: No. 1–13. (T200.B.2)

236 Youth / edited by Stephen McKenna. London: Youth, Vol. 1 no. 1 (Feb. 1922)–no. 3 (June 1922)

"The authors' magazine" according to the sub-title. A general literary magazine. Contributors included Walter de la Mare, Betty Pyke, Alfred Noyes, W. Somerset Maugham, W. H. Davies, A. A. Milne, Laurence Housman, and E. Hamilton Moore.

BL: P.P.5938.dda
CUL: L727.B.32
TCD: Vol.1 no.2 (Mar. 1922)–no. 3. (106.a.82, Nos.19–20)

Chapter B: 1940–1949

Wartime

THE CLOSE OF the 1930s had seen the rise of the New Apocalyptic poets through magazines such as *Seven* and *Kingdom Come*. During the Second World their work flourished. They were marshalled together in no less than three anthologies by J. F. Hendry and Henry Treece, the first giving them their name *The New Apocalypse* and assembling Dorian Cooke, J. F. Hendry, Norman MacCaig, Nicholas Moore, Philip O'Connor, Henry Treece and the honorary elder, Dylan Thomas. They can be seen as a group operating within the wider trend of neo-romanticism. Apocalyptic poetry is open to the bardic, the prophetic, and to high registers of rhetoric and attentive to sound. It can have a disarming earnestness as if the poets are offering much of their work as attemptive. To some a 'Celtic' element quickly became clear: partly because of Dylan Thomas's influence on the group and partly because of strong Scottish representation (MacCaig and Hendry and, later, W. S. Graham). This drew a counter-attack on the basis of ethnicity: by 1944 John Atkins' *The New Saxon Pamphlets* was asserting that "the point of the new saxon is this: he won't subscribe to the view that to write good poetry you must be a celt". Other disagreements would base themselves, at least outwardly, on aesthetics, with England's Movement poets emerging in the 1950s with the assertion of a quieter, apparently undemonstrative verse.

One physical outcome of the War was the relocation of British poets to overseas. Several magazines were produced in Cairo, including *Personal Landscape*, *Citadel* and *Salamander*. Sometimes these published Greek poems in translation, Greek poetry being a significant element of literature in Egypt at that time. If British poets found themselves abroad, foreign nationals found themselves in England. London-based magazines devoted to French, Belgium and Norwegian culture were the result, often with British authors as contributors. The Anglo-French Surrealism of the previous decade continued in *Arson: an ardent review* [1942] and *Free Unions – Unions Libres* [1946] but new influences were appearing, too. Indian literature was represented with *Indian Writing* (1940–42) running for five issues and Fredoon Kabraji's *This Strange Adventure* which had a single issue in 1947. The Ceylonese editor (i.e. Sri Lankan) J. M. Tambimuttu ran the eclectic *Poetry London* from which grew the imprint Poetry Editions London, publisher of several poetry collections and Henry Moore's London Underground sketchbook.

American poetry continued to be welcomed in English little magazines with the publication of Wallace Stevens, William Carlos Williams and E. E. Cummings (no strangers to English magazines in previous years) and the relatively early appearances by John Berryman, Elizabeth Bishop, Kenneth Patchen, William Everson and the Anglo-American Denise Levertov. Pound's voice was much less frequent, however, presumably because of distaste for his opinions and allegiance: he was, after all, a fiercely anti-Semitic propagandist who was actively supporting Mussolini. Interest in his work would only be revived towards the end of the decade with the advent of Peter Russell's *Nine* (1949). American culture of another kind, jazz, is marked as an influence in the publication of *Jazz Forum: a quarterly review of jazz and literature* [1946]–(1947). Post-war reconstruction led to at least one Anglo-German magazine, *The Gate* (1947–1949).

The geographical distribution of British magazines changed in the 1940s. Although many will associate this period with Cyril Connolly's London-based *Horizon* (1940–1950), London was losing its grip as the natural place of publication for a literary magazine. In the previous period London had been the place of publication for approximately 50% of all the literary magazines in our survey; in the 1940s this had been reduced to 41%. The temporary importance of Cairo as a publication centre has already been noted, but of longer lasting significance were the appearance of new Scottish and Welsh titles, with the publisher William MacLellan in Glasgow emerging as a key publisher of Scottish literature. In Wales the appearance of Raymond Garlick's review *Dock Leaves* (1949)–[1957] marks a key foundation in the building of a Welsh literary infrastructure.

Cambridge and Oxford remained relatively quiet as publishing centres, each producing less than a new magazine per year, a yearly rate similar to the previous decades. There were no Oxbridge groups to rival either the 1930s Auden Generation, broadly Oxford-linked, or the New Apocalyptics, educationally unaligned (except, perhaps, to the Scottish education system).

Substantial and eclectic magazines in Dublin such as *The Bell*

(1940–1954) and *Envoy* (1949–1951) suggest that the censorship of the previous two decades did not triumph in the long run. However, Dublin was producing proportionally fewer new magazines per year than in the period 1914–1939: perhaps the success and aesthetic range of *The Bell* put off prospective editors.

Regionalisation within England and Scotland is particularly noticeable in this period, especially immediately post-war. The decreasing dominance of London as a place of publication and the advent of magazines such as *The New Shetlander*, *The West Country Magazine*, *The Cornish Review* and *Leeds University Poetry* suggest a significant cultural readjustment taking place. In this way not only did the "home colonies" of Britain, including England itself (hence the explicitly titled *The New Saxon Pamphlets*), continue to assert themselves but emerging self-identifying cultures within these countries began to do the same.

1 Adam International Review / edited by Miron Grindea. London: St. Clements Press, No. 152 (Sept. 1941)–499 (1988). ISSN: 0001-8015

Note: The numeration continues that of the periodical of the same name formerly published at Bucharest. After no. 153, published by Adam International Review. A volume designation was also sometimes given, independent of the issue number, e.g. the last issue was vol. 49 no. 499
Index: An index for nos.152–200 was published with no. 200
Profiled in: Stanton; Sullivan 1914–1984
Related Work: Vanessa Davies (ed.), *Miron Grindea MBE, OBE, 1909–1995, editor of Adam International Review: a celebration*. London: Centre for Twentieth-century Cultural Studies, King's College London, [1996?]. Includes "Cultivating one's garden : on being a literary editor", the inaugural Adam lecture given by Miron Grindea in King's College London in 1985. BL: YK.1997.a.2396

Adam is an acronym for Arts, Drama, Architecture, Music. A very eclectic, international general literary review, publishing articles, artwork, music and drama. Notable for its European contributors including Thomas Mann, Georges Duhamel, Stefan Zweig, Jean Cocteau, André Gide, Paul Claudel, Jean-Paul Sartre, Picasso, Tzara, Chagall, Miró, and Georges Simenon. T. S. Eliot contributed a number of essays including "Reflections on the Unity of European Culture" and "The Aims of Poetic Drama". British authors included Auden, MacDiarmid, Graham Greene and many others. King's College London holds the Adam archives within its College Archives and a statement about the archive is given within the archives section of the King's website www.kcl.ac.uk.

BL: 152–201; 204–207; 212–321; 328–497. (P.P.5938.bbs)
NLS: 152–157; 174–192;195–196; 199–298; 337–348; 364–366; 370–400; 404–499. (NF.1571 PER)
TCD: 152–499. (47.bb.60–62 1941–1961; PER 71–80 1962–1988)
UCL: 196, 214–230; 300–499

2 Air Force Poetry / edited by John Pudney and Henry Treece. London: John Lane, 1944

Profiled in: Hoffman, Allen, & Ulrich
BL: 11605.cc.16

3 Alba: a Scottish miscellany in Gaelic and English / edited by Malcolm MacLean and T. M. Murchison. Glasgow: William MacLellan for An Comunn Gaidhealach, No. 1 [1948]

Related Imprint: MacLellan was one of the key post-war publishers in Scotland, publishing fiction, social analysis, art criticism and theory, and poetry. The Poetry Scotland Series, published by William MacLellan, featured collections by Hugh MacDiarmid, Sydney Goodsir Smith, George Bruce, Adam Drinan, Ruthven Todd, and W. S. Graham (BL: W.P.1989).

A cultural review with the emphasis on Highlands and Islands culture. Many contributions are in Gaelic, including those by Somhairle MacGilleathain (Sorley Maclean), Deorsa Caimbeul Hay (George Campbell Hay), and Ruairidh MacThòmais (Derick Thomson), but there are also items in Scots (notably Douglas Young's translation of some Campbell Hay poems) and in English.

BL: X.908/298

Albion *See* The New Saxon Pamphlets B84

4 Angus Fireside. Arbroath: Angus Fireside, Vol. 1 no. 1 (Oct. 1948)–no. 10 (Winter 1949/50)

Articles, short fiction, news, reviews and poems. The texts are almost as conservative as the title suggests and the subject matter is Angus and Scotland in general. Contributors include Lewis Spence, the novelist Neil M. Gunn (on the role of new magazines), Quentin Crisp (a short story), Maurice Lindsay (on the composer F. G. Scott) and Hugh MacDiarmid (on Angus literature). There is poetry by Maurice Lindsay, William Montgomery, and others.

BL: P.P.6203.aap
NLS: 5.1538 PER

5 Anvil: life & the arts: a miscellany / edited by Jack Lindsay. London: Meridian Books, Book 1 (Spring [i.e. Autumn] 1947)

Note: An erratum slip corrects the publication date to Autumn 1947

Contributors included: Joseph MacLeod on "Poet and People (with special reference to Scotland)", Adam Drinan (pseudonym of MacLeod), Louis Aragon on Mallarmé, George Barker, Apollinaire translated by W. J. Strachan, and Mulk Raj Anand on Tagore.

BL: W.P.8202

6 Arena: a literary magazine / edited by Jack Lindsay, John Davenport and Randall Swingler. London: Arena Publications, [Vol. 1] no. 1 (1949)–[vol. 2. no. 9] (1952)

Note: Vol. 2 no. 8 and 9 bear neither the title nor numeration. Variant subtitle: a magazine of modern literature
Profiled in: Stanton; Sullivan 1914–1984

Contributors included: Albert Camus, Paul Eluard, Eugenio Montale and Louis Aragon, as well as Hugh MacDiarmid and Edith Sitwell. One theme in many of the essays was Romantic poetry and literature following on from the ideas of Romanticism. Lindsay, Davenport and Swingler edited the first volume but Lindsay edited the second. The last two issues were centred on conferences Lindsay had organised, "Britain's Cultural Heritage" and "The American Threat to British Culture" respectively.

BL: P.P.5939.cba
NLS: P.213.PER
TCD: 37.q.61–

7 Arson: an ardent review. London: Toni del Renzio, Part 1 [1942.]

Profiled in: Hoffman, Allen & Ulrich

"Part one of a surrealist manifestation", includes two essays on surrealism by André Breton and Nicholas Calas respectively. There appear to have been no more issues.

BL: P.P.1931.ubh
CUL: T735.B.1

8 The Arts / edited by Desmond Shawe-Taylor. London: Lund Humphries, No. 1 [1946]–2 [1947]

Large format illustrated review of the arts, including poetry. No. 1 features a collaboration between the poet W. R. Rodger and the artist Duncan Grant, "Europa and the Bull"; no. 2 a collaboration between Kathleen Raine and Robert Medley, "The Four Elements".

BL: P.P.1931.pdm
CUL: L400.B.97
NLS: 6.458

9 Babel: a multi-lingual critical review / edited by Peter G. Lucas, John Fleming and G. Gordon Mosley. Cambridge: Bowes & Bowes, Vol. 1 no. 1 (Jan. 1940)–no. 3 (Summer 1940)

Profiled in: Hoffman, Allen & Ulrich

An interesting attempt to publish French, Italian, Spanish and other continental European language texts with, usually, their translations, alongside English language work. Babel published essays on various aspects of national literatures as well as poems by Luis Cernuda, Eugenio Montale, Alfonso Gatto, David Gascoyne, and others.

BL: P.P.6109.bb
CUL: CAM.C.231.18
NLS: 5.999
TCD: 133.n.111, nos.5–7

10 The Bell: a survey of Irish life / edited by Sean O'Faolain, then Peader O'Donnell. Dublin: Cahill and Company, Vol. 1 no. 1 (Oct. 1940)–vol. 19 no. 11 (Dec. 1954)

Note: Imprint and subtitle vary
Index: Rudi Holzapfel, An Index of Contributors to The Bell (Dublin: Carraig Books, 1970), BL: 2713.m.4
Anthology: Geoffrey Taylor (ed.) Irish Poems of Today, Chosen from the First Seven Volumes of The Bell (London: Secker & Warburg, 1944), BL: 11605.aa.31
Profiled in: Hoffman, Allen & Ulrich; Sullivan 1914–1984; Princess Grace Irish Library Electronic Irish Records Dataset, www.pgil-eirdata.org; Tom Clyde, Irish Literary Magazines: an outline and descriptive bibliography (Dublin: Irish Academic Press, 2003), BL: 2725.g.3414; Gerry Smyth, Decolonisation and Criticism: the construction of Irish literature (London: Pluto Press, 1998), pp.113–117, BL: YC.2001.a.4091

An impressive literary and cultural review which published an eclectic range of Irish writers and provided serious comment and debate on Irish social, political, and artistic issues. Sean O'Faolain was editor from October 1940 to March 1946; O'Donnell from April 1946 to December 1954. Publication was suspended between April 1948 and November 1950.

BL: P.P.5938.bcq. Lacking: Vol. 4 no. 2; vol. 18 no. 5, 8–11; vol. 19 no. 5–7, 9. These are however available in the microfiche set (Mic.F.132)
CUL: Vol. 1 no. 2–vol. 18 no. 4. (L900.C.197)
NLS: HP1.91.2187
TCD: Vol.1 no.1–vol.19 no.10. Lacking: Vol.11 no.2 (Nov. 1945) and vol.12 no.1 (Apr. 1946). (OLS L–2–50–69)

11 **Blaze** / edited by Reginald Moore. London: [Blaze], No. 1 [1940]

One of Reginald Moore's numerous war-time magazines. Poems and short stories, Jack Carney on T. S. Eliot, Paul Verlaine translated by M. Hillyer. Production values are low, with the use of a poor-quality stencil process. The British Library has a substantial Reginald Moore archive within the Department of Manuscripts.

BL: Imperfect copy: Lacking pp. 27–34. Pp. 21–2 substituted with typescript. (YA.1992.a.8746)

12 **Bless 'Em All** / edited by Derek Stanford. [Virginia Water: No. 6 Company NCC, 1940?]

A magazine that appears to have been suppressed by the War Office. Stanford soon began work as editor of X–6. No holdings known.

13 **The Bridge** / edited by Geoffrey Moore. Cambridge: Geoffrey Moore, at Emmanuel College, Vol. 1 no. 1 (Apr. 1946)

Hamish Henderson contributes a poem, "Written at a Conference". There is literary criticism on Louis Aragon and T. F. Powys and a short story by Raymond Williams. The editor cites the pre-war Fords and Bridges as a model.

BL: P.5938.cas
CUL: CAM.C.31.63

14 **Bristol Packet:** West of England writings. Bristol: Rankin Bros. for the Bristol Writers Association, [1944]

A one-off, publishing poetry, short fiction and articles. Foreword by Reginald Moore. Contributors include: Keidrych Rhys, Jack Lindsay, Idris Davies and others.

BL: 12298.bb.31
NLS: 1946.8

15 **Bugle Blast: an anthology from the Services** / edited by Jack Aistrop and Reginald Moore. London: Allen & Unwin, No. 1 (1943)–4 (1947)

Profiled in: Hoffman, Allen & Ulrich

Fiction and poetry, the latter including work by Henry Treece, Keidrych Rhys and others. Julian Maclaren-Ross, H.E. Bates and Alun Lewis contribute prose pieces, and there is "My First Day on Tarawa" by Carl Jones, an eyewitness account of a U.S. attack on a Pacific island.

BL: W.P.889
NLS: 1. (R.41.f) ; 2. (R.41.g) ; 3. (R.40.i) ; 4. (Vts.173.b.38)
TCD: Gall.RR.21.91–

16 **Cambridge Writing** / edited by William Watson, and others. Cambridge: The Young Writers' Group, [No. 1] (Easter Term 1948)–8 [1952]

Short stories, general arts articles, and poetry. Poets include Eric Mottram, Donald Davie, an article by Donald Davie on "Recent Cambridge Writing" (no. 4), and a review by Davie of issues of Nine and Poetry London (no. 5).

BL: [1]–6. (P.P.6109.be)
CUL: CAM.C.31.70
TCD: 125.a.190, nos.1–8.

17 **Caseg Broadsheet** / [edited by Brenda Chamberlain, Alun Lewis and John Petts]. Llanllechid: Caseg Press, No. 1 (1942)–6 (1942)

Study: Brenda Chamberlain, Alun Lewis & the Making of the Caseg Broadsheets, with a letter from Vernon Watkins and a checklist of the Broadsheets (London: Enitharmon Press, 1970), BL: X.981/3813.

No editors are stated but Brenda Chamberlain's memoir suggests that the broadsheets were produced by Chamberlain, John Petts and Alun Lewis. Contributors were: Alun Lewis, John Petts (illustration), Brenda

Chamberlain (illustration and poems), Taliesin (trans. H. Idris Bell), Lynette Roberts, and Dylan Thomas. The first issue has two versions with the same illustration but with different typefaces.

BL: Cup.501.k.48
CUL: 864.B.143

18 The Catacomb / edited by Rob Lyle and Roy Campbell. London: The Forty-Five Press, [No. 1] (April 1949)–14 (May 1950). Then, New Series, Vol. 1 no. 1 (Summer 1950)–vol. 2 no. 4 (Winter 1951/52)

A cultural review with a particular interest in poetry. Includes an anti-MacDiarmid poem by Roy Campbell, "Ska-Hawtch Wha Hae!", and poems and articles displaying an enthusiasm for Lorca and Apollinaire.

BL: P.P.5938.cae
CUL: L533.C.23
NLS: R.211
TCD: 140.b.14, nos.1–21

19 The Changing World / edited by Bernard Wall and Manya Harari. London: Harvill Press, No. 1 (Summer 1947)–7 (Feb./Mar./Apr. 1949)

Related Imprint: The Changing World Series, published by Harvill, was a short-lived series of books on art, poetry, history and philosophy, BL: W.P.2360

A general literary review with some coverage of European and American literature. Contributors included: David Jones, Giuseppe Ungaretti, Auden, Pierre-Jean Jouve, Nicholas Moore, G. S. Fraser, Roy Campbell, Herbert Read, Guillaume Apollinaire (in French, and trans. Rayner Heppenstall), Ramon Gomez de la Serna, Eugenio Montale (in Italian, and trans. Bernard Wall), D. S. Savage, Ezra Pound and Peter Russell.

BL: P.P.5939.bet
CUL: Q900.C.207
NLS: 1951.43
TCD: 47.cc.30

20 Chapbook: the magazine of Scottish achievement / edited by Alec Donaldson. Glasgow: Scoop Books, then A. & J. Donaldson, No. 1 (Jan. 1946)–12 [1947]

Related Imprint: Scoop Books had a short-lived Modern Scots Poets series, which published collections by John

Kincaid and Edward Boyd respectively.

By its own admission aimed at a popular market (which, nevertheless, did not materialise), this included articles on Scottish culture past, present and future; reviews; Gaelic lessons for beginners; some short fiction; correspondence; and poems. Poets included Edward Boyd, Robert McLellan, George Campbell Hay, Hamish Henderson, Alexander Scott, Maurice Lindsay. Contemporary poems were generally published in a section called "Scottish Heritage" which also showcased poems from centuries earlier. Prose contributors included Naomi Mitchison, Joseph MacLeod, Alexander Scott (on contemporary Scottish poetry), Charles Graves (on the poetry of Marion Angus), and the artist J. D. Fergus[s]on. Maurice Lindsay's article on the controversy over the use of 'plastic' or synthetic Scots in poetry started what would dominate the last few numbers: exchanges between the art critic Frederic Quinton and Hugh MacDiarmid on the nature of modernity within Scots language writing. Donaldson signed off with a familiar lament: "... the publisher was confident that the co-operation CHAPBOOK could expect from the many thousands of intelligent and progressive people in our country would both lighten his labour and conserve, as far as possible, the limited financial resources at his disposal. This confidence has proved to have been misplaced."

BL: P.P.6203.laa

21 Citadel: literature, criticism, reportage, stories, poetry / edited by R. D. Smith. Cairo: The British Institute [i.e the Anglo-Egyptian Institute], 1942–[194?]

Profiled in: Tolley 1940s

May 1942 issue includes "A Note on Cavafy" by George Seferis, with a translation of Cavafy's "Waiting for the Barbarians", and a note on Cavafy by someone who had known him, Timos Malanos. The Dec. 1942 issue includes poems by Lawrence Durrell, Peter Davies, and John Penderill. Hamish Henderson and Olivia Manning also contribute to the magazine, and Terence Tiller's essay "Modern English Poetry" is serialised over three issues.

BL: Dec. 1942 only. (P.901/1246)

Civvy Street see Khaki and Blue B62

22 Convoy / edited by Robin [i.e. Robert] Maugham. London: Collins, No. 1 (1944)–7 [1947]

Note: No. 2 was entitled *Convoy File*. No. 6 was published as *Christmas Convoy*
Profiled in: Hoffman, Allen & Ulrich

A miscellany of non-fiction prose, short stories and a small number of poems, e.g. by Roy Fuller, Alun Lewis, Mary Ellis, Nina Kaplan, Nancy Spain, Maurice Lindsay. Produced for those serving in the forces. Often with charming line drawings.

BL: 1 (W.P.772), 2 (12354.f.22), 3–4 (W.P.772)
CUL: 1–4. (Lg00.D.84)
NLS: HP1.78.3135
TCD: 1–4. (118.e.81. nos. 1–4)
UCL: 1, 3

23 The Cornish Review / edited by Denys Val Baker. Hayle, Cornwall: Denys Val Baker, No. 1 (Spring 1949)–10 (Summer 1952). New Series, No. 1 (1966)–16 (1970)

Study: Tim Scott, *Cornish Review magazine* (Newlyn: Hare's Ear, 1995)

A general cultural review focused on Cornwall, and including photographs of sculpture and art produced in Cornwall, many of which are associated with St. Ives. Poets included A. L. Rowse, Jack R. Clemo, Anne Treneer, Ronald Duncan, Gladys Hunkin, Ronald Bottrall, W. S. Graham, Allen Curnow, Charles Causley, John Heath-Stubbs, Erma Harvey James, Norman Levine and Arthur Caddick.

BL: 1–10. (P.P.6049.ibb). New Series, No. 1. (ZA.9.a.11235)
CUL: 1–2; 8. New Series, No. 12; 16 (L479.C.47)
NLS: 1–2; 8. (1952.34)
TCD: 1–8. (PER 80–212)

24 Counterpoint / edited by Conrad Senat [i.e. Ronald Senator]. Oxford: Counterpoint Publications, Vol. 1–2 [1945?]

Profiled in: Ronald Senator, *Requiem Letters* (London: Marion Boyars, 1996), BL: Nov.1996/230, pp.57–63
Related Imprint: Counterpoint also published a booklet by the artist Paul Nash, *Aerial Flowers* (1947), BL: YA.1994.b.8930, and Vera Leslie's translations of Kafka, *The Country Doctor* , BL YD.2005.a.2563

An art and literary review, which used black and white and full-colour reproduction to publish the painters Paul Nash, Michael Ayrton, Mervyn Peake, Lucien Freud, John Minton, Robert Colquhoun, and others, as well as Lawrence Durrell, George Barker, Roy Campbell, Walter de la Mare, John Heath-Stubbs, and R. S. Thomas. In vol. 2 Henry Treece is taken to task by Geoffrey Grigson in a letter complaining about Treece's misrepresentation of Grigson's pre-war magazine *New Verse*. There were also articles on music, for example a study of Egon Wellesz by W. H. Mellers, and a study of William Walton by Nigel Townshend. Ronald Senator would later be better known as a composer.

BL: X.435/707
CUL: Lg99.B.1.15
TCD: Vol. 1 (1946). (24.ee.84, no.20)

25 The Critic: a quarterly review of criticism / edited by Wolf Mankowitz, Clifford Collins and Raymond Williams. Mistley: The Critic Press, Vol. 1 no. 1 (Spring 1947)–[no. 3, 1947]

Note: Vol. 1 no. 2 was published in London. Incorporated by *Politics and Letters*
Profiled in: Tolley 1940s

Includes no poetry but does have articles on poetry, e.g. D. J. Enright on "The Significance of *Poetry London*" (no. 1), and B. Rajan on Georgian Poetry (no. 2). *Politics and Letters* was focused even further outside of poetry and is out of scope for this bibliography.

BL: Lacking: Vol. 1 no. 3. (P.901/771)
CUL: Lacking: Vol. 1 no. 3. (Lg00.C.298)
NLS: Lacking: Vol. 1 no. 3. (6.469)

26 The Crown and the Sickle: an anthology / edited by J. F. Hendry and Henry Treece. Westminster, London: P. S. King & Staples, [1945]

Profiled in: Tolley 1940s

The third and last anthology of the New Apocalypse. The contents were: essays on war by J. F. Hendry and Terence White; stories and other prose by Alex Comfort, F. J. Brown, Fred Marnau, Terence White, Stefan Schimanski and Denys Val Baker; poems by Treece, Hendry, Comfort, Peter Wells, Gervase Stewart, Leslie Phillips, Robert Herring, Robert Greacen, Wrey Gardiner, Ian Bancroft, Dorian Cooke, John Gallen, Maurice Lindsay, and Seán Jeannett; and a conclusion by Terence White. The other anthologies were *The New Apocalypse*, and *The White Horseman*.

BL: 12299.b.30
NLS: Vts.175.h.13

27 Crux: controversial, constructive, critical / edited by Alastair M. Mowat. Glasgow: William McLellan, [No. 1] (May 1940)

"Crux is designed to gather constructive Christian thought upon the future of Scotland, to give it the publicity it sometimes fails to get, and to crusade for a New Spirit in every department of life – religion, economics, social life, industry, education and art." A general cultural review, but with a poem by William Soutar and one by Albert Mackie.

BL: P.P.6203.aag

28 Danta Ard-teistimeireachta... / edited by Donncha A. O Croinin and others. Baile Atha Cliath: Brun agus O Nuallain, 1946/47–1982

Note: In Irish

BL: Lacking: 1972/73, 1975/76–1982. (P.P.5126.kac)
NLS: 1946/47–1974/74. (P.med.1992)
TCD: PR 3587

29 Danta Mean-teistimeireachta... / edited by Peadar O hUallachain and others. Baile Atha Cliath: Brun agus O Nuallain, 1946/47–1982

Note: In Irish.

BL: Lacking: 1972/73, 1976/77–1982 (P.P.5126.kab)
NLS: 1946/47–1974/75. (P.med.1981)
TCD: 1953/54–1971/72. (PR 3585 1946/47–1982)

30 Daylight: European arts and letters yesterday, to-day, to-morrow / edited by John Lehmann. London: Hogarth Press, Vol. 1 (1941)

Note: Subsequently combined with Folios of New Writing to form New Writing and Daylight
Profiled in: Hoffman, Allen & Ulrich; Tolley 1940s

BL: 12359.e.22
CUL: L700.C.32
NLS: Y.190
TCD: 92.p.75.

31 Delphic Review. an anarchistic quarterly / edited by Albert J. McCarthy. Fordingbridge: Vol. 1 no. 1 (Winter 1949)–no. 2 (Spring 1950)

Related Imprint: Delphic Press

A general cultural review with anarchist leanings. Each issue had a poetry section, with e.g. Kenneth Patchen, Alex Comfort, Dachine Rainer and Eithne Wilkins.

BL: P.P.5938.cao
CUL: L900.C.307
NLS: 6.592

32 Dint: anthology of modern poetry / edited by Feyyaz Fergar and Sadi Cherkeshi. London: Feyyaz Fergar and Sadi Cherkeshi, No. 1 [1944]–2 (Autumn 1944)

From the first issue: "DINT is experimental in aim. It is to provide the poets with some more shouting area and a means of communication amongst themselves and their readers. DINT is not intended to be commercial." Despite the intent the poems are generally not experimental. Contributors include the editors and many of the widely published poets of the 1940s. In the first issue: Henry Treece, Hardiman Scott, Wrey Gardiner, Nicholas Moore, James Kirkup, Robert Greacen, Edwin Allan, John Atkins, Denton Welch, Roy McFadden, Valentin Iremonger. The second issue had a section guest-edited by Ross Nichols, and structured round the ideas of Man Symbolic (with John Heath-Stubbs, Hardiman Scott, and James Kirkup), Portraits (John Heath-Stubbs, Wrey Gardiner, Morwenna Donnelly, James Kirkup), Landscape (Rolf Gardiner, Roy McFadden, Denton Welch, Edwin Allan), and Lyrics (Morwenna Donnelly and Iain Fletcher). The second half of the magazine returned control to the editors and included contributions by Brian Allwood, Henry Treece, Maurice Lindsay, L. E. Leaper, R. Crombie Saunders, John Atkins, Simon Watson Taylor, Ross Nichols, Sylvia Read, John Christian, David Matthews (age 8), Hermann Peschmann, and others. It also included some translations of tiny poems by Melih Cevdet and Oktay Rifat, originally in Turkish. Fergar contributes one poem in French, and also lists new French books and periodicals of interest.

BL: W.P.6203
CUL: L727.C.124
NLS: P.sm.1382

33 Dock Leaves / edited by Raymond Garlick. Pembroke Dock: Dock Leaves Press, [Vol. 1. no. 1] (Christmas 1949)–vol. 8. no. 22 [Winter 1957]

Note: Continued as: The Anglo-Welsh Review
Profiled in: Sullivan 1914–1984; Sam Adams, Roland Mathias (Cardiff: University of Wales Press, 1995), BL:

YK1996.a.2281
Related Imprint: Dock Leaves Pamphlets published two
Raymond Garlick collections and Peter Preece's *The Ringing
Stone* (1954). BL: Pamphlet series at: W.P.D.209
Related Work: Garlick also guest-edited a "Poetry from
Wales" special issue of the *The Poetry Book Magazine*,
published in Brooklyn, New York (vol. 6 no. 5 (Fall 1954)),
BL: P.P.5126.gda.

A key magazine of Welsh literature in English. Raymond
Garlick was appointed as an assistant English master by
Roland Mathias to Pembroke Dock Grammar School, and
Mathias encouraged him to set up *Dock Leaves*.

BL: P.P.5938.bdh
CUL: L727.C.142
NLS: Lacking Vol. 1 no. 2. (NF.1549.PER)
TCD: 86.gg.45

34 English Folios: an anthology of contemporary English prose and verse / edited by Patrick Dudgeon. Buenos Aires: La Asociación ex Alumnas del Instituto Nacional del Profesorado en Lenguas Vivas "Juan R. Fernandez", I (1947)–III (1948)

Each issue has a generous selection of work by the
individual writers concerned. The magazine declares itself
deliberately biased towards poetry. The contributors are:
Kathleen Raine, Alex Comfort, Peter Wells, Nicholas
Moore, John Hall, Howard Sergeant, Roy Campbell,
Ruthven Todd, Douglas Nicholls, Lawrence Durrell,
Margaret Crosland, Hugo Manning, Muriel Spark, John
Symonds, Hubert Nicholson, and Ross Nichols.

BL: Tambi.104

35 Envoy: a review of literature and art / edited by John Ryan, with Valentin Iremonger as poetry editor. Dublin: Envoy, Vol. 1 no. 1 (Dec. 1949)–vol. 5 no. 20 (July 1951)

Index: Hayes
Profiled in: Tom Clyde, *Irish Literary Magazines: an outline and
descriptive bibliography* (Dublin: Irish Academic Press, 2003),
BL: 2725.g.3414; Gerry Smyth, *Decolonisation and Criticism:
the construction of Irish literature* (London: Pluto Press, 1998),
pp.117–119, BL: YC.2001.a.4091
Related Imprint: Envoy published Valentin Iremonger's
Reservations. Poems (Dublin: Envoy, 1950), BL: 11659.bb.8.
Related Work: John Ryan, *Remembering How We Stood:
Bohemian Dublin at the mid-century* (Dublin: Gill and
Macmillan, 1975), BL: X.809/40226

Arts articles, short fiction, poems, reproductions of
paintings, and reviews, with a significant element of
modernist work and material from overseas. Poets included
John Hewitt, Roy McFadden, Patrick Kavanagh (who con-
tributed a regular, provocative diary), Brendan Behan,
Blánaid Salkeld, Denis Devlin, Anthony Cronin, Ewart
Milne, Maurice Farley, Máire MacEntee, Claire McAllister,
Hölderlin (trans. Michael Hamburger), Howard Sergeant,
Pearse Hutchinson, John Montague, as well as prose by
Samuel Beckett, Gertrude Stein and even Martin Heidegger.
Other pieces include a translation of an extract from
Chekhov's "Sachalin Island" (trans. Hubert Butler),
Anthony Cronin on "Guilty Poetry", and an essay on "The
Age of Suspicion" by Nathalie Sarraute. A lengthy farewell
editorial sums up its achievements and describes the
causes for its demise which include "that semi-illiterate
organ of bad criticism, and outpost of British literary impe-
rialism, *The Times Literary Supplement*").

BL: P.P.6189.eba
CUL: L727.C.112
NLS: R.211
TCD: 125.g.161–163.
UCL

36 Exe / edited by John Hocknell and then others. Exeter: The Literary Society in the University College of the South West of England, No. 1 (Winter 1947)–5 (Autumn 1950)

An eclectic magazine of essays, short fiction and occasional
poems. Articles cover such topics as "The Medieval
Undergraduate", "The Semantic Problem", "Some
reflections on West Indian poetry" (by Glorria Cummins),
"Some notes on Anglo-Welsh poetry" (by Gwyn Oliver
Jenkins), "Yoruba Wisdom", "Marvell's Hero", and "A New
Zealander in the English landscape". The last issue was
edited by Glyn Court, with Norma L. Segeal as assistant
editor.

BL: P.P.6152.clh
CUL: L985.B.37
TCD: 32.tt.66, nos.1–5

37 Facet: arts magazine of the West / edited by P. Britten Austin, then Ergo Jones and Jack Knapman. Bristol: Quest Publications, Vol. 1 no. 1 (Oct. 1946)–vol. 3 no. 4 (Autumn 1949)

Index: Indexes for vol. 1 and 2 were advertised

A general arts review focussed on south west England but

not exclusively so. Poets included Charles Morgan, Alan Ross, John Waller, John Heath-Stubbs, Quentin Crisp, Judith Buckland, Elizabeth Louch, Jack Clemo, Ronald Duncan, John Atkins, and others. Essayists included Quentin Crisp (on Mervyn Peake), Raoul Dufy (half-tones), John Heath-Stubbs (on Literature in the eighteenth century), Alan Ross (on the poet and society), and others. From vol 2 no 3 *Facet* was edited by Jones and Knapman.

BL: P.P.5939.caw
CUL: L400.C.65
TCD: PER 75–893

38 Fantasia. Worthing: Fantasia, No. 1 [1946]–2 [1946].

Note: Continued by: *Fantasma*
Anthology: *Left-Wing Verse* (Worthing: Fantasma, [1947]), BL: 11657.ff.55.
Related Imprint: Fantasia also associated with *Fantasma Miscellany, Fantasma Parade* and *Fantasma Supplement*

BL: P.P.5939.bgx

39 Fantasma. Worthing: Fantasia, No. 3 (Mar./May 1947)–22 (Autumn/Winter 1952)

Note: Continues: *Fantasia*
Anthology: *Left-Wing Verse* (Worthing: Fantasma, [1947]), BL: 11657.ff.55.
Related Imprint: Fantasia was also associated with *Fantasma Miscellany, Fantasma Parade* and *Fantasma Supplement*

BL: P.P.5939.bgx

40 Focus / edited by B. [i.e. Balachandra] Rajan and Andrew Pearse. London: Dennis Dobson, [Vol.] 1 (1945)–5 (1950)

Profiled in: Hoffman, Allen & Ulrich; Tolley 1940s

Essentially an annual, each issue being built around a symposium, although also including miscellaneous poetry, fiction, and criticism. The symposia topics were, in order of appearance, "Kafka and Rex Warner", "The realist novel in the Thirties", "T. S. Eliot", "The novelist as thinker", and, lastly, "Modern American Poetry". Andrew Pearse ceased to co-edit after the second volume. Poets included George Barker, W. S. Graham, John Heath-Stubbs, Louis Adeane, Vernon Watkins, George Woodcock, Kathleen Raine, Nicholas Moore, Norman Nicholson, Kenneth Patchen, E. E. Cummings and others. The American issue includes poems by James Laughlin, Robert Lowell, Norman Macleod, Marianne Moore, Wallace Stevens, William

Carlos Williams and others, as well as questionnaire on American poetry answered by some American poets themselves.

BL: W.P.927
CUL: L700.C.38

41 Folios of New Writing / edited by John Lehmann. London: Hogarth Press, Vol. 1 (Spring 1940)-4 (Autumn 1941)

Note: Continues: *New Writing*; continued by: *New Writing and Daylight*
Index: Sader
Profiled in: Hoffman, Allen & Ulrich; Stanton; Sullivan 1914–1984; Tolley 1940s
Reprint: New York: Johnson Reprint [undated]

Mostly a publisher of prose, but poets include Nicholas Moore, Stephen Spender, David Gascoyne, Goronwy Rees, C. Day Lewis, Laurie Lee, Rex Warner, Adam Drinan, Louis MacNeice, and Allen Curnow.

BL: PP.5938.bbd
CUL: L727.C.23
NLS: Y.190
TCD: 33.aa.71–89

42 Forum: Stories and Poems / edited by Muriel Spark and Derek Stanford. London: Forum Stories and Poems, Vol. 1 no. 1 (Summer 1949)–no. 2 [1950]

Interview: with Derek Stanford in Gortschacher I

A literary review produced in the aftermath of Spark's controversial departure from the Poetry Society (as editor of *Poetry Review*). Poems by John Waller, Herbert Palmer, Lorca (trans. Roy Campbell), Iris Birtwistle, Alec Craig, Kathleen Raine, Weston McDaniel, Wrey Gardiner, Hugo Manning, John Bayliss, and Iain Fletcher. Other contributions include Henry Treece on the prose poem, and G. S. Fraser on the Classical and Romantic. Muriel Spark edited the first issue; Spark and Stanford co-edited vol. 1 no. 2.

BL: P.P.5938.bdk
CUL: L999.C.3.42
NLS: 1954.1

43 La France Libre / edited by André Labarthe. London: Hamish Hamilton, Vol. 1 no. 1 (nov. 1940)–vol. 13 no. 75 (jan. 1947)

Related Imprint: *La France Libre* teamed up with *Horizon* to produce the Francophile Horizon imprint, publishing a series of books which included Aragon's *Le Crève-Coeur* and Sartre's *Huis Clos*.

A French exile cultural review. Texts are in French. Articles on French and francophone life and culture, and occasional essays from English authors e.g. H. G. Wells, and Aldous Huxley. Actual poems are rare, e.g. "Timgad" by Vita Sackville-West (fév. 1941) and poems by Kathleen Raine (nov. 1946).

BL: P.P.3555.ahl
CUL: Q560.C.5
NLS: NJ.712
TCD: Vol. 10 no. 55 (June 1945)–vol. 13 no. 74 (Jan. 1947). (36.nn.52, Nos.10–24; 36.nn.53)

44 Free Unions – Unions Libres / edited by Simon Watson Taylor. London: Simon Watson Taylor in association with the Surrealist Group in England, [1946]

A large format illustrated one-off. Surrealism is the keynote (including an errata slip confusing de Gaulle with Bonaparte and Hitler by turns), with translations from the French and Portuguese. Contributors include Lucien Freud, E. L. T. Mesens, Alfred Jarry, and the Marquis de Sade in a new translation, and there are poems from George Melly, Patrick Waldberg, Jeanne Santerre, Eduoard Helman, Serge Ninn, Jacqueline Darras, Sadi Cherkeshi, Jean L. Davy and others.

BL: 12298.k.6
CUL: L999.B.1.37

45 Gambit / edited by G. L. J. Engle and P. A. Mulgan; then Michael Shanks, C.A. Cooper and Mitchell Raper. Oxford: 1949–50

Profiled in: Tolley 1940s

Included work by John Bowen, Martin Seymour Smith, and Mitchell Raper. No holdings known.

46 Gangrel / edited by J. B. Pick. London: [J. B. Pick], [No. 1, 1945]–no. 4 (1946)

Profiled in: Hoffman, Allen & Ulrich; Sullivan 1914–1984

A cultural review with sections on general literature, poetry, philosophy, and music. Contributors include Henry Miller, Alfred Perlès, John Gawsworth, Kenneth Patchen, Nicholas Moore, George Orwell, Denise Levertoff [i.e. Levertov], James Kirkup, and Neil M. Gunn.

BL: 2–4. (P.P.5938.cap)
CUL: L900.C.282
NLS: 1951.34
UCL

47 The Gate: international review of literature and art in English and German / edited by Margaret Greig, Rudolf Jung and Howard Sergeant. London: The Gate, Vol. 1 no. 1 (Jan./Mar. 1947)–vol. 3 no. 1 [1949]

Note: The first issue also bore the German title, *Das Tor*. Publisher and place of publication vary. From vol. 1 no. 4, published in Oxford by Pen-in-Hand
Related Imprint: Pen-in-Hand, a general press that published a wide variety of books

A general literary review with a particular interest in German, often publishing articles and poetry in that language. Contributors included: Stephen Spender, C. Day Lewis, Herman Hesse, Rilke (trans. Vita Sackville-West and Vernon Watkins, and by R. F. C. Hull), Jack Lindsay, Wrey Gardiner, J. B. Pick, George Woodcock, Michael Hamburger, and Muriel Spark. The issue for March–May 1948 describes a circulation of 20,000, a figure A.T. Tolley suggests, in an unpublished account of the 1940s, was likely the result of distribution to a post-war Germany under reconstruction. Perhaps this also implies British government assistance.

BL: Vol. 1 no. 1–vol. 2 no. 3/4. (P.P.5939.r)
CUL: L700.C.50
NLS: NF.1572
TCD: Vol. 1 no. 1 (PL–140–605) Vol. 1 no. 2. (PL–140–606); Vol. 1 no. 3. (PL–140–607); Vol. 2 no. 1. (PL–140–608); Vol. 2 no. 2. (PL–140–609); Vol. 2 no. 3 (PL–140–610); Vol. 3 no. 1 (PL–140–611)

48 Gemini: a pamphlet magazine of new poetry / edited by Frederic Vanson. Derby: Frederic Vanson, No. 1 (May 1949)–5 (Sept. 1950)

Related Imprint: Gemini Press, presumably belonging to Vanson himself, published his *The Furious Finding. Fifteen sonnets* (1950, BL: 11658.b.39) and his *Four Holy Sonnets* (1955, BL: 11660.e.13)

Contributors to this typescript magazine included Muriel Spark, Robert Greacen, Ian Hamilton Finlay, Raymond

Tong and Derek Stanford. "During the late war a number of young men were brought together by the blind decrees of the War Office and soon discovered common interests – among them poetry. [...] In one sense GEMINI is a result of those associations." Vanson would also publish The Christian Poet in 1953.

BL: P.P.5126.bbl

49 The Glass / edited by Antony Borrow and Madge Hales. Lowestoft: Antony Borrow, No. 1 (1948)–11 (1954)

Publishing mainly poetry, including prose poems. Borrow's interest was in literature that proceeded by "dislocating the ordinary". The magazine included work by Henri Michaux (trans. James Kirkup), T. E. F. Blackburn, A. S. Thwaite (i.e. Anthony Thwaite), Bernard Bergonzi, Christopher Middleton, Yves Bonnefoy, Derek Stanford, Henry Treece, Oswell Blakeston, Harold Pinta (i.e. Pinter). Issues 1–7 were edited by Borrow, 8–11 by Borrow and Hales. The last issue was devoted to contemporary French poetry.

BL: P.P.5938.bde

50 Greek Horizons / edited by Derek Patmore. Athens: Icaros Publishing Co., No. 1 (Sept. 1946)

Contributors include the artists Nikoi Engonopoulos and Osbert Lancaster, and Rex Warner, Lawrence Durrell, I. Scott-Kilvert and the editor.

BL: Cup.410.f.121

51 Harlequin / edited by Oliver Carson & Anthony Blond. Oxford, then London: Harlequin, No. 1 (Winter 1949)–2 (1950)

Note: Continued by: Panorama.

A glossy magazine for students and in part by them. Essays by Enid Starkie on Verlaine and Mallarmé at Oxford, and Compton Mackenzie on Oxford literary magazines; poems by John Betjeman.

BL: P.P.6118.hga
CUL: No. 2. (L999.B.1.46)
NLS: No. 2. (6.631)

52 Here and Now: a group production: poetry-prose-drawing / [edited by Sylvia Read]. London: Favil Press, [No. 1] (1941)–5 (1949)

Note: Imprint varies. Nos. 4 and 5 were published by Falcon Press. Variant title: Here and Now Miscellany
Profiled in: Hoffman, Allen & Ulrich; Tolley 1940s

Emerged from a pre-war "group of young people [who] met regularly to share their common interest in poetry, drama and music. Significantly all were under twenty-five and already felt the need for a changed world in which the delights of music, colour and words would form an integral part of the lives of its people. Came the war. Our group was dispersed by the forces of this new destruction, but, determined to beat the cultural "black-out", we kept in touch by a type-written quarterly passed among our members. Here and Now is the best of all that appeared in that "periodical" in 1940.'"– Introduction in first issue. Sylvia Read and Peter Albery co-edited nos. 4–5. Contributors included: Francis King, Anne Ridler, Alex Comfort, Nicholas Moore, Henry Treece, Eleanor Farjeon, Howard Sergeant, Patric Dickinson, and C. Day Lewis.

BL: [1], 2; 4; 5. (12298.eee.29)
CUL: [1], 2; 4; 5. (L727.C.83)
TCD: [1]–2 (1943). (PER 75–971)

53 Here To-day / edited by Pierre Edmunds and Roland Mathias. Reading: No. 1 (1944)–4 (1945).

Profiled in: Hoffman, Allen & Ulrich
Related Work: Sam Adams, Roland Mathias (Cardiff: University of Wales Press, 1995), BL: YK.1996.a.2281

BL: [An unnumbered issue published in 1945]. (YD.2005.a.3848)

54 Horizon: a review of literature and art / edited by Cyril Connolly. London: Horizon, Vol. 1 no. 1 (Jan. 1940)–vol. 20 no. 120/121 (Dec. 1949/Jan. 1950)

Note: The issue for March 1946 appears not to have been published
Index: Sader. A separate index was published by Horizon for Jan. 1940–Dec. 1948. An index for Jan. 1949–Jan. 1950 was published with no.120/121
Profiled in: Hoffman, Allen & Ulrich; Stanton; Sullivan 1914–1984; Tolley 1940s
Study: Ian Hamilton, "Style of Despair", in Hamilton, The Little Magazines: a study of six editors (London: Weidenfeld and Nicolson), 1976, BL: X.989/50900; Michael Shelden, Friends of Promise: Cyril Connolly and the world of Horizon (London: Hamish Hamilton, 1989), BL: YH.1989.b.317
Related Imprint: Horizon, a Francophile imprint, was founded on Horizon teaming up with La France Libre to

publish translations of Apollinaire, Sartre, Proust, Gide, Malraux, Michaux and others.

Anthology: Cyril Connolly (ed.), *The Golden Horizon* (London: Weidenfeld and Nicolson, 1953), BL: 12298.ff.19; Cyril Connolly (ed.), *Ideas and Places* [a selection of editorial comments by Connolly] (London: Weidenfeld and Nicolson, 1953), BL: 12298.ff.14

Related Work: Clive Fisher, *Cyril Connolly: a nostalgic life* (London: Macmillan, 1995), BL: YC.1995.b.3657; Jeremy Lewis, *Cyril Connolly: a life* (London: Jonathan Cape, 1997), BL: YK.1998.b.3622; Cyril Connolly, *Enemies of Promise* (London: Routledge, 1938), BL: 11860.f.27; 2nd ed., 1949, BL: 11868.aa.43

Reprint: New York: Johnson Reprint Corp, [undated]

Microfilm: New York: New York Public Library, [undated]; Millwood, New York: KTO Microform, [undated]

A general literary review, which also published poetry.

BL: P.P.5939.car
CUL: Q718.C.16
NLS: Y.139
TCD: 100.u.5;100.u.1–20; CUNN 488 no.13 v.1 nos.1–6 (1940)

55 Imprint / edited by J. M. Grundy. Cambridge: [J. M Grundy, at Caius College], Vol. 1 no. 1 (Oct. 1949)–no. 5 (Summer 1950)

Index: Contents of vol.1 (i.e. all issues) are listed in issue 5.

The editor would later be better known as Milton Grundy, author of *Venice Recorded: a guidebook and anthology* which, like his classic tax law text *Grundy's Tax Havens*, has gone through many editions.

BL: P.P.5938.bdi
CUL: CAM.C.31.67
NLS: 1954.22

56 Indian Writing / edited by Iqbal Singh, Ahmed Ali, K. S. Shelvankar, and A. Subramaniam. London: No. 1 (Spring 1940)–5 (Summer 1942)

Profiled in: Hoffman, Allen & Ulrich

A general cultural review which published short stories and very little poetry, e.g. by Peter Blackman and Bharati Sarabhai. An extract from Tagore's eightieth birthday speech is reprinted in no. 4 (Aug. 1941).

BL: P.P.5939.cas
CUL: L900.D.78
NLS: 5.1182
TCD: 31.nn.60, nos.7–11

57 Irish Bookman / edited by Seamus Campbell, and others. Dublin: Seamus Campbell, Vol. 1 no. 1 (Aug. 1946)–vol. 3 no. 1 (Dec. 1948).

Index: Hayes
Profiled in: Tom Clyde, *Irish Literary Magazines: an outline and descriptive bibliography* (Dublin: Irish Academic Press, 2003), BL: 2725.g.3414

Book notes, articles, short fiction, snippets from other journals, quotations and occasional, rather old fashioned, poems (e.g. by Padraic Fiacc, Celia Randall, Padraic Gregory and others). Thomas MacGreevy contributes a short article about an Italian Mass composed in honour of Daniel O'Connell, and Robert Greacen also contributes prose. Evelyn Waugh is provoked in the last issue to contribute a letter on the question of being a Catholic writer.

BL: PP.6158.dd
TCD: 104.r.1–

58 Irish Harvest: a collection of stories, essays, and poems / edited by Robert Greacen. Dublin: New Frontiers Press, 1946

BL: 12299.c.22
NLS: 1947.11

Irish Voices *See* Ulster Voices B136

59 Irish Writing: the magazine of contemporary Irish literature / edited by David Marcus and Terence Smith; then S. J. White. Cork, then Dublin: Trumpet Books, No. 1 (1946)–37 (1957)

Note: Some issues have *Poetry Ireland* as a supplement
Index: Hayes
Profiled in: Tom Clyde, *Irish Literary Magazines: an outline and descriptive bibliography* (Dublin: Irish Academic Press, 2003), BL: 2725.g.3414

A general literary magazine focusing mainly on Ireland. Contributors included Samuel Beckett, Teresa Deevey, Robert Greacen, Patrick Kavanagh, John Montague, Thomas Kinsella, and Donald Davie. S. J. White took over editorship with no. 29 in 1954. No. 33 was a special issue devoted to the "A representative selection of the modern Gaelic revival presented in translation." Revived as *New Irish Writing* in 1968, a supplement within the Saturday edition of the newspaper *Irish Press*, and then, after a brief absence in 1988, as a supplement within the *Sunday Tribune*.

BL: 1–29; 31–34. (P.P.6158.de)
CUL: 1–34; 37. (L996.C.72)
NLS: P.sm.1591
TCD: 102.r.41–;OLS L–6–672 No.10; OLS L–7–251 No.1

60 Jabberwock: Edinburgh University review / edited by Dick Scott [and others, including Iain Ferguson]. Edinburgh: Edinburgh University Liberal Club, then Edinburgh University Scottish Renaissance Society, Vol. 1 no. 1 (Summer 1945)–vol. 6 no. 1 [1959?]

Note: Issues may be unnumbered. Continued by: *Sidewalk*

The magazine maintained a Scottish focus, with contributors such as Hugh MacDiarmid, Compton Mackenzie, Norman MacCaig and Alan Jackson until late in its existence. An unnumbered issue of 1959 includes work by William Burroughs, Allen Ginsberg, Jack Kerouac, Gregory Corso, Gary Snyder, Robert Creeley and other American writers. Its successor, *Sidewalk*, continued and widened the internationalist interest.

BL: Summer 1957. (P.P.6199.bde)
NLS: NH.289
UCL: Vol. 5 no. 1 (1958)–vol. 6 no. 1 (1959?)

61 Jazz Forum: quarterly review of jazz and literature / edited by Albert J. McCarthy. Fordingbridge, Hampshire: Delphic Press, No. 1 [1946]–5 (Autumn 1947)

Profiled in: Hoffman, Allen & Ulrich
Related Imprint: Delphic Press published Louis Adeane, *The Night Loves Us* (1946), BL: YA.1992.a.19963; Raymond Tong, *Salute to Greece* (1946), CUL: Uc.8.7991; William Everson, *Poems MCMXLII* [1946?] and Kenneth Patchen, *Double Header* [1946?] were also advertised but may not have appeared from Delphic.

Mostly articles about jazz, but with poems by Langston Hughes, George Leite, Raymond Tong, Kenneth Patchen, Eithne Wilkins, Aimé Césaire, W. S. Graham, Louis Adeane, and Howard Sergeant, and articles by Patchen, George Woodcock and Nicholas Moore. William Everson contributes a letter on Bunk Johnson's records.

BL: P.P.1945.sbb

62 Khaki and Blue: the younger

writers in battledress / edited by Peter Ratazzi. [In the field]: Peter Ratazzi, distributed by Staples and Staples (Slough), [No. 1, 1944–no. 3, 1946]

Note: Editor and publisher vary. Continued by *Civvy Street*?
Anthology: Peter Ratazzi (ed.) *Little Anthology: the first girl writers in battledress* (London: Staples & Staples, [1944]), BL: 12298.d.52.
Related Imprint: Peter Ratazzi published several books using his own name as the imprint. These included poems by Arthur Ball, *Sea Acres* (1947), BL: 11658.aaa.153.

Short stories and poems. Ratazzi was wounded so did not edit no. 2, which was edited by P. L. H. Smith and published by Pan Press, but he was fit enough to resume control of the remaini͠g issue. Poets included Maurice Lindsay, Emanuel Litvinoff, Henry Treece, Derek Stanford and Molly Francis. In no. 3 it published the manifesto of the Front Line Generation, P.H.L. Smith, Howard Sergeant and Peter Ratazzi, whose poetry was then released in *New Generation*. The successor to *Khaki and Blue* appears to have been *Civvy Street*, edited by F. T. Tubes, but it was more of a magazine devoted to giving ex-service personnel practical help, a political voice, and to helping them keep in touch with each other (BL: Vol. 1 no. 1 [1947], P.P.4050.clc). From the evidence of the first issue, it did not publish poetry.

BL: 12299.a.28

63 Lagan: a miscellany of Ulster writing / edited by John Boyd. Lisburn: The Lagan Press, No. 1 [1943]–no. 4 (1946)

Note: No. 4 was also referred to as Vol. 2 no. 1

Index: Hayes
Profiled in: Tom Clyde, *Irish Literary Magazines: an outline and descriptive bibliography* (Dublin: Irish Academic Press, 2003), BL: 2725.g.3414

Short stories, poems and other texts. Founded with a specifically Northern Irish focus by Sam Hanna Bell, John Boyd, and Bob Davison. Contributors include May Morton, John Hewitt, Roy McFadden, Louis MacNeice, and Robert Greacen. John Hewitt contributes a discursive essay, "The Bitter Gourd: Some Problems of the Ulster Writer" in no. 3.

BL: 3–4. (ZA.9.a.11237)
CUL: 3–4. (L900.C.290)
NLS: 3–4. (1970.257)
TCD: 3–4. (126.b.27, Nos.18–19)
Princess Grace Irish Library of Monaco

Chapter B: 1940–1949

64 Leaven / edited by John Bate. Croydon: Ditchling Press, Easter 1946

Profiled in: Hoffman, Allen & Ulrich

John Bate's attempt to move on from *Oasis* after the war: "We would not have men listen to our voice, but to still themselves within, so that they may hear the Voice that has never been silent, or, if you like, the Silence that has never been voiced" (from the Editorial). Includes poems by Bate, Norman Nicholson, an anonymous pantomime ("The Walter-Kelpie Princess"), D. S. Savage on "Socialism and the Problem of Evil", and Sid Chaplin's "North-Countryman's Journal".

BL: YD.2004.a.902
NLS: HP.1.79.1191
UCL

65 Leeds University Poetry / edited by Robin Skelton, then W. A. Hodges and others. Leeds: Lotus Press, 1949–1950, 1954–1956

Anthology: A. R. Mortimer and James Simmons (eds.), *Out on the Edge* (Leeds: Dept. of English Literature [Leeds University], 1958), BL: YA.1995.a.22540. Includes work by Tony Harrison. See also Debjani Chatterjee and Barry Tebb (eds.), *Sixties Press Anthology of Gregory Fellows' Poetry* (Sutton: Sixties Press, 2005)

Contributors included James Kirkup and Robin Skelton. Bonamy Dobrée contributed a preface to the 1949 and 1950 volumes. The 1956 issue contains poems by Thomas Blackburn, James Simmons, John Heath-Stubbs, Geoffrey Hill and others.

BL: 1949–1950; 1956 (P.P.5126.bbs)
CUL: L727.D.103

66 Life Line / [Staff of R.A.F. Coastal Command], dates unknown

A poster magazine, noted by A. T. Tolley in an unpublished account of magazines in the 1940s.
No holdings known.

67 London Forum: a quarterly review of literature, art and current affairs / edited by Peter Baker and Roland Gant. London: Falcon Press, Vol. 1 no. 1 (Winter 1946)–no. 4 (Christmas 1947)

Almost no poetry itself though e.g. one poem by Wrey Gardiner, but includes articles on poetry and the arts, e.g. by John Heath-Stubbs, Kathleen Nott (on verse drama), Jack Lindsay, and Henry Miller (on Kenneth Patchen).

BL: Vol. 1 no. 1–no. 2. (P.P.5938.caa)
CUL: L.900.C.266
NLS: 1950.48
TCD: PER 91– 84

68 Lyra: an anthology of new lyric / edited by Alex Comfort and Robert Greacen. Billericay: Grey Walls Press, 1942

Profiled in: Tolley 1940s
Related Imprint: Wrey Gardiner's Grey Walls Press published numerous poetry collections and other books in the 1940s and 50s

Describing itself as a publication of "new romanticism", this anthology included work by Henry Treece, Nicholas Moore, G. S. Fraser, Norman Nicholson, Anne Ridler, Francis Scarfe, Vernon Watkins, Alex Comfort, Emanuel Litvinoff, John Bayliss, Tambimuttu and Wrey Gardiner. Grey Walls' *New Road* is loosely a continuation of *Lyra*.

BL: 11605.b.15
NLS: T.31.e.

69 Mandrake / edited by John Wain, then Arthur Boyars and Audrey M. Arnold, then Arthur Boyars and John Wain, then Arthur Boyars. Oxford: Arthur Boyars Vol. 1 no. 1 (May 1945)–vol. 2 no. 11 (Winter 1956)

Profiled in: Sullivan 1914–1984

Started by John Wain when he was an undergraduate at St. John's College Oxford, this was a general arts review, with poetry, short fiction and arts essays. Contributors included: John Atkins, Audrey Beecham, William Bell, Alexander Blok, Philip Larkin, C. M. Bowra, Georg Büchner, Roy Campbell, Neville Coghill, Patric Dickinson, Geoffrey Dutton, David Gascoyne, Michael Hamburger, John Heath-Stubbs, J. B. Leishman, C. Day Lewis, Lorca, Boris Pasternak, Pierre Reverdy and others. Notable for its early publication of Larkin in no. 3.

BL: P.P.5939.cat
CUL: Vol. 1 no. 4–vol. 2 no. 11. (L727.C.417)
NLS: NH.290

70 **Manuscript** / edited by C. P. Billot, A. D. Walters, Peter Dunn, and others. Southampton: Vol. 1 no. 1 (June 1941)–no. 3 (Nov./Dec. 1941)

A general literary review. There was a deliberate attempt to publish younger writers but most are still unknown today. Poets included Idris Parry and Wrey Gardiner, and there was a short story by A. H. Teece.

BL: P.P.5938.bbr
CUL: L999.C.3.75

71 **Message: Belgian review** / edited by Paul Weyember. London: Message, No. 1 (nov. 1941)–55 (juin 1946)

A Belgian exile cultural review. Among the obviously more pressing articles on the war, and proposals for life after the war, there are articles on Belgian culture and occasional essays from non-Belgians, e.g. Michael Roberts on "Poetry and war" (April 1942) and Herbert Read on "The freedom of the artist" (Dec. 1942). Actual poems are rare.

BL: P.P.4480.i
NLS: Y.180
TCD: 130.p.41–47

72 **Mid-Day** / [edited by Antoinette Pratt Barlow]. Oxford: Mid-day Publications, No. 1 (Winter 1946–7)

Short stories, miscellaneous arts articles, and poems by Hugh Popham and Stevie Smith.

BL: P.P.6004.gre
CUL: L999.C.3.49
NLS: 6.2131

73 **Middle East Anthology** / edited by John Waller and Erik de Mauny. London: Lindsay Drummond, 1946

BL: 12299.c.18
NLS: Vts.175.g.21

74 **Million: new left writing** / edited by John Singer. Glasgow: William Maclellan, No. 1 [1943]–3 [1946]

Profiled in: Hoffman, Allen & Ulrich
Related Imprint: MacLellan was one of the key post-war publishers in Scotland, publishing fiction, social analysis, art criticism and theory, and poetry. The Poetry Scotland Series, published by William MacLellan, featured collections by Hugh MacDiarmid, Sidney Goodsir Smith, George Bruce, Adam Drinan, Ruthven Todd, and W. S. Graham. BL: W.P.1989

Short stories, literary criticism, and poems, the latter from: Langston Hughes, Joe Corrie, Maurice Lindsay, Sydney Tremayne, Hugh MacDiarmid, Sydney Goodsir Smith, Brecht (trans. Honor Arundel), John Singer himself, Sid Chaplin, Jack Lindsay, Honor Arundel, Nicholas Moore, Patricia Ledward, and others. John Singer also contributes an article on "Literature and the War" (no. 1).

BL: W.P.7447
CUL: L900.C.276
NLS: 1951.12

75 **The Mint. A miscellany of literature, art and criticism** / edited by Geoffrey Grigson. London: Routledge, [No. 1] (1946)–2 (1948)

Profiled in: Sullivan 1914–1984

A general cultural review, which also published poetry.

BL: W.P.1353
CUL: L727.C.72
NLS: 1. (Vts.175.f.52); 2. (1968.119)

76 **Modern Reading** / edited by Reginald Moore. London: Staples & Staples [and subsequently other publishers], No. 1 [1941]–23 (1953)

Profiled in: Hoffman, Allen & Ulrich
Related Imprint: Modern Reading Library

The focus was on short fiction, but Modern Reading did publish just a few poems, e.g. by Idris Davies and Frederic Prokosch.

BL: X.989/709 and W.P.5180/22.
CUL: Lacking no. 2 and no. 23. (L996.D.12)
NLS: Lacking no. 2, 16, 18–19, 21, and 23. (P.med.2271)
TCD: 21–22. (PAM K.34 no.22–23)

The New Alliance & Scots Review See The New Alliance A134

77 The New Apocalypse: an anthology of criticism, poems and stories / [Edited by J. F. Hendry.]. London: Fortune Press, [1940]

Profiled in: Tolley 1940s

The anthology that, building on 1930s magazines such as *Seven* and *Kingdom Come*, gave the name to the "New Apocalypse" poets. The contributors were Dorian Cooke, J. F. Hendry, Norman MacCaig, Robert Melville, Nicholas Moore, Philip O'Connor, Dylan Thomas and Henry Treece. There was a frontispiece by Pablo Picasso. Further anthologies were *The White Horseman* and *The Crown and the Sickle*.

BL: 12299.b.11
NLS: T.239.b

78 The New Athenian Broadsheet / edited by Winifred Binning. Edinburgh: New Athenian Broadsheets, No. 1 (Aug. 1947)–16 (Christmas 1951)

Note: No. 2 (Christmas 1947) was reprinted for Christmas 1950, but bears the same number.

Publishing solely poetry, occasionally reprinted from earlier collections or magazines, this began with the Edinburgh Festival in 1947. The emphasis was on Scottish poetry, but not exclusively so. Contributors included: Lewis Spence, Hugh MacDiarmid, Sydney Goodsir Smith, George Campbell Hay, Naomi Mitchison, Maurice Lindsay, Marion Angus, Helen B. Cruickshank and others. The rather Victorian A. V. Stuart was particularly well represented. The editor was not always indicated, but Winfred Binning appears to have edited nos. 1–13 and 15. R. Ogilvie Crombie was designated the Interim Editor, and edited nos. 14 and 16.

BL: P.P.5126.gbu. (No. 2 is supplied in reprint only, P.P.5126.gbu.(2))
CUL: L727.C.121
NLS: 5.1716
TCD: 69.n.111, nos.3–20

79 New Generation / edited by Peter Ratazzi. London: No. 1 (Spring/Summer 1946)–2 (Winter 1947)

Apparently intended as the magazine of the Front Line Generation, P.H.L. Smith, Howard Sergeant and Peter Ratazzi, whose manifesto was published in the third issue of Ratazzi's magazine *Khaki and Blue*. Also includes a poem by Dannie Abse.

BL: P.P.5938.cad

80 The New Meridian Magazine / edited by Robert Muller, David Hack and Harry Klopper. London: Alan Neame Publications, Vol. 1 no. 1 (Jan/Feb. 1947)–no. 3 (June/July 1947)

Related Imprint: Meridian Books issued at least two poetry collections in its Garrick Poets series, by Randall Swingler, *The Years of Anger* (1946), BL: W.P. 1744/1, and Maurice Carpenter, *The Tall Interpreter* (1946), BL: W.P.1744/2

A general cultural review, with considerable interest in foreign affairs and countries overseas. Each issue had a "World Poetry" section where untranslated poems from other countries were presented. Poets included Erich Kästner, Paul Eluard, Jules Supervielle, Ernst Wiechert and Andre de Rache, as well as, e.g. Patric Dickinson. Jack Lindsay was brought in to co-edit with Muller, Hack and Klopper for the second issue; the third and last issue was edited by Klopper and Muller alone.

BL: P.P.5939.cax
CUL: L999.B.1.22
NLS: 5.1278 PER

81 New Poetry / edited by Nicholas Moore. London: Fortune Press, No. 1 [1946]–2 [1946]

Profiled in: Hoffman, Allen & Ulrich; Stanton; Sullivan 1914–1984

Contributors included Lawrence Durrell, G. S. Fraser, Nicholas Moore, Ruthven Todd, Wallace Stevens, Conrad Aiken, W. S. Graham, Elizabeth Bishop, Allen Tate, Christopher Middleton and Hamish Henderson.

BL: W.P.1743
CUL: No. 1. (L999.C.3.77)

82 New Road: new directions in European art and letters / edited by Alex Comfort and John Bayliss, then Fred Marnau, then Wrey Gardiner. Billericay: Grey Walls Press, [No. 1] (1943)–5 (1949)

Profiled in: Hoffman, Allen & Ulrich; Sullivan 1914–1984
Related Imprint: Wrey Gardiner's Grey Walls Press published numerous poetry collections and other books in the 1940s and 50s
Reprint: Nendeln, Liechtenstein: Kraus Reprint, 1969

A substantial general cultural review with a particular interest in continental literature, published in translation.

Contributors included: David Gascoyne, J. F. Hendry, Nicholas Moore, Anne Ridler, André Breton, Aimé Césaire, Lawrence Durrell, Norman McCaig, John Singer, Dylan Thomas, Ruthven Todd, Vernon Watkins, Robert Greacen, Delmore Schwartz, Elizabeth Bishop, Carlos Drummond de Andrade, Hugh MacDiarmid, Hamish Henderson, Georg Trakl, Paul Eluard, Henri Michaux and Jean Cocteau. Articles included those by: Kathleen Raine, James Kirkup, George Orwell, Derek Stanford. Comfort and Bayliss edited from 1943–44, Fred Marnau from 1944–46 and Wrey Gardiner the last issue (1949).

BL: X.989/38704
CUL: L727.C.60
NLS: T.32.c.

83 The New Savoy / edited by Mara Meulen and Francis Wyndham. London: New Savoy Press, 1946

Short stories, articles, poems and other texts. Contributors include: Betty Miller, Olivia Manning, George Orwell, Inez Holden, Stevie Smith, J. F. Hendry, Elizabeth Berridge, Hesketh Pearson, Isobel Strachey and Arthur Koestler.

BL: YA.1992.a.8747
CUL: L900.D.66

84 The New Saxon Pamphlets / edited by John Atkins. Prettyman Lane, Kent: John Atkins, No. 1 [1944]–3 [1945]. Then as The New Saxon Review, 4 [1945]–5 [1946]. Then as Albion, 6 [1947]–7 [1947].

Note: Place of publication varies. No. 6 is numbered Vol. IV no. 6
Profiled in: Hoffman, Allen & Ulrich; Stanton

A magazine produced in reaction to the New Apocalypse poets, and to the assumption that poetry is essentially a Celtic form. John Atkins's first editorial spells out the policy: "the point of the new saxon is this: he won't subscribe to the view that to write good poetry you must be a celt." The emphasis is on prose, but each issue does carry some poetry, e.g. by Patric Dickinson (verse drama), Stevie Smith, and John Singer. George Orwell contributes an article on "Poetry and the Microphone" in no. 3, and no. 4 carried work by the poet Brian Allwood, killed in action in Italy in 1944.

BL: W.P.967
CUL: L727.C.95
NLS: 1957.7

The New Saxon Review See The New Saxon Pamphlets B84

85 The New Scot / edited by Norrie Fraser and A. I. Milton, then R. G. MacMillan and Norrie Fraser. Glasgow: Golden Eagle Press for the Scottish Reconstruction Committee, [Vol. 1 no. 1, 1945]–[vol. 5 no. 1, Jan. 1949?]

A general cultural magazine focussed on Scotland. Occasional poems and short fiction. Contributors included Maurice Lindsay, Naomi Mitchison, William Soutar, Douglas Young, T. S. Law, and Hugh MacDiarmid (e.g. an article, "What's wrong with the 'Songs of the Hebrides'" and, with Douglas Young, a defence of the synthetic nature of the Scots language in poetry). Vol. 2 no. 1 included an open letter by Lindsay to Mitchison, defending the editorial policy of Poetry Scotland.

BL: Vol. 2 no. 1 (Jan. 1946)–vol. 5 no. 1 (Jan. 1949) (P.P.6223.bc)

86 The New Shetlander. Lerwick: The New Shetlander, No. 1 (Mar. 1947)– . ISSN: 0047-987X

A cultural review with a focus on Shetland. However, many of the contributors are from further afield. For example, in the first few years contributors included Orcadian poet George Mackay Brown (poetry, plays, articles, fiction), Hugh MacDiarmid (poetry, and an essay on 25 years of the modern Scottish Renaissance), Naomi Mitchison, Maurice Lindsay, T. S. Law, John J. Graham, J. T. Hughson (both poets writing in a Shetland dialect). Many of the local poems in the early issues are signed only by a pseudonym. The New Shetlander continues to publish new poetry to this day.

BL: P.P.6203.oa
CUL: 2– .(L486.B.24)
NLS: 1. (6.2395). 2– . (QJ9.797 PER). Lacking: No. 9 (1948); 15 (1949); 45 (1957); 178 (1991).
TCD: 2–43. (PER 81–333)

87 New Writing and Daylight / edited by John Lehmann. London: Hogarth Press, Vol. 1 (Summer 1942)–vol. 7 (1946)

Note: Continues: Folios of New Writing and Daylight; continued by: Orpheus
Index: Sader
Anthology: John Lehmann (ed.), Poems from New Writing (London: Lehmann, 1946), BL: 11606.b.13; John Lehmann

Chapter B: 1940–1949

(ed.) *Pleasures of New Writing: an anthology of poems, stories and other prose pieces from the pages of New Writing* (London: Lehmann, 1952), BL: 12299.ee.27
Profiled in: Hoffman, Allen & Ulrich; Stanton; Sullivan 1914–1984; Tolley 1940s

BL: P.P.5938.bbd
CUL: L727.C.23
NLS: Y.190
TCD: 33.aa.71–89

88 Nine / edited by Peter Russell and others. London: Peter Russell, Vol. 1 no. 1 (Autumn 1949)–vol. 4 no. 2 (Apr. 1956)

Index: UK Little Magazines Project
Profiled in: Stanton; Sullivan 1914–1984; Tolley 1940s; UK Little Magazines Project
Interview: with Peter Russell, in Görtschacher 2
Related Work: James Hogg (ed.), *The Road to Parnassus: homage to Peter Russell on his seventy-fifth birthday* (Salzburg: University of Salzburg, 1996), pp.269–80, BL: X.0909/611 (101) includes Wolfgang Görtschacher's essay '"Continuing the Dances of the Ages": Peter Russell's Literary Magazine Nine', pp.269–80.

A literary review, with the emphasis on poetry and a particular emphasis on Poundian modernism and classical traditions of verse. Russell had a number of co-editors: G. S Fraser and Iain Fletcher from Autumn 1949 to Spring 1950; Fletcher, Ian Scott-Kilvert and D. S. Carne-Ross from August 1950 to Autumn 1951. Russell edited alone from April 1952 to April 1956.

BL: PP.5126.bbk
CUL: P727.C.16
NLS: NF.1561
TCD: 133.a.38–39

89 The Norseman: an independent literary and political review / edited by Jac. S. Worm-Müller, then H. L. Lehmkuhl. London: Lindsay Drummond Ltd, then the Norseman, Vol. 1–no. (Jan. 1943)–vol. 16 no. 6 (Nov./Dec. 1946)

Index: An index to vols. 1–16 was published in Oslo in 1960, BL: P.P.4811.n.(1)

A Norwegian exile cultural review. Articles on Norwegian (and Scandinavian) culture, short fiction and occasional poems. Occasional pieces by British authors, e.g. Derek Stanford on John Masefield, Neville Braybrooke on T. S. Eliot, Gilbert Murray, Herbert Read, and a short story by

Muriel Spark. In vol. 1 no. 6 (Nov. 1943) Eliot contributes an article on "The Social Function of Poetry" and a chorus from *Murder in the Cathedral*. Texts are in English. There are short valedictory accounts of the magazine in the last issue.

BL: P.P.4811.n
CUL: P593.C.11
NLS: NH.672

90 Northern Review: the magazine of the North / edited by W. B. de Bear Nicol and Kenneth Severs. Pontefract: Vol. 1 no. 1 (June 1946)–vol. 2 no. 3 (Jan./Feb./Mar. 1948). New Series, No. 1 (May 1948)–no. 9 (Summer 1950)

Note: Absorbed by *The Dalesman*

A general cultural review with a northern England focus. Publishes three or four poems each issue. Contributors include Vernon Scannell, Wilfred Childe, Howard Sergeant, and James Kirkup. W. B. de Bear Nicol edited the magazine on his own from vol. 1 no. 7 onwards, when he also began to refer to himself as Bernard de Bear Nicol.

BL: P.P.5939.bga
CUL: L900.C.274
NLS: New series only. (5.1411)

91 Now / edited by George Woodcock. Maidenhead: M. C. Pitts, No. 1 (Easter 1940)–7 (Fall 1941). Then, New Series, No. 1 (1943)–9 (July/Aug. 1947)

Note: Place of publication and imprint varies
Profiled in: Hoffman, Allen & Ulrich; Stanton; Sullivan 1914–1984; Tolley 1940s
Reprint: Nendeln, Liechtenstein: Kraus Reprint, 1968

Started by Woodcock when he was a conscientious objector, working as an agricultural worker. The earlier issues included other conscientious objectors, such as D. S. Savage and Julian Symons, and was largely a political magazine. The new series had higher profile contributors such as George Orwell on "How the Poor Die", Herbert Read on "The Cult of Leadership", and Alex Comfort on "Art and Social Responsibility", while poets included W. S. Graham and George Barker. Towards the end of its run, there were more American contributions, e.g. by Kenneth Rexroth and William Everson.

BL: P.P.6033.gda
CUL: 3–7. New Series, 1–9. (L.900.C.304)
NLS: 1–7. New Series, 1–7. (1948.29)
TCD: New Series, 1–7. (110.s.1)

92 Now-a-days: book reviews, theatre, music, poetry, art / edited by Cyril Stone. Brighton: Crabtree Press, Vol. 1 no. 1 (Spring 1947)–no. 5 (Spring 1948)

A general cultural review, which published very little poetry. "Poetry" was dropped from its masthead in the last issue.

BL: P.P.5938.bdd
CUL: L400.C.54
NLS: 6.395

93 Oasis / edited by John Bate. Sonning: John Bate, March 1942–[Summer 1944?]

Note: Unnumbered. Subsequently published at Oxford, Lettcombe Bassett, and Croydon. Continues: X6; continued, in spirit at least, by: *Leaven*
Profiled in: Hoffman, Allen & Ulrich

A miscellany of short fiction and poetry, and some reviews. Poets included John Bayliss, Baudelaire translated by Edith Davis, Wrey Gardiner, and Boris Pasternak translated by J. M. Cohen. Conan Nicholas joined Bate as co-editor for the Summer 1944 issue. Derek Stanford contributed reviews. Not to be confused with *Oasis: the Middle East anthology of poetry from the Forces* (Cairo: Salamander, 1943), BL: Cup.410.d.86.

BL: Mar. 1942, Apr. 1942, June 1942, July 1942, Aug. 1942, Sept. 1942, Oct. 1942, [Nov. 1942], [1943], Spring 1944, and Summer 1944. (YA.1989.b.2)
NLS: Summer 1944 only. (1948.42)

94 Opus / edited by Denys Val Baker. London: [Denys Val Baker] no. 8 (Autumn 1941)–14 (Spring 1943)

Note: From no. 10 (Spring 1942) published at Tring
Profiled in: Hoffman, Allen & Ulrich; Stanton
Anthology: Robert Atthil et al., *Preludes: an anthology of wartime poetry* [1943], BL: YA.2003.a.35462.
Related Imprint: Opus Press published Nicholas Moore's short but early study, *Henry Miller* (1943), BL: 11869.dd.21. From 1943 Baker published *Voices* from his Opus Press

A general cultural review, which also published poetry. It began with no. 8, probably to avoid looking like a new little magazine, since war restrictions designed to limit paper consumption forbade new magazines starting up. Baker contributes a short survey of the "Britain's culture press in wartime" in no. 8. Most of the poets are now little known, though it did publish Nicholas Moore, Maurice Lindsay, Wrey Gardiner, and Henry Treece.

BL: P.P.5938.caq
NLS: 11 (Summer 1942)–14. (5.1104)

95 Orientations / edited by G. S. Fraser, then D. J. S. Thomson, then J. M. MacKechnie, then Raymond Nunn. Cairo: Victory Club, [Spring? 1942]–no. 29? 1945

Profiled in: Tolley 1940s

Founded by a group originally working at the Headquarters of British Troops in Egypt, specifically to give ordinary soldiers a voice. However, most contributors were fairly experienced writers, including John Waller, Lawrence Durrell (writing under the pseudonym Charles Norden), Hamish Henderson, Tambimuttu and Nicholas Moore. Despite publishing as many as twenty nine issues, copies are now extremely rare. The editors are grateful to A. T. Tolley for information on this title.

Imperial War Museum

96 Orion: a miscellany / edited by Denys Kilham Roberts and others. London: Nicholson and Watson, Vol. 1 ([Spring] 1945)–4 (Autumn 1947)

Profiled in: Hoffman, Allen & Ulrich; Sullivan 1914–1984

The first two volumes were edited by Rosamond Lehmann, Edwin Muir, Denys Kilham Roberts, and C. Day Lewis; Muir was no longer an editor by vol. 3, and vol. 4 was edited by Roberts alone.

BL: W.P.1288
CUL: L727.C.69
Poetry Library: 1–3

97 Orpheus: a symposium of the arts / edited by John Lehmann. London: John Lehmann, Vol. 1 (1948)–vol. 2 (1949)

Note: Continues *New Writing and Daylight*

BL: W.P.2388
CUL: L727.C.24
NLS: T.145
TCD: 33.aa.90–91

98 Our Time / edited by Beatrix Lehmann, John Banting, Birkin Haward, Ben Frankel, Randall Swingler and others. London: Newport Publications then Fore Publications, Vol. 1 no. 1 (Feb. 1941)–[vol. 8 no. 8] (July/Aug. 1949)

Note: Incorporates *Poetry and the People* and *New Theatre*.

Editors and imprint vary
Profiled in: Hoffman, Allen & Ulrich; Sullivan 1914–1984
Reprint: Nendeln, Liechtenstein: Kraus Reprint, 1976

A general cultural review, occasionally publishing poetry
and articles on poetry.

BL: P.P.5126.bo
CUL: L727.B.25
NLS: Y.149
TCD: 26.bb.222–223

99 **Outposts** / edited by Howard Sergeant,
then Roland John. Blackpool: Howard
Sergeant, No. 1 (Oct. 1943)–? ISSN:
0030–7297

Note: Location and imprint varies. Originally bore the
subtitle: *poems, articles and reviews*. Anna Martin was also
involved editorially. From no. 133 (Summer 1982) the title
changed to *Outposts Poetry Quarterly*
Profiled in: Görtschacher 1; Hoffman, Allen & Ulrich;
Stanton; Sullivan 1914–1984; Tolley 1940s; Wolfgang
Görtschacher and James Hogg (eds.), *Salute to Outposts on its
Fiftieth Anniversary*, Salzburg: University of Salzburg Press,
1994, BL: X.0909/611(110)
Interview: with Roland John in Görtschacher 1
Anthology: Howard Sergeant (ed.), *For Those Who Are Alive*
(London: Fortune Press, 1946), BL: 11605.a.21
Related Imprint: Outposts Publications; Outposts Modern
Poets Series; Hippopotamus Press
Reprint: Nos. 1–75 (1944–77), Nendeln, Liechtenstein:
Kraus Reprint, 1972

BL: 1–184. (W.P.747)
CUL: 1–184. (L727.D.66)
NLS: 1–5; 24–132. (5.3167)
TCD: 1944–1977. (PER 94–938 1944–1977)
Poetry Library: 14; 25–26; 28–54; 56–65; 73–184

Oxford and Cambridge Writing *See* Z: Oxford
and Cambridge Writing B152

100 **Parade.** Cairo: [Parade], 1940?–1948?

NLS: No. 18, vol.2 (Dec. 14, 1940)–Feb. 28, 1948. Includes
European Victory number for 1945. (8.40)

101 **Penguin New Writing** / edited by
John Lehmann. Harmondsworth and New
York: Allen Lane, Vol. 1 (Dec. 1940)–40 (1950)

Profiled in: Stanton; Sullivan 1914–1984; Tolley 1940s

Anthology: John Lehmann and Roy Fuller (eds.) *The Penguin*

New Writing 1940–1950 (Harmondsworth: Penguin, 1985),
BL: X.958/33163
Reprint: Nendeln, Liechtenstein: Kraus Reprint, 1976

BL: P.P.5938.bbp
CUL: L727.D.37
NLS: 5.1366–1367
TCD: No.16 (1943); 25 (1945)–40 (1950). (85.h.290–305)

102 **Personal Landscape** / edited by
Lawrence Durrell, Robin Fedden, and Bernard
Spencer. Cairo: Bernard Spencer, [Vol.1], no.1
(Jan. 1942)–vol.2 no.4 (1945)

Anthology: *Personal Landscape: an anthology of exile* (London:
Editions Poetry London, 1945), BL: 12299.e.2.
Profiled in: Tolley 1940s
Study: Roger Bowen, *Many Histories Deep: the Personal
Landscape poets, 1940–1945* (Madison, N.J.: Farleigh
Dickinson University Press, 1995), BL: Durrell 156; Robin
Fedden, *Personal Landscape* (London: Turret Books, 1966),
BL: Cup.510.dak.48.
Reprint: Nendeln, Liechtenstein: Kraus, 1969. BL: Durrell 90.

Poems include those by George Seferis, Keith Douglas, G.
S. Fraser, Ellie Papadimitriou, and the editors. Durrell sets
out a manifesto in the first issue, including "Neither poet
nor public is really interested in the poem itself but in
aspects of it."

BL: Durrell 89

103 **Phoenix: a literary journal** / edited
by Norman Swallow, then Nigel Storn. Lewes:
Furze Press, [No. 1] Spring 1946–[2] (Autumn
1946)

Profiled in: Hoffman, Allen & Ulrich

Contributors included Mervyn Peake and Edmund Blunden
as well as Arturo Barea and Ramon Gomez de la Serna.
Swallow edited the first issue, Storn the second.

BL: P.P.5938.ca
CUL: L999.C.3.59
NLS: 1949.19

104 **Phoenix Quarterly: a journal
directed towards the recovery of
unity in religion, politics and art** /
edited by Maurice Cranston. London: Jason
Press, Vol. 1 no. 1 (Autumn 1946)–no. 3
(1948)

Related Imprint: Jason Press

Essays on religion, e.g. by C. S. Lewis, a "Letter from Sweden" by Vera Brittain, and poems by Denton Welch and Alan Rook.

BL: Vol. 1 no. 1. (P.P.5939.cau)
CUL: Vol. 1 no. 1–no. 2. (L900.D.81)
NLS: 5.1364
UCL: Vol. 1 no. 2 (L Housman Coll), vol 1 no. 3 (Little Magazines Coll)

105 The Pleasure Ground: a miscellany of English writing / edited by Malcolm Elwin. London: Macdonald & Co, 1947

Subsections were: Stories and sketches, Travel, Reflection and reminiscence, Philosophy, Historical comment, The Theatre, Literary criticism, and Poems. Notable articles included J. C. Trewin's "The post-war theatre: a survey", John Atkins' "Above the neck: an approach to contemporary poetry", Patricia Johnson's "The younger women writers of to-day", Sylvia Townsend Warner's "A writer's dream". The poems include those by Morchard Bishop, Henry Treece, John Atkins, and Gilbert Phelps (the latter contributes a poem about a conversation he had with Roy Campbell and Edmund Blunden). Other contributors include Llewelyn Powys, T. F. Powys, Henry Williamson, and J. Middleton Murry.

BL: 12298.bbb.24
NLS: Vts.175.h.56

PL Pamphlets *See* Poetry London A173

106 Ploy / edited by R. Crombie Saunders. Glasgow: William MacLellan, [No. 1, 1946]–14 (June 1959)

Cartoons and gentle humour, including light verse by Douglas Young.

BL: P.P.6018.fep

107 Poems for Christmas and the New Year. Ilfracombe: Arthur Stockwell, 1946/47–[1960?]

Note: Variant titles: *Poems Christmas, Poems for Christmas*

Annual anthologies of perhaps rather old-fashioned poetry. Edited anonymously.

BL: 1946/47, 1948/49, 1950/51, 52/53, 53/54; 1957, 1958; 1960. (P.P.5126.bbn)

TCD: 1946–1947. (PAM POEMS 18.20); 1947–51.(PAM POEMS 24. 27, 39. 2, 3, 54. 27); 1954–1955. (PAM POEMS 119 no.28); 1960.(PAM Poems 152.5).

108 Poetry and Poverty / edited by Dannie Abse, Elwyn Jones, Molly Owen, and Godfrey Rubens. London: Vol. 1 no. 1 [1949]–no. 7 [1954]. ISSN: 0477–0897

Profiled in: Tolley 1940s
Anthology: Howard Sergeant and Dannie Abse (eds.), *Mavericks: an anthology* (London: Editions Poetry & Poverty, 1957), BL: 11604.ff.20
Reprint: Nendeln, Liechtenstein: Kraus Reprint, 1968, BL: P.901/925

Contributors include: Emanuel Litvinoff, John Heath-Stubbs, Michael Hamburger, Louis Adeane, Norman Kreitman, Herbert Read, Lawrence Durrell, Kathleen Raine, Lynette Roberts, Jacques Prévert, Georg Trakl, Charles Madge, Sydney Tremayne, Jon Silkin and Stephen Spender. The *Mavericks* anthology, which published several of the poets from the magazine, was designed to present "individual poets who are not connected with 'The Movement', but whose work should not be overlooked on that account."

BL: Lacking: 7. (P.P.5126.gcd)
CUL: L727.C.166
NLS: 6.697
UCL

Poetry Library: Reprint set; and an individual issue, no. 4

109 Poetry Commonwealth / edited by Lionel Monteith. London: Poetry Commonwealth, No. 1 (Summer 1948)–8 (Spring 1951)

Profiled in: Sullivan 1914–1984

BL: P.P.5126.gbw

110 Poetry Folios / edited by Alex Comfort and Peter Wells, except Summer 1951, edited by James Kirkup. Barnet, then Forest Hill, London: The Editors, [No. 1, 1942]–10 (1946). New series: Summer 1951 only.

Profiled in: Hoffman, Allen & Ulrich
Related Imprint: Poetry Folios published *The Song of Lazarus* by Alex Comfort in 1945. BL: 11657.d.23

Poetry Folios's purpose is "to present outstanding verse,

selected as far as possible without literary prejudice, to a small interested public." – Back cover, no. 2 (Winter 1942/43). "The editors of this Anthology have no enemies. We uphold the neutrality of poetry in precisely the same spirit as we uphold its liberty. German writers are welcomed by us on exactly the same terms as we welcome everyone else. The only poets whom we exclude are the acquiescent writers of all countries. Send us your work.' – Inside front cover of no. 8 (1945). Contributors included: Henry Treece, Nicholas Moore, Kathleen Raine, Feyyaz Fergar, John Hall, Fred Marnau, James Kirkup, Peter Wells, Ian Serraillier, Keidrych Rhys, George Woodcock, Roy McFadden, Charles Wrey Gardiner, Brenda Chamberlain, Anne Ridler, Joaquin Gomez Bas, Robert Greacen, John Bayliss, Maurice Lindsay, Adolpho Perez Zelaschi, W. S. Graham, Brian Allwood, Stephen Spender, Emanuel Litvinoff, Ruthven Todd, Paul Potts, E. E. Cummings, Kenneth Patchen, Sylvia Read, Louis Adeane, Judith Wright, Luis Merino Reyes, D. S. Savage, John Heath-Stubbs, Alex Comfort, John Atkins, Antonio de Undurraga, Gerardo Diego (trans. Harold Morland), Vincente Huidobro (trans. Morland), Luis Cernuda (trans. Morland), Manuel Machado (trans. Morland), Kenneth Rexroth, Pierre Seghers, Howard Sergeant, John Waller and others. The new series was intended to consist of short single collections with illustrations, but only the first, by Iris Orton, seems to have been published.

BL: [2] (Winter 1942/43)–10 (1946); Summer 1951. (X.989/38700)
CUL: [2]–10. (L727.D.69)
NLS: 5.1385
TCD: 5 (Winter 1942/43), Summer, Autumn 1943; nos. 7–10 (1945–46). (131.d.33, nos.14–20)
UCL: [1]–10
Poetry Library: 8

111 **Poetry Ireland** /edited by David Marcus. Cork: Trumpet Books, No. 1 (Apr. 1948)–19 (Oct. 1952)

Note: After no. 19, issued as an occasional supplement within *Irish Writing*. A journal with the title *Poetry Ireland* was also published from 1962–1968 and another from 1978–1980
Index: Hayes
Profiled in: Tom Clyde, *Irish Literary Magazines: an outline and descriptive bibliography* (Dublin: Irish Academic Press, 2003), BL: 2725.g.3414
Related Imprint: Trumpet Books published e.g. R. M. Fox's *Years of Freedom. The story of Ireland 1921–1948* (1948), BL: 9508.b.33.
Reprint: Nendeln, Liechtenstein: Kraus, 1970

Contributors include: Robert Greacen, Padraic Colum, C. Day Lewis, John Hewitt, Roy McFadden, Myles na gCopaleen, Samuel Beckett, Lord Longford, Peter Russell, Denis Devlin, Ewart Milne and Thomas Kinsella. An American issue (no. 7) featured E. E. Cummings, William Carlos Williams, Kenneth Patchen, and others; no. 12 was devoted entirely to translations of Columbanus.

BL: P.P.5126.ka
CUL: L727.C.118
NLS: P.53
TCD: 131.r.20 1948–1952
Poetry Library: Reprint set

112 **Poetry Nottingham.** Nottingham: Nottingham Poetry Society, [1946]– .
Numbers: [Vol. 1 no. 1] [1946?]–vol. 49 no. 1 (Spring 1995). Then, as *Poetry Nottingham International*, Vol. 49 no. 2 (Summer 1995)– .
ISSN: 0143–3199

Related Imprint: The Nottingham Poetry Society published collections in the series Poetry Nottingham Publications, e.g. Tony Lucas, *A Private Land* (1980), BL: X.950/1380

BL: Vol. 29 no. 4 (Dec 1975), vol. 30 no. 2 (June 1976), vol. 4 [i.e. 31] no. 2 (April 1977), vol. 33 no. 1 (Jan 1979)–vol. 49 no. 1. Then, as *Poetry Nottingham International*, Vol. 49 no. 2–. (P.901/3174)
CUL: Vol. 34 (1980)–vol. 49 no. 1 (1995). Then, as *Poetry Nottingham International*, Vol. 49 no. 2– .(L727.C.793)
NLS: Vol. 34 no. 1 (Winter 1980)– . Lacking Vol. 45 (1991). (HJ4.1551 PER)
TCD: Vol.34 no. 1 (Winter 1980)–. (PER 83–214)
Poetry Library: Vol. 32 no. 2; vol. 34 no. 3; vol. 36 no. 1, 4; vol. 37 no. 1–vol. 38 no. 2; vol. 38 no. 4; vol. 40 no. 2, 4–vol. 43 no. 3; vol. 44 no. 1–vol. 47 no. 3; vol. 48 no. 1–4; vol. 50 no. 3– .

113 **Poetry Scotland** / edited by Maurice Lindsay. Glasgow: William MacLellan, 1 [1943]–4 (1949)

Note: No. 4 was published in Edinburgh by Serif Books
Profiled in: Hoffman, Allen & Ulrich, Tolley 1940s
Related Imprint: MacLellan was one of the key post-war publishers in Scotland, publishing fiction, social analyis, art criticism and theory, and poetry. The Poetry Scotland Series, published by William MacLellan, featured collections by Hugh MacDiarmid, Sidney Goodsir Smith, George Bruce, Adam Drinan, Ruthven Todd, and W. S. Graham. BL: W.P.1989.

Poems, and some reviews. Published many of the poets of

the second wave of the modern Scottish Renaissance, including Norman MacCaig, W. S. Graham, Sorley Maclean, Derick Thomson, George Bruce, Robert Garioch, J. F. Hendry, Sydney Goodsir Smith, Tom Scott, Adam Drinan, Alexander Scott, Deorsa Caimbeul Hay (George Campbell Hay), and Hamish Henderson, as well as Edwin Muir, William Soutar and Hugh MacDiarmid. The final issue was guest edited by Hugh MacDiarmid.

BL: ZC.9.a.3700
CUL: L727.C.74
NLS: P.la.829
Poetry Library: 1–2, 4

114 Poets Now in the Services / edited by A. E. Lowy. London: Favil Press: No.1 [1942]–2 [1943]

Profiled in: Hoffman, Allen & Ulrich
BL: 11606.b.39
CUL: L727.D.55
NLS: 5.1207

115 Polemic / edited by Humphrey Slater. London: Rodney Phillips & Co, No. 1 [1945]–8 [1947]

Profiled in: Hoffman, Allen & Ulrich, Stanton

Later subtitled, "A magazine of philosophy, psychology, and aesthetics," it published next to no poetry – only two poems by Dylan Thomas, which appear in no. 7 – but a number of poets wrote essays for it, including Stefan Themerson ("Circles and Cats", with special regard to Ben Nicholson's paintings, in no. 4) Geoffrey Grigson ("On a present kind of poem", in no. 7), Stephen Spender ("Writers in the world of necessity" in no. 1; "Thoughts in an aeroplane over Europe", in no. 8). George Orwell and Bertrand Russell contribute several essays as well.

BL: P.971/28
CUL: L180.C.39
TCD: No. 2 (1946)–8 (1947).(PER 75–850)

116 The Portsmouth Quarterly / edited by Gordon Jeffery. Portsmouth: [Portsmouth Quarterly]. Vol. 1 no. 1 (Autumn 1946)–no. 3 (Summer 1947)

Related Imprint: The Pastoral Press (almost certainly the author himself) published Jack Shepherd's *Fugitive Pieces* in 1947. This was the only publication from the press.

A cultural review focused on the Portsmouth area. Very few poems, but the last issue published a poem by Jack Shepherd and one by Ailsa Aneurin. Jeffery's Book Pages were unusual in reviewing literary magazines.

BL: P.P.3610.gs

117 Prospect: the voice of the younger generation of poets / edited by Edward Toeman and others. Little Chalfont: The Claremont Press [printed by Lawrence Werner, Hinckley], Vol. 1 no. 1 [1945]–vol. 3 no. 1 (1950)

Note: Numbered both in terms of issues (nos. 1–13) and vols (Vol. 1 no. 1 etc). Editors and place of publication vary. Nos. 2–6 were published in Birmingham, nos. 7–12 in Worcester. From vol. 2 no. 9, it incorporated *Resistance* Profiled in: Hoffman, Allen & Ulrich, Stanton Anthology: Barry Keogan and James Welch (eds.), *The Heart of England. An anthology of Midlands verse* (London: Mitre Press, [1946], BL: 11605.b.39. An advert in *Prospect* states that many of the contributors in this anthology were from the magazine.

Although he was the first editor, several other co-editors joined Edward Toeman over the course of the magazine: Barry Keogan, James Welch, F. S. Round, Gladys Keighley, Harold F. Bradley, David West. Contributors included John Atkins, Cyril Hughes, Howard Sergeant, Raymond Tong, Wolf Mankowitz, Nicholas Moore, James Kirkup, John Gawsworth, Aneurin Rhys, Kathleen Raine, Norman Nicholson, Christopher Fry, John Bayliss, George Woodcock, Muriel Spark, and Donald Davie ("Towards a New Poetic Diction", vol. 2 no. 11).

BL: Lacking: Vol. 3 no. 1. (P.P.5126.br)
CUL: Vol. 1 no. 2– vol. 3 no. 1. (L727.C.145)
TCD: No.2 (1944) 12 (Christmas 1949); Vol.3 no.1(1950). (32.tt.66, nos.21–31)

118 Psyche. [Birmingham]: [Hollymoor Hospital], No. 1 (May 1943)–?

Poems and short articles by military patients at Hollymoor Hospital.

BL: 1. (YA.1992.b.2682)

119 Rann: a quarterly of Ulster poetry edited by Barbara Hunter and Roy McFadden. Lisburn: Lisnagarvey Press, No. 1 (Summer 1948)–20 (June 1953)

Note: From no. 13 published in Belfast by H. R. Carter Publications.

Index: Hayes

Profiled in: Tom Clyde, *Irish Literary Magazines: an outline and descriptive bibliography* (Dublin: Irish Academic Press, 2003), BL: 2725.g.3414; Gerry Smyth, *Decolonisation and Criticism: the construction of Irish literature* (London: Pluto Press, 1998), pp.119–120, BL: YC.2001.a.4091

Related Imprint: The Lisnagarvey Press published several books, including the collections: Jack McQuoid, *Followers of the Plough* (1949), BL: 11658.b.48; Roy McFadden, *Elegy for the Dead of the Princess Victoria* (1953), BL: 11658.f.61; and May Morton, *Masque in Maytime* (1948). H. R. Carter Publications was a less specialised and much more prolific publisher.

Poems by John Hewitt, Robert Greacen, Padraic Colum, as well as John Wain, Norman Nicholson, Maurice Lindsay, Dannie Abse, Henry Treece, Idris Bell, Vernon Watkins, and R. S. Thomas. No. 19 was a Welsh number. No. 12 features an essay by Daphne Fullwood and Oliver Edwards on "Ulster poetry since 1900"; an essay by John Hewitt on "The Course of Writing in Ulster"; and bibliographic and biographical information concerning Ulster writers, 1900–1953.

BL: P.P.5126.kaa
CUL: L727.C.129
NLS: 1954.24
TCD: 136.b.126

120 Resistance: a social-literary magazine / edited by Derek Stanford and David West. London: Derek Stanford and David West, No. 1 (Oct. 1946)

Interview: with Derek Stanford in Görtschacher I

Prose by C. S. Lewis, Derek Stanford and even Charles Baudelaire. Poems by Apollinaire (trans. Margaret Howorth), John Bayliss, Wrey Gardiner, Howard Sergeant, and Nicholas Moore.

BL: P.P.5938.car

121 Resurgam Younger Poets. London: Favil Press, No.1 [1940]–10 [1944]

Profiled in: Hoffman, Allen & Ulrich
Related Imprint: Favil Press, established in the 1920s, published many collections of poetry over the decades, but appears to have ceased in the 1980s. Resurgam seems to have been a Favil Press imprint, which also included Resurgam Library, BL: 012213.bb.4.

More a series of small poetry collections than a magazine, each publication was taken up by one poet only, including

John Atkins, Patricia Ledward, Alex Comfort, and Emanuel Litvinoff.

BL: 11613.d.3

122 Review 43 [Review 45, Review 46] / edited by Walter Berger and Pavel Tigrid, and then Walter Berger and E. Osers. London: Allen & Unwin, Vol. 1 no. 1 (Spring 1943)–vol. 3 no. 1 (Summer 1946)

Note: No *Review* 44 was produced
Profiled in: Hoffman, Allen & Ulrich

A literary review focusing on European literature, especially from Czechoslovakia. There are features on Norwegian, Slovakian, Polish, and Soviet contemporary poetry. Also includes Edwin Muir's essay "A Note on the English Romantic Movement" (vol 1. no. 2), and T. S. Eliot's "Cultural Diversity and European Unity" (vol. 2 no. 2). Pavel Tigrid's last issue as co-editor was vol. 2 no. 2; E. Osers, who had been an assistant editor previously, became a co-editor from vol. 3 no. 1.

BL: P.P.5939.bgp
CUL: Q900.C.206
NLS: P.210.

123 Salamander / edited by Keith Bullen. Cairo: [The Salamander Society], [Folio 1] (Sept. 1942)–Folio 5 [1945?]

Note: Publisher varies
Profiled in: Tolley 1940s
Anthology: *Oasis: the Middle East anthology of poetry from the Forces* (Cairo: Salamander, 1943), BL: Cup.410.d.86; Keith Bullen and John Cromer (eds.) *Salamander: a miscellany of poetry* (London: Allen & Unwin, 1947), BL: 11605.a.30.
Related Imprint: Salamander published several poetry collections, including John Waller's *Spring Legend* [1945?], BL: 11658.c.37, and Albert Samain, trans. Keith Bullen, *Un Pastelliste Exquis: selected poems and prose* [1945?], BL: YA.1995.a.23853

Poems and articles on poetry. Contributors included the editors, John Cromer, Raoul Parme (who contributed his own poems, and translated English language verse into French), G. S. Fraser, John Gawsworth, Hamish Henderson, Ahmed Rassim, and others.

BL: RF.1999.a.26

The Scots Review *See* The New Alliance A134

124 Scots Writing / edited by P. McCrory and Alec Donaldson. Glasgow: Scoop Books, No. 1 [1943]–4 [1947?]

Related Imprint: Scoop Books had a short-lived Modern Scots Poets series, which published collections by John Kincaid and Edward Boyd respectively.

Mostly short stories, though there were poems by: Naomi Mitchison, Joe Corrie, Maurice Lindsay, John Kincaid, Margaret Ross Mitchell and others.

BL: 1; 3–4. (W.P.11672)
CUL: Upper Library
TCD: 1–3 (1945). (31.ff.52, nos.5–7)

125 Scottish Art and Letters / edited by R. Crombie Saunders. Glasgow: William Maclellan, No. 1 (1944)–5 (1950)

Profiled in: Hoffman, Allen & Ulrich; Tolley 1940s

Related Imprint: MacLellan was one of the key post-war publishers in Scotland, publishing fiction, social analyis, art criticism and theory, and poetry. The Poetry Scotland Series, published by William MacLellan, featured collections by Hugh MacDiarmid, Sidney Goodsir Smith, George Bruce, Adam Drinan, Ruthven Todd, and W. S. Graham. BL: W.P.1989.

BL: P.P.6203.le
CUL: L727.B.19

126 The Seagull: stories, poems, general interest. West Worthing: Fantasma, Summer 1949.

"If you are on holiday at Worthing, or elsewhere, we wish you a pleasant holiday. If you are a writer, you may find our publications interesting; we particularly try to encourage and aid new writers." Short fiction, general articles, and a few poems.

BL: P.P.5939.bha

127 Sheaf / edited by B. Rajan and Wolf Mankowitz. Cambridge: Cambridge Undergraduate Council, [1, 1943?]–Michaelmas [1943?]

A general arts review with essays (A. I. Doyle on John Cornford and Rupert Brooke; B. Rajan poking fun at Bloomsbury; B. Rajan on T. S. Eliot's "escapism"; anonymous unflattering notes on William Saroyan, Isherwood and *Poetry London*) and poems (Lorca,

Mankowitz, Phyllis Thomas, Rajan, and Michael Barad).

BL: [1, 1943?]–Michaelmas [1943?]. (P.901/1417)
NLS: [1, 1943?]. 1951.13
UCL

128 Stand-by / [Manchester: Staff of the National Fire Service, dates unknown]

Noted by A. T. Tolley in an unpublished account of magazines in the 1940s.
No holdings known.

129 Stroud Anthology. London: Stroud Poetry Society, 1948–1949

Edited anonymously.

BL: P.P.5126.bbm

130 Tempest / edited by John Leatham and Neville Braybrooke. London: First series (1943).

Profiled in: Hoffman, Allen & Ulrich

Edited by the same team who edited the literary review *The Wind and the Rain*, *Tempest* was an attempt to encourage experimental short prose: "It exists for the writers and readers of some sadly neglected trends in present literature: the fantasy, the allegory, the letter and the creative essay." In the first and only issue the contributors were Denys Val Baker, Anna Kavan, Alan Storey, W. S. Graham, Leslie D. Knights, Peter S. Dickens, and Eric Nixon.

BL: 12650.aaa.120
CUL: L999.D.1.7

131 This Strange Adventure / edited by Fredoon Kabraji. London: New India Publishing Co. Ltd., Spring 1947

Related Imprint: New India Publishing Co. Ltd. published a small number of books of Indian fiction, non-fiction and poetry in the late 1940s, including a translation of Rabindranath Tagore's *Sesha Kavita*, translated as *Farewell, my Friend* (14127.g.79)

The first and perhaps only issue comprises *An anthology of poems in English by Indians, 1828–1946*, edited with an introduction and notes by Fredoon Kabraji.

BL: P.P.5126.gby

132 **Three** / edited by Joan Cooper and Cedric Dover. Chisledon: No. 3 Formation College, No. 1 (Mar. 1946)–4 (July 1946)

A general arts review with contributions by students and staff of the college, including poems (and translations of poems). The students appear to have been ex-service personnel.

BL: No. 1, 2. (Tambi.224). No. 2; 4. (P.P.6146.af)

133 **Transformation: prose, poetry, plays** / edited by Stefan Schimanski and Henry Treece. London: Victor Gollancz, [No. 1] (1943)–4 [1947]

Note: Published by Lindsay Drummond in 1947
Profiled in: Hoffman, Allen & Ulrich; Tolley 1940s
Related Imprint: Transformation Library

General cultural review that also published poems. Contributors included Herbert Read, Alexander Blok, Henry Treece, J. F. Hendry, G. S. Fraser, Anne Ridler, Boris Pasternak, Alan Ross, Michael Hamburger, Brenda Chamberlain and Kenneth Patchen; in no. 3, Stephen Spender and Robert Herring contribute surveys of Poetry 1919–1939 and 1939–1944 respectively; in no. 4 Oscar Williams edits an American poetry feature, with poems by Marianne Moore, E. E. Cummings, John Berryman, Wallace Stevens, and Delmore Schwartz.

BL: W.P.2869
CUL: L718.C.30
Poetry Library: [1]

134 **Translation (London)** / edited by Neville Braybrooke and Elizabeth King. London: Phoenix Press, First Series (1945)–Second Series (1947)

BL: X.989/38855
TCD: PAM POEMS 47.4
UCL

135 **Ulster Parade.** Belfast: Quota Press, No. 1 [1942]–12 [1946]

Index: Hayes
Profiled in: Tom Clyde, *Irish Literary Magazines: an outline and descriptive bibliography* (Dublin: Irish Academic Press, 2003), BL: 2725.g.3414
Related Imprint: Quota Press published many collections of poetry and playscripts in the 1920s, 30s and 40s, usually with an Ulster theme.

Mainly short stories, though some drama and poetry, and some articles on literary topics. The motto was "with humour to the fore"; some texts use Ulster dialects.

BL: X.989/26115
CUL: No. 2–12. (L900.D.53)
TCD: No. 2–12. (125.t.21–22)

136 **Ulster Voices** / edited by Roy McFadden and Robert Greacen. Belfast: [Ulster Voices], No. 1 (Spring 1943)–3 (Autumn 1943). As *Irish Voices*, No. 4 (Dec. 1943)

Profiled in: Hoffman, Ulrich and Allen; Tom Clyde, *Irish Literary Magazines: an outline and descriptive bibliography* (Dublin: Irish Academic Press, 2003), BL: 2725.g.3414.

CUL: L999.D.1.4
TCD: 138.b.60, nos.17–19
UCL: 1–2
Linen Hall Library

137 **The Verist.** Cardiff: The Verist, [No. 1 vol. 1, 1946?]–no. 1 vol. 2 (Spring 1947)

Poets included Katharine Ryan, Aneurin Rhys and Anne R. Weston. A note from the British Museum Copyright Receipt Office suggests that no.1 vol. 1 was not published. No editors are identified on the item, but an advert in *Prospect* (no. 7/8) suggests that the editor was Cyril Hughes. It also suggests that earlier roneoed issues of *The Verist's* predecessor were circulated only among "The Poet Pilgrim Society".

BL: No. 1 vol. 2 (Spring 1947). (P.P.5126.gbp)

138 **Verse** / edited by J. C. Murgatroyd. [Middlesex]: Author's Guild, Vol. 1 no. 1 (1945)

Bodleian: Per. 2805 e.1164 (vol. 1, no. 1)

139 **Verse** / edited by Dannie Abse. London: Deacon Press, No. 1 (Winter 1947)

The first and apparently only issue contained work by James Kirkup, Denise Levertov, John Singer, and John Heath-Stubbs (on Hart Crane).

BL: P.P.5126.bce
Poetry Library

140 Verse Lover / edited by Neville Armstrong. London: Spearman [for Verse-Lovers' Guild], No. 1 (Spring 1947)–3 (Autumn 1947)

Poems of the Verse-Lovers' Guild, formed in 1938 but not able to publish until after the War. The first issue has articles on Dylan Thomas and Hugh MacDiarmid respectively.

BL: P.P.5126.bbh

141 Vistas: a literary and philosophical review / edited by Donald Mullins. Taunton: Donald Mullins, Vol. 1 no. 1 (Summer 1946)–no. 2 [1949?]

No poems but the first issue has an essay by Laurence Housman on "The Necessity of Doubt", and Joseph Wicksteed on "William Blake's Eternal River".

BL: P.P.5939.bgs

142 The Voice of Youth: the Poetry Society's junior quarterly / edited by John Graddon, then Kennedy Williamson. London: The Poetry Society, Vol. 1 no. 1 (Spring 1951)–vol. 7 no. 11 (Autumn 1963)

Note: The subtitle changed to The Poetry Society's Quarterly for Associate Members with the vol. 3 no. 4 (Winter 1955)

Aimed to begin with at younger readers (Enid Blyton contributed an article and poem in the first issue), but then widened to include Associate Members of the Society. Graddon edited until vol. 7 no. 2, after which Williamson was sole editor.

BL: P.P.5126.bbu
CUL: L727.C.132
NLS: NF.1548
TCD: PER 94–739

143 Voices / edited by Denys Val Baker. London: Opus Press, First series (1943)–Fourth series (1945); New series no. 1 (Autumn 1946)–no. 2 (Winter 1946–47)

Profiled in: Hoffman, Allen & Ulrich

A slim but general literary review. Baker had previously edited the magazine Opus.

BL: P.P.5938.cab
NLS: No. 3 (1944)–no. 2 (1947) only. (1978.30)

Wales: Wartime Broadsheet see Wales A227

144 The West Country Magazine / edited by Malcolm Elwin, then J. C. Trewin. Denham, Buckinghamshire, then London: Westaway Press, No. 1 (Summer 1946)–vol. 7. no. 3 (Autumn 1952)

Note: Possibly revived as The New West Country Magazine C66

Short stories, articles and poems. The emphasis is, as the title suggests, on celebrating and increasing knowledge about the West Country. Poets include John Betjeman, Patric Dickinson, Dorothy Wordsworth (a previously unpublished poem), A. L. Rowse, Anne Treneer, Jack R. Clemo, and others. Other contributors (of prose) include: Ronald Duncan, Henry Williamson, Sean O'Casey, Llewelyn Powys, T. F. Powys, Geoffrey Grigson, and Arthur Caddick, among many.

BL: P.P.6049.ik
CUL: L478.C.17
TCD: 104.p.106–108

145 The White Horseman: prose and verse of the New Apocalypse / edited by J. F. Hendry and Henry Treece. London: Routledge, 1941

Profiled in: Tolley 1940s

The second New Apocalypse anthology. An introduction by G. S. Fraser suggests the New Apocalypse is the next dialectical stage from Surrealism and highlights the work of J. D. Hendry, Henry Treece and Nicholas Moore. As well as the work of these four, the anthology includes verse by Norman MacCaig, Tom Scott and Vernon Watkins, an essay by Robert Melville on "Apocalypse in Painting", an essay by Hendry on "Myth and Social Integration" and some fiction by several of the poets. The other anthologies were The New Apocalypse and The Crown and the Sickle.

BL: 12299.b.18
NLS: X.184.l

146 The Wind and the Rain / edited by Michael Allmand, Neville Braybrooke and others. London: Phoenix Press, Vol. 1 no. 1 (Jan. 1941)–vol .7 no. 2/3 [April/July 1951]. Then, New Series: Easter 1962

Index: Sader
Profiled in: Hoffman, Allen & Ulrich, Stanton, Tolley 1940s
Related Imprint: Phoenix Press

Founded by Michael Allmand. An account of this general literary review is given by Braybrooke in the Easter 1962 issue.

BL: Lacking: vol. 1.no. 1; vol. 2 no. 1. Main sequence: P.P.5938.bbt. New Series: P.P.5126.nv.
CUL: Lgoo.C.223
TCD: Vol. 2 no. 3 (1944)–Vol. 7 no. 2/3. (110.s.20a–23)

147 The Windmill: being a selection of essays, papers, stories and verses... / edited by Reginald Moore and Edward Lane. London: Heinemann, 1944–48

Profiled in: Hoffman, Allen & Ulrich; Sullivan 1914–1984
Reprint: Millwood, New York: Kraus Reprint, 1967

Perhaps more significant for its fiction, this commercial magazine did however publish poetry including Wrey Gardiner, Kenneth Patchen, Stevie Smith, Kathleen Raine, and F. T. Prince. Moore and Lane co-edited from 1944–46, but from 1947–48 Lane edited alone.

BL: 12360.g.2
CUL: Lgoo.C.238
TCD: (132.t.38–40)

148 Writers of the Midlands / edited by Stanley Derricourt. Birmingham: [Stanley Derricourt; then Thomas's Publications], No. 1 [1946]–2 [1948?]

A modest attempt to build a cultural critical mass in the Midlands, publishing short fiction, articles on Midlands arts (e.g. on theatre and broadcasting), and a poem per issue (James Kirkup and W. H. Boore respectively). Although a commercial publisher was used for the second issue, with letters of support from Derek Stanford and J. B. Pick (the latter welcoming the magazine, but questioning the idea of "Midland writing"), the magazine appears to have ceased after that.

BL: 011840.m.75

149 Writers of Tomorrow: new sketches by soldiers and workers of to-day / edited by Peter Ratazzi. London: Resurgam Books, No. 1 (1945)–5 (Summer 1948)

Note: From no. 3 onward published by Clark's Publications (Bristol).
Related Imprint: Resurgam Books (apparently an imprint of Favil Press) published a small number of poetry

collections as well as the anonymously edited *Today's New Poets: an anthology of contemporary verse* [1944] BL: 11606.b.38.

Largely short fiction but with poems by for example Raymond Tong, John Bate, Derek Stanford, Sydney Tremayne, John Atkins, John Bayliss, Margaret Stewart, Lucy Worth, Howard Sergeant. J. F. Hendry contributes a prose "Letter to Sarah Bernhardt"; Aneurin Rhys contributes an essay, "What Shall We Write". See also *Resurgam Younger Poets*.

BL: W.P.1359
CUL: 2–4. (L727.D.78)
TCD: 2–3. (PAM K.7 no.8–9)

150 Writing Today / edited by Denys Val Baker and Peter Ratazzi. London: Staples & Staples, No. 1 (Oct. 1943)–4 (Winter 1946)

Short stories and poems, including W. S. Graham, Robert Greacen, Nicholas Moore, Sylvia Read, Hugh MacDiarmid, John Heath-Stubbs. From no. 2 onward, Baker edited the magazine on his own.

BL: 12299.e.20
CUL: (L996.D.6)

151 X6 / edited by Derek Stanford and John Bate. [Croydon]: [Derek Stanford for the Army Bomb Disposal Squad], [No. 1 (1940?)]–6 (Nov. 1941)

Note: Continued by: *Oasis*

Typewritten miscellany of short fiction, poems, articles and reviews. Poets include Bate, Nicholas Moore, and Jack [i.e. John] Bayliss.

BL: No. 2 (Jan 1941), no. 3 (Mar 1941), no. 6 (Nov 1941). (YA.1989.b.1)

152 Z: Oxford & Cambridge writing / edited by Donald Bain, Antony Brown, Mark Roberts, John Croft, Patrick Gardiner, and Francis King. Cambridge: Anthony Brown & Donald Bain, [No. 1] (1942)

Profiled in: Tolley 1940s

Short fiction and poetry. Contributors include Michael Hamburger, John Heath-Stubbs, and Sidney Keyes. Sometimes referred to simply as *Oxford & Cambridge Writing*.

BL: 12362.aa.18
UCL

Chapter C: 1950–1959

Movements

THE 1950S CAN BE characterised as the decade in which the poets of the Movement found recognition. Robert Conquest's first anthology of these poets *New Lines* (1956) identified them: Elizabeth Jennings, John Holloway, Philip Larkin, Thom Gunn, Kingsley Amis, D. J. Enright, Donald Davie, John Wain, and Conquest himself.

Hindsight emphasises the individuality of Jennings and Larkin even if they are likely to be always identified as writing from within the Movement's values: that is, an apparently undeceived temperament, a quiet tone, a technical achievement within regularly rhymed and metred forms and a mapping of all these qualities onto an idea of essential Englishness. Thom Gunn's later poetry suggests a distance from his Movement roots almost as large as the Atlantic that soon separated him from England. Enright's poetry would come to have a subject matter derived from his experience of the Far East, where he taught for many years. Wain and Amis were already better known as novelists and would continue to be. Similarly, it was not as a poet but as the author of the literary study *Purity of Diction in English Verse* (1952) that Davie was better-known at this point in his career; arguably literary criticism remained his greatest strength. Conquest is remembered for little more than his editing of *New Lines* and John Holloway is hardly remembered at all.

In this way, if the Movement was a poetry grouping it was already one in which most of its members were not primarily poets at the time and would not be remembered especially as poets in the future. Of those who are remembered first and foremost for their poetry several are not now seen as typical Movement poets at all. To borrow a Movement emphasis on rationality, on this basis it does not seem reasonable to characterise the Fifties by the Movement not least because the Movement itself dissolves quickly on examination. The evidence of the literary magazines shows that much more was happening in this decade, too.

Take for example John Sankey's magazine *The Window* which

began in 1950, running for nine issues over the next six years. Here early work by very individual authors Roy Fisher, Gael Turnbull, Patricia Beer, and Harold Pinter (publishing as Harold Pinta) is published within the pages of a magazine also open to the American Black Mountain poets Charles Olson and Robert Creeley and to the translation of French modernists René Char, Pierre Reverdy, Robert Desnos, and Francis Ponge. This is in continuity with the internationalist magazines of the 1940s such as *Focus* edited by Balachandra Rajan and Andrew Pearse (1945–1950) and *The Changing World* (1947–1949) edited by Bernard Wall and Manya Harari. In these magazines an evenhanded interest in European and American literature is balanced with a confidence in the variety of different kinds of British poetry that will stand comparison with the best of other cultures' writing. There is no sense that there is a Movement line to be observed in the name of what is quintessentially English (or, elidingly, "British") but neither is there a surrender to the overwhelming magnificence of all things foreign.

There is, however, a shift overall in the way that the little magazines were responding to overseas literature that makes *The Window* an exception rather than the rule. Firstly, the deliberately Europhile magazines of the Forties, partly a result of the then displaced foreign nationals in England, have closed. They are not being replaced by similarly country-focused new titles. Secondly, while Britain's decades-long openness to American literature and its avant-gardes continues with the Black Mountain poets and the Beats finding publication here, *The Window* and the Francophile *Chanticleer* and *Merlin* notwithstanding, there appears to be less interest in Western European literature. Britain's position as a bridge or lookout between America and Western Europe is no longer maintained so evenly.

However, while our survey appears to show a decline in the focus on Western Europe, with the publication of Albanian, Czech, Polish, Russian and other Eastern European poems a small but perceptible refocussing takes place towards the Eastern Bloc. It is as if the spirit of Janko Lavrin and Edwin Muir's pre-war *European Quarterly* was gently being revived. This usually amounted to only a light peppering of translations in any given magazine but at least one title, *Dialogue* (1959–1960), edited by Alasdair Clayre and Peter Jay, had more than a passing interest in the countries behind the Iron Curtain. It published translations of Russian prose, an article on Eastern European poetry by Julian Mitchell, and some other work related to the Eastern Block.

One magazine, *Samovar* (1954)–[1959], the largely Cyrillic

magazine of the Joint Services School for Linguists at Bodmin, demonstrates one of several ideological undercurrents. The School may have produced writers Alan Bennett, Michael Frayn, and others with a less than straightforward political perspective but it was founded in direct response to a perceived Soviet threat. By the same token *Encounter* (1953–1990), secretly underpinned by CIA funds, disseminated British and American literature in an effort at soft propaganda (apparently unbeknownst to one of its editors, Stephen Spender, and certainly to most of its contributors). Similarly, the private funds of the American Ford Foundation made sure that James Laughlin's *Perspectives* (1952–56) exported American poetry to Britain via its assisted London edition, published by Hamish Hamilton.

No such sponsorship appears to have underwritten a never-theless American-friendly magazine, *The Poet* [1952]–(1956), edited by W. Turner Price. Price's example of publishing new British writers such as Anne Ridler, Iain Crichton Smith, Edwin Morgan, Gael Turnbull, Burns Singer, and Roy Fisher alongside new American ones such as Robert Creeley, Cid Corman, and Kenneth Patchen would be followed by Gael Turnbull's briefer but better-known *Migrant* (1959–60). *Migrant* published many of *The Poet*'s authors as well as Ian Hamilton Finlay, Charles Tomlinson, Ed Dorn, and Robert Duncan. Perhaps more significantly the Migrant imprint would go on to publish early books by Creeley, Finlay, Fisher and others. Production values may have been plain for these two magazines, but it is difficult to characterise a decade as dull in which these writers, all very broadly speaking within the spectrum of late modernism, were being read for the first time.

The Fifties do, however, mark a striking downturn in the number of new titles being published: 125 new titles in our survey compared to 152 in the previous decade, an 18% falling off. This statistic is deceptive, however, and its interpretation as a measure of the austerity of the decade, against which the undeniable pro-duction and aesthetic fecundity of the 1960s is then seen as a revolutionary release, is simplistic. The demise of many magazines in the late 1940s and the failure of many new ones to be founded at all is usually seen as a byproduct of the 'peace dividend'.

Certainly the war encouraged a natural thirst for literature – as solace, as a personal commitment to and interest in the cultural values Britain was fighting to defend, and as a way of distracting particular thoughts – and this appears to have declined sharply as a less intense period began on the close of hostilities. Moments of forced solitariness as combatant or civilian in wartime and the relative lack of other mass entertainment media in wartime suggest material reasons behind the popular appeal of reading, too, and the improvements in these circumstances help to explain the consequent decline in peacetime. Those living in a country still using ration books long after the war, it can be argued, simply didn't have the cash to spend on literary magazines; would-be editors themselves may have been too involved in the ordinary work of reconstruction to dwell on the world of literature. These arguments may ring true but the apparent decline in magazines is not what it seems even if it has proven a useful concept against which to base a "revival" in the proceeding decades. In the Fifties the world of the little magazine was much more complicated than that.

One striking trend is just how many magazines begun in the 1950s lasted for years and years. *Gairm, Lines, Stand, Delta, Encounter, The London Magazine, Poetry & Audience, Envoi, Gambit, Threshold, The Anglo-Welsh Review, Agenda* and *Ambit* would each go on for another three decades and half continue to this day. Many of the longest surviving magazines are anchor titles, strongly associated with a linguistic, regional or national locus (*Gairm* for Gaelic readers, *Lines* for Scotland, *Threshold* for Northern Ireland, *London Magazine, The Anglo-Welsh Review*, etc.) or a university constituency (*Poetry & Audience* for Leeds; *Delta* for Cambridge; *Gambit* for Edinburgh). They are eclectic within admittedly an often mainstream spectrum and were certainly publishing work from well beyond their declared boundaries.

As with the few but broad-ranging magazines in Ireland in the 1940s what might have been happening here is that these titles were for a time "category-killers". They were likely sufficiently meeting or exceeding a need within a fragile economy and their presence may have initially discouraged others from starting another magazine. Longevity particularly characterises this period: many of the magazines that didn't last for thirty years still lasted for ten, fifteen, or twenty years instead. Rather than seeing this as a low-key decade it might be more accurate to see it as one of cultural reconstruction with foundations that were usually pretty solid, even to the point of becoming Establishment or simply over-familiar titles of later years. In later years there would be relatively lower start-up costs as print technology changed and markets in fact "grown" by the anchor titles could be exploited by new, less labour-intensive magazines. Importantly, the idea of what the literary journal's expectations should be would later be recon-figured, with an increasing specialisation of aesthetics and a sense of the little magazine more as a circular among like-minded practitioners than as a review for non-practicing readers. In the 1950s, however, the concept of the common reader was not entirely forgotten.

Nor was it just the stolid magazines that proved to have staying power. The New Apocalyptics were generally scattered now, their individual poets stronger than the sum of the group, Norman MacCaig and W. S. Graham in particular publishing significant early collections, but a series of new English avant-gardes was emerging. Some experimental groups would be supported by what came to be long-standing magazines and their associated publications. Born in the 1950s *And* and *Ore*, for example, would each last for at least decades (a further Boolean operator, *Not*, sadly failed to materialise). *And* was edited by Bob Cobbing and others within the London-based organisation Writers Forum who placed an emphasis on sound and visual poetry. *Ore*, edited by Eric Ratcliffe, was variously interested in magic, ancient Britain and a kind of neo-paganism. These long-stayers, albeit with very sporadic publication patterns, each gradually fostered a distinctive strand in English poetry. Another English avant-garde was beginning to emerge, too. *Prospect* (1959)–[1964], founded by Elaine Feinstein in Cambridge and later edited by J. H. Prynne, would publish Prynne's essay "Resistance and Difficulty" as if to announce the beginning of the Cambridge School.

In fact, following a long relatively dormant period, the university towns began to publish more titles and more interesting work in the Fifties. Our survey shows many of these towns buck the overall trend by publishing more titles this decade than they did in the last: these include Belfast, Keele, Hull, Newcastle upon Tyne, Manchester, Liverpool, and Oxford, all with slight increases and several, such as Keele and Hull, with their first appearance in the survey to date. Cambridge had ten new titles compared to six the previous decade; Edinburgh had seven new titles compared to only two before.

These two cities, especially, were qualitatively interesting, too. In Cambridge *Prospect* began publishing at the end of the decade, but David Ross's *Saint Botolph's Review* (1956) had already published Ted Hughes and, at the launch party, introduced Hughes to Sylvia Plath. Earlier, Rodney Banister and Peter Redgrove's *Delta* (1953–1981) had started and was publishing the intense work of Hughes and Plath. As editorships changed *Delta* would soon be associated with the gifted workshop leader, critic and poet Philip Hobsbaum.

While Glasgow's publishing breakthrough in the 1940s, essentially the work of William McLellan, proved shortlived (three new titles compared to nine, albeit *The Poet* and *Gairm* among them), its sister city fared much better. In Edinburgh *The Saltire Review* (1954–1961) published a cross-section of contemporary Scottish writers while a less traditionally Scottish focus occurred in *Extra Verse* (1959)–[1966], *Lines* [1952]–(1998) and *Gambit* (1957–1965; as *New Gambit*, 1966–[1986]). These magazines published distinctive and quietly experimental writers who did not feel bound to Scottish subjects, including D. M. Black, Alan Riddell, Edwin Morgan, and Ian Hamilton Finlay. One or two were particularly open to American avant-garde work. As *Prospect* in Cambridge published Ed Dorn, Paul Blackburn, Charles Olson, and Lawrence Ferlinghetti, *Jabberwock*, an Edinburgh university magazine begun in the 1940s, dramatically Americanised its contents with an unnumbered issue of 1959 that featured the work of William Burroughs, Allen Ginsberg, Jack Kerouac, Gregory Corso, Gary Snyder, Robert Creeley, and other American writers.

London, already declining (by the measure of new titles) as a literary centre in the 1940s, fell further: only 24% of the titles in our survey were published from London, compared to 41% previously. It may be that this decline is why the 1950s is remembered in such bleak terms. If so, it rather flatters London as the arbiter of cultural production: what was happening across the country was in fact the growth of university towns as engines of poetry and (as the interest in Western European literature appears to have fallen) as places of American influence. In this light, the Fifties appear more of a prelude to the Sixties than a decade against which to react. The Fifties were, after all, the decade when a zine-ish sense of humour started to affect the titles of magazines, sometimes that being the best thing about the journal: credit where credit is due for the unidentified editors of *Suppose Pig Walk* [1950] and *Dejected Nurses* (1959).

1 4: a review of the visual arts, literature, music and drama / edited by Garry Denbury. Glastonbury: [Garry Denbury], Vol. 1 no. 1 (Oct. 1952)

The first and probably only issue contained one poem only, by Edgar Martin.

BL: P.P.5938.bds
NLS: 6.598

2 Agenda / edited by William Cookson, then co-edited with Peter Dale, then edited by Patricia McCarthy. London: [printed by Poets and Painters Press], Vol. 1 no. 1 (Jan 1959)- . ISSN: 0002-0796

Index: Sader (Vol. 1 (1959)–8 (1970) only; Little Magazine Project, Vol. 1 (1959)–4 (1966) only
Profiled in: Görtschacher 1, Sullivan 1914–1984
Interview: With Peter Dale, in Görtschacher 1; with Patricia McCarthy, in *Poetry News: the Newsletter of the Poetry Society*, Winter 2003/4, p.8
Anthology: William Cookson (ed.), *Agenda: an anthology: the first four decades (1959–1993)* (Manchester: Carcanet, 1994), BL: YC.1994.a.2124. Includes an introduction by Cookson
Related Imprint: Agenda Editions
Reprint: Nendeln, Liechtenstein: Kraus Reprint, [undated]. (Vols. 1–5 only)
Microform: University Microfilms International, [undated]

An advocate of Ezra Pound's poetry and ideas, but also of a wide range of poetry informed by an understanding of poetry's formal qualities, by the history of poetry and by modernism. Special issues have focused on Thomas Hardy, Pound, David Jones, H.D., Wyndham Lewis, Hugh MacDiarmid, Basil Bunting, Louis Zukofsky, Giuseppe Ungaretti, Ronald Duncan, Stanley Burnshaw, Robert Lowell, Geoffrey Hill, Peter Levi, and others.

BL: P.P.5109.aac
CUL: P727.C.36
NLS: Lacking: Vol. 17 no. 3–4 (1979); vol. 28 no. 4 (1990);

vol. 31 no.1 (1993); and vol.36 no.1 (1998). (HJ4.1268 SER)

3 Ambit: a quarterly of poems, short stories, drawings and criticism / edited by Martin Bax. London: No. 1 (Summer 1959)–. ISSN: 0002-6772

Indexes: *Ambit* 101 (1985) was the index to 1–100; 100–150 were published by Ambit in 1999
Profiled in: In Martin Bax's introduction to *Ambit* 101
Interview: With Martin Bax, *3 a.m. magazine*, June 2002, www.3ammagazine.com/litarchives/2002_jun/interview_martin_bax.html; with Martin Bax, *Poetry News: the Newsletter of the Poetry Society*, Spring 2003, p.8
Related Imprint: Ambit have occasionally published books, e.g. Anselm Hollo's collection *Faces & Forms* (1965), BL: X.909/6673, and E. A. Markham's short story collection *Something unusual* (1986) BL: YH.1987.a.230
Website: www.ambitmagazine.co.uk

Modelled to some degree on John Middleton Murry's pre-First World War magazine *Rhythm* (BL: P.P.5938.de), the look and format of this magazine was established from the first issue, in part because it used the typesetting machine the Variotyper which allowed the integration of visual work. Reproductions of sketches and other black and white drawings intersperse poetry, short stories and comment from the word go, and there is an independent tone to the editorial and content, characterised in the first issue by an attack on John Betjeman's poetry. In later years colour plates were also used and the magazine acknowledged "the [editorial] assistance" of J. G. Ballard and Carol Ann Duffy among others, both of whom had contributed work to the magazine early on. There is a sensuous hedonism to the production and editorial values, and it has been controversial. It famously ran a competition for work produced under the influence of drugs (illegal or otherwise), and contributions by Ballard, David Hockney and others have sometimes lent to calls for its funding to be withdrawn. Its 2003 submission guidelines list the following types of work that should *not* be sent for consideration: "indiscriminately centre-justified or italicised poems; parochial "bed-sitter", life is grim, I've got no

money poems; self-consciously poetic poems; poems
aspiring to Keats or Wordsworth; that man (or woman)
done me over poems; sweeping generalisation poems; why
are we here, what is it all about poems; [and] horror / ghost
/ fantasy stories."

BL: P.P.7612.aaz
CUL: 8 (1961)– . (L727.C.259)
NLS: 1–6, 8–81 (Y.4); 82–97, 99–114 (HJ4.463 PER);
115–163, 165– . (HJ8.114 SER)
TCD: 8–118, 136– . (PER 82–25)
UCL
Nottingham Trent University
Poetry Library: 8, 11, 37, 39– .

4 And / edited by Bob Cobbing, Mary Levien, John Rowan, and Adrian Clarke. [London]: Arts Together, then Writers Forum, No. 1 (July 1954)–

Note: The alternative title and sub-title *Hendon Arts Review*
was used only for the first issue. No. 6 is also described as
WF [i.e. Writers Forum] 100
Interview: With Bob Cobbing, Görtschacher 2
Website: pages.britishlibrary.net/writersforum

A very occasional magazine, e.g. the second issue did not
appear until February 1961. The first issue was edited by
Bob Cobbing and Mary Levien, the second by Cobbing and
John Rowan. Further details, including contributors, are
given at the Writers Forum website.

BL: 2–5; 7–11. (ZA.9.b.2079)
UCL
Poetry Library: 2; 4–6

5 The Anglo-Welsh Review / edited by Raymond Garlick, then Roland Mathias, then Gillian Clarke, and others. Pembroke Dock: The Dock Leaves Press, vol. 9 no. 23 (1958)–no.88 (1988). ISSN 0003–3405

Note: Imprint varies. Continues: *Dock Leaves*
Profiled in: Sullivan 1914–1984; Sam Adams, *Roland Mathias*
(Cardiff: University of Wales Press, 1995), BL:
YK.1996.a.2281
Anthology: Vera Rich (ed.) *Healing of the Nations*, Dock
Leaves Press, 1965. An Anglo-Welsh Review Supplement.

A key magazine of the Welsh literary scene for three
decades, the magazine published essays, reviews, and
poems. The editors of the last issue, Greg Hill and Huw
Jones, suggested that "Anglo-Welsh" may no longer be an
appropriate term for work produced by Welsh authors
writing in English.

BL: P.P.5938.bdh
CUL: L727.C.142
NLS: 24–88. (NF.1549 (No.23–no.56) and PER HJ2.47
(No.57–88))
Poetry Library: 44–47, 64–65, 70–80, 85–87

6 Anthology of the Gwent Poetry Society. Newport: Gwent Poetry Society, 1 (1956/7)– .

BL: 1 (YA.1995.a.16057); 41 (1996/97)– . (ZK.9.a.5902)
CUL: 28(1983/84)– . (L727.c.871)
NLS: 28 (1983/84)– . (HP.sm.437)

7 Arbiter / edited by George Bull, Peter Mansell-Moullin, Sebastian Kerr and Jeremy Mitchell. Oxford: The Editors, at Brasnose College, No. 1 (Winter 1952)–2 (Spring 1953)

Mostly poetry, but some short fiction and articles.
Contributors included Donald Hall, Roy Campbell
(translating Lorca), Elizabeth Jennings, George MacBeth,
Lucien Stryk, Neville Braybrooke and others. After the four
co-editors of issue one, Jeremy Mitchell edited the second
issue alone.

BL: P.901/1579

8 Artisan. Liverpool: Heron Press, [1, 1953?–5, 1954?]

Related Imprint: Heron Press also published the
anonymously edited pamphlet, *Nine American Poets* [1953],
BL: YA.1992.a.1182, and *timeo hominem unius mulieris* by
Vincent Ferrini was advertised in *Trace* in 1954, but no copy
is as yet known.
No. 4 was Hugh Creighton Hill's *Some Propositions from the
Universal Theorem*; no. 5 was the single collection *Travellers
Alone* by Alan Brownjohn. Listed in *Trace*, which describes it
as having an interest in metrical invention.
BL: 4. (YA.2003.a.11049). 5. (YA.1988.a.4116)
CUL: 4–5. (Upper Library)
UCL

9 The Arts and Philosophy / edited by Sidney Arnold. London: Candlelight Press, No. 1 (Summer 1950)–3 (Spring 1962)

As its title suggests, a general arts and philosophy review.
Includes some discussion of poetry, and two poems (in
French) by Marian Arnold.
BL: P.P.5938.bdl
CUL: L500.C.139

10 The Aylesford Review / edited by Father Brocard Sewell. Aylesford: The English Carmelites, Vol. 1 no. 1 (Autumn 1955)–vol. 9 no. 1 (Autumn 1967). New Series: Vol. 1, no. 1 (Summer 1968)

Index: Colin Stanley (compiler), *The Aylesford Review 1955–1968: an index*, with a preface by its editor, Brocard Sewell (Nottingham: Paupers' Press, 1984), BL: Cup.510.dop.1
Related Imprint: Aylesford Review Poets

A Carmelite general literary review with material that went far beyond conventional religious interest. Poems included those by Angela Carter, Gregory Corso, Ruth Fainlight, Anselm Hollo, dsh [Dom Sylvester Houédard], Stevie Smith, Thomas Merton, Ian Hamilton Finlay, Harry Fainlight, Michael Horovitz, Frances Horovitz, Elizabeth Jennings, Peter Levi, John J. Sharkey, Penelope Shuttle, D. M. Thomas, Jack Clemo, and Stefan Themerson. Fred Uhlman's prose fables were also regularly included. Houédard contributes a note on 'Carmel: Renewal and Reform' but also "Beat and Afterbeat: a parallel condition of poetry and theology?" and "to freshen our sense of the language we do have". George Bowering contributes "Universal and Particular: An Enquiry into a Personal Esthetic", and there were also essays on Frederick William Rolfe (Baron Corvo), John Gray, John Cowper Powys, M. P. Shiel, Henry Williamson, William Morris and others.

BL: P.P.210.lae
CUL: L100.C.42
NLS: Vol. 1, no. 2, 3, 5–7 ; vol. 2, no. 5 ; vol. 3, no. 2 ; vol. 9, no. 1. (HP1.78.4410 (Vol. 1–2 and P.80 (Vol.3–9))
UCL: Vol. 1–9 (incomplete). New Series: Vol. 1 no. 1.

11 The Bullring. West Worthing, then Liverpool, 1953–195?

Listed in *Trace* as "largely devoted to comments on the literary scene." No holdings known.

Camobap *See* Samovar C103

12 Chance: new writing and art / literary editors: Peter Marchant, Robin Scott-Smith, Colin Haycraft; art editor: Jack Stafford. London: Jack Stafford, 1st Chance (Oct. 1952)–4th Chance (Autumn 1953)

The literary editors seem to have edited on a rotating basis. *Chance* published short stories, artwork, book reviews and poetry (the latter usually contained in sections printed on

blue-grey coloured paper). Poets included Claire Delavenay, Alistair Reid, Thom Gunn, Hilary Corke, Anthony Thwaite, and Donald Hall, with essays by Cecil Day Lewis ("On Translating Poetry") and Ronald Duncan on Alun Lewis.

BL: P.P.5938.bdq
CUL: L999.C.3.78
NLS: NJ.300 PER

13 Chanticleer / edited by Patrick Galvin and Gordon Wharton. London: Chanticleer, Vol. 1 no. 1 (Autumn 1952)–no. 4 (Spring 1954)

After the first issue, Galvin edited alone. Though some fiction and reviews were published, this was mainly a poetry magazine with a particular interest in French poetry in translation. Contributors include: Sydney Goodsir Smith, James Kirkup, Cecil Day Lewis, Peter Russell, Robert Desnos, Jon Silkin, Robert Greacen, Gael Turnbull, G. S. Fraser, Jacques Prévert, Raymond Queneau, John Gawsworth, W. Price Turner, Muriel Spark, and Oswell Blakeston.

BL: P.P.5938.bdr
CUL: L727.C.178
NLS: 6.461 PER

14 Chequer / edited by Harry Guest, Ronald Hayman, Malcolm Ballin and Paul McQuail. Cambridge: Trinity Hall, No. 1 (1953)–11 (Winter 1956/56)

Contributors included Anne Stevenson, Ted Hughes, Sylvia Plath and Christopher Levenson.

BL: 2 (May 1953) and 11 only. (P.P.5939.bhi)
CUL: (1953)–7 (1954). (CAM.C.31.82)

15 The Christian Poet / edited by Frederic Vanson. Spondon, Derby: [Frederic Vanson], No. 1 [1953]

Related Imprint: Gemini Press, presumably belonging to Vanson himself, published his *The Furious Finding*. *Fifteen sonnets* (1950, BL: 11658.b.39) and his *Four Holy Sonnets* (1955, BL: 11660.e.13)

The first and probably only issue consisted of three foolscap, typewritten, duplicated leaves of very poor production quality. It consisted solely of poems by Marjorie Bunt, Gilbert Matthers, Maureen Duffy, Olive Culshaw, Douglas Lord, and others. Matthers had published a collection of poems, *My Thoughts*, in 1919; BL: 011649.de.127. Maureen Duffy would later be known as a novelist and editor as well as a poet. Olive Culshaw published two collections from Outposts: *Silver Wyre* in 1959, BL: 11662.ee.12; and *We Are Not Extinguished* in 1976, BL: X.909/41013. Vanson, who had edited *Gemini* a few years earlier, went on to have his own collections of poetry published by several different publishers over the decades.

BL: P.P.5126.fa

15a Cinquième Saison / edited by Raymond Syte, then Henri Chopin. Toulouse, then Paris, then, as OU, Ingatestone: [1, Spring 1958]–42/43 (1974). ISSN: 0529-777X

Note: The magazine changed title to OU with no. 20/21, also described as vol. 1/2. The new magazine had variant titles including *Revue OU* and *Review OU* and the previous *Cinquième Saison*, and sometimes had the subtitle, *revue de poèsie évolutive*

Anthology: *OU Sound Poetry: An Anthology* (Alga Marghen, 2002); 5 vinyl discs of material originally included with *OU* and an additional Henri Chopin disc (British Library Sound Archive: 1SS0004009)

Related Imprint: Collection OU

Interview: with Henri Chopin, by Nicholas Zurbrugg, in *Art & Design*, Vol. 10 no. 11/12 (1995), Profile No. 45: The Multimedia Text; BL: P.425/151

Concrete poetry, especially visual poetry, and sound poetry, with other experimentation. Syte founded the magazine in Toulouse, Chopin being a contributor from the first issue and becoming editor from no. 4 (1959), with Syte still "directeur". By no. 10 Chopin was in sole control of the magazine and moved it to Paris. He moved to Ingatestone in Essex in the late 1960s, with the first issue published from there being no. 34/35 (1969). Contributors included Michel Seuphor, Raoul Hausmann, Stefan Themerson, Paul de Vree, Bob Cobbing, Bengt Emil Johnson, Francois Dufrêne, Brion Gysin, Jochen Gerz, Sten Hanson, and others. Earlier issues were conventional in format but the issues published in England involved loose sheets, posters, and sound recordings etc., contained in folders.

TCD: 26/27, 28/29, 33. (OLS X–2–121 no.1–4)
UCL: 22, 25, 33, 34/35–40/41

16 Circus: the pocket review of our time. London: Hubbard Publications, Vol. 1 no. 1 (Apr. 1950)–no. 3 (June 1950)

A general review which also published fiction, poems, and cartoons; popular in intention, but short-lived. With articles by Jack Lindsay and Dylan Thomas, poems by Gavin Ewart, Norman Cameron, and reviews by Angus Wilson, Oswell Blakeston, and others. Edited anonymously.

BL: P.P.7616.uf
NLS: No. 1. (HP1.79.747)

17 Colonnade: a journal of literature and the arts / edited by Iain Fletcher, Ian Scott-Kilvert, D.S. Carne-Ross. London, Vol. 1 no. 1(1952)–no. 2 (1952). ISSN: 0531-1136

Note: Absorbed by *Adam International Review*, where it became a column.

CUL: L700.C.48
NLS: 1961.7
UCL

18 Concern: a literary magazine / edited by Harold Silver, then Norman Buller. Cambridge: [Concern], No. 1 (Apr. 1951)–3 [1953]

Essays, short fiction, and poems: e.g. Chris Busby contributes an essay on Salvatore Quasimodo, with translations of his poems, Harold Silver assesses Herbert Read's work, Doris Lessing contributes a short story, and there are poems from Montagu Slater, Ewart Milne, the editors, and others.

BL: P.P.6058.hfa
CUL: 1–2 (1952). (L999.C.3.99)

19 Couth: a magazine of new writing, gaiety and good living / edited by Richard Cox and others. Oxford: [Holywell Press for Couth], [No. 1] Spring, [1954]–[3] Summer, [1955]

BL: P.901/1243
CUL: L727.C.217
NLS: [1]–[2]. (5.2289)

20 Crescent / edited by R. Brian de L'Troath. Leicester: [Crescent], Vol. 1 no. 1 (Nov. 1959)–no. 3 (Summer 1960)

The first issue's subtitle, "A Leicester magazine devoted to the arts and matters of topical interest", illustrates the locus of interest here. In the first issue there's a memoir of W. H. Davies by Samuel J. Looker, an article on the patronising nature of the Soviet Union's alleged implementation of arts programmes, short stories, a review of Leicester-born Colin Wilson's *Age of Defeat*, artwork from local artists, an "abstract" poem by R. O. M. Bayldon, and a free verse poem by the editor. Production values went up a notch from a typed stencil to commercial vari-typing with the last issue.

BL: P.P.4881.td

21 The Criterion. Galway: Arts Society, University College Galway [1953–1984?]

Profiled in: Tom Clyde, *Irish Literary Magazines: an outline and descriptive bibliography* (Dublin: Irish Academic Press, 2003), BL: 2725.g.3414
Anthology: Gerald Dawe, *Criterion 1953–1983: An Anthology* (1983)

TCD: 1973; May 1984 (PER 90–464)

22 Critical Quarterly / edited by C. B.Cox and A. E. Dyson, and others. Bangor and Hull, then London, then Manchester. Vol. 1 no. 1 (Spring 1959)– . ISSN 0011–1562

Index: Michael Freeman, *Critical Quarterly: Index to Volumes 1–25, 1959–83* (Manchester University Press, 1984), BL: YC.2001.a.15777
Profiled in: Sullivan 1914–1984
Related Imprint: Anthologies of new poetry were published first as *Critical Quarterly Supplement*, no. 1 (1960), then as *Critical Quarterly Poetry Supplement* nos. 2–16 (1962–1975), both BL: ZA.9.a.9651. A Critical Quarterly Poetry Pamphlet was published by Manchester University Press, *Poetry Now*, edited by Brian Cox [1982?], containing poems by twelve poets. BL: X.950/14134.
Reprint: Millwood, New York: Kraus Reprint, [undated]

As its title suggested, dedicated to literary criticism but between the essays (whose authors included Raymond Williams, Bernard Bergonzi, and Malcolm Bradbury) there were in the early years poems by Ted Hughes, Charles Tomlinson, Thom Gunn, Sylvia Plath, R. S. Thomas, Philip Larkin, and others. A sister journal with shorter articles and reviews, *The Critical Survey*, was published from 1962, as the "journal of the Critical Quarterly Society", based at Hull.

BL: P.P.4881.sct
CUL: P700.C.220
NLS: Vol. 1–21 (NJ.321/2 SER) then vol. 22– . (HJ3.703 SER)

23 Crux. Spondon, Derby, [1953]

Listed in *Trace*, but perhaps this was a pre-publication announcement for what was actually published as *The Christian Poet*.

24 Dejected Nurses / edited by Fred Leavings. Bristol: [Dejected Nurses], [No. 1] (Spring 1959)

Probably a one-off, this appears to be an unofficial student magazine from Bristol University. It consists solely of fabricated testimonials in praise of the magazine, an editorial by Leavings (real name?), four anonymous parodic poems (Eliot and Arnold are sources), and an agony column which suggests that Empson's salts will purge your ambiguities.

BL: P.P.5126.0

25 Delta: a literary review from Cambridge / edited by Rodney Banister and Peter Redgrove, and others. Cambridge: [Delta], No. 1 (1953)–62 (1981)

Index: Sader (No 1 (1953)–47 (May 1970) only).
Related work: John Kinsella, "Peter Porter – 1998" [Interview with Porter], www.johnkinsella.org/interviews/porter2.html

Later editors included Philip Hobsbaum, Christopher Levenson, and Simon Gray. No 8 (Spring 1956) and no. 10 (Autumn 1956) were special issues on the Movement. Contributors included Sylvia Plath, Ted Hughes, Thomas Kinsella, Thom Gunn, Peter Porter, Donald Davie, Roy Fisher, and others. In an interview conducted by John Kinsella, cited above, Peter Porter remarks of Peter Redgrove: "He actually founded a magazine here called *Delta* which operated for quite some time. Its subsequent editors included not only Hobsbaum but also a man who became a very famous playwright later, Simon Gray. But they all believed in the principle that literature was discussable. They believed more or less I suppose what people believed in Ancient Greece, a sort of peripateia where you wandered around and discussed things." Merged with *Argo* in 1981.

BL: P.P.5126.bcd
CUL: CAM.C.41.3
NLS: 1–3; 5–16; 18–62. (NH.290 PER)

26 Departure: a magazine of literature and the arts / edited by John Adlard, Alan Brownjohn, Bernard Donoughue and Dennis Keane. Oxford: O.U.E.A.C, Vol. 1. no. 1 [1953?]–vol. 4 no. 11 [1957]

Note: The volume designation runs independently of the individual number, i.e. there were 11 issues in total, collected in four volumes. Editors varied
Reprint: Nendeln, Liechtenstein: Kraus Reprint, 1968

Chapter C: 1950–1959

A magazine based at Oxford University and publishing mainly but not wholly Oxford undergraduates' poetry. Contributors included: Vernon Watkins, Kathleen Raine, Martin Seymour-Smith, J. E. M. Lucie-Smith [i.e. Edward Lucie-Smith], James Kirkup, Norman Nicholson, Sydney Tremayne, John Heath-Stubbs, Geoffrey Hill, George MacBeth, Jenny Joseph, Anthony Thwaite, Elizabeth Bartlett, Lotte Zurndorfer, Alex Comfort, Adrian Mitchell, Karen Loewenthal, Donald Hall, W. Price Turner, Nicholas Moore, Elizabeth Jennings, Mary Lomer, Jon Silkin, Philip Larkin, Peter Redgrove, Donald Davie (who responds in rhyme in no. 8 to an essay by Seymour-Smith in no. 7), William Empson, Richard Eberhart, and Bernard Bergonzi. Loosely, a predecessor of *New Departures*.

BL: Vol. 1 no. 2 [1953?]–vol. 3 no. 9 [1955?]. (P.P.5938.caw)
CUL: Vol. 1 no. 3; vol. 3 no. 7–vol. 4 no. 10 (Autumn 1956). (L727.B.241)
NLS: Vol. 3 no. 7 (Spring 1955)–vol. 4 no. 10 (Autumn 1956). (1910.20)
UCL: Reprint
Oxford University Library Services: Per. 2705.d.597
Poetry Library: Vol. 2 no. 5–6; vol. 3 no. 9

27 Deuce / edited by Gog and Magog. Cheltenham: [Deuce], Pack 1 no. 2 (Nov. 1957)–Pack 2 (Dec. 1959). New Series, No. 1 (Spring 1960)–no. 9 (Spring 1962)

Related Imprint: Deuce Publications published at least four books, including collections by Yann Lovelock and David Holliday.

"Centred on, but not limited to, Cheltenham, it is intended as a forum for argument, a rostrum for the opinionated, a platform for prophets, a shooting box for critics, as well as a place of publication for worthwhile stories, essays, poems and articles."- editorial in the first issue. Seems to have worked in association with the Cheltenham Theatre and Arts Club. Until the New Series, launched in Spring 1960, the same small number of contributors recur. That issue, however, seems to mark a widening of intake. Contributors include David Holliday, F. J. Bradley, Peter J. Dale, Ian (i.e. Yann) Lovelock, Frances Harland, David Tipton, Ross MacAulay, D. M. Black, Marion Schoeberlein, Ena Hollis, Tom Malcolm, Geoffrey Holloway, R. L. Cook, Eric Hermes, Ruth Raymund, Vera Rich, and others. One of the best pieces is a (doggerel) Drinker's Alphabet, by Mark Black, in the March 1958 issue. According to Yann Lovelock, in Görtschacher 2, David Holliday seems to have be one of the editors, or the editor.

BL: P.P.4881.scf
CUL: New Series. 3–9. (L.727.c.244)
NLS: New Series. 3–9. (6.988)

28 Dialogue / edited by Alasdair Clayre and Peter Jay. Oxford: Dialogue, Vol. 1 no. 1 (March 1959)–vol. 3 no. 3 (Summer 1960). ISSN: 0433–2989

Note: Merged with *Gemini* to become the alternating *Gemini / Dialogue*.

A general cultural review, with political essays e.g. by Denis Healy, a review essay on East European poetry by Julian Mitchell, articles on War Crimes by Leszek Kolakowski and the philosopher Alasdair MacIntyre, and translations from contemporary Russian prose (fiction and non-fiction). See also entry for *Gemini*.

BL: Vol. 1 no. 1 only. (PP.7615.bw)
NLS: Vol. 1 no. 3 (Autumn 1957)–vol. 2 no. 8 (Autumn 1959), but lacking Vol. 1 no. 4 (Winter 1957)–vol. 2 no. 5 (Winter 1959). (6.920)

29 Elegreba / edited by Roye McCoye. Abergele: [Roye McCoye], No. 1 (Spring 1958)–3 (1959). ISSN 0420–9834

Related Imprint: Elegreba Press published the anthology *Five: new poems*, by Philip Callow, Ronald Hall, Leonard Kendall, Roye McCoye, and Edward Storey (Chippenham: Elegreba Press, 1961), BL: YA.1997.a.10117. The editor had published his own collection *Not to Lethe* in c.1956., BL: 11660.f.26

Poems by Paul Casimir, Corinne Sherman, Gael Turnbull, W. Price Turner, Edward Storey, R. L. Cook, Geoffrey Holloway, Gordon Harris, Ewart Milne, and others. Reviews by W. Price Turner, Roye McCoye, Eric Ratcliffe, Derek Maggs, and others. Probably inspired by Dylan Thomas's backwards town Llareggub in *Under Milk Wood*, the title of the magazine is Abergele in reverse.

BL: 1–2. (P.P.5126.nab)
CUL: 1–2. (L999.c.3.151)

30 Encounter / edited by Irving Kristol and Stephen Spender, and others. London: Martin Secker for the Congress for Cultural Freedom, [Vol. 1] No. 1 (1953)–[Vol. 75] no. 427 (1990)

Index: Every volume was issued with an index (i.e. every six issues of this monthly)
Profiled in: Sullivan 1914–1984
Related imprint: Encounter Pamphlet Series
Reprint: New York: AMS Press, 1969

Well-funded cultural review of considerable longevity and a circulation in the tens of thousands, making it hardly a "little magazine". Many of its contributors were unaware that it was part funded by the Central Intelligence Agency of the United States as a soft propaganda weapon against the Soviet Union. Nevertheless, it published some interesting if well-established poets and other literary figures. Auden, Betjeman, Creeley, Hughes, Robert Lowell, and Christopher Middleton withdrew after the revelations in 1967.

BL: P.P.5938.can
CUL: P900.B.40
NLS: Vol. 1–49. (P.65 PER); Vol. 50–75. (QJ9.149 PER).

31 **Envoi** / edited by J. C. Meredith Scott; Robert Wesley, then Bob Castle, then Anne Lewis-Smith, then Roger Elkin. Cheltenham, then Newport, then Ballachulish, then Stoke-on-Trent, then Newport, No. 1 [1956]– . ISSN: 0013–9394

Anthology: Eg. *Envoi Spring Anthology* (Newport: Envoi Poets, 1988), BL: PP.5126.naf/3; *Envoi Summer anthology*, (Newport: Envoi Poets, 1989), BL: PP.5126.naf/3
Related Imprint: Envoi Poets

BL: P.P.5126.naf
CUL: 15–16; 1980– . (L727.C.301)
NLS: 9–103, but lacking 11–13. (P.126.PER). 104– . (HJ4.1357 PER)
PL: 33; 41–59; 76–82; 88– .
UCL: 3; 8; 10–12; 14– .

32 **Extra Verse** / edited by A. G. Hill, then Peter Williams, then D. M. Black. Birmingham, then Edinburgh: Extra Verse, No. 1 [Summer 1959?]–17 (1966). ISSN: 0531–6243

Contributors included Anthony Edkins, Philip Hobsbaum, David Tipton, Roy Fisher, Anselm Hollo, Yevgeni Yevtushenko, Andrei Voznesensky, Jim Burns, Penelope Shuttle, D. M. Thomas, Giles Gordon, Vernon Scannell, George Mackay Brown, Robin Fulton, Yann Lovelock, Libby Houston, George Macbeth, Robert Garioch, Edwin Morgan, and Ernst Jandl. D. M. Black edited issues 12–16, when the magazine moved to Edinburgh; these included the special Ian Hamilton Finlay number (no. 15).

BL: 1 [Summer 1959?]–5 (Spring 1961), 7 (Summer 1962), 10 (Summer 1963)–17 (1966). (P.P.5126.0a)
CUL: 3–16. (L727.C.304)
NLS: 2 (Autumn 1959)–17 (1966), but lacking: 9 (1963) and 11 (1963). (5.5946)

33 **Fantasma Miscellany** / edited by J. V. Jones. Worthing: Fantasma, [No. 1, 1951]–7 [1954]

BL: Lacking: 2. (012359.a.55)

34 **Fantasma Parade**. Worthing: Fantasma, 2 [1951]

Note: Continues: *Fantasma Supplement*
BL: W.P. 2444

The Fantasy Poets *see* New Poems C64

35 **Fantasma Supplement**. Worthing: Fantasma, [No.1, 1951]

Note: Continued by: *Fantasma Parade*.
BL: W.P.2444

36 **FDARTS**. Rhu, Ullapool, by Garve, Ross-shire. 1952?

Noted in *Gargoyle* as a "critical literary newsletter".

Four *see* 4: a review of the visual arts, literature, music and drama C1

37 **Friday Market** / edited by A. L. Shearn. [Thames Ditton]: [Ember Press], No. 1 (1956)–15 (1961)

CUL: 13–15. (L999.C.3.154)
UCL: 1–14

38 **Gairm: an raitheachan Gaidhlig** / edited by Ruaraidh MacThomais and Fionnlagh Domhnullach. Glaschu [Glasgow], 1952– .

Related Imprint: Gairm published collections by Anne Frater, Iain Mac a'Ghobhainn (Iain Crichton Smith), Maoilios M. Caimbeul, Ruaraidh MacThomais (Derick Thomson) and others.

A long–standing Scottish literary magazine, publishing to this day. Devoted to Gaelic literature, language and the arts, and published entirely in Scottish Gaelic. All of the major modern writers in Gaelic have had their work published in *Gairm*.

BL: P.P.8004.dh.
CUL: Lacking: 48–49. (L900.C.21)
NLS
UCL

39 Gambit: Edinburgh University review / edited by Peter T. Froestrup; Tom Scott, Mike Shea, Donald MacArthur, Bill McArthur, Douglas Eadie, Arthur Smyth... and others. Edinburgh: Edinburgh University, 1957–Autumn 1965. Then, as *New Gambit*, Vol. I no. 1 (Spring 1966)–vol. 11 no. 42/3 [1986]. ISSN: 0016–4283

A literary review. Contributors included: in *Gambit*, Ian MacArthur, Robin Fulton, George Mackay Brown, Sydney Goodsir Smith, Tom Scott, Ian Hamilton Finlay, Norman MacCaig, Alan Jackson, Iain Crichton Smith, Anselm Hollo, Alan Riddell, George Campbell Hay, Edwin Morgan, Ken Morrice, Hugh MacDiarmid, Alan Bold, D. M. Black, and others and in *New Gambit*, Alan Jackson, Adrian Henri, Brian Patten, D. M. Black, Robert Garioch, Malcolm Rifkind (an essay on democracy and responsibility), Roger McGough, Ian Hamilton Finlay, Anselm Hollo, Tom Pickard, Pete Morgan, and others.

BL: From *Gambit*, lacking: 1957, Spring-Summer 1958, Autumn 1960, Autumn 1961, Spring 1963, Spring and Summer 1964. (P.P.6150.mbd). From *New Gambit*, lacking: all except Vol. 1 no. 1 (Spring 1966), Festival 1966, Spring 1967, Summer 1967, and Winter 1967.
CUL: *Gambit* only (imperfect set). (L985.C.112)
NLS: From *Gambit*, lacking: 1957; Spring-Summer 1958; Autumn 1960; Summer 1961; Spring 1963; 1964; Spring-Summer 1965. (P.76 PER). From *New Gambit* Lacking: Vol. 2, no. 6. (Y.106 PER)
UCL: Spring 1960, Spring 1962, Autumn 1962, Spring 1964 only.

40 Gargoyle / [edited by Kenneth Nobes and Christopher Logue]. Northolt Park, Middlesex: [Gargoyle], Nov. 1951–Oct. 1952?

A little magazine with a satirical tone. The editors' manifesto begins: "Our purpose is truly charitable: the Enlightenment of the Unenlightened and the Dissemination of Culture to the Poor and the Needy. As if that was not sufficient, another modest object will be to provide an outlet for the Creative Writer (hallelujah!) – we are compelled to include this immortal phrase for without it no little magazine manifesto would be complete – thus satisfying the flank scratching borborygmics of Kensington, the bard of Winchelsea, and sparing geniuses the need to contract consumption before attaining recognition. Contributions are invited for which we offer fame." Most contributions in these slender magazines are in fact pseudonymous poems, but presumably Nathaniel

Bloodwhisker and Cornelius Grogpot etc are the editors. Patrick Brangwyn and Pauline Roberts have poems signed with their real names.

BL: Nov. 1951, Feb. 1952, Oct. 1952. (P.P.6018.pdg)

41 Gemini: the Oxford and Cambridge magazine / edited by William Donaldson, Julian Mitchell, Graeme McDonald, Christopher Levenson, Dom Moraes, David Howell, David Cammell, Nicholas Tanburn, James Cornish and Peter Ridout. Cambridge: [Gemini], Vol. 1. no. 1 Spring 1957–[vol. 2 no. 8 (Autumn 1959)?]. Then, as *Gemini / Dialogue*, [Vol. 3 no. 2?] Jan. 1960–vol. 3 no. 3 (Summer 1960)

Contributors included Auden, Philip Hobsbaum, Dom Moraes, Paul Potts, Vernon Scannell, Peter Levi, Gregory Corso, Peter Redgrove, Christopher Logue, and others; the cover of Autumn 1959 is artwork by W. S. Graham. The magazine merged and alternated with *Dialogue* in its last year.

BL: Vol. 2 no. 6 (Spring 1959)–no. 8 (Autumn 1959); Jan. 1960–vol. 3 no. 3. (P.P.4881.tar)
CUL: Nos 1–2, 6–8. (L985.b.96)
UCL: Vol. 1 no. 1–no. 5, vol. 2 no. 6, vol. 3 no. 2.

Gemini / Dialogue *See* Gemini C41

42 Gorgon / edited by Seamus Heaney [and others?]. Belfast: [English Society, Queen's University, [No. 1, 1959?]–5 (Hilary 1961)

Profiled in: Tom Clyde, *Irish Literary Magazines: an outline and descriptive bibliography* (Dublin: Irish Academic Press, 2003), BL: 2725.g.3414

The last issue is edited by Seamus Heaney, who signs his editorial off as "an ex-poet". It also includes early poems by him including under the nom-de-plume Incertus. Hilary is the January –March term in the old academic year.

BL: Hilary 1961. (Cup.410.f.750)
Queen's University, Belfast: 3–5. (876)

43 Grid / edited by Peter Greene. London, 195–?

Mentioned in *Deuce*.

44 Grub Street / edited by R. D. E. H. and R. C. F., then John Parry. London: Grub Street, Edition 1 (Aug. 1953)–no. 5 (May/ June 1954)

Short fiction, poetry and reviews. Contributors of poetry included Jon Silkin, James Kirkup, Alan Brownjohn, Ithell Colquhoun, H. R. Bramley, Oswell Blakeston, Karen Loewenthal, Patrick Garland, Arthur Moyse and Meredith Roberts. Ian Norrie contributed theatre reviews. The first editors are not identified; John Parry took over from issue 3.

BL: P.P.5938.bcm
CUL: L727.C.172
NLS: 1950.58
UCL: No. 3–4 (1954)

45 The Guild Broadsheets / edited by John Hoffman. Hull: Guild Press, No. 1 (1956)–[no. 9?, 1958?]

Related imprint: The Guild Press, imprint of the Poetry Guild, which also published the Guild Poets series of poetry pamphlets and *We Offer*.

Each featured a single poet, namely Frederic Vanson, J. Phoenice, Pamela Page, Alexander Clarke, Ruth Partington, Frances Porteous, Patricia Howe, Eric Ratcliffe and Penelope Anne Bennett.

CUL: 1–8. (L727.C.226)
UCL: 8 (1957)

Gwent Poetry Society Anthology *See* Anthology of the Gwent Poetry Society C6

46 Icarus / edited by Cecil Jenkins, Rosalind Brett-Jones and Peter Devlin; and others. Dublin: Trinity College, Vol. 1 no. 1 (1950)– . ISSN: 0019–1027

Note: Volume numbers are generally independent of the issue number, e.g. vol. 7 no. 22 was the twenty-second issue of the whole run. The exceptions are vol. 44 no. 1 (Feb 1994) and vol. 44 no. 2 (Apr. 1994). March 1959 is wrongly numbered no. 28 (it should be no. 27) and there are two issues numbered 29.

Index: Goode

Profiled in: Tom Clyde, *Irish Literary Magazines: an outline and descriptive bibliography* (Dublin: Irish Academic Press, 2003), BL: 2725.g.3414

Anthology: No. 98 was *The Worst of Icarus: an anthology of poor quality student verse* [1993]

Poetry, articles, and short fiction. Contributors came to include Donald Davie, Thomas Kinsella, Eavan Boland, Michael Longley, Derek Mahon, Brendan Kennelly and, in the mid-sixties, Iain Sinclair, and William Burroughs. Pauline G. Bewick provided the cover and other illustrations for no. 15 (Feb 1955) and 16 (May 1956). No. 46 (1965) has a long editorial by Sinclair which includes the suggestion that *Icarus* should be like the "good bad taste" of the cartoon strip *Peanuts*.

BL: 1–23; 25–58; 91–98; vol. 44 no. 1; 2; 102–105. (P.P.4970.eca)
CUL: 1–57; 76 [1980]; 1984– . (L727.B.337)
TCD: IN.C.TRI
UCL

47 Ideogram: poetry, prose, criticism / edited by David Kosubei, Alfred Manley, Charles Orwell and Ben Sands. London: [The Editors], No. 1 [1952]

BL: P.P.5126.gcb

48 Impact / edited by Francis Cabuche. Dulwich, London: Dulwich Branch of the British Poetry Association, Vol. 1 no. 1 [195?]–?

Mostly poems, with some reviews. Produced from a typewritten stencil. Contributors included Wrey Gardiner, Hardiman Scott, Hugh Creighton Hill. The poetry of Marie Stopes is reviewed enthusiastically by Madeleine D'Avy in vol. 1 no. 2. Presumably the British Poetry Association was a rival to the Poetry Society. The BPA also had their own, main, magazine simply called *Poetry*.

BL: Vol. 1 no. 2 only. (ZA.9.a.2214)

49 Interlude. Loughton, Essex, 1958–?

Listed in *Trace* as covering all the arts (including poetry?), but especially theatre.

No holdings known.

50 Kavanagh's Weekly: a journal of literature and politics / edited by Patrick Kavanagh. Dublin: Peter Kavanagh, Vol. 1 no. 1 (Apr. 12 1952)–no. 13 (July 5 1952)

Profiled in: Tom Clyde, *Irish Literary Magazines: an outline and descriptive bibliography* (Dublin: Irish Academic Press, 2003), BL: 2725.g.3414; Gerry Smyth, *Decolonisation and Criticism: the construction of Irish literature* (London: Pluto Press, 1998), pp.103–113, BL: YC.2001.a.4091

Reprint: The Curragh, Co. Kildare: Goldsmith Press, 1981; BL: L.45/3099

Next to no actual poetry in this provocative journal with a wide cultural agenda, but still very much part of the poetry world: edited by the poet Patrick Kavanagh and published by his brother. The last issue reveals the pseudonyms used for the previous issues' articles.

BL: P.P.6193.kdd
CUL: Q700.A.7
TCD: Gall.BB.11b.40

51 Key Poets. London: Fore Publications, No. 1–10 (1950). Then, New Series, London: Fore, No. 1 (1951)

Note: Variant title: *Key Poet*

Related Imprint: Fore Publications published a number of books on various topics from the 1930s to the 1950s, often related to central and eastern Europe.

A pamphlet series, each pamphlet containing a collection by a single author. These were often poets who had been better-known before the War. In the first series the poets were: Edith Sitwell, George Barker, Randall Swingler, Jonathan Denwood, Stanley Snaith, Dorian Cooke, Jack Lindsay, Maurice Carpenter, Jack Beeching and Norman Cameron. The new series seems to have contained only one publication, a translation of a Vítězslav Nezval poem by Jack Lindsay and Stephen Jolly.

BL: W.P.8498. New Series: W.P.8498.a.

52 Lines / edited by Alan Riddell. Edinburgh: Poetry Edinburgh, [No. 1, 1952]–no. 3 (Summer 1953). Then as *Lines Review*, Edinburgh: Macdonald, no. 4 (Jan. 1954)–144 (March 1998). ISSN 0459–4541

Index: *Scottish Poetry Index Vol. 3* (Edinburgh: Scottish Poetry Library, 1995; all issues indexed) BL: ZC.9.b.6227; Robin Fulton, *Lines Review Index* (Loanhead: Macdonald, 1978), indexes 1–60

Profiled in: Sullivan 1914–1984

Related Imprint: M. Macdonald published two poetry collections in its first full year, 1953, Alan Riddell's *Beneath the Summer*, BL: 11659.cc.23, and Sidney Goodsir Smith's *Cokkils*, BL: 11660.bb.8. Many more would be published during *Lines Review*'s life.

Reprint: 1–25, New York: Johnson Reprint Corp, 1972; 1–6, Millwood, New York: Kraus Reprint, [undated]

Poems and reviews and articles concerning poetry.

Scottish-based, but not limited to Scottish poetry. The first issue of what would become, as *Lines Review*, one of the longest running poetry magazines in Scotland, was published during the 1952 Edinburgh Festival in honour of Hugh MacDiarmid who celebrated his 60th birthday that year. No. 3 was a Sidney Goodsir Smith number. That issue was published by M. [i.e. Callum] Macdonald, who would publish all future issues of *Lines Review* as well. After Riddell's departure in 1954, the editors were Sydney Goodsir Smith, Tom Scott, J. K. Annand, Albert Mackie, Alan Riddell again (from 1962–1967), then Robin Fulton (1967–1977), Robert Calder, William Montgomerie (1977–1982), Trevor Royle and Tessa Ransford. Robin Fulton's editorship was especially noteworthy for its numbers given over to contemporary poetry in Europe.

BL: 3–144. (P.P.5126.bcf)
CUL: 3–144. (L727.C.190)
NLS: NH.290
UCL: Johnson Reprint

Lines Review *see* Lines C52

53 Listen / edited by George Hartley. Hessle, East Yorkshire: [Listen] [Vol. 1 no. 1 Spring 1954]–vol. 4 no. 1 (Autumn 1962)

Related Work: Jerry Bradley, *The Movement: British poets of the 1950s* (New York: Twayne, 1993), BL: YC.1996.a.818; Blake Morrison, *The Movement: English poetry and fiction of the 1950s* (Oxford: Oxford University Press, 1980), BL: X.989/88175; Mohan Ramanan, *The Movement: a study of contemporary poetic tradition* (Delhi: B.R. PublishingCorp, 1989), BL: YA.1990.a.15972; Charu Sheel Singh, *Auguries of Evocation: British poetry during and after the Movement* (New Delhi, Associated Publishing House, 1987), BL: YA.1988.a.16569

A little magazine associated with the Movement poets, but not in fact confined to them. A significant number of American writers were among the contributors. Poets include: Philip Larkin, John Wain, Kingsley Amis, Anthony Thwaite, Elizabeth Jennings, Roy Fuller, W. S. Merwin, Thom Gunn, Adrienne Cecile Rich, James Merrill, James Wright, Martin Seymour Smith, Edwin Morgan, Donald Davie, Charles Madge, Tom Scott, George MacBeth, W. H. Auden, G. S. Fraser, Thomas Kinsella, R. S. Thomas, Alan Brownjohn, Stevie Smith, J. E. M. Lucie-Smith, Geoffrey Hill, Richard Wilbur, Ezra Pound, W. D. Snodgrass, and Norman MacCaig. As critics: Charles Tomlinson, Frank Kermode, Philip Hobsbaum, and Malcolm Bradbury (e.g. a review article on the Movement, in vol. 2 no. 2).

BL: P.P.5126.gci
CUL: Vol. 1–3 (L727.C.187)
NLS: P.210
UCL

54 The London Broadsheet. London:
[The London Broadsheet], then Kenneth Coutts-Smith, No. 1 [Dec. 1954]–5 (June 1955). ISSN: 0456–4898

From no. 1: "The broadsheet tradition is a subversive one, and this broadsheet exists to subvert you. We wish to reintroduce a healthy anger at bad art and bad government. Poetry is retreating to provincial universities, criticism has grown mealy-mouthed, honest bawdy is censored, and every real political opposition is watched by the police. We solicit serious comment on any of the above tendencies; and also satire, cartoons and ballads on contemporary events (which may be doggerel, but must have bite); as well as creative writing and line drawings." Edited anonymously. Contributors included Ithel Colquhoun (poems, and an article on Austin Osman Spare), Oswell Blakeston, Thomas Blackburn, Paul Potts, Bernard Kops, Raymond Tong, Antony Borrow (e.g. an article on Thomas Blackburn), Michael Ivens, Robert Greacen (translating an anonymous Albanian poem), Ewart Milne, and others. Sold by subscription and also at the Harlequin Coffee House in Fulham.

BL: P.P.7001.ap. Also, 1–3 on microfilm Mic.32035 (no. 1–3)
UCL: 3–5

55 The London Magazine: a monthly review of literature / edited by John
Lehmann, then Alan Ross, then Sebastian Barker. London: Chatto and Windus, Vol. 1 no. 1 (Feb. 1954)–vol. 8 no. 3. (Mar. 1961). New series. Vol. 1 no. 1 (April 1961)– . ISSN 0024–6085

Note: Imprint varies. From 1971 published by London Magazine itself.
Index: Each volume had its own index
Profiled in: Görtschacher 1; Sullivan 1914–1984
Related Imprint: From c.1966 to the 1980s London Magazine Editions published poetry, fiction and other texts, notably collections by Roy Fuller, Brian Jones, and Tony Harrison and anthologies such as Robin Fulton (ed. and trans.) An Italian Quartet (1966), BL: X.908/9492; Maureen Ahern and David Tipton (eds. and trans.), Peru: the new poetry (1970), BL: X.989/6564 and Alan Riddell (ed.), Typewriter art (1975), BL: X.421/10167
Anthology: Hugo Williams (ed.), London Magazine poems, 1961–66, (London: Alan Ross, 1966), BL: X.908/9488; Alan Ross (ed.), London Magazine 1961–85, (London: Chatto & Windus, 1986), BL: YC.1986.a.1646; Alan Ross (ed.), Signals: thirty new stories to celebrate thirty years of the London

Magazine, (London: Constable, 1991), BL: Nov.1991/2129
Reprint: Nendeln, Liechtenstein: Kraus Reprint, [undated]

A commercial-looking magazine (in fact subsidised by private and public funds) which began as a general literary review, publishing and reviewing poetry as well as other literature, but which under Alan Ross's editorship broadened its remit to include the arts in general. Alan Ross edited London Magazine from the beginning of the new series, in 1961, until his death in 2001. An offshoot was the non-poetry series, London Magazine Stories (BL: X.0909/321) which ran from 1964 to 1979.

BL: P.P.5939.cbg
CUL: L900.C.324
NLS: Vol. 1 no. 1–vol. 21 no. 12. Lacking: vol. 21 no. 11. (NF.1603.SER) Vol. 22 no. 1.– . Lacking various issues. (HJ3.588. SER)
UCL: Vol.1–20. (Rare Arts Pers) Vol.1 no. 4, vol. 7 no. 1, vol. 16 no. 1, vol. 20 no. 1–2. (Little Magazines Collection)

56 Man!: the measure of all things: an
Anglo-American anarchist publication. London: S. E. Parker, New series, Vol. 1 no. 1 (May 1955)–no. 6 (Mar/Apr. 1957)

Anthology: Marcus Graham (ed.), Man! An anthology of anarchist ideas, essays, poetry and commentaries (London: Cienfuegos Press, [1974]), BL: X.808/9448. An anthology which relates to the American journal of this title, but which nevertheless had an oblique relationship with the British periodical.

A general cultural and political review that published occasional poetry and reviews of poetry. Poems by Robinson Jeffers and Eric Ratcliffe and others. Edited anonymously. Its American predecessor, of which it was not officially a continuation, ran from 1933 to 1940.

BL: P.P.3554.eny

57 Merlin: a collection of contemporary writing / edited by
Alexander Trocchi. Limerick, Me., then Paris: Alice Jane Lougee, Vol. 1 no. 1 (1952)–vol. 2 no. 4 (Spring/Summer 1955). ISSN: 0543–5277

Reprint: Nendeln, Liechtenstein: Kraus Reprint, 1973

Robert Creeley was on the Committee for vol. 2 no. 4. The journal published Beckett, Ionesco (the first printing in any language), Sartre, Genet, Neruda, Henry Miller, Trocchi himself and others. It was apparently in order to fund the magazine that, among a number of casual jobs, Trocchi wrote pornographic books for the Olympia Press.

BL: Lacking: vol. 1 no. 1. (P.P.4881.say)
CUL: [1973 Reprint]. (Q700.c.67)
NLS: 6.2067
UCL: Lacking: vol. 2 no. 4

58 Migrant / edited by Gael Turnbull.
Ventura, Ca. and Worcester: Migrant Press,
No. 1 (July 1959)–8 (Sept. 1960). ISSN:
0540–004X

Profiled in: *Chapman* 78–79 (1994), BL: P.901/945

Related Imprint: Migrant Press published poetry
collections over a period of thirty years by Robert Creeley,
Ian Hamilton Finlay, Edwin Morgan, Roy Fisher, Hugh
Creighton Hill, Omar Pound, Anselm Hollo, Pete Brown,
Matthew Mead, Michael Shayer, Gael Turnbull, Tony
Harrison, Adele David, and others.

Published Roy Fisher, Edwin Morgan, Robert Creeley, Cid
Corman, Charles Olson, Larry Eigner, Ian Hamilton Finlay,
Denise Levertov, Anselm Hollo, W. Price Turner, Robert
Duncan, Edward Dorn, Charles Tomlinson, and others.
The influence of or affinity with Turnbull's friend W. Price
Turner, who edited *The Poet* earlier on in the decade, is felt
in the understated design and the transatlantic spread of
the contributors. Michael Shayer was a contributing editor.

BL: P.P.4881.sdy.
CUL: L727.c.229
NLS: NJ.704
UCL

59 New Broom / edited by Anne Turner.
Glasgow: [New Broom]. No. 1[1953]–3 [1955]

Satirical poetry and editorials, with an anti-establishment
flavour. Contributors included Tom Wright, William Price
Turner, Hyacinthe Hill, Eric Nixon, Hugh Creighton Hill
(poem: "A critical note on the little magazines"), Gael
Turnbull, Sydney Tremayne, Christopher R. Levenson
(poem: "The Poetry Society") and others.

BL: P.901/822

60 New Chapter: a quarterly
magazine of literature / edited by Robert
Bruce and Leslie Candappa. London: New
Chapter, Vol. 1 no. 1 (May 1957)–no. 3 (Sept.
1958). ISSN: 0467–1945

Short fiction, and articles on fiction, drama, travel and
poetry. Poems by: Edmund Blunden, Elizabeth Jennings,
Jon Silkin, Owen Thomas, Hilary Crusz, Christopher

Levenson, Richard Drain, Vernon Scannell, Alan
Brownjohn, John Smith, Eric Ratcliffe, Paris Leary,
Geoffrey Holloway, Gael Tunrbull, Gene Baro, Charles
Duranty, P. A. T. O'Donnell. The last issue had a John
Cowper Powys feature, with contributions by Angus
Wilson, Raymond Garlick, and others.

BL: P.P.5939.bhh.
CUL: L727.C.250
NLS: 1961.28
UCL

61 New Departures / edited by Michael
Horovitz and David Sladen. South Hinksey:
[New Departures], No. 1 (1959)– .

Note: No. 5 was also vol. 2 no. 12 of *Resurgence*. No. 6
consists of a booklet of poems by Frances Horovitz, *The
High Tower*
Profiled in: Görtschacher 1; Sullivan 1914–1984
Interview: With Michael Horovitz, Görtschacher 1
Anthology: Michael Horovitz (ed.), *Children of Albion: poetry
of the underground in Britain* (Harmondsworth: Penguin,
1969), BL: X.908/18647; Michael Horovitz (ed.),
*Grandchildren of Albion: an illustrated anthology of voices and
visions of younger poets in Britain* (Stroud: New Departures,
1992), BL: YK.1993.a.10246; Michael Hulse and Inge Elsa
Laird (eds.) POP!: *the poetry olympics party anthology*
(London: New Departures, 2000), BL: YK.2000.a.12681

Loosely, a successor to *Departure*. An eclectic, erratically-
published magazine with a strong visual presence (photos,
collage, typography). A relatively early publisher of the
Beats in England. Contributors include Alan Brownjohn,
Patrick Bowles, Bernard Kops, John McGrath, Stevie Smith,
Gregory Corso, Donald Davie, Allen Ginsberg, Eugene
Ionesco, Jack Kerouac, Jon Silkin, W. H Auden, John
Berryman, Paul Celan, Austin Clarke, Langston Hughes,
Pablo Neruda, Kenneth Patchen, Charles Olson, Ezra
Pound, Anne Sexton, Ted Hughes, Stephen Spender,
Samuel Beckett, and Frances Horovitz. Sladen was
co-editor only for no. 1, after which Horovitz generally
edited alone (though Roger Franklin co-edited no. 5). *New
Departures* is strongly associated with live events including
the "Poetry Olympics" readings organised by Michael
Horovitz.

BL: P.P.4881.sdg.
CUL: L727.B.241
NLS: 1 (Summer 1959)–2/3 (1960) (Y.217 PER); 7/8, 10/11
(1975) (1975.179 PER); 12 (1980)–13 (1981), 15 (1983); 16
(1984) (HP4.87.906)
UCL
Poetry Library: 1–7/8, 10/11–15, 17/18/19/20/21/22, 25/26

62 **New Helios** / edited by Peter Jones.
London: New Helios, Vol. 1 no. 1 (Oct.
1956)–no. 3 (1958). ISSN: 0467–2860

With poems by H. R. Bramley, Philip Crick, Geoffrey
Hazard, Peter Jones, and others.

BL: Vol. 1 no. 1. (Pressmark pending)
UCL

63 **New Lines** / edited by Robert Conquest.
London: Macmillan, [I] (1956)–II (1963)

Related Work: Jerry Bradley, *The Movement: British poets of the
1950s* (New York: Twayne, 1993), BL: YC.1996.a.818; Blake
Morrison, *The Movement: English poetry and fiction of the 1950s*
(Oxford: Oxford University Press, 1980), BL: X.989/88175;
Mohan Ramanan, *The Movement: a study of contemporary poetic
tradition* (Delhi: B.R. PublishingCorp, 1989), BL:
YA.1990.a.15972; Charu Sheel Singh, *Auguries of evocation:
British poetry during and after the Movement* (New Delhi,
Associated Publishing House, 1987), BL: YA.1988.a.16569
Reprint: New Lines [I] was reissued by Macmillan in 1967,
BL: X.989/37000

The first of these two anthologies heralded The Movement
poets. Contributors included: Elizabeth Jennings, John
Holloway, Philip Larkin, Thom Gunn, Kingsley Amis, D. J.
Enright, Donald Davie, Robert Conquest, and John Wain.
The later volume added James Michie, Hilary Corke, John
Fuller, Francis Hope, Jonathan Price, Ted Hughes, Anthony
Thwaite, Hugo Williams, Vernon Scannell, George
MacBeth, Thomas Blackburn, Laurence Lerner, Edwin
Brock, Thomas Kinsella, and Edward Lucie-Smith.

BL: 11606.bb.36
NLS: [I] (NE.116.h.39), II (NG.1599.e.11)
TCD: [I] (150.f.100)
UCL: ENGLISH S 40 CON

64 **New Poems** / edited by Donald Hall, and
others. Eynsham: Fantasy Press, Vol. 1 no. 1
(Autumn 1952)–vol. 2 no. 2 [1954]. ISSN:
0467–5118

Note: Editors vary
Related Imprint: Oscar Mellor's Fantasy Press issued the
Fantasy Poets series (BL: W.P.B.649), which published collections, each of six pages only, from many of those
featured in *New Poems*. It also featured some, like Philip
Larkin, who were not actually in the magazine. The Press
published more substantial individual collections, and
printed the longstanding *Oxford Poetry* from 1953 to 1960.
Bibliography: John Cotton, *Oscar Mellor: The Fantasy Press: A*

Memory (Hitchin: Dodman Press, 1977), BL: 2725.d.858.
Includes a brief memoir of Oscar Mellor and a four-page
checklist of Fantasy Press publications.

Vol. 1 no.–vol. 2 no. 1 were edited by Donald Hall, then at
Christ Church, Oxford University. Jonathan Price and
Geoffrey Hill edited the last issue. Each number was 12
pages in extent and published only poetry. The contributors
were: Robert Bly, Martin Seymour-Smith, Simon
Broadbent, Elizabeth Jennings, Michael Shanks, A. Alvarez,
Jenny Joseph, F. George Steiner, Alistair Elliott, Donald
Hall; Adrienne Cecile Rich; Geoffrey Hill, Anthony
Thwaite, Brian Morris, Michell Raper, Don Collis; Thom
Gunn, Alan Brownjohn, John Bayley, David Mitchell;
Jonathan Price, Will Morgan, Margaret Strahan, J. E. M.
Lucie-Smith, George MacBeth; Andrew Anderson, Jeremy
Brooks; John Holmstrom, Donald Davie, Richard Selig,
and Brian Aldiss. Not to be confused with the *New Poems*
anthology issued by the writers' organisation P.E.N. in 1952
and subsequent years (BL: P.P.5126.bcb)

BL: P.P.5126.gce
CUL: L727.C.148
NLS: 1955.21
UCL: Vol. 1 no. 1–no. 2

65 **New Rooster** / edited by Ben Howard.
195–?

Mentioned in *Deuce*. Oddly, appears to have become *Rooster*.
No holdings known of either.

66 **The New West Country Magazine.**
Stratton St. Margaret, Wiltshire. 1957?

Listed in *Trace*. Presumably an attempt to revive the work of
West Country Magazine (B144).
No holdings known.

67 **Nightwatchman** / edited by I. R. Orton.
Leicester: I. R. Orton, No. 1 (Winter
1950/51)–6 [1953]

Poems, with poetry notices and short articles. Typewritten.
Contributors included: Danny Abse, James Kirkup, Nissim
Ezekiel, John Heath-Stubbs, Anne Tomlinson, Bernard
Kops, Paul Potts, Jane Lunt, Jon Silkin, W. Price Turner,
Antony Borrow, and others. Iris Orton published several
collections of her own poetry, including *The Dreamer and the
Sheaves* (Oxford University Press, 1955) and *A Man Singing*
(Scorpion Press, 1962).

BL: P.P.5126.bbo
CUL: 2/3–6. (L999.B.1.55)
UCL

68 Nimbus / edited by Tristram Hull and others. London: [Nimbus], [Vol. 1] no. 1 (Dec. 1951)–vol. 4 no. 2 (Feb. 1958). ISSN: 0549–4931

Profiled in: Sullivan 1914–1984
Related Imprint: The Westminster Press published a poetry collection by Ivo Jarosy, The Ascent (1951), BL: 11657.l.36

The first issue had a rather poorly-composed cover design credited to Terence Conran. Nimbus was at first a modest magazine, publishing poetry, fiction and essays, with poetry mainly from the British Isles, e.g. Ruth Bulman, R. F. C. Hull, Frances Bellerby, John Heath-Stubbs, George Barker, Vernon Watkins, Patrick Galvin, and Vernon Scannell. The range increased with the June/Aug 1953 issue and the magazine went on to feature contributors as various as C. J. Jung (R. F. C. Hull being his translator), Alexander Trocchi, D. J. Enright, James Kirkup, Herbert Read, Bertolt Brecht, Christopher Logue, Conrad Aiken, Jean Cocteau, W. S. Graham, Paul Eluard, MacDiarmid, Patrick Kavanagh, Geoffrey Hill, Roy Campbell, Stevie Smith, Richard Wilbur and, in the final issue, Auden, George Mackay Brown, Danny Abse and William Empson. Some of its reviews took exception to the poetry of the Movement. Ivo Jarosy joined Tristam Hull as co-editor from vol. 2 no. 1 (June/Aug. 1953), from when it was published by John Trafford but printed at the Westminster Press. From vol. 3 no. 2 Jarosy was no longer co-editor; David Wright took his place from that issue.

BL: Vol. 1 no. 1– vol. 3 no. 3 (Summer 1956). (P.P.5938.bdp)
CUL: Vol. 1 no. 1– vol. 3 no. 3 (Summer 1956). (L727.C.196)
NLS: Vol. 1 no. 1– vol. 3 no. 3 (Summer 1956). (6.774)
UCL: Vol. 1 no. 1–vol. 2 no. 1; vol. 4 no. 2.

69 Ninepence / edited by Patrick Brangwyn, Charles Fox and Christopher Logue. Bournemouth: [Ninepence], No. 1 (Sept. 1951)–3 (Autumn 1952). ISSN: 0468–2696

'To the editors the character of this circular is one of resistance – resistance to liars and fools who whine that poetry is dead, yet whose bony elbows guard the bread and butter. They consider the muses creatures of similar appetite and fail to discriminate between belch and song. May we tangle with their guts, cloud their urine and generally irritate their solemn toilet.' – from the editorial of the first issue. There were poems, an article by Charles Fox on poetry and theatre, and reviews. Contributors included Logue, Charles Causley, Robert Duncan, and Alexander Trocchi.

BL: PP.5126.faa

CUL: L999.B.1.63
NLS: 6.742
UCL: 2–3.

70 Nonplus / edited by Patricia Murphy. Dublin: Nonplus, then Irish Channels Ltd., No. 1 (Oct. 1959)–4 (Winter 1960)

Profiled in: Tom Clyde, Irish Literary Magazines: an outline and descriptive bibliography (Dublin: Irish Academic Press, 2003), BL: 2725.g.3414

A cultural review with professional production values. It published, for example, prose and poetry by Patrick Kavanagh, essays on Max Jacob, Albert Camus and Francis Ponge, and reprinted work by Myles na gCopaleen. Printed, but not published, by the Dolmen Press.

BL: P.P.4881.sdu
CUL: L900.D.108
NLS: P.212
TCD: PER 91–483

71 Northern Broadsheet / edited by Dorothy Una Ratcliffe. Edinburgh: [Northern Broadsheet], No. 1(Summer 1956)–6 (Spring 1960). ISSN: 0468–6896

Poetry only, except for an illustration on the first page of each issue. Some poems were in dialects of the Northern counties of England, including Lancashire, Wensleydale, and various regions within Yorkshire. Similar to The Microcosm which Ratcliffe had edited decades earlier. The magazine seems to have had a connection with the Yorkshire Dialect Society whose adverts it displays and whose President was the editor. Poets in the Broadsheet included: James Kirkup, Herbert Read, Anthony Thwaite, Kathleen Stark, Phoebe Hesketh, Wilfrid Gibson, and others. A supplement, a poem by the editor about St John's Cross, Iona, was published in Autumn 1957.

BL: Ac.9941/5
CUL: L727.C.268
NLS: 5.467
UCL

72 Oasis / edited by David Stone and Geoffrey Roughton, and others. Cambridge: [The Editors], No. 1 [1951]–5 [1952]

Began in the first two issues as reprinting relatively contemporary poems; the third issue published new work from Cambridge undergraduates; the fourth issue was a special Yeats number.

BL: 1–4. (X.909/10852)
CUL: L999.c.3.607
UCL: 1–2; 5.

73 Ore / edited by Eric Ratcliffe. Teddington, then Stevenage: Ore, No. 1 [1954]–50 (1995). ISSN: 0030–459X

Anthology: Eric Ratcliffe and Wolfgang Görtschacher (eds.) *Veins of Gold: Ore 1954–1995* (Salzburg, Austria: University of Salzburg, 1997), (Salzburg studies in English literature: Poetic drama & poetic theory , vol. 105), BL: 8071.854 vol 105. Includes an interview with the editor, articles by Brian Louis Pearce, Penelope Shuttle, Steve Sneyd, and others, a bibliography of poems, essays and reviews published, and photographs. A large selection of poetry from *Ore* is reprinted in the anthology.
Interview: With Eric Ratcliffe, Görtschacher 2
Related Imprint: Ore Publications published a poetry series in the 1970s and 80s, Chariot Poets, whose authors included Helen Shaw, Olive Bentley, Tony Rowe, Ithell Colquhoun, and Frederic Vanson.

Poetry, articles on poetry, and reviews, especially reflecting the editor's concern with magic, ancient Britain, and Arthurian legend. Poets in the first few years included Geoffrey Holloway, Olive McAllan, Peter Redgrove, Robert Nye, J. Phoenice, W. Price Turner, Raymond Tong, Hugh Creighton Hill, Edward Storey, and others. Ratcliffe espoused a 'neo-pagan' approach to life in general, as witnessed by his editorials and other prose interventions. Later catch-phrases were "The magazine which remembers the island of Britain and those who first came to it" and "For Arthur's Britain". No. 9 includes "The Poet in the imaginary prop-loft" by Derek Stanford, an article arguing against Donald Davie's allegedly over-sophisticated approach to understanding poetry. No. 28 was a special issue devoted to the late nineteenth century poet W. E. Henley. No. 30 is a Brian Louis Pearce special issue. Frederic Vanson contributed to many of the later issues which also included work by Penelope Shuttle, Jay Ramsay, James Kirkup, William Oxley, Margaret Toms, Jenny Johnson, Ian Caws, Raymond Tong, Geoffrey Holloway, Ithell Colquhoun, Rupert M. Loydell, Stephen C. Middleton, and Kenneth Steven. The last issue included work by John Greening, Peter Russell, Angela Topping, Jon Silkin, Steve Sneyd, and others. Publication was suspended between no. 10 (1959) and no. 11 (1968).

BL: 1 (1954)–9 (1959). (P.P.5126.fab). 21; 22; 27–32. (P.901/3181)
CUL: 15 (1971)–? (L727.B.158)
NLS: Lacking: 26; 29; 35; 40. (HP.med.355 PER)
UCL: 4–50.
Poetry Library: 1; 20; 22–24; 28–30; 32–34; 36–50

74 Oxford Left / edited by Stanley Mitchell, then Phyllis Kline, Gabriel Pearson and Ralph Samuel. Oxford: Oxford University Socialist Club, [1953?]–[195–]. Then, [New series], No. [1] (Michaelmas 1965)–9 (1969)

As it suggests, a socialist student magazine. Poetry and articles on poetry were published, however, and contributors included: Geoffrey Richman, Anthony Thwaite, Jim Fitton, Gabriel Pearson, A. N. Kaul, and Adrian Mitchell. The latter also contributed an article on "Poetry and Society" and Gabriel Pearson contributed a response to it in the same issue (Michaelmas 1954). The New Series was published under the auspices of the renamed Oxford University Socialist Group and was much more of a politics-focused magazine.

BL: Michaelmas [ie Autumn] 1953, Hilary [i.e. Spring] 1954, Michaelmas 1954. (ZA.9.a.6661). New Series, [1]–4. (P.701/48)
London School of Economics: New Series, [1]–6. (Main collection, HX3); also, New Series, 2–9. (Reserve Periodicals, LB3610)

75 Oxford Opinion: art, literature, music, poems, philosophy, politics, travel / edited by Ian Downing; and others. Oxford: [Oxford Opinion], [Vol. 1. no. 1, 1955–no. 46, 1961]. New Series, No. 1 [Autumn 1965]–4 [Summer 1966]

Note: Volume numbering ceases after vol. 4 no. 11 (Mar. 1960), the next issue being no. 38 (30th Apr. 1960); no. 45 was a joint issue with *Granta*
BL: [Vol. 1] no. 4 (25 Oct. 1956)–vol. 3 no. 6 (22 Nov. 1958)–no. 45. New Series, No. 1–4. (P.P.6118.ke)
CUL: Vol. 4 no. 4–vol. 4 no. 11; no. 39–[46]. (L985.B.93)
NLS: Vol. 4 no. 4–no. 44. (6.1186)

76 Pawn / edited by John Blackwood; Charles Harrison; Christopher Dougherty, Clive Wilmer; Leslie Bell and Robert Wells; Kevin Stratford and Charles Nicholl. Cambridge: [Pawn, c/o King's College], No. 1 (1956)–39 (1972)

Note: Several issues are unnumbered

Poems, often by those who went on to be better known in other fields, e.g. Angus Calder, Jenni Daiches, Alexis Lykiard, Howard Brenton, Clive Wilmer, Terry Eagleton, Clive James, Richard Burns, Simon Jervis, and others.

BL: 17 (Nov. 1960), March 1961, 21 (Mar. 1962), Michaelmas 1962, Easter 1963, 28 (May 1965), 33 (Lent 1967), 36 (Summer 1969). (ZA.9.a.4737)
CUL: CAM.C.72.28
UCL

77 PEN in Exile / edited by T. Zavalani. London: P.E.N. Centre for Writers in Exile, No. 1 [1954?]–27/28 (October 1960)

Note: Related to *Arena* (1961–1967): produced by the same organisation and probably *Arena*'s predecessor
Anthology: P. Tabori (ed.) *The Pen in Exile* (London: International P.E.N. Club Centre for Writers in Exile, 1954), BL: 12299.ee.33; and P. Tabori (ed.) *The Pen in Exile: a second anthology* (International P.E.N. Club Centre for Writers in Exile, 1956), BL: 12300.cc.17

BL: 25–27/28. (PP.7615.ir)

78 Perspectives / edited by James Laughlin, then Lionel Trilling, then Jacques Barzan, then Malcolm Cowley, then R. P. Blackmur, etc. London: Hamish Hamilton, No. 1 (Autumn 1952)–16 (Summer 1956). ISSN: 0553–7495

Index: Index to whole series published with final number
Related Imprint: Intercultural Publications published a number of Perspective anthologies on different countries around the world, e.g. Carleton Sprague Smith (ed.), *Perspective of Brazil* [1956], BL: X.802/3856.(5). They also published *The Atlantic Monthly*.

Made possible by a grant from the Ford Foundation to promote American culture, this British edition of the American general arts journal was lavish for a literary publication: elegant understated typography and design, black and white and colour illustration, and many of the distinguished U.S. critics and writers of the day contributed, including William Faulkner, William Carlos Williams, Marianne Moore, and many others. Each was edited by a single editor but Laughlin acted as managing publisher-editor within the U.S. firm of Intercultural Publications. Literary rather than little.

BL: P.P.6392.eci.
CUL: L900.C.313
NLS: NJ.710 PER
UCL: No. 1–2

79 Phoenix. Edinburgh: George Watson's College Literary Club, Summer 1950–[1974?]

BL: P.P.6203.bin.

80 Phoenix: a poetry magazine / edited by Harry Chambers; and others. Liverpool: [Phoenix], No. 1 (1959)–11 (Winter 1964). New series, No. 1 (Mar. 1967)–13 (Spring 1975). ISSN: 0031–8345

Poems and reviews, with a focus on the quieter, formally conservative poets, e.g. Seamus Heaney and Philip Larkin. In the new series the first issue was devoted to the new Ulster poets, such as Heaney and Michael Longley, no. 5 was devoted to American poetry and no. 11/12 was a special Philip Larkin issue.

BL: 8 (Autumn 1962)–11 (Winter 1964); New Series, 1–13. (P.901/1493)
NLS: New Series, No. 1 (6.1937). New Series 3–13. (NH.589 PER)
UCL: 6 (1961)–11 (Winter 1964). New Series, 1–13
Poetry Library: New Series, 1; 3–13

81 Platform / edited by Frederick Woods. London: [Platform], No. 1 [Spring 1953]–4 [Autumn 1955]

Related Imprint: Platform Poets was a series that published at least one (untitled) collection, by E. L. Mayo, c.1954, BL: X.950/37423. Not to be confused with the Platform Poets series of the 1970s.

Poems included those by Maureen Duffy, W. Price Turner, Bernard Bergonzi (who was also associate editor), Christopher Goodwin, E. L. Mayo, G. S. Fraser, Elizabeth Jennings, Robert Garioch, Paul Valéry (trans. Charles Higham), William Carlos Williams, Sydney Goodsir Smith, Peter Russell, Kingsley Amis, Philip Larkin, Alan Brownjohn, and Norman MacCaig, as well as reprinted poems (E. E. Cummings, Wallace Stevens). Nicholas Moore contributes an article in no. 3, "John Peale Bishop and the classic virtues".

BL: P.P.5126.bna.
CUL: L727.C.181
NLS: 1950.58
UCL: No. 3–4

82 Poems in Pamphlet / edited by Erica Marx. Aldington, Kent: Hand & Flower Press, No. 1–12 (1951); no. 1–12 (1952)

Anthology: Barry Newport (ed.) *A Hand and Flower anthology: poems and fables commemorating Erica Marx and the Hand and Flower Press* (No place or publisher given, 1980), BL: YA.1991.a.18158
Related Imprint: The Hand & Flower Press published

fiction and drama as well as poetry, the latter including collections by Muriel Spark, Michael Hamburger, and Joseph Chiari, and *Beowulf* (trans. Edwin Morgan)

Each monthly issue published the work of usually one poet only, building up to a yearly anthology. In the first year the poets included: Gwyneth Anderson, Robert Waller, Charles Tomlinson, Peter Russell, John Alden, Charles Higham, Arthur Constance, Rob Lyle, Charles Causley, John O'Hare, Thomas Blackburn, and Robert Manfred. In the second year the poets included: Frederick Pratt Green, Arthur Joseph Bull, Michael Hamburger, Juanita Peirse, Frederic Vanson, R. L. Cook, Alan Barnsley, Ursula Wood, Richard Heron Ward, and Jocelyn Brooke.

BL: P.P.5126.bbt.
CUL: L727.D.60

83 The Poet / [edited by W. Price Turner]. Glasgow: Venture, No. 1 [1952]–15 (1956)

Anthology: [W. Price Turner, ed.?] *A Venture of Poets*, Glasgow: Venture, [1952] (BL: 11606.aaa.17); W. Price Turner (ed.), *Eleven Scottish Poets: a contemporary selection* (Glasgow: The Poet, 1954)
Related Imprint: The Poet also published the Poet Cameo Series, which published collections by Eric Nixon (*Statements of Love*, [1956], BL: W.P.3658), Gael Turnbull (*A Libation*), and Hyacinthe Hill (*Promethea*).

Poets included: Derek Stanford, Tom Wright, Sydney Tremayne, E. E. Cummings (reprinted from another magazine, but with a new appreciation of his poetry by Price Turner), Margaret Crosland, John Atkins, Kathleen Raine, Anne Ridler, Hugh Creighton Hill, W. S. Merwin, John Heath-Stubbs, Kenneth Patchen, Bernard Bergonzi, Geoffrey Holloway, Norman Nicholson, Iain Crichton Smith, Karen Loewenthal, Cid Corman, Gordon Wharton (issue 8 was entirely given over to his work), Francis Scarfe, Carol Hogben, J. F. Hendry, Robinson Jeffers, Tom Buchan, Norman MacCaig, Merrill Moore (issue 10 was entirely given over to Moore's work), Edwin Morgan, Donald Davie, Eric Ratcliffe, Charles Edward Eaton, Gael Turnbull, J. Phoenice, Roy Fisher, Robert Creeley, Laurie Lee, Donald Hall, William Carlos Williams, and Burns Singer. Reviews were issued as a separate supplement to the magazine.

BL: P.P.5126.bbz
CUL: L727.D.81
UCL: No. 3, 7
Poetry Library: No. 8

84 Poetry / edited by Hardiman Scott. Birmingham: The British Poetry Association, [Vol. 1 no. 1 (1950)?–1951?]

The BPA appears to have been a rival to the Poetry Society, and *Poetry* was its house magazine. James Brockway, in Görtschacher 2, suggests that Howard Sergeant helped found it in reaction to Muriel Spark's departure from *The Poetry Review*. Brockway, then living in Holland, contributed Dutch poems in translation. Location varied: advertisements from different sources suggest London, Liverpool, Petersfield, and Birmingham.

CUL: Vol. 2 no. 8 (1951), vol. 3 no. 9 (1951), no. 11 (1951). (L999.C.3.297)

85 Poetry & Audience. Leeds: University of Leeds Student Union, [Vol. 1 no. 1] (30 April 1954)– . ISSN: 0032–2040

Anthology: A. R. Mortimer and James Simmons (eds.), *Out on the edge* (Leeds: [University of Leeds Department of English Literature], 1958), BL: YA.1995.a.22540; A. R. Mortimer [et al.] (eds.) *Poetry and Audience, 1953–1960: an anthology*. [Leeds: University of Leeds Student Union, 1961], BL: 11663.i.3.; *Leeds Undergraduate Poetry from the First Ten Years of Poetry & Audience*. (Leeds: [University of Leeds Student Union], 1963), BL: X.908/4381; Tom Wharton and Wayne Brown (eds.), *21 years of Poetry & Audience* (Breakish: Aquila, 1976), BL: X.908/40673
Related Imprint: The Poetry & Audience Pamphlet imprint published at least one collection, by Brian Oxley, *Poems*, [1967?], BL: YA.2003.b.3781

In the early years, usually edited for an academic year by a single editor. In the first eight years these included James Simmons, A. R. Mortimer, T. W. Harrison (i.e. Tony Harrison), and Desmond Graham. From vol. 33 no. 1 [1991?] published by the Leeds University Poetry Society.

BL: Lacking: [Vol. 1.] no. 1–14; vol. 1 no. 20; vol. 2. no. 10, 18, 20–22; vol. 3. no. 1, 5, 10–12, 14–16, 18, 24, 25; vol. 4. no. 2, 4, 5, 9, 10, 14, 17; vol. 5. no. 1–5, 7; vol. 6 no. 23; vol. 7 no. 5, vol. 11 no. 7, vol 11 nos. 13–17, vol 13 no. 14, no. 19, vol. 14 nos. 6–9, no. 14, and all to vol. 29 no. 1 except vol. 15 no. 2. (P.P.5126.nag)
CUL: Vol. 5(21), 1958– .(L727.B.35)
NLS: Lacking: Vol. 11 no. 1, 11, 17; vol. 13 no. 19; vol. 14 no. 3; all between vol. 14 no. 5–vol. 16 no. 1; vol. 16 no. 8; vol. 17 no. 13; vol. 19 no. 2; vol. 19 no. 7; vol. 20 no. 4–vol. 21 no. 1; vol. 21 no. 4–vol. 28 no. 1; all between vol. 29 no. 1–vol. 31 no. 1; vol. 33 1991. (HJ8.1204 PER)
UCL: [Vol. 1] no. 7– . Incomplete.
Poetry Library: Vol. 17 no. 2; vol. 20 no. 9; vol. 21 no. 1–vol. 22 no. 5; vol. 23 no. 2–4; vol. 27 no. 3; vol. 28 no. 2–3; vol. 30 no. 1; vol. 31 no. 1; vol. 32 no. 1–[2?]; vol. 35 no. 1– .

86 Poetry Broadsheets / Cambridge: Poetry Broadsheets, No. 1 (Feb. 1951)–?

Index: 6 (July 1951) contains an index for the preceding issues

BL: 2 (Mar. 1951), 6 (Jul. 1951)–10 (Nov. 1951). (ZD.9.b.54)

87 Poetry London-New York / edited by Tambimuttu. New York, Vol. 1 no. 1 (Mar./Apr. 1956)–no. 4 (Summer 1960)

Note: Continues: *Poetry (London)*. Continued by: *Poetry London / Apple Magazine*.

Tambimuttu's New York continuation of his earlier London title, included here for its association. Two decades later it would be resurrected in another form, even briefer than this one.

BL: P.P.7615.ma
UCL: Vol. 1 no. 1–no. 3

88 Poetry Manchester / edited by Doreen Taylor, Brian Wright, Peter Robins and Harry Webster. Leigh: Poetry Manchester, [No. 1] (Autumn 1951)–5 [1953]. ISSN: 0477–0951

Note: Editors change over the course of the run Anthology: Doreen Taylor and Brian Wright (eds.), *Poetry Manchester* (Leigh: Poetry Manchester, 1951), BL: 11606.bb.16.

Poetry by Robin Skelton, Norman Nicholson, James Kirkup, Eric Nixon, Kathleen Raine, Peter Russell, Gordon Wharton, Jon Silkin, John Heath-Stubbs, and others. Peter Russell contributes an essay on Edith Sitwell in the first issue.

BL: [1]–[2]; 4–5. (P.P.5126.bca)
CUL: [1]–[2]; 5. (L999.C.3.112)
NLS: 6.739
UCL: [2]; 4–5

89 Poetry Midlands. Derby: [1950?]

Listed in *Trace*.
No holdings known.

90 Poetry of the Soho Festival. [London]: Soho Association, [1], 1955

Note: Variant title: *Poetry Broadsheet Soho Fair*
BL: YA.2003.a.37328

91 Poetry Periodical / edited by Irene Coates. Cambridge: Irene Coates, No. 1 (Autumn 1952)–3 (Summer 1953)

"*Poetry Periodical* has come into being because of the need for a magazine which will publish more forthright, satirical, or experimental poetry than is in vogue at the present day." Poems by Ted Waring, John Holmstrom, K. W. Gransden, Peter Daw, Alan Fowles, Frederick Woods, Todja Tartschoff (trans. Leopold Sirombo), Gordon Wharton, Peter Craig Raymond, James Boyer May, David Stacton, Lucien Stryk, Marion Deschamps, Norman Helm, Derek Maynard, Robert Ivy, Evathia Mowle, Enes Ramos, Keith M. Sagar, Victor Musgrave, Anthony Bailey, Glynne Hughes, Rosamund Stanhope, Alec Craig, Rodney Banister, Seymour Gresser, and the editor.

BL: P.P.5126.bcc.
CUL: Periodicals Depts

92 The Poetry Year Book / edited by G. B. Spencer and P. B. Godfrey Bartram. London: Citizen, 1958

Intended as an annual to encourage a greater readership for unknown poets, but appears to have failed after first volume. Two poems are tributes to Ezra Pound and Sydney Keyes respectively.

BL: P.P.5126.nae.

93 Promenade / edited by Ben Howard. Cheltenham, 195–?

Most significant for no. 65, which is entirely by W. S. Graham and includes his own drawings and prose work. It is bound with no. 66 (which is mainly about W. S. Graham).

BL: 65–66. (Pressmark Pending)
NLS: 65–66. (6.1579)

94 Prospect / edited by Elaine Feinstein, then Tony Ward, then Jeremy Prynne. Cambridge: [Prospect], [No. 1] (Summer 1959)–[6] [1964]

A magazine that could be seen as an early Cambridge School journal. Friendly towards American experimental poetry, publishing e.g. Paul Blackburn, Charles Olson, Lawrence Ferlinghetti, Ed Dorn, and Arthur Freeman, it also published short stories by Harold Pinter, Tony Ward, and Robert Creeley, and poems by Denise Levertov, Charles Tomlinson, Donald Davie, Desmond McCarthy, Jeremy

Prynne, and others. Donald Davie also contributes, e.g. an article on the problems of The Movement, and Prynne's essay "Resistance and Difficulty" is published here for the first time.

BL: P.P.7616.pz.
CUL: L727.C.271
NLS: 5. (DJ.m.442(5) PER)
UCL
Poetry Library: [1?]

95 Q / edited by H. A. Barrington and Victor Price; and, later, others. Belfast: Students' Representative Council of the Queen's University of Belfast, No. 1 (Michaelmas 1950)–[no. 19?, 1960?]

Note: Continued as: Q Review
Profiled in: Tom Clyde, Irish Literary Magazines: an outline and descriptive bibliography (Dublin: Irish Academic Press, 2003), BL: 2725.g.3414

Trundling cheerfully along with only occasional surprises, e.g. under the editorship of T. Alan Bennett, no. 7 (Michaelmas 1952), at which point a couple of translations from Prévert appeared (trans. A. W. Burrowes) and Philip Larkin contributed a book review. Larkin would later contribute poems and an assessment of Betjeman's poetry (all in no. 11, Hilary 1955, edited by Wesley Burrowes), and contributors would also include John Hewitt. Betjeman, returning Larkin's compliment, reviewed The Less Deceived in no. 14 (Hilary 1957). Hilary is the second term (January to March) in the old academic year.

BL: 1–11 (Hilary 1955). (P.P.6180.cgc)

Linen Hall Library, Belfast

96 Q Review. Belfast: [Students' Representative Council of the Queen's University of Belfast, No. 1, 1960?–1961?]

Note: Continues: Q. Because of the doubt over the start date, and its continuation of Q, this title has been placed in this section rather than a later one.
Profiled in: Tom Clyde, Irish Literary Magazines: an outline and descriptive bibliography (Dublin: Irish Academic Press, 2003), BL: 2725.g.3414

Linen Hall Library, Belfast

97 Quarto: a quarterly broadsheet of new poetry / edited by James Reeves. Dorchester: Friary Press for Quarto, No. 1 (Spring 1951)–8 (Winter 1952). ISSN: '

0481–2220

Published solely poetry, including Norman Cameron, Donald Davie, Martin Seymour-Smith, Robert Graves, F. T. Prince, Lynette Roberts, Elizabeth Jennings, Charles Madge, Michael Hamburger, D. J. Enright, and Donald Hall.

BL: P.P.5126.bbw.
CUL: L999.b.1.24
NLS: P.la.1339 PER
TCD: 147.a.67, Nos.1–8
Poetry Library: 1, 3, 5, 7–8

98 Quixote / edited by Jean Rikhoff Hills and others. Cornwall-on-Hudson, New York State, and Stockton Heath, Cheshire: Quixote, No. [1] (Spring 1954)–24/25 (Winter/Spring 1960)

Short fiction, a little poetry, and some essays on aspects of general culture. Despite the two locations, essentially a US magazine that was just printed for the most part in England. From 1959 published in the United States only. An account of the magazine's demise, involving the printer moving from England to Gibraltar, is given in the last issue. Contributors of poetry included May Swenson, John Lucas, Charles Bukowski, Jerome Rothenberg, Ronald Tamplin, and others.

BL: [1]–3, 5–24/5. (P.P.5939.bhf)
CUL: L727.C.157

99 Review Fifty: a quarterly synthesis of poetry and prose / edited by Edmund Cooper. Botesdale, via Diss, Norfolk, [No. 1] Winter 1950–[3] (Summer/Autumn 1951)

Short fiction, poems and reviews. Poets included: R. L. Cook, Friedrich Hölderlin (trans. Vernon Watkins), Gunnar Ekelöf (trans. Bertil Lange and Terence Heywood), Bernard Bergonzi, Joseph Joel Keith, Eric Nixon, Lionel Monteith, Iris Birtwistle, Mervyn Levy, Gilbert Phelps, Howard Sergeant, Marjorie Boulton, Vernon Watkins, J. M. Calder, Takis Hagipanayotis (trans. Mabel and Terence Heywood), Anthony Garwood, T. H. Jones, Clarence Alva Powell, Phoebe Hesketh, Kenneth Lawrence Beaudoin, Antony Borrow, Lucile Coleman, Edmund Cooper, Jack Dalglish, Charles Duranty, Martin S. Dworkin, D. E. Edgley, Howard Griffin, Ralph Houston, Henny Kleiner, S. E. Laurila, W. McDermott, John Barron Mays, Philip Murray, E. H. Ray, Bernard Raymund, Peter Robins, Hardiman Scott, Raymond Tong, and Anne Turner.

BL: P.P.5126.gcc.
UCL

100 Reynard: the magazine of the Quaker Fellowship of the Arts / edited by Katharine M. Wilson, and others. Reading: The Gower Press, Vol. 1 no. 1 (Sept. 1955)–? .

Note: Each issue received a running number independent of its volume and issue number, and later issues were designated only by a date
Related Imprint: The Quaker Fellowship of the Arts published occasional collections, such as the anonymously edited anthology of poems by older poets, *Vintage Voices* (South Croydon, [1977]), BL: X.909/41963

A Quaker magazine, which publishes poetry, fiction, and arts articles. Contributors include: Christopher Fry, Laurence Housman, Laurence Lerner, Katherine Herbert, and others.

BL: P.P.5939.cbh.
CUL: 32 (1978)–[34]; [44] (1990). (L400.c.566)
NLS: Lacking: 1961, 1962, 1963, 1965, 1966, Winter 1968/69, 1979–1980. (P.sm.3420 SER)
UCL: Vol. 2 no. 1–vol. 3 no. 2; 1959; 1964–1967; Spring 1968; Winter 1968/69; Autumn 1969; 23–30, 32, 1979–1980

Rooster *See* New Rooster C65

101 Saint Botolph's Review / edited by David Ross. Cambridge, [No. 1], 1956

Profiled in: Elaine Feinstein, *Ted Hughes: the life of a poet* (London: Weidenfeld & Nicolson, 2001), BL: YC.2002.a.11716

A magazine with a significance far beyond its pages. It was named after the rectory outside college limits where a small number of undergraduates and others associated with Cambridge University took lodgings. Several of Hughes's poems were included in the only issue of the magazine, and it was at the launch of the *Review* on 26th February 1956 that Hughes first met Sylvia Plath. The other contributors were Daniel Huws, Daniel Weissbort, George Weissbort, David Ross, and Lucas Myers. A commemorative issue was published in 2006.

CUL: Cam.c.211.40
UCL

102 Saltire Review: of arts, letters and life / edited by Alexander Scott, and others. Edinburgh: The Saltire Society, Vol. 1 no. 1 (April 1954)–vol. 6 no. 23 (Winter 1961)

Note: Continued by: *New Saltire*. The issue numbering is

consecutive, so that vol. 6 no. 23 is the twenty-third issue of the whole run
Profiled in: Sullivan 1914–1984

A general cultural review, with a strong interest in poetry, publishing poems and articles about poetry. Many of the Scottish writers of the day and of later days appear in its pages including Edwin Muir, Sydney Goodsir Smith, Tom Scott, Burns Singer, Joseph Macleod, R. Crombie Saunders, Robert Garioch, Alan Riddell, Edwin Morgan, Norman McCaig, Naomi Mitchison, Alexander Scott, George Bruce, Hugh MacDiarmid, William Montgomerie, Maurice Lindsay, W. Price Turner, Alexander Reid, Iain Crichton Smith, Derick Thomson, Sydney Tremayne, Robin Fulton, and others. Includes signficant literary criticism by Edwin Morgan on Scottish poetry.

BL: Lacking: Vol. 2 no. 1– vol. 3 no. 6. Ac.9945.b/2.
CUL: L727.C.160
NLS
Poetry Library: 10–11; 13; 16; 18–19; 22

103 Samovar: the magazine of the Joint Services School for Linguists / [edited by Michael Frayn, Eric Korn and others]. Bodmin, then Crail: Joint Services School for Linguists, No. 7 (April 1954)–25 [1959]

Note: Continues: *Teapot and Samovar*, and takes up its numbering. No. 15 was not published. No. 16 was published in Crail, Scotland
Profiled in: D. M. Thomas's introduction, *Secret Classrooms: An Untold History of the Cold War*, by Geoffrey Elliott and Harold Shukman (London: St Ermin's Press, 2002), BL: YC.2002.a.20997

The Joint Services School was designed to meet the Cold War challenge by teaching British servicemen Eastern Bloc languages, especially Russian. Alan Bennett, D. M. Thomas, Michael Frayn, and Eric Korn went through the School as part of their National Service. It usually appeared in Cyrillic, although there were also Czech and Polish poems in at least one issue. D. M. Thomas recalled that it "served up an eclectic diet of gentle mockery, short stories, anecdotes, reviews and essays on topics from the learned to the seriously abstruse." In Russian, the title is written *Самовар*. *Teapot and Samovar*, [1] (Whitsun 1952)–2 (July 1952), is held by the British Library and shelved with *Samovar*.

BL: 7; 9–11; 14; 16; 18–25. (ZA.9.a.11851)

104 **Scorpion** / edited by Ian Hamilton. Darlington: Ian Hamilton, [No. 1–2, c.1954.]

Interview: Dan Jacobson interviews Ian Hamilton in *London Review of Books*, 24th January 2002.

Edited by Hamilton as an anti-school magazine, the school being Darlington Grammar School. The first issue had a foreword by John Wain. Noted in the *London Review of Books* interview.
No holdings known.

105 **S.D.'s Review** / edited by Sean Dorman. [Fowey?]: [Sean Dorman?], [1959–196?]

Note: Continued by: *Writing Published*

The predecessor of a number of magazines, *Writing Published*, *Writing*, and *Writers News*, which encouraged co-operation among writers, self-help, and published short fiction and poems of an unassuming kind.
No holdings known.

105a **Seed** / edited by Peter Ferguson and Liam Hudson. Oxford, [1?, 1955]–?

Contributors include: Dannie Abse, Oliver Sacks, Peter Levi, Christopher Levenson, and Alan Bennett

BL: [1?. 1955]. (Pressmark pending)

106 **Sky-Line** / edited by Derek Townsend. Tipton: Edition 1 (Feb/April 1955)

Short fiction, a few poems, jokes, plans for an agony column and children's page. Popular in tone, but seems not to have survived first issue. Poems by Eric James, Mary Ward, Joyce Dunkley, and Clare Withers.

BL: P.P.5938.cax

St. Botolph's Review *See* Saint Botolph's Review C101

107 **Stand** / edited by Jon Silkin, and others. Newcastle upon Tyne, and other locations: [Stand], [Vol. 1] no. 1 (1952)–vol. 40 no. 2 (Spring 1999). New series, Vol. 1 no. 1 (Mar. 1999)– . ISSN: 0038–9366, for years 1952–1983. From 1983, ISSN: 0952–648X

Note: Absorbed: *3 Arts Quarterly* and *North East Arts Review*.
Title variant: From 1983 entitled *Stand Magazine*

Index: Sader (Vol. 1 (1952)–11 (1970) only)
Profiled in: Görtschacher 1, Sullivan 1914–1984
Interview: with Jon Glover, Matthew Welton and John Whale, in *Poetry News: the Newsletter of the Poetry Society*, Winter 2002/3, p.8
Anthology: Jon Silkin (ed.) *Poetry of the Committed Individual: a Stand anthology of poetry* (London: Gollancz, 1973), BL: X.989/20509
Reprint: New York: Johnson Reprint, [undated] (Vols. 1–12 only)

Poems, short fiction and reviews. Special issues include: vol. 4 no. 3, The War Poets; vol. 7 no. 2, East European Issue; vol. 22 no. 2, In Memory of Nadezhda Mandelstam; vol. 23 no. 3, Modern Norwegian Writing; vol. 23 no. 4, Christina Stead: a celebration; vol. 33 no. 3: New African Writing. When Jon Silkin died in 1997, *Stand* continued for two years under the co-editorship of Rodney Pybus and Lorna Tracy before being relaunched and edited by John Kinsella and Michael Hulse, basing it at the University of Leeds. Following in turn their departure, Jon Glover became editor. Others involved editorially have been: Gordon Wharton, T. Heaton, Jack Kohn, Stanley Chapman, Gene Baro, Ken Smith, Tony Harrison, Catherine Lamb, Merle Brown, Michael Blackburn, Brendan Cleary, Evangeline Paterson and others.

BL: [Vol. 1] no. 2 (1952)– . (P.P.5938.cau)
CUL: [Vol. 1] no. 3 (1952)– . (L727.C.193)
NLS: HJ4.1328
UCL
Poetry Library: [Vol. 1] no. 2–3; [vol. 2]–vol. 4 no. 1, 3; vol. 5 no. 3; vol. 6 no. 2, 4; vol. 7 no. 1–2, 4; vol. 10 no. 2; vol. 11 no. 1, 3; vol. 12 no. 1–vol. 35 no. 2; vol. 37 no. 1–vol. 38 no. 4; vol. 39 no. 3–vol. 40 no. 2; New Series: vol. 1 no. 1, 3; vol. 2 no. 1– .

108 **Suppose Pig Walk.** West Worthing: Fantasma, [No. 1, 1950]

Apparently only one issue published, edited anonymously. An 'open forum' of pre-election political comment. Includes a little poetry by Claude Len O'Shea, and J. Halsen. Typewritten format.

BL: P.P.5939.bhd

The Teapot and Samovar *See* The Samovar C103

109 **Thames** / edited by Arthur Hammond, then Michael Craton, then Bryan Johnson and Muriel Starkey. London: The University of London Literary Society, [Vol. 1 no. 1]

(1953)–no. 2 (1954); Then, London: King's College Literary Society, [no. 3] (1958)

Poems only. Contributors included Frank Lissauer, Maureen Duffy, the Polish poet Cyprian Norwid (trans. Adam Czerniawski), and Gordon Wharton. Maureen Duffy was the assistant editor for the second issue.

BL: P.P.5126.gch
UCL: Vol. 1 no. 1–no.2

110 The Threshold / edited by Alec Smith. Mytholmroyd, Yorkshire (printed by Lawrence Warner, Hinckley): Alec Smith, No. 1 [1952].

The apparently sole issue had poems by Kuo Ching Té (trans. John Brun), R. L. Cook, Charles Duranty, Albert Greenwood, Geoffrey Johnson, Joseph Joel Keith, John Barron Mays, Eric Nixon, Cecily Pile, and Alan Smith.

BL: P.P.5126.bby

111 Threshold / edited by Mary O'Malley; poetry editor: John Hewitt; and others. Belfast: The Lyric Players, Vol. 1 no. 1 (Feb. 1957)–no. 38 (1987). ISSN: 0040–6562

Note: After Vol. 5 no. 1, numeration changes form to no. 18, 19, etc.
Index: Hayes
Selected contents are listed by EirData (http://www.pgil-eirdata.org).
Profiled in: Tom Clyde, *Irish Literary Magazines: an outline and descriptive bibliography* (Dublin: Irish Academic Press, 2003), BL: 2725.g.3414

General literary review, with Ulster focus. John Boyd edited from 1971.

BL: Vol. 1 no. 1–4, vol. 2 no. 1–4, vol. 3 no. 1–4, vol. 4 no. 1–2, vol. 5 no.1, no. 18 (1964)–no. 26 (Autumn 1975), no. 28 (Spring 1977)–no.32 (Winter 1982), no. 34 (Winter 1983/84)–no.36 (Winter 1985/86). (P.P.5196.hb)
CUL: L900.c.349
TCD: Lacking: Vol. 4 no. 1. (OLS L–2–189–192)
UCL: Vol. 1 no. 2–vol. 5 no. 1; vol. 5 no. 18–no.38

112 Tomorrow / edited by Ian Hamilton and Susil Pieris. Oxford: The Editors, No. 1 (June/July 1959)–4 [1960]. ISSN: 0495–8349

Interview: Dan Jacobson interviews Ian Hamilton in *London Review of Books*, 24th January 2002.

Contributors to this poetry review included: Roy Fuller, Michael Hamburger, Michael Horovitz, Roger McGough,

Christopher Middleton, Edwin Morgan, Ronald Duncan, D. J. Enright, Elizabeth Jennings, A. Alvarez, John Fuller, Francis Hope, Bernard Kops, Oscar Mellor, Richard Adams, Tayner Baybars, Thomas Blackburn, Alan Brownjohn, Caryl Churchill (a poem), Peter J. Dale, Harold Pinter (a short play), J. H. Prynne, Robin Skelton, and others. Susil Pieris co-edited for the first two issues, after which Hamilton edited alone.

BL: P.P.4881.sr
CUL: 2–3. (L727.C.247)
NLS: 5.6538
UCL: 2–4
Poetry Library: 1–3

113 The Transatlantic Review / edited by J. F. McCrindle. London and New York: Transatlantic Review, No. 1 (Summer 1959)–60 (1977). ISSN: 0041–1078

Drawings, prose, playscripts, and poetry. Eclectic, with work by Ted Hughes, C. Day Lewis, Robert Graves, Muriel Rukeyser, George Barker, Eugenio Montale, Austin Clarke, Jeni Couzyn, Stewart Conn, Maureen Duffy, Ruth Fainlight, Zulkifar Ghose, Giles Gordon, Jeff Nuttall, Lou Reed, Peter Redgrove, Vernon Scannell, D. M. Thomas, and others. Also involved editorially were Eugene Walter, Heathcote Williams and B. S. Johnson. Not to be confused with Ford Madox Ford's journal of 1924.

BL: P.P.7617.br.
CUL: P727.C.41
NLS: 2–60. (NJ.670 PER)
UCL
Poetry Library: 7–8; 10; 14–20; 22–23; 25–28; 30–35; 39–47; 49–50; 52–57

114 Trio / edited by John Bingham, George MacBeth and Anthony Thwaite. Oxford: No. 1 (1952)–7 (1955). ISSN 0493–9883.

Reprint: Nendeln, Lichtenstein: Kraus Reprint, 1972

A magazine that published the work of Oxford students. Contributors included Alan Brownjohn, Thom Gunn, Alistair Elliott, Jonathan Price, Adrian Mitchell, and others.

BL: 1–2; 5. (ZD.9.a.171)
CUL: L727.D.109
UCL

115 Troubadour / edited by Raymond Buxton, then Buxton and Mavis Heath-Miller, then Kennedy Williamson. London: The Writers' Guild, [No. 1, 1950–no. 4, 1955]

Poems only. Contributors included Lionel Monteith, Terence Heywood, R. L. Cook, Elizabeth Douglas, Kennedy Williamson, Henny Kleiner, and many others.

BL: [1]–[3]. (W.P.A.141)
CUL: L727.D.100
UCL

116 Tydfil: a Merthyr Tydfil miscellany / edited by John Fletcher and Harri Webb. Merthyr Tydfil: Eisteddfod Merthyr Tydfil A'r Cylch, No. 1 (Spring 1959)

A magazine linked to the Merthyr Tydfil Eistedfodd, publishing winning poems and prose but also offering itself as a "sounding board for the distinctive thoughts and voices of our community."

BL: P.P.4881.sck.

117 Umbrella / edited by W. F. Holland, then T. C. Watson, John F. West. Coventry: The Umbrella Club, Vol. 1 no. 1 (Oct. 1958)–vol. 2 no. 8 (Summer 1962)

The Umbrella Club was set up as "an independent, non-political, non-profitmaking organisation for encouraging interest in art, music, literature, the theatre and kindred subjects. It arranges lectures, recitals, dramatic performances and many related activities." The magazine was a general arts review with occasional poems, e.g. by Owen Leeming, George MacBeth, Ian [i.e. Yann] Lovelock, Bryan Johnson, Zulkifar Ghose, Vera Rich, Taner Baybars, Herbert Read, and others; other contributions included essays by John Hewitt, Philip Larkin, Zulkifar Ghose, and others.

BL: P.P.4881.scp.
CUL: L900.C.352

118 Universities' Poetry / edited by Bryan A. Reed and R. Bryan Tyson, and others. Keele: University College of North Staffordshire, 1 (March 1958)–7 (1965)

Profiled in: Sullivan 1914–1984

The intention was for this to be a representative sample of student poetry from the universities across England, Scotland, Northern Ireland and Wales, but from issue two onwards there was a strong English bias and arguably an Oxbridge influence, too. Poets included: Malcolm Bradbury, Meic Stephens, John McGrath, Pat Rogers, Bryan Johnson, Dom Moraes, John Fuller, Jon Silkin, W. Price Turner, Christopher Levenson, Angus Calder, Alexis

Lykiard, Derek Mahon, T. W. Harrison (i.e. Tony Harrison), Ken Smith, Peter Dale, Philip Hobsbaum, Ian Hamilton, Iain Sinclair (apparently his first published poem, 'Cockling' in no. 7), Angela Carter, Stephen Mulrine, Paul Merchant, and others. The other editors included: Zulkifar A. Ghose, Anthony Smith, John Fuller, Bryan Johnson, Edward Lambton, Andrew Roberts, Christopher Williams, Dax MacColl, Anthony Tillinghast, Clive Jordan, and Peter Redgrove.

BL: 1–4; 7. (P.P.5126.na)
CUL: 1–3. (L727.C.286)

119 Vril / edited by Michael Hales, then others. Old Windsor, Berkshire: Beaumont College Poetry Society, No. 1 (July 1956)–4 (July 1959)

Short fiction, articles on just about anything, and poems. The third issue declared that it was now the journal of the Quodlibetarian Society.

BL: P.P.5126.naa.

120 We Offer: prose and verse of the Poetry Guild / edited by John Hoffman and Joan Haddock, then John Hoffman with assistant editors. Chesterfield: The Guild Press, Vol. 1 no. 1 (Autumn 1951)–[1959?]. Then, New Series, Vol. 1 no. 1 (Jan/Mar. 1963)–no. 3 (July/Sept. 1963). ISSN: 0508–1858

Related Imprint: The Guild Press, imprint of the Poetry Guild, which also published the Guild Poets series of poetry pamphlets, and The Guild Broadsheets.

Contributors may have had to belong to the Poetry Guild itself, founded by John Hoffman in 1951, which was a "fellowship of men and women whose lives and talents are deciated, sensitively, sacramentally and humbly, to the apprehension and to the expression of the Greater Spirit." Contributors included Hugh Creighton Hill, on bridging the gap between The Prelude and The Pisan Cantos, and R. L. Cook, Edward Storey, Geoffrey Holloway, Helga Petersen, Vernon Scannell, John Hoffman, Roye McCoye, Brian L. Pearce, Phoebe Hesketh, and others.

BL: Vol. 1 no. 1–no. 3 (Spring 1953); vol. 2 no. 1 (Autumn 1953); vol. 4 no. 2 (Oct/Dec. 1958). New Series, Vol. 1 no. 1–no. 3. (P.P.5126.gca)
CUL: Vol. 1 no. 1–vol. 2 no. 1 (Autumn 1953). (L727.C.175)
UCL: Vol. 1 no. 1; New Series, Vol. 1 no. 3–4.

121 **Windfall** / [edited by R. L. Cook, Michael Levy, and George Kay]. [Edinburgh]: Poetry Society of the University of Edinburgh, No. 1 (June 1954).

Probably a one-off, this published poems by the editors, Alan Riddell, Antonia Sansica Scott, Kirsty Ross, Hamish Henderson, and others.

BL: YA.1989.a.9557
UCL

122 **The Window** / edited by John Sankey. London: Villiers Publications, No. 1 [1950]–9 [1956]

Related Imprint: Villiers published a number of single-author collections, including those by Joseph Chiari, W. Price Turner, and Jean Overton Fuller.

Poems and short reviews. Jean Andrews was also involved editorially. Contributors included: I. R. Orton, Margaret Crosland, Michael Hamburger, Terence Heywood, Nicholas Moore, Arthur Boyars, Eric Nixon, Harold Pinta (i.e. Harold Pinter), W. Price Turner, Robert Creeley (reprinted), Charles Olson (reprinted), Kay Johnson, John Heath-Stubbs, R. L. Cook, Martin Seymour-Smith, Vernon Scannell, Thomas Blackburn, Alan Brownjohn, A. J. Bull, Patricia Beer, Gael Turnbull, Roy Fisher, and others. No. 7 was a French number, with translations of René Char, Pierre Reverdy, Robert Desnos, Francis Ponge, and others, with translators including David Gascoyne, Michael Hamburger, Philip Inman, and James Kirkup. No. 8 was guest-edited by Philip Inman.

BL: Lacking: 8. (P.P.5126.bbp)
CUL: 2–9. (L727.C.169)
UCL
Poetry Library: 7–8

123 **Writing Today.** London: Villiers, No. 1 (July 1957)–12 (Mar. 1962). ISSN: 0509–3910
Profiled in: Sullivan 1914–1984

A general literary review, edited anonymously. Despite never extending beyond twelve pages and generally publishing poems that were reprints from recent collections it reviewed poetry collections (e.g. Peter Porter's appalled review of Judith Wright's anthology, *New Land, New Language*) and conducted profile-style interviews with John Betjeman, Roy Fuller, and Herbert Read. The magazine also carried general articles (such as Vernon Dodds on the effect of the contemporary paperback revolution on poetry, or Philip Hobsbaum on William Empson). The writers Bernard Bergonzi, Ann Thwaite, and A. C. [i.e. Alan] Brownjohn

were among the review contributors.

BL: P.P.5939.bhk
CUL: 11–12. (L999.C.3.187)
UCL

124 **X: a quarterly review** / edited by David Wright and Patrick Swift. London: Barrie and Jenkins, Vol. 1 no. 1 (Nov. 1959)–vol. 2 no. 3 (July 1962). ISSN: 0512–6576

Index: With vol. 1 only
Profiled in: Sullivan 1914–1984
Reprint: London: Barrie and Jenkins, 1961 (Vol. 1 only, with index); Nendeln, Liechtenstein: Kraus Reprint, [undated]

A general arts review, which, apart from its considerable interest in contemporary art and fiction, specialised in publishing longer examples of poets' work, often with links back to the early generations of modernists. *X* included work by Ezra Pound, Hugh MacDiarmid, Stevie Smith, George Barker, Patrick Kavanagh, Vernon Watkins, David Gascoyne, Samuel Beckett, C. H. Sisson, and Geoffrey Hill, as well as Robert Graves, Anthony Cronin, Robert Nye, Boris Pasternak, Martin Seymour-Smith, Malcolm Lowry, Nathaniel Tarn, Dannie Abse, Philippe Jaccottet, Dom Moraes, and others.

BL: P.P.5977.ae.
CUL: P727.B.11
UCL
Poetry Library: Vol. 1 no. 1–vol. 2 no. 1, 3. Note: vol. 1 no. 3 and vol. 2 no. 3 are reprints

125 **Zebra** / edited by Derek Maggs. Bristol: Derek Maggs, [Vol. 1] no. 1 (Jan. 1954)–vol. 2 no. 3 (Winter 1955/56)

Note: The magazine became quarterly with vol. 2
Related Imprint: Derek Maggs published collections in the Zebra Poets series by W. Price Turner, Derek Parker, Paul Casimir, Richard Easton.

Poetry, short fiction, literary articles. Contributors include: Denys Val Baker (on the need for Little Magazines), Derek Maggs (on the first issue of Lehmann's *London Magazine*), Brian Jones, W. Price Turner, Edward Storey, Roye McCoye, Eric Ratcliffe, Paul Casimir, Richard Easton, Derek Parker, Tom Wright, Eric Nixon, Hugh Creighton Hill, Ian Crichton Smith, John Manson, Geoffrey Holloway, Elizabeth Louch, Robert Nye, Raymond Tong, and others.

BL: P.P.5939.bhe
CUL: L727.c.154
UCL: Vol. 1 no. 6, 10–12; vol. 2 no. 1–no. 3
Poetry Library: Vol. 1 no. 8–vol. 2 no. 3

Chapter D: 1960–1975

The Sixties and After

THE 1960s SAW A RENEWED interest in the Modernism of poets such as Ezra Pound, Louis Zukofsky, Basil Bunting, David Jones, and Hugh MacDiarmid. These years also witnessed the growth of contemporary approaches stemming in part from the influence of these older poets, many of them (including those named above) still active, partly through interaction with recent American and, to a somewhat lesser extent, European poets. However, the seeds of these developments were sown in the 1950s by magazines such as John Sankey's *The Window* [1950–1956], Bob Cobbing and others' *And* (1954–), and Brocard Sewell's *The Aylesford Review* (1955–68). As Wolfgang Görtschacher has pointed out in *Little Magazine Profiles* (1993), a number of significant magazines that presaged the Sixties started in 1959, including *Agenda*, *New Departures*, *Migrant*, and *Ambit*. If Gael Turnbull's *Migrant* (1959–1960), an especially important bridge between contemporary American and British poetry, lasted only briefly, *Agenda*, *New Departures* and *Ambit* have all been long-term survivors, though arguably most important in their earlier years. *Agenda*, in particular, is significant for its championing of Modernist poets including Pound, Jones, MacDiarmid, Bunting, and Zukofsky, through various features and special issues in the 1960s and 1970s.

What is even more important to note is the greatly increased number of magazines in the 1960s disseminating the work of experimental or exploratory American and European poets – Black Mountain, New York School, and Concrete poets, amongst others – often alongside their British counterparts. By "exploratory" we can perhaps point to the tendency to explore the possibilities of the material medium of poetry, in relation to possibilities of imagination, thought, emotion and perception or, in some cases, primarily as an exploration of language itself. We can also point to a desire to discover and deal with the unfamiliar, in various ways. This tendency has usually been in distinction to working with conventional modes and forms. However, there has also been the possibility of working with, especially re-thinking, older forms, as with the sonnets of Edwin Denby, Ted Berrigan, and Bernadette Mayer – poets associated with the New York School. The terms "experimental" and "innovative" are more commonly used than "exploratory" – with considerable overlap, at least, even if the former terms are often employed with a more exclusive emphasis on formal experimentation.

Concrete poetry emerged most clearly in the early 1950s (though with some notable antecedents). It's possible to distinguish two main strands within Concrete poetry: a more minimalist or perhaps constructivist poetry, represented by Eugen Gomringer, Ian Hamilton Finlay, and the 'Noigandres' poets, and the often more maximalist approach of such visual poets as Carlfriedrich Claus, Bob Cobbing, Henri Chopin, and dom Sylvester Houédard. (Visual poets like Cobbing, Claus, and Chopin were also very involved with sound poetry.) These distinctions sometimes break down – Houédard, in particular, also produced some very spare poetry – but basically there is a reductive tendency (in a non-pejorative sense) on the one hand, and a much more expansive one on the other. Concrete poetry was truly international, with representatives in the UK, Brazil, Germany, Austria, France, Australia, the USA, and Mexico, amongst other places.

Working from a Scottish base, *Poor. Old. Tired. Horse* (1962–1967), under Ian Hamilton Finlay's editorship, published independent and distinctive American poets Robert Lax and Ronald Johnson, alongside the Brazilian 'Noigandres' poet Edgard Braga and the Austrian Concrete poet Heinz Gappmayr. Though strongly drawn towards poetry that was linked, in one way or another, to Concrete poetry, Finlay published various other poets, including Robert Creeley and Pete Brown, as well as the writings of the American abstract artists Ad Reinhardt and Charles Biederman,

Other magazines representing various aspects of Concrete poetry and related work included Henri Chopin's *OU* (196?–1974), Cavan McCarthy's *Tlaloc* (1964–70), Simon Cutts and Stuart Mills' *Tarasque* [1962/63–1972], Thomas A. Clark's *Bo heem e um* [1967–1968], Michael Gibbs' *Kontexts* (1969–76/77), Nicholas Zurbrugg's *Stereo Headphones* (1969–1982), and Dom Sylvester Houédard's *Kroklok* (1971–1973?). Again, it should be made clear that while *Stereo Headphones*, for example, maintained an emphasis on Concrete poetry, it also published a varied range of experimental or exploratory poetry and art in its later issues. The final issue, no. 8/9/10 (1982), included visual work by Barry McCallion with no connection to Concrete, as well as a text by Samuel Beckett and translations of the German poet Fredericke Mayröcker – alongside Henri Chopin and also Robert Lax.

Concrete poetry drew antagonism from various sources, including the editors of *Agenda*, William Cookson and Peter Dale. Cookson and Dale were equally hostile to Beat poetry and to at least some of the Black Mountain poets. Surprisingly, Ian Hamilton's magazine *The Review*, which especially promoted the poetry of Michael Fried, Colin Falck, Douglas Dunn, and David Harsent, devoted a feature in 1964 to Black Mountain poetry, guest edited by Charles Tomlinson. The issue brought together various poets associated with Robert Creeley's *Black Mountain Review*, including Charles Olson, Louis Zukofsky, Robert Duncan, Denise Levertov, Gary Snyder, Allen Ginsberg, Paul Blackburn, and Creeley himself. (Poets such as Olson, Duncan, and Creeley can be seen as affirming the modernism of Pound and William Carlos Williams, while developing their work in distinctive directions.) However, *The Review*'s editor, Ian Hamilton, found it prudent to state that "The editorial motive of *The Review* in this project has been a documentary rather than, necessarily, a critical one. We believe the movement ought at least to be known about."

This cautious attitude was not shared by an increasing number of magazines in the period, enthusiastically embracing innovative or exploratory US poetry, Black Mountain and New York School in particular. Tom Raworth's *Outburst* (1961–1963) was publishing Snyder, Creeley, Blackburn, Edward Dorn, and Philip Whalen, together with Gael Turnbull and Christopher Logue, and the singular poet Piero Heliczer. *New Departures*, principally edited by Michael Horovitz, in its earlier years gave attention to American Beat poetry, but together with a wider range of innovative writers, artists and composers, including Heliczer, Charles Olson, Robert Creeley, Stefan Themerson, George Brecht, and John Cage. *Resuscitator*, later more of a platform for the Cambridge School, included Zukofsky, Oppen, Creeley, Eigner, Snyder and others in its first series (1963–1966). Cambridge School magazines such as *The English Intelligencer* [1966–1968], Wendy Mulford's *The Anona Wynn* (1969) and John James's *The Norman Hackforth* [1969] put their main emphasis on a distinctive tendency (or network of tendencies) in English innovative poetry developing from the work of J.H. Prynne, Andrew Crozier, and others. The first series of The *English Intelligencer* was edited by Andrew Crozier, the second series by Peter Riley, and the third series by James, Crozier and J. H. Prynne. Peter Riley's *Collection* (1968–70) printed Cambridge

School poets alongside US poets (including Charles Olson, Jack Spicer, Robin Blaser, John Wieners, and Frank O'Hara) as well as Lee Harwood, Tom Raworth, and the Scottish poet Thomas A. Clark. The latter's namesake, the New York School poet Tom Clark, was another important source of UK/US interaction, through his involvement with *The Wivenhoe Park Review* (1965–1968) and his editorship of *Once* [1965?–1966?]. Tim Longville's *Grosseteste Review* (1968–1983/84) also promoted a confluence of US and UK poets, publishing Louis Zukofsky, Cid Corman, James Koller, Anthony Barnett, Roy Fisher, John Riley and Gael Turnbull, amongst others, as well as European poets in translation.

Controversially, *The Poetry Review* under Eric Mottram's editorship (1971–1977) became a focus for experimental or innovative poetry, with a strong emphasis on US as well as UK poets. *The Poetry Review*, as the official organ of The Poetry Society, had been (and would revert to being) a conservative literary journal, although Derek Parker had pursued an eclectic line and published Gael Turnbull and Anselm Hollo, as well as Concrete poetry, during his years as editor (1966–1970). Mottram's intense commitment to innovative poetic tendencies may have alienated some readers, but helped enormously in disseminating US poetry (of this kind) in particular. In retrospect, his editorship of the magazine has gained an almost legendary reputation.

Another editor who deserves special mention is the poet Lee Harwood. From around 1963 to 1969, Harwood edited or co-edited several important magazines, including *Night Scene* [1963?], *Night Train* (1964), *Horde* (1964), *Soho* (1964) and *Tzarad* (1965–1969). Harwood (with his collaborators) published Anselm Hollo, Harry Guest, Pete Brown, and Libby Houston, but he also brought attention to European poets. *Soho* was a bi-lingual magazine, co-edited by the French poet Claude Royet-Journoud, and included Michel Couturier, Alain Bosquet, Jean Fanchette, and others. *Tzarad* (which was incorporated with Peter Riley's *Collection* for its final two issues) had translations of Tzara, Reverdy, Cendrars, Apollinaire, Soupault, Hugo Ball, and Max Jacob in its pages, as well as poetry by John Ashbery, Dom Sylvester Houédard, Brian Patten, Paul Evans and Chris Torrance.

Julliard (1968–1972), edited by Trevor Winkfield, also included translations of French poets, such as Breton, Cendrars, Reverdy, and Michaux. Anthony Rudolf and Peter Hoy's *The Journals of Pierre Menard* (1969) and *The Notebooks of Pierre Menard* (1969–1970) focused on translation, including English versions of poems by Stramm, Pessoa, Char, Ponge, Paz, Takahashi, Pavese, and others.

The Menard Press, founded by Rudolf in 1969, has shown a similarly strong – though not exclusive – emphasis on poetry in English translation. Paul Buck's *Curtains* (1971–1978) explored contemporary French writing, often of a transgressive nature, as well as publishing innovative English-language poetry. In particular, *Curtains* made available work by Bataille, Blanchot, Noël, Jabès, Faye, and Deguy. More generally, *Modern Poetry in Translation*, which was started in 1966 by Daniel Weissbort and Ted Hughes, has published numerous special issues on non-English poetry from around the world in English translation. Anthony Barnett's *Nothing Doing in London* (1966–1968), with Claude Royet-Journoud as its editor for France, should also be mentioned here, as it published an interesting array of English, French and Portuguese texts (as well as music and artwork).

With a strong interest in publishing visual art and illustration, *Ambit*, principally edited by Martin Bax, has published a wide range of poets, including Jeff Nuttall, Jim Burns, Edwin Morgan, Henry Graham, Florence Elon, George MacBeth, Alan Brownjohn, and Gavin Ewart. Jon Silkin's strongly independent magazine *Stand* (1952–) also continued to publish a variety of poets, with Roy Fisher, Ronald Johnson, Frances Horovitz, and Ken Smith appearing alongside Michael Hamburger and Geoffrey Hill. More consistently concerned with exploratory poetry, though still eclectic, *Oasis* (1969–), principally edited by Ian Robinson, published an extraordinary number of fine poets, including Lee Harwood, Roy Fisher, Christopher Middleton, Peter Dent, David Chaloner, Alan Halsey, Brian Louis Pearce, Frances Presley, Yann Lovelock, Tony Lopez, Ken Edwards, and Robert Sheppard. Michael Schmidt and C. B. Cox's *Poetry Nation* (1973–1976), while mostly publishing more formally conservative poets, included essays on William Carlos Williams, Louis Zukofsky, and Roy Fisher, as well as poems by W. S. Graham, who was beginning to re-emerge as a significant figure in Scottish and British poetry.

It is impossible to discuss all of the more important English magazines, but it would be remiss not to at least mention a few more: notably Richard Downing and Andi Wachtel's *Sesheta* (1971–1974), Stuart Brown and Jim Burns' *Palantir* (1973)–[1983], Ken Edwards, Robert Hampson and Peter Barry's *Alembic* [1973]–(1979), Stuart Mills' *Aggie Weston's* (1973–1984) and Allen Fisher's *Spanner* (1974–). *Great Works* (1973–1979), edited by Peter Philpott and Bill Symondson, spawned the Great Works Editions imprint, which published Andrew Crozier, Allen Fisher, John Hall, Michael Haslam, Paul Green, John Freeman, and John Welch. The magazine was later resurrected on the Web as an e-zine. David Wright and Patrick Swift's *X* (1959–1962) helped to bring attention to older poets such as Pound, MacDiarmid, David Gascoyne, and George Barker. There was also *New Measure* (1965–1969), edited by Peter Jay and John Aczel. Jay established the related Anvil Press Poetry in 1968, over the years publishing Harry Guest, Peter Whigham, Gavin Bantock, and many others, as well as significant collections of non-English language poetry in translation.

In Scotland, Alex Neish's *Sidewalk* [1960] published American poets such as Ginsberg, Olson, Creeley, and Snyder, and French writers Michel Butor and Alain Robbe-Grillet, as well as Scottish and English poets (Edwin Morgan, Ian Hamilton Finlay, Christopher Logue). Finlay's own highly significant magazine, *Poor. Old. Tired. Horse*, has already been discussed. *Lines Review* (1954–1998) displayed an interest in Concrete poetry during Alan Riddell's second period as editor, in the 1960s (Riddell wrote Concrete poetry himself), while Robin Fulton (in 1967–1977) steered it towards modern European poetry; more generally, it remained a major forum for contemporary Scottish poetry. Duncan Glen's *Akros* (1965–1983) was another important magazine for Scottish poets, in particular championing Hugh MacDiarmid and also publishing Norman MacCaig, Iain Crichton Smith, Edwin Morgan, Tom McGrath, Tom Leonard and others. Glen also maintained a small press, Akros Publications. *Chapman* (1970–), *Scottish Poetry* [1966–1976], David Morrison's *Scotia* (1970–1972) and *Scotia Review* (1972–), *Gallimaufry* (1974–1993), and the Scots language poetry journal *Lallans* (1973–) should also be mentioned. So should some general arts magazines with a concern with contemporary Scottish poetry: *The Scottish Review* (1975–1985), *New Edinburgh Review* (1969–1984) and Robert Garioch and Edwin Morgan's *Scottish International* (1968–1974).

Peter Finch's *Second Aeon* [1966]–(1975), based in Wales, disseminated UK, American and European experimental or exploratory poetry in this period. In addition, it included extensive listings of small press and little magazine publications. Finch also edited *No Walls Broadsheet* (1968–1970), with a mix of Welsh, English and Irish poets. Other Welsh magazines with an emphasis on innovative poetry include poet Philip Jenkins' *Quickest Way Out* (1969) and Ruthi Blackmore's more eclectic *Paperway* (1968; with Jaci Wilde) and *Oyster* [1968]–(1969). *The Anglo-Welsh Review* (1958–1988) was an important forum for Welsh poets, while maintaining a more mainstream focus. Much the same can be said of *Poetry Wales* (1965–), publishing R. S. Thomas, Harri Webb,

Sheenagh Pugh, Gillian Clarke, and others, though with an avowed concern with situating Welsh poetry in an international context. Planet (1970–), a general cultural review, has also published the work of Welsh poets. Vaughan Hughes' Pair (1972–1973) was a magazine devoted to Welsh language poetry (including visual pattern poems).

Michael Smith and Trevor Joyce's The Lace Curtain [1969]–(1978) explored the legacy of Irish modernist poetry (Brian Coffey, Denis Devlin, Thomas McGreevey), with contributors including Coffey, Samuel Beckett, and the editors, as well as John Montague, Eiléan Ni Chuilleanáin, Macdara Woods, and Anthony Kerrigan. Hayden Murphy and Benedict Ryan's Broadsheet (1968–1983?) brought together Irish, Scottish and English poets, including experimental writers such as Bob Cobbing and Dom Sylvester Houédard. Poetry Ireland (1962–1966), edited by John Jordan and then Theo Dorgan, and John Montague and Thomas Kinsella's The Dolmen Miscellany of Irish Writing (1962), were publications of the legendary Dolmen Press (1951–1987); with Liam Miller as its guiding spirit, Dolmen published John Montague, Thomas Kinsella, Richard Murphy, Austin Clarke, and Anthony Kerrigan, as well as Beckett's translation of Apollinaire (Zone) and Coffey's of Mallarmé (Un Coup de Dés – Dice Thrown Never Will Annul Chance). All of these magazines were Dublin-based, as were such other notable journals as Brian Lynch's The Holy Door (1965–1966) and Eamon Carr and Peter Fallon's Capella (1969–[1971], while James Liddy, Liam O'Connor and Michael Hartnett's Arena (1963–1965) was published from Co. Wexford.

Turning to Northern Irish poetry magazines, The Honest Ulsterman (1968–), founded by James Simmons, has been an influential and enduring publication; its contributors have included Seamus Heaney, Derek Mahon, Bernard McLaverty, Michael Longley, Brendan Kennelly, Paul Muldoon, and John Montague. Amongst other Northern Irish magazines that deserve to be mentioned here are Patrick Lynch and Michael Mitchell's The Northern Review (1965–1967) and Robert Johnstone, Trevor McMahon and William Peskett's Caret (1972–1975). Although not an Irish magazine – it has always been based in London – Eddie Linden's Aquarius (1969–) also championed Irish poetry; otherwise, it has been especially active in focusing attention on such poets as W. S. Graham, George Barker, and John Heath-Stubbs.

Many of the little magazines of the period were directly linked to small presses. In many cases, magazines and books were published concurrently, or alternatively a magazine might prefigure the setting-up of a poetry press. Amongst others, there were *Migrant* and Migrant Press, *Poor. Old. Tired. Horse* and Wild Hawthorn Press, *Tarasque* and Tarasque Press, *Grosseteste Review* and Grosseteste Press (later Gr / ew Books), *Oasis* and Oasis Books, *Joe di Maggio* and Joe di Maggio Press, *Schmuck* and Beau Geste Press. Other notable small presses active in this period include Fulcrum Press, Trigram Press, Gaberbocchus Press, and Goliard (later Cape Goliard) Press.

Little magazines and small press publications were disseminated through a number of significant bookshops, including Better Books, Indica, Turret Bookshop, Unicorn Bookshop, and Compendium. Bill Butler's Unicorn Bookshop in Brighton opened around 1966 and closed in 1973; Lee Harwood ran the shop in the winter of 1967/1968. Better Books was in operation from the early 1960s until the early 1970s; in its heyday it was staffed by a number of poets, writers and editors associated with little magazines, including Lee Harwood, Paul Buck, Anthony Barnett, Paul Selby, David Kosubei, and Barry Miles, with Bob Cobbing running it from 1964–1967. During Cobbing's time there, it was a focus for alternative tendencies in literature, film, theatre and art, with readings, exhibitions and performances – as well as making relevant magazines and books available. Indica Bookshop and Gallery was started by Barry Miles with John Dunbar and Peter Asher in 1965, and the bookshop existed until 1970 (the gallery closing a year earlier). (Miles also published Lovebooks, with John Hopkins, and edited *Long Hair* magazine with Ted Berrigan, as well as being involved with *International Times*.) Compendium, which started in 1968 and remained open until 2000, benefited in its earlier years from the presence of little magazine editor Nick Kimberley, who had previously worked at Indica. Opening in the early 1960s, Bernard Stone's Turret Bookshop was another long-running shop with a strong interest in small presses and little magazines: it only closed in 1994. Stone was also involved in running small presses, including Turret Books, with George Rapp and Edward Lucie-Smith. Turret published a variety of poets, including Louis Zukofsky, Robert Creeley, Ernst Jandl, Harry Fainlight, Stuart Mills, D. M. Black, and Michael Hamburger.

This period is characterised perhaps most of all by the sheer number of little magazines that were produced. The increase in numbers was partly enabled by the availability of inexpensive print technology, especially mimeograph (a form of printing that used a typed stencil as its master). *Migrant, The English Intelligencer, Tzarad, Once,* Jeff Nuttall's *My Own Mag* [1963]–(1966), *The Curiously Strong*

(1969–1975), *Curtains*, John Robinson's *Joe di Maggio* [1971–1975], *Alembic*, *Spanner* and the various titles from Brian Marley's Laundering Room Press (such as *Loaded Drum* (1974)) were just a few of the significant magazines produced in this way.

The total figure of new magazines is not the thousands of titles that are sometimes imagined to have appeared in this sixteen year period. Our survey finds considerably less than 600 across this time span. While likely to be an underestimate given the fleeting nature of little magazines, it is probably not a figure out by an order of thousands.

Nevertheless a yearly average of just under thirty–four new titles (non-net) per year is an extraordinary figure compared to the meagre twelve new titles produced on average each year in our survey of the 1950s. The Sixties had a slow start: a closer look at the year-by-year birth rate of new titles suggests that 1963 was the key year, with twenty new titles in those twelve months, as opposed to just ten new titles in 1962. So many magazines closed between 1960 and 1962 inclusive that there was a net loss of six magazines across those first years. In 1963 the trend was reversed (twenty magazines opened, fourteen closed) and no further year in this chapter's period registered a net loss of titles. The boom years for new titles began in 1966 (39 new titles; 20 net) and ended in 1972 (47 new titles; 11 net), with 1970 being the highpoint for both number of new titles and number of title closures (54 new titles; 43 closures; so 11 net). A vision of many short-lived magazines fluttering out year after year into the light is not far off the mark. By 1975, however, the numbers appear to have declined: our survey records 28 new titles that year which, although a substantial figure, when closures are taken into account, gives only a net increase of 2 new titles for that year. The data from our last period, 1976–2000, suggests, however, that the following years consolidated and gently increased the growth of new titles in the 1960s and 70s, with a net average rise of new titles of just under 4 titles per year, rather than the decline that is sometimes imagined (more details are given in the following chapter).

As our survey of the 1950s shows, the numerical domination of the little magazines scene by London titles had been broken in that decade: only 24% of titles were produced from London addresses. In the period 1960–1975, the message is substantially the same: only 23% of new titles came from the capital. The now traditional association of the Sixties with "Swinging London" on first sight seems to take a knock under this analysis. However, the lesser importance of literary texts compared to the more London-based non-literary alternative press, commercial music, performance, fashion and the established print and broadcast media may suggest why London has a lasting place in memories of the Sixties and its aftermath. Of course, this percentage still represents 125 new titles from London: the nearest to that figure is the 25 titles produced by Oxford.

Like Oxford in this period the other university towns continued to produce at the improved rates of the 1950s or higher, notably Belfast (12 new titles from 1960 to 1975), Edinburgh (13), and Cambridge (17). Newcastle (10), Birmingham (14), and Dublin (18) emerge strongly from a previously low publication base in the 1950s, a general decentralising trend that can be detected to a lesser extent in Cardiff (5 new titles), Exeter (5), Huddersfield (5), Nottingham (5), Bristol (6), Leicester (6), Leeds (7), Liverpool (7), Glasgow (9), and Manchester (9). Places of publication that registered for the first time in our survey, but which would take on significance in the following period, included Norwich, Maidstone, Sheffield, Huddersfield, Hebden Bridge, and York. Editors in the towns and cities of Yorkshire seem to have been particularly involved in the publication of little magazines compared to previous years.

Given the importance of the "Cambridge School" poets it is surprising that Cambridge as a place of publication was barely producing more magazines per year than it had in the 1950s (1.06 per year compared to 1 per year). A closer look shows that in that decade Cambridge had been producing the highest number of magazines per year after London, so any increase would be from an already rather high base. A breakdown of publication dates also shows that most new Cambridge magazines were published from 1966 to 1972, arguably the heyday of the first wave of Cambridge School poets. Magazines in London, Hove, and Hastings during this period also published the Cambridge poets. Conversely, Oxford, producing on average the 1.56 new titles per year in this chapter's period, the highest behind London's 7.8 per year, failed to produce any comparable creative movement.

This was a period in which strong specialisation occurred in magazines. Beat-style poetry and the slower, more clipped tones of Movement-influenced verse were strong default strands, but magazines emerged which followed neither, as we have seen in relation to Concrete, New York School, and Black Mountain poetry. Although the seeds were sown in the previous decade, our survey suggests that the publishing of American poetry and the translation of European languages may each have more than doubled their yearly rate across this period compared with the 1950s. Magazines that devoted special issues to women's literature, as a self-conscious movement or tendency, also began to appear, including Valerie Sinason's *Gallery* and the Caribbean-orientated *Savacou*; *Women's Liberation Review* devoted all its pages to feminism and feminist literature.

Perhaps the most important 'poetry-demographic' story for the Long Decade of this chapter is not, however, to do with the urban clusters, aesthetic schools or the politics of this remarkable period, although these trends may be connected to each other. Rather, there is the statistic that people in over four hundred places up and down the country – nearly 80% of the whole survey of this period – published small numbers of magazines (between one and four titles each). Many of these locations were small towns or villages. From Aberdeen to Zennor, a radically decentralised form of publication had arrived. Together, this represents a considerable cottage industry, an often mimeograph revolution that set some of the ground rules for the successive publishing changes from photocopy to desktop publication and on into the internet world of e-zines.

3 Arts Quarterly *See* Three Arts Quarterly D478

60s *See* The Sixties D446

11th finger *See* Eleventh Finger D150

365 Days of the year *See* Three Hundred and Sixty Five Days of the Year D479

2000 *See* Two Thousand D499

1 A: a magazine of visual poetry / edited by Jeremy Adler. London: Jeremy Adler, No. A (1971/2)–ABCD (1977)

Note: The numbering followed the form A, Ab, ABC, and ABCD

Edited from the premises of the Poetry Society. Contributors include Bob Cobbing, Peter Finch, Paula Claire, Jeremy Adler, Betty Radin, Dom Sylvester Houédard, Bill Griffiths, Clive Fencott, Lawrence Upton, bp Nichol, Jackson Mac Low, Sylvia Finzi, cris cheek, Alaric Sumner, P. C. Fencott, Michael Gibbs, and Peter Mayer. Issue Ab features poets associated with the Visual Poetry Workshop.

CUL: ABC (1975). (L999.B.1.596)
UCL

2 Abandoned Notebook / edited by Magnificent Goldberg. Brighton: [Magnificent Goldberg, 1970?]

Noted by UK Little Magazines Project. No holdings known

3 Abject / edited by Jeff Cooper, Seān O'Reilley, and Bob Tedder. London: Abject, [c/o] North–Western Polytechnic School of Librarianship, [1, 1968?]–? Then New Series, 1

(May 1969)–3 (June 1970)

Poems, short fiction, and illustrations. An article by Richard Downing on little magazines in libraries is in New Series no. 3.

BL: New Series, 1–3. (P.901/588)

4 About This: an occasional publication of poetry by members of Chichester Poets Co-operative / edited by John Bennett and Kevin Kewell. Chichester: Chichester Poets Co-operative, Vol. 1 (1968)–4 (1971)

UCL

5 Accent / edited by Donald Cross and Fred Sedgwick. Exeter: St. Luke's College, 1 (1967)–14 (1973). ISSN: 0001–4486

Note: At least four supplements were published.

BL: All issues, and four supplements. (P.901/334)
UCL: 1–9, 14

6 Acorn / edited by Alan Warner. Derry: English Department, Magee University College, Vol. 1 no. 1 (1961)–no. 17 (1972)

Index: Hayes
Profiled in: Tom Clyde, *Irish Literary Magazines: an outline history and descriptive bibliography* (Dublin: Irish Academic Press, 2003), BL: 2725.g.3414

CUL: Vol 1. No. 1 (1961)–no. 2 (1962). (L980.c.170)
NLS: No. 17 (Spring 1972). (1976.66 PER)
TCD: IN.C.MAG

7 Acorn / edited by Gary Wilson. Huddersfield: [Acorn, No. 1, 1968?]
Noted by UK Little Magazines Project. No holdings known.

8 Aegis / edited by Richard Landy and Andrew Hall. Cambridge: Emmanuel College, No. 1 (1973)–2 (1973)

CUL: 2. (L999.B.1.411)
UCL: 2

9 Afrasian / edited by Nathanial Tarn. London: School of Oriental and African Studies Students Union, University of London, No. 1 (1968). ISSN: 0307–9953

Afrasian was the student paper of the School of Oriental and African Studies and for many years had covered other topics apart from poetry. This issue was guest-edited by the American poet Nathaniel Tarn, however, and was devoted solely to poetry from Latin America, Africa, and the Middle East. The holding statements below refer only to this issue.

BL: P.P.7611.el.
CUL: L999.C.3.420
UCL

10 Aggie Weston's / edited by Stuart Mills. Belper, Derbyshire: Stuart Mills, No. 1 (Winter 1973)–21 (1984). ISSN: 0140–9352

Index: UK Little Magazines Project
Profiled in: a note attached to the index produced by the UK Little Magazines Project
Related Imprint: Aggie Weston's Editions

A statement carried in each issue: "The name of this magazine comes indirectly from a work by Kurt Schwitters; 'A Small Home for Seamen'. I have been told that it was one Agnes Weston who founded the seamen's homes in this country and I hope this magazine will likewise provide some sort of refuge." A good-looking, even beautiful, magazine, with an interest in photography, and typically setting out poems with generous white-space around them. Contributors included: Thomas Meyer, Ian Hamilton Finlay, Thomas A. Clark, Stuart Mills, Simon Cutts, Trevor Winkfield, Andrew Crozier, Gael Turnbull, Richard Long, Robert Lax, and others. No. 14 reprints two letters from the East Midlands Art Association to Stuart Mills, the first setting out the terms of grant for any successful application, and the second turning Mills's application down on the grounds of its luxurious minimalism: "the selling price was too low for the lavishness of production but unless the area of print in each publication was increased the public would not feel inclined to pay any more."

BL: P.611/770

CUL: 1–11, 13–21. (L727.C.865)
NLS: 13–16. (P.med.3262 PER)
UCL
Poetry Library: 2, 5–7, 10, 12–14, 17, 19.

11 Agog / edited by Alan Kerr and M. Gibson... and others. Bothwell, Lanarkshire: [Agog], Vol. 1 (1972)

UCL

12 Akros / edited by Duncan Glen. Bishopbriggs, near Glasgow, then Penwortham, Preston, then Radcliffe-on-Trent, Nottingham, No. 1 (1965)–51 (1983). ISSN: 0002–3728

Note: A supplement, Knowe, was published from No. 1 (Jan. 1971)–3 (Apr. 1971), BL: P.903/91
Index: Scottish Poetry Index Vol. 1 (Edinburgh: Scottish Poetry Library, 1994), BL: ZC.9.b.6227
Anthology: Duncan Glen (ed.), Akros verse, 1965–1982: an anthology from Akros nos. 1–49 (Nottingham: Akros, 1982), BL: X.950/17840
Bibliography: Akros: check-list of books and magazines published by Akros Publications, and earlier imprints owned by Duncan Glen, 11th August 1962 to Spring 2000 (Kirkcaldy: Akros, 2000), BL: 2708.e.2522
Profiled in: Sullivan 1914–1984; Duncan Glen, Introduction to Scottish Poetry Index Vol. 1 (Edinburgh: Scottish Poetry Library, 1994), BL: ZC.9.b.6227
Related Imprint: Akros publish many mainly Scottish poets, z20, and Scottish interest books
Reprint: Nendeln, Liechtenstein : Kraus Reprint, [undated] (1–22 only).

A key Scottish literary magazine, publishing poems, reviews and essays, in distinctively designed issues. The magazine championed Hugh MacDiarmid, but was also a great encourager of younger poets.

BL: P.901/1
CUL: L727.C.354
NLS: NB.77
TCD: PER 85– 34
UCL
Poetry Library: 11–51 (incomplete)

13 Albion / edited by Steve [Stephen] Pank. London: Albion, No. 1 (May 1968)

Note: Includes a Supplement, Albion Awakes, dated March 1968.

Designed to "spread the new awareness." Contributors included Michael Horovitz, Jane de Mendelson, Dave Tomlin, Brian Patten, Pete Brown.

BL: P.973/72
CUL: L999.B.1.134
NLS: 6.1780 PER
UCL

14 Albion / edited by David Kay and D. Robinson. Manchester: [The Editors], 1 [1970?]–6 [1974]

CUL: L900.B.394
NLS: 7.148 PER
UCL: 1–5

15 Alembic: a magazine of new poetry, prose and graphics / edited by Ken Edwards, Peter Barry and Robert Hampson. London, then Orpington, Kent: Grasshopper, No. 1 [1973]–8 (1979). ISSN: 0140–5136

Interview: with Ken Edwards, in Görtschacher 2; with Robert Hampson, in Görtschacher 2
Related Imprint: Alembic Editions published Ken Edwards, *Lorca: an elegiac fragment* (1973), BL: Cup.407.p.14.

The first issue consisted of poems by the editors, plus Jim Stewart, and various illustrations. These were printed on different colours and sizes of paper, and simply placed in a plastic bag. It was sold at the Edinburgh Festival in the summer of 1973, in association with a sound and vision ensemble known to Hampson, called Zoom Cortex. This loose leaf "bag mag" physical presentation, with a couple more poets added to the original editorial line up, continued only for no. 2, the next issue adopting a stapled card cover. The intention was announced in no. 3 (Spring 1975) to concentrate more on "one area of contemporary creative practice" and to represent the range of poetry being written in England. Further contributors to this issue, which seems to take a significant leap towards the more difficult and the avant-garde, included Paul Brown, Lee Harwood (poems, and an essay on "Surrealist Poetry Today"), Ulli McCarthy, Paul Matthews, Jeff Nuttall, Boudewijn Wegerif, Heathcote Williams, and others. No. 4, edited solely by Robert Hampson, included work by Allen Fisher (and an interview with him), Jeremy Hilton, Bernard Kelly (including his compilation of quotations from American poets about Open Field poetry), Roy Fisher, Eric Mottram, Ulli McCarthy, Alan Davies, Mike Dobbie, Richard Miller, Emanuel Ro, and the three editors. No. 5

(Autumn 1976), edited by Ken Edwards, focused on prose poetry, contributors including David Miller, Nicki Jackowska, Opal L. Nations, Ian Robinson, Steve Snider, and others. That issue also marked a change from the mimeograph stencil production to commercial printing, presumably offset litho. No. 6 (Summer 1977), edited by Hampson, includes further work by earlier contributors as well as by Rosmarie Waldrop, Tom Leonard, Robert Lax, Sarah Lawson, James Sherry, Elaine Randell, and Barry MacSweeney. With No. 7 (Spring 1978), edited by Hampson and Edwards, a more visually and physically elaborate issue was produced. This, the "Assemblage Issue", included the specially-mounted, blind-embossed booklet *Honour can be bought & sold like...* [by Tony Ward?], E. E. Vonna-Michell's poem about glass-paper, which included two inserted sheets of that material, and many works of poetry, usually with a strong visual emphasis, e.g. by Peter Finch, Glenda George, Robert Sheppard, Alaric Sumner, Herbert Burke, Paula Claire, Jeremy Adler, Bob Cobbing, P. C. Fencott, cris cheek, Lawrence Upton, and other poets published in previous issues. Edwards's acquaintance and correspondence with the Language poet James Sherry was one of the Anglo-American meeting points of the respective avant-gardes.

BL: 1–7 (ZK.9.b.1596)
UCL
Poetry Library: 2–8

16 All In / edited by Nina Steane and Nina Carroll. Kettering [and Oxford?]: Nina Steane, [1968–1972?]

Related Imprint: Nina Steane published: *All in Poetry Wallsticker* (Kettering, 1968), BL: Cup.21.g.15.(19.); Ted Hughes, *Autumn Song from 5 Poems for Children* (Kettering, ca.1970), BL: Cup.648.k.16.; and Gerda Mayer's *Library folder: poems for our bookcase* (Kettering, 1972), BL: X.909/42874

The UK Little Magazines Project notes that at least three numbers were issued. Unless *All In Poetry Wallsticker* (see Related Imprint note above) is in fact *All in*, there are no holdings known.

17 Almer Parkes / edited by Alan Gardner. London, [1975?]

Noted by UK Little Magazines Project.

No holdings known.

18 **Alpha: a magazine of poetry and criticism** / [edited by Clive Allison]. Oxford: [Alpha], No. 1 (1966)–3 (1966)

Edited anonymously from Trinity College Oxford, but ascribed to Allison by Chris Torrance, writing in *Origins / Diversions* 6/7. Relatively large samples of work from a few poets each issue, including Jim Burns and Marion Knell. Illustrated. A heated correspondence in no. 2 about modern poetry and editorial policy demonstrates that even the quite innocuous poetry it had published in no. 1 was, for some, a challenge.

BL: ZA.9.a.11668
UCL: No. 3

19 **Alta: the University of Birmingham Review** / edited by Peter Davison. Birmingham, No. 1 (1966)–11 (1970)

A general review, reflecting the varied interests of the university, but poems were occasionally included, e.g. A. C. H. Smith's long poem "Structures of a Cancer", and others.

BL: 1–7. (P.521/273.)
CUL: L985.B.134
NLS: P.82 PER
TCD: PER 80–54 1966–1970

20 **Amalgam** / edited by John M. Wallace and Wendy Rosier. Hounslow: [Amalgam], No. 1 [1967?]–5 (1971)

UCL: 2–5

21 **Amarinth** / edited by Criton Tomazos. London: [Amarinth], 1 (1966)-2 (1966)

Contributors include Jeff Nuttall, Bob Cobbing, Keith Musgrove, and Bill Butler.

UCL

22 **Amazing Grace** / edited by Jennifer Pryke [i.e. Pyke] and Elaine Randell. London: Institute for Research in Art and Technology, Vol. 1 [1969?]–6 [1972?]

Note: Continued as: *Harvest*

Illustrated in a fairly hippyesque style, with poems by the editors, Barry MacSweeney, John Harvey, James Kirkup, Denise Deegan (later the author of the play *Daisy Pulls It Off*), Michael Horovitz, Anthony Rudolf, Francis Ponge

(trans. Peter Hoy), Peter Finch, Doug[las] Oliver, John James, David Grubb, Nicholas Moore, Tom Pickard, Jeff Nuttall, and others. Elaine Randell edited alone from the second issue.

BL: 1–4; 6 (ZA.9.a.3059)
UCL

23 **Amoeba Broadsheet** / edited by Robin E. Wild. Weston-super-Mare: Quickbeam Enterprises, No. 1 (1970)–25 (1979)

UCL: 4–24
Poetry Library: 21

24 **The Anona Wynn: a magazine** / edited by Wendy Mulford. Cambridge: [The Anona Wynn], No. 1 (1969)

Contributors to this "Cambridge School" magazine include: Peter Riley, Pete Bland, Nick Totton, Anthony Barnett, Ian Patterson, John James, Jeremy Prynne, Ian McKelvie, Elaine Feinstein, Jeremy Mulford, Douglas Oliver, Barry MacSweeney, and Andrew Crozier, with visuals by Peter Riley, Sarah Braun and Sophie Grillet. Anona Wynn was a singer, and also a panellist in the radio show *Twenty Questions* from which the magazine *The Norman Hackforth* also took its name.

BL: YA.1992.b.7479
CUL: 1993.11.230
UCL
Poetry Library

25 **Anthology** / edited by Janet Z. Gordon. Beaconsfield: [Janet Z. Gordon, 1971–1972?]

Noted by UK Little Magazines Project. No holdings known.

26 **Antiphon** / edited by Melville Hardiment and Caroline Benn. Glasgow, then London: National Association for School Magazines, Vol. 1 no. 1 (Autumn 1964)–vol. 2 no. 1 (1966)

Note: Vol. 1 no. 3 has the date Spring 1965 on the cover, but the Winter 1964/65 on the title page. Continues: *Hightime Anthology*: Melville Hardiment (ed.), *From Under the Desk: poetry and prose from school magazines* (London: Max Parrish, [1964]), BL: X.900/580.
Related works: Melville Hardiment would later have a poetry collection published by Migrant Press, *Doazy Bor* (1978), BL: X.950/9420. Caroline Benn, whose husband is the politician Tony Benn, has published works which

include the book, co-written with Clyde Chitty, *Thirty Years On: is comprehensive education alive or is it struggling?* (London: Penguin, 1997), BL: YC.2001.a.11411.

Set up, in the words of the first issue's editorial, to "consolidate the work already done by the Association and give notice of coming projects – whether literary competitions, conferences, courses, exhibitions or lectures. It will keep members in touch with each other's work and advise on many aspects of school magazine production." Each issue included a selection of poetry and prose from school magazines, and essays and other work by much more established poets, critics, and other writers, often giving a campaigning and intellectual framework to the project of empowering students through school magazines. Contributors included Anselm Hollo, Eric Mottram, Herbert Read, Alan Sillitoe, Robert Penn Warren, Michael Shayer, Gael Turnbull, J. B. Priestley, Michael Hamburger, Arnold Wesker, and others. Vol. 1 no. 3 also had a listing of school magazines. The Association had a "Magazine Centre" in Paddington, open from 11 a.m. to 6 p.m. on a Saturday where members could see other magazines and monthly special exhibitions.

BL: Vol. 1 no. 1–no. 3 (Spring 65). (PP.8004)
CUL: Vol.1 no.1–no.2 (1964). (L999.B.1.109)
NLS: Vol.1 no.1–no.2 (1964). (5.3673)
TCD: Vol.1 no.1–no.2 (1964). (PER 81–130)
UCL: Vol. 1 no. 1–vol. 2 no. 1 (1966)

27 **Ape.** Kingston-upon-Hull, No. 1 [1971]
Noted by *Headland 8.* No holdings known.

28 **Apex One** / [edited by Geoffrey Barrow and Gabriel Beaumont?] London: Inca Books, No. 1 (Sept. 1973)–4/5 (1975). ISSN: 0308–2814

Related Imprint: Inca Books published a small number of pamphlet collections, printed by Covent Garden Press, including Hugh MacDiarmid, *Song of the Seraphim* [1973], BL: X.989/22350

Inca Books were essentially a second-hand bookselling company from Lewisham. They produced bookselling catalogues issued in their own right, until catalogue no. 11 which was featured as the middle pages of *Apex One* no. 1. Contributors included: Katherine Tynan (a selection of her letters from 1884–5 are published in no. 1), Stefan Martin, Guy Horton, Jack Lindsay, Yann Lovelock, Richard Sylvester, and others.

BL: P.901/1325
CUL: L727.C.607

NLS: 1–2 (Feb. 1974). (HP.1.79.4554)
UCL

29 **Aplomb** / [edited by Charles Verey] [Sherborne: South Street Publications?, 1969?]
Note: Continued by: *Aplomb Zero*
Noted by UK Little Magazines Project. No holdings known.

30 **Aplomb Zero** / edited by Charles Verey. Sherborne: South Street Publications, 1 (1969)–3 (1970)
Note: Continues: *Aplomb*
Related Imprint: South Street also published the magazine *Bo heem e um* and the anthology of work by Thomas A. Clark, Neil Mills, and Charles Verey, *Statements: an advertisement for experiments in disintegrating language* [1971], BL: YA.1994.b.9302

No. 1 was Dom Sylvester Houédard's *12 dancepoems from the cosmic typewriter*, and no. 2 was Thomas A. Clark's *The secrecy of the totally: collage and chance poems*

BL: 1. (RF.2005.b.61); 3. (RF.2005.b.34)
NLS: 2 (FB.m.521(53))
TCD: 2 (OLS X–2–114 no.6)
UCL

31 **Apocalypse** / edited by Frank Flynn and David Sharkey. Liverpool: [Apocalypse], No. 1 (1968)–3 (1968). ISSN: 0570–4677

Poems, short stories, essays, line drawings. Contributors included the editors, Dermot Joseph, D. Black and others.

BL: P.901/343
CUL: L999.C.3.328
NLS: 6.1923 PER
TCD: PER 80–807
UCL

32 **Apprentice: Oxford and Cambridge poetry** / edited by Lawrence Stone, Stephen Fraser, Jeremy Helm. Cambridge: Apprentice, c/o Magdalene College, 1 [1970]–3 (1971)

BL: 2 (Jan. 1971) (P.901/845)
CUL: 2–3. (L999.C.3.426)
NLS: 1; 3. (5.5807 PER)
TCD: PER 90–528

33 Approach Magazine / edited by Phillip Hodson and Trevor Pateman. Oxford: St. Peter's College, No. 1 (June 1967)–2 (1968). ISSN: 0003–7125

Essays on topics across the academic range, but including, e.g. on Shelley and Concrete Poetry.

BL: P.971/38
CUL: L999.C.3.296
NLS: 6.1761 PER
TCD: PER 80–47 1967–1968
UCL

34 Aquarius / edited by Eddie S. Linden. London: [E.S. Linden], No.1 (1969)– .

Profiled in: Görtschacher 1
Related Works: Eddie Linden has been portrayed in a number of fictionalised accounts and/or novels, including Sebastian Barker, *Who is Eddie Linden?* (London: Jay Landesman, 1979), BL: Nov.40392), a book which was made into a play by William Tanner, and as the character Sammy Giffen in Alan Sharp, *The Wind Shifts* (London: Michael Joseph, 1967), BL: Nov.10708

Strong on essays and tributes to British poets, especially though not exclusively those who emerged just before and during the 1940s, e.g. John Heath-Stubbs, W. S. Graham, and George Barker. Another strength has been the Irish poets it has published, including Paul Durcan, Seamus Heaney, Michael Longley, Derek Mahon, Medhb McGuckian, Paul Muldoon, Eiléan Ní Chuilleanáin, Eithne Strong, Matthew Sweeney, and others. Linden has often used the device of guest editor to take advantage of particular expertise. There can be a considerable time lag between issues, e.g. four years between 23/24 (1998) and 25/26 (2002).

BL: 1–18; 23/24–. (P.901/516)
CUL: 1–5; 9–11. (L727.C.402)
NLS: 1–5; 11; 15–16; 21–. (HP2.78.810 PER)
TCD: 1–5. (PER 81–146)
UCL: 1–8; 10; 11; 15–17/18
Poetry Library: 1–13/14; 17/18–

35 Aquarius: an annual religio-cultural review / edited by Cyril Farrell. Benburb, Co. Tyrone: Servite Priory, No. 4 (1971)–7 (1974)

Note: Continues: *Everyman: an annual religio-cultural review*
Profiled in: Tom Clyde, *Irish Literary Magazines: an outline history and descriptive bibliography* (Dublin: Irish Academic Press, 2003), BL: 2725.g.3414

With a stronger literary content than its immediate predecessor, poets included Harry Clifton, John F. Deane, Seamus Heaney, John Montague, James Simmons, and Eithne Strong. Short stories and non-fiction were an important part of the magazine, too, including articles by Joan Baez, Estyn Evans, and John Hewitt.

BL: P.801/1245
CUL: L900.C.421
NLS: Y.131.PER
TCD: Per 80–206

36 Arc / edited by A. Ward [i.e. Tony Ward]. Gillingham, Kent: Arc, No. 1 [1969]–14 (1972)

Note: Two different issues each numbered no. 13 were published.

Related Imprint: Arc Publications went on to become a publisher of many collections, usually with high production values
Website: www.arcpublications.co.uk

The first in this series of pamphlets was a sequence by Donald Gardner. Later contributors included: Alan Palmer (no. 2); Tristan Tzara, translated by Lee Harwood (no. 3); Ken Smith (no. 4–5); Christopher Hall (no. 6); Francis Bellerby (no. 7); Charles Verey, Thomas A. Clark, John S. Sharkey (no. 8); Paul Evans (no. 9); Adrian Henri (no. 10); Bob Cobbing (no. 11); Paul Jenkins (no. 12); Brian Jones (no. 13); Peter Riley (no. 13); and David Chaloner (no. 14). It is often difficult to tell what number a particular issue is and there appear to be two no. 13s. In some catalogues the number is not given.

BL: 1 (X.900/20456); 2 (X.900/21025); 3 (X.909/808415); 4/5 (X.909/80416); 6 (X.909/80460); 7 (Cup. 503.m.12.); 8 (X.909/80839); 9 (YA.1993.a.23540); 10 (Cup.510.alb.3); 11 (X.909/80665); 12 (Cup.510.alb.1); 13 Jones (Cup.510.alb.2); 13 Riley (X.909/23762); 14 (X.900/10570).
CUL: 2 (1993.9.2448); 4/5 (1993.9.2448); 7 (864.a.115(51)); 13 Jones (864.a.115(2))
NLS: 8 (6.1816); 9 (6.1915); 10 (6.1911); 12 (6.1816); 13 Jones (6.1879); 13 Riley (6.2073); 14 (6.2126)
TCD: 8 (OLS X–1–428 no.2); 12 (OLS X–1–428 no.8); 13 Jones (OLS L–4–351 no.10); 13 Riley (OLS L–4–606 no.7); 14 (OLS L–4–407 no.10)
UCL: 1–5, 9, 11, 14.

37 Arcade / edited by Martin Leman. London: [Arcade], No. 1 (1964)–5 (1967). ISSN: 0570–6017

Largely visual, i.e. photographs, graphics, and some visual poetry. William Burroughs contributed several short prose pieces to the first issue.

BL: 1, 2, 4, 5. (Cup. 805.ff.1)
CUL: L992.D.6
NLS: 1968.89
UCL

38 Arcadian Guild Newsletter / edited by M. D. Hammond. London, No. 1 (Autumn 1968)–?

A conservation pressure group's newsletter which also published conservative poetry and light verse, e.g. the editor's "To those who take transistor radios into public places".

BL: 1–4 (Summer 1969). (P.905/10.)

39 Arcanum / edited by James Goddard. Salisbury: [Arcanum, 1970s; final issue, 1974?]

Note: Related to *Cypher*

Noted by UK Little Magazines Project.
No holdings known.

40 Arena / edited by a committee of K. A. Jelenski, Ivan Jelinek, Velta Nikere and Paul Tabori, and then others. London: P.E.N. Centre for Writers in Exile; printed by the Poets and Painters Press, [No. 1, 1961]–26 (Mar. 1967). ISSN: 0570–7439

A significant outlet for writers in exile or regarded as dissidents, especially those exiled from Eastern Europe. Although the first issue does not mention it, it is probably a continuation of *Pen in Exile* produced by the same organisation. There were poems, stories and essays, and often a feature themed by country of origin, e.g. Estonians, Ukrainian, Bulgarian literature, etc. Texts are in English and other languages, and not usually parallel text. Contributors include: Czeslaw Milosz, Aleksis Rannit, George Faludy, Jean Schlumberger, Marina Tsvetayeva, Boris Pasternak, Vladimir Nabokov, as well as Vera Brittain (writing in no. 4 about the importance of exiles to Britain), and others. Elizabeth Jennings contributes a review of a Lithuanian anthology in no. 6. Stephen Spender and Nicholas Nabokov contribute a libretto in no. 15, and T. S.

Eliot "A Note on Translation" in no. 19. *Arena* appeared in a small attractive pocketbook format (18cm tall, 12.5cm wide).

BL: [1],2–12, 14–22. (ZA.9.a.2148)
CUL: 15 (Sept. 1963)–26. (L700.D.11)
NLS: 15 (Sept. 1963)–26. (P.157 PER)
TCD: 15 (Sept. 1963)–26. (PER 80–34 1963–1967)

41 Arena / edited by James Liddy and Liam O'Connor and Michael Hartnett. Coolgreany, Co. Wexford, Republic of Ireland: No.1 (Spring 1963)–4 (Spring 1965). ISSN: 0570–7404

Index: *This Was Arena* (see below); Stephen H. Goode, *Index to Commonwealth little magazines* (New York: Johnson Reprint, 1966), BL: HUR011.3409171; Hayes
Profiled in: Tom Clyde, *Irish Literary Magazines: an outline history and descriptive bibliography* (Dublin: Irish Academic Press, 2003), BL: 2725.g.3414
Reprint: *This Was Arena*, [a facsimile] introduced by James Liddy, (Naas: Malton, 1982), BL: L.45/3456
Microfilm: New York: New York Public Library, [undated]

Contributors included Austin Clarke, Patrick Kavanagh, Thomas Kinsella, Mary Lavin, Derek Mahon, Paul Durcan, Anthony Cronin, Pearse Hutchinson, and John Montague, as well as Eugenio Montale (trans. Desmond O'Grady), Penelope Shuttle, Bertold Brecht, Miguel de Unamuno, C. H. Sisson, and others. Hartnett joined as an editor after the first issue edited by Liddy and O'Connor.

BL: PP.8001.gk
CUL: L999.A.1.8
NLS: P.el.58 PER
TCD: Per 80–35. Also, *This was Arena* facsimile. (Lecky Library, HIB 820.5 K3)
UCL

42 Arena: an independent student publication / edited by Paul Daniel Schedl and Anthony Fiennes Trotman. Cottingham, East Yorkshire: [Arena], No. 1 (1966)

UCL

43 Arkwright's First Magazine / edited by Chris Meade, Keef Green, Jon Arnold and Nick Dalziel. London: Arkwright, No. 1 (1973)

Naïve poems and short fiction. Three of the editors played with the band Edge of August, and Arkwright itself seems to have been the name of a band.

BL: P.901/1208.
CUL: L999.C.3.602
NLS: HP3.78.1469 PER
UCL

44 Arlington. Arlington Mill, Bibury, Glos.: [Arlington], Une (1966); Two (1967), [Three] (1967/68), Quadlog / Quadro (1968)

Note: The last issue was published in Sherborne by South Street Publications.
Related Imprint: South Street also published the magazine Bo heem e um and Thomas A. Clark, Neil Mills and Charles Verey, Statements: an advertisement for experiments in disintegrating language (London: South Street, [1971]), BL: YA.1994.b.9302

Each issue accompanied an exhibition of concrete poetry and was itself an anthology of concrete poetry. The first exhibition was arranged by Ken Cox, John Furnival, Dom Sylvester Houédard, and Charles Verey; the last by E.M. de Melo e Castro and Verey. As well as the organisers, contributors included Ian Breakwell, Thomas A. Clark, Bob Cobbing, Simon Cutts, Tom Edmonds, Ian Hamilton Finlay, John Hall, Roy Hewish, Brian Lane, Liliane Lijn, Andrew Lloyd, Peter Mayer, Cavan McCarthy, Stuart Mills, Edwin Morgan, Hayden Murphy, Tom Phillips, John J. Sharkey, Trevor Wells, Abilio-José Santos, António Aragão, Ana Hatherly, José-Alberto Marques, José Viale Moutinho. There are original contributions, sometimes in colour, photographs of exhibits, and background information on the poets. Naturally, given the concrete poetry focus, there is a strong Brazilian contingent.

BL: Quadlog / Quadro. (YA.2003.b.1648)
CUL: Une. (1989.11.1659)
NLS: Quadlog / Quadro. (HP4.88.1143)
UCL: Quadlog / Quadro.
Leeds University, Brotherton Library: Une; Quadlog / Quadro. (Special Collections General Literature D–6 ARL)

45 Arnold Bocklin / edited by Mike Davies and Kathy Chater. Birmingham: Flat Earth Press, No. 1 [1974?]–7 (1976). ISSN: 0307–6148

Related Imprint: Flat Earth Press published: Mike Davies (ed.) Conversations (Flat Earth Press, 1975), BL: X.909/31388

BL: 4. (Pressmark pending)
UCL: 4 (1975)–7 (1976)

46 Artery / edited by Leslie Daly and John Brown. Kirkintilloch: Artery, [No. 1 (1968?)–2 (1969?)]

Related imprint: Ethos Publications published Doubts & Memories by Stephen Morris (Glasgow, 1969), BL: X.909/39868

Poetry and the then alternative music scene, e.g. review of a Pink Floyd concert. Contributors included Peter Finch (reviewing Adrian Henri) and Stephen Morris (poems).

BL: 2. (P.971/128)
UCL: 2.
Poetry Library: 2

47 Artery / edited by Colin Bibby, then Jeff Sawtell. London: Artery, [No. 1, 1971]–Vol. 8 no. 1/2 (issue 28/29) [1984]. ISSN: 0144–8412

Related Imprint: Artery published at least six books in the Artery Poets series, which ran in the 1980s, and included collections by Arthur Clegg, Keith Armstrong, and others.

Left-wing general arts review, often publishing poetry, especially poetry in translation, and often giving over essay space to discussion of poets and poetry. For a short time, Jack Lindsay and Hugh MacDiarmid were on the editorial board, although this may have been honorary only. Poets included: Mayakovsky, Brecht, Volker Braun, Louis Aragon, Gioconda Belli, Ernesto Cardenal, Pablo Neruda, and a number of British poets associated with the magazine, Arthur Clegg, Chris Searle, John Green, and Keith Armstrong. There was also a collaboration between Alan Bush and Hugh MacDiarmid (a cantata), and poetry features from various countries, e.g. from South Africa and Mozambique.

BL: No. 4 [1972]–Vol. 8 no. 1/2 (issue 28/29). P.971/128
CUL: No. 6 (1973), 13–16, 26/27 (1983). (L231.b.300.)
NLS: No. 13 (Autumn/Winter 1977)–no. 16 (1978). (P.la.6998 PER)
TCD: No. 13 (Autumn/Winter 1977)–no. 16 (1978). (PER 92–428)
UCL: No. 4 [1972]–27 (1983)

48 Arts Club Magazine / edited by Rod Brookes. Birmingham: [Midland Arts Centre for Young People], [No. 1, 1966]

Some poems, short fiction and illustrations. None of the contributors seem to have gone on to publish more poetry or fiction.

BL: P.901/171
UCL

49 The Arts in Ireland / edited by Charles Merrill. Dublin: Trinity Publications, Vol. 1 no. 1 (Autumn 1972)–vol. 3 no. 2 (1977)

BL: DSC 1736.650000
CUL: Vol. 1 no. 2 (1972)–vol. 1 no. 4 (1972); Vol. 2 no. 2 (1973). (L400.B.315)
NLS: Vol. 1 no. 1–vol. 2 no. 3 (1974), but lacking vol. 2 no. 1 (1974). (Y.100 PER)
TCD: PER 94–657 1972–1977
UCL: Vol. 2 no. 1 (1973)

50 As It Is / edited by Steve Saunders. Spalding: Steve Saunders, [No.1, 1974]–? ISSN: 0305–053X

Short fiction, some poetry, reviews of books, films and albums, and comment about local events in Lincolnshire.

BL: [1]. (P.903/269)

51 Ashes / Newcastle upon Tyne: P. Laver [with financial assistance from the Students' Representatives Council, Newcastle University], [No. 1] (1970)–3 (1972)

Edited anonymously, but Peter Laver appears to have been one of the editors. Contributors to this magazine included Tony Harrison, Barry Cole, Richard Caddel, Koef Nielsen, Alistair Elliot, Tom Pickard, David Constantine, Rodney Pybus, and others.

BL: ZA.9.a.10835
UCL

52 Asphodel. London: [Asphodel], No. 1 [1968?]

UCL

53 Assassinator Broadsheet / edited by Chris Torrance and Bill Wyatt. Croydon: [Assassinator Broadsheet], No. 1, 1967

Note: Continues: Origins/Diversions. Continued by: Broadsheet (D88). Related to: Maya. Variant title: Assassinators Broadsheet.
UCL: No. 1 (1967)

54 Assegai / edited by Alex Smith, Tully Potter, and A. H. Snow. Hornchurch, London: Poetry One, Vol. 1 (1974)–2 (1976). ISSN: 0308–5449

Note: Continues: Poetry One.
Related Imprint: Poetry One published e.g. Tully Potter's The Emigrant, and other poems (1975), BL: X.908/40265

Assegai is the name of a Zulu spear. The magazine was based around the Poetry One workshop, which met fortnightly at the Arts Centre on Billet Lane, Hornchurch.

BL: 1. (X.0909/725)
CUL: L727.C.339
NLS: PER
TCD: PER 90–718
UCL
Poetry Library

55 Asylum /edited by Tony Dash and Brian Wake. Bootle: Asylum Publications, No. 1 [1967]–7 [1968?]?

Note: Related to Driftwood Quarterly
Related Imprint: Asylum Publications published Tony Dash (ed.) Anthology of Little Magazine Poets (Bootle: Asylum, 1968), BL: YA.1995.b.7249. This included poets from many other little magazines, and sports a cover pinpointing the names and locations of magazines on a map of England, Scotland and Wales.

Contributors include: Tina Morris, Barry McSweeney, Alan Jackson, Dave Cunliffe, George Dowden, David Chaloner, Anselm Hollo, Peter Cundall, Alan Plater (a play, "The Rainbow Machine"), Pete Morgan, Jim Burns, Chris Torrance, and others.

BL: 4 (Mar. 1968); 5 (June 1968). (ZA.9.a.12101)
CUL: 4 (Mar. 1968). (L999.C.3.288.)
NLS: 4 (Mar. 1968). (1970.78.PER)
TCD: 4 (Mar. 1968). (PER 81–195)
UCL: 3–6.
Liverpool University Library: 4–6. Two copies of no. 6 with variant covers. (SPEC Merseyside Poets III.A86 4–).

Athlone Poets *See* Poem–sheet: Athlone poets
D355

56 Atlantis / edited by Seamus Deane, Derek
Mahon, Hugh Maxton, Augustine Martin,
Michael Gill. Dublin: [Atlantis], No. 1 (Mar.
1970)–6 (Winter 1973/74)

Index: Enda P. Guinan,
www.may.ie/academic/english/atlantis.htm;
index to nos.1–4 in *Atlantis* 6.
Profiled in: Tom Clyde, *Irish Literary Magazines: an outline
history and descriptive bibliography* (Dublin: Irish Academic
Press, 2003), BL: 2725.g.3414

Broad cultural review with articles on the arts and politics.

BL: P.701/390
CUL: L900.C.457
NLS: NH.587 PER
TCD: Per 81–195

The August August *See* Collection D117

57 Avellenda / edited by Robin E. Wild.
Croydon: Quickbeam Enterprises, 1 (1972)–4
(1974)

UCL: 1, 2, 4.
Poetry Library: 1

58 Aventine / edited by Patrick Galvin and
Peter Gee. Brighton: [Aventine, 1969?]

Noted in *Gaga* 1. This Patrick Galvin, born in Dublin, is not
to be confused with the better-known Irish poet, born in
Cork in 1927. No holdings known.

59 Axis / edited by Barry Fitton. Rochdale:
[Axis], No. 1 (1970)–2 (1970)

Note: Related to *Axis Bag*

Associated with this magazine, which published poems
and short fiction, as well as debate about the arts, there was
The Axis Experimental Poetry Theatre, comprising Barry
Fitton, Michael George, Doug Kippon, C. B. Bostock, and
Kath Richardson.

BL: 2. (ZD.9 a.237)
UCL

60 Axis Bag / edited by Mike George.
Rochdale: [Axis Bag, 1969?]

Noted by UK Little Magazines Project. No holdings known,
but related to *Axis*.

61 Axle Quarterly / edited by Alan Blaikley,
Ken Howard and Paul Overy. London and
Bromley, No. 1 (Autumn 1962)–4 (Summer
1963)

BL: 1. (PP.8000.gd.)
CUL: L900.c.388
NLS: 6.1361
TCD: PER 80–796

62 Bad News / edited by Dave Wood.
Nottingham, Dave Wood, No. 1 [1966]

Duplicated from typewritten stencil. Arts reviews and some
poems, all in a jokey style.

BL: P.901/122

63 Bananas / edited by Emma Tennant, then
Abigail Mozley. London: Bananas Publishing,
No. 1 (Jan./Feb. 1975)–26 (April. 1981). ISSN:
0308–3381

An eclectic general literary magazine publishing essays and
short fiction (e.g. J. G. Ballard, Angela Carter) and poetry.
No. 18 was a special German number, guest-edited by Iain
Galbraith. No. 20 had a special African writing feature; no.
23 was devoted almost entirely to poetry, guest-edited by
David Sweetman; no. 24 had a special French number,
guest-edited by Adam Feinstein and Nicole Ward Jouve; no.
26 had a Dublin writing feature, guest-edited by Dennis
O'Driscoll. Emma Tennant edited from no. 1 until no. 11,
Abigail Mozley from 12 to 26. It had a broadsheet format
from 1–16, then became a stapled magazine. Poets
included: Ted Hughes, Ruth Fainlight, Libby Houston,
Peter Redgrove, Henri Michaux, Frances Horovitz, Carol
Rumens, Wes Magee, Harold Pinter, Ken Smith, Elaine
Feinstein, Maura Dooley, Pete Morgan, Kit Wright,
Penelope Shuttle, Jenny Joseph, Tony Curtis, Gillian
Allnutt, Seamus Heaney, Thomas Kinsella, Douglas Dunn,
Iain Crichton Smith, Tom Pow, Brian McCabe, Ron Butlin,
Robert Creeley, Robert Minhinnick, Jeremy Hooker, and
others.

BL: P.2000/379
CUL: 1–25. (L727.B.223)
NLS: DJ.1.118

Chapter D: 1960–1975

TCD: 1–25. (PER 94–177 1975–1981)
UCL
Poetry Library: 1–25

64 Barwell Broadside / [edited by Toni Savage?]. Aylestone: [Printed by Patricia Green and Rigby Graham at the] Cog Press, No. 1 [1975]–22 (1977)

Note: Continues: Cog Broadsheet
Study: Derek Deadman and Rigby Graham, A Paper Snowstorm: Toni Savage & The Leicester Broadsheets (Oldham: Incline Press, 2005). This book also tips in many examples of broadsheets and other printing, and comes with a portfolio of further examples.
Related Imprint: Cog Press published a number of poetry and art-related books, including the Maltese poet Victor Fenech's London Pictures, and other poems (1976), BL: Cup.510.cod.10

These one-sided broadsides were single poems printed on coloured paper, each with an illustration by Graham. They were given out at the Ampersand Folk Club which then met at the Three Crowns pub in Barwell, Leicestershire. The poems could be contemporary, e.g. by William Oxley, or historical, e.g. by Oliver Goldsmith, and there were a number of translations by Richard O'Connell, too.

BL: 2, 5, 6, 8, 9, 11, 12, 13, 15, 16 (two printings, each on a different colour of paper), 17, 19, 20, and 22 (July 1977). (ZA.9.d.557)

65 Bath Children Write. Bath: Bath Library and Art Gallery Committee, 1966–1985

Note: Continued by: Young Bath Writers

Annual volume of poetry and short fiction by children and teenagers.

BL: P.901/75.
CUL: 1969–1985. (L990.B.199.)
NLS: 1969–1985. (P.la.4152 PER.)
TCD: 1969–1985. (PR 758 1969–1985)
UCL

66 Bean Train. [Vol. 1 no. 1– vol. 3 no. 1?] [London: c.1963]

Note: Appears also to have been known as Bean Train Express and Bean Train Press
Related Imprint: Bean Train Press published Spike Hawkins, Too Few Moats and Old Bridges [1963], BL: Cup.21.g.26(22), and co-published the magazine Night Train.

Anthology: Bean Train Press Readings: selected poems, by crew of the Bean Train (London: Bean Train Press, 196?), BL: LB.31.b.27930

BL: Vol. 3 no. 1 (YA.2003.b.4780)

67 "Before Your Very Eyes!" / [edited by Charles Olson]. London: Goliard, [No. 1], 1967

Edited anonymously by Olson. High production values, with strong visual presence. Contributors were Charles Olson, Anselm Hollo, Aram Saroyan, Tom Raworth, Ron Padgett, James Koller, and Jack Hirschman.

BL: Cup.510.dak.11
CUL: L999.B.1.191
NLS: 6.2063
UCL

68 Big Camel / edited by Nick Kimberley. London: [Nick Kimberley], 1 (1969)

Related Imprint: Kimberley published Big Venus under the Big Venus imprint.

Noted by the UK Little Magazines Project. No holdings known.

69 Big Venus / edited by Nick Kimberley. London: Big Venus; [printed by Roy and Erica Eden], 1 (1969)–4 (1970)

Note: No. 2 is entitled Big Big Venus, no. 3 is Big Big Big Venus, and no. 4 is Queen Camel, Sister to Big Venus.
Related Imprint: Big Venus published a number of pamphlets including Larry Eigner's Valleys, Branches (1969), BL: X.950/5215 and Dody Pitter's The Face in the Tear [1969] (no known holdings, but advertised in no. 3).

Almost wholly poetry with a very small amount of visual work; no reviews. Stapled, mimeographed text, with soft card covers. Contributors include: John Ashbery, Clayton Eshleman, Andrew Crozier, Bob Cobbing, Stuart Montgomery, Peter Riley, Bill Butler, George Dowden, Allen Fisher, Tom Raworth, Anselm Hollo, Barry MacSweeney, John James, Fred Buck, David Chaloner, Daphne Marlatt, Kris Hemensley, Larry Eigner, and Gerard Malanga (in conversation with Andy Warhol and others). Paul Buck contributes the violent rape text "a cunt not fit for the queen" in no. 2. This appears to have attracted very little attention until republished in the Manchester counterculture magazine Corridor in 1971, when it caused the printers to refuse to print it. Nick Kimberley worked in the famous Compendium bookshop in Camden, where he developed a strong emphasis on contemporary American poetry as well as avant-garde British texts. Later, he would be as well known as a classical music and opera critic.

BL: 1 (X.902/2151); 2 (X.900/16118); 3 (X.900/16117); 4 (X.900/16116)
CUL: L727.b.364
UCL
Poetry Library: 4

70 Black Columbus / edited by John Akeroyd, Nick Toczek and others. Birmingham: University of Birmingham Students' Union, Vol. 1 (1971)–5 (1972)

Black Columbus was the name of a group of poets based at the university, and who included the editors, Sue Hicks, and others.

UCL: Vol. 1, 3; 5.

71 Black Country Meat Chronicle / edited by Richard Miller. Edgbaston, Birmingham: BMC Press, No. 1 (1969)–17 (1970)

Concrete and visual poetry as well as more conventional work. No. 17 was a "bag mag" or "assemblage", i.e. loose leaf in a plastic folder. Contributors included Jeff Nuttall, Thomas A. Clark, Bill Butler, Jim Pennington, Peter Finch, Paul Brown, and others.

BL: 2 (Sept. 1969); 17 [1970]. (ZA.9.ad.623)
TCD: 2 (Sept. 1969) (OLS X–2–121 no.6,7 Copy A); 17 [1970] (OLS X–2–121 no.8 Copy B)
UCL: 2 (Sept. 1969)
King's College London, Eric Mottram Archive: 17. (7/85/1 [1969])

72 Black Eggs / edited by Pat Waiters, Duncan Tweedale, Paul Smith and Gabrielle Hinton. Winchester: Blue Dog Publications, No. 1 (1971)–3 (1972)

UCL
Poetry Library: 1

73 Blackburn Barker / edited by Ian Ross and Dave Cunliffe. [Blackburn, c.1974]

Note: Related to Global Tapestry Journal

Noted by the UK Little Magazines Project. No holdings known.

74 Blue Food / edited by John Lyle. Sidmouth, Devon: Transformaction, 1 (1970)–3 (1970)

Related Imprint: Transformaction's main publication was the surrealist magazine Transformaction

Contributors included Ian Breakwell and others.

UCL

75 The Blue Front Door / edited by George English. [Durham]: [George English], [No. 1, 1972–no. 2, 1972]

A general arts magazine for the county of Durham. Issue 2 contained concrete poetry by Robin Crozier and poems by E. Taylor, R. I. Caddel [i.e. Richard Caddel] and J. W. McCracken.

BL: 2 [1972]. (P.971/418)
Durham University Library: L 050 BLU // Nos.1–2; [1971–72]

76 The Blue Tunnel / edited by Ian Gardner. Bradford: Ian Gardner, [No. 1, 1973–17, 1979?]

Note: Continued by: [New Arcadian Broadsheet]
Related Imprint: Blue Tunnel published Patrick Eyres' Happy Valley, concerning the landscape gardens of Culzean Castle (1978), BL: YD.2004.b.1115

Very close in style to Tarasque Press's Private Tutor of a few years earlier, this also has a one A4 sheet format and the emphasis on minimalism. As well as Gardner, contributors included: Astrid Wilson, Anne Gardner, Simon Cutts, Pete Wall, Edward Lucie-Smith, Rod Gathercole, and others. It was issued free to those who expressed an interest in it.

BL: RF.2005.b.21
UCL: Fourteen unnumbered issues from c.1974–1976

77 Blueprint: annual magazine of the Cambridge Poetry Society / edited by Richard Tabor, then an editorial board of Tabor, Peter Robinson and Aidan Semmens; then Richard Tabor alone; then Tabor and Edward Fox. Cambridge: c/o Jesus College, Cambridge, Cambridge Blue Room Poetry Workshop (later known as the Cambridge Poetry Society), [No. 1, Spring 1975]–[5, 1979]

Not to be confused with the magazine of the Cambridge

University Conservative Association, also called *Blueprint*. The complex editorial succession seems also to have involved Chris Goode; a chronology in no. 5 setting out the magazine's history does not wholly clarify the process or to what extent the Cambridge Poetry Society was involved. Contributors included Rod Mengham, Geoffrey Ward, Allen Fisher, Glenda George, Ulli McCarthy, Lynn Moore, Edwin Morgan, Tom Raworth, Carlyle Reedy, Alaric Sumner, and others.

BL: 1; 5. (P.901/1299)
CUL: CAM.B.21.51
NLS: 1–3 (Mar. 1977). (HP3.80.2129 PER)
TCD: 1–3 (Mar. 1977). (PER 81–225)
UCL: 4–[5], 1978–1979

78 Bo Heem E Um / edited by Thomas A. Clark. [Sherborne]: South Street, 1 [1967]–5 [Dec. 1968] ISSN: 0523–7726

Related Imprint: South Street also published the exhibition anthology series *Arlington* and Thomas A. Clark, Neil Mills and Charles Verey, *Statements: an advertisement for experiments in disintegrating language* [1971], BL: YA.1994.b.9302

Some issues would be a single author's collections, e.g no. 3 was Charles Verey's *An Explosion Without a Fuse*, and no. 5 was Thomas A. Clark's *Alexander's Gaze*.

BL: 3–5. (ZA.9.a.11214).
CUL: 3–5. (L727.c.390)
NLS: 3–5. (6.1923 PER)
TCD: 3–5. (PER 81–217)
UCL: 1, 3–5.

79 Bogg / edited by George Cairncross and Trevor Greenley, John Elsberg and others. Leeds: Fiasco Publications, No. 1 [1968?]– . ISSN 0882–648X

Related Imprint: Bogg Free-For-Postage Publications; and Fiasco Publications which published George Cairncross, *A Friend of the People: being one man's saga of the sixties and dedicated to all those who were there* [1977], BL: X.900/25357

Contributors in the early days included the editors, Lawrence Upton, Gerald England, Steve Sneyd, Colin Nixon, and others. Many of the poems imply a sexual libertarianism. Later co-published in Vermont.

BL: P.905/16
CUL: 35 [1977]– . (L727.B.198.)
NLS: 35 [1977]– . Lacking 57 (1987). (HJ9.2227 PER)
TCD: 35 [1977]–67 (1995). (PER 77–467 1977–1995)
UCL: 1, 3– .
Poetry Library: 40 [197–?], 44 (1980), 63 (1990)– .

80 The Book of Invasions / edited by Eamon Carr and Peter Fallon. Dublin: Tara Telephone, Chapter 1 (1969)–4 (1970)

Profiled in: Tom Clyde, *Irish Literary Magazines: an outline history and descriptive bibliography* (Dublin: Irish Academic Press, 2003), BL: 2725.g.3414
Related Imprint: Tara Telephone also published *Capella* and a number of poetry collections, e.g. from Gerald Smyth and Brendan Kennelly respectively.

Folded broadsheet format. Contributors included the editors, Brendan Kennelly, Roger McGough, Sue Evans, Wes Magee, Jim Burns, Adrian Henri, and others.

BL: 2–4. (P.901/713.)
CUL: 2–4. (L727.C.435)
NLS: 1972.297
TCD: 194.p.10
UCL

81 Both Sides Now / edited by Robert King. Belfast: Northern Ireland Small Press Syndicate, [No. 1] (1974)–2 [1974]

Free to all subscribers of *Id* and *Ego* and to members of the Northern Ireland Small Press Syndicate. Contributors included: Peter Fallon, William Oxley, Colin Nixon, George Cairncross, Steve Sneyd, and others. Terri Hooley was also associated with the magazine.

BL: X.0902/118
TCD: OLS X–2–158 no.15–16
UCL

82 Breakfast / edited by Brian Marley. Heaton, Newcastle upon Tyne: Laundering Room Press, [1] First Quarter 1974

Note: Continued by: *Loaded Drum*
Related Imprint: Laundering Room also published several pamphlet collections, e.g. by Elaine Randell and by Jeremy Reed.

Contributors: Asa Benveniste, Tony Jackson, David Miller, Spike Hawkins, Elaine Randell, Andrew Crozier, Bockris-Wylie, Tim Reynolds, Barry MacSweeney, Martin Thom, Tom Raworth, Ulli McCarthy, Paul Gogarty, and Opal L. Nations.

BL: RF.2005.b.92
CUL: 864.a.174(3)
UCL

83 Breakthru International Poetry Magazine / edited by Ken Geering. Lindfield: Ken Geering, Vol. 1 no. 1 (Nov./Dec. 1961)–vol. 11 no. 57 (Autumn 1972)

Note: The volume designation is independent of the number designation.
Related Imprint: Breakthru Publications
Anthology: Ken Geering (ed.), *It's World That Makes The Love Go Round: modern poetry selected from* Breakthru international poetry magazine (London: Corgi, 1968), BL: X.908/16767

Typed foolscap format, publishing reviews and a vast number of poets each issue (regularly, well over a hundred). Almost all the poets (with the exception of D. M. Black and a few others) appear never to have gone on to have their own collections.

BL: Vol. 2, no. 8 (Jan./Feb. 1962)–vol. 2, no. 12 (Sep./Oct. 1963); vol. 5, no. 30 (Sep./Oct. 1966); vol. 6, no. 33 (Mar./Apr. 1967), no. 35 (Jul./Aug. 1967); vol. 7, no. 37 (Nov./Dec. 1967), no. 40 (May/June 1968), no. 42 (Sept./Oct. 1968); vol. 8, no. 43 (Nov./Dec. 1968), no. 45 (Mar./Apr. 1969)–vol.11, no. 57 (Autumn 1972). (P.905/13)
CUL: Vol. 1 no. 4 (May/June 1962)–vol. 11 no. 57 (Autumn 1972). (L727.B.41.)
NLS: Vol. 1 no. 4 (May/June 1962)–vol. 11 no. 57 (Autumn 1972). Library lacks: Vol. 5 no. 28 (Mar./Apr. 1966) ; vol. 11 no. 56 (Summer 1972). (P.99 PER)
TCD: PER 80–93 1962–1972
UCL: 9, 11–12, 16–17, 19–22, 34–53, 57

84 Breath of Fresh Air. [Belfast]: Inner City Publications, [1] [1972?]–2 [1973?], and poetry supplement [1974?]

Note: Imprint varies: Fresh Garbage was also one of its publishers.

Contributors included Steve Sneyd, Tina Fulker, Opal Nations, Gerald England, Colin Nixon, and others. Edited anonymously. Dedicated in the first editorial, "to the people of Belfast who may not know but they are beautiful, if only they would wave their own flags, and not the flags of the power structure (the people who are keeping them down)".

BL: [1] [1972?]–2 [1973?], and poetry supplement [1974?]. (P.975/47.)
TCD: 16 sheets loose in cut-out folder with red rubber balloon. (OLS X–2–158 no.14)
UCL: [1] [1972?]–2 [1973?], and poetry supplement [1974?].

85 Brecht Times / edited by Peter Langford. Welwyn: Brecht Times Press, 1 [1973]–[1974]

The first issue's editorial declared: "The aim of this magazine is to publish the work of socialist poets. Contributions need not be directly political, but should reflect Marxist thought in some sphere." The poets included: Chris Searle, Norman Hidden, Kim Howells, Stan Trevor, Peter Langford, Andrew Salkey, David Craig, Keith Armstrong, Jamal Ali, Cecil Rajendra, and others. Kim Howells, later a minister in the Blair Government's Department of Culture, Media and Sport, includes two poems which anticipate the ministerial theme: "Open Your Eyes Fat Man Minister" and "The Minister's Goodbye."

BL: 1–2. (P.901/949)
CUL: L727.b.116
NLS: 6.2660
UCL
Poetry Library

86 Brief / [edited by Alasdair Aston]. Dulwich, London: Dulwich Poetry Group, No. 1 (Nov. 1970)–[39] (March 1976)

Contributors included: Anthony Barnett, Edwin Brock, Ruth Fainlight, and others.

BL: Lacking Dec. 1974. (P.903/324.)
CUL: L727.B.161
UCL

87 Broadsheet / by Philip Ward. North Harrow: Philip Ward, No. 1 (1961)–3 (1962)

Poems solely by Philip Ward.

BL: P.P.7616.no

88 Broadsheet / edited by Richard Downing; also with Chris Torrance, Andi Watchel and Bill Wyatt. Sutton and Bristol: Broadsheet, No. 1 (Nov. 1967)–4 (Sept. 1970). ISSN: 0007-2044

Note: Continues: *Assassinator Broadsheet*. Continued by *Sesheta*.
Related Imprint: Broadsheet published Roger Yates, *The Blind Charioteer: poems* (1968), BL: X.908/82149, and Bill Wyatt, *Wind Blown Cloud Poems* [1969], BL: X.908/83945

Contributors included: Paul Evans, Paul Green, Lee Harwood, Roger Yates, Bill Wyatt, Andrew Crozier, Dave

Cunliffe, Tina Morris, Peter Riley, and others.

BL: 1, 3–4. (P.905/22)
CUL: 3–4. (L727.A.1)
NLS: 1, 3–4. (6.2094)
TCD: OLS Papyrus Case 2 no.1
UCL: 1, 3–4
Poetry Library: 3–4

89 Broadsheet / Hayden Murphy and Benedict Ryan. Dublin: [Broadsheet], No. 1 (Feb. 1968)– 26/30 (June 1978); [31?] [1983?]

Note: No. 26/30 published by Martin, Brian & O'Keeffe, London
Index: Indexed in *Broadsheet 1967–1978* (see below)
Profiled in: Tom Clyde, *Irish Literary Magazines: an outline history and descriptive bibliography* (Dublin: Irish Academic Press, 2003), BL: 2725.g.3414
Exhibition catalogue: Hayden Murphy (ed.), *Broadsheet 1967–1978: poetry, prose and graphics* (Edinburgh: National Library of Scotland, 1983), BL: X.950/22265; Hayden Murphy, *Broadsheet Retrospective: introduction: making an exhibition for myself* (Edinburgh: [Hayden Murphy], 1985)

A great variety of poetry from a magazine that, as its title implies, was seldom more than a single sheet. Contributors included: Dom Sylvester Houédard, Edwin Morgan, Norman MacCaig, Bob Cobbing, Michael Hartnett, Macdara Woods, Sara White, Marina Tsvataeva, Colm Toibín, Geoffrey Thurley, John Heath-Stubbs, Francis Stuart, Eithne Strong, Iain Sinclair, James Simmons, Mícheál Ó hUanacháin, Desmond O'Grady, Eiléan Ní Chuilleanáin, John Montague, Sorley Maclean, Patricia McCarthy, Gerald Mangan, Derek Mahon, Tom Leonard, Liz Lochhead, Michael Longley, James Kirkup, Thomas Kinsella, Brenden Kennelly, P. J. Kavanagh, Michael Horovitz, John Hewitt, Hamish Henderson, Seamus Heaney, Peter Fallon, Paul Durcan, Thomas A. Clark, the editors, and others. After the first issue Murphy edited the magazine alone.

BL: 3; 26/30. (P.2000/654.)
NLS: 1–26/30. (FB.el.106)
TCD: 1–26/30. (OLS Papyrus Case 2 no.1.)
UCL: 3, 4, 6–10.
Poetry Library: 10–26/30 (incomplete), [31?].

90 Broadsheet / edited by W. J. Barnes. Orpington: Poetry Workshop, Society of Civil Service Authors, No. 1 (Jan. 1971)–6 (Jan. 1976)

Note: Continued as: *Focus* and then as *Waves*

BL: P.901/3067

UCL: 1–[3?]
Poetry Library: 1

91 Broadsheet / edited by Gerard Fanning. Dublin: Poetry Workshop, University College Dublin, [No. 1, 1974?–?]

Profiled in: Tom Clyde, *Irish Literary Magazines: an outline history and descriptive bibliography* (Dublin: Irish Academic Press, 2003), BL: 2725.g.3414

National Library of Ireland: No. 5 (1975). (LO LB 99)

92 Brooklyn Manuscript. Birmingham: Brooklyn College of Technology, c.1974

Mentioned in *Muse* 5 as a student poetry magazine. No holdings known.

93 Bump. [Edinburgh University Student Publications Board], No. 1 [1972]–[no.7, 1976]

The pages of the earlier issues were printed by typewritten stencil. Robert Garioch contributes a poem essentially dedicated to the magazine in the first issue, and contributors include Brian McCabe, Andrew Greig, Ronald Y. Butlin (i.e. Ron Butlin), Mario Relich, Maureen Sangster, and others.

BL: 1–4, and an unnumbered issue. (P.523/332)
NLS: HP3.80.269 PER

94 Byways / edited by Gerry Loose. Saffron Walden: Gerry Loose, No. 5 [1972?]–6? [197?]

Note: Continues: *Haiku Byways*
Related Imprint: Byways Press published at least one pamphlet, *Thistle Brilliant Morning: Shiki, Hekigodo, Santoka, Hosai* [translations from the Japanese by William J. Higginson] [197?], BL: YA.1996.a.19834

Haiku and minimalist poetry, presented in an understated, white-space way. Contributors include Larry Butler, Michael McClintock, Christopher Gray Hulse, Virginia Baltzell, Virginia Brady Young, Larry Gates, Geraldine Little, James Evetts, Takuboku Ishikawa, David Lloyd, M. Pace, and Cid Corman, whose *A Language Without Words* takes up all of *Byways* no. 6.

BL: 5. (ZD.9.a.65). 6. (YA.2003.a.50300)

95 Canards du Siècle Présent / edited by Anthony Barnett. Nivaa, Denmark: Anthony Barnett, 1970

A one-off, with contributions by a number of those associated with 'The Cambridge School' (though not exclusively so), e.g. Anthony Barnett, Andrew Crozier, Lee Harwood, John James, B. S. Johnson, Douglas Oliver, J. H. Prynne, Tom Raworth, Peter Riley, Nick Totton, and others.

BL: X.902/1604
UCL

96 Candelabrum / edited by Dale Gunthorp and M. L. McCarthy. London: Red Candle, Vol.1 no.1 (Apr. 1970)– . ISSN: 1470–8493.

Index: With last number of volume 1
Related Imprint: Red Candle Press published a number of anthologies as well as collections by authors particularly associated with *Candelabrum*, e.g. R. L. Cook, Roy Harrison, M. L. McCarthy, Helen Tudor Morgan, and others.
Website: www.members.tripod.com/redcandlepress

Longstanding magazine publishing just poetry (no reviews). The aesthetic is unexperimental. Contributors to the early issues included William Oxley, Doris Lessing, W. H. Auden, Peter Scupham, Jack Clemo, R. L. Cook, and others.

BL: P.901/594
CUL: Vol. 1 no. 2– . (L727.C.562.)
NLS: Vol. 1 no. 2– . (HJ4.904 PER)
TCD: Vol.1 no. 1–vol.4 no.5/6 (1983) .(PER 71–785)
UCL

97 Capella / edited by Eamon Carr and Peter Fallon. Dublin: Tara Telephone, No. 1 (April 1969)–8 [1971]

Profiled in: Tom Clyde, *Irish Literary Magazines: an outline history and descriptive bibliography* (Dublin: Irish Academic Press, 2003), BL: 2725.g.3414
Related Imprint: Tara Telephone also published *The Book of Invasions* and a number of poetry collections, e.g. by Gerald Smyth and Brendan Kennelly.

This poetry-only magazine makes connections across the Irish Sea, publishing Liverpool poets Adrian Henri, Roger McGough, and Brian Patten alongside the editors, Seamus Heaney, Brendan Kennelly, Eiléan Ní Chuilleanáin, and others. John Lennon contributes a line drawing to no. 3.

BL: 1–3 (Dec. 1969); 5/6 [Apr. 1971]; 8. (ZA.9.a.10836)

CUL: 3–8. (L727.C.438)
NLS: 3–8. (NH.578 PER)
UCL: 1–2, 4–8.

98 Carcanet / edited by Farrukh Dhondy and Diane Troy. Oxford: Carcanet, [1962]–[1970]. ISSN: 0008624X

Interview: with Michael Schmidt, in Görtschacher 1
Related Imprint: Carcanet

The magazine that would inspire the well-known poetry imprint. The main archive of Carcanet is held at the John Rylands Library, Manchester University. Contributors include: Adil Jussawalla, John Birtwhistle, Adi Katrak, Clive Wilmer, Peter Jay, Clive James, and others.

BL: Jan. 1963; Winter 1966/67; Winter 1967/8; Spring 1969–Winter 1969/70; Summer 1970. (P.901/528.)
CUL: 1962–1970. (CAM.B.41.39)
NLS: Winter 1969/70; Summer 1970. (1974.207 PER)
UCL: Winter 1966–Summer 1970

99 Caret: a poetry magazine / edited by Robert Johnstone, Trevor McMahon and William Peskett. Belfast and Cambridge: [Caret], No. 1 (Autumn 1972)–8/9 (Spring/Summer 1975)

Profiled in: Tom Clyde, *Irish Literary Magazines: an outline history and descriptive bibliography* (Dublin: Irish Academic Press, 2003), BL: 2725.g.3414

A publisher of several of the Northern Irish poets who would be prominent in the decades that followed, namely Michael Longley, Paul Muldoon, and Tom Paulin. Short stories and line drawings also featured. Others included Philip Hobsbaum, Elaine Feinstein, Stewart Conn, Michael Schmidt, C. H. Sisson, Douglas Dunn, Peter Porter, Gavin Ewart, and Val Warner. Robert Johnstone's last issue was no. 3; William Peskett continued until no. 7; the last issue, 8/9, was edited by Trevor McMahon alone.

BL: P.901/946
CUL: L727.C.516
NLS: DJ.s.167 PER
TCD: PER 81–766
UCL

100 Catacomb Poets / edited by Rev. Alastair Osborne. [Edinburgh]: [Catacomb Press], No. 1 [1972]–4 [1975]

Poems mainly by students connected with New College, Edinburgh.

CUL: L727.d.177.1
NLS: P.med.1453
TCD: P 25783
UCL

101 Centre 17 / edited by Stanley J. Thomas. [Walthamstow, then Thaxted]: Walthamstow Poetry Group, No. 1 (Summer 1971)–6 (1973)

"Centre 17 is a magazine loosely formed around the Walthamstow Poetry Group which meets during term time on the first Thursday of each month at 7.30pm in the Green Room of the Walthamstow Adult Education Centre." Contributors include Gerda Mayer, George Cairncross, Geoffrey Holloway, Lawrence Upton, Steve Sneyd, and others.

BL: 1–2. (P.901/805)
CUL: 3–6. L727.C.604)
NLS: 3, 4, 6. (HP3.79.662 PER)
UCL

102 Ceolfrith. Sunderland: Ceolfrith Press, No. 1 (1970)–? [198?]

Index: A listing of Ceolfrith Press publications is given in *Ceolfrith Press: list of publications 1970–1978* [1978], BL: YD.2005.a.3329
Related Imprint: Ceolfrith Press also published individual poetry collections.

Sometimes regarded as a little magazine, but generally treated by libraries as a series of individual works and so catalogued individually. It is not always clear what number the item is so that libraries may have more in the series than is clear from the catalogue. Holdings are therefore not given here. Associated with the Ceolfrith Arts Centre, there is often a focus on visual poets and artists who work with text, including Dom Sylvester Houédard, John Furnival, Robin Crozier, Bob Cobbing, Henri Chopin, Ian Hamilton Finlay, Layton Ring, and others. Ceolfrith was the name of the eighth-century Abbot of Jarrow. There are over seventy publications in the series.

103 Cerddi / [edited by] Gwilym Rees Hughes and Islwyn Jones [and others]. Llandysul: Gwasg Gomer, 1969–1975; 1977; 1979 .

Roughly annual volumes of contemporary poetry in Welsh.

BL: 1969–1977 (P.901/535). 1979 (X.950/8015)
CUL: L733.C.37
NLS: 1969 (NG.1525.e.27). 1970 (NG.1525.g.45)
TCD: 1969 (HL– 74–420). 1970 (HL– 74–421), 1971 (HL–74–422), 1972 (HL– 74–423), 1973 (HL– 74–424), 1974 (PL– 96–859), 1975 (PL– 96–860), 1977 (PL– 96–861), 1979 (PL– 96–862)

104 Chapbook / edited by Arthur Argo. [Aberdeen: Waverley Press, Vol. 1 no. 1, 1967?]–vol. 5 no. 3 [1969]

A magazine devoted to Scottish folk music, printing songs and reviewing records and performances. The crossover in Scotland between poets and other writers and the folk scene was significant and contributors include Hamish Henderson (songs, and articles, e.g. on William McGonagall), Carl McDougall, Stuart MacGregor, Matt McGinn, Sheila Douglas, Adam McNaughton, Ewan McColl, Peggy Seeger, Duncan Williamson, Billy Connolly, and others.

BL: Vol. 2 no. 2–vol. 5 no. 3. (P.901/239)
CUL: Vol. 3–vol. 5 no. 3. (L409.D.87)

105 Chapman / edited by George Hardie and Walter Perrie, then Joy Hendry. Hamilton, then Edinburgh: The Chapman, No.1 (1970)– . ISSN 0308–2695

Note: Variant title: *The Chapman*
Index: *Scottish Poetry Index vol. 4* (Edinburgh: Scottish Poetry Library, 1996)
Profiled in: Görtschacher 1
Interview: with Joy Hendry, in Görtschacher 2
Related Imprint: Chapman has published a number of individual poetry collections, e.g. by George Gunn and Janet Paisley.
Website: http://www.chapman-pub.co.uk/

A major Scottish literary review publishing articles, poems and short reviews. Most contemporary Scottish poets are featured. Issues often have a feature on a particular Scottish author or theme, e.g. on women's contribution to twentieth century culture (27–28 double issue), on Kenneth White (59), on Iain Crichton Smith (71), on Ian Hamilton

Finlay (78–79) etc. Many of the covers have been illustrated by Alasdair Gray. Although founded by Hardie and Perrie, Hendry has edited for the vast majority of its numbers.

BL: P.901/945
CUL: L727.C.444
NLS: HJ4.449 PER
TCD: PER 72–720
UCL

106 **Chase: a quarterly review of new writing** / edited by S. Newman, L. W. Lawson Edwards, and A. E. Dudley. Hednesford: Cannock Chase Literary Society. 1 (June 1963)–5(Nov. 1965). ISSN: 0577–5701

BL: P.P.8003.ls.
CUL: L727.C.313
UCL

107 **Chesil: the magazine of Chesil Poets.** Weymouth: Word and Action, No. 1 (1973)–6 (1975)

The Chesil Poets were David Boadella, Elsa Corbluth, Chris Fassnidge, R. G. Gregory, and Jon Robbins, and this A4 mimeographed magazine published their work only. Issues 2 to 5 invoke pagan festivals or seasons, e.g. Midwinter Feast, Spring Sacrifice, etc., as the timing and theme of their work.

BL: P.903/168
CUL: L727.b.119
TCD: PER 81–931
UCL

108 **Chicago. European Edition** / edited by Alice Notley. Wivenhoe, Essex, [1, 1973?–3, 1974?]

BL: 2. (ZD.9.b.52)
UCL: 2 (1974)–3 (1974)

109 **Christian Poetry.** London: Fellowship of Christian Writers, 1975–?.

BL: 1977. (YA.1990.a.12443)

110 **Circle in the Square Broadsheet** / edited by Bill Pickard. [Bristol: Circle in the Square, c.1966?]

Note: Continued by: *Poetry of the Circle in the Square*

The magazine of the Circle in the Square group, much later known as the Polygon Poets.
No holdings known.

111 **Circuit** / edited by Stephen Heath, David Bieda and Robert Wistrich. Cambridge: Circuit Magazine, [No. 1] (Summer 1965)–11 (1969). ISSN: 0578–3127

Related Work: A supplement of philosophical essays entitled *Language* was issued by Circuit and Cambridge Opinion and numbered no. 1 (Summer 1969), BL: P.983/17.

"We wish CIRCUIT to enable the student mind to escape from the imprisonment of the narrow compass of academic degree requirements." – from the editorial in no. 1. A broad-ranging magazine, with an interest in many of the arts and with a certain philosophical outlook. Essayists included: Roger Scruton, Terry Eagleton, and Feliks Topolski; Peter Brook gives an interview on his opposition to the American war in Vietnam; J. G. Ballard contributes "Love and Napalm: Export USA" and Situationniste Manifesto Strasbourg publishes "How to Smash A System". The magazine deliberately tried to keep the number of poets featured down to a low number, for more concentrated reading. Contributing poets included Pete Brown (who also contributed a piece on American Beats in Britain), Dick Davis, Simon Barnard, Gillian Barron, Spike Hawkins, Ted Milton, Brian Patten, Carlyle Reedy, Adrian Mitchell, Richard Holmes, and Maureen Duffy. Tall, thin format, professionally printed with collage-style graphic design in later issues.

BL: 1–5 (Winter 1968). (P.523/3)
CUL: 1–5 (Winter 1968). (L985.B.125)
UCL

112 **City of Tears** / edited by Chris Torrance. London: Origins Diversions, [1, 1963?]

Note: Continued by: *Diary of an Assassin and Other Documents*

UCL

113 **Civil Service Poetry** / edited by Ernest Meadowcroft and Mabs Allen. Brentwood, then Walton-on-Naze: EMMA, [Issue 1] (1968)–12 (1979)

BL: P.901/453
CUL: L727.d.139
NLS: P.med.1283 PER
TCD: PR 338 1969–1979
Poetry Library: 6

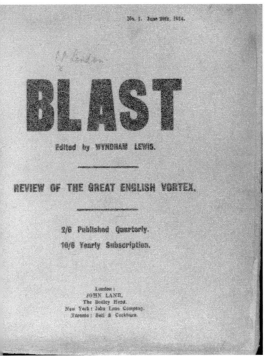

last: review of the great English vortex, London 1 (June
1914), front cover. A15. BL: Cup.410.g.186

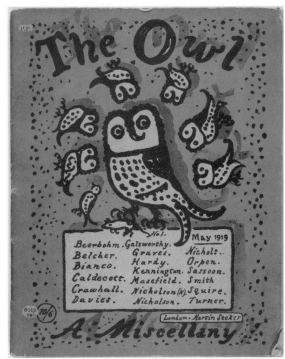

2. The Owl. London Vol. 1 no. 1 (May 1919), front cover
[by William Nicholson]. A157. BL: P.P.6018.oab.

e Scottish Chapbook, Montrose. Vol. 1 no. 3 (Oct.
). A192. BL: P.P.6203.l.

4. Germinal, London. Vol. 1 no. 1 (July 1923), front cover
by Ludovic-Rodo Pisarro. A78. BL: P.P.6018.oac

5. The Klaxon, Dublin, Winter 1923/4, front cover. A103. BL: P.P.4881.tc.

6. Experiment, Cambridge. No. 1 (Nov. 1928), front cover by Misha [Black]. A64. BL: P.P.6119.crb.

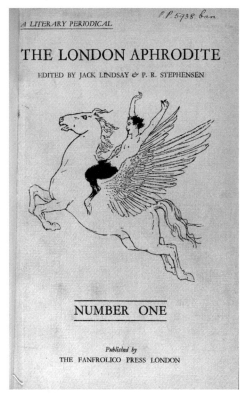

7. London Aphrodite, London. No. 1 (Aug 1928), front cover. A115. BL: P.P.5938.ban

8. The Modern Scot, Dundee. Winter Number, Jan. 1 front cover by Edwin Calligan. A126. BL: P.P.6197.ff.

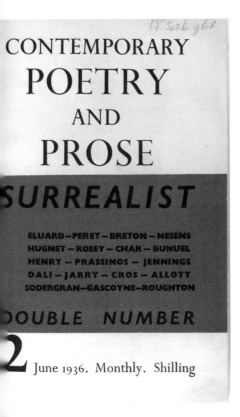

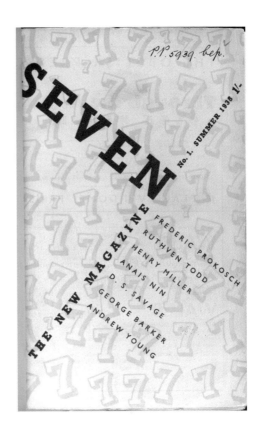

Contemporary Poetry and Prose, London. No. 2 (June 6), front cover. A41. BL: P.P.5126.gbf

10. Seven, Taunton. [Vol. 1] no. 1 (Summer 1938), front cover. A197. BL: P.P.5939.bep

Kingdom Come, Oxford. Vol. 2 no. 3 (Spring 1941), front cover by Baptista Gilliat-Smith. A102. BL: 118.hk.

12. Poetry London, London. No. 14 (Nov.-Dec. 1948), front cover by Henry Moore. A173. BL: P.P.5126.bbi

13. The Glass, Lowestoft. No. 6 (Spring 1951). Cover, by Arthur Phelps. B49. BL: P.P.5938.bde

14. Gairm: an raitheachan Gaidhlig, Glaschu [Glasgow] [No. 1] (1952), front cover. C38. BL: P.P.8004.dh

15. Delta: a literary review from Cambridge, Cambridge. No. 2, front cover by James Fitton. C25. BL: P.P.5126.bcd

16. Agenda, London. Vol. 5 no. 1–3 (1967). Front cover drawing by David Jones. C2. BL: P.P.5109.aac

Prospect, Cambridge. [No. 4] (Winter 1960), front cover. C94. BL: P.P.7616.pz

18. And, London. No. 3 [196?], title page. C4. BL: ZA.9.b.2079

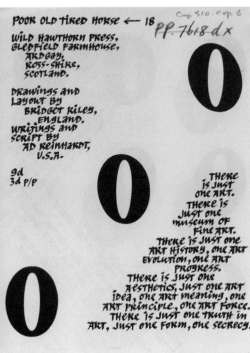

Poor. Old. Tired. Horse, Edinburgh. No. 18 [1966?], front cover: text by Ad Reinhardt, design by Bridget Riley. 5. BL: Cup.510.cop.6

20. Underdog: English poetry scene, Liverpool. No. 8 (1966), front cover: "Death of a bird in the city" by Adrian Henri. D504. BL: P.P.8005.iu

21. Soho: bi-lingual review, revue bilingue, London. No. 1 (1964), front cover, by Nick Tidnam. D451. BL: P.903/193

22. The English Intelligencer, London. ['Telegram' issu[e] 1967], front cover. D153. BL: P.905/20

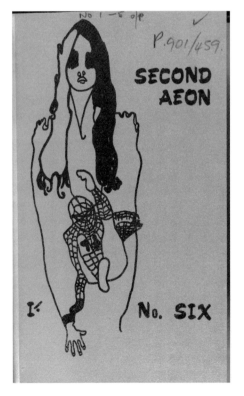

23. Second Aeon, Cardiff. No. 6 [1968], front cover. D434. BL: P.901/459

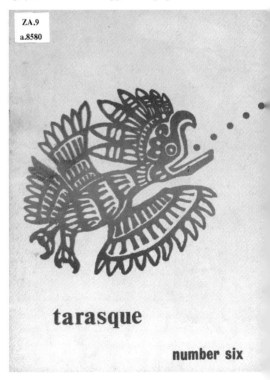

24. Tarasque, Nottingham. No. 6, undated, front c[over] D473. BL: ZA.9.a.8580

. The Honest Ulsterman, Castlerock. No. 4
ug. 1968), front cover. D212. BL: P.801/433

26. Modern Poetry in Translation, London, No. 6
(1970), front cover. D285. BL: ZD.9.a.122

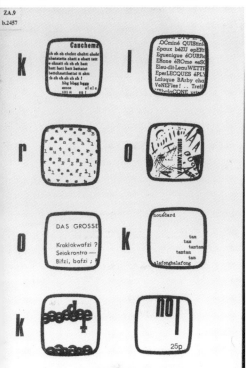

Kroklok, London. No. 1 [1971], front cover. D245.
ZA.9.b.2457

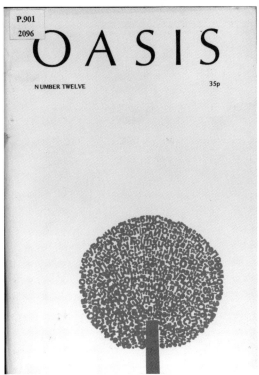

28. Oasis, London. No. 12 (1974), front cover, production
and design by Ian Robinson and Ray Seaford. D318. BL:
P.901/2096

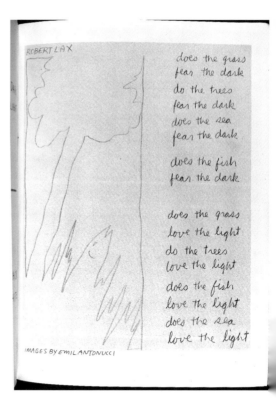

29. Schmuck, Cullompton. No. 5 (1974). D425. BL: ZD.9.a.62

30. Stereo Headphones: an occasional magazine of the new poetries, Kersey. No. 7 (1976), p.37: poem by Robert Lax, drawing by Emil Antonucci. D460. BL: P.431/100

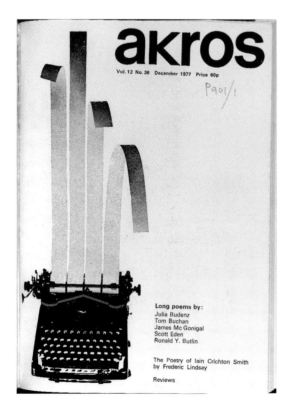

31. Akros, Bishopbriggs [then other locations]. Vol. 12 no. 36 (Dec. 1977), front cover. D12. BL: P.901/1

32. Ludd's Mill, Ossett. No. 15 [1979?], front cover. D. BL: P.903/110

114 Cleft: a university quarterly / edited by B. [i.e. Bill] McArthur. Edinburgh: Edinburgh University, 1 (June 1963)–2 (May 1964). ISSN 0529–9330

Includes work by Henry Miller, William Burroughs, Michael McClure, Anselm Hollo, Norman Mailer, Gary Snyder, Andrei Vosnesensky, Jonathan Williams, Ian Hamilton Finlay, Louis Zukofksy, and others.

BL: P.P.8003.jy
NLS: 5.3017
UCL

115 Clump. [1974]

Describing itself as "not a school magazine" but giving no publication details.

King's College London, Eric Mottram Archive: 7/148/1 [1974]

115a Cog Broadsheet / [edited by Toni Savage?]. Leicester: [Cog Press], No. 1 (1973)–22 (1975)

Note: Continued by: Barwell Broadsides
Study: Derek Deadman and Rigby Graham, A Paper Snowstorm: Toni Savage & The Leicester Broadsheets (Oldham: Incline Press, 2005). This book also tips in many examples of broadsheets and other printing, and comes with a portfolio of further examples.
Related Imprint: Cog Press published a number of poetry and art-related books, including the Maltese poet Victor Fenech's London Pictures, and other poems (1976), BL: Cup.510.cod.10

For distribution at the Ampersand Folk Club, Barwell. No holdings known.

116 Collection / [edited by Eric Ratcliffe]. Whitton: Whitton Poetry Group, No. 1 (June 1962)–2 (Feb. 1963)

Note: Continued by Expression
Interview: with Eric Ratcliffe, in Görtschacher 2

Contributors included Eric Ratcliffe, Brian Louis Pearce, and one of the first appearances of work by Penelope Shuttle, described as a "Staines schoolgirl".

BL: 11397.bb.2
CUL: L727.C.310
NLS: 5.3074 PER

117 Collection / edited by Peter Riley. Hove, Sussex, then Odense, Denmark: Collection, 1 (Mar. 1968)–7 (Autumn 1970). ISSN: 0529–9330

Note: Collection 4 (April 1969) is a co-publication with Tzarad 3 and Collection 6 is a co-publication with Tzarad 4 with the individual title The August August: a special seaside bucket-and-spade issue. Five supplements to Collection 7 were issued in a limited edition of perhaps forty copies, including work by Mark Hyatt, Fred Buck, Michael Haslam, and Donald Haworth. Haworth's Ambivalent Propaganda (1971), BL: YA.1997.b.4059, was a further, unnumbered, supplement to the magazine.

 Among the contributors to the magazine were: Andrew Crozier, Lee Harwood, John James, Tim Longville, Chris Torrance, David Chaloner, Barry MacSweeney, Stephen Rodefer, Fred Buck, Wendy Mulford, J. H. Prynne, Douglas Oliver, Tom Raworth, Paul Evans, Ian Patterson, Thomas A. Clark, and others. No. 4 included, in the Tzarad section, translations of Tristan Tzara, Pierre Reverdy, Blaise Cendrars, Apollinaire, Hugo Ball, René Magritte, Michel Couturier, Max Jacob, and Philippe Soupault, as well as, in the Collection section, a translation of a Francis Ponge piece. There was also work from Robin Blaser, Jack Spicer, Charles Olson, Ron Padgett, Tom Clark, Anne Waldman, John Wieners, and Frank O'Hara. Peter Riley also posted out works not necessarily connected to Collection, such as Fred Buck's The Hair on the Face of the Dog Moon issued at about the same time as Collection 7. The last issue was co-edited with John James. Essentially a "Cambridge School" magazine.

BL: 1–4, 6–7. (P.903/46.)
CUL: L727.B.80
NLS: 6.2110 PER
TCD: 1–2. (PER 90–33 1968)
UCL: Lacking nos. 5–6
Poetry Library: Lacking nos. 5–6.

118 Collection. Huddersfield: Straight Enterprises, 1 [1973]–3 [1974]

Each issue comprised the poetry and fiction of a single author. In order of appearance: Alex Kernaghan, Andrew Darlington, and David Ward.

BL: P.903/201
UCL: 1 only

119 **Concept Poetry** / edited by David Rees; then David Black, David Hamilton, Marigold Popplewell and others. Whipsnade: Concept, No.1 (1970)–6 [1972]

Free verse by Sebastian Horn, David Rees, David J. Black (and also David Black, presumably the same person), Steven Douglas, Maria Harper, Peter Orla-Bardzki, Richard Plewes, Roger McGough, and others.

BL: 1 and a further unnumbered issue. (ZA.9.a.11451)
CUL: L727.C.754
NLS: 1976.245 PER
TCD: Lacking 2. (PER 81–945)
UCL: Lacking 2
Poetry Library: 3–4.

120 **Concern (Faroes)**. 1 (1960)

CUL: L999.C.3.145

121 **Context** / edited by James F. Porter. Westgate-on-Sea, Kent, [c. 1970]

Winter 1970 issue noted in *Headland* 8. No holdings known.

122 **Continuum** / edited by Gray Austerberry, then Brendan Cronin and Rick Lyon. Lancaster: Bowland College, University of Lancaster, No. 1 [1966]–7 (1970)?

BL: P.901/116
CUL: L900.C.427
NLS: 5.5761 PER
TCD: PER 81–584
UCL

123 **Contrasts: a magazine of new poetry** / edited by Russell Pemberton. New Milton, Liverpool: Russell Pemberton, No. 1 (1970)–9 (1972)

Eclectic range of contemporary poems and reviews and short unusual articles, e.g. on the historical context for tonal and atonal music, an appraisal of minor Elizabethan poets, on the medievalism of William Morris and Rudyard Kipling, on F. R. Leavis, on the science fiction author Ray Bradbury, and other topics. Bob Cobbing's visual (and other) poetry could as well appear as work by Barry MacSweeney, Brian Patten, Robin Fulton, Nina Steane, David Chaloner, Adrian Henri, and many others; translations included renderings of French, Greek, Dutch

and Aztec poems.

BL: 1–7, 9. (P.901/544)
CUL: 6. (L999.C.3.822.)
UCL

124 **Corridor.** Manchester, Vol. 1 (1971)–5 (1975)

Note: Continued by: *Wordworks*

A 'vehicle for new and experimental writings'.

CUL: May 1971–June 1971. (L999.B.1.179)
UCL

125 **Cosmos** / edited by Steve MacDonogh and Michael Gray. York: Cosmos, 1 (Sept. 1969)–4 (August 1972)

Contributors include Michael Horovitz and Jeff Nuttall.

BL: 1. (P.901/474)
CUL: L727.c.465
NLS: 5.4958 PER
TCD: PER 90–57 1969–1972
UCL: 1–3
Poetry Library: 1

126 **Crab Grass: poetical sonatas** / edited by John Gilbert and Marcus Patton. Belfast: [No. 1, 1969–5?, 1972?]

Note: No. 2 included *The Crabgrass Music Dropout: a supplement of avant-garde music.*
Profiled in: Tom Clyde, *Irish Literary Magazines: an outline history and descriptive bibliography* (Dublin: Irish Academic Press, 2003), BL: 2725.g.3414

Sound, visual and found poetry from: Abraham Klax-Williams, Spencer Megahey, Charles Patton, Marcus Patton, Philip Jenkins, Roger Armstrong, Nancy Noble, Henry Tonk, Peter Fallon, and others.

BL: [1]– 2 [1970]. (P.901/587.)
Queen's University Belfast: [1–5]. (hAP4.C9)

127 **The Curiously Strong** / edited by Fred Buck, then Ian Patterson. Cambridge: Fred Buck, Vol. 1 no. 1 (Feb. 24, 1969)–vol. 4 nos. 9/10 (1975). ISSN: 0011-3077

Related imprint: Curiously Strong
Note: Vol. 3 no. 8 was not published because two issues were numbered vol. 3 no. 7, Elaine Randell's *Songs of*

Hesperus and Peter Riley's *Five Sets.* However, some copies of the latter were renumbered by hand. Vol. 4 no. 8 appears not to have been published either.

A classic "Cambridge School" magazine. Contributors include: Barry MacSweeney, Peter Riley, Jim Burns, Thomas A. Clark, Paul Evans, David Chaloner, Elaine Feinstein, John James, Wendy Mulford, Paul Green, Paul Wheeler, J. H. Prynne, Nick Totton, Peter Ackroyd, Andrew Crozier, Elaine Randell, and others. The last issue included contributions by Anthony Barnett, Allen Fisher, Roy Fisher, Lee Harwood, Michael Horovitz, Michael Haslam, Pierre Joris, Tim Longville, Matthew Mead, Jeff Nuttall, Douglas Oliver, Peter Philpott, John Seed, Ian Sinclair, Chris Torrance, David Tipton, and John Welch, as well as several of the magazine's regulars.

BL: Vol. 1 no. 1–vol. 3 no. 7, vol. 3 no. 9–10, vol. 4 no. 1–no. 3/4, no. 6–9/10. (Cup.410.c.28)
CUL: Vol. 3 no. 2, no. 4; vol. 4 no. 2, no. 6, and no. 7 only. (SCERR)
UCL
Poetry Library: Vol. 3 no. 3, no. 7, no. 9–10; Vol. 4 no. 1, no. 3–4, no. 9–10

128 Curlew / edited by Jocelynne Precious. Kettlesing, Harrogate: Curlew Press, 1 (Jan 1975)–9/10 (Oct/Nov 1975). ISSN 1463–8347

Note: No. 6 was entitled *Curlew Circular.* Continued by: *Poetry Quarterly,* then *The Singing Curlew.*
Related Imprint: Curlew Press have published a number of individual collections by Jocelynne Precious and Steve Sneyd

Contributors include: Steve Sneyd, Colin Simms, Nicki Jackowska, Harry Guest, George Cairncross, Tom Raworth, and others. The last issue, no. 9/10 is an anthology of "Small Press Poets of the mid 70s."

BL: ZC.9.a.1028
UCL

Curse of Babel (June Diary of Pierre Menard) *See* The Journals of Pierre Menard D327

129 Curtains / edited by Paul Buck. Hebden Bridge, then Maidstone: Paul Buck, No. 1 (1971)–18/21 (1978)

Note: Most issues are unnumbered and have alternative titles based on the Curtains theme.
Related Imprint: Pressed Curtains

Especially strong in translation of contemporary French literature. The titles were: *Curtains* (1971), *Safety Curtain* (1971), *Curtain Raiser* (1972), *Curtains in the Meantime* (1972), *Curtains no. 4* (1972), *French Curtains* (no. 5, 1973), *A Range of Curtains* (1973), *Upside Down Curtains & Appendages* (1974), *Drawn Curtains* (1974), *Velvet Curtains* (1974), *Split Curtains* (1975), *Curtains: le prochain step* (nos. 14–17, 1976), and *Bal:le:d Curtains* (18/21, 1978). *Drawn Curtains* featured poems by Paul Auster.

BL: *Curtains* (1971), *Safety Curtain* (1971), *Curtain Raiser* (1972), *Curtains* (no. 4, 1972), *Curtains in the Meantime* (1972), *French Curtains* (no. 5, 1973), *A Range of Curtains* (1973), *Drawn Curtains* (1974), *Velvet Curtains* (1974), *Split Curtains* (1975), and *Curtains: le prochain step* (nos. 14–17, 1976) (P.973/116). *Bal:le:d Curtains* (Cup.815/38)
CUL: 1–4; 14/17–18/21. (L727.B.167)
NLS: 14/17–18/21. (DJ.m.1027 PER)
TCD: 18/21. (PER 90–251)
UCL
Poetry Library: [3?]–[6?]; 14/17; Undated supplement featuring *scarlet opening: poems* by Geraldine Monk and prose by Glenda George

130 Cutely / edited by Chrissie Smith. Talybont-on-Usk: Mainly, No. 1 (1966)

Probably a one-off, as a special issue of *Mainly.*

UCL

131 Cyclops / edited by Pat Williams and Dan Franklin. Norwich: [printed by the Wild Pigeon Press for Cyclops], No. 1 (Nov. 1968)–5 (Spring 1970)

Poems, illustrations and photographs. Contributors include Peter Riley, Jeff Nuttall, Nina Steane, Pete [i.e. Peter] Hoida, Paul Evans, and others. Marc Bolan contributes to the first number.

BL: 1–2, 4. (ZA.9.a.6134)
CUL: 1, 4. (L999.C.3.695)
TCD: 3, 5. (OLS X–2–116 no.24, 25)
UCL

132 Cyphers / edited by Leland Bardwell, Eiléan Ni Chuilleanáin, Pearse Hutchinson and Macdara Woods; associate editor, Peter Fallon. Dublin: Elo Press, No. 1 (June 1975)– . ISSN: 1393–2985

Index: UK Little Magazines Project

Profiled in: Tom Clyde, *Irish Literary Magazines: an outline history and descriptive bibliography* (Dublin: Irish Academic Press, 2003), BL: 2725.g.3414

Poetry, fiction, reviews, and art-work, with some texts in Irish. Associated in particular with Paul Durcan's poetry.

BL: 25; 49/50–. (ZC.9.a.6495)
CUL: L727.C.622
NLS: HJ4.1141 SER
TCD: 1975–1983 (OLS L–4–9); 1983–1990 (OLS L–4–10); 1991–2001 (OLS L–4–639); 2001– . (OLS L–7–597)
UCL
Poetry Library

133 DADD Magazine / edited by Piers Martens, Lala Anya Wade, Logan Finlayson and David Graham. London: DADD Magazine [No. 1, 1970]

A visual arts magazine consisting of loose sheets, printed professionally. It could be argued that the text-based works share something with poetry, e.g. the exam-style questions laid out on the plan of a cube, as well as the relatively more straightforward texts by Dylan Kaplan, Richard Godden, and Adrian Barlow. Anna Bowman contributes an essay on Richard Hamilton's use of women in his art, as compared to the same subject in Willem de Kooning's.

BL: P.883/6
UCL

134 DATR: Sussex's only literary mag / edited by John Noyce. Brighton: John Noyce, 1 (1971)–3 (1974)

Note: "A Smoothie Publication"
Related imprint: Smoothie published a number of poetry collections, including K. J. Flint's *Backwards (but effortlessly Miss Inchcape)*, 1971 (BL: X.908/27388)

BL: P.901/1058
CUL: L999.B.1.312
NLS: 1–2. (HP1.77.3710 PER)
UCL: 1–2.

135 Y Ddraig: cylchgrawn llenyddol myfyrwyr Aberystwyth. Aberystwyth: Undeb Myfyrwyr Cymraeg Aberystwyth, Rhif 1 (1965)–5 (1970); 1971–1976; 1980; 1984–1993; 1996–

The student literary magazine of the University College Wales, Aberystwyth.

BL: 1–2. (P.901/90.)

UCL: 1–4.
National Library of Wales

136 Diary of an Assassin and Other Documents / edited by Chris Torrance. Carshalton, Surrey: Origins Diversions, [1, 196?]

Note: Continues: *City of Tears*
UCL

137 The Disinherited / edited by Peter Hoida. Cheltenham: Vol. 1 (1965)–vol. 6 (1969)

Note: Variant title: *Disinherited*. Continued as: *Inherited*
UCL

138 Diversion / edited by Milford Harrison. Northallerton: Milford Harrison, [No. 1, Spring 1972]–12 (1983). ISSN: 0144–5413

Note: *Messages to the Void* was issued as a companion volume to no. 10.

Strong emphasis on visuals. Poems by Gerda Mayer, Keith Jafrate, and others.

BL: [1]–3, 5–12. (P.901/3187)
CUL: 6–12. (L727.C.832)
NLS: 7–12 (HP2.85.4691 PER)
TCD: 7–12. (PER 90–911)
UCL

139 Documento Trimestral / edited by Felipe Ehrenberg. Cullompton, Devon: Beau Geste Press, No. 1, vol. 1 (Nov. 1971/Jan.1972)

Related Imprint: Beau Geste Press produced a number of visual poetry and artists' books, including Allen Fisher's *Taken The Days After We Had Beef Curry Between 28.7.72 & 28.10.72* (1974), BL: Cup.510.amf.7.

The now well-known Mexican artist Felipe Ehrenberg went on in the late 1970s to be a member of Grupo Processo Pentagono, which directed the painting of hundreds of murals across Mexico. See also the entry for *Schmuck*. No holdings known.

140 Dodo / edited by Steve Kuttner. Manchester: Manchester University Poetry Society, [No. 1, 1970?]–6 (1972)

UCL: 2 (1970)–6 (1972)

Leeds University, Brotherton Library: Oct. 1970. (Special Collections English Q-1 DOD)

141 The Dolmen Miscellany of Irish Writing / edited by John Montague; poetry editor, Thomas Kinsella. Dublin and New York: Dolmen Press and Oxford University Press, No. 1 (1962)

Index: Rudi Holzapfel, *A Survey of Irish Literary Magazines from 1900 to the present day*, M Litt thesis (Trinity College Dublin, 1964)

Profiled in: Tom Clyde, *Irish Literary Magazines: an outline history and descriptive bibliography* (Dublin: Irish Academic Press, 2003), BL: 2725.g.3414; James Liddy, "How we stood with Liam Miller: The Dolmen Miscellany, 1962", in *New Hibernia Review* Vol. 2 no. 3 (Autumn 1998), pp.9–15, BL: DSC 6084.235720

Related Imprint: Dolmen was a key literary press in Ireland from the 1950s to 1970s, publishing many poetry-related titles. It appears to have stopped publishing after 1986. The Michael Freyer Collection at Trinity College Dublin contains a substantial archive of the Dolmen Press.

Related Work: Maurice Harmon (ed.) *The Dolmen Press: A Celebration* (Dublin: Lilliput Press, 2002), BL: 2708.e.2634

This magazine, intended to go further than one issue, presented the Dolmen Press stable of new Irish writers especially to an American audience, hence co-publication by the New York branch of Oxford University Press. It had contributions in prose by e.g. Aidan Higgins, John McGahern, Brian Moore, and John Jordan (who soon edited Dolmen's *Poetry Ireland*); and poetry by Thomas Kinsella, James Liddy, and others.

BL: P.P.8000.dk.
CUL: L999.C.3.343
NLS: 6.1620
TCD: Press A DOL 1962 12 Copy A
UCL

142 Dragoncards / [edited by John Mole and Peter Scupham?]. Hitchin: Mandeville Press, [No. 1, 1974]–?

Related Imprint: Mandeville Press published many short collections by authors who included Anthony Hecht, George Szirtes, Neil Astley, Freda Downie, Peter Porter, Christopher Levenson, the editors, and others.

An envelope of a dozen or so cards, each with a poem on it. The poems are generally genial and straightforward, and many of the contributors were later featured in short collections published by the press. An archive of

correspondence and manuscript poems of the Mandeville Press is held by the British Library's Department of Manuscripts.

BL: 3 (1975), *Nine Muses* (1975), 4 (1976), 5 (1978), Winter [1978], 6 (1979), Christmas [1979], 7 (1980), 8 (1980), 11 (1981), 12 (1982), Christmas [1982], and an unnumbered set dated 1984. (Cup.900.t.21)
CUL: Winter [1978] (864.a.169(137); 11 (1981) (864.a.169(180–); 12 (1982) (864.a.169(244)); Christmas [1979] (864.a.169(165); Christmas [1982] (864.a.169(231)
NLS: Winter [1978] (L.198.b.3 (38)); 5 (1978) (L.198.b.3 (24)); Christmas [1979] (L.198.b.4(49)); 7 (1980) (L.198.b.4 (50)); 11 (1981) (L.195.b.4 (52)); Christmas [1982] (HP1.83.2016); and an unnumbered set dated 1984 (HP1.85.397).
TCD: *Nine Muses* (1975) (Press B MAND 1975 8); *Nine Muses* 2 (Press B MAND 1975 9); 5 (1978) (PRESS B MAND 1978 4); Winter [1978] (PRESS B MAND 1978 5); 6 (1979) (Press B MAND 1978 3); Christmas [1979] (Press B MAND 1979 6); 7 (1980) [Press B MAND 1979 2); 12 (1982) (Press B MAND 1981 5); and an unnumbered set dated 1984 (Press B MAND 1984 1)

143 Driftwood Quarterly / edited by Brian Wake. Bootle: Driftwood Quarterly, No. 1 [1968]

Contributors include: Marguerite Edmonds, Spike Milligan, Roger McGough, Michael Horovitz, Alan Plater, David Chaloner, Rosemarie Strebe (trans. Michael Bullock), Brian Patten, Jim Burns, Wes Magee, Anselm Hollo, Paul Matthews, and Peter Cundall.

BL: ZD.9.a.75
Leeds University, Brotherton Library: Special Collections English Q-1 DRI
Liverpool University: SPEC Merseyside Poets III.D77

144 The Dublin Magazine / edited by Rivers Carew and Timothy Brownlow; then John Ryan. Dublin: New Square Publications, Vol. 4 no. 1 (Spring 1965)–vol. 10 no. 4 (Spring / Summer 1974). ISSN: 0012–687X

Note: Continues *The Dubliner*
Index: To 1969, Hayes
Profiled in: Tom Clyde, *Irish Literary Magazines: an outline history and descriptive bibliography* (Dublin: Irish Academic Press, 2003), BL: 2725.g.3414
BL: Vol. 4 no. 1–vol. 5 no. 3/4; vol. 6 no. 2–vol. 7. no. 2/3/4; vol. 8 no. 3–vol. 10 no. 4. (PP.7617.rn)
CUL: L727.C.283
NLS: 1965–1967. (P.66 (1965–1967) PER). 1968–1974. (Y.86

(1968–74) PER)
TCD: Gall M.37.57–63
UCL

145 The Dubliner / edited by Donald Carroll; then Bruce Arnold; then Rivers Carew and Timothy Brownlow. Dublin: New Square Publications, Vol. 1 no. 1 (Nov./Dec. 1961)–vol. 3 no. 4 (Winter 1964)

Note: Continued as: The Dublin Magazine

Index: David Elyan and Rudi Holzapfel, The Dubliner, Vol. 1 no. 1–Vol. 3 no. 4: an index to contributors (Dublin: New Square Publications, 1965), BL: P.P.7617.rn; Stephen H. Goode, Index to Commonwealth little magazines (New York: Johnson Reprint, 1966), BL: HURO11.3409171; Hayes

Profiled in: Tom Clyde, Irish Literary Magazines: an outline history and descriptive bibliography (Dublin: Irish Academic Press, 2003), BL: 2725.g.3414

BL: Vol. 1 no. 2 –vol. 3 no. 4 (Winter 1964). (P.P.7617.rn)
CUL: L727.C.283
NLS: P.66 PER
TCD: OLS L–3–731, no. 5
UCL

146 The Ear in a Wheatfield / edited by Kris Hemensley. Hawthorn, Australia: K. Hemensley, No. 1 (1973)–17 (1976)

Note: Continues Earth Ship.

Anthology: Kris Hemensley (ed.) The Best of the Ear: the Ear in a wheatfield 1973–76: a portrait of a magazine (Melbourne: Rigmarole Books, 1985), BL: YA.1989.b.7287

Contributors included: Anthony Barnett, David Bromige, Paul Buck, Charles Bukowski, Clark Coolidge, Cid Corman, Laurie Duggan, Larry Eigner, Ulli Freer, Edmond Jabès, Tim Longville, Bill Manhire, David Miller, Francis Ponge (trans. Peter Riley), John Riley, Peter Riley, John Tranter, Rosmarie Waldrop, and others.

BL: 1. (ZA.9.b.1024)
UCL: 3–17

147 Earth Ship / edited by Kris Hemensley. Southampton: [Earth Ship], No. 1 (Oct. 1970)–13 (Oct. 1972)

Note: Continued as: The Ear in a Wheatfield.

BL: 1 (Oct. 1970)–4/5 (Sep. 1971), 7 (Dec. 1971/Jan. 1972)–9 (April 1972), 13 (Oct. 1972). (ZA.9.c.36)
UCL

148 Ego / [edited by Hastings Donnan with Terri Hooley?, then 'The Tribe']. Belfast: ID Publications, No. 1 [1971]–6 [1971?]

Profiled in: Tom Clyde, Irish Literary Magazines: an outline history and descriptive bibliography (Dublin: Irish Academic Press, 2003), BL: 2725.g.3414

Related to Id and Both Sides Now. A general arts and politics review for Belfast but with poems by George Cairncross, William Oxley, and others. The last issue was edited anonymously under the collective name The Tribe.

BL: 5, 6. (P.903/253)
TCD: 2–6 (OLS X–1–612 no.2)

149 Eikon Review / edited by Paul Horne. Chelmsford, Printed by the Poets' and Printers' Press [for Paul Horne], No. 1 (Jan. 1965)

The first and only issue included short fiction and satire, and poems by Beatrice Mayor.

BL: P.901/87
CUL: L999.C.3.610
NLS: 1973.107
TCD: PER 81–226
UCL

150 Eleventh Finger / edited by Paul Evans and Paul Matthews. Brighton: Paul Evans and Paul Matthews, 1 (1965)–4 (Spring 1968)

Note: No. 3 was the poetry collection by George Dowden, Because I Am Tired of the Night.

Related Imprint: Eleventh Finger collaborated with the imprint Ant's Forefoot to produce several pamphlets, including Paul Evans, True Grit (1970), BL: YA.1993.a.25074; and Tristan Tzara, trans. Lee Harwood, Destroyed Days: a selection of poems 1943–55 (1971), BL: YA.1998.a.11937

Contributors included Günter Grass, George Dowden, Tristan Tzara (trans. Lee Harwood), Brian Patten, James Koller, Michael Shayer, Jan Arb, Chris Hebron, Eric Mottram, Michael McClure, Harry Guest, Georg Trakl (trans. various), and others. Issue 2 has correspondence between Robert Kelly and Jerome Rothenberg about Deep Image poetry.

BL: 2. (ZD.9.a.83). 3 (YA.1994.a.20109). 4. (ZD.9.a.83)
UCL

151 Embryo: the poetry of Oundelians / edited by Nick Pritchard and others. Oundle, Peterborough: Oundle School, No. 1 (1964)–11 (June 1968)

BL: 11. (P.901/1623.)
UCL: 1–8, 10.

152 The Enchanted Moan. Vol. 1 no. 1 (1975)–?

The title is taken from a phrase in Tennyson's poem "Maud". No holdings known.

153 The English Intelligencer / edited by Andrew Crozier (Series 1); Peter Riley (Series 2); and Andrew Crozier, John James, and J. H. Prynne (Series 3). Hastings: Series 1 [1966]–3 [1968]

Profiled in: The description of the Fales Library, New York University archive at: www.nyu.edu/library/bobst/research/fales/coll_mss/englishint.html

A key magazine of "The Cambridge School". Typed foolscap format, sent out to a select number of contributing poets, with surprising frequency: on average, the thirty-six issues of the whole run appeared at a rate of an issue about every three weeks. Contributors included the editors, Barry MacSweeney [as Barry McSweeny], Elaine Feinstein, Lee Harwood, Anselm Hollo, Gael Turnbull, Donald Davie, Paul Evans, John James, Ed Dorn, Wendy Mulford, Jon Silkin, Tony Rudolf (translating a number of French poets, including Apollinaire and Mallarmé), Jules Laforgue (trans. MacSweeney), Francis Ponge, Gill Vickers, Chris Torrance, Tim Longville, and others. The magazine's archive is held by the Fales Library, New York University

BL: P.905/20
CUL: Series 1–2. (T727.A.31.)
UCL

154 Enigma / edited by Jessica A. Burgess [later known as Jessica A. Gorst-Williams]. Pembury, Kent, then London: Enigma, Vol. 1 no. 1 (1968)–vol. 2 no. 2 (1970). ISSN: 0013–8428

BL: Vol. 1 no. 1–vol. 2 no. 1. (P.901/333)
CUL: Vol. 1 no. 3 (1968)–vol. 2 no. 2 (L727.C.571)
NLS: Vol. 1 no. 3 (1968)–vol. 2 no. 2 (HP2.77.323 PER)
UCL
Poetry Library: Vol. 2 no. 1

155 Enigma / edited by Rigby Graham. Leicester: Cog Press, 1 (1969)–4 (1971)

Related Imprint: Cog Press published a small number of art and poetry-related books including Leon Spiro's *Cobwebs from California* (1973), BL: Cup.510.cod.9, as well as *Barwell Broadside*

The texts were typewritten and mimeographed. The use of coloured paper, the considerable space given to each writer and each artist, and the interspersal of striking prints of a range of styles made this magazine visually very attractive. Poets included: John Cotton, Patrick Bridgwater (two "typograms" or concrete poems), Oliver Bayldon, and Leon Spiro. Artists included Graham himself, John Minton, Margaret McCord, Anne Palmer, Elizabeth Dowling, Paul Peter Piech, John Farrington, and John Piper. There were articles on John Cotton's magazine *Priapus* (to which *Enigma* was a spiritual successor), Robert Graves and Laura Riding's Seizin Press, Nicolas de Stael as a book illustrator, printing *Fishpaste*, Rilke's influence on English poetry, and other topics.

BL: Cup.510.cod.4.
CUL: T727.c.51

Enock's Fatal Bile Beater *See* Ludd's Mill D260

156 Envelope: a magazine of visual poetry. Birmingham: No. 1 [1969?]

UCL

157 Equator: Liverpool University poetry magazine / edited by Veronica Forrest [–Thomson]. Liverpool: Liverpool University, No. 1 (1966)–5 (1967)

Edited by a figure who would soon become a significant poet and theoretician within the "Cambridge School" grouping, this magazine survives, as far as is known, only in one, late, issue.

UCL: 5 (1967)

158 Era / edited by Desmond Egan. Castleknock, Dublin: Goldsmith Press, 1 (Spring 1974)–6 (1982)

Profiled in: Tom Clyde, *Irish Literary Magazines: an outline history and descriptive bibliography* (Dublin: Irish Academic Press, 2003), BL: 2725.g.3414
Related Imprint: The Goldsmith Press published work by e.g. Michael Hartnett, Desmond Egan, and Desmond O'Grady.

Poems, short fiction, articles and reviews. Contributors included Patrick Kavanagh (posthumously), Thomas Kinsella, Michael Hartnett, Desmond O'Grady, John Hewitt, Paul Durcan, Padraic Fallon, Yannis Ritsos, and others.

BL: 1–4. (P.901/3013)
CUL: L727.B.250
NLS: HP4.86.1388 PER
TCD: OLS L–2–71 no.2 nos.1–6
UCL: 1–4.
Poetry Library: 1–2, 4–6.

159 **Euphoria** / edited by Paul J. Green. Peterborough: Paul J. Green, No. 1 (1966)–5 (1968)

Note: Continues: *Target*

UCL: 5

160 **Everyman: an annual religio-cultural review** / edited by Cyril Farrell, Edmund Haughey, Gerard McCreesh, Denis Haughey, and Seamus Heaney. Benburb, Co. Tyrone: Servite Priory, No. 1 (1968)–3 (1970)

Note: Continued as: *Aquarius: an annual religio-cultural review*
Index: To 1969, Richard. J. Hayes, *Sources for the History of Irish Civilization: Articles in Irish Periodicals*, (Boston: G. K. Hall, 1970), BL: HUL941.5
Profiled in: Tom Clyde, *Irish Literary Magazines: an outline history and descriptive bibliography* (Dublin: Irish Academic Press, 2003), BL: 2725.g.3414

BL: P.801/1245
CUL: L900.C.421
NLS: 2–3. (NB.126 PER)
TCD: Per 80–206

161 **Excello & Bollard Annual** / edited by Paul Lamprill, Paul Bura, John Rice, Graeme Carter and others. Canterbury: Excello & Bollard, 1974–1978

Related Imprint: Excello and Bollard published *Sandwiches* and a range of books, including single-author collections, e.g. by George Cairncross, Tina Morris, Steve Sneyd, and Paul Lamprill.
Related Work: Paul Lamprill, *The British Excello & Bollard Company Chronicle*, 1973–4–5 (King's Lynn: Excello & Bollard, 1976), BL: YC.1989.b.5557

BL: LB.31.c.9105

CUL: L727.B.170
NLS: 1976 (HP1.77.988), 1977 (HP4.79.104), 1978 (HP3.78.1530)
TCD: 1976–1978. (PR 4729 1976–1978)

162 **Exit** / edited by John Hall, Ian Breakwell and Cliff Harris. Risley, Derby: Exit Publications, 1 (1965)–6 (1968). ISSN: 0531–5409

Related Imprint: Exit Publications

Contributors include John Stevens Wade, Shimpei Kusano, Henny Kleiner, Lee Harwood, Kevin Coyne, John Sharkey, Tom Phillips, Edwin Morgan, Cavan McCarthy, Andrew Lloyd, Dom Sylvester Houédard, John Furnival, and Bob Cobbing. Nos. 5 and 6 constituted a double issue of coloured sheets "bag mag" style, devoted to British visual poetry. No. 7 was planned as a readers' Do-It-Yourself issue, and no. 8 to be guest-edited by Paul Matthews. Publicity about Exit and Exit Publications was contained in *Exit News* (BL: No. 2 only, pressmark pending).

BL: 2–6. (ZA.9.c.44).
CUL: 1–4. (L727.B.68)
NLS: 1–4. (5.357)
TCD: 1–4. (PER 90–93 1967)
UCL

163 **Expression** / edited by Eric Ratcliffe, Brian Louis Pearce, Robert Druce and Les Surridge. Whitton: Whitton Poetry Group, then New Richmond Poetry Group, No. 3 [1965]–14 (April 1968). Then as *Expression One*, No. 15 (July 1968)–32 [1973]

Note: Continues: *Collection* (1962–63)
Interview: With Eric Ratcliffe in Görtschacher 2

Contributors included Eric Ratcliffe, Penelope Shuttle, Brian Louis Pearce, William Oxley, and others. After a two year gap, following the closure of *Expression One*, the group renamed itself again and "The Richmond Poetry Group" issued the annual anthology *Richmond Poets*. Not to be confused with Michael Bullock's magazine *Expression*, publishing at the same time.

BL: 3–23. (11397.bb.2.)
CUL: L727.C.310
NLS: 3–25, 28–32. (P.med.1264 PER)
TCD: 28–32. (PER 71–793)
UCL: 3–29.
Poetry Library: 15–16, 28, 29, 32

164 Expression / edited by Michael Bullock, then Ian Robinson. Harrow: No. 1 [1966]–12 (1970). ISSN 0014–5319

Note: Absorbed by: *Oasis*

Ian Robinson edited the last issue of this magazine, when Michael Bullock moved to Canada. Not to be confused with the Whitton/Richmond Poetry Group's magazine *Expression*, publishing at the same time.

BL: P.901/76.
CUL: L727.D.136
NLS: NG.728 PER
TCD: PER 81–706
UCL
Poetry Library: 2–5, 7, 8, 10–12

Expression One *See* Expression D163

165 Face North: Review of Northern Arts & People / edited by Mark Featherstone-Witty. Durham: Face North, Vol. 1 no. 1 (Oct./Nov. 1972)–no. 4 (Apr./May 1973)

A general arts review which always gave space to local schoolchildren's poetry. No. 2 carries an autobiographical account by Norman Nicholson, no. 3 carried an interview with Tony Harrison, and the last issue has an interview with Jon Silkin about *Stand*.

BL: P.803/345

Fenice Broadsheet *See* Phoenix Broadsheet D347

166 Fire / edited by Joseph Berke. London: Fire, 1 (1967)–[11–15, 1972]

Note: Nos. 3–9 were issued as a single volume *Counter Culture: the creation of an alternative society*, London: Peter Owen, 1969; nos. 11–15 were issued as the poetry collection by Roberta Elzey Burke, *Sphere of Light*, co-published with Trigram, 1972

The editor founded the Free University of New York, was involved in the Antiuniversity of London, and organised the radical international conference, The Dialectics of Liberation. Gary Snyder contributed the prose piece "Buddhism and the Coming Revolution" to no. 1. Included in no. 2 are another prose piece by Snyder, "Passage to More Than India", Ferlinghetti's performance piece "Fuclock", and an interview with Julian Beck, "Dialectics of Liberation on the Theatre".

BL: 1–2, 10. (PP.7611.tl.), 3–9 (X.525/394), 11–15 (X.981/9218).
CUL: 2–10. (9200.B.222.)
NLS: 7.99 (Nr. 2 (Mar. 1968) ; Nr. 10) PER; NG.1329.d.8 ([Nos. 2–9]) PER; H3.75.84 ([Nos. 11–15]) PER
TCD: 2 (Press B POET 1968+1 no.2 (1968)); 10 (Press B DAE 1970+13 no.10 (1970))
UCL: 1

167 Fireweed / edited by David Craig, Nigel Gray and Graham Taylor. Lancaster: Fireweed, No. 1 (Spring 1975)–12 (Apr. 1978). ISSN: 0307–2961

Related Imprint: Fireweed published some fiction and some single-author collections, including works by David Craig and by Nigel Gray

"A quarterly magazine of working-class and socialist arts." Many photographs and other visual material; song lyrics and accompanying music notation; essays; and poems, e.g. from Brecht, Neruda, Erich Fried and José Emilio Pacheco in translation, as well as Edward Bond (better known as a playwright), Ferlinghetti, Denise Levertov, Adrian Mitchell, Joyce Carol Oates, and others. Alan Dent was an editorial assistant.

BL: P.901/1354
CUL: L727.c.598
NLS: DJ.s.313 PER
TCD: PER 75–924
UCL
Poetry Library: 1, 3–11

168 Fishpaste / produced by Rigby Graham, Peter Hoy and Toni Savage. Leicester, then Oxford: Graham, Hoy and Savage, No. 1 (Feb. 1967)–22 (May 1968); hors-série 1 (May 1968)–3 (Aug. 1968); 2nd series. no. 1 (Feb. 1967)–5 (Dec. 1969). ISSN: 0015–3087

Note: The numbering is eccentric: in the first series, 4? appears between 4 and 5; an issue numbered 6A similarly appears between 6 and 7; and issue "Umpteen" appears between 19 and 20.
Profiled in: *Enigma* (ed. Rigby Graham), [No.] 2 [1969], BL: Cup.510.cod.4.
Study: Derek Deadman and Rigby Graham, *A Paper Snowstorm: Toni Savage & The Leicester Broadsheets* (Oldham: Incline Press, 2005)

Each issue was one postcard, with a drawing or other artwork on one side and generally a poem or other text on the other. The poets included: René Char (translated by

Paris Leary and Peter Hoy), Alan Riddell, Adrian Henri, John Birtwhistle, Lyman Andrews, Adrian Wright, John Cotton, Gillian Fidler, Francis Ponge (translated by Peter Hoy), Carmela Moya, Anthony Conran, Yvonne Caroutch (translated by Raymond Federman), and John Mole.

BL: Cup.503.a.18
CUL: Imperfect set. (L727.e.1)
NLS: 1–17, 19–20, 22; hors-série 1 (May 1968)–3 (Aug. 1968); 2nd series, 1–5. (5.4898 PER)
UCL: 1

169 Fish-sheet / [edited by Ian Hamilton Finlay]. [Edinburgh: Wild Hawthorn Press], 1 [1963]

Poems, including shaped poems, by Pete Brown, J. F. Hendry, Spike Hawkins, Ian Hamilton Finlay, Anselm Hollo, and Edwin Morgan.

BL: HS.74/1570/77
NLS: 6.1990 (7)

170 Fix / edited by Mike Dobbie. Hayes: Poet & Peasant Books, No.1 (1974)–3 (Summer 1976)

Related Imprint: Poet & Peasant Books published a number of single author pamphlets and seemed also to have acted as an agent for other small presses.

Mike Dobbie had previously published and edited *Streetword* magazine. For this title Ulli McCarthy and Bernard Kelly assisted with editing. Contributors included Bill Griffiths, Pierre Joris, Robert Vas Dias, Jeff Nuttall, Cecil Helman, Allen Fisher, Anna Banana, Eric Mottram, David Miller, Opal Nations, Ken Edwards, and others. The last issue reproduced for the first time some of the collages made by Joe Orton and Kenneth Halliwell out of stolen library books.

BL: 3. (ZA.9.a.8908)
UCL
Poetry Library: 2–3

171 Flame / edited by Alistair Wisker; and James F. Peck, Chris Mullins and Mike Loftus. Colchester: Colchester School of Art, then University of Essex, No. 1 (1966)–6 (1969)

Anthology: *Some Flame Poetry* (Colchester: University of Essex, [1967]), BL: X.902/452

Some illustrations and other visuals, but the emphasis is on poetry. Contributions include: poems by Barry McSweeney,

Chris Mullins, Michael Hamburger (who is also interviewed), Ed Dorn, Jim Burns, Andrew Crozier, Dannie Abse (also interviewed), Peter Riley, Tom Clark, David Chaloner, Lee Harwood, Brian Patten, Tom Raworth, Larry Eigner, Elaine Feinstein, David Tipton, Chris Torrance, Wes Magee, Martin Booth, José Emilio Pacheco (in translation) and others

BL: 2–5. P.903/23
CUL: 1–5. (L985.B.122)
UCL

Fo Po *See* Folk and Poetry D172

172 Folk and Poetry / edited by Margaret Tunstall, David Miller, Mike Simmons and Jill Doncaster. Luton: Margaret Tunstall, No. 1 (Dec. 1967)–18 (June 1969)

Note: Variant title: Fo Po
Profiled in: David Miller, "A whole year's FoPoing", in *Folk and Poetry* 12 (Dec. 1968)

Typewritten stencil format. First issue foolscap, then subsequent issues A4. The magazine was designed "to foster young creative talent. Many of the people in this edition will be well known to you through their appearances at the Folk and Poetry clubs in Luton and Harpenden." – from the first issue. Poems and songs (with sheet music) from those associated with the clubs, and very occasional articles and reviews of records

BL: P.905/9

173 Form / edited by Philip Steadman, Mike Weaver and Stephen Bann. Cambridge: Philip Steadman, No. 1 (Summer 1966)–10 (Sept. 1969). ISSN: 0532–1697

Note: Subtitle: a quarterly magazine of the arts
Related Imprint: Motion Books, which operated from the same address as Philip Steadman in Cambridge, published *Four Essays on Kinetic Art*, by Frank Popper, Philip Steadman, Reg Gadney, and Stephen Bann.

A magazine interested in literary and other arts theory. Professionally printed with high design and production values that matched its impressively intellectual remit. As well as theoretical articles, the magazine published poems, especially visual and sound poetry. Contributors included: Roland Barthes on "The Activity of Structuralism", Pedro Xisto, William Carlos Williams on Emanuel Romano (posthumously, but for the first time), Ian Hamilton Finlay, Eugen Gomringer on "The first years of Concrete Poetry",

Raoul Hausmann on "Meaning and Technique in Phonic Poetry", David Chaloner, Simon Cutts (poems, as well as an essay on "The Aesthetic of Ian Hamilton Finlay") and others. Each issue featured extracts from what it considered to be a "Great Little Magazine", as well as notes and an index to it. Apart from *Ray* (London, 1927–28), the featured magazines were almost all published outside of the British Isles: *Secession, Blues, G, Mecano, Ray, De Stijl, SIC, Kulchur* and *LEF*. The latter, though profiled in issue 10, had its index delayed until the intended issue 11, an issue which seems never to have appeared. The importance to contemporary practitioners of visual and sound poetry of placing and asserting their work within a documented historical context, also demonstrated in magazines such as *Kroklok*, is perhaps no better illustrated than in *Form*.

BL: P.421/41
CUL: L400.B.153
NLS: 2–10 (Sept. 1969). Q.133 PER
TCD: PER 90–132 1966–1969
UCL

174 Form / edited by A. S. Martin. Campeltown, Argyll: Form Publications, No.1 (Summer 1969)

Contributors included: Nathaniel Tarn, Peter Porter, Stephen Mulrine, David Harsent, Tom Buchan, Wes Magee, Iain Crichton Smith, Douglas Dunn, Thomas Kinsella, Naomi Mitchison, Robin Fulton, Edwin Morgan, Edward Lucie-Smith, Jon Stallworthy, Jon Silkin, Robin Hamilton, Robert Nye, and others.

BL: YA.1989.a.9565
CUL: L727.D.171
NLS: 5438 PER
TCD: PER 92–310
UCL

175 Format. Stroud: Alan Tucker, No. 1 (1966)–9 (1971). ISSN: 0015–7740

"This is less a magazine than a group anthology." – editorial in first issue. The poets featured throughout the series were Morris Cox, T. R. Glover, Brian Morse, and Alan Tucker.

BL: 1–2 (Mar. 1967), 5 (Jan. 1968)–9. (P.901/178.)
CUL: 1–8. (L727.B.71)
NLS: 1–4 (Sep. 1967) (5.4434). 5–8 (1970). (5.5674)
TCD: 1–8. (PER 90–132 1967–1969)

176 Fortnight / edited by Tom Hadden and others. Belfast: Fortnight Publications, Issue 1 (25th Sept. 1970)–

Index: Bill Rolston, *The Index 1970–1987, Nos. 1–250* (Belfast: Fortnight Publications, 1987)
Profiled in: Tom Clyde, *Irish Literary Magazines: an outline history and descriptive bibliography* (Dublin: Irish Academic Press, 2003), BL: 2725.g.3414

Cultural and political review with a significant publication of poetry.

BL: Newspaper Library
CUL: 1–133[1976]; 141 [1977]– . (L488.B.22)
NLS: QJ9.815
TCD: Per 72–467

177 Full House Poetry / edited by Pat Williams. Hemel Hempstead: Full House Poets, No.1 [1974]–10 [1984]

Note: From no. 6, the magazine had the variant title: *Full House Poets*

Anthologies of poems by the Full House Poets group.

BL: 4 (1977)–10. (P.901/3087)
CUL: 4 (1977)–10. (L727.C.700)
NLS: 4 (1977)–10. (DJ.s.13 PER)
TCD: 4 (1977)–6. (PER 94–223 [1976–1977])
UCL: 1–8 [1981]
Poetry Library: 1 [1974]–6 (1977)

178 Fuse / edited by David Templer, David Thomas and Paul Johnstone. Cambridge: [Fuse], No. 1 (June 1972)–4 (Nov. 1973)

"FUSE came into being as a result of a feeling that confrontation should evolve in the context of communication. We feel that Cambridge needs a magazine which presents the work of undergraduates beside that of graduates and senior members, while at the same time placing University work in a wider perspective. It is important not to see such work in terms of divisions of any kind; although FUSE is primarily concerned with literature, we want to set up a focus for a wide range of creative thought, and to provide the charge for a response." – the editorial in no. 1. Contributors included Iain Crichton Smith, Stephen Poliakoff (short fiction), R. S. Thomas, Peter Levi, John Harvey, Veronica Forrest-Thomson, J. H. Prynne, Charles Tomlinson, Philip Hobsbaum, John Mole, John Wilkinson, George Steiner, Jane Rogers, Jon Silkin, Alan Brownjohn, Anthony Burgess, D. J. Enright, Nathaniel Tarn, Raymond Williams, Peter Redgrove, Christopher

Logue, Martin Thom, Nigel Wheale, Seamus Heaney, Al Alvarez, Edwin Morgan, and others. The last issue was edited by Thomas and Johnstone only.

BL: P.903/179
CUL: CAM.B.31.65

179 Futura. [Stuttgart]: Hansjorg Mayer, No. 1 (1966)–26 (1968). ISSN: 0532–9019

Folded sheets of (mostly) concrete poetry, each issue solely featuring a single poet's work. Contributors include Bob Cobbing, Ian Hamilton Finlay, Edwin Morgan, Louis Zukofsky, Augusto de Campos, Edward Lucie Smith, Jonathan Williams, and others.

BL: RH.9.x.1300
NLS: 7 (HP2.86.2240); 20 (HP2.77.225) only
UCL: 5, 10

180 Gaga / edited by Paul Brown. London: Gaga Bureau, Issue 1 [1969]–4 (1970)

Note: Issue 3 came with a large poster, depicting President Kennedy, which was used, somewhat obliquely, to advertise the Unicorn Bookshop, Brighton. Issue 4 bore the cover title *Purple Ga*, and was indeed purple.

A hippy, psychedelic atmosphere to this magazine. The first issue has an eighteen-point declaration by the "Bureau of Surreal Activities" – eg. "9. There are no Virgin Marys… 10. We are the factors determining the velocity of angels…13. In Britain there are no demilitarised zones…" Contents included poems, comic strip art, advice on what to do if arrested, listings of other little magazines, and collages. Despite *Gaga* stating leftist aspirations, pictures of near-naked women appear in ways that seem untroubled by their objectification; a collage announcing "smash the bourgeoisie" uses photos of what appear to be several Chinese civilians and one Chinese soldier. Poets included Lawrence Upton, Libby Houston, Helen Fletcher, Peter Finch, Julian Elliot, the editor, and others.

BL: P.901/567
UCL
Poetry Library: 3 [1970]

181 Gallery: an illustrated poetry magazine / edited by Valerie Sinason. London: Valerie Sinason, No. 1 (Autumn/Winter 1974)–5/6 (1978). ISSN: 0306–1256

As the name suggests, this magazine had an *Ambit*-like interest in showing art as well as poetry. Contributors

included Penelope Shuttle, Ruth Fainlight, Nicki Jackowska, Fleur Adcock, Jim Burns, and others. No. 3 was entitled "Women's poetry".

BL: 1–4. (P.901/1288)
CUL: 1–4 (L727.C.592)
NLS: 1–2. (HP2.78.2170 PER)
TCD: 1–2 (PER 75–948)
UCL
Poetry Library

182 Gallimaufry: Dundee University arts magazine / edited by Brian McGlynn and Felicity Berry, and then others. Dundee: Dundee University, No. 1 (1974)–20 (1993). ISSN 0306–445X

Note: Continued by: Eric

Anne Stevenson, when Fellow in Creative Writing at Dundee, helped create this long-running magazine, and the poet provides a preface (and some poetry) in the first issue. Other contributors include G. F. Dutton, Ellie McDonald, Bill Duncan, A. D. Foote, Maurice Lindsay, Norman MacCaig, Iain Crichton Smith, Gerald Mangan, Carl MacDougall, Andrew Greig, Val Warner, Douglas Dunn, John Greening, Peter Porter, Peter Redgrove, Penelope Shuttle, Margaret Gillies Brown, George Bruce, Tracey Herd, James Hall Thomson, Sean O'Brien, Kathleen Jamie, Gerald Dawe, Christopher Rush, Edwin Morgan, and others.

BL: ZK.9.a.1948
CUL: L985.C.127
NLS: HJ4.1361 PER
UCL: 1–4.

183 Gandalf / edited by Neil Palmer, Tony Quinn, [Mike Williams?]…and others. [Plymouth, No. 1, 1969?–?]

UCL: 4 [1969?]–8 [1970]

184 Gandalf's Garden / edited by Muz Murray. London: Gandalf's Garden, No. 1 (1968)–6 (1969). ISSN: 0016–4429

A counterculture magazine that mixed do-it-yourself mysticism with thoughts of peace and love. It carried very few poems, but these included work by Christopher Logue, Peter Finch, Adrian Mitchell, and Marc Bolan. John Peel contributed a prose meander. Muz Murray later issued the one-off *Gandalf's Inner Garden Newsletter* (1971), a copy of which is held at UCL.

BL: P.905/12
CUL: L900.B.302
NLS: 7.148 PER
TCD: PER 90–205

185 **Gargantua** / edited by Robert Ensor. Birmingham: Gargantua, No. 1 [1971]–3 [1973?]

Contributors include Lawrence Upton, Geoffrey Holloway, visual poetry by Stephen Morris, Opal L. Nations, Nina Steane, and others.

BL: 1–2. (P.901/760)
UCL
Leeds University, Brotherton Library: 2–3. (Special Collections English Q–1 GAR)

186 **Genera** / edited by Colin Simms. Kirbymoorside, Yorkshire: Colin Simms, [No. 3? 1975?–?]

Note: Continues: *North York Poetry*

Each issue was given over to the work of a single writer, e.g. no. 13 was Eric Mottram's *A Faithful Private*.

BL: 13. (YA.2003.b.3674)
UCL

General Schmuck *See* Schmuck D425

187 **George: son of My Own Mag** / edited by Jeff Nuttall. [London]: Jeff Nuttall, 1 [Nov. 1969]–7 (Sept. 1970)

Note: Continues: *My Own Mag*

Nuttall is the only contributor. Largely pictorial and sexually explicit.

BL: RH.9.x.1310
CUL: L400.B.651
UCL: 1–3

188 **Gervase** / edited by James Whitaker, E. Seffen and Clive H. Morris. [Thurrock]: Thurrock Literary Society, 1 (1971)

Named after Gervase of Tilbury, this magazine collects poems by members of the Thurrock Literary Society.

BL: P.901/806

189 **Ginger Snaps: a collection of cut-ups / machine prose / word & image trips** / edited by Michael Gibbs and Hammond Guthrie. Exeter: Kontexts Publications, Mar. 1972

Related Imprint: Kontexts Publications published the magazine *Kontexts* devoted to visual and experimental poetry, and various one-off publications

Contributors include William Burroughs, Tom Phillips, Allen Ginsberg, Brion Gysin, and Claude Pelieu.

Edinburgh University Library: CS.82191 Gin
King's College London, Eric Mottram Archive: 7/253/1
1971–1972

190 **The Glasgow Review** / edited by Joseph Mulholland. Motherwell: Joseph Mulholland, Vol. 1 no. 1 (Spring 1964)–vol. 5 no. 1 (Summer 1974)

Essays on Scottish arts, history and politics, and more general articles, too; poetry and reviews.

BL: Vol. 1 no. 1–vol. 1 no. 3. (PP.8004.aa)
CUL: Vol. 1 no. 1–vol. 2 no. 1. (L900.C.394)
NLS: P.175 PER
TCD: Vol. 1 no. 1–vol. 2 no. 1. (PER 81–706)
UCL: Vol. 1 no. 1–vol. 2 no.2. [Flaxman Periodicals]. Vol. 3 no. 1–vol. 4 no. 4. [Little Magazines Collection]

191 **Glass Onion** / edited by Roger Edwards. Tondu, Glamorgan: No. 1 (1972)–2 (1973)

CUL: 2. (L999.C.3.752)
NLS: 2. (5.6406 PER)
UCL

The Global Moon-Edition Long Hair Times North Atlantic Turn-On *See* Long Hair D258

192 **Global Tapestry and Vegan Action** / edited by Dave Cunliffe and Tina Morris. Blackburn: BB Books, Thunderskyglow issue [No. 1, 1970]–[5, 1974]. Then as *Global Tapestry Journal*, 6– . ISSN: 0141–1241

Note: Absorbs: *PM Newsletter* and *Vegan Action*. From no. 6 title changed to *Global Tapestry Journal*. PM Newsletter

sometimes appeared as the name of the magazine's listings section.
Related Imprint: BB Books have published e.g. Tina Morris and Dave Cunliffe (eds.), *Thunderbolts of Peace and Liberation*, [1969], BL: X.900/3837; and Maggie Finn, *Selections from Maggie Finn's Dirty Panties*, [1980], BL: X.909/45019. George Dowden's *Waiting at the Traffic Lights: British poetry stop or go into the 1990s* (1991), BL: YA.1997.a.13986, was issued as a supplement to issue 21.
Microfilm: *The Underground & Alternative Press in Britain* (Hassocks: Harvester Press, 1974–), BL: Mic.F.19(2)

Beginning as much as a magazine of counterculture as a literary magazine, *Global Tapestry* was against the Vietnam War and for general peaceful revolution, love and veganism, and it published the manifesto of the Love & Peace Freak Party in the second issue. Work by Kenneth Patchen was published in its pages, and Patchen seems to have been a key figure for the magazine in the early years; it soon published more poetry, with work from the editors, Jim Burns, Andrew Darlington, David Tipton, Vivienne Finch, Steve Sneyd, Michael Horovitz, and many others. After a few years, Dave Cunliffe edited the magazine alone. It was produced in mimeograph format until 1991, when it closed for nearly ten years, re-launching with what looks like desk-top camera-ready copy in 2000, with issue no. 22.

BL: [1]–[2]; [4?, "Homage to Patchen Issue"]; 6–. (P.971/124)
CUL: [1]–[2]. (Microfiche 014)). 3. (L900.B.375]. 5 [1974]–. (Microfilm P106(34–)).
NLS: [1]–[3], 5 [1974]– . (HJ8.762 SER)
TCD: PER 91–770 1970–1991
UCL: [4?, "Homage to Patchen Issue"]–21 (1991)
Poetry Library: 7–11, 13, 15, 16, 18–21

193 Good Elf / edited by Lawrence Upton. Streatham: Lawrence Upton, No. 1 (Sept. 1970)–5/6 (1977)

Related Imprint: Good Elf published work from, e.g. Lawrence Upton, Don Jarvis, Tom Leonard, and Bob Cobbing
Related Publication: *The Great Good Elf Fiasco: poetry reading on Tuesday 30th October1973 at 8pm at Wolsey's Wine Bar, readers: George Cairncross …[et al.]*, (London: Good Elf Reading Group, [1973]), BL: YA.1993.b.11407

BL: 1–Interregnum issue [issued in 1972 following the 4th issue]; Supplement (June 1973). (P.901/661)
UCL: 1–4.
King's College London, Eric Mottram Archive: 5/6. (7/256/1 1977)
Poetry Library: 4.

194 Great Works / edited by Bill Symondson and Peter Philpott. Stoke-on-Trent and Bishop Stortford: Great Works Editions, 1 (1973)–7 (May 1979)

Related Imprint: Great Works Editions
Website: www.greatworks.org.uk/

From the website, June 2005: "Great Works published seven issues of a magazine, and a small number of books, aiming at surprise, innovation and delight in writing, especially poetry, hovering on that unstable cusp between modernism and postmodernism." Contributors included Peter Riley, Douglas Oliver, Andrew Crozier, John James, John Welch, Iain Sinclair, Wendy Mulford, Barry MacSweeney, Lee Harwood, Anthony Barnett, Richard Caddel, Elaine Randell, Ian Tyson, David Miller, Jeremy Harding, John Wilkinson, Nigel Wheale, Rod Mengham, David Chaloner, and others. The website is essentially an electronic continuation of the magazine.

BL: 1–3, 5–7. (P.903/559)
CUL: L727.b.164
NLS: 6–7. (6975 PER)
TCD: 6–7. (PER 80–135)
UCL

195 Greedy Shark / edited by Ian Patterson and Barry MacSweeney. [London]: [Greedy Shark], [No. 1, 1973]

Contributors include Peter Ackroyd, Douglas Oliver, Tom Pickard, Anthony Barnett, and Jeff Nuttall.

BL: YA.1991.b.1966
CUL: L999.B.1.2345
Poetry Library

196 Green Island: an occasional magazine / edited by David Kilburn. London: David Kilburn, 'Abstract Poem' [undated], 'You will dissolve...' (1970); 'Poem' [1972?], 'Shower Girl Song' [1972?], 'Rosebud is' [1976?], 'The Port Was Longing' (1984). ISSN 0307–7918

Note: Unnumbered and largely undated.

Appears to have been devoted solely to the publication of Robert Lax's poetry, with accompanying photographs. The ISSN UK Centre dates the magazine as beginning in 1967.

BL: 'Abstract Poem' [undated], 'Poem' [1972?], 'Shower Girl Song' [1972?], 'Rosebud is' [1976?]. (P.903/151)

UCL: 'Poem' [1972?], 'Shower Girl Song' [1972?], 'Rosebud is' [1976?], 'The Port Was Longing' (1984)
Poetry Library: 'You will dissolve...' (1970); 'Rosebud is' [1976?]; 'The Port was Longing' (1984)

197 Grosseteste Review / edited by Tim Longville. Lincoln: Grosseteste Press, Vol. 1 no. 1 (Spring 1968)–vol. 15 (1983/1984). ISSN: 0017–4637

Index: Tim Longville, *Seven Years of Grosseteste, 1966–1973: An Index to Grosseteste Review, Vols. 1–6, Issues 1–22* (Pensnett: Gr/ew Books, 1973), BL: YA.2003.a.8197
Anthology: Andrew Crozier and Tim Longville (eds.) *A Various Art* (Manchester: Carcanet, 1987), BL: YC.1987.a.11887
Related Imprint: Grosseteste Press, and its other name, Gr / ew Books, published collections by David Chaloner, William Bronk, Peter Philpott, Thomas A. Clark, Ralph Hawkins, Peter Riley, Gael Turnbull, and others.

Short prose and poetry, with a substantial American content, including: Denise Levertov, Cid Corman, Louis Zukofsky, Jonathan Williams, and Larry Eigner. Vol. 1 no. 2 (Autumn 1968) includes poems by "members and associates of the *Migrant* magazine and press of the 1950's. This covers the contributions by Gael Turnbull, Michael Shayer, Roy Fisher, Matthew Mead, and Hugh Creighton Hill." Vol. 3 no. 4 (Winter 1970) is devoted to the translations of Catullus by Celia and Louis Zukofsky. A selection is published, and there is comment by Cid Corman, Hugh Creighton Hill, and Richard Emil Braun. Vol. 4 no. 2 (Summer 1971) is devoted to Guillaume Chpaltine and Liliane Lijn. Vol. 5 no. 1 (Spring 1972) is a William Bronk special issue. Vol. 7(4), 1974: "Shannon, Who Was Lost Before" by James Koller (co-published by *The Ear in a Wheatfield*, Australia). Vol. 8 includes the following booklets: Anthony Barnett, "Titular I–VI", 1975; Roberto Sanesi, "A Selection" (with translations by William Alexander, Vernon Richards, Richard Burns, Cid Corman), 1975; "19 Poems & an Interview" by Roy Fisher, 1975; "An Alleghany Star Route Anthology", ed. Franco Beltrametti, 1975; "Residues: Down the Sluice of Time" by Gael Turnbull, 1976. Vol. 9 includes the following booklets: "To intimate distance" by Tim Longville, 1976; "Promenades" by Michael Chamberlain, 1976; "Brown Smoke and Dark Amber" by Elizabeth Rothwell, [9(3)], 1976; "Lime Tree Notes" by Philip Garrison, [9(4)], 1976; "Between the river and the sea" by Tim Longville, [9(5)], 1976. Vol. 11 includes the following booklets: "Eastwyke Farm" by Michael Chamberlain, 1978; "Exile Within" by Owen Davis, 1978; "Meaning Insomnia" by John Hall, 1978. John Riley was closely associated with the magazine (and with Grossesteste Press), and was listed as Business Manager

from 1971. Gordon and H.J. Jackson were involved with publishing the magazine from 1968–1971.

BL: Vol. 1–7, 10, 12–15. (P.901/319). Collections issued as part of vol. 8, 9, and 11 are held, but catalogued and shelfmarked separately.
CUL: Vol. 1–7, 10–15. (P727.C.46).
NLS: Vol. 7 no. 4–vol. 15. (P.sm.1616 (Vol. 7–12) PER); (P.med.4053 (Vol. 13–15) PER)
TCD: Vol.10–15. PER 92–436
UCL
Poetry Library: Vol. 1 no. 1; vol. 2 no. 1–2; vol. 3 no. 4; vol. 4 no. 1–3; vol. 5 no. 1, 3–4; vol. 6; vol. 8–10; vol. 12–15

198 H& / [edited by Ted Kavanagh?] Hove: Caliban Press, Feb. 1970

A one-off? Contributions by Jim Duke, Lee Harwood, Ted Kavanagh, Jeff Keen, Barry MacSweeney, and Peter Riley. Perhaps the title would be read as *Hand*.

UCL
Poetry Library

199 Haiku Byways / edited by Gerry Loose. London: Shan Press, [No.1] [1970]–3/4 [1972?]. ISSN 0046–6719

Note: Continued by *Byways*

Haiku and minimalist poetry, presented in an appropriate understated, white-space way. Contributors include Tony Hicks, Bernard Leach, Cid Corman, W.J. Higginson, John Wills, Chris Torrance, Tom Raworth, Gerry Loose, and translations from Chinese and Japanese writers (e.g. Basho, Chuang Tzu.)

BL: ZA.9.a.11547
UCL

200 The Hallamshire & Osgoldcross Poetry Express / edited by Gerald England. Sheffield: Headland Poetry, Vol. 1 no. 1 (Jan. 1972)–? Then as *New Hope*, (Spring 1978). Then as *New Hope International*, no. 1 (1980)–5; New Series, no. 1–12, vol 13 no. 1– vol.19 no.5 (1997). ISSN: 0260–7948. Then as *New Hope International Review*, Vol.20 no. 1 (1998)–no.3 [1999?]. ISSN: 1465–6868. Then as *New Hope International Review Online* (www.nhi.clara.net/online.htm)

Note: The first title was abbreviated as H.O.P.E., hence the

names of the continuations. Title variants: *New Hope Iinternational Zine*, *New Hope International Writing*. Includes several review supplements. Issue A of *Aabye* is also referred to as *New Hope International* vol. 20(3). Gladys Mary Coles was also involved editorially. Continued by: *Aabye*
Interview: with Gerald England in *Poetry Today Online*, www.poetrytodayonline.com/ JANpub.html
Related Imprint: New Hope International have published various single author collections, and after the closure of *New Hope International Review* these were issued on a subscription basis, as well as available individually. Other related magazines include *Osgoldcross Review*, *Headland*, and *New Headland*.

Related Work: Gerald England, *Editor's Dilemma: 20 years of small press publishing* (Hyde: New Hope International, 1990), BL: YK.1998.a.12604.
Website: www.nhi.clara.net/online.htm

BL: *H.O.P.E*: Vol. 1 no. 1–no.6 (Jan. 1974); no. 8 (Jan. 1975). (P.905/60). *New Hope International* and *New Hope International Review*: lacking Vol. 20 no. 2–3. (P.901/3250)
CUL: *New Hope International*. (L727.C.781)
NLS: *New Hope International*: 1980/81–no. 9 (1987). (P.1a.9072 PER)
TCD: *New Hope International*: 1980/81–no.9 (1987); Vol.15, no.6 (1993). (PER 92–731 1980–1993)
UCL: *New Hope International*: Vol.16 no. 6 (1993) only.
Poetry Library: *New Hope International*, no. 1–3, 5; New Series, vol. 1–vol. 7 no. 1; vol. 8–vol. 9; vol. 11–vol. 12; vol. 13 no. 2; vol. 14 no. 2–3; vol. 15 no. 1–vol. 16 no. 1; vol. 16 no. 3–vol. 17 no. 1; vol. 17 no. 3–5; vol. 18 no. 2–3, 5; vol. 19 no. 1, 3–5, vol. 20 no. 1, 3

Hand *See* H& D198

201 Hapt. Bournemouth, [1, 1969?–?]

UCL: 4, 23 and two unnumbered others
King's College London, Eric Mottram Archive: 16. (7/263/1 (1970))

202 Harvest / [edited by Elaine Randell?], c.1970

No holdings known.

203 Headland / edited by Gerald England, then William Oxley. Sheffield: Gerald England, No. 1 (Jan. 1970)–10 (April 1972). Then, as *New Headland Poetry Magazine*, Epping: Ember Press, 1 (Aug. 1972)–7 (Oct. 1974)

Index: Index to no. 1–4 published alongside no. 4

Interview: with Gerald England in *Poetry Today Online*, www.poetrytodayonline.com/ JANpub.html; with William Oxley in Görtschacher 1
Related Imprint: Headland Publications published collections by e.g. Colin Simms, James Kirkup, David Jaffin, Edna Bartholomew, Nicki Jackowska, and Penelope Shuttle. Ember Press published works by e.g. William Oxley, and Tom Scott, and also the magazines *Acumen* and *Littack*.
Related Work: Gerald England, *Editor's Dilemma: 20 years of small press publishing* (Hyde: New Hope International, 1990), BL: YK.1998.a.12604.

Soon after William Oxley took over editorship the magazine was developed as a miscellany to complement the more pointed aesthetic programme of his other magazine *Littack*. In Görtschacher 1 (p.224) *Headland* is reported as being relaunched by Gerald England in 1989, but no holdings are known.

BL: *Headland*. (P.901/539). *New Headland*, 1–4, 7. (P.901/1530)
CUL: *Headland*. (L727.B.86). *New Headland*, 1–4, 7. (L727.C.643)
NLS: *New Headland*. (NHP1.78.154 PER)
TCD: *Headland*. 1–8. (PER 81–970)
UCL
Poetry Library: *Headland*. 1–7. *New Headland*: 3

204 Henry Glasgow / [edited by Alan Spence?]. Glasgow: [Alan Spence?], 196–?

UCL: 3 (1969)

205 Here Now: South Tyneside arts quarterly / edited by Tom Kelly. Hebburn: Here Now, Vol. 1 no. 1 (Spring 1972)–vol. 3 no. 2 (Spring 1975). [New Series, edited by Terence Kelly and Peter Dixon], Jarrow, No. 1 [198–]–3 (1982/83). ISSN: 0046–7294

Related Imprint: Here Now became a poetry book imprint at the time of the new series, and published collections by Terence Kelly and Tom Kelly respectively.

Associated with the Bede Gallery in Jarrow. Poems, poetry debate, profiles of past master poets (e.g. Shelley, Tagore), and reviews, including early work by F. George Charlton (i.e. before he dropped the "F."), as well as by Peter Finch, Geoff Holland, Eleanor Makepeace, William Oxley, John Seed, T. S. Law, Stephen Mulrine, Colin Simms, Rodney Pybus, David Jaffin, J. D. Beardsley, Vivienne Finch, Frederic Vanson, Derek Stanford, Cal Clothier, Stephen Wade, and others.

BL: Vol. 1 no. 2–vol. 3 no. 2. (P.421/395)
CUL: Vol. 2 no. 1–vol. 3 no. 2. (L727.C.553)
NLS: Vol. 2 no. 1–vol. 3 no. 2. (NH.577 PER)
TCD: [New Series] No. 3. (PER 90–449)
UCL: Vol. 1 no. 1.
Poetry Library: Vol. 1 no. 1–no. 5; [New Series] No. 2

206 Hiatus: a poetry, prose and graphics magazine / edited by Stanley Engel. London: Oasis, No. 1 (1970)–2 (1972)

Related Imprint: Oasis published many single author collections, as well as the magazine *Oasis*.

Eclectic. Contributors included Ian Robinson, Betty Berenson, Owen Davis, Ulli McCarthy, Pier Paolo Pasolini, Joyce Kahn, Steve Sneyd, Raymond Queneau (trans. Marcus Cumberlege), Opal Nations, and others.

BL: P.903/136
UCL

207 Hightime. Harlow?, c.1964

Note: Continued by *Antiphon*

Noted by the UK Little Magazines Project. No holdings known.

208 The Hillingdon Writer / edited by Richard Wakely; John C. Keeble. [Hillingdon etc.], [No. 1, 1963?–25, 1975]

From no. 5 (Winter 1964) to no. 8 (Summer 1966) sponsored by the Yiewsley & West Drayton Arts Council. From no. 11 (Summer 1968) to no. 17 (Spring 1971) published by the West Drayton Literature Group. Nos. 18–25 were published by the Hillingdon Writer Group. The place of publication varies.

BL: No. 5–25 [1975]. (P.901/500.)
UCL: No.6–25 [1975]

209 Holy Cow / edited by Logan Finlayson. London, No. 1 (1973)

Noted by the UK Little Magazines Project. No holdings known.

210 The Holy Door / edited by Brian Lynch. Dublin: [1] (Summer 1965)–3 (Spring 1966). ISSN: 0441-1013

Index: Stephen H. Goode, *Index to Commonwealth Little Magazines* (New York: Johnson Reprint, 1966), BL: HUR011.3409171; Hayes

BL: HUL941.5
Profiled in: Tom Clyde, *Irish Literary Magazines: an outline history and descriptive bibliography* (Dublin: Irish Academic Press, 2003), BL: 2725.g.3414

Contributors included Pearse Hutchinson, Patrick Kavanagh, Paul Durcan, Anthony Cronin, Thomas Kinsella, Michael Hartnett, John Montague, and Desmond O'Grady as well as W. H. Auden, George Barker, Edward Dahlberg, Pablo Neruda (translated by Robert Bly), C. H. Sisson, and Andrei Voznesensky (in translation). Manuscripts relating to *The Holy Door* are held at Southern Illinois University at Carbondale, U.S.A.

BL: P.P.8007.ey.
CUL: Summer 1965. (L999.B.1.135)
NLS: P.la.295
TCD: OLS X–2–225
UCL

211 The Holy Eye / edited by Ian Vine. Bristol: Ian Vine, c.1964

Noted in *Origins Diversions* 4. No holdings known.

212 The Honest Ulsterman / edited by James Simmons; Frank Ormsby and Michael Foley; Robert Johnstone and Ruth Hooley; Tom Clyde. Castlerock then Belfast: [Ulsterman], No. 1 (May 1968)– . ISSN: 0018-4543

Note: For the first twenty issues had the sub-title: *Handbook for a Revolution*. Variant title: *H.U.*
Index: Tom Clyde, *H.U.: an author index to issues 1–99* (Belfast: HU Publications, 1995); Tom Clyde and Andreas Schachermayr, *H.U.: an author index to issues 100–107* (Belfast: HU Publications, 1999)
Interview: with Tom Clyde in Görtschacher 2
Profiled in: Tom Clyde, *Irish Literary Magazines: an outline history and descriptive bibliography* (Dublin: Irish Academic Press, 2003), BL: 2725.g.3414
Related Imprint: Ulsterman published a number of poetry pamphlets, e.g. by Harry Clifton, Derek Mahon, Tom Paulin, Ciaran Carson and Paul Muldoon

Essays, reviews, and poems. The first issues had an editorial by James Simmons entitled "Revolutionary Advice", the cause of one consignment being seized by the police. Over the years it has published poems and reviews across the range of Northern Irish poetry, as well as work, including translations, from further afield.

BL: P.801/433
CUL: L727.C.393

NLS: HJ4.101
TCD: PER 73–479
UCL
Poetry Library: 28, 31, 35, 18–40, 42–66, 68–88, 90–

H.O.P.E. *See* Hallamshire & Osgoldcross Poetry Express D200

213 Horde / edited by Johnny Byrne, Lee Harwood, Roger Jones and [Barry] Miles. London: Horde, No. 1 (Dec. 1964)

Note: Continues: *Night Train*

Contributors included Pete Brown, Mal Dean and Libby Houston, described as "now working on a series of 'goings-on' (free experiments in jazz, poetry, drama, etc.) at the Mercury Theatre, Notting Hill Gate." Two of the contributors seem to have been work acquaintances of Lee Harwood, then employed as a packer, including Mal Dean, and Geoffrey Hazzard. Byrne and Jones were interested in and wrote science fiction; another contributor, Paul Pignon, was described as a "poet, jazz musician, composer, & ex-atomic physicist." This was clearly a magazine about cross-over and experimentation; now better-known poets also appeared in its pages, including Harry Guest, Spike Hawkins, Anselm Hollo, and Penelope Shuttle. A second issue was advertised on the last page of the first issue, to be guest-edited by Anselm Hollo, but seems not to have materialised.

BL: P.903/1a
UCL

214 How: international poetry magazine / edited by Andrew Lloyd and others. Cheltenham, then Leeds, No. 1 (Feb. 1964)–7 [1966?]

Note: Only the first issue was dated; the last 2 issues were joint productions with *Tlaloc*

Contributors include Peter Hoida, Tom McGrath, Chris Torrance, Andrew Lloyd, Penelope Shuttle, and many others.

BL: P.P.8006.ot.
CUL: No. 3 (1965); 5 (1965). (L999.C.3.355)
NLS: No. 3 (1965)–No. 5 (1965). (5.676 and 5.076)
UCL

215 The Human Handkerchief / edited by Simon Pettet, Ralph Hawkins and Douglas Oliver. Colchester: [The Human Handkerchief c/o University of Essex], [No.1 (1972?)]–[197?]

Contributors included the editors, Iain Sinclair, Clark Coolidge, David Chaloner, Gordon Brotherston, Anne Waldman, Jeff Nuttall, John Seed, George Oppen, Barry MacSweeney, Andrew Crozier, Wendy Mulford, Alice Notley, Anselm Hollo, John James, Michael Haslam, Nigel Jenkins, and others. No. 4 was a collaborative work, with text by Paul Evans and drawings by Peter Bailey.

BL: 2–5. (ZA.9.b.2734)
UCL

216 The Human World: a quarterly review of English letters. Swansea: No. 1 (Nov. 1970)–15/16 (1974)

Note: Continued by: *Gadfly*.

A general review. Edited anonymously.

BL: P.901/692
CUL: P900.C.192
NLS: Y.105 PER
TCD: PER 81–943

217 Hydromel: the Oxford poetry magazine / edited by D. A. Freud. Oxford: Merton College, [No. 1, 1971]

CUL: L999.C.3.525
NLS: 6.2743 PER
TCD: PER 81–383

218 Iconolâtre: poetry, painting, jazz / edited by Alex Hand and Alan Turner. [West Hartlepool, No. 1, 1963?–24, 1969]. ISSN: 0019–1140

Related Imprint: Iconolâtre published C. C. Hebron's *Scavengers* (noted in *Broadsheet*, ed. Torrance)

Contributors included Brian Patten, Tina Morris, Geoffrey Holloway, Penelope Shuttle, Jim Burns, Vera Rich, Dave Cunliffe, and others. "Iconolâtre the Image-worshippers: Poetry, Visual Art, Jazz. No slither! Pound's dictum and ours." – from the first issue's editorial.

BL: 1; 3–12; 14/15. (P.P.8005.mc.).
CUL: 18/19–21; 24. (L999.C.3.376)
NLS: 18/19–21; 24. (5.5030)

219 Icteric / Trevor Winkfield, David Wise, Ronald Hunt, Stuart Wise and John Myers. Newcastle upon Tyne: Icteric, No. 1 (Jan.1967)–2 (June 1967)

BL: 2. (YA.1995.a.16414)
TCD: 1. (OLS L–6–145 no.11)
UCL

220 ID / edited by Terri Hooley. Belfast: Eye Publications, No. 1 [1970]–5 [1973?]; Souvenir issue: *The Rise and Fall of Id* (Belfast: Belfast Index, 1973)

Profiled in: Tom Clyde, *Irish Literary Magazines: an outline history and descriptive bibliography* (Dublin: Irish Academic Press, 2003), BL: 2725.g.3414

Related to *Ego* and *Both Sides Now*, this magazine's expressed aim was to "enlight and ignite you [...and to establish] a small, independent press." It published anti-Vietnam War political cartoons, comic strips, sound and visual poetry, more conventional poems, a song (with sheet music), an interview with an Irishman sent to a mental hospital in Epsom after being unable to pay a bill at a well-known venue in London, an account of someone being imprisoned for nine years for possession of a very small amount of marijuana, short fiction, an article on the evolution of rock music, and a brief attack on Irish Prime Minister Jack Lynch following the British Army killings on "Bloody Sunday". Issue two reveals an acknowledged affinity with the London Arts Lab: Hooley had tried to establish an equivalent centre in Belfast, but had been thwarted by the police. By issue three it described its circulation as 2000, and explained that it was part of the Queen's University student scene without being formally connected to it. Overall, there is a gentle sense of humour to this counter-culture magazine but nevertheless a determination to avoid and challenge political and religious divisions in Belfast and Northern Ireland. Judging from the high proportion of pages given over to poems, poetry was central to it. Contributors included Steve Sneyd, Denis Greig, George Cairncross, Claire Winston, Robert Johnstone, George Dowden, and others.

BL: 1–5, and Souvenir issue. (P.973/137)
TCD: 1–5. (OLS X–1–612 no.1)
UCL: 1–5, and Souvenir issue.

221 Ikon / edited by Doug Sandle. Leeds: Leeds University Student Union, [Vol. 1] No. 1 (Autumn 1964)–4 (March 1966)

Note: Continued by *M.O.M.A: magazine of modern arts*

BL: [Vol. 1] 1–2. (P.P.8007.eg.)
CUL: [Vol. 1] 3–4. (L999.c.3.356)
TCD: [Vol. 1] 3–4. (PER 81– 65)
UCL

222 Imprint / edited by John Clement and Derek Telling. Bristol: Bridgewest Publications, 1 (1967)–6 (1970). ISSN: 0019–3038

Related Imprint: Bridgewest Publications published, for instance, Nicki Jackowska's *The Words that Manda Spoke* (1974), BL: YA.1993.a.26152

CUL: 1 (1967)–5 (1969). (L727.C.396)
NLS: 1 (1967)–5 (1969). (6.1923 PER)
TCD: PER 81–227
UCL
Poetry Library: 5 (1969)

223 In The Night Of / c.1969

Note: Merged with *McCarthy's Technicolour Dream Pie* to become *Gaga*

No holdings known. Noted in *Gaga* 1.

224 Incept / [edited by Eric Harrison]. Shalford, Surrey: Eric Harrison, [No.1, 197?–?]

Related Imprint: Eric Harrison appears later to have established the Guildford Poets Press, which published John Emuss's *Affirmation* (Shalford, 1978), BL: X.909/43290

BL: 2. (ZA.9.a.5629)

225 Indigo Lumus / edited by Liam Maguire. Harlow: Harlow Writers, [1, 1966?]–7 (1969)

The group associated with this magazine appears to be different from The Harlow Writers Workshop, set up in 1990s and with its own imprint.

UCL

226 The Informer: the international poetry magazine / edited by Keith Armstrong and David Gill. Oxford: Circle Books, [No. 1, 1966?]–9 (1971)

Note: Loosely inserted in no. 7 is *Now: a minipoempoester* by Keith Armstrong (Circle Books, 1969). A volume designation was given to some issues, independent of the issue number, e.g. the last is referred to as no. 9 vol. 2 Related Imprint: Circle Books published several poetry pamphlets, e.g. Keith Armstrong, *Dreams* (1968), BL: YA.1996.a.4602

A stylistically eclectic magazine, publishing sound, visual, and more conventional poems alongside each other. Contributors included: Bob Cobbing, David Chaloner, Deirdre Farrell, Dom Sylvester Houédard, Nina Carroll, Peter Hoida, Roger Garfitt, R. G. Gregory, Edward Lucie-Smith, and others. Bruce Ross-Smith was also involved editorially.

BL: 9. (YA.1995.a.22861)
UCL: 2 (1966); 4–9
Poetry Library: 7 [1969]

227 Inherited / edited by Peter Hoida. London, then Cheltenham: Peter Hoida, [No. 1, 1965?]–7 [1971?]. ISSN: 0020–1332

Note: Continues: *The Disinherited*

A poetry magazine interspersed with psychedelic cameo drawings, photographs, and other visuals. Contributors included: Jeff Nuttall, Margaret Randall, Dave Cunliffe, Barry Edgar Pilcher, Lee Harwood, Frances Horovitz, Mike [i.e. Michael] Horovitz, the editor, and others.

BL: 6 (1969). (ZA.9.a.7514)
UCL: 4, 7
Poetry Library: 6–7

228 Innti / edited by Michael Davitt, Gabriel Rosenstock and Louis De Paor. Corcaigh: Innti, [No. 1, 1971]–?

A key magazine for modern Irish-language poets, originally founded at University College Cork; the most well-known have even been referred to as "the Innti poets", including Michael Davitt, Nuala Ní Dhomhnaill, Liam Ó Muirthile, and Gabriel Rosenstock. No. 4 came with a translation supplement, i.e. English translations of a selection of poems from that issue.

BL: 2 (aib. 1971)–4 (feabh. 1980). (P.905/209)
CUL: 3 (aib. 1973). (L733.C.43)

NLS: 3 (aib. 1973). (DJ.m.143(3) PER)
TCD: PER 79–217 1971–1996
UCL

229 InsideOut: monthly magazine for Scotland / edited by Chrissy McKean, Tony Stark, Geoffrey Andrews and Drew Clegg. Dundee, Vol. 1 (1973)–5 (1974)

CUL: Microfilm P106(15)
NLS: 6.2538 PER

230 Interest: an independent university magazine / edited by Stewart Parker and others. Belfast: Interest Publications, Vol. 1 no. 1 (Nov. 1960)– vol. 6 no. 1 (May 1966); unnumbered issue (May 1969)

Profiled in: Tom Clyde, *Irish Literary Magazines: an outline history and descriptive bibliography* (Dublin: Irish Academic Press, 2003), BL: 2725.g.3414

Articles, short stories, poetry. Includes poems by Seamus Heaney, Philip Hobsbaum, James Simmons, Joan Watton, and others.

Linen Hall Library, Belfast: Incomplete set

230a Iron / edited by Peter Mortimer. Cullercoats, North Shields: Iron Press, No. 1 (Spring 1973)–81/82 (1997). ISSN: 0140–7597

Anthology: Peter Mortimer (ed.), *Iron Age Anthology* (Iron Press, 1983), BL: YC.1989.a.2800
Related Imprint: Iron Press
Website: www.ironpress.co.uk

BL: P.903/548
CUL: 2–56, 58–81/82. (L727.b.188)
NLS: 11–50; 52–56, 58–81/82. (HJ9.90 PER)
TCD: 48, 75. (PER 95–342 1986 & 1995)
UCL: 7, 11–81/82
Poetry Library: 1–2, 5, 7, 9, 11, 21, 24–57, 59–81/82

231 The Iron Flute: a magazine for poetry / edited by Tony Coles and David Chapman. London: Iron Flute, [1964]

Contributors included Asa Benveniste.

BL: YA.1989.a.9558
UCL

232 Iron Hog. London: [Arkwright?], No. 1 [1972]–?

Appears to have been produced by the publishers of *Arkwright's First Magazine*.

CUL: 1. (L999.C.3.598)

233 Ishmael: a quarterly review of literature an[d] art / edited by Francis Boylan. Paris: Ishmael [at Librarie du Luxembourg], Vol. 1 no. 1 (Nov./Autumn 1970)–no. 3 (1972)

Multilingual, with contributions by Philippe Jaccottet, José Maria Velazquez, Manuel Salinas and Felix Grande, this very solid review, edited by perhaps an Irish emigré (since he contributes an extract of a play about the Easter Rising) looks more like a work of the 1950s. A fair proportion of the very well represented English language contributors did indeed first come to light much earlier including Kathleen Raine, C. H. Sisson (who writes on W. B. Yeats), R. S. Thomas, John Heath-Stubbs, George Barker, Peter Levi, and others.

BL: Vol. 1 no. 1. (Pressmark pending)
CUL: L727.B.382
UCL

234 Itch / L. Miller. Uxbridge, No. 1–7 [1970?]

Noted in *Gaga* 3 as "perhaps the best all-round magazine around."

UCL

235 It's: The Wimbledon School of Art Magazine / edited by Ariel Whatmore; Sarah Read; Geoffrey Toy, Alexa Smith, and David Burrows; George Foster, and others. Wimbledon: Wimbledon School of Art, No. 1 (Summer Term 1964)–?

A highly visual magazine, as you'd expect from an art school, but with a great deal of poetry. An outstanding issue was no. 2 (Summer 1965) which featured "A Survey of Some Aspects of Contemporary Poetry" presented by Ann Robinson and including sound and concrete poetry. Historical figures' work was included and presented beautifully (George Herbert, Kurt Schwitters, Apollinaire) and contemporary work and some comment by Ian Hamilton Finlay, Anselm Hollo, Henri Chopin, John Furnival,

Houédard, Eugen Gomringer and others. Issue no. 3 also had a feature by Robinson (who worked in Wimbledon's Dept. of Painting), this time on "Three Phonetic Poets", Bob Cobbing, Ernst Jandl and Henri Chopin. The same issue publishes Adrian Mitchell's collaboration with Anne Davison, "Nostalgia now 3d off".

BL: 1–3 (1966); 5 [1967?], 6 [1968?]
UCL: 5.
Leeds University, Brotherton Library: 3 (Special Collections General Literature D–6 ITS)

236 Joe DiMaggio / edited by John Robinson. Bexleyheath: John Robinson, No. 1 [1971]–[9, 1975?]

Related Imprint: Joe DiMaggio Press

This magazine often published an issue devoted solely to a single author's work, e.g. Robert Lax, Tom Raworth, Asa Benveniste, Ulli McCarthy, Victor Bockris, and others.

BL: 1, 3, 4, 9, 11, 12. (LB.31.c.5770)
CUL: 4. (L999.B.1.1266)
UCL: 1–3

237 The Journals of Pierre Menard / edited by Anthony Rudolf and Peter Hoy. Oxford: [Anthony Rudolf and Peter Hoy], No. 1 (Jan. 1969); 3 (July 1969); 4 (Oct. 1969)

Note: No. 2 was never issued. A one-off, *June Diary of Pierre Menard (The Curse of Babel)* was essentially an issue of this magazine. The *Notebooks of Pierre Menard* were issued as a supplement, but are listed separately in this sequence
Interview: with Anthony Rudolf in *Görtschacher* 2
Related Imprint: The Menard Press grew out of *The Journals of Pierre Menard*, and is profiled in Anthony Rudolf's *From Poetry to Politics: The Menard Press, 1969–1984* (London: Menard Press, 1984), BL: YC.1987.a.5410

A significant magazine devoted to poetry in translation, which takes its title from the Borges story, "Pierre Menard, Author of *Don Quixote*". The first issue was devoted to translations by Michael Hamburger. Poets covered in the whole run include Goethe, Hölderlin, German Poets of the 1914–18 War, René Char, Neruda, Pessoa, and others. *June Diary of Pierre Menard*, dated June 1970, included Octavio Paz translated by Charles Tomlinson, and translations of Shinkichi Takahashi (trans. Lucien Stryk), George Oppen (trans. into French by Claude Royet-Journoud), Francis Ponge (trans. Rudolf and Hoy respectively), Pavese (by Richard Burns).

BL: P.901/468. *June Diary of Pierre Menard*. (X.900/5597)

CUL: 1, 3. (L700.C.143)
NLS: 1, 3. (5.5404 PER). *June Diary of Pierre Menard.* (5.4815)
TCD: 1, 3. (PER 90–834). *June Diary of Pierre Menard.* (p 11363)

238 Juillard / edited by Trevor Winkfield. Leeds, then New York: Trevor Winkfield, [No. 1?] (Spring 1968)–9 (Spring 1972)

Website: http://www.trevorwinkfield.com/

There is a strong French and mainland Europe element to this mimeographed magazine, with contributions from: Louis Aragon, André Breton, Francis Picabia, Yves Klein, a spoof Situationist interview with "Brigitte Bardot", Blaise Cendrars, Cavan McCarthy, Henri Michaux, Tristan Tzara, Pierre Reverdy, Philippe Soupault, Alfred Jarry, and Apollinaire, as well as Gertrude Stein, Laura Riding, Paul Auster, Lewis Carroll, Anne Waldman, Clark Coolidge, and others. Winkfield moved to New York in 1969, from where he continued to edit *Juillard*.

BL: 7 (1970). (ZD.9.b.36).
TCD: [No. 1?] (Spring 1968); Winter 1968–9. (OLS L–6–145 no.9–10)
UCL: 7–8
King's College London, Eric Mottram Archive: 6–9. (7/327/1–4 1972)
Poetry Library: [7?] (1970)

June Diary of Pierre Menard *See* The Journals of Pierre Menard D237

239 Junk / Greenwich, 1–? [c.1970]

Gaga 3 notes the existence of an issue no. 4 of this magazine, and that it in part published poetry. There may be a connection to *Junk* by Dada Lee (presumably a pseudonym), "A Johnny Lee Publication", 1970, BL: X.0615/118, which is a collage work. No holdings known.

240 The Kilkenny Magazine: an all-Ireland literary review / edited by James Delahanty. Kilkenny: Kilkenny Literary Society, No. 1 (Summer 1960)– 18 (Winter 1970). ISSN: 0453–8757

Index: To 1969, Hayes
Profiled in: Tom Clyde, *Irish Literary Magazines: an outline history and descriptive bibliography* (Dublin: Irish Academic Press, 2003), BL: 2725.g.3414

Contributors included: John Banville, Padraic Colum, Monk Gibbon, Pearse Hutchinson, Patrick Kavanagh,

Thomas Kinsella, Ewart Milne, John Montague, Frank O'Connor, Desmond O'Grady, Seamus Heaney, Brendan Kennelly, and others.

BL: ZA.9.a.4596
CUL: 1–10. (P718.c.485)
NLS: 1–15, 18. (HP.1.78.5463)
TCD: PER 78–455
UCL

241 Kleek-Poemz. Birmingham: Birmingham Peace Centre, No. 1 [1975?]

Mentioned in *Muse* 8 as containing poems by Sandra Mullen, Ankaret Shakti, Caroline Begley, Shirley Paul, Keith Thoth, and Tenebris Light: "Birmingham's new Beat Generation, but only if you're prepared to be shaken."

West Midlands Creative Literature Collection, Shrewsbury Library

Knowe *See* Akros D12

242 Kolokon / edited by Peter Lattin with Rodney Coward, then with Raymond Anderson. Durham: Kolokon, [Vol. 1] no. 1 (Spring 1966)–vol. 2 no. 1 (Spring 1967) ISSN: 0454–238X

John Fletcher's articles, especially, made this a very Francophile magazine, with pieces on Apollinaire, Proust, and "From Sade to Genet". Fletcher was a lecturer of French at Durham University. There were short stories, and articles on music, art and philosophy, but poetry featured large. Contributors of poetry included Kenneth White, who also published an essay on "The Phoney University" in vol. 1 no. 3.

BL: [Vol. 1] no. 1–no. 3. (P.901/119)
CUL: L900.D.99
NLS: 6.1815
TCD: PER 81–706
UCL

243 Kontexts: an occasional review of concrete, visual, experimental poetry / edited by Michael Gibbs. Leamington Spa, then Exeter, then Amsterdam: [Michael Gibbs], [1] (1969)–9/10 (1976/77)

Related Imprint: Kontext Publications produced books by Robert Lax, Jiri Valoch, Michael Gibbs, Jackson Mac Low, Jan Voss, and others. It also produced *Ginger Snaps*, and

Michael Gibbs (ed.) *Kontextsound* (Amsterdam: Kontext Publication, 1977), a compilation of sound poetry activity published to coincide with the 10th International Festival of Sound Poetry, Stockholm, Amsterdam and London, 1977. A copy of this is held at Cambridge (1999.13.3); at UCL (Poetry Store Quartos KON:GIB); and in the Poetry Library. Website: http://www.xs4all.nl/ffinondes/kontexts.html

Contributors included Bob Cobbing, Dom Sylvester Houédard, Paul de Vree, Nicholas Zurbrugg, Robert Lax, Clark Coolidge, John Giorno, bp Nichol, Jonathan Williams, William Burroughs, Brion Gysin, Jackson Mac Low, Henri Chopin, Dick Higgins, Robin Crozier, and others. At least one issue, no. 5, was printed at the Beau Geste Press in Cullomptom, Devon where *Schmuck* and other Fluxus publications were produced.

BL: 5. (ZD.9.a.184)
NLS: HP1.78.5499
TCD: 2? (OLS X–1–650 no.12)
UCL: 2–9/10
Leeds University, Brotherton Library: 1–2 (Special Collections General Literature D–6 KON); 3 (Special Collections English Q–1 KON)
Poetry Library: 1–2, 6/7, 9/10

244 Krax / edited by Andy Robson, David Pruckner and Graham Rhodes. Leeds: Krax, No. 1 (1971)–

Related Imprint: Krax have published a number of poetry collections, especially in the *Rump* numbered series.

The main focus of this long-lived magazine is on humorous, light-hearted and whimsical poetry. Graham Rhodes seems to have ceased co-editing by issue no. 6 and Andy Robson would later become the solo editor.

BL: P.901/3120
CUL: 11 (1977)– . (L727.C.1273)
NLS: 12 [1978]– . (HJ4.1223.SER)
TCD: 12 [1978] only. (PER 90–376)
UCL
Poetry Library: 7, 13–18, 23–26, 28– .

245 Kroklok / edited by Dom Silvester [i.e. Sylvester] Houédard. London: [Writers Forum], No. 1 [1971]–4 [1973?]

Dedicated to sound poetry, encouraging and publishing new works, but also reclaiming older texts as sound poems. Contributors include Christian Morgenstern, Raoul Hausmann, Ernst Jandl, Lewis Carroll (and the connection between 'Jabberwock' and an Austrian ballad), Filippo Tommaso Marinetti, Paul Scheerbart, Bob Cobbing, Paul de

Vree, Jack Kerouac (a reprint), Man Ray (from 1924), Henri Chopin, Pierre Albert-Birot, Eugen Gomringer, Theo van Doesburg, Gino Severini, Hugo Ball, Charles Verey, Neil Mills (four number poems in issue 2), Peter Meyer, François Rabelais, Antonin Artaud, Kurt Schwitters, Raoul Hausmann, François Dufrêne, Michel Seuphor, Peter Finch, Jeremy Adler, Michael Chant, Peter Greenham, Brion Gysin, Ilya Zdanevich, Thomas A. Clark, Helmut Heissenbüttel, August Stramm, Bill Bissett, Paula Claire, Lawrence Upton, bp Nichol, and others. The editor is sometimes referred to simply as d.s.h.. Bob Cobbing and Peter Mayer were also involved editorially.

BL: ZA.9.b.2457
UCL
Poetry Library: 1–3

246 The Lace Curtain: a magazine of poetry and criticism / edited by Michael Smith and Trevor Joyce. Dublin: New Writers' Press, No. 1 [1969]–6 (1978). ISSN: 0460–1084

Index: Eoin Meegan, at www.may.ie/academic/english/laceinto.htm. An issue by issue listing of contributors is also given at http://indigo.ie/ffitjac/Publishers /nwp_publications.htm
Profiled in: Tom Clyde, *Irish Literary Magazines: an outline history and descriptive bibliography* (Dublin: Irish Academic Press, 2003), BL: 2725.g.3414
Related Imprint: New Writers Press, a key small press for Irish modernist poetry, helping to refocus attention on Thomas McGreevey and Brian Coffey, as well as publishing younger poets who took their bearings from modernism

Contributors included: Patrick Galvin, Anthony Kerrigan, Thomas Kinsella, Niall Montgomery, Michael Smith, Trevor Joyce, and others. No. 4 (Summer 1971) was a special issue on the Thirties, with contributions from Samuel Beckett, Austin Clarke, Brian Coffey, Denis Devlin, Arthur Power, George Reavey, and Mervyn Wall. Smith and Joyce co-edited until issue 3; Smith and Brian Coffey issue 4; after which Smith edited alone.

BL: YA.1989.b.1905
CUL: L727.C.946
NLS: 1–5. (HP2.79.2184)
TCD: Press A New W 1970 LAC 1–6 1970–1978
UCL: 1–4

247 Laissez Faire / [edited by J. D. Beugger]. Esher: Ember Press, Sheet 1 (Dec. 1971)–6 (Mar. 1975)

Related Imprint: Ember Press also published *Acumen*, *Headland*, *Littack* and various single-author collections.

Solely devoted to reviewing little magazines.

BL: P.905/55
CUL: L727.B.113
NLS: 7.144 PER
TCD: PER 81–680
UCL

248 Lallans / J. K. Annand, and others. Edinburgh: Lallans Society [later renamed Scots Language Society], No. 1 (Mairtinmas 1973)–

Index: *Scottish Poetry Index Vol. 5* (Edinburgh: Scottish Poetry Library, 1996)
Anthology: Neil R. MacCallum and David Purves (eds.), *Mak It New: an anthology of twenty-one years of writing in Lallans* (Edinburgh: Mercat Press, 1995), BL: YK.1996.a.1070
Website: www.lallans.co.uk/

"Atween the batters o *Lallans* ye'll finnd a wheen guid poetry, stories an airticles wrutten in the Scots leid; aa reflectin the tungs o Scots fowk fae Shetland til the Mairches." – from the Scots Language Society website. Annand was editor for the first ten years of the magazine. Later editors have included the playwright Donald Campbell, Willian Neill, David Purves, Neil R. MacCallum, J. Natanson, Mary McIntosh, and K. Armstrong.

BL: 3 (1974)– . (P.901/1853)
CUL: 3 (1974)– . (L718.C.211)
NLS: HJ8.567 PER
TCD: 3 (1974)– . (PER 77–20)

Language *See* Circuit D111

249 The Lesser Known Shagg / edited by Tony Jackson and Tom Pickard. Newcastle-upon-Tyne: Ultima Thule Bookshop, [1, 1969?]

Contributors include Ed Dorn, Barry MacSweeney, Gael Turnbull, and Bill Butler.

BL: YA.1995.b.7246
CUL: 1997.10.772
UCL

250 Limestone / edited by Geoffrey Adkins. London: Limestone, c/o The City Lit, [1] (June 1974)–10 [1980]. ISSN: 0308–4787

Note: Merged with *Strange Fruit* to become *Strange Lime Fruit Stone*. However, No. 3 of *Strange Lime Fruit Stone* was described as *Strange Fruit* no. 8 and *Limestone* no. 13
Related Imprint: Limestone published the anthology, the first of its kind, James Berry (ed.), *Bluefoot Traveller: an anthology of West Indian poets in Britain* (1976), BL: X.909/40918. A revised edition was later published by Harrap in the 1981, BL: X.950/4200, and reprinted by Nelson in 1985

Although it described itself as a "poetry and short fiction magazine" the emphasis was very much on poetry. It often published four or five poems of an author at a time, including James Berry, John Welch, Antonio Cisneros (trans. David Tipton), David Jaffin, E. A. Markham, and Ted Burford. Tim Longville, Edwin Morgan, Peter Redgrove, Judith Kazantsis, Maggie O'Sullivan, Yann Lovelock, and others also appeared. It carried reviews of poetry and reviewed the small presses.

BL: P.901/1289
CUL: L727.D.195
NLS: 6216 PER
TCD: PER 75–672
UCL

Lincolnshire Writers *See Proof* D395

251 Lines / edited by Geoff Holland. North Shields: Elpar Poem Productions, [No. 1, 1969?]–13 (1972)

BL: 13. (ZD.9.a.85)
UCL: 8 (1971), 13 (1972)

252 The Literary Supplement / edited by Anthony Barnett. London (printed in Norway): Nothing Doing (formally In London), No. 1 (Sept. 8th 1972)–21 (Dec. 1975)

Anthology: *The Literary Supplement Writings 1: Answer to a letter* / [by] Edmond Jabès ; version in English by Rosmarie Waldrop ; [and], *Es lebe der König* / [by] J.H. Prynne; [and], *Conversation in the mountains* / [by] Paul Celan; version in English by Rosmarie Waldrop. (London: Nothing Doing, 1973). BL: RF.2000.a.30
Related imprint: Nothing Doing also produced *Nothing Doing in London*

"Gratis to persons". On no. 20 a doctored *Times Literary*

Supplement masthead was used to emphasise the joke in the title. Contributors to no. 1 include Anthony Barnett, Nick Totton, J. H. Prynne, Jakob Paulsen (trans. Anthony Barnett), and Helmut Heissenbüttel (trans. Rosmarie Waldrop); to no. 2: Anthony Barnett, Edmond Jabès, Joseph Guglielmi, Claude Fain, Paul Buck, Mark Hyatt, David Ball; to no. 3: John Wieners and Tom Ahern; no. 8 is devoted to *18 Poems from Nothing Has Changed* by Rosmarie Waldrop; no. 9 is a prose piece by Jorge Luis Borges and Adolfo Bioy Casares translated by Merle Ruberg; no. 10 is a prose piece by Richard Grossinger; no. 11 is the poem "Postponement" by André du Bouchet, translated by Paul Auster; contributors to no 12 include Peter Riley and Peter Philpott; no. 13 is "from The Book of Questions..." by Edmond Jabès, trans. Rosmarie Waldrop; no. 14 is *The Triangle of Velocities* by Michael Haslam; no. 15 is an untitled poem beginning "From foetal slime" by Barry MacSweeney; no. 20 has contributions by Martin Thom, Terry Stokes, Alan Davies, Denise Riley, Nick Totton, Gary Gach, and Wilson Stapleton; no. 21 is *Etat* by Anne-Marie Albiach, translated by Keith Waldrop. A magazine associated with the "Cambridge School" poets.

BL: 1–16, 20, 21. (P.901/1109)
CUL: L727.B.131
NLS: HP3.78.596 PER
TCD: PER 73–630

253 Littack / edited by William Oxley. Esher: Ember Press, Vol. 1 no. 1 (1972)–vol. 4 no. 2/3 (1976)

Note: Continued as: *Littack Supplement*. Two number sequences were used, so that vol. 4 no. 2/3 is also designated no. 11/12.
Profiled in: Görtschacher 1
Interview: with William Oxley in Görtschacher 1
Related Imprint: Ember Press also published *Acumen*, *Headland*, *Laissez Faire* and various single-author collections

From the last issue: "LITTACK is ceasing because it is undeniable that it has made its fundamental point – namely, it has asserted – and re-iterated over a period of time – the constant need for a tensional base for poetry, a polemical climate for the, often violent, exchange of ideas about the craft. But, as LITTACK has striven to emphasise, such 'exchange' cannot confine itself, any more than poetry can, to a discussion of technicalities. It is easy, in retrospect, to see the damage that has been done by the modernist's obsession with technique – the direct cause of such present-day absurd notions as 'the poem's proper subject is language itself'. Of course, this is false – a poem's proper subject is life, words but forming an artifact for the expression of the subject. Equally absurd has been the imposed fiction, traceable to Pound, that all attempted

expression be limited or restricted to the object. [...] It was out of such a realization that LITTACK created a polemical forum to allow discussion and controversy, to permit the pubication of various manifestos, to offer a philosophy of poetry (neo-vitalism) and, above all, to make the point that life must be let into poetry all the time." Contributors included: Kathleen Raine, Hugo Manning, Tom Scott, Hugh MacDiarmid, Martin Booth, Stephen Wade, Ian Hamilton Finlay, and others. Peter Russell acted as Overseas Editor.

BL: P.901/825
CUL: L727.C.522
NLS: P.168 PER
TCD: PER 81–702
UCL

254 The Little Word Machine / edited by Nick Toczek. Shipley: Nick Toczek, No. 1 (1972)–11 (1979)

An eclectic magazine that deliberately published a cross-section of contemporary poetry rather than a particular group or style; included translations from across the world. Yann Lovelock became assistant editor from the seventh number.

BL: P.901/3229
CUL: 1–8/9. (L727.C.583)
NLS: 1–10. (DJ.s.452 PER)
UCL: 2–11

255 Living Arts. London: Institute of Contemporary Arts, 1 (1963)–3 (1964)

Covering the arts generally, but notable for publishing Roy Fisher's long poem "City" in the first issue (a revised, longer version, differing from the text originally published in *Migrant*) and for reprinting nine poems from the Nigerian magazine *Black Orpheus* in the second issue. Other poetry contributors include Geoffrey Hill and Patrick Fetherston.

BL: P.P.8001.bj
CUL: L999.c.3.224
NLS: 5.3360
TCD: PER 80–509
UCL: 1–2

256 Llanfairpwllgwyngyllgogerych wyrndrobwllllantysiliogogogoch / edited by Peter Hoy. Oxford: Peter Hoy. 2 (13th June 1972)–22 (7th July 1973)

Note: There appears to have been no issue no. 1 (advice

from Peter Riley).

The title is taken from the village in Wales whose railway station has the longest name of any in Britain, and perhaps the world. Because of its length, library catalogues sometimes replace the title with the abbreviation Llanfair P.G. Contributors to this generally one-sheet per issue, largely French language magazine included Claude Royet-Journoud, Claude Faïn, Joseph Guglielmi, Lars Fredrikson, Roger Laporte, Rosmarie Waldrop (a poem printed so that it could only be read faintly through the other side of the page), Edmond Jabès, Anthony Barnett, Roger Giroux, Jean Daive, Keith Waldrop, Hoy himself and others. There was a strong visual element to many of the texts, using drawn lines, handwriting, and the whole whitespace of the page.

BL: 2–20; 22. (ZA.9.b.2708). 21 (HS.74/1056(58)).

257 Loaded Drum / edited by Brian Marley. Heaton, Newcastle upon Tyne: Laundering Room Press, No. 2 (1974)

Note: Continues: Breakfast
Related Imprint: Laundering Room also published several pamphlet collections, e.g. by Elaine Randell and by Jeremy Reed.

BL: X.902/2156
CUL: L999.b.1.463
NLS: 6.2597
TCD: OLS L–4–456 no.1
UCL

258 Long Hair: North Atlantic Turn-on / edited by Barry Miles, and Ted Berrigan in New York. London and New York: LoveBooks Ltd, No. 1 (1965)– [2, April 1966]. ISSN: 0459–7613

Note: The second issue was unnumbered but given the designation "The Global Moon-Edition", and with a further variation to the title, which was now Long Hair Times. It is sometimes cited as a separate title, The Global Moon-Edition Long Hair Times North Atlantic Turn-on
Profiled in: Andrew Wilson, "Spontaneous Underground: an introduction to London psychedelic scenes, 1965–1968" in Summer of Love: the Art of the Psychedelic Era (Liverpool: Tate Liverpool, 2005
Related Imprint: LoveBooks was set up by Miles and John Hopkins ("Hoppy")

Contributors include Allen Ginsberg, Ted Berrigan, Ron Padgett, Gerard Malanga, Lawrence Ferlinghetti, and others. Ginsberg declined payment for his poem "Ankor Wat" and his money was divided among the other

contributors. There was more of a news element to the second issue of the magazine, for example the drug experimentalist Timothy Leary's arrest was reported, as was the founding of the London Free School, and there were pieces by Tom Wolfe and Harry Fainlight. Long Hair can be regarded as a precursor of the underground press, outside the scope of this bibliography, such as International Times (BL: Newspaper Library).

BL: 1. (Cup.802.ff.3)
UCL: 1

259 Loudspeaker. London: Loudspeaker, No. 1 [1968?]

Contributors included Tony Dash, Steve Morris, Clive Williams, and others.

UCL

260 Ludd's Mill / edited by Steve Sneyd and Gary Wilson; then Andrew Darlington. Huddersfield: Eight Miles High Publications, No. 1 [1971]–no. 18 [1983?]. ISSN: 0047–5157

Note: A single review supplement, Enock's Fatal Bile Beater, was issued in March 1975 for subscribers. As well as issue 13 and 14 there was an issue 13?.
Related Imprint: Hilltop Press

Intended to have a Huddersfield focus, it was associated in the beginning with the local live reading series Inner Circle. The magazine had a large visual content – poems typewritten and handwritten, and many cartoons and collages – and with a particular interest in Beat literature, with fantasy and science fiction poetry elements.

BL: P.903/110
CUL: 3 (1971)–18 [1983?] (L727.B.143)
NLS: Lacking 12 [1975]. (HP4.85.853 PER)
UCL: 1

261 Lycidas / edited by Henry Hardy and then others. Oxford: Wolfson College, No. 1 (1972/73)–15 (1988)

An annual college magazine recording the activities of the College and publishing essays, reviews and creative writing by college members and those associated with the college. Contributors of poetry include: Philip Larkin, Bertolt Brecht in translation, Peter Redgrove, Zaituna Umer (with Elizabeth Jennings), Ruth Padel, Helen Kidd, and others.

BL: 1–14 (P.903/225)
NLS: HJ8.748 PER

262 Mabon / edited by Alun R. Jones and Gwyn Thomas. Bangor: Cymdeithas y Celfyddydau yng Ngogledd Cymru / North Wales Association for the Arts, Vol. 1 no. 1 (1969)–no. 9 (1975/6)

Note: Produced in a Welsh and an English edition.

BL: English edition: P.901/465. Welsh edition: P.901/466
CUL: English edition: Vol. 1 no. 1–5; vol. 1 no. 7. (L727.c.547.1)
NLS: English edition: Vol. 1 no. 1–no. 7. (DJ.s.347 PER). Welsh edition: Cyfr. 1, rhif. 1 (1969)–cyfr. 1, rhif. 9 (1975/76)
TCD: English edition: Vol. 1 no. 1–no. 7. (PER 90–806)
UCL: Welsh edition: Vol. 1 no. 1–no. 7
Poetry Library: English edition: Vol. 1 no. 2

263 Magazine / [edited by Opal L. Nations?]. Oxford, 197?

Advertised in *Transgravity Advertiser* no. 5. No holdings known.

264 Mainly / edited by Chrissie Smith. Talybont-on-Usk: Mainly, No. 1 (1965)–4 (1966). ISSN: 0025–0848

Note: The magazine *Cutely* was issued as an apparently one-off special issue. Also related to *Nicely*.

CUL: L727.C.625
UCL

265 Maio / edited by Alberto de Lacerda. No. 1 (1973)

BL: 1. (ZD.9.a.128)

266 Make / edited by Sheila Hope then Martin Bradbrooke, then Alan Codd. Newcastle-upon-Tyne: Authors & Critics Society at the University of Newcastle upon Tyne, No. 1 (1964)–8 (1969)

Related Imprint: A number of initially untitled Make Pamphlets were issued, e.g. no. 1 (by John Rocha and Philip Sharpe); no. 2 (*Angel Beak Poems*, by Bill Welch); and no. 3 (*Icarus and other birds*, by Richard Caddel), all BL: P.901/674b

Mostly students' work, but in no. 4 (1965) Basil Bunting contributed an eight line poem, "Who sang sea takes", which would be changed and become part of *Briggflatts*.

Later issues included work by Tony Harrison, John Wilkinson, John Rocha, Richard Caddel, and others.

BL: 1–4, 6–8. (P.901/674)
UCL: 1–7

267 Malenka / edited by Brian Moses and Jeffrey S. Bleakley; then Pie Corbett. Eastbourne: Eastbourne College of Education, No.1 (197?)–?

Earlier issues appeared as unbound pages in an envelope. Contributors included John Rice, Steve Sneyd, Alexis Lykiard, Wes Magee, Frances Horovitz, Michael Horovitz, Martin Booth, Barry MacSweeney, William Oxley, and others.

BL: 4, 5, 6, 10. (Cup.410.g.282.)
UCL: 5.

268 Mañana / edited by Peter Ryan and Eli Renn. Dublin: The Phrynge, No. 1 (May 1963)

Index: Rudi Holzapfel, *A Survey of Irish Literary Magazines from 1900 to the present day*, M Litt thesis (Trinity College Dublin, 1964)
Profiled in: Tom Clyde, *Irish Literary Magazines: an outline history and descriptive bibliography* (Dublin: Irish Academic Press, 2003), BL: 2725.g.3414

BL: P.P.8001.cf.
CUL: L999.B.1.111
NLS: 6.1046

269 Manifold / edited by Vera Rich. London: Vera Rich, No. 1 (1962)– . ISSN: 0025–2166

Related Imprint: Manifold have published several pamphlets, including Vera Rich and Elizabeth Harvey (eds.), *Sonnetarium: a chapbook of sonnets*, [1962], BL: 011498.a.45, and *Laudamus Te: a cycle of poems to the praise and the glory of God* (1967), BL: YA.1994.a.17939

Began with and maintained a distinctly anti-academic stance in the poetry it published, though also interested in translation. A little magazine with a surprisingly long break between two of its issues: nearly thirty years, between no. 28, in 1969, and no. 29, in 1998. Also involved editorially: Elizabeth Harvey, Graziella Sara Cacace, Alison Cameron, and Hilary Sheers.

BL: ZK.9.a.6262
CUL: Lacking 29. (L727.C.262)
NLS: HJ8.1635 SER
TCD: 6–28. (PER 80–513 1963–1969). 30– . (PER 101–520

1989/99–)
UCL
Poetry Library: 23, 25–

270 Mansfield Mixture / [edited by J. Sim?]. Mansfield: British Amateur Press Association, [No. 1, 1973?]–?

BL: 2, 4, 5, 7, 8, 9, 12, 15, 17–22. (ZK.9.b.2199)

271 Manuscript / edited by C. J. Luke. Dagenham: West Essex Writers' Club, No. 1 (July 1967)–6 (Oct. 1968/Jan. 1969)

Short fiction, debate, some reviews and poetry. Perhaps most notable for Sir Compton Mackenzie's letter in no.3 suggesting that transferring an interest from smoking to drug taking might not be a good idea. In issue no. 5 and no. 6 a section called "Explosion" was devised for poetry only. Its pages were of a different colour and were paginated differently.

BL: P.901/3320
CUL: 1–5. (L727.C.429)
NLS: 1–5. (6.2056 PER)
TCD: 2–5. (PER 90–855)
UCL: 1

272 Maquis. London, c.1964

Noted in *How* 5 as a "new libertarian poetry magazine". No holdings known

273 The March Hare / edited by Nigel McGilchrist. Winchester: Winchester College, [No. 1] (Autumn 1973)–?

A general arts magazine that included some poetry, including a poem by Brian Patten and one by Peter Levi in the first and possibly only issue.

BL: [1]. (P.901/1119)

274 Masque / edited by Jane E.M. Cronin, H. Walton, A. Barton... and others. Leicester: The Aurata (Leicester City Grammar Schools), Vol. 1 no. 1–no. 3 [1969?]

"Leicester's Inter-Sixth Form Magazine."

UCL
Poetry Library

275 Masques / edited by Paul Darby. Kingswinford, Brierly Hill: Paul Darby, [No.]1 (Dec. 1975)–?. ISSN 0307–9988

Devoted to the poetry of its editor.

BL: 1 (X.0900/1009)
CUL: 1 (L999.B.1.472)
NLS: 1 (HP3.79.1525 PER)

276 Matrix / edited by Liam Maguire and Carol Burns. London: The City Literary Institute, No. 1 [197–?]–6 (1974)

UCL: 2–4
Poetry Library: 5–6

277 McCarthy's Technicolour Dream Pie / edited by Paul Brown. London: [Paul Brown], [No. 1, 1969]

Note: Merged with *In The Night Of* to become *Gaga*.

UCL

278 Medley / edited by Douglas Priestley. Potters Bar: Douglas Priestley, No. 1 (Sept. 1962)–2 (Dec. 1962)

An early backlash against mimeographed magazines: the idea, as stated in the first editorial, was to produce a magazine *not* printed by typewritten stencil and duplicator. Instead it was "to introduce poets to people who matter, because it will present their work in normal book style." Contributors included many who remain obscure, but also (presumably) Penelope Shuttle (writing as P. D. Shuttle) and D.M. Black.

BL: P.P.8000.ag.
CUL: L727.C.298
NLS: 1965.60

279 Mentor / edited by R. Tomlinson. Newton Aycliffe: R. Tomlinson, No. 1 (Mar. 1975)–5 (Mar. 1976). ISSN: 0306–4239

Size A5, stencil-printed: mostly short stories and *Reader's Digest*-like talking-point articles ("Pity the dumb animal"; "Is an intelligent machine possible?"; "The evils of black magic"), but with poems interspersed. An open letter issued after the final number reveals that the magazine had been printed on a Roneo 250 Duplicator. In trying to trade up to a Gestetner 300 , a part-exchange deal had gone wrong and only a Roneo 450 had been delivered. Because of difficulties with the new Roneo, the editor explains, the magazine has had to close.

BL: P.901/1316
CUL: 2–5. (L727.c.613)
NLS: 2, 3, 5. (1977.33 PER)

280 Meridian Poetry Magazine / edited by Trevor Kneale. Liverpool: Rondo, Vol. 1 no. 1 (Autumn 1973)–no. 15 (1975). ISSN: 0306–3461

Related Imprint: Rondo published a number of anthologies, including Trevor Kneale (ed.), *Contemporary Women Poets* (1975), BL: X.909/40556; Trevor Kneale (ed.), *Poetry in the Seventies* (1976); and, e.g., Thomas Blackburn's collection *Post Mortem* (1977), BL: X.909/41745; Penelope Shuttle, *Autumn Piano* (1974)

Quietly eclectic. Poems and a very occasional essay, e.g. Douglas Dunn on "Traditional Dangers" (no. 11), Peter Redgrove on science and poetry (no. 13), and Gladys Mary Coles on "The Poetry of Mary Webb" (no. 15).

BL: YA.1994.a.6906
CUL: Vol. 1 no. 1–8; 14. (L727.C.534)
NLS: Vol.1 no.1–7; 14. (DJ.s.442)
UCL: Vol.1 no. 1 only.

281 Metron / edited by Brenda Cook, Sally Maclachlan, Carol White, David Smith and Martin White. Farnham: The Editors, c/o Farnham College of Art, No. 1 (Mar. 1965)–2 (July 1965)

Devoted to the contemporary arts, including some poetry.

BL: P.901/11
UCL

282 Midland Read: an omnibus of local poetry / edited by Paul Humphries, Maralyn Heathcock and Nick Tozcek. Stafford: West Midlands Arts Association, No. 1 [1973]

BL: X.0958/138
CUL: 1998.8.5684
UCL

283 Minerva / edited by Padraic Mac Anna, Janet Cole and others. London: Birkbeck College, [No. 1, 1973]–? ISSN: 0143–9820

Note: Seems to have quickly become an annual, issued in the first half of the year.

BL: 2 (Jan. 1974), 1975 (no. 1), 1976, Spring 1977, Spring 1978, June 1981, 1982, 14 (1988). (P.901/1148)
Poetry Library: May 1982

284 Minerva: a magazine of modern poetry / edited by Patrick Murray, Colm Holmes and David Kane. Dublin: [Minerva], No. 1 [1972]–4 (1973)

Profiled in: Tom Clyde, *Irish Literary Magazines: an outline history and descriptive bibliography* (Dublin: Irish Academic Press, 2003), BL: 2725.g.3414

Typed production, perhaps not even mimeographed stencil. Murray and Holmes edited the first two issues, Murray and Kane the last two. Contributions by the editors, as well as Brendan Kennelly, Pete[r] Fallon, and others.

TCD: 2–4. (Per 81–789)

285 Modern Poetry in Translation / edited by Ted Hughes and Daniel Weissbort; and others, London: Modern Poetry in Translation, No. 1 [1966]–44 (Winter 1981/82); [45](1983). ISSN: 0026–8291. Then, as *Poetry World*, edited by Peter Jay, London: Anvil Press, No. 1 (1986)–2 (1988). ISSN: 0268–1390. Then, as *Modern Poetry in Translation*, New Series, edited by Daniel Weissbort, London: King's College London, No. 1 (Summer 1992)–[Unnumbered issue](2003). Then, as Series 3, edited by David and Helen Constantine, Oxford: Queen's College, distributed by Inpress Books London, Series 3 no. 1 (2004)– .ISSN: 0969–3572

Note: Numbering of individual issues ceased with no. 44 (Winter 1981–1982)
Index: An index of authors from no. 1–25 is published with no. 25. An index of translators for 1–25 was published in no. 26.
Profiled in: Ted Hughes, [Introduction], *Modern Poetry in Translation*, [45] (1983)

The major journal for translation of poetry into English.

The archive is held at King's College London.

BL: First Series: 1–3 (Spring 1967); 8 (1970)–[45] (1983). (ZD.9.a.122) Poetry World: ZC.9.a.6970. New Series: ZC.9.a.3315.
CUL: First and New Series: L727.b.62.31– ; Poetry World: L727.b.62.24–
NLS: First Series: P.la.3776 PER. Poetry World: HJ4.1494 PER. New Series: HJ4.1494 SER
TCD: First and New Series: 1; 8 (1970)–. (PER 71–836). Poetry World: PER 91–737
UCL
Poetry Library: 1–[45]; Supplement: Poetry International '71 Programme; New Series, 1–

286 Mofussil / edited by Joan Murphy. Kettering: No. 1 [1968]–4 (1969). ISSN: 0026–8860

BL: P.901/353
UCL

The Mongol Review See Residu D409

287 Mothra / London: Mothra Press Ltd, Vol. 1 (Spring 1975).

Poetry, adult cartoon strip, short story. Various modes of presentation: calligraphy, typescript, various kinds of artwork. Includes poetry by Carlyle Reedy and a Kenneth Rexroth translation of a Li Ch'ing Chao poem.

BL: P.901/1293

288 Motus: periodical of the arts / edited by Roderic Campbell. Cork: Arts Society, University College Cork, Issue 1 (Summer 1968)–4 (Spring 1970)

Profiled in: Tom Clyde, Irish Literary Magazines: an outline history and descriptive bibliography (Dublin: Irish Academic Press, 2003), BL: 2725.g.3414

Mimeograph type-written production. From no. 2 Gabirel Rosenstock was associate editor. No. 4 had assitant editors Nuala Nì Dhomhnaill and Peter Denman.

BL: 1. (ZD.9.a.113)
UCL
National Library of Ireland: Ir 82191 p50
Queen's University Belfast: hAP4.M9

289 Move / edited by Jim Burns. Preston: Jim Burns, No. 1 (Dec. 1964)–no. 8 (Apr. 1968). ISSN: 0580–0854

Related Imprint: Move published Kirby Congdon (ed.), Thirteen American Poets in 1966 (BL: P.901/163a)

"There are no subscription rates. Anyone wishing to receive the next issue should send 6d to the address given above. This amount may be sent in stamps." – from the first issue. Contributors include Andrew Crozier, Larry Eigner, David Chaloner, Daphne Buckle, Wes Magee, Michael Horovitz, Joan Gilbert, Thomas Clark (i.e. Thomas A. Clark), Gael Turnbull, John James, Paul Evans, Chris Torrance, Anselm Hollo, Tina Morris, Roy Fisher, Dave Cunliffe, Lee Harwood and others. Robin Blaser, Jack Spicer and other west coast poets were published, too, "netted from Open Space magazine" in San Francisco, though these were not included in the Move anthology of American poets.

BL: 1–8. (P.901/163)
CUL: 5–8. (L727.C.408)
NLS: 5–8. (P.med.398 PER)
TCD: 5–7. (56.a.)
UCL

290 The Moving Times / edited by Alexander Trocchi and Jeff Nuttall. London: Moving Times, No. 1 (1964)–?

Some numbers of Sigma Portfolio were issued as a supplement to The Moving Times, and the first issue of Sigma Portfolio, which was poster-size, bore the title The Moving Times. This poster was in turn cut up and a piece of it used for a later unidentified issue of The Moving Times itself.

BL: [An un-numbered issue]. (ZA.9.d.465)
NLS: 1. (7.87)

291 Mult / edited by Phil Cooper. Ealing: Mult, 1 (1968)–3 (1970)

Contributors include Libby Houston and Peter Finch. According to Gaga 1, to which Cooper contributes, the editor was an electrical engineering student at Brunel.

UCL

292 Muse / edited by Mary Beaman, Jeff Charlton, John Dalton, Jim Green, Brendan Hogan and Helen Medley and others. Birmingham: Birmingham Poetry Centre, No. 1 (1971)–8 (1976)

Related Imprint: The Birmingham Poetry Centre also published *Poetry News*

The first issue featured poets from the Second City Poets group, including Nick Toczek. Other contributors included Martin Booth, Nina Steane, Stephen Morris, Stephen Morris, Yann Lovelock, Peter Finch, Steve Sneyd, and others. There was a brief controversy among correspondents in issue 2 and 3, concerning Peter Cash, the use of obscenities, and Cash's magazine *Gong*. Jeff Charlton was the most long-standing editor.

BL: P.901/732
CUL: L727.C.577
NLS: HP3.79.663 PER
TCD: PER 81–904
UCL
Poetry Library: 4

293 My Own Mag / edited by Jeff Nuttall. Barnet: Jeff Nuttall, No. 1 [1963]–17 (1966). ISSN: 0580-3799

Note: Continued by *George: Son of My Own Mag*. Editor's name for no. 16 is given as Clifton DeBerry.
Related Work: Jeff Nuttall, *Bomb Culture: Pop, Protest, Art, Sick, The Underground* (London: MacGibbon & Kee, 1968), BL: X.529/9994

Contributors included Nuttall, William Burroughs, Allen Ginsberg, Robert Creeley, Michael McClure, Alexander Trocchi, Anselm Hollo, Brian Patten, B. S. Johnson, Tom McGrath, and others. The format was usually mimeographed stapled foolscap, with texts stapled on, and gaps cut into the text; Burroughs's *Moving Times* appeared as an occasional column within it, too.

BL: [7, Oct 1964?], 11 (Feb. 1965), 12 (May 1965), 14 (Dec 1965), 15 (1966), 16, and a further unnumbered and undated issue, probably of 1964. On order: 13 (Aug 1965), (P.P.8005.ig)
CUL: 1 [1963]–17 (1966). (L400.B.651)
UCL
Poetry Library: [10], 12–16

294 Naissance / edited by P. Smith. Winchester, No. 1 [1970?]–6 (1971)

UCL: 3 (1970)–6 (1971)

The N.A.P.M. *See* The New Age Poetry Magazine D299

295 Nebulum / edited by Glyn Pursglove and Phillip Hodson. Oxford: Two Birds Press, c/o St. Peter's College, No. 1 (1966)

Note: In 1966, Phillip Hodson in part continued the magazine with *Ubullum*, while in the same year Glyn Pursglove began *Olive Dachsund*

BL: Pressmark Pending
UCL
Brotherton Library, Leeds University: 2. (Special Collections General Literature D–6 NEB)

296 Nemo / edited by David John Ward. Towcester, Northamptonshire, [No. 1, 1968?–1971?]

UCL: 4 (1968)

297 Neoeil / edited by John Upton-Prowse, and others. Amersham: John Upton-Prowse, No. 1 [1970]–5 [1971?]

Started by John Upton-Prowse when he was "(nearly) seventeen". To begin with the magazine had poorly produced mimeograph stencil production but legibility did improve slightly in later issues. Variety of poetry styles, notably Peter Finch's work. Finch also pens the article "Concrete poetry: a brief outline" in the final issue, which is guest-edited by Charles Turnbull.

BL: 1, 2, 4, 5. (P.903/81)
UCL: 4–5.

298 Neptune's Kingdom: poetry broadsheet / edited by Martin Gleeson. Kilkee, Co. Clare: Neptune's Kingdom, No. 1 (1972)–3 (Winter 1974)

Profiled in: Tom Clyde, *Irish Literary Magazines: an outline history and descriptive bibliography* (Dublin: Irish Academic Press, 2003), BL: 2725.g.3414

Poems, reviews, and notices of little magazines. Poets included: Peter Fallon, James Liddy, Steve Sneyd, Anthony Cronin, and others. In an open letter in the third issue Liddy attacks both John Montague's and Thomas Kinsella's poetry as too academic.

BL: P.905/49
CUL: L727.B.122
NLS: HP4.80.125 PER
TCD: 1. (194.u.15 no. 15). 2. (OLS L–4–203 no.16). 3. (178.n.13 no.10)
UCL

299 New Age Poetry Magazine / edited by H.A.Weir. Rye, [Vol. 1 no. 1]–vol. 1 no. 12 (1975).

Note: Variant title: *The N.A.P.M.*

Poetry Library

300 New Edinburgh Review / edited by David Cubitt, then others. Edinburgh: Edinburgh University Students Publications Board, No. 1 (Feb. 1969)–66 (Summer 1984). ISSN: 0028–4645

Continued by: *Edinburgh Review*
Index: The Scottish Poetry Library plan to publish an index; their catalogue indexes the poems and poetry-related articles issue by issue at http://www.spl.org.uk/
Anthology: James Campbell (ed.), *New Edinburgh Review Anthology* (Edinburgh: Polygon, 1982), BL: X.950/19232
Related Imprint: Edinburgh University Students Publications Board published a number of social and economic documents about contemporary Scotland, and also Pat Arrowsmith, *Breakout: poems & drawings from prison* (1975), BL: X.909/41565

A cultural, political and even philosophical review with an international scope (Gramsci, Northern Ireland, West Africa...). Alongside a very eclectic range of essays, articles, photos and reviews it published poems in a fair number of its issues. In the early years Robin Fulton then Robert Garioch was its poetry editor, and the poets it published included Hugh MacDiarmid, Edwin Morgan, Norman MacCaig, Thomas A. Clark, D. M. Black, Brian McCabe, Kathleen Jamie, and many others. Writers who would come to rank among the leading commentators of their day, such as Neil Ascherson and Tom Nairn, made contributions which could be seen as significant precursors of the consti-tutional change in Britain and Scotland much later. Subsequent editors included Julian Pollock (1970), Paul Atkinson (1971), C.K. Maisels (1973), James Campbell (1978–1982) and Allan Massie (1982–1984).

BL: 1–2; 4–66. (P.523/237)
CUL: L900.B.338
NLS: HJ10.108 PER
TCD: PER 74–558
UCL

New Headland Magazine *See* Headland D203

301 New Measure / edited by John Aczel and Peter Jay. Oxford, then Northwood, Middlesex: Donald Parsons, then Peter Jay, No. 1 (Autumn 1965)–10 (1969). ISSN: 0548–5940

Index: UK Little Magazine Project (adapted from an original index by Glyn Pursglove)
Profiled in: Notes attached to the index by the UK Little Magazines Project
Related Imprint: Peter Jay's Anvil Press appears to have grown out of his experience as editor of *New Measure*, and poets in Anvil Press's catalogue were featured in no. 9.

Eclectic poetry magazine, with next to no reviews or criticism. Contributors included Gavin Bantock, Adrian Husain, John Wheway, Tom Raworth, Christopher Middleton, W. H. Auden, Matthew Mead, Harry Guest, Louise Glück and others, and, in translation, Boris Pasternak, Anna Akhmatova, and Salvatore Quasimodo. No. 1 was jointly edited by John Aczel and Peter Jay; no. 3 by Gavin Bantock and Peter Jay; no. 6 was edited by Stuart and Deirdre Montgomery of Fulcrum Press. This issue featured American poets Larry Eigner, Ed Dorn, Jerome Rothenberg, Gary Snyder, and others, and a piece by Gael Turnbull on Robert Duncan. All other issues were edited by Peter Jay alone, the first six from Oxford (where Jay was an undergraduate) and published by Donald Parsons. Nos. 7–10 were edited from Northwood in Middlesex, and published by Jay himself.

BL: P.901/36
CUL: L727.C.324
NLS: Y.98 PER
TCD: PER 80–555
UCL
Poetry Library 1, 3–10

302 New Poet Magazine. Leicester: New Poets' Club, No. 1 (Feb. 1960)–18 (July 1961)

Related Imprint: New Poets' Club published some pamphlets, including an anthology of poems about friendship, *A Measure of Fulfilment*, [1961], BL: 11454.n.37.

Issued free to members of the New Poets' Club. Traditional verse, mainly by members of the club. Edited anonymously.

BL: P.P.5126.nn

New Poetry (ed. Norman Hidden) *See* Writers' Workshop D533

303 New Poetry: a publication in 'The grand anthology of poetry series'.
London: Cathay Books, 1/2 (1971)–3/4 (1971)

Large anthologies of well-meaning but old-fashioned verse.

BL: P.903/103
CUL: L727.b.101.1– // Nos 1–4
NLS: 6.2764 PER
TCD: PER 81–632

304 New Poets: an anthology of contemporary verse. London: Regency Press, 1969–1979

An annual volume of work, but the word "contemporary" should not be taken to indicate modernity.

BL: Lacking 1973 and 1974. (P.901/379)
CUL: Lacking 1969. (L727.C.489)
NLS: Lacking 1969. (NE.1024.e.)
TCD: Lacking 1969. (DIR 1551 1970–1979)

305 The New Review / edited by Ian Hamilton: London: New Review Ltd., Vol. 1 no. 1 (April 1974)–vol. 5 no. 2 (Autumn 1978). ISSN: 0305–8344

Note: Continues: *The Review*
Index: According to Sullivan, Vols. 1–3 were indexed.
Profiled in: Sullivan 1914–1984 (under *The Review*)
Anthology: Ian Hamilton (ed.), *The New Review Anthology* (London: Heinemann, 1985; repr. Paladin, 1987), BL: YC.1987.a.6993
Interview: Dan Jacobson interviews Ian Hamilton in *London Review of Books*, 24th January 2002

Poems, short fiction, articles, reviews and interviews. Most of the British writers were drawn from the established London publishing houses, but many European authors appeared in translation as well.

BL: Lacking the Index to vols 1–3. (P.903/223.)
CUL: P727.B.16
NLS: HJ8.121 PER
TCD: PER 81–697 1974–1978
UCL

306 Nicely / edited by Lyndon Puw. Talybont-on-Usk: Mainly, No. 1 (1966)

Note: Related to *Cutely* and *Mainly*

UCL

307 Night Scene / edited by Lee Harwood. London: Lee Harwood, c.1963?

Note: Related to *Night Train, Soho: bilingual review, Tzarad,* and *Horde*

Noted in *Origins/Diversions* 4. No holdings known.

308 Night Train / edited by Johnny Byrne, Lee Harwood, Roger Jones and [Barry] Miles. London: [Beantrain, *Night Scene* and *Tree* magazines], [No. 1] (May 1964)

Note: Continued by: *Horde*. Related to *Night Train, Soho* and *Tzarad*, and co-published by three other magazines

Contributors included: Pete Brown, Tristan Tzara (trans. Harwood), Anselm Hollo, Harry Guest, Spike Hawkins, Libby Houston, Tina Morris, Neil Oram, and others. Mimeograph production inside, black and white primitivist cover by Nick Tidnam.

BL: P.903/1
UCL

309 No Walls Broadsheet / edited by Peter Finch. Cardiff: [Peter Finch, No. 1 (1968)–18 (1969)]

Bibliography: An issue by issue contents listing is given at Peter Finch's website (see below)
Interview: Peter Finch interviewed by Andy Brown, in Brown (ed.) *Binary myths 2: correspondences with poet-editors* (Exeter: Stride, 1999), BL: YA.2001.a.16411
Website: http://dspace.dial.pipex.com/peter.finch/2ndaeon.htm

"A 340 x 400 mm poetry sheet was published between 1968 and 1970 as part of the *No Walls Poetry Readings* held in the Marchioness of Bute, The Blue Anchor, The Moulders Arms, and other Cardiff public houses." – From Peter Finch's website. Contributors included: Fred Daly, John Tripp, Alan Jackson, Jim Burns, Adrian Henri, Brian Patten, Huw Morgan, Tony Curtis, Bob Cobbing, Thomas A. Clark, Harri Webb, and others. Number Fourteen featured *The Swansea Poets* including Leonard Griffin, W.M.Goulding, Paul Botham, Tony Curtis, Mike Evans, Tony Thomas, and Chris Dix.

BL: 2–18. (P.2000/64)
CUL: 8–10, 16–18. (L727.b.89)
NLS: 5–18. (7.103 PER)
TCD: 11–16. (202.v.1 no.11 (a–f))
UCL: 2–18

310 The Norman Hackforth / edited by John James. Cambridge: [The Norman Hackforth], [1969]

A typed foolscap one-off magazine from the Cambridge school poets. Contributors were: J. H. Prynne, Nick Totton, Wendy Mulford, Gill Vickers, Fred Buck, Ian Patterson, Anthony Barnett, Douglas Oliver, and Elaine Feinstein; with illustrations by Penny Bovill. Norman Hackforth was one of Noel Coward's accompanists on piano, and the Mystery Voice of the radio programme Twenty Questions, from which the magazine The Anona Wynn also took its name.

BL: YA.1993.c.8
CUL: L727.b.83.1
NLS: 6.1657
UCL

311 North [Poetry Edition] / edited by Norman Smithson. Leeds: Norman Smithson, No. 1 (Winter 1973/74)–7/8 (1977)

This appears to have been a special edition of a magazine not normally devoted to poetry. No. 1 of the Poetry Edition publishes the poems of "a group of Manchester poets and friends [who] came to Leeds for a 'Little Magazine' Conference at Swarthmore College," namely, Johnny McDonald, Jack Marriott, Derek Ridge, David Dunn and David Ward, as well as Mike Haywood, who the editor notes has sadly recently died. Not to be confused with the later The North.

BL: 1. (P.901/1111)
UCL: 1–3, 4, 7/8.

North York Poetry See York Poetry D539

312 The Northern Review: a quarterly magazine of the arts / edited by Patrick Lynch and Michael Mitchell. Comber, Co. Down: Eusemere, Vol. 1 no. 1 (Spring 1965)– no. 3 (1967)

Profiled in: Tom Clyde, Irish Literary Magazines: an outline history and descriptive bibliography (Dublin: Irish Academic Press, 2003), BL: 2725.g.3414

A magazine associated with Philip Hobsbaum's Belfast Group, Hobsbaum being on the editorial board from the first issue. The poets published in the magazine included Seamus Heaney, Derek Mahon, and Michael Longley, as well as Ted Hughes, Peter Redgrove, and others. There were also short stories and reviews; Anthony Burgess contributed an essay on Aldous Huxley, Hobsbaum one on Joyce Cary, George MacCann on MacNeice, and Denis Ireland on W. B. Yeats.

BL: Vol. 1 no. 1. (ZA.9.a.4451)
NLS: 5.5297
UCL: Vol. 1 no.2–vol. 1 no. 2
Queen's University Belfast: hAP4.N8

313 The Notebooks of Pierre Menard / edited by Peter Hoy and Anthony Rudolf. Oxford, No. 1 (15 Sept. 1969); no. 8 (15 April 1970).

Note: Nos. 2–7 were never published. A supplement to The Journals of Pierre Menard, which is listed separately in this sequence.
Interview: with Anthony Rudolf in Görtschacher 2
Related Imprint: The Menard Press grew out of The Journals of Pierre Menard, and is profiled in Anthony Rudolf's From Poetry to Politics: The Menard Press, 1969–1984 (London: Menard Press, 1984), BL: YC.1987.a.5410.

Intended to cover translations of poems that were work in progress: In no. 1: Hölderlin (trans. Lane England; Roger Poole; Ted Walker), Rimbaud (trans. Alan Bold; Elizabeth Jennings; Jonathan Griffin); Anthony Rudolf's translations of Raymond Queneau, Guillaume Apollinaire, Jacques Dupin, and Thomas Wilson. No. 8 was devoted to poems by Michael O'Brien, Nicholas Moore (sixteen pages), and a bibliography of recent translations of Baudelaire.

BL: P.901/541
CUL: (L700.C.144)
NLS: HP3.85.1020 PER
TCD: PER 91–12
UCL: 1

314 Nothing Doing in London / edited by Anthony Barnett; editor for France, Claude Royet-Journoud. London: Nothing Doing, No. 1 (1966)–2 (1968) ISSN: 0029–411X

Related Imprint: Nothing Doing also produced The Literary Supplement

English, French and Portuguese texts; artwork; music. Contributors were: Anne-Marie Albiach, Samuel Beckett, Paul Joyce, Jean Cocteau, Michel Deguy, Alberto De

Lacerda, Thomas Livingston, Harold Norse, António Sena, John Tchicai, Nick Totton, Homero Aridjis, Gwen Barnard, Carla Bley, F. Castillo, Michel Couturier, David Coxhead, Andrew Crozier, Stephen Dwoskin, Jacques Garelli, Edmond Jabès, Stuart Montgomery, Yoko Ono, George Oppen, Tom Pickard, and the editors.

BL: P.901/233
CUL: L999.C.3.443
NLS: NG.1593.a.12 PER
UCL

315 Novice: a free magazine/outlet for unsung writers and poets / edited by Robert Bowe. Manchester: [Novice], [1, 1973]–?

UCL: 5–7 (1973)

316 Nucleus: PV anthology of poetry / edited by Malc Payne. Crowborough: PV Publications, 1 [1972]–4 (1975)

Related Imprint: PV Publications also published single-author collections, e.g. David Calcutt, *Savage Portrait* (1975), BL: X.909/31123, as well as the magazine *Radix*. PV stands for Poet's Vigilantes.

BL: 2 (1973). (ZA.9.a.2454)
UCL: 2–4 (1975)

317 Number: a bi-monthly journal of the arts, architecture, society, graphics, poems etc / Publishing Editor: Ken Baynes; Editor: Gerald Nason. London: Number, No. 1 (Feb. 1961)–4 (1962)

A strongly visual magazine, with engravings and photographs and essays with an emphasis on public art and architecture. The third issue takes a historical and philosophical view of toys; the fourth issue, which breaks from the larger square format of all previous issues, is a booklet of poems and drawings by Gerald Nason, *Songs of An Amateur Rake*.

BL: PP.7615.dx

318 Oasis / edited by Ian Robinson. London: Oasis, No.1 (Nov. 1969)– . ISSN 0029–7410

Note: Absorbed *Expression*. *Oasis* was incorporated with *Shearsman* and the U.S. *Atlantic Review* into *Ninth Decade* from 1983-1991. From 1991 *Oasis* separated out from *Ninth Decade* (which had become *Tenth Decade*) and began to publish in its own right again.
Index: An index of 1–10 was issued to subscribers, and this was repeated for 11–15, 31–65, and 66–99 (and probably 16–30)
Related Imprint: Oasis Books published many single–author collections, including work by Robin Fulton, Frances Presley, Harry Gilonis, Martin Booth, Judith Kazantzis, Tomas Tranströmer, and others, as well as the magazine *Telegram* (with Oxus Press) and *Ninth Decade* and *Tenth Decade*.
Interview: with Ian Robinson in Görtschacher 2; with Yann Lovelock in Görtschacher 2
Website: A number of issues are presented digitally at www.poetrymagazines.org.uk

A very eclectic magazine, publishing poems from many different traditions. Contributors include: Peter Dent, Tom Lowenstein, Matthew Sweeney, John Perlman, Pierre Joris, Peter Manson, Andrew Duncan, and many others. Often illustrated by Robinson's line drawings and those of others. Occasional reviews. Strong on the prose poem. Others involved editorially include Michael Bullock, Gail Howell-Jones, Yann Lovelock, Tony Lopez, John Stathatos, and Ray Seaford. Ian Robinson died in May 2004 and the future of the magazine is uncertain.

BL: 5, 6, 8, 10, 12–19, 23–31, 35, 36, 39–53, 65, 67, 69– . (P.901/2096).
CUL: 11, 17, 20–21, 23, 27, 29, 80– . (L727.d.186)
NLS: 11, 20–21. (HP2.87.3157 PER)
UCL
Poetry Library: 5–32, 35–98, 100–

319 Oasis / edited by Vincent Mills, Gerry McCarthy, David Neilson and others. Glasgow: [Students' Representatives of] Glasgow University, [Vol. 1 no. 1, 1975]–vol. 2 no. 7 (April 1979). ISSN 0309–9091

Note: Continues the more general *Glasgow University Magazine (GUM)*. Continued by: *Written in Ink*.

Poems, short fiction, and some reviews. Contributors included several of the poets associated with Glasgow's literary rise: Tom Leonard, Liz Lochhead, Edwin Morgan, Alan Spence, Philip Hobsbaum, and Stewart Conn (later the Poet Laureate of Edinburgh). Hamish Whyte, also known as editor, librarian and publisher (Mariscat Press) also contributes poems, as does the historian of music, John Purser. Alasdair Gray publishes an extract from *Lanark*, and Iain Crichton Smith has poems, too.

BL: Vol. 1 no. 1 (1975)–vol. 2 no. 7 (April 1979). (P.901/3061)
NLS: Vol. 1 no. 1 (1975)–vol. 2 no. 7 (April 1979). (P.el.280)

320 Oddments / by Gerda Mayer. London: Gerda Mayer, [No. 1–2, 1973?]

The first issue consists entirely of poems by Gerda Mayer. Mimeograph stencil production. "*Oddments* appears at odd intervals and is added to or subtracted from according to the mood of the author & the availability & behaviour of duplicators." The second issue bore the title, *Poet Tree Centaur: A Walthamstow Group Anthology*.

BL: [1]. (YD.2005.b.983)
UCL

321 Okike / edited by Chinua Achebe. Enugu, Nigeria and Canterbury: Okike, No. 1 (April 1971)– . ISSN 0331–0566

Note: Subtitle varies: *a Nigerian journal of new writing*; then an *African journal of new writing*
Related Imprint: Okike also published anthologies of poetry and short fiction.

A key African literary review. Poems, fiction, interviews, essays and reviews. Also published an occasional *Educational Supplement* featuring background essays on British, African and other authors.

BL: 1 (1971)–24 (June 1983). (P.901/1340). Another set: 7 (1975)–33 (1996) (DSC 6252.860000)
CUL: 14 (Sept. 1978)– .(L700.c.224.5–)
NLS: 14 (Sept. 1978)–15 (Aug. 1979). (HP2.80.3879 PER)
UCL

322 Olive Dachsund / edited by Glyn Pursglove. Oxford: Two Birds Press, No. 1 (Sept. 1966)–3 (Apr. 1968)

Note: In part, continues *Nebulum*

The first issue, published c/o Glyn Pursglove at St. Peter's College, Oxford, contains a brief anthology of Czechoslovakian concrete poetry, with work by Jiri Valoch and Ladislav Novak, as well as poetry from Germany, France, the USA and the UK.

BL: 1 (ZD.9.b.147)
Brotherton Library, Leeds University: Special Collections General Literature D–6 OLI

323 Omens / edited by G. S. Fraser, with Sam Brown, Robert Duxbury, John Martin and David Timms. Leicester: Omens, Vol. 1 no. 1 (Nov. 1971)–vol. 9 no. 1 (Mar. 1980)

Related Imprint: The Omens Poetry Pamphlet series published several single-author collections including, Veronica Forrest-Thomson, *Cordelia, or, 'A poem should not mean but be'* (1974), BL: X.909/40589; and Nicki Jackowska, *The Bone Palaces* [1977], BL: YA.1997.a.15670

Set up by G. S. Fraser as general editor with co-editors who took over from him after vol. 4 no. 2. Contributors were (presumably) Leicester University students and poets from further afield, notably Veronica Forrest-Thomson, Nicki Jackowska, Yann Lovelock, Tom Paulin, David Miller, Matthew Sweeney, E. A. Markham, Penelope Shuttle, Valerie Sinason, Maggie O'Sullivan, and Martin Stannard.

BL: Lacking Vol. 1 no. 2. (P.901/1435)
CUL: L727.C.706
NLS: Vol. 5 no. 2 (Jan. 1976)–vol. 9 no. 1 (Mar. 1980), but Lacking Vol. 8 no. 1 (1978)–vol. 8 no. 2 (1979). (DJ.s.366 PER)
UCL: Vol.2 no. 1 (1971)–vol. 7 no. 3 (1978)
Poetry Library: Vol. 1 no. 2; vol. 3 no. 1–vol. 9 no. 1

324 Once: a one-shot magazine / edited by Thomas Clark. Brightlingsea, Essex, [1965?]. Then *Twice*, then *Thrice*, then *Thrice and a 1/2*, then *Frice*, then *Vice*, then *Spice*,then *Slice*, Vol. 1 no. 1–no. 2, then *Ice*, then *Nice*, then *Dice*, then *Lice* [1966?]

Related Imprint: Once Books published Thomas Clark's *Airplanes* (1966), BL: Pressmark pending; and Ron Padgett's *Tone Arm* (1967), BL: YA.2001.b.4030
Interview: Tom Clark is interviewed by Kevin Ring in *Beat Scene* 42 (Autumn 2002), an interview re-issued in the online magazine *Jacket* 21 (Feb 2003), jacketmagazine.com

Edited by the American poet Thomas [i.e. Tom] Clark while he was living in England. Contributors include Robin Blaser, Ed Dorn, Ron Padgett, Tom Raworth, Ted Berrigan, Gregory Corso, Larry Eigner, and others. Stapled foolscap.

BL: *Once* (Cup.805.n.2), *Twice* (LD.31.b.97), *Thrice and a 1/2* (LD.31.b.98), *Frice* (LD.31.b.99), *Vice* (LD.31.b.100), *Slice* (LD.31.b.101), *Ice* (LD.31.b.104), *Nice* (LD.31.b.103)
UCL: *Once, Twice, Thrice and a 1/2, Frice, Slice, Ice and Nice*

325 **One** / edited by David Chaloner and Barry Dixon. Cheadle Hulme, [No. 1, Summer 1971]–5 (Spring 1981)

Note: The fifth issue was a merger with the last issue of *Vanessa* to form *Vanessa and One*.

From the second issue, David Chaloner was sole editor, and the magazine moved to London from the third issue, published in Spring 1976.

BL: 1–4 (P.903/208). 5 (P.903/508)
CUL: 1–4 (L727.B.152). 5 (L727.B.152)
NLS: 1–4 (P.la.9433 PER). 5 (P.la.9433)
UCL: 1–3, 5
Poetry Library: 4

326 **Open Space** / edited by Linda Anderson and others. [Aberdeen]: [c/o Department of English, Taylor Building, University of Aberdeen, Old Aberdeen]: [Open Space], No.1 (Autumn 1974)–[10] (Spring 1980)

Mostly poetry, but some short fiction. Some poems in Gaelic and in Scots. Contributions included poems by: Tom Leonard, G. F. Dutton, Cairns Craig (later better known as a literary critic and academic), Robert Garioch, Tom Buchan, Nan Shepherd (a poet and novelist more normally associated with the interwar years), Olga Wojtas (later better known as a *Times Higher Educational Supplement* correspondent), Robin Robertson, Ken Morrice, Angus Calder, and others.

BL: P.901/3427
CUL: 4–[10]. (L727.C.628)
NLS: HP3.82.3445 PER
UCL

327 **Orbis** / edited by Mike Shields, then Carole Baldock. [Youlgreave, Derbyshire]: [Hub Publications], 1 [1969]–? ISSN: 0030–4425

Note: Publisher and subtitle varies. Absorbed: *Scrip*.
Profiled in: Görtschacher 1
Interview: with Mike Shields, in Görtschacher 1

Poems, reviews, and listings. Readers' comments to previous issues are relayed in subsequent numbers. The magazine announced in issue 119 (Winter 2000) that its last issue would be 120, but Carole Baldock took over with issue 121, continuing the magazine. Robin Gregory, John Waddington-Feather, Cal Clothier, Mabel Ferrett, and

Rupert M. Loydell were also involved editorially. Special issues have included: no. 58/59, a Scottish issue, with guest editor Joy Hendry; no. 69/70, an Irish issue, guest editor John F. Deane; and no. 86, an American issue.

BL: 7, 8, 68–. (P.901/1041)
CUL: L900.B.332
NLS: Lacking: 4 [1970], 12 [1972] 20–21 (1975). (HJ6.37 PER)
TCD: [1988]–. (PER 85–750)
UCL
Poetry Library: 10/11–12; 15–16; 20, 30–

328 **Origins/Diversions** / edited by M. J. Dyke and C. J. [i.e. Chris] Torrance. Carshalton then Sutton, Surrey: No. 1 (Nov. 1963)–12 (1966)

Note: Continued by *Assassinator Broadsheet*
Related Imprint: Origins/diversions published at least one pamphlet, Bill Wyatt's *Songs of the Four Seasons* (1965), BL: YA.1993.a.2416

A magazine with an interest in poetry and jazz. Contributors included Dave Cunliffe, Tina Morris, Mike [i.e. Michael] Horovitz, Bill Wyatt, Steve Sneyd, Jim Burns, Penelope Shuttle, Lee Harwood, and others.

BL: 3 (Jan. 1964)–10 (Apr./Aug. 1965). (PP.8006.pz.).
CUL: 4 (Mar. 1964); 10–11 (1966). (L727.C.375)
NLS: 4 (Mar. 1964); 6/7 (July/Aug. 1964)–8 (Oct./Nov. 1964); 10 (Apr./Aug. 1965)–12 (Summer/Autumn 1966). (6.1496)
UCL: 2 (1963)–12 (Summer/Autumn 1966)

329 **Origo** / edited by Philip Carr, then Paul–René Sieveking. Cambridge: [Origo], c/o Queens' College, then Cambridge Black Cross c/o Jesus College, 1 (Spring/Summer 1968)–?

The first issue includes a short story by Graham Swift, but most of the contributions to this and other issues are poetry, including work by Julian Nangle and Nigel Wheale. No. 3, much taller and thinner, has a cover by Antony Gormley depicting a swan and perhaps Leda, and the rest of that issue bears illustrations by him.

BL: 1; 3 (ZA.9.c.35)
CUL: 1. (Apply to Periodicals Librarian)

330 Osgoldcross Review / edited by
Gerald England. Ackworth: Poets' Press of
Osgoldcross, No. 1 (1973).

Interview: with Gerald England in *Poetry Today Online*,
www.poetrytodayonline.com/ JANpub.html
Related Work: Gerald England, *Editor's Dilemma: 20 years of
small press publishing* (Hyde: New Hope International, 1990),
BL: YK.1998.a.12604.

UCL

331 Ostrich / edited by Keith Armstrong.
Newcastle upon Tyne, then Whitley Bay: IRD
Arts Club, then Erdesdun Pomes, [No. 1] (June
1971)–18/19 (Sept./Oct.1976). ISSN:
0307–0786

Related Imprint: Erdesdun Pomes published some single-
author collections, as well as local history.

Began life as an A4 typescript anthology of the work of four
poets – Barry Cole, John White, Daphne Waters, and Keith
Armstrong – but later increased its production values,
greatly extended the number of poets appearing in its
pages, and carried short fiction, reviews and articles.
Malcolm Povery, Gordon Phillips, and Paul Lester were also
involved editorially.

BL: Lacking 2–3. (P.903/169)
CUL: L727.B.140
NLS: Lacking 1–3. (HP3.79.2244 PER)
TCD: Lacking 1–3. (PER 81–705)
UCL
Poetry Library: [3?], 6–10, 12–13, 15–18/19

332 Other Times / edited by Mr. E.
(Fiction, Portfolio), Paul Brown (Faction,
Poetry & Film), and Andrew Brown (Music,
Letters, Cartoons). London: P.P. Layouts, Vol. 1
no. 1 (Nov.1975–Jan. 1976)

"Other Times is an international *speculative* quarterly. Sad as
this thin word seems, it at least defines our vices. Like Jean
Harlow in McClure's 'The Beard' we have to say to you,
"Before you can pry any secrets from me, you must first
find the real me! Which one will you pursue?" We offer you
in every issue some tactics, some strategy, some method of
inquiry. We offer you in every issue new destinations, some
diversions, some dead-ends. Which one you pursue is a
matter of beautiful indifference to us. We shall continue to
massage the organs of this media before your very eyes. We
intend that something should happen between your ears

rather than the lobotomy others seek to engineer." – from
the editorial, signed by "The Editors". The magazine has
fairly high production values for its time, using black and
white visuals creatively and with a black, blue and white
glossy cover. As the editorial suggests it is characterised by
eclecticism and it looks both to America and the Continent,
with not a little nod to Surrealism. Items include a cartoon
strip, short fiction, Eric Mottram on "Dionysus in
America", an essay on the film-maker Georges Méliès and
poems by Blaise Cendrars translated by Peter Hoida. The
name of the publisher, P.P. Layouts, is a jokey reference to
the sinister corporation in Philip K. Dick's novel *The Three
Stigmata of Palmer Eldritch*. Perhaps the editor's name, "Mr.
E.", is also an in-joke of this kind.

BL: ZA.9.b.500

OU *See* Cinquième Saison C15a

333 Outburst / edited by Tom Raworth.
London: No. 1 (1961)–2 (1963). ISSN:
0474–9111

Related Imprint: Matrix Press

Contributors include: Outburst 1: Tom Malcolm,
Christopher Logue, Tram Combs, Gary Snyder, Gael
Turnbull, Fielding Dawson, Edward Dorn, Pete Brown,
Michael Horovitz, Robert Creeley, Anselm Hollo, Piero
Heliczer, Cha Tze-Chiang (translating Tu Fu), Maurice
Capitanchik, Nigel Black, Denise Levertov; Outburst 2:
Douglas Woolf, Paul Klee, Paul Blackburn, David Ball,
Pentti Saarikoski, Phillip Whalen, Leroi Jones, Fielding
Dawson, Allen Ginsberg, Cha Tze-Chiang (translating Tu
Fu), Piero Heliczer, Edward Dorn, David Meltzer, Larry
Eigner, Ruth Weiss, Gregory Corso, Carol Bergé, Alan
Sillitoe, Anselm Hollo. "After all this time and with a crate
of letters still waiting to be answered. To be use at all, it
should appear regularly so something must change. And
now the type is too worn to use again. Who has ten pounds
to spare? But subscribe" – Back cover of last issue. Raworth
hand-set each issue. *Outburst: The Minicab War* was also
published (no date of publication) on the theme of
minicabs versus taxis. This featured imaginary interviews
with Bertrand Russell, Harold Macmillan, George Barker,
John Betjeman and T. S. Eliot.

BL: Lacking *Outburst: The Minicab War*. (P.P.7616.ft.)
CUL: Lacking *Outburst: The Minicab War*. (L727.C.319)
NLS: Lacking *Outburst: The Minicab War*. (1967.52)
TCD: 1. Lacking *Outburst: The Minicab War*. (VP 27303)
UCL: Lacking *Outburst: The Minicab War*

334 The Oxford Literary Review /

edited by R. H. Silvertrust and Ian B. Owen; and others. Oxford: Oxford Literary Review, c/o University College; [No. 1] (Trinity term, 1973)– . ISSN: 0305-1498

Almost entirely literary criticism. It may have started as 'little' – and in the early issues a poem occasionally strayed in, e.g. by Nick Totton – but it soon became essentially an academic journal.

BL: P.903/231
CUL: L700.B.60
NLS: HJ8.647
TCD: Vol.7 (1985)– . (PER 73–137)

335 The Oxford Poetry Magazine /

[edited by "Adrian"?]. Oxford: Oxford University Poetry Society, c/o Adrian, Balliol College, 1 (1973)

BL: P.421/298
CUL: L999.c.3.452
NLS: 1975.27 PER
TCD: PER 81–964
Poetry Library: 1

335a Oxymoron / edited by Peter Adamson.

Oxford: Oxymoron, No. 1 (1965)–7 [1967].

Contributors include: Peter Jay, Sally Purcell, John Birtwhistle, and others.

BL: [Unnumbered issue, 1967?]
CUL: 1–4, [7]. (L985.b. 119)

336 Oyster / edited by Ruthi Blackmore.

Cardiff: Oyster Publications, [I, Nov. 1968]–III (1969)

Note: Continues: *Paperway*

Very similar to its predecessor, but with an added featured poet element, in a different colour of pages: in the first issue Jeni Couzyn: in the second, Kevin Hanson. Contributors included George MacBeth, Peter Levi, Eddie Linden, Christopher Logue, Dinah Livingstone, Peter Porter, Roger McGough, Nina Stene, Elizabeth Jennings, Tina Morris, Mike [i.e. Michael] Horovitz, Peter Redgrove, Vernon Scannell, Brian Patten, Alan Brownjohn, Edward Lucie-Smith, and others. John Horder was the guest editor for III.

BL: I. (ZA.9.a.6256 (1)); II. (ZA.9.a.6256 (2))

TCD: III. (OLS X–2–116 no.3)
UCL: I–II
Poetry Library: III

337 P. Coleraine: New University of Ulster, [1, 1970?–24, 1972?]

Profiled in: Tom Clyde, *Irish Literary Magazines: an outline history and descriptive bibliography* (Dublin: Irish Academic Press, 2003), BL: 2725.g.3414

Typed mimeograph production, with striking covers. Edited anonymously, although Kevin Durham is named as an editor for one issue. Clyde notes a connection with James Simmons, who contributes stories and poems, and whose Resistance Cabaret events were running at the university, where he was teaching.

University of Ulster: PN 1010 P2

338 Pages: international magazine of the arts / edited by David Briers.

Berkhamsted, then London: HRS Graphics, No. 1 (Autumn 1970)–3 (1972)

Related Imprint: Pages published, in an edition of 22 copies, A.D.4 (1972), a boxed collection of original works by Robin Crozier, Dick Higgins, Tom Phillips, Emmett Williams, and others

A magazine very interested in the visual arts, with a related interest in concrete poetry and text used in art. Hence work, for example, by Jindrich Prochazka and Jiri Valoch, John Furnival, Richard Demarco, Ian Breakwell, and Joseph Beuys, and an article by Nicholas Zurbrugg, "Towards the Death of Concrete Poetry" (no. 2, Winter 1970).

BL: (Pressmark Pending)
CUL: L999.b.1.190
NLS: 6.2239 PER
TCD: OLS X–1–650 no.27–28

339 Pair: cylchgrawn barddoniaeth /

edited by Vaughan Hughes. Llandybie: Christopher Davies, Rhif 1 (Haf 1972)–Rhif 3 (1973)

Related Imprint: Christopher Davies Publishers publishes general and history titles, but also occasionally produces poetry collections and poetry-related books. Most titles are in English.

Welsh language poetry and reviews. Contributors included: Aneirin Talfan Davies, J. M. Edwards, John Eilian, Siôn Eirian, Dewi Jones, Eluned Phillips, Tom Parri Jones (poem in the shape of Wales), Haydn Lewis (poem in the shape of a question mark), John Llewelyn Roberts, Wyn Roberts, Eluned Williams, Stanley Williams, Euros Bowen, and others.

BL: 1. (P.901/919)
CUL: L733.C.52
NLS: HP1.77.1099 PER
UCL

340 Palantir / edited by Stuart Brown, then Jim Burns. [Preston]: Palantir, c/o Preston Polytechnic, No.1 (Winter 1973)–23 [1983]

Eclectic. Poets included Robert Sheppard, Adrian Clarke, Edwin Morgan, Hamish Whyte, Duncan Glen, David Tipton, Gavin Ewart, Roy Fisher, Lee Harwood, Andrew Crozier, Matthew Mead, Valerie Sinason, Rafael Alberti (trans. Henry Probyn), Douglas Dunn, Christopher Middleton, Peter Riley, Alexis Lykiard, Jeremy Reed, David Chaloner, Yann Lovelock, John Welch, and others. Jim Burns, who took over editorship with issue 3, sets out a short survey of little magazines in issue 2.

BL: 1–21, 23. (BL: P.901/3185)
CUL: 1–12 [1978]; 15 [1980]; 17 [1981]–23 [1983]. (L727.C.853)
NLS: 17–23. (6449/A PER)
UCL
Poetry Library: 1, 3–23

341 Paperway / edited by Ruthi Blackmore and Jaci Wilde. Cardiff: Paperway Publications, I (June 1968)–II (Aug. 1968)

Note: Continued by *Oyster*

"...we want ALL poetry, somehow, to exist in harmony." – from the editorial in the first issue. Poems, some comment, and in the second issue an interview with Dannie Abse. Poets included: Peter Finch, David Chaloner, Jim Burns, Wes Magee, Paul Green, Adrian Henri, Herbert Lomas, Brian Pearce, Mike [i.e. Michael] Horovitz, Tina Morris, Dave Cunliffe, Peter Hoida, Frances Horovitz, Anselm Hollo, Brian Patten, and others.

BL: I. (ZA.9.a.6256(4)); II. (ZA.9.a.6256 (3)).
UCL

The Park *See* The Wivenhoe Park Review D525

342 Pause / edited by Deirdre Farrell. Monmouth: Pause, 1 (1969)–?

Stapled, mimeographed production, with presumably

litho-printed card cover. There were reviews and listings of other magazines. Contributors included: Dave Cunliffe, George Dowden, Harry Guest, Frances Horovitz, Michael Horovitz, Barry MacSweeney, Tina Morris, Kenneth Patchen, Ahmed Rashid, Tom Phillips (translating *The Seafarer*), Charles Bloomfield (translating Guillevic), Peter Hoy (translating Francis Ponge), Paul Brown, Peter Finch, Eric Ratcliffe (writing in no. 2 on "The Ratcliffe Plan: the nine aspects of love and discipline"), and others.

BL: 2. (ZD.9.a.72)
UCL: 1
Poetry Library: 2–3

343 Pax / [edited by Jim Bamber]. Preston: Pax Publications, No. 1 (Jan. 1969)–2 (May 1969)

Related Imprint: Pax also published the anonymous poetry collections *Keep It in the Family; or, Pax is a Place Called Home* (1969), BL: Cup.900.w.46

Reproduced from a typed stencil; stapled format. Contributors include Jim Burns.

BL: P.901/403
Poetry Library: 1

344 Peacock: a new Oxford literary magazine / edited by Sebastian Brett and Crispin Hasler Oxford: [Peacock. c/o Trinity College], [No.1, 1965?]. ISSN: 0553–4321

Poems and short stories, and an essay on the painter Victor Vasarely; all in a handsomely designed square format, designed by Jules Goddard. Contributors included George Barker, D.J. Enright, Matthew Mead, Patrick Bowles, Anselm Hollo, Craig Raine, Peter Redgrove, Nathaniel Tarn, and a small number of undergraduates, including Kit Wright. There were a number of translations of Latin American and German poetry.

BL: YA.1991.a.6596
CUL: L999.C.3.1077
NLS: 6.366
UCL

345 Pennine Platform / edited by Mabel Ferrett, Brian Merrikin Hill, Ken Smith, Jez Colclough, Ed Reiss, Nicholas Bielby. Heckmondwike [and subsequent locations, including Wetherby, Huddersfield, and Bradford]: Pennine Platform, Spring

1973–1980. New Series, No. 1 (April 1981)– .
ISSN: 0306–140X

Note: Continues: *Platform*. Early issues are unnumbered, and bear only the season and year. Issues 4–[8] are numbered as No. 1, 1979, No. 2, 1979, No. 3, 1979, No.1, 1980, etc. The pivotal issue had the numbering of both the original series and the new series, expressed as "New Series No. 1 (1980– Three) (April 1981)".
Profiled in: Görtschacher 1
Interview: with Brian Merrikin Hill, in Görtschacher 1
Related Imprint: Pennine Platform have published e.g. Steven Zivadin's *Metre, Rhyme & Freedom* [1976], BL: X.900/25141

Associated with the Pennine Poets Group.

BL: Spring 1973–Winter 1973/4. (P.901/537). Spring 1974–. (P.901/1273).
CUL: Spring 1975– . (L727.C.595)
NLS: Spring 1975– . Lacking New Series no. 1 (1981). (HJ4.753SER).
UCL: Spring 1973–New Series no. 17 (1987).
Poetry Library: 1 (1979)–[8], New series, 1–46, 48–

346 Phase / edited by Mike Hall. Exeter: [Phase, at Exeter University], [No. 1, 1967?]

BL: P.901/167
CUL: L999.C.3.260
UCL

347 Phoenix Broadsheet / [edited by Toni Savage]. [Leicester]: [Toni Savage], No. 1 (1971)–

Note: Continued as *Fenice Broadsheet*, edited by Cynthia Savage, following Toni Savage's death
Study: Derek Deadman and Rigby Graham, *A Paper Snowstorm: Toni Savage & The Leicester Broadsheets* (Oldham: Incline Press, 2005). This book tips in many examples of broadsheets and other printing, and comes with a portfolio of further examples.
Related Imprint: New Broom Press

Each issue devoted to a poem; illustrated. Phoenix authors include: Arthur Caddick, Shirley Toulson, John Adlard, Spike Milligan, Edward Lowbury, Yann Lovelock, Brian Patten, Count Potocki of Montalk, Robin Alston, Alix Weisz, John Clare, Roger McGough, and others.

BL: 38, 40, 44, 45, 50, 53, 54, 56, 58, 80, 87, 91, 92, 94–100, 103, 104, 106, 200, 205–215, 217–229, 231–282, 284–313, 315–338, 345–360, 366–410. With three unnumbered broadsheets. (X.0900/1043)
NLS: 100–. Lacking 107–145, 147–221. (HP.sm.132.)
TCD: Each broadsheet, if held, catalogued individually.

348 Pick: a magazine of contemporary poetry [edited by Brian Dann; Jerry Orpwood, Michael Rose, Carol Rumens, Jonathan Finch]. London: Pick Publications, Vol. 1 no. 1 (Autumn 1974)–vol. 3 no. 10 (Summer 1978). ISSN 0305–652X

Note: Variant titles: *Poetry Pick, Pick Poetry*. Also numbered: no. 1–12

Edited anonymously at first because "the poems are more important than the names of those who selected them." Poets included Peter Porter, Carol Rumens, John Welch, Gavin Ewart, John Heath-Stubbs, Ivor Cutler, Ruth Fainlight, Edwin Morgan, Norman MacCaig, Fleur Adcock and others.

BL: Lacking 9–10. (P.901/1285)
CUL: L727.C.610
NLS: DJ.s.370
TCD: PER 75–126
UCL
Poetry Library: Vol. 1 no. 1–vol. 3 no. 4

349 Pink Peace / edited by John Rice. Folkestone: Aten Press, 1 [197?]–9 [1974]

Contributors include: Tony Curtis, Jim Burns, Nick Toczek, Martin Booth, and others.

BL: 2 (Nov. 1971). (6501.507570). 5 (Autumn 1972) (ZA.9.a.2455).
NLS: 2 (Nov. 1971). (1976.170)
UCL: 1–9
Poetry Library: 3, 9

350 Plain Poetry / edited by Nicholas Zurbrugg. Norwich: Poetry Society of the Students Union of The University of East Anglia, No. 1 [1968?]–?

BL: 6 (Summer 1969). (Pressmark Pending)

351 Planet: the Welsh internationalist / edited by Ned Thomas, then John Barnie. Tregaron, then Aberystwyth: Planet, 1 (Aug./Sept. 1970)– . ISSN: 0048–4288

Index: An index to no. 51–100 was compiled by Mary Madden, and an index to 1–50 was probably issued to subscribers. If received, libraries may shelve these with the run of the magazine
Anthology: Janet Davies (ed.), *Compass Points: Jan Morris*

introduces a selection from the first hundred issues of Planet (Cardiff: University of Wales Press, 1993), BL: YC.1993.b.8137

Related Imprint: Planet publishes an eclectic and international list of short stories, non-fiction and poems, including work in translation by the Swedish poet Werner Aspenström

Website: www.planetmagazine.org.uk/

"*Planet* is a bi-monthly magazine covering the arts, culture and politics in Wales and beyond. In addition to features on and interviews with contemporary Welsh artists and writers, it includes political analysis, both of Welsh affairs and international issues. Several poems and one short story are published in every issue of the magazine." – from *Planet*'s website, Oct. 2002.

BL: P.901/975
CUL: 4 (Feb./Mar. 1971)– . (L900.C.448)
NLS: 4 (Feb./Mar. 1971)–49/50 (U.478.SER); 51– . ((QJ2.95 PER)
TCD: 4 (Feb. Mar. 1971)– . (PER 72–717)
UCL: 1–43 (1978); 72 (1988)–
Poetry Library: 68–98, 100–

352 Platform / edited by Joan Lee. Halifax, then Luddenden Foot, Yorkshire: Halifax and District Poetry Society, [1] (Sept 1966)–22 (1972)

Note: Began numbering issues in 1972. Continued by *Pennine Platform*

Emerged from the Halifax and District Poetry Society (later the Pennine Poets group).

BL: [1] (Sept. 1966)–Jan. 1970. (P.901/537)
UCL

353 Platform / edited by Andrew and Jim Cozens, Paul Robinson and Cynthia Corres. Stockbridge, Hampshire: No. 1 (1972)–7 (1974) ISSN: 0032–1389

Related Imprint: Platform's book imprint was Green Horse, which published (for example) Larry Eigner, *Suddenly It Gets Dark and Light in the Street: poems 1961–74* (1975), BL: YA.1986.a.11060

BL: 5, 6. (ZA.9.a.2470)
UCL

354 Platform: East Midlands / edited by Alexander Thomson. Nottingham: Arts Province, Vol. 1 no. 1 [1971?]–?

A general arts magazine, with events listings for the East Midlands area. Some space is given to poetry, e.g. vol. 2 no. 2 has "A Poetry Causerie: Home Thoughts on Ireland" by G. S. Fraser, poems by Pat McGrath, and an article about Coleridge visiting Derby.

BL: Vol. 2 no. 1, vol. 2 no. 2 [1972?]. (Pressmark pending)

PM Newsletter *See* Poetmeat D359

355 Poem Sheet: Athlone poets. Athlone, Westmeath: Kincora Poetry, 1 (1974)–2 (1975)

Contributors were: Gearoid O'Brien, Wm. Colm Nolan, Paul Hoare, Frank Bannon, Conleth Ellis, Peter Fallon, Frances Gwynn, Brendan Kennelly, and James Liddy.

BL: 1. (X.0900/400) 2. (X.0900/417)
NLS: 6.2591
TCD: 1. (194.0.71 no.2.) 2. (178.n.13 no.4)

356 Poems / St. Albans: Ver Poets, 1973?–?

Anthology: May Badman and Margaret Tims (eds.), *Ver Poets' Voices: thirtieth anniversary anthology* (St. Albans: Brentham, 1996), BL: YK.1996.a.19404

Website: http://www.hertsnews.com/arts/ver.htm

An anthology of poems selected from those entered for the Michael Johnson Memorial Poetry Competition. Ver Poets also issued *Poetry Post* and *Ver Poets Voices*. *Poems 2000*, an anthology issued by Ver Poets to mark the eponymous year, is not an issue of *Poems*.

BL: 1973, 1974. (P.901/1411)

357 Poems '69 [etc.] / edited by John Stuart Williams, and others. Llandysul: Gomer 1969–1974; 1976; 1978.

Anthologies of contemporary poetry from Wales: began as an annual, but became less frequent towards the end.

BL: P.901/689
CUL: 1978 (1978.8.2212)
NLS: 1969 (NE.1020.f.18); 1970 (NE.1020.a.43); 1971 (NE.1022.e.30); 1972 (NE.1022.e.30); 1973 (NE.1022.e.30); 1974 (6.2886); 1976 (HP2.79.1594); 1978 (HP2.79.957)
TCD: PR 3830 1969–1978

358 Poet / edited by Alan Tarling. London: Derek Maggs, 1 (Autumn 1972)–2 (1974?)

Related Work: Alan Tarling, *Titles from a Poetry Press: an* account of small-press publishing at Poet & Printer, 1965 to 1990 (Hatch End: Poet & Printer, 1990), BL: YK.1991.a.7625

BL: 1. (P.901/970)
CUL: 1. (L999.D.1.26)
NLS: 1. (5.6444 PER)
UCL
Poetry Library: 1

359 Poetmeat / edited by David Cunliffe, Tina Morris and Kirby Congdon. Blackburn: Screeches Publications, [No. 1, 1963]–no. 13 (1967). ISSN: 0554-3886

Profiled in: John Sutherland, *Offensive Literature: decensorship in Britain, 1960–1982* (London: Junction Books, 1982), BL: YA.1989.a.20398

Related Imprint: Screeches Publications published Anselm Hollo (ed. and trans.), *Word from the North: new poetry from Finland* (1965) (YD.2005.b.147), Arthur Moyse (ed.) *The Golden Convolvulus* (1965), 2nd printing, BL: YA.2003.b.3955; and Ian Vine, *Cascades* (1965), BL: X.900/8797, a small volume of poems which also contains Ian Vine's appeal for financial support for Screeches as it faces prosecution over the explict anthology *The Golden Convolvulus*. BB Books was another imprint associated with *Poetmeat* and issued *Global Tapestry* and *PM Newsletter*, "free to BB Bks subscribers, as a service to little mag editors, small press book publishers, collectors & readers", carrying reviews and listings concerning the small press world. UCL holds nos. 15 (1967)–19 (1969) of *PM Newsletter*, which later became the name of the listings section of *Global Tapestry*. Poetmeat and Strangers Press co-published Anselm Hollo's anthology of Finnish poetry *Word from the North* (1965), BL: YD.2005.b.147

For publishing and distributing the sexually explicit anthology *The Golden Convolvulus*, David Cunliffe was prosecuted for sending indecent material in the post (found guilty) and for obscene publication (found innocent). *Poetmeat* itself published counter-culture manifestoes, as well as poetry. There are no British locations known for the first edition of *The Golden Convolvulus*, but it did escape England and there appear to be copies at Harvard University, University of Michigan, University of California at Berkeley, and Northwestern University Library.

BL: 1; 2; 4–9; 11–13. (Cup.700.f.18.)
CUL: 11–13. (L727.B.56.)
NLS: 11–13. (5.3673.)
TCD: 11–13. (OLS X–2–116 no.11–13 Copy A). Second set, 11–13. (UB Per 2nd copy nos. 11–13)
UCL: 4–13
Poetry Library: 6; 12

360 Poetrait: free digger poetry magazine. [1968]

Advertised in the first issue of *Gandalf's Garden* as available at the "FREE BOOKSHOP", but no address is supplied. No holdings known.

361 Poetry Anthology. Zennor: United Writers, No. 1 [1972]

A 130-page anthology, edited anonymously. Contributors included Vivienne Finch.

BL: X.0709/566
NLS: P.sm.295
TCD: P 27022

362 Poetry Dimension / edited by Jeremy Robson then Dannie Abse. London: Abacus then Robson Books, 1 (1973)–7 (1980)

Poems, essays, interviews, letters and a "Lives of the Poets" feature, in which a poet reflects about a subject that concerns them: most culled from the year's publications (magazines and books) and broadcasts, but some specially commissioned.

BL: P.901/1095
CUL: L727.D.192
NLS: 1 (5.5785); 2 (NE.1021.e.45); 3 (5.6490); 4 (HP1.77.776); 5(HP1.78.1030); 6 (HP1.79.4656); 7 (HP1.80.4262)
TCD: DIR 2832 1973–1980

363 Poetry Essex. Harlow: Olive Bentley, 1 (Autumn 1975). ISSN: 0308-2768

BL: P.901/3010
CUL: L999.c.3.601
NLS: P.sm.1406 PER

364 Poetry Forum. Farnborough: Green and Williams Associates, No. 1 ([1970])–5 (Winter 1971)

Light, traditional verse. A ten guinea prize (later, £5) is offered by the unnamed editor for the best poem published.

BL: P.903/82
CUL: L727.b.128
NLS: 6.2489 PER
TCD: Lacking 3. (PER 81–361)

365 Poetry in the Circle in the Square / [edited Bill Pickard?] Bristol: Bristol Arts Centre, No. 1 (1966)–20 (1976)

Note: Continues: Circle in the Square Broadsheet. Variant title: Poetry of the Circle in the Square
Related Imprint: Circle in the Square published Terence Dooley's House of Cards (1969), BL: YD.2005.b.20

The magazine of the Poetry in the Circle group, later known as Polygon Poets.

UCL
Poetry Library: 13–14

366 Poetry Information / edited by Peter Hodgkiss and others. Newcastle-upon-Tyne, then London: Peter Hodgkiss, then Association of Little Presses, No. 1 (Jan. 1970)–20/21 (Winter 1979/80). ISSN: 0048–4598. Then as Poetry and Little Press Information, No. 1 (May 1980)–no. 12 (Nov. 1984), ISSN: 0260–9339. Then as PALPI, Issue 13 (Oct. 1985)–37 (Mar. 1997). ISSN: 0260–9339

BL: Poetry Information, 3–20/21. (P.903/74). Poetry and Little Press Information, and PALPI. (P.903/685)
CUL: Poetry Information, Imperfect set, 1970–80. (L727.b.98); Second set, 16–21 (English Faculty Library). Poetry and Little Press Information, and PALPI. (L727.b.238)
NLS: Poetry Information. (P.la.4811 PER). Poetry and Little Press Information. (HJ8.854 PER). PALPI. (HJ8.767 PER)
TCD: Poetry Information (PER 91–307 1970–1980)
UCL: Poetry Information
Poetry Library: Poetry Information, 4–20/21

367 Poetry International: an anthology of contemporary verse. London: Regency Press, 1970–1978

An annual volume of work, but the word "contemporary" should not be taken to indicate modernity. Not related to the Poetry International festival on London's South Bank.

BL: 1970–71, 1973–76, 1978
CUL: 1970–74, 1976, 1978. (L727.c.447)
NLS: 1970–74, 1976, 1978. (NE.1022.f)
TCD: DIR 1253 1970–1978

368 Poetry Ireland / edited by John Jordan; editorial board: James Liddy, James J. McAuley,

Richard Weber. Dublin: Dolmen Press, No. 1 (Autumn 1962)–7/8 (Spring 1968)

Profiled in: Tom Clyde, Irish Literary Magazines: an outline history and descriptive bibliography (Dublin: Irish Academic Press, 2003), BL: 2725.g.3414
Interview: with Theo Dorgan, in Görtschacher 2
Related Imprint: Dolmen was a key literary press in Ireland from the 1950s to 1970s, publishing many poetry-related titles. It appears to have stopped publishing after 1986. The Michael Freyer Collection at Trinity College Dublin contains a substantial archive of the Dolmen Press
Related Work: Maurice Harmon (ed.) The Dolmen Press: A Celebration (Dublin: Lilliput Press, 2002), BL: 2708.e.2634

A self-conscious refounding of the Poetry Ireland of the 1950s. John Montague compiled the last issue.

BL: P.P.8000.nd.
CUL: L727.C.118
NLS: 1974.48 PER
TCD: PER 75–123 1962–1968; also, a second full set in the Freyer Collection, with the addition of prospectus, invitation to the launch, and Irish Times cuttings relating to the magazine.
UCL
Poetry Library: 1–2, 7/8

369 Poetry Letter / edited by Colin R. Fry. London, Issue 1 [196?]–2 (June 1969)

BL: 2. (ZD.9.a.151)
UCL: 2
Poetry Library: 2

370 Poetry Loughborough: a periodical collection of verse written at Loughborough University of Technology. Loughborough: Loughborough University of Technology, Student Arts Centre, No.1 (April 1974)–no.4 (1977)

CUL: L727.b.149
NLS: HP4.82.748 PER
UCL: No.2 (1975)–4 (1977)

371 Poetry Market: a magazine for poets and poetry lovers. Nottingham, 1 (1965)–3 (1967). ISSN: 0032–2083

BL: P.905/1
UCL

372 Poetry Nation / edited by C.B. Cox and Michael Schmidt. Manchester: Department of English, Manchester University, 1 (1973)–6 (1976). ISSN 0308–2636

Note: Continued by PN Review
Index: Mark Beech, Poetry Nation I–VI and PN Review 1–110: index (Manchester: Carcanet, 1997), BL: YK.1997.b.3628
Profiled in: Görtschacher 1
Interview: with Michael Schmidt, in Görtschacher 1
Related Imprint: Carcanet
Website: Digitized copies at www.poetrymagazines.org.uk

Stout hardback format; poetry and essays. The first editorial suggests a seeking of consensus for British poetry on the basis of "the necessary intelligence that must be brought to the poetic act (whether of writing or reading), the shaping of adequate forms, and, equally important, the responsibilities to a vital linguistic and formal heritage, to a living language, to a living community." Contributors included: Kingsley Amis, James Atlas, Ted Hughes, Michael Longley, Elizabeth Jennings, Michael Hamburger, Elaine Feinstein, Terry Eagleton, Roy Fuller, Douglas Dunn, W. S. Graham, Donald Davie, Val Warner, Peter Scupham, C. H. Sisson, Peter Porter, Stewart Conn, James Aitchison, Christopher Middleton, Tom Paulin, and others. Important for its in-depth essays, which remain a significant part of its successor, P.N. Review. Michael Schmidt's papers, and those of Carcanet, are held at the John Rylands Library, Manchester University.

BL: 1; 3–6. (P.901/1153)
CUL: P727.C.31
NLS: Y.49 PER
TCD: PER 77–705
UCL
Poetry Library

373 Poetry News Birmingham: Birmingham Poetry Centre, No. 1 (1971)–10 (Dec. 1973)

Related Imprint: The Birmingham Poetry Centre also published Muse

News about activities associated with the Poetry Centre, some reviews, and considerable discussion about the role and profile of poetry in society. The Birmingham Poetry Centre was founded by John Dalton, Nina Weddell and George MacBeth, whose names are used in the last issue of Poetry News to implore more members to turn up to events, presumably in vain.

BL: 7 (Jan. 1973)–10. (P.903/207)
CUL: L727.B.125

NLS: 7 (Jan. 1973)–10. (HP1.77.4121 PER)
TCD: 7 (Jan. 1973)–10. (PER 81–745)

374 Poetry North East / edited by Alan Brown, Gordon Phillips and Keith Armstrong. Whitley Bay: Tyneside Poets, No. 1 (1974)–? ISSN: 0307–0263

Related Imprint: Tyneside Poets also published Keith Armstrong (ed.) Return to Cherryburn: the life and work of Thomas Bewick (1753–1828), with new poems by the Tyneside Poets, and photographs by Alan C. Brown and Tony Whittle (1978), BL: X.908/42324; the small press Erdesdun Pomes published A portrait of Grainger Market, by the Tyneside Poets (1973), BL: YA.1995.a.19322

Appearing once or twice a year. Intended to publish not just from the Tyneside Poets group, but from poets across the North East.

BL: 2 (1975)–3 (1976). (P.901/3004)
CUL: 2 (1975)–7 (Summer 1980). (L727.B.195)
NLS: 2 (1975)–7 (Summer 1980). (HP4.83.922 PER)
UCL: 2 (1975)–8 (undated).
Poetry Library: 3

375 Poetry One [Poetry Two] / edited by Adrian West, Tom Corbett, Harold Wood, Jill Potter, Lis Holloway, Stuart Ogilvy and others. Upminster: Havering Poetry Group, 1966–1973

Note: Continued by: Assegai.
Related Imprint: Poetry One became an imprint in its own right, and as well as publishing the magazine Assegai published e.g. Tully Potter's The Emigrant, and other poems (1975), BL: X.908/40265

Each year, two issues were produced, one entitled Poetry One and the other Poetry Two. Havering Poetry Group was a workshop that renamed itself to Poetry One and continued to meet every fortnight. The contributors came from the workshop and from further afield and included: Hugo Williams, A. Alvarez, Frances Horovitz, Wes Magee, Gerda Mayer, Vernon Scannell, Dannie Abse, Nick Toczek, Tully Potter, Alan Bertolla, and others.

BL: Poetry One 1966, Poetry One 1967, Poetry One 1969, Poetry One 1970, Poetry Two 1970–71, Poetry One 1971, Poetry Two 1971–72, Poetry One 1972. (P.901/144.)
CUL: 1966–1973. (L727.C.339)
NLS: Poetry One 1966. (P.med.1993.) Poetry One 1970 (P.sm.2309), Poetry Two 1970–71 (P.sm.2308), Poetry One 1971 (P.sm.2309), Poetry Two 1971–72 (P.sm.2308), Poetry One 1972 (P.sm.2309), Poetry One 1973 (P.sm.2309)
TCD: Poetry One 1966–Poetry One 1973. (PER 90–718)

UCL
Poetry Library: *Poetry Two* 1972. *Poetry One* 1973.

Poetry Pick *See* Pick D348

376 Poetry Post / edited by M. E. Badman.
St Albans: Ver Poets, [No. 1, 197?]– ?

Note: Variant title: *Ver Poets Poetry Post*
Anthology: May Badman and Margaret Tims (eds.), *Ver Poets' Voices: thirtieth anniversary anthology* (St. Albans: Brentham, 1996), BL: YK.1996.a.19404
Related Imprint: Ver Poets also published the magazines *Ver Verse*, *Ver Poets*, and *Ver Poets Voices*, the newsletter *Ver Poets Poetry World*, the *Vision On* anthologies, c.1980–1997, and individual collections of poetry
Website: http://www.hertsnews.com/arts/ver.htm

Poems, reviews, and "Ver Poets in action – news of members". Ver Poets take their name from the River Ver, and also Verulamium, the Roman town of St. Alban's. A short history of the group is given in Badman and Tims.

BL: 4 (Oct. 1973)–6 (Nov. 1974). (P.901/3047)
CUL: 5 [1974]–6 [1974]; 9 [197?]; 11 [1978]–?. (L727.B.191)
NLS: 11 (1978)–13, 15–17, 20–26. (HP.1a.476 PER)
TCD: 11 (1978)–26 (1994). (PER 92–449 1978–1994)
UCL: 3 (1972)–6 (1974)
Poetry Library: 17 [1980?]–22, 24

377 Poetry Presented by Transgravity.
London: Transgravity, with the assistance of the London Poetry Secretariat and Camden Council. 1 [Sept. 1967?]–?

A magazine, A4 typescript with stapled coloured card covers, given out at *Transgravity* readings, and which comprised the text of poetry by the featured speakers. Contributors included Lee Harwood, Eric Mottram, Pierre Joris, and others.

BL: 2 (Sept. 26, 1967), 4 (Oct. 17 1967). (ZD.9.b.8)

378 Poetry Quarterly / edited by Jocelynne
Precious. Harrogate: Jocelynne Precious, 1 [1975?]–?

BL: 18/19, 20/22, 25. (P.903/713)

379 Poetry St. Ives / edited by Nicki Tester.
St. Ives: Nicki Tester, No. 1 [1968?]–?

Note: Imprint varies. No. 3 published by Tower of Babel (Zennor)

Contributors included W. S. Graham, John Clark (visual poetry), Peter Redgrove, Penelope Shuttle, and Nicki Jackowska (who edited no. 3 – a change of name from Nicki Tester?).

BL: 2 (1968) (YA.2001.a.23538); 3 (May 1971) (YA.2001.a.23118)
UCL
Poetry Library: 2–3

Poetry Student *See* PS: poetry student D398

Poetry Two *See* Poetry One D375

380 Poetry Wales: Cylchgrawn cenedlaethol o farddoniaeth newydd / edited
by Meic Stephens, and others. Merthyr Tydfil [and later locations]: Triskell Press, then Poetry Wales, then Seren, Vol. 1 (1965)– . ISSN: 0332–2202

Anthology: Cary Archard (ed.), *Poetry Wales 25 years* (Bridgend: Seren Books, 1990), BL: YC.1991.a.3943
Related Imprint: Poetry Wales Press, later Seren
Website: www.serenbooks.com

One of the main Welsh poetry reviews but with interests much wider than Wales. In *Poetry Wales 25 years*, Cary Archard summarised the magazine's purpose: "to encourage poets in Wales by printing their poetry and reviewing their books, to inform English readers about poetry in the Welsh language, and to place the poetry of Wales in a broader international context." Later editors included: Gerald Morgan; Sam Adams; Mike Jenkins; J.P. Ward; Cary Archard; Richard Poole; Bryan Aspden; Paul Henry; Duncan Bush; and Robert Minhinnick. Numerous special issues have appeared, including those on R.S. Thomas, Vernon Watkins, Idris Davies, Henry Vaughan, David Jones, Lynette Roberts, Chris Torrance, and John Tripp. Seren is a major publisher of poetry from Wales.

BL: P.P.8007.jg
CUL: L727.B.216
NLS: HJ4.749 PER
TCD: Vol. 1 (1965)–vol. 16 no.3 (1981). (PER 90–846)
UCL: Vol. 1 no. 2 (1965)–vol. 24 no. 4 (1989)
Poetry Library: Vol. 3 no. 3; vol. 5 no. 3; vol. 7 no. 4; vol. 8 no. 2; vol. 9 no. 1–2; vol. 10 no. 3–vol. 22 no. 3; vol. 25 no. 1–4; vol. 26 no. 2–vol. 27 no. 4; vol. 29 no. 1–

381 Poetry Workshop / edited by Stephen
Morris. Wolverhampton: Wolverhampton

College of Art, Dept. of Art History and Contemporary Studies, No. 1 (1967)–5 (1973)

UCL
Poetry Library: Summer 1973

382 Poetry Workshop / edited by Harold Massingham. Manchester: Department of Extra–Mural Studies, University of Manchester, Spring 1973

BL: P.901/1049
NLS: 5.5748
TCD: P 34426

383 Poets & Poetry / edited by M.A. Gettisburg and A. Markievicz. Colchester: Poetry Press, No. 1 (1973)–?

UCL: 1, 2, 6 (1976)

Poets' Workshop Readings *See* Readings D408

383a Poets Eye: a Hull University poetry magazine / edited by Colin Ward and Steve McCaffery. Hull: Hull University, No. 1 [Dec. 1966]

Philip Larkin contributes a foreword.

BL: 1. (Pressmark pending)

384 Poetsdoos / edited by Jeff Cloves. St. Albans: Jeff Cloves, then Ourside Press, No. 1 (1966)–?

CUL: 11 (1971). (1995.11.398)
UCL: 1 (1966)–7 (1969)
Poetry Library: 9–10

385 Poor. Old. Tired. Horse. [Edited by Ian Hamilton Finlay]. Edinburgh, then Ardgay, Ross-shire, then Ceres, Fife, then Dunsyre, Lanark: The Wild Hawthorn Press, No. 1 (1962)–25 (1967)

Note: Variant titles: POTH; *Teapoth*
Index: Sader. The contents are also listed issue by issue in *Ian Hamilton Finlay & The Wild Hawthorn Press: a catalogue raisonné [1958–1990]* (Edinburgh: Graham Murray, 1990), BL: 2708.e.2072

Profiled in: Edwin Morgan, "Early Finlay", in *Ian Hamilton Finlay & The Wild Hawthorn Press 1958–1991* (Edinburgh: Graham Murray, 1991), BL: YK. 1993.b.14835
Related Imprint: The Wild Hawthorn Press published many books, booklets, cards and other productions by poets, many of whom were also published in *Poor. Old. Tired. Horse.*

An extraordinarily international poetry magazine, including work from Brazil, Russia, Cuba, the United States, France, England, and Scotland: at turns interested in sound, visual, futurist, objectivist, concrete and minimalist poetry, not to mention art and photography; and, as with almost all Finlay productions, executed with style and a light touch. The first issue was edited by "J. McGuffie and P. Pond", and subsequent issues anonymously, but it is assumed that Finlay was the main editor. There appear to have been two different versions of no. 2, both of which are held by the National Library of Scotland. As well as Finlay himself, contributors include George Mackay Brown, Robert Garioch, Douglas Young, Tom McGrath, Helen Cruickshank, Edwin Morgan, Crombie Saunders, J. F. Hendry, D. M. Black, Mayakovsky, Attila József, Robert Lax, Ronald Johnson, and Edgard Braga, as well as the artists Ad Reinhardt, Charles Biederman, Bridget Riley, John Furnival, and Emil Antonucci. Reinhardt and Biederman are both represented by art theory.

BL: Cup.510.cop.6
CUL: Lacking 22–23. (L727.B.47.)
NLS: (P.1a.3513). A second set lacks no. 8 but includes two versions of no. 2. (FB.m.285(72))
TCD: 25. (OLS L–6–483 no.4)
UCL
Poetry Library: 4, 10–15, 17–19, 21–25

386 Portents / [edited by Samuel Charters?]. London: [No. 1, 197?–?]

No. 23 consisted of instructions for a treasure hunt, involving fifteen poems hidden in boxes in various places across London on a particular day in 1973.

BL: 23 (Pressmark pending)

387 Potwick Papers / edited by Peter R. Butcher. London: [Potwick Papers], 196?–?

Mentioned in *Deuce*. No holdings known.

388 Preface / [edited by Harry Nash then Peter Luke then Colin Luke?]. Ilford: Preface, 1964?

Noted in *Origins / Diversions 3*, in 6–7 (July/Aug. 1964) and in

8 [Nov 1964]. Peter Luke appears to have been a new editor to a magazine that had already been running for some time. *Preface* is described as having 'strong links with *Origins / Diversions* now' in issue 8. Described in *Origins / Diversions* as "the oldest duplicated magazine in the country". No known holdings.

389 Priapus / edited by John Cotton.
Denham then Berkhamsted: [Priapus], 1 (Autumn 1962)–23 (Dec. 1972). ISSN: 0032–8146

Index: A simple list of all the contributors to the complete run is given in the last issue

Profiled in: Sullivan 1914–1984; John Cotton, "Priapus: the growth of a magazine" in *Enigma*, ed. Rigby Graham, [No.] 1 [1969], pp.a–[l], BL: Cup.510.cod.4. and reprinted as *Priapus: the growth of a magazine* [John Cotton, 1969], BL: YA.1996.b.6352

Related Imprint: Priapus published several single-author poetry collections before the magazine closed, and then many collections in the 1970s, 80s, and 90s.

"PRIAPUS, a magazine of poetry and art, was begun in 1962 by John Cotton and Ted Walker, who were working at that time in Southall at the Grammar Technical School. [...] In its time PRIAPUS printed the first published poems of its two founders and the first or early poems of D. M. Thomas, Miles Burrows, Gerda Mayer, Norman Jackson, Sally Purcell, Peter Jay, Paul Coltman, Peter Cundall, John Mole, Peter Scupham, Wes Magee, W. G. Shepherd, Christopher Pilling, Roger Iredale and others now well known in their own right. [...] Covers were designed and printed by Oscar Mellor at his Fantasy Press and by Alan Tarling at the Poet and Printer Press, and art work was supplied by Oscar Mellor, Michael Markham, Heinke Jenkins and Jack Yates amongst others. Then with PRIAPUS 9, in the Summer of 1967, Rigby Graham joined forces with us and the art began to rival the poetry as our reason for existence." – John Cotton, from the last issue.

BL: P.901/212
CUL: 4 (Autumn 1965)–23. (L727.B.65)
NLS: 3 (Autumn 1964)–22 (Spring 1972). (NG.725 PER)
TCD: 4 (Autumn 1965)–22 (Spring 1972). (PER 91–343)
UCL: 1–22 (Spring 1972).
Poetry Library: 4–23

390 Prism / edited by Wes Magee.
No known holdings

391 Prison Clothes Press / edited by Jeff
Nuttall and Ulli McCarthy. London: No. 1

(1970)–7? (1974?)

Halfway between a magazine and a pamphlet series, each issue with its own title. After the first two issues, which had a selection of different authors, no. 1 titled *Tramps*, no. 2 *Zusammen*, issues tended to be given over to a single author's work, e.g. no. 3 was McCarthy's *Erire*, with drawings by Nuttall.

BL: 1. (YA.1996.b.5266). 2. (YA.1993.c.21). 7 (*Junk Sculptures*, by Mike Dobbie). (YA.2003.b.538)
CUL: 2. (2002.12.183) Also, two unnumbered Prison Clothes Press books: Kris Hemensley's *The Soft Poems* (1971) (Ub.8.1544), and Allen Fisher's *5 Plages from 10* (1974) (Ub.8.1584)
UCL: 1–6

392 Private Tutor. Nottingham: Tarasque
Press, No.1 (Aug. 1967)–12 (Sept. 1970)

Related Imprint: Tarasque published small single-author collections such as Roy Fisher, *Ten Interiors with Various Figures* (1966), BL: YA.1987.a.9983. It also published the more substantial magazine *Tarasque*.

Many of these one-sheet issues took the form of instructions and exercises, adopting the tone of the first issue which declared, "Assuming from the onset that the reader has little or no grounding in literature we will commence and continue in a very direct manner." This was matched by the design of the masthead which featured a red L sign for Learner. The intention seems to have been to encourage poets to read more poetry and to read more critically. By issue four, the lessons on Hopkins and Logue etc. had been replaced by a sole photograph of some rocks; issue five was a poem by Edwin Morgan about "Making a Poem"; later numbers had texts by Stephen Bann, Ian Hamilton Finlay, Simon Cutts, and Stuart Mills. Edited anonymously, from the Trent Book Shop.

BL: YA.1992.b.7484
UCL

393 Promenade Poetry Magazine /
edited by Michael Thomas. Cambridge: Quill Books, No. 1 (Winter 1964)

Related Imprint: Quill Books issued the anonymously edited anthology *The 12 days of Christmas* [1970], BL: X.900/21197

Related to the longer running Quill.

BL: P.901/531
CUL: L999.B.1.98
NLS: 5.3028

394 Promontory: a magazine of progressive poetry / edited by Gerald England. New Malden: Headland, No.1 (1974)–3 (1976). ISSN: 0306–1310

Related Work: Gerald England, *Editor's Dilemma: 20 years of small press publishing* (Hyde: New Hope International, 1990), BL: YK.1998.a.12604

UCL

395 Proof / edited by Norman Jackson, Christopher Scott, Gerry Wells, Allen Prowle and others. Scunthorpe: Lincolnshire Writers' Workshop, then Lincolnshire and South Humberside Arts, [No. 1, 1965]–3 [1966?]. Then as *Lincolnshire Writers*, no. 4 (Summer 1967)–17 (Winter 1973/Spring 1974). Then as *Proof*, no. 1 (July 1974)–13 [1978]. Then, new numbering: Vol. 1 no. 1 (May 1979)–vol. 10 no. 4 (Winter 1989). ISSN: 0305–7992

Anthology: Simon Williams (ed.) *Proof: an anthology of new writing from Lincolnshire and Humberside collected in 1979* (Lincolnshire and Humberside Arts, 1979), BL: YA.2002.b.3030; Patrick O'Shaughnessy (ed.) *Proof anthology 2: new writing from Lincolnshire and Humberside collected in 1980*, (Lincolnshire and Humberside Arts, 1980), BL: X.955/346

Essentially a magazine for Lincolnshire and Humberside writers; in the last five years it would feature in each issue one invited better-known poet as well, e.g Oliver Reynolds, Selima Hill, F. T. Prince, Peter Levi, Douglas Dunn, Roger Garfitt, Ian McMillan, Kevin Crossley-Holland, and U. A. Fanthorpe.

BL: *Proof* [first series], No. 1–3. *Lincolnshire Writers*; *Proof* [second series], No. 1 (July 1974)–11 (1978); New numbering: Vol. 1 no. 1–vol. 10 no. 4 (Winter 1989) (P.901/441)
CUL: *Proof* [first series], No. 1–3; *Lincolnshire Writers*; *Proof* [second series], No. 1 (July 1974)–11 (1978); New numbering: Vol. 1 no. 1. (L727.C.399)
NLS: *Proof* [first series], No. 1–3 (5.4097 PER); *Lincolnshire Writers* (Y.165 PER); *Proof* [second series], No. 1 (July 1974)–13 (1978); New numbering, Vol. 1 no. 2 (1980). (HP3.82.5.1253 PER)
TCD: *Proof* [first series], No. 1–3. *Lincolnshire Writers*; *Proof* [second series], No. 1 (July 1974)–13 (1978); New numbering: Vol. 1 no. 1–no.2 (1980). (PER 90–803 1966–1980)
UCL: *Proof* [first series], No. 1–3; *Lincolnshire Writers*, 4; *Proof* [second series], No. 1–3 (1975).
Poetry Library: *Proof* [second series], No. 1 (July 1974); 3–4; 8; New numbering, Vol. 8 no. 1–3; vol. 9 no. 1–3; vol. 10 no. 2–4

396 Prospect: a new arts magazine / edited by Philip Turner and others. Swansea: The Literary Magazine Society, University College of Swansea, No. 1 (May 1974)–4 (Oct. 1975). ISSN: 0306–5529

"This magazine intends to pursue the policy of a broad, non-specialist and non-sectarian interest in art and culture. Its object is to be both critical and creative." - from the editorial in the first issue. The final issue includes several poems by John Welch.

BL: P.901/1152
CUL: L727.C.543
NLS: HP2.81.1109 PER
Poetry Library: 3

397 Prospice / edited by J. C. R. Green and others. Solihull, then Breakish, Isle of Skye: Aquila, Vol. 1 (Nov. 1973)–no. 25 (1988). ISSN 0308–2776

Profiled in: Görtschacher 1
Interview: with J. C. R. Green, in Görtschacher 1
Related Imprint: Aquila published collections by Peter Finch, Martin Booth, Alison Bielski, and others, as well as anthologies, e.g. of Mexican poetry and of Portuguese poetry

International and quietly modernist. Various special issues included "Through an Orchard" by Philippe Jaccottet, tr. with an essay by Mark Treharne; "Raymond Queneau", ed. Michael Edwards; "Directions in Italian Poetry", ed. Michael Edwards, Giuliano Dego, and Margaret Straus; and "Fernando Pessoa: the genesis of the heteronymns" by J.C.R. Green. Also involved editorially were Martin Booth and Roger Elkin.

BL: 1–5, 7–10, 12–14, 16–22. (P.901/1116); Another set: 6935.160000
CUL: 1–22. (L727.D.180)
NLS: 1–17, 20–22. (HJ2.340 PER)
TCD: PER 73–355
UCL: 1–25
Poetry Library: 1–12, 15–25

398 PS: poetry student / edited by Paul Merchant, Godfrey Rust, Toby Sachs. Leamington Spa: Warwick University, No. 1 (1975). ISSN: 0306–171X

Intended for school, college and university students. With an eight-page "Centrepiece" of sound and visual poetry, guest-edited by Bob Cobbing and featuring work from Germany, Sweden, Japan, Brazil and Britain. Also articles by Eric Mottram defending Writers Forum poetic practice, Lawrence Upton on William McGonagall, Kit Wright on the Poets in Schools scheme, and an interview with John Heath-Stubbs.

BL: P.903/267. Another copy: 6541.781000
CUL: L999.B.1.413
NLS: HP3.78.1366 PER
TCD: PER 90–388
UCL

Purple Ga See Gaga D180

399 Quarto / edited by George A. Smith. Bradford: Bradford Writers' Circle, [1, 197?]–14 (Sept. 1974)

Short fiction, puzzles and some poems from the members of the Circle.

BL: [5] (June 1972)–14 (Sept. 1974). (P.901/850)
CUL: [5] (June 1972)–14 (Sept. 1974). (L727.C.486)
NLS: [5] (June 1972)–14 (Sept. 1974). (HP3.78.2125 PER)
TCD: [6] (Sept. 1972)–14 (Sept. 1974)

400 Quarto: new poetry & prose from the University of Ulster at Coleraine. Coleraine: The Literary Society, c/o Department of English, Media & Theatre Studies, University of Ulster, [Vol.1, 1974]–10 (1978); vol. 11 (1991)–13 (1992)

Profiled in: Tom Clyde, Irish Literary Magazines: an outline history and descriptive bibliography (Dublin: Irish Academic Press, 2003), BL: 2725.g.3414

One of the highlights was the publishing of Heaney's worksheets for North.

BL: Vol. 11 only. (ZC.9.b.4957)
CUL: Vol. 2 no. 1 (Nov. 1975)–vol. 4 no. 3 (May 1978); vol. 11 (Summer 1991). (L895.C.166)
NLS: Vol. 2 no. 1 (Nov. 1975)–vol. 4 no. 3 (May 1978); vol. 11 (Summer 1991). (DJ.m.1805(4) PER)
TCD: Vol.2 no.1 (Nov.1975)–vol. 13 (1992). (PER 91–646

1975–1992)
Poetry Library: Vol. 4 no. 3

Queen Camel, Sister to Big Venus see Big Venus D69

401 Quickest Way Out / edited by Philip Jenkins. Tredegar: Quickest Way Out, No. 1–2 (1969)

Related Imprint: Quickest Way Out Publications published Peter Finch's An Alteration In The Way I Breathe (1970), BL: YA.2003.a.49971

BL: 2. (ZD.9.a.130)
UCL

402 Quill / edited by Michael Thomas. Cambridge, then Welwyn, then Hitchin. No. 1 [1963]–40 (1970)

Note: Some issues also had a volume designation, e.g. no. 40 was vol. 7 no. 40
Related Imprint: Quill Books issued the anonymously edited anthology The 12 Days of Christmas [1970], BL: X.900/21197

Especially keen on letters – more of a letter magazine than a magazine of poetry, the latter often in a direct or even naïve vein. Related to Promenade Poetry Magazine.

BL: 37 (1969)–39 (Spring 1970) (P.901/532)
CUL: 21 (1965)–40. (L727.B.74)
TCD: 21 (1965)–40 (1970). (178.a)
UCL: 10 (1964)–40

403 Quill / edited by Jim Grant and Mary Reed. Christchurch, Hampshire and Banbury: Quill, 1 [Sept./Oct. 1966]

BL: P.901/155

404 Radix / general editor Malc Payne; co-editors William Kent and Brian Moses. Crowborough: PV Publications, [1, 1971?]–?

Related Imprint: PV Publications published single-author poetry collections by, e.g. Malcolm Payne and David Watkin Price. The PV stands for Poet's Vigilantes, also the publisher of the Nucleus magazine anthology.

BL: 2, [3], 4. (ZA.9.a.3001)
UCL: 3 (1973)–8 (1975)
Poetry Library: 4

405 Rainbow: a quarterly of verse / edited by Joan Muir. London: Phoenix Publications, 1 (Autumn 1965)–20 (Summer 1970). ISSN: 0033–9059

BL: P.901/72
CUL: L727.D.130
NLS: Y.107 PER
TCD: PER 94–744
UCL: 1–18

406 Rainbow Manuscripts / edited by John Coburn. Dublin: Rainbow Manuscripts, No. 1 (1972)–2 (1973)

CUL: L727.B.110
NLS: P.la.5259
TCD: VP 30027

407 Ram / edited by Jeremy Hilton. Bangor: Ram Poetry Society, University College of North Wales, [No. 1] (1972)–6 [1978]

Note: According to the NLS catalogue, no. 3 was not published.

BL: 4–5. (P.901/941.)
CUL: L727.B.207
NLS: 6.2782 PER
UCL: 5

408 Readings. Frensham, Farnham: Poets' Workshop, 1968?–1979?

Typed, foolscap texts of poems read at Poets' Workshop events, many of which were held at the Poetry Society's premises in Earls Court, although unconnected to the Society. Poets included: Christopher Hampton, Elizabeth Cottle, Philip Hobsbaum, Peter Porter, Alan Brownjohn, George Macbeth, Fleur Adcock, Katharine Gallagher and others.

BL: 4th Oct./20th Dec. 1968–11th Apr./25th July 1969; 3rd Oct. /19th Dec. 1969; 8th Jan./2nd Apr. 1971; 24th Sept./17th Dec. 1971. (P.905/11.)
NLS: 4th Oct./20th Dec. 1968–11th Apr./25th July 1969; 2nd Jan./20th Mar. 1970; 8th Jan./2nd Apr. 1971; 24th Sept./17th Dec. 1971. (6.2783 PER)
UCL: Jan. 1970–Autumn 1979

409 Residu / edited by Daniel Richter. Athens, then London: Residu / Daniel Richter, then c/o Trigram Press, No. 1 (Spring 1965)–2 (Spring 1966). ISSN: 0486–5421

English language journal with substantial American content (Allen Ginsberg, William Burroughs) originating in Greece then distributed by Trigram for its second issue, when the British contributions increased, e.g. Alexander Trocchi, Jeff Nuttall, Michael Horovitz, and others, as well as Americans living in England, such as Henry Fainlight and Asa Benveniste. A number of examples of collage and visual poetry. Other contributors included Anselm Hollo, Gregory Corso, Harold Norse, Gerard Malanga, Olivia de Haulleville. No. 2 also included a magazine-within-a-magazine, *The Mongol Review*, No. 1 (1966), edited by John Esam, printed on a different coloured paper and with contributions by Brian Patten, Nick Shoumatoff, and others.

BL: P.901/1219
NLS: 5.4220
UCL
Poetry Library: 2

410 Response. Manchester: Pyamid Press [for St. John's College of Further Education], [No. 1, 1964?]–?

Fiction and other prose and a little poetry from students of the college. Edited anonymously.

BL: 4. (1965) (P. 901/320)

411 Resuscitator / edited by John James, C. I. McNeill and Nick Wayte. Paulton, Somerset, then Cambridge, then Pampisford, Cambridgeshire; and Cheltenham: [John James and Nick Wayte], Vol. 1 no. 1 (Autumn 1963)–no. 7 (1966); Second Series, No. 1 (Jan. 1968)–no. 3/4 (Jan. 1969). ISSN: 0486–5677

Related Imprint: R Books published, e.g., John James, *Trägheit* (Pampisford, [1968]), BL: X.902/2962; J. H. Prynne, *Day Light Songs* (Pampisford, 1968), BL: X.439/4804

A magazine whose first series published several significant American poets – Zukofsky, Olson, Corman, Oppen, Eigner, Creeley, Thomas [i.e. Tom] Clark, and Gary Snyder – as well as Charles Tomlinson, Gael Turnbull, Anselm Hollo, Roy Fisher, Jim Burns, Paul Evans, Barry McSweeny [as printed], Gill Vickers, and Tom Pickard. The short-lived second series published from Cambridge had a greater 'Cambridge school' focus, with poets including Peter Riley, Douglas Oliver, Wendy Mulford, Gill Vickers, J. H. Prynne, John James, Tim Longville, Andrew Crozier, David Chaloner, John Riley, Chris Torrance, Tom Raworth, and others. An archive of poems and correspondence relating to the second series is held at Lilly Library, Indiana University. The cover design of most issues in both series involved a striking use of black and white: this was a stylish little magazine, inside and out. C. I. McNeill was only editorially involved in the first issue of the first series; James and Wayte were co-editors for the whole run.

BL: P.P.8005.wx
CUL: Vol. 1 no. 1–no. 7; Second series, no. 2–3/4. (L727.C.333.)
NLS: Vol. 1 no. 1–no. 7. (P.148 PER); Second series, no. 2–3/4. (1970.187 PER)
UCL: Vol. 1 no. 1–no. 7; Second series, no. 2–3/4
Poetry Library: 5–6

412 The Review / edited by Ian Hamilton. London: Nexus Publications, 1 (Apr./May 1962)–29/30 (Summer 1972). ISSN: 0034–6330

Note: The editorial address was in Oxford, though the publisher was in London. Continued by *The New Review*
Profiled in: Sullivan 1914–1984
Interview: Dan Jacobson interviews Ian Hamilton in *London Review of Books*, 24th January 2002
Reprint: Nendeln, Liechtenstein: Kraus Reprint, [undated]
Related Work: Ian Hamilton (ed.), *The Modern Poet: Essays from The Review* (London: Macdonald, 1968), BL: P.901/407

Poems, short fiction, articles, reviews and interviews. Like its successor, *The New Review*, most of the British writers were drawn from the established London publishing houses. Nevertheless, many European authors appeared in translation in it, and indeed the first poems published were four prose poems by Zbigniew Herbert; it also had a number of special issues, e.g., on Eliot (no. 4, Nov. 1962), on William Empson (no. 6/7, June 1963), on the Black Mountain poets (no. 10, Summer 1964), and the last issue published the contributions of many poets on the theme, "The State of Poetry – A Symposium". Some issues were part of a Pamphlet Series, e.g. no. 13 comprises Antonio Machado, *The Garden in the Evening*, tr. Colin Falck. Also involved editorially: Colin Falck, Michael Fried, John Fuller, Francis Hope, Clive James, Gabriel Pearson, and Stephen Wall.

BL: PP.7618.ky
CUL: L727.D.118
NLS: 1–18, 22. (NH.581 PER)
TCD: 1–22. (PER 81–697 1962–1968)
Poetry Library: 1–9, 11–17, 19–20, 22–29/30

413 Richmond Poets / edited by Brian Louis Pearce and Colin Nixon; then Brian Louis Pearce; then Joe Cousins and William Lindsay; then Brian Louis Pearce. Twickenham: Richmond Poetry Group, 1975–?

In a sense, a continuation of *Expression One*: annual anthologies from the members of the associated poetry workshop, "which meets for monthly readings, talks and discussions at a private house not far from Twickenham station." Better-known poets include the editors, Eric Ratcliffe, Penelope Shuttle, Martin Booth, Duncan McGibbon, and others. An account of the Richmond Poetry Group is given in the 1983 issue. Eric Mann and Doreen Titler were also involved editorially.

BL: 1975, 1976, 1977, 1983, 1984. (P.901/1287)
CUL: 1975, 1976. (L727.d.189)
NLS: 1975, 1976, 1984. (P.med.1707)
TCD: 1975–1984. (PR 3464 1975–1984)
UCL: 1975, 1976, 1977
Poetry Library: 1975–1978

414 Riding West / edited by Steve Sneyd. Huddersfield: Riding West, Vol. 1 no. 1 [1966]–no. 8 (1968)

The first three issues were typewritten foolscap, with collages and cartoons, opinion and poetry. The poetry is folk and Beat influenced, and there is a strong anti-Vietnam War stance.

BL: Vol. 1 no. 1–[no. 4, Christmas 1966]. (P.975/1)
UCL

415 Rocket / edited by Alan Bold. Edinburgh, then London: Alan Bold, then Peter Moran, [No. 1, 1964]–11 (1965)

Related Work: *Rocket Booster* [Edinburgh: Alan Bold, 1965?], BL: P.901/1326.

Contemporary art criticism

BL: P.901/1322
CUL: No. 8 (1965)–9 (1965). (L999.C.3.230)
NLS: No. 7 (Aug. 1964)–11. (P.la.2446 PER)
UCL

416 Ronald Reagan: the magazine of poetry / edited by John Sladek. London, [1] (1968)–2 (1970)

Contributors include J. G. Ballard ("Why I Want to Fuck

Ronald Reagan"), Thomas M. Disch, John Giorno, Lee Harwood, Ron Padgett, Anne Waldman, and others.

BL: YK.1994.b.839
UCL

417 Root / edited by Noreen Lynch. Cardiff: English Dept, University College Cardiff, Vol. 1 (1974)
Poetry Library

Rump *See* Krax D244

418 Rumpus / edited by Cris [i.e. Christopher] Morgan. Swansea: [Rumpus], [No. 1, 196?]– 5 (1971). ISSN: 0035–9858

UCL: 2 (1969)–3 (1969)
Poetry Library: 5

419 The Running Man / edited by Christopher Kypreos. London: Running Man Publications, Vol. 1 no. 1 (May/June 1968)–no. 3/4/5 (1969). ISSN 0557–4889

BL: Vol. 1 no. 1. (Cup.805.ff.9)
CUL: L900.C.418
NLS: 5.4318 PER
TCD: Vol. 1 no. 3/4/5. (PER 91–396)

420 Sad Traffic Barnsley: Sad Traffic, Vol. 1 no.1 (Dec. 1969)–[197–]

BL: Vol. 1 no. 1–no. 5 (1971). (ZA.9.a.5532)
UCL: Vol. 1 no. 1–no. 5 (1971)

421 Samphire / edited by Michael Butler and Kemble Williams. Ipswich: Samphire, [Vol. 1] No. 1 (Jan. 1968)–vol. 3 no. 8 (1981)

Note: A running number was also kept, so that the last issue was no. 40 as well as vol. 3 no. 8
Index: An index to the first two volumes was issued in 1977 with vol. 2 no. 16. An index to the third volume was contained within vol. 3 no. 8.

A magazine which began with an East Anglian focus, but soon moved on to a British and wider remit. Contributors included: Taner Baybars, Yves Bonnefoy, Martin Booth, Alison Brackenbury, Jim Burns, Philip Crick, Gavin Ewart, Roy Fisher, Peter Forbes, Ida Affleck Graves, Geoff

Holloway, Frances Horovitz, Michael Horovitz, Michael Hulse, Nicki Jackowska, Judith Kazantzis, Alexis Lykiard, Wes Magee, E. A. Markham, Robin Maunsell, Gerda Mayer, Matthew Mead, John Mole, Edwin Morgan, Keith Please, Peter Redgrove, Jeremy Reed, Penelope Shuttle, Gael Turnbull, W. Price Turner, and others.

BL: [Vol. 1] no. 1; [vol. 1] no. 5–vol. 3 no. 8. (P.901/1369)
CUL: L727.D.147
NLS: Library lacks: [Vol. 1] no. 4 ([1968]); [vol. 1] no. 8 ([1970]); and all issues between [vol. 1] no. 11 (1971) and vol. 2 no. 9 (1975). (HJ3.105 PER)
UCL
Poetry Library

422 Sandwiches / edited by Mark Williams. Canterbury: Excello & Bollard, No. 1 (Mar. 1973)–21 [1978]

Related Imprint: Excello and Bollard published *Excello & Bollard Annual* and a range of books, including single-author collections, e.g. by George Cairncross, Tina Morris, Steve Sneyd, and Paul Lamprill.
Related Work: Paul Lamprill, *The British Exello & Bollard Company Chronicle, 1973–4–5* (King's Lynn: Excello & Bollard, 1976), BL: YC.1989.b.5557

Faintly printed A4 typescript for most issues, with occasionally a photolitho cover. Poems, correspondence, notices of other little magazines.

BL: 2 [1974]–21. (P.903/215)
CUL: No. 7 (1975)–21 [1978]. (L727.B.226)
NLS: 7 (1975)–21 [1978]. (HP4.82.117 PER)
UCL: 1–19 (July 1976)

423 Satis / edited by Matthew Mead. Newcastle upon Tyne: Malcolm Rutherford, No. 1 (Autumn 1960)–5 (Spring/Summer 1962). ISSN: 0558–7107

Related Imprint: Satis also published a number of single-author collections, e.g. Matthew Mead's *Kleinigkeiten* (1966), BL: YA.1993.a.1872, and Gael Turnbull's *Finger Cymbals* (1971), BL: YA.1994.a.16118

A rather restrained magazine, as perhaps the title suggests (just "enough", and no more): understated photolitho printed A5 format, with pagination usually only 24pp. Poems by: John Heath-Stubbs, Anne Cluysenaar, Gael Turnbull, Michael Shayer, Anselm Hollo, Larry Eigner, Bernice Ames, J. H. Prynne, and others. Each issue had one essay, e.g. Matthew Mead on Alun Lewis; Gael Turnbull on William Carlos Williams.

424 Savacou: a journal of the Caribbean Artists Movement. / edited by Edward Kamau Brathwaite, Kenneth Ramchand, Andrew Salkey, and others. Kingston, Jamaica and London: The Caribbean Artists Movement; Savacou Publications, Vol. 1 no. 1 (June 1970)–14/15 (1979)

Note: After Vol. 1 no. 1, each successive issue was simply numbered 2, 3, 4... etc.
Related Imprint: Savacou also publishes poetry collections, bibliographies and critical texts, some of which continue the numbering of the magazine

"Our purpose is to bring together the work of creative writers, academics and theoretical thinkers and so provide a forum for artistic expression and thought in the Caribbean today" – from the first issue. Contributors include C. L. R. James, Mervyn Morris, Aimé Césaire, Derek Walcott, James Berry, John Figueroa, Linton Kwesi Johnson, E. A. Markham, Judy Miles, Stuart Hall, V. S. Naipaul, and others. The gathering of dub poetry, emphasising Creole and oral forms, published in no. 3/4 has been seen as a breakthrough in the recognition of Caribbean poetry's qualities. Special issues included: 6, the collection *Reel from "The Life Movie"* by Anthony McNeil; 13, *Caribbean Women*; and 14/15, *New Poets from Jamaica*.

BL: P.901/1308
CUL: 5; 7/8–13. (RCS.Per.2243)
UCL: 2; 7/8
Poetry Library: 7/8–9/10

425 Schmuck. Cullompton, Devon: Beau Geste Press, etc., [No. 1, 1972?]–8 (1976) ISSN: 0301–5769

Note: Title varies with each issue, e.g. *French Schmuck, General Schmuck, Teutonic Schmuck, Aktual Schmuck Czechoslovakia, Schmuck Iceland, Hungarian Schmuck, Japanese Schmuck*. Some issues appear to have formed part of a wider monographic series "Schmuck anthological".

A note on the website of the Department of Special Collections and University Archives, Stanford University Libraries, Stanford, California, where a Beau Geste Press archive is held, summarises the project: "The Beau Geste Press existed in England between 1971–1974. It was founded by Felipe Ehrenberg, David Mayor, Chris Welch, and Martha Hellion. It printed the works of visual poets, conceptualists, and neo-dadaists, many of whom were closely tied to the Fluxus movement. The press printed artist books using inexpensive materials, such as mimeograph machines, cheap paper, and staples." *Schmuck* itself seems to have been a project to collect avant-garde poems and other short texts, especially visual and paper-engineered work from the particular country named in the title. The primary Beau Geste archive is held in the archives of Tate Britain, London.

BL: [1]; 6–8. (ZD.9 a.62)
CUL: 5–8. (L400.b.303)
NLS: [4]–8. (HP3.79.726 PER)
UCL: 2–8

426 Scotia / edited by David Morrison. Lyth, Caithness: David Morrison, No. 1 (Jan. 1970)–28 (Apr. 1972)

Note: Continued by *Scotia Review*
Index: *Scottish Poetry Index* Vol. 6 (Edinburgh: Scottish Poetry Library, 1997), BL: ZC.9.b.6227
Profiled in: David Morrison, "*Scotia*, and *Scotia Review*" in *Scottish Poetry Index* Vol. 6, p.7

David Morrison traces his interest in Scottish poetry to being introduced to the poets frequenting Milne's Bar in Ediburgh and to Alan Bold's magazine *Rocket*. *Scotia* published many of the Scottish poets of the day, with a particular interest in poets writing in Scots, but not exclusively so.

BL: P.701/474
NLS: RB.s.1233 PER
UCL

427 Scotia Review / edited by David Morrison. Wick: Scotia Review, No. 1 (Aug. 1972)–. ISSN: 0306–316X

Note: Continues: *Scotia*. Suspended between 1979 and 1998. No. 20 entitled: *Shetland Review*
Index: No. 1–20 are indexed in *Scottish Poetry Index* Vol. 6 (Edinburgh: Scottish Poetry Library, 1997), BL: ZC.9.b.6227
Profiled in: David Morrison, "*Scotia*, and *Scotia Review*" in *Scottish Poetry Index* Vol. 6, p.7
Related Imprint: Pulteney Press

Contributors included poets from across Scotland. Also notable for features on Northern Scottish writing, Orkney and the Shetlands.

BL: P.701/715

CUL: 1–15; 18–20. (L727.C.510)
NLS: 1–20; 23– . (HJ8.2342)
UCL: 1–20

428 Scottish International / edited by Robert Garioch and Edwin Morgan (managing editor: Robert Tait; then Tom Buchan). Edinburgh: No. 1 (Jan. 1968)–vol. 7 no. 2 (Mar. 1974)

Note: Continues: *Feedback*, a current affairs magazine out of scope for this guide. Variant title: *Scottish International Review*.
Index: *Scottish Poetry Index Vol. 6* (Edinburgh: Scottish Poetry Library, 1997), BL: ZC.9.b.6227
Profiled in: Bob Tait, "Scottish International: a brief account", *Scottish Poetry Index Vol. 6*. pp.63–65

"Scotland 1968. Mainly urban population, sharing with the rest of Britain a Government, mass media, and much of the available Press and publishing – among other things. There is discontent with the consequences of this situation for Scotland. As witness Hamilton and other SNP successes. One must neither underrate nor exaggerate what this unease means. The shared interests and culture form part of the terms within which people are now living in Glasgow, Edinburgh, Aberdeen, Dundee and other places. It is with these people, defined in these terms, that our story begins." – from the first editorial. Open to all the issues and arts in Scotland and with a very strong poetry presence. Contributors included: Liz Lochhead, Alan Jackson, Tom Leonard, George Mackay Brown, Robin Fulton, D. M. Black, Andrew Greig, Anne Stevenson, Tom McGrath, Norman MacCaig, Iain Crichton Smith, Peter Morgan, Ian Hamilton Finlay, George MacBeth, Robert Garioch, Edwin Morgan, and others. An archive of *Scottish International* is held at the Library of the University of St. Andrews.

BL: P.803/167
CUL: L900.B.323
NLS: NB.55.PER
TCD: Per 90–117 1971–1974
UCL

Scottish International Review *See* Scottish International D428

429 Scottish Poetry / edited by George Bruce, Maurice Lindsay and Edwin Morgan [and others], Edinburgh, then Glasgow, then Cheadle: Edinburgh University Press, then

Glasgow University Press, then Carcanet, 1[1966]–9 [1976]. ISSN: 0080–8156

Index: Scottish Poetry Library Catalogue at www.spl.org.uk/ indexes individual contributors and poems, and gives an author listing for each volume

A self-conscious attempt to revive the ideals of the 1940s *Poetry Scotland*, these annual volumes published an eclectic mix of Scottish poetry. Most of the significant Scottish poets of the time appeared within its pages. The little hardbacks in the Edinburgh University Press phase are particularly attractive and pleasing to hold.

BL: P.901/97
CUL: P727.D.17
NLS: NG.1166.e PER
TCD: 1–2 (HB–58–214 Vol.1); 3 (HB–58–215 Vol.3); 4 (HB–58–216 Vol.4); 5 (SHL–36–771); 6 (SHL–36–772); 7 (HB–58–217); 8 (SHL–36–773); 9 (SHL–36–774)
UCL

430 The Scottish Review: arts and environment / editorial board: Lindsey MacLeod (Managing Editor), George Bruce, A. C. Davis, Gordon Huntly, Maurice Lindsay, Lorn M. Macintyre, Tom Markus, Alexander Scott; also, James Aitchison, Roger Billcliffe, Douglas Gifford, Hugh Leishman, Marista Leishman, Craig Lindsay, Charles McKean, Findlay McQuarrie, Christopher Rush, and Paul Scott; Managing Editors later included Julie Horwood and Kirsteen Stokes. Glasgow: Scottish Civic Trust; and Edinburgh: Saltire Society, in assocation with the Scottish Arts Council, No. 1 (Winter 1975)–37/38 (Feb./May 1985). ISSN: 0140–0894

Index: *Scottish Poetry Index Vol. 8* (Edinburgh: Scottish Poetry Library, 1999), BL: ZC.9.b.6227
Profiled in: Maurice Lindsay's introduction in *Scottish Poetry Index Vol. 8* (see above)

Bruce, Lindsay, and Scott were the permanent co-editors. A general review which published many poems.

BL: 1–6 (Spring 1977). (P.801/3103)
CUL: 4 (1976)–37/38. (L727.C.712)
NLS: HJ2.192 PER
TCD: 4 (1976)–37/38. (PER 77–149)

431 **Scree Poetry.** King's Lynn: Scree Publications, No. 1 (1974)–10 (May 1978). ISSN 0141–4313

BL: P.903/553
CUL: 5 (1976)–10 (1978). (L727.B.232)
NLS: HP4.82.513 PER
UCL
Poetry Library: 10

432 **Scribblers** / edited by Margaret Beat. Ampthill, near Milton Keynes: Scribblers Magazine Club, [1, 1974]–50 (May 1979). ISSN: 0308–2806

BL: 12–50. (P.901/1426)
CUL: 18–50. (L727.c.637)
NLS: 18–50. (DJ.s.336 PER)
Poetry Library: 44 (1978), 50 (1979)

433 **Scrip: a quarterly magazine of recent poetry** / edited by David Holliday. Southhall, then Chesterfield, No. 1 [1961]–44 (1973). ISSN: 0036–9659

Note: Absorbed by Orbis

BL: P.P.7617.ex.
CUL: L727.c.277
NLS: P.196 PER
TCD: PER 80–632 1962–1972
UCL: 7–43
Poetry Library: 12, 18, 20, 29, 31–33, 36, 43–44

434 **Second Aeon** / edited by Peter Finch. Cardiff: Peter Finch, No.1 [1966]–19/21 (1974). ISSN: 0037–0525

Anthology: Peter Finch (ed.), Second Aeon Travelling Circus Sampler (Cardiff: Second Aeon Publications, [1970]), BL: X.908/84379
Bibliography: An issue by issue contents listing (not all contributors are named) is given at website (see below)
Profiled in: Website (see below)
Interview: Peter Finch interviewed by Andy Brown, in Brown (ed.) Binary myths 2: correspondences with poet-editors (Exeter: Stride, 1999), BL: YA.2001.a.16411
Website: http://dspace.dial.pipex.com/peter.finch/2ndaeon.htm
Related Imprint: Second Aeon Publications published around fifty books, including single author collections and anthologies such as Peter Finch (ed.) Typewriter Poems

(1972), BL: RF.2000.a.26

"Peter Finch's journal of contemporary poetry, graphics, fiction and reviews ran from late 1966 to early 1975. Issue 1 was 6 pages of foolscap (a kind of early A4) with a circulation of a hundred copies. Issue 21 ran to 268 in B-format with a circulation of 2,500. It was the British poetry magazine of the period featuring most UK writers and leavened with Americans and with Europeans in translation. The magazine had a strong leaning towards the innovative and regularly included concrete and experimental works in its pages. A great strength was The Small Press Scene, a vast and comprehensive round-up of activity among poetry and alternative publishers world-wide." – from Peter Finch's website, noted above. Issue 10 (Dec. 1969) included a plastic bag containing concrete poem cards from John Furnival, Edwin Morgan, Will Parfitt, Peter Finch, and Bob Cobbing. Huw Joshua was also involved editorially.

BL: P.901/459
CUL: 6–19/21. (L727.c.456)
NLS: 6–19/21. (Y.128 PER)
TCD: 12. (OLS L–6–145 no.8)
UCL
Poetry Library 7–9, 12–19/21

435 **Sefton's Empire Monolith** / edited by Pete Bryan. Belfast: [Pete Bryan], No. 1 [1971?]

Advertised in Id no. 3. No holdings known.

436 **Self Expression.** Hemel Hempstead: EPT Associates, Autumn 1971–Winter 1971

Edited anonymously. Traditional poetry and very short fiction, mainly from Hertfordshire.

BL: P.903/120
UCL

437 **Sesheta** / edited by Richard Downing and Andi Wachtel. Sutton: Sesheta Press, No. 1 (Winter 1971)–6 (1974)

Continues: Broadsheet

Contributors include Peter Philpott, Andrew Crozier, Chris Torrance, David Chaloner, Gerard Malanga, Peter Riley, Lee Harwood, Ron Padgett, John Riley, Myra Klah, Kris Hemensley, Clark Coolidge, Larry Fagin, Barbara Guest, Donald Hall, Barry MacSweeney, David H. W. Grubb, Victor Bockris, John James, Harry Guest, James Schuyler, Tom Raworth, Douglas Oliver, Ron Loewinsohn, Elaine Randell,

Robert Bly, Peter Ackroyd, Michael Palmer, Peter Schjeldahl, Jeremy Hilton, Tom Disch, Opal L. Nations, Clayton Eshleman, Paul Buck, Gael Turnbull, Gerry Loose, Frances Horovitz, César Vallejo (trans. Eshleman), Michael Haslam, Paul Selby, and others. Two issues of the magazine were given over to single-author collections: *The Whole Band* by Peter Riley (no. 3), and *Fox Houses* by Jeremy Hilton (no. 6).

BL: P.901/807
CUL: L727.B.286
NLS: 1973.33 PER
UCL
Poetry Library: 2, 5

Shetland Review *See* Scotia Review D427

438 The Shore: the magazine of the Cleveleys Poetry Circle / Thornton-Cleveleys: Cleveleys Poetry Circle, No. 1 (197?)–?. Then Blackpool: [New series], No. 1 [198?]–5 [1984?]

The New series was edited by Olive Dewhurst.

Brotherton Library, Leeds University: 7 (Christmas 1972); 13 (Christmas 1975). (Special Collections English Q–1 SHO)
Poetry Library: [New series], 5

439 Sidewalk: Scotland's quarterly review / edited by Alex Neish. Edinburgh: [Sidewalk]; Printed by Macdonald, Vol. 1 no. 1–no. 2 [1960]

Note: Continues: *Jabberwock*

The magazine whose one-word mission statement was "Anti-parochialism" included many contributions from America and Europe, including work by William Burroughs, Robert Creeley, Gary Snyder, Michael McClure, Allen Ginsberg, and Charles Olson, and translations of Marguerite Duras (on Georges Bataille), Alain Robbe-Grillet, Michel Butor, Tristan Corbière, and Salvatore Quasimodo. Scottish poets included J. F. Hendry, Edwin Morgan, Ian Hamilton Finlay, W. Price Turner, James Aitchison, and others; Christopher Logue also contributes a poem; and Edwin Morgan writes on Jean Genet. The third issue was advertised but apparently not published.

BL: P.P.8005.rn
CUL: L727.c.238
NLS: 1961.10
TCD: PER 81–130
UCL

440 Sigma Portfolio / edited by Alexander Trocchi. London: Project Sigma, [No. 1 (1964)–39 (1967)]

Related Work: Alexander Trocchi (ed. Andrew Murray Scott), *Invisible Insurrection of a Million Minds: A Trocchi Reader* (Edinburgh: Polygon, 1991), BL: H.91/2049; Allan Campbell and Tim Niel, *A life in pieces: reflections on Alexander Trocchi* (Edinburgh: Rebel Inc, 1997), BL: YC.2002.a.2324; Andrew Murray Scott, *Alexander Trocchi: The Making of the Monster* (Edinburgh: Polygon, 1991), BL: YC.1991.a.2522

The first issue folds out to become a poster or broadsheet. Apart from Trocchi himself, contributors include William Burroughs, Robert Creeley, R. D. Laing, and others. Some numbers were issued as a special supplement to Trocchi and Jeff Nuttall's *The Moving Times*.

BL: [1]. (HS.74/1373). 2–7, 9–14, 16–19, 21–23, 25, and 26. Nos. 14, 2, 5, and 12 have been stapled together, in that order. (RF.1999.c.15)
NLS: 28 pts. (issue numbers not identified on catalogue record). (6.1825)
UCL

441 Silence / [Students of Sculpture Dept., St Martin' School of Art, No. 1, 1964?–16, 1965]

Included visual, concrete and sound poetry.

BL: 14. (ZD.9.a.189)
UCL: 3–16.

442 Silyn: a collection of writings by WEA students / edited by Rufus Adams. [Bangor, Gwynedd]: Workers' Educational Association [North Wales Branch], No.1 (1974)–? ISSN 01413481

An annual with articles, short stories and a little poetry.

BL: 1–3. (P.901/3095)
CUL: 3–?. (L727.c.685)
NLS: 3–10. (DJ.s.587 PER)
TCD: 3–10. (PER 78–703)

443 Singe / [edited by Asa Benveniste?] Newcastle-upon-Tyne and London: [Laundering Room Press?], 1 [197?]–?

Contributors include Tom Raworth, Edwin Morgan, Louis Zukofsky and others.

UCL: 5
King's College London, Mottram Archive: 5 (1976/77). (7/584/1 1976–1977)

444 Siren / [Sussex University]. [1968]

King's College London, Mottram Archive: [1968]. (7/585/1 [1968])

445 Sixpack / edited by Pierre Joris. London (then London and Lake Toxaway, North Carolina): Lame Duck Press, 1 (May 1972)–9 (Fall 1975)

Heavily US-influenced magazine. Contributors include William Burroughs, Paul Blackburn, Ted Berrigan, Allen Ginsberg, Jerome Rothenberg, Ed Dorn, Charles Olson, Jonathan Williams, and others. In the first issue Joris translates six poems by Paul Celan. No. 5 was guest edited by Bill Sherman. No. 7/8 is a special Paul Blackburn issue. W. R. Prescott was also involved editorially.

BL: 1 (P.901/51). 2–9. (ZA.9.a.6123)
UCL
Poetry Library: 5–9

446 The Sixties / edited by Maureen Duffy and John Ackerman. London, [1] Spring 1960–[3] Spring 1961

Note: Variant title: 60s

Not to be confused with the American magazine of the same title, edited by William Duffy and Robert Bly. Poetry only, except for an editorial by Maureen Duffy in each issue engaging with issues in contemporary verse. Contributions include poems by Bryan [i.e. B. S.] Johnson, Arnold Wesker, Edwin Brock, David Tipton and others.

BL: P.P.5126.nc
CUL: [1]. (L999.c.3.191)
NLS: [1]. (1965.52 PER)
Poetry Library: [1]

447 Skylight / edited by Peter Baker. Manchester: Peter Baker, [1] (Spring 1971)–. 2 (Winter-Spring 1972)

A fairly broad church: contributors included Paul Evans, David Chaloner, John Cooper-Clark, Andrew Crozier, Peter Hoida, Jim Burns, Barry MacSweeney, Elaine Feinstein, Paul Green, Tina Morris, Chris Torrance, John James, Peter Riley, Nick Totton, Douglas Oliver, Peter Finch, John Riley, Kris Hemensley, Michael Haslam, and others.

BL: P.801/820
UCL

448 Slugs / edited by Rob Earl. Maidstone: Outcrowd, [1975]–?

Related Imprint: Outcrowd published several later magazines, and pamphlet collections such as Steve Sneyd, Prug plac gamma [1983], BL: X.958/17257

An annual. Poems and some graphics. A5 typescript format.

BL: [1975], [1976], [1977]. (P.901/3160)
NLS: [1975] (HP2.78.2562) ; [1977] (HP2.78.1925); [1979] (HP2.79.1007)
TCD: 1977 (PL– 20–852); 1979 (PL– 31–916)

449 Smoke / edited by David Ward and others. Liverpool: Windows Project, [No. 1, 1974]– . ISSN: 0262–852X

Related Imprint: The Windows Project publishes a number of collections, including those in the Merseyside Poetry Minibooks Series and published Write Away
Website: www.windowsproject.demon.co.uk/index.htm

Each issue selected by a different editor, including Nigel Crisp, Tim Gunton, Tom McLennan, Dave Calder, Paul Donnelly, Dave Symonds, Joan Poulson, and Jean Sprackland.

BL: 8– . (P.901/3168)
CUL: 10– . (L727.d.303)
NLS: 10– . (P.la.7954)
TCD: 1979– . (PER 79–378)
UCL
Brotherton Library, Leeds University: 2–3 (1975–6); 5 (1976); 7–12 (1978–1980); 20 (1984); 22–26 (11/84–1/87); 30–32 (4/89–8/90); 35–36 (7/92–3/93). (Special Collections English Q–1 SMO)
Poetry Library: [1]; 9–11; 13– .

450 Snow. London: X Press, 1968

Apparently a one-off magazine or anthology. Edited anonymously. Contributors were: Andrew Crozier, David Coxhead, Brian Patten, Jeff Nuttall, Rick Sanders, Bob Cobbing, Stephen Vincent, Penelope Shuttle, John Brown, Harold Norse, Christine Bowler, Pete Brown, and Richard Sylvester.

BL: YA.1990.b.8682
CUL: L999.C.3.1294
NLS: 5.4318
UCL
Poetry Library

451 Soho: bi-lingual review / revue bilingue / edited by Lee Harwood and Claude Royet-Journoud. London: Night Scene Publications, No. 1 (1964)

Note: Continues: Night Scene. Continued by: Tzarad

Contributors were: Tristan Tzara (trans. Lee Harwood), Anselm Hollo, Christine Agius, Mary Lucraft, Spike Hawkins, Pete Brown, Johnny Byrne, Jean-Louis Avril, Neil Oram, Lee Harwood, Harry Guest, Barry Parr, Christine Billson, Roger Jones, Dave Cunliffe, Denise van Dyck, Ian Vine, Peter Jay, Michael Wilkin, Kirby Congdon, Michel Couturier, Peter Vigar, Jean l'Anselme, Mohammed Khai r-Eddine, Henri Maisongrande, Tootsie Barbault-Guéra, Pierre Dargelos, Michel Dansel, Jean Fanchette, Guy Chambelland, Bernard Jakobiak, Claude Royet-Journoud, and Alain Bosquet. Typescript mimeo inside; an arresting white-on-black lino-cut of cow skeleton on the cover, by Nick Tidnam.

BL: P.903/193
UCL

452 Sol / edited by Tony Burrell and "Polly" and "Matthew"; then Malcolm E. Wright; then Adrian Green; then Malcolm E. Wright. Clacton-on-Sea [and then other locations in Essex]: [Sol], No. 1 [1971]–? ISSN: 0951–0362

Note: Occasional subtitle: A magazine of fancy and imagination
Index: An index and a contents listing is provided on the website
Website: www.solpubs.freeserve.co.uk/solmagazine.htm
Related Imprint: Sol Publications (single author collections and anthologies)

Fiction, poems, letters and articles. Favourite contributors appear to have been: Michael Daugherty, Frederic Vanson, Margot K. Juby, Derek Adams, and Steve Sneyd. A long gap between 19 (Summer 1980) and 20 (Spring 1986), and another long gap between 28 (Summer 1995) and 29 (July 1997). Monica Aldous was also involved editorially.

BL: 1, 2, 3, 6–22, 29. (P.901/3105)
CUL: 7, 9–18, 20, 21. (L727.c.718)
NLS: 12 (Mar. 1977)–15 (Autumn 1978). (3823 PER)
UCL: 1
Poetry Library: 9, 13–17, 19, 22–25

453 Solstice / edited by Phil Short, and others. Cambridge: Solstice, No. 1 [Mar. 1966]–9 [1969]. ISSN: 0038–1225

"Our critical standards are derived from criteria common to the evaluation of any art form: That it should present original thought in a new form; or utilize an accepted form in such a way as to give it new meaning." – from the first issue. Contributors include: Howard Brenton (a short story), Jim Burns, Celia Williams (translating Vasko Popa), Tom Raworth, Louise Glück, Anselm Hollo, Iain Sinclair, John James, Peter Jay, Roger Garfitt, Harry Guest, Spike Hawkins, Clive James, Brian Patten, David Chaloner, Edward Dorn, Ken Smith, D. M. Thomas, John Furnival, Bob Cobbing, John Welch, Veronica Forrest[-Thomson], Christopher Pilling, Nick Totton, and others. The last issue is edited by John Cook and Graham Swift, the latter, well-known later as a novelist, contributing an early short story.

BL: P.901/69
CUL: L727.c.336
NLS: NB. 120 PER
TCD: PER 81–968
UCL

454 Somethings / edited by Rosemarie Bayley and John Pardoe, then Dave Austin and Kay Anderson, then G. Charlton. [Shropshire, then Birmingham: Somethings], No. 1 (1967)–15/16 (1971)

BL: One unnumbered issue. (P.901/198.)
UCL

455 Soundings: an annual anthology of new Irish poetry / edited by Seamus Heaney, then James Simmons. Belfast: Blackstaff, [No. 1] (1972)–3 (1976)

Profiled in: Tom Clyde, Irish Literary Magazines: an outline history and descriptive bibliography (Dublin: Irish Academic Press, 2003), BL: 2725.g.3414
Related Imprint: Blackstaff

Heaney edited the first two volumes, after which the subtitle changed the word "poetry" to "writing", to accommodate short fiction. Contributors included: Eavan Boland, Ciaran Carson, John Hewitt, Brendan Kennelly, Thomas Kinsella, Michael Longley, Derek Mahon, John Montague, Paul Muldoon, Eiléan Ni Chuilleanáin, Dermot Healy, Michael Hartnett, Harry Clifton, Frank Ormsby, Michael Foley, and others.

BL: P.901/948
CUL: L727.c.483
NLS: P.med.3259
TCD: 1. (OLS L–4–203 no.120). 2. (OLS L–6–548 no.10). 3. (OLS L–4–532 no.9)
UCL: 2–3.

456 Spanner / edited by Allen Fisher. London, then Hereford: Spanner, 1 (Nov. 1974)–

Interview: Bill Griffiths interviews Allen Fisher at the Lollipop website, www.indigogroup.co.uk/llpp/interview1.html
Website: www.shadoof.net/spanner/ and www.indigogroup.co.uk/llpp/spanner.html
Related Imprint: Aloes Books
Reprint: Nos. 1–20 were reprinted bound together in two volumes under the title *Spanual* and *Spanual 2*

Each issue tends to be devoted to a single author or topic. Contributors include John Cage, Eric Mottram, David Miller (on Paul Goodman), Ken Smith, Bill Sherman, Dick Higgins, John Welch, Michael McClure, Clive Bush (on Muriel Rukeyser), Paul Buck, Ralph Hawkins, Anthony Barnett, cris cheek, J. H. Prynne, Gilbert Adair, Bill Griffiths, Lawrence Upton, Pierre Joris, Spencer Selby, Ira Lightman, Rob Holloway, Martin Thom, Bern Porter, J. Christopher Jones (i.e. John Chris Jones), and others. *Spanner* 35 was a festschrift for Howard Skempton. Topics included Fluxshoe work, i.e. Fluxus-related texts, and "Speech Poetry". Earlier issues also occasionally had listed works from small press poetry imprints. *Spanner* published supplements, single-author works by e.g. Bill Sherman, Ulli Freer, and Allen Fisher.

BL: 1–20 (Reprint ed.), 21–26, 31– (P.903/846)
CUL: Imperfect set. (L727.b.289)
NLS: 11– . (HJ9.578 SER)
TCD: 11–20. (Reprint ed.). (PX– 37–849)
UCL
Poetry Library: 2, 4–7, 10, 12, 14–

457 Spindrift: poetry of a new generation / edited by A. S. Martin. Campbelltown, Argyll: Campbelltown Courier, No. 1 (1968)

NLS: 1970.134
UCL

458 Stable / edited by Rupert Mallin and Keith Dersley. Sudbury: The Stable Press; Syntaxophone Publications (The Oak Arts Workshop Ltd.), [No.] 1 [1975?]–5 (1979)

BL: 5. (ZA.9.a.10610)
CUL: L999.b.1.340
Poetry Library: 1–2; 5

459 Stepney Words / edited by Chris Searle. London: Reality Press, [No. 1, 1971]–2 (Sept. 1971).

Reprint: *Stepney Words I & II* (London: Centerprise, 1976)

The first volume consists of poems by Stepney children, aged 11–15 years; the second by adults and children. Strong visuals: photographs and illustrations. Arnold Wesker contributes a poem of his from 1953 in the second issue.

BL: X.0902/50
NLS: 6.2199
TCD: [1] (P 15213)

460 Stereo Headphones: an occasional magazine of the new poetries / edited by Nicholas Zurbrugg. Kersey, near Ipswich; then c/o The School of Humanities, Griffith University, Brisbane, Australia: Nicholas Zurbrugg, Vol. 1 no. 1 (Spring 1969)–no. 8/9/10 (1982)

Related Work: Nicholas Zurbrugg, *The Parameters of Postmodernism* (London: Routledge, 1993), BL: YC.1993.a3557; obituary of Nicholas Zurbrugg, *The Guardian*, Oct. 26th 2001.
Note: Volume numbers were only used for the first few issues. Only the final issue, 'Time and Space Fictions', was published from Griffith University in Brisbane, Australia.

Minimalist, sound, visual and concrete poetry, with provocative essays on these topics. Contributors include Anselm Hollo, Stephen Bann, Thomas A. Clark, Dick Higgins, Robert Lax, bp Nichol, Eugen Gomringer, Dom Sylvester Houédard, Henri Chopin, Bob Cobbing, Ernst Jandl, Edwin Morgan, Steve McCaffery, Glyn Pursglove, Ian Hamilton Finlay, Tom Phillips, Ed Ruscha, Edgardo Antonio Vigo, Nicholas Zurbrugg, Samuel Beckett, John Christie, John Furnival, Brion Gysin, Raoul Hausmann, Franciszka Themerson, Stefan Themerson, and others. No. 2/3 has a feature on new French poetries against concrete poetry (as, it is argued, a fundamentally reactionary form). Bob Cobbing and Peter Mayer contribute an outline of the history of concrete poetry in no. 5, which takes to task a number of the alleged myths surrounding this form (and which generates correspondence in no. 6).

BL: Vol. 1 no. 1–no. 7 (Spring 1976). (P.431/100)
CUL: Vol. 1 no. 1–no. 7 (Spring 1976). (L727.c.474)
NLS: Vol. 1 no. 1–no. 7 (Spring 1976). (P.med.456 PER)
TCD: Vol. 1 no. 1–no. 7 (Spring 1976). (PER 81–356)
UCL
Poetry Library: Vol. 1 no.1–no. 4; no. 6–no.7

461 The Stony Thursday Book / edited by John Liddy and Jim Burke, then John Liddy, Liam Liddy and Miguel Ortega, then Mark Whelan. Limerick, then Madrid: Treaty Press Ltd, then Archione Editorial, No. 1 (1975)–8 [1980?]. Then, as *The Stony Thursday Book / Cuaderno de Madrid: a bilingual literary magazine / Revista literaria bilingüe*. Madrid, No. 1 (1991)– .

Profiled in: Tom Clyde, *Irish Literary Magazines: an outline history and descriptive bibliography* (Dublin: Irish Academic Press, 2003), BL: 2725.g.3414

Poetry, some fiction, and reviews. An Irish focus, with an interest in Spanish literature following the move to Spain. With the Spanish poet Miguel Ortega, John Liddy and his brother Liam co-edited bilingual editions which appear to have added the title *Stony Ediciones* to the banner. Special issues included no. 7 on Kate O'Brien (guest edited by John Jordan), and no. 8, "American Odyssey". *The Stony Thursday Book* also published *Penumbra: a poetry broadsheet*, edited by John Kelly, in the late 1980s.

BL: 2 (Winter 1976), 4 (Spring 1977). (P.901/3084)
NLS: 2 (1976)–8 [1982]. (DJ.m.161 PER)
TCD: 1–8 [1982]. (OLS L–4–474 1976–1982)
UCL: 7 (1981)
Poetry Library: 2–8

462 Strange Faeces / edited by Opal and Ellen Nations. London, then Cambridge, Mass., then Vancouver: [Strange Faeces], No. 1 [1971?]–[198?]. ISSN: 0362-1871

Note: No. 14 and no. 19 were apparently never published
Related Imprint: Strange Faeces also published several books, including work by Allen Fisher and by Opal Nations

Mimeographed A4 format. 'Unintentionally a literary magazine' – Title page verso, no. 7. No. 2 includes a concrete poem by P. J. O'Rourke; no. 3 is a Ron Padgett issue, with all its poems by him; no. 5 ("Goodies from Anne Waldman") was guest edited by Anne Waldman; no. 6 was a Larry Fagin issue; no. 10A is edited by Allen Fisher and Dick Miller; no. 17 was devoted to experimental Canadian poetry.

BL: 2 (1971), 3 (1971), 7 (1972), 10 (1972), 10A (1972), 17(1975), 20 (Mar. 1980). (ZA.9.b.1485)
UCL: 3 (1971)–20 (1980). Lacking 9, 11, and 15.
Poetry Library: 4–7

463 Strath / Neil McNeil, then Michael Park, then these editors alternately. Bletchley: Rannoch Gillamoor Poets, No. 1 (1971)–11 (1976).

Related Imprint: Rannoch Gillamoor Poets survived the demise of the magazine and published e.g. Michael Park's collection *Arabian snapshots* (1981), BL: X.950/4127. As "Rannoch Gillamoor" the press also published at least one selection of radio plays.

A magazine that grew out of the poetry workshop, "Rannoch Gillamoor Poets" – the Rannoch comes from the Rannoch Close of the magazine's first address, but Neil McNeil also gives a Scottish element to the poems, some of which, e.g. by David Angus, are in Scots. Other poets include Steve Sneyd, Colin Nixon, Jocelynne Precious, and others. Also carried reviews.

BL: 1–9. (P.901/907)
CUL: L727.C.559
NLS: NH.575 PER
UCL: 3–11

464 Street Poems / edited by Derek Kitchen. Birmingham: West Midlands Arts Lab, 1970s

UCL
Poetry Library: 2 (1975)

465 Streetword / edited by Mike Dobbie. Hayes, Middlesex: Streetword, No. 1 (1972)–6 (1973)

Related Imprint: Streetword also published several poetry pamphlets, e.g. Barry Edgar Pilcher's *Black Tulips* [1973], BL: X.907/12100

Contributors included: Jocko Lekutanoy, Jeff Nuttall, Michael Horovitz, Roger McGough, Will Cowburn, Niall Duggan, Alan Brownjohn, David Gill, Trevor Reeves, Richard Marcus, Nick James, Jeff Cloves, Dave Calder, Peter Finch, Adrian Mitchell, and others. Although typewritten stencil, uses different colour paper, folding, cutting-out and different textured covers (e.g. wallpaper) for a very busy effect. Streetword also was associated with live readings actually in the street. Mike Dobbie soon went on to set up Poet & Peasant Books and to publish *Fix* magazine.

BL: P.901/1062
CUL: 1–2; 4–5. (L727.C.580)
UCL

466 Structure: a magazine of art and thought / edited by Michael Kane. Dublin: Michael Kane, Vol. 1 no. 1 (Spring 1972)–vol. 3 no. 2 (Winter 1978)

Related Work: Michael Kane, *Works, 1985–2001* (London: Artspace Gallery, 2001). Contains an essay on Kane by Anthony Cronin, and Kane interviewed by Marianne O'Kane

The long opening editorial in the first issue draws on Cézanne, Léger, Jack and W. B. Yeats, and especially Anthony Cronin. The magazine is characterised by fairly long essays on all the arts, including architecture, and plenty of space is given to generally figurative artwork, some of the latter by the editor, an artist. This is an urban, modernist magazine which, taking its cue from Anthony Cronin's suspicion of the use of pastoral in Irish writing, pitted itself against what it called "Bogolatory".

BL: P.905/43
CUL: L400.B.285
NLS: HP4.82.746 PER
TCD: Vol.1 no.1–vol. 3 no.1 (Summer 1975). (PER 81–633)

Surrealist Transformaction *See*
Transformaction D487

467 Suzanne / edited by J. Harrison. Exeter: J. Harrison, No. 1 [1971?]–4 [1972]

CUL: 4. (L999.B.1.225)

468 Sycamore Broadsheet / [edited by John Fuller]. Oxford: Sycamore Press, No. 1 (1968)–?

Profiled in: John Fuller, "The Sycamore Press 1968–1993", in *Oxford Poetry* vol. 8 no. 1 (Summer 1994), BL: P.901/3428

Each broadsheet usually consists of a folded sheet of poems by one poet only. Poetry tends to be formally conservative work in the tradition of the Movement poets, some of which it includes. Contributors include: Roy Fuller, Douglas Dunn, Peter Porter, James Fenton, Thom Gunn, Alan Hollinghurst, Gavin Ewart, Peter Redgrove, Craig Raine, Michael Schmidt, Philip Larkin, N. K. Sandars, Alan Brownjohn, Peter Scupham, John Mole, Peter Levi, and others. The first twenty-four issues were also published in sets that collected a dozen broadsheets within an envelope. Libraries can catalogue these erratically: sometimes as a series, sometimes as individual items, sometimes both.

BL: 1–30 (1983). (Cup.503.n.36).
CUL: 864.A.91 (30–)
NLS: Each broadsheet catalogued individually
TCD: Each broadsheet catalogued individually
UCL

469 Tagus / edited by John Blackwood and Peter Shingleton; then Shingleton alone. Oxford, then Peterborough, Tagus Poetry, Vol. 1 no. 1 (Winter 1970)–no. 2 (1972). ISSN: 0039–8950

Contributors include: Richard Burns, Peter Finch, Anne Ridler, Kathleen Raine, Michael Horovitz, Gerda Mayer, John Heath-Stubbs, Thomas Blackburn, Edward Lucie-Smith, C. Day Lewis, Peter Redgrove, Michael Hamburger, Roy Fuller, G. S. Fraser, Sally Purcell, Ann Born, Boris Pasternak, Marine Tsvetayeva, Anna Akmatova (all three trans. Lydia Pasternak Slater), and others. Gerald Killingworth, Susan Jones, and Ronald Bury were also involved editorially.

BL: ZA.9.a.2183
CUL: Vol. 1 no. 1. (L999.B.1.284)
NLS: Vol. 1 no. 1. (HP3.85.1018 PER)
TCD: Vol. 1 no. 1. (PER 81–394)
UCL: Vol. 1 no. 1.
Poetry Library: Vol. 1 no. 2

470 Tamarisk / edited by Terry Kingham. Erith: [1, 1968–2, 1968]

Note: Incorporated by *Tracks*.

UCL

471 Tangent / edited by Vivienne Finch, then Vivienne Finch and William Pryor. New Malden: Tangent Books, 1 (Winter 1975/76)–7 (1981). ISSN 0307–546X

Related Imprint: Tangent Books

Poems, short fiction, articles, reviews, graphics, and listings. The fourth issue was the collection *Away* by William Pryor.

BL: 1–4. (P.901/3083)
CUL: 1–6. (UC.8.7437)
NLS: HP4.86.141 PER
TCD: PER 91–514

472 Tantalus / edited by Roy Laberc; then D. J. Buckman and John Sanson.. London: Tantalus Press, No. 1 (Winter 1963)–4 [Sept. 1964]

With the strap line "Poetry, essays, criticism, short stories" was a general literary review featuring just one or two poems each issue, e.g. by Bill Butler, Barry Cole, Alan Crang, Christopher Levenson, Charles Tomlinson, and others. It also published a short story by Roy Fuller and an interview with Laurie Lee.

BL: P.901/1143
CUL: 1–2. (L999.c.3.353)
UCL

473 Tarasque / edited by Stuart Mills and Simon Cutts. Nottingham: [Tarasque Press], [No. 1, 1962/63–?, 1972]. ISSN: 0039–9647

Related Imprint: Tarasque published small single-author collections such as Roy Fisher, *Ten Interiors with Various Figures* (1966), BL: YA.1987.a.9983. It also published the magazine *Private Tutor*

Minimalist, concrete, sound and visual poetry. Contributors included the editors, Ian Hamilton Finlay, Oliver Folkard, Ian Gardner, Stephen Bann, Anselm Hollo, Gael Turnbull, Robert Lax, and others.

BL: 2–7, 8 (signed by Hugh Creighton Hill), 9–11/12. (ZA.9.a.8580)
CUL: 2–9 (L727.C.378)
NLS: 2–9 (6.2175); 11/12 (IHF.m.1(10) PER)
TCD: 2–8 (PER 92–310 1966–1968)
UCL
Poetry Library: 2–7; 9–11/12

474 Target / edited by Paul J. Green. Gunthorpe, Peterborough: Paul J. Green, No. 1 [1965?]–4 [1967?]. ISSN: 0082–1721

Note: Continued by: *Euphoria*

Typewritten mimeographed magazine. Poets included Anselm Hollo, Brian Patten, Jim Burns, Dave Cunliffe, Tina Morris, David Chaloner, Larry Eigner, d.a. levy, John James, Joan Gilbert, Bill Wyatt, Barry McSweeney, Alan Dixon, George Dowden, Mile Hall, Diane Wakoski-Sherbell, W. Price Turner, Paul Matthews, and others. The magazine changed its title to *Euphoria* to avoid confusion with *Target*, the monthly journal of the British Productivity Council.

BL: 2–4. (P/901/333)
UCL

475 T.A.S.C. in Poetry. Horsforth, Leeds: Trinity and All Saints' Colleges Poetry Society, Vol. 1 no. 1 [Dec. 1969]–?

Poetry from students of the colleges. Vol. 3 no. 7 (Nov. 1971) was a single-author collection by Coventry College of Education student Richard Green.

BL: Vol. 1 no. 1 [Dec. 1969]–vol. 5 no. 1 (Jan. 1973). (P.901/546)

Teapoth *See* Poor. Old. Tired. Horse. D385

476 Thames Poetry / edited by A. A. Cleary. Harrow: Thames Poetry, Vol. 1 no. 1 (Winter 1975/6)–Vol. 2 no. 17 [1990]. ISSN: 0307–9562

Note: There were seventeen issues in total: the volume numbers are independent of the issue numbers.
Index: Nos. 1–12 are indexed in no. 12.

Poems, reviews, essays. Contributors included: Alan Brownjohn, Douglas Dunn, D. J. Enright, Gavin Ewart, John Fuller, Roy Fuller, Thom Gunn, Seamus Heaney, Peter Howe, Michael Hulse, Michael Longley, Peter Porter, Peter Redgrove, John Wain, and others.

BL: 1–10; 12–16. (X.0909/2021).
CUL: L727.c.913
NLS: 1–16. (HJ3.484 PER)
TCD: 1–16. (PER 76–38)
UCL

477 Thistle / [edited by Tom Malcolm]. Glasgow: [Tom Malcolm], No. 1 [1961]– 4 [1962]

Printed badly by typewritten stencil, with faint illustrations. Very much a mixture of styles, from traditional forms to more avant-garde work. Contributors included: Tom Raworth, W. Price Turner, D. M. Black, David Holliday, Peter [i.e. Pete] Morgan, Vera Rich, Yann Lovelock, R. L. Cook, Frederick Brockway, and others.

BL: PP.5126.NJ
CUL: L727.C.289
NLS: 6.1180
TCD: PER 81–525
UCL

478 Three Arts Quarterly / edited by Frederick Palmer. London: Woodstock Gallery, No. 1 (Spring 1960)–4 (Winter 1960)

Note: Absorbed by *Stand*

Devoted to the arts: visual art, poetry, and drama in particular. Contributors included Henry Moore, Jean Cocteau (a drawing, and a poem, trans. Sheila Mann), Eugene Ionesco, Mervyn Peake, C. Day Lewis, Edwin Brock, Michael Horovitz, Paul Potts, A. Alvarez, Gregory Corso, Jenny Joseph, and others.

BL: 1, 2; 4. (PP.1932.se)
CUL: L727.c.742
NLS: 1. (1963.8.)
UCL

479 Three Hundred and Sixty-Five Days of the Year: independent poetry review / edited by Tom Bamford. Rontswood, Worcester: 365 Days of the Year, No. 1 (1969)

UCL

480 Throb / [edited by G. Harrison]. Edinburgh: University of Edinburgh Student Publications Board, 1 (Feb. 1972)

A "bag mag" in which individually printed sheets of paper were put into a plastic envelope. Probably a one-off.

CUL: L999.B.1.217
NLS: 6.2148
UCL

481 The Time Machine: a magazine devoted to literature and the arts / [edited by Stephen Leanse]. London: Stephen Leanse Publications, [No. 1, Spring 1970]–2 (Summer 1970)

"Our aim is to provide a medium to stimulate new writing; poetry, experimental work, reviews, articles and short stories." A foolscap format with illustrations largely made from cut-outs. Poems included those by George Barker, D. J. Enright, Christopher Logue, and George MacBeth.

BL: P.905/29
CUL: L999.b.1.203
NLS: [1]. (6.1960 PER)
TCD: PER 81–385
UCL

482 Tlaloc / edited by Cavan McCarthy. Leeds, No. 1 (1964)–22 (1970)

Related Imprint: Location Press

An emphasis on concrete and visual poetry. Contributors included: Anselm Hollo, Edwin Morgan, Gael Turnbull, bp Nichol, Dom Silvester Houédard, Roy Fisher, Veronica Forrest [-Thomson], Bob Cobbing and others. An archive of correspondence and manuscripts concerning *Tlaloc* is held at UCL. Andrew Lloyd was also involved editorially.

BL: P.P.8005.zl
CUL: L727.c.366
NLS: 6.1982 PER
TCD: 22. (OLS X–1–650 no.29)
UCL
Poetry Library: 21

483 Tomorrow / edited by Alan Evison. Oxford: New College, Oxford University, Vol. 1 no. 1 (Oct. 1970)–Vol. 2 no. 1 (1971–2)

John Fuller is listed as a Senior Member.

BL: ZA.9.a.10747
Poetry Library: Vol. 1 no. 2 (1971–2)

484 TR: a magazine of Arabic and English literature. London: TR Press, [Vol. 1] no. 1 (Winter 1974)–vol. 2 no. 1 (Jan. 1979). ISSN 0306–9117

Note: Vol. 2 no. 1 is also described as no. 4. The subtitle was only used for the first issue.
Related Imprint: TR Press published e.g. several collections by Abdullah al-Udhari, and the anthology *Dust and Carnations: traditional funeral chants and wedding songs from Egypt* [translated from the Arabic by John Heath-Stubbs and Shafik H. Megally] (1977), BL: X.907/25620

"The main function of TR is to introduce British poetry to Arab readers and Arabic poetry to British readers" – from no. 3. Sometimes had parallel Arabic and English texts, sometimes Arabic alone (e.g. an interview with Hugh MacDiarmid by William Oxley). Contributors included: Samuel Beckett, Muhammad al-Maghut, Jon Silkin, Geoffrey Hill, Ibn Zaidun, Abu Mihjan, Majnun Laila, Buland al-Haidari, John Heath-Stubbs, Urw Ibn al-Ward, Arji, Abu al-Shamaqmaq, Smih al-Qasim, Peter Porter and others. In no. 3 Heath-Stubbs gives an account of the Arab world (as a subject) in English literature.

BL: [Vol. 1] no. 2–vol. 2 no. 1. (P.903/556)
CUL: L830.C.96
NLS: HP2.82.3442 PER

TCD: PER 92–319 1974–1979
Poetry Library: [Vol. 1] no. 1; 3– vol. 2; no. 1

485 Track: new poetry and prose quarterly / edited by Peter Armstrong and Ian Vine. London: Peter Armstrong and Ian Vine, No. 1 [1966]–2 (Feb.1967)

Poetry, prose, drawings and some reviews. Contributors include Gael Turnbull, Jim Burns, and others.

BL: 2. (ZD.9.a.84)
UCL: 1–2

486 Tracks / edited by Neil Powell. Coventry: c/o University of Warwick, No. 1 (Summer 1967)–8 (Summer 1970). ISSN: 0041–0349

Note: No. 8 incorporated *Tamarisk*

A general arts review with a considerable amount of poetry and poetry-related articles and interviews. Philip Larkin is interviewed at length in the first issue. Included poetry by J.H. Prynne, John Temple, John Hall, Andrew Crozier, John James, Peter Riley, Elaine Feinstein, John Mole, Martin Booth, and others. Independent of the university.

BL: P.901/534
CUL: L985.c.115
NLS: P.sm.2482 PER
TCD: 2–5. (OLS L–6–495 no. 1–5)
UCL
Poetry Library: 2; 6–8

Tramps *See* Prison Clothes Press D391

Transformation *See* Transformaction D487

487 Transformaction / edited by John Lyle. Harpford, [nr.] Sidmouth, Devon: Transformaction, No. 1 [1967]–10 (Oct. 1979). ISSN: 0039–6168

Note: First issue is sometimes recorded by libraries as *Transformation*; the cover and title page could be taken to read *Surrealist Transformaction*
Related Imprint: Transformaction also published the magazine *Blue Food*

"Founded by Jacques Brunius, E. L. T. Mesens and John Lyle in 1967 to provide a forum for the Surrealist movement in Britain." Contributors include: Ian Breakwell, André Breton, Luis Buñuel, René Magritte, Philippe Soupault,

George Melly, Conroy Maddox, Ken Smith, Alan Burns, and others. Included with no. 2 is a loosely inserted pamphlet by Eric Thacker, *Aerojack: an illustrated novel*. John Lyle's Devon bookshop specialised in surrealism from across the world. Conroy Maddox was also involved editorially.

BL: 2 (Oct. 1968)–8 (1977); 10 (Oct. 1979). (P.901/1132)
CUL: 1; 4–10. (L700.c.269)
NLS: 10. (P.la.9080 PER)
TCD: 10. (PER 90–103 1979)
UCL
Poetry Library: 2

488 Transgravity. London: Paul Brown, 7 [1972]–15 (1980)

Note: Continues: *Transgravity Advertiser*
Related Imprint: Transgravity also published single-author collections in the Transgravity Publication series, and e.g. Paul Brown, Peter Nijmeijer and David Cevet (eds.), *These Are Also Wings: a dada/surreal anthology* (1972), BL: YA.1993.a.24641

Visual and minimalist poems, but not exclusively so, with contributors such as Robin Crozier, Djamila Boupacha, and others. See also *Poetry Presented by Transgravity*.

BL: 7; 10, 11; 13, 14. (ZA.9.d.389)
UCL: 7 [1972]–15 (1980)

489 Transgravity Advertiser. [London]: [Paul Brown], [No. 1]–6 (1971)

Note: Continued by: *Transgravity*
Related Imprint: Transgravity also published single-author collections in the Transgravity Publication series, and e.g. Paul Brown, Peter Nijmeijer and David Cevet (eds.), *These Are Also Wings: a dada/surreal anthology* (1972), BL: YA.1993.a.24641

An A4 sheet intended to sell advertising space to like-minded projects, with artwork and a few poems, e.g. by John Robinson, Gillian Jones, Alison Dunhill, and others. See also *Poetry Presented by Transgravity*.

BL: 3/4–6. (ZA.9.d.388)
UCL

490 A Treasury of Modern Poets: an anthology of contemporary verse. London: Regency Press, [1970]–1978

BL: 1971–1976. (P.901/733)
CUL: [1970], 1972–78. (L727.c.519)
NLS: NE.1024.a.
TCD: 1973–1978. (DIR 2115 1973–1978)

491 Tree / edited by Barry Miles. Cheltenham and Stroud: Barry Miles, [No. 1–2, 1960?]

UCL: 2

492 The Tree: an illustrated arts magazine / edited by Gregory Spiro. Cambridge: c/o Emmanuel College, [No. 1, Summer 1966]–?

Related Work: Gregory Spiro (ed.), *Shade Mariners: Dick Davis, Clive Wilmer, Robert Wells*, with an introduction by Tony Tanner (Cambridge: G. Spiro, 1970), BL: YA.1997.a.10253

Landscape format, high production values. Poems, reviews, an extract of a new Swedish novel by Eion Hanski, music and libretto, graphics. Poets included Thomas Blackburn, Gregory Spiro, and others.

BL: P.901/237

493 Trend / edited by Brian Woods. Dovercourt, Essex: Woods Publishing, Vol. 1 no. 1 [July 1971]–vol. 2 no. 1 [Dec. 1971]

BL: P.901/761

494 Troll: a magazine of articles, reviews, stories, illustrations, poems and letters. Beckenham, [1, 1965]–?

From schools in South London, mainly teenagers. Nick Totton, age 17, contributes an article, "The British Peace Campaign – A Biased Analysis" in issue 2.

BL: 2 (Mar. 1966). (P.P.8007.lj)

495 Troubadour / edited by Malcolm Peltu and Adel Hamadi. London, No. 1 [1970?]

A magazine of poets associated with London's Troubadour Coffee House.

Poetry Library

496 Turpin / edited by Jeremy Helm, Jeremy Harding, Maurice Slawinski, and Martin Thom. Cambridge: Turpin, c/o Magdalene College, [No. 1, 1972]–9 (1979)

"We're trying to break down the idea that you have to be a 'writer', 'artist', 'media man', 'business freak', etc. There is no cast list. If you like what we're doing then you are a part

of it." – from the first editorial. Earlier issues folded out to become posters of poetry and graphics. No. 2 included Eugenio Montale on painting, translated by Maurice Slawinski. No. 3 was written, designed, and produced by pupils from schools in Cambridge. No. 5 was the single poetry collection, *Just Twenty Two and I Don't Mind Dying: the official poetical biography of Jim Morrison – rock idol*, by Barry MacSweeney. This is different from the edition published as an issue of *The Curiously Strong*. No. 6 was devoted to the following small collections: *all blue chickens go to goodgold* by Michael Haslam, *The last 10 poems of marine life*, by Peter Riley, and an untitled prose work by Martin Wright. Other contributors included: Michael Horovitz, Leigh Hughes, Blaise Cendrars (trans. Peter Hoida), Ian Patterson, David Chaloner, John Welch, Iain Sinclair, Peter Philpott, and others.

BL: 1–4; 6–9. (ZA.9.b.829); 5 (YA.1992.a.19527.)
CUL: L727.b.146
UCL: 1–8

Twice (ed. Tom Clark) *See* Once D324

497 Twice: magazine for the once bitten ... / edited by Pat and Sidney Parker. London: [Pat and Sidney Parker], No. 1 (1963)–?

Related Imprint: S. E. Parker also published Émile Armand, *Anarchism and Individualism: three essays* (1962), BL: 08074.m.26

Not related to Tom Clark's *Once* etc. Typescript format; short drama, poetry, fiction, comment. "In the main *Twice* will be a contraceptive against the self-destructive spirit of the age."

BL: 1 (P.901/146.)

498 Twice: UEA student paper. Norwich, No. 1 [1971]–42 (1972)

UCL

499 Two Thousand / edited by Philip Snow. Oxford, then London: [Two Thousand], 1971–1976.

Note: The magazine also bore the title 2000 on each issue.

A political and cultural review which was very international in outlook and this is reflected in a large number of poems in translation.

BL: Feb 1973; Winter 1976.(P.903/275)

Chapter D: 1960–1975

CUL: June 1971–Winter 1976. (L900.B.473)
NLS: June 1971; Nov. 1971; Feb. 1972; June 1972.
(QP1.77.67 PER)

500 Tzarad / edited by Lee Harwood. London: Night Scene, No. 1 (August 1965)–4 (1969)

Note: Continues: *Soho: a bi-lingual review*. Related to: *Night Train* and *Horde*. No. 3 was co-published as *Collection* (ed. Peter Riley) 4. After this, *Tzarad* 4 was co-published as *Collection* 6.
Related Work: [Barry] Miles (ed.) *Darazt* (London: Lovebooks, 1965), BL: YA.2003.b.3656. An anthology containing work by Lee Harwood, William Burroughs, Miles, and photographs of Gala Mitchell by John Hopkins. The anthology was inspired by *Tzarad*, whose title it reverses. A copy is also held by UCL.

Included John Ashbery, Michel Couturier, Brain Patten, Dom Sylvester Houédard, Paul Evans, Chris Torrance, John Newlove, and the editor's translations of Max Jacob and Tristan Tzara.

BL: 1. (ZD.9.b.138). 3, 4 shelved with *Collection* (P.903/46)
CUL: 1. (L727.b.81). 3, 4. (L727.b.80)
NLS: 3, 4. (6.2082)
UCL: 1–3
Poetry Library: 1

501 Ubu 8 / edited by Graham Passmore. Newport: Ubu Publications, [1, 1970]

UCL

502 Ubulum / edited by Phillip Hodson. Oxford: c/o St. Peter's College, [No. 1, 1967?]

Note: In part a continuation of *Nebulum*

UCL

503 Ugly Duckling: poetry magazine / edited by Keith Richmond and Susan Jane March. High Wycombe; Oxford: Urban Refugee Press, No. 1 (1975)–8 (1977)

Included supplements (e.g. *Oil Slick*, which appeared with no. 7 and 8).

UCL: 4–7
Poetry Library: 6–8; *Oil Slick* supplement

504 Underdog: English poetry scene / edited by Brian Patten (sales editor, Eddie O'Neill). Liverpool: Citybird Press, 1 [1963]–8 (1966).

The first few issues were foolscap with the pages printed by typewritten stencil. Later issues were professionally printed throughout, and were illustrated with photos of some of the poets. This was the primary magazine of the Liverpool poetry scene, with contributors who included Roger McGough, Brian Patten, Pete Brown, and Adrian Henri (who also contributes a piece "Schwitters, the 'Nowness' of Rauschenberg and the Portobello Road School" to the first issue), as well as Spike Hawkins, Michael Horovitz, Harry Fainlight, Allen Ginsberg, Adrian Mitchell, Anselm Hollo, Robert Creeley, Libby Houston, and others. Brian Patten was only fifteen when he started it.

BL: 1–2; 5; 8. (P.P.8005.iu)
UCL: 5–8
Poetry Library: 5; 8

505 Unicorn: a magazine of poetry and criticism / edited by Norman Harvey. Bath: South Western Arts Association, No. 1 (Winter 1960/61)–12 (Autumn 1963)

BL: ZA.9.a.10098
CUL: L727.C.256
TCD: PER 80–716
UCL: 1–4
Poetry Library: 6

506 The United Scotsman / edited by Michael Donnelly. Glasgow: [The United Scotsman], Vol. 1 no. 1 (Oct. 1972)–?

A "journal devoted to promoting the unity of workers in both the highlands and the lowlands in the cause of an Independent Scottish Workers Republic", in the words of the first issue's editorial. There was a strong literary focus, with poetry and other texts by Hugh MacDiarmid, Andrew Tannahill, Susan Fromberg, John Manson, and others.

BL: Vol. 1 no. 1; vol. 2 no. 2 (Feb. 1973)–no. 4 (Apr./May 1973). (Pressmark pending)
NLS: Vol. 1 no. 1–vol. 2 no. 5 (May/June 1973). (HP4.79.66 PER)
UCL: Vol. 1 no. 1–no. 2

507 The Urbane Gorilla. [Sheffield]: Raven Publications, [Vol.1] [1970]–13 (Spring 1981). ISSN: 0142–128X

Edited anonymously then possibly pseudonymously (by "Ed Tork"). Appears not to have thought of itself as a magazine to begin with: the first issue was an anthology of poems by Joe Warrington, Rik Kavanagh, and Tom Owen.

BL: 1–7; 10. (P.901/3138)
CUL: 3–13. (L727.B.176)
NLS: 7–13. (P.sm.962 PER)
TCD: 7–13. (PER 92–418)
UCL
Poetry Library: Vol. 6–9

Urge *See* Yam D537

Ver Poets Poetry Post *See* Poetry Post D376

508 Viewpoints / edited by Lynn Carlton and Fred Cosgrove. Newton Heath, Manchester: [Folio 1, 1962?]–?

Poems and reviews within a friendly, chatty context. Aesthetically conservative. In no. 60 (Autumn 1966), which marks an upgrade in production values to a commercially printed format, it is described as the "oldest duplicated magazine in the U.K." The earliest issues were described as "folios", and the magazine as being "the organ of the Outsiders Forum". More well-known contributors include: Peter Finch, Eric Ratcliffe, Terry Kingham, Tony Curtis, R. L. Cook, Wes Magee, Lawrence Upton, Steve Sneyd, and Brian Louis Pearce. Regular contributors who seem particularly associated with the magazine include: Ken Price, Ian Caws, Doris Corti, Honor Butlin, Helen Shaw, and John Wiltshire.

BL: 60–80. (P.901/579)
CUL: 74–80. (L727.c.459)
NLS: 74–80. (5.5638 PER)
TCD: 74–80. (PER 81–383)
UCL: 37–81

509 The Village Review. Newport, Essex: Newport Press, Vol. 1 no. 1 [Spring 1972]–no. 4 [Winter 1973]

UCL

510 Vision. Torbay: Torbay Diary of Arts Association, [1961?]

Mentioned in *Umbrella*. No holdings known.

510a Vision / edited by Angela Carter and Neil Curry. [Bristol: Bristol University, No. 1, 1963]

Angela Carter co-edited this 8-page poetry magazine while studying psychology and anthropology at Bristol, and contributed two poems under the name Rankin Crowe.

BL: Pressmark pending

511 Vision & Voice. Sunderland: Sunderland Polytechnic School of Art & Design, No. 1 (1969)

A visual arts magazine, which appears to have been a one-off. The sixteen-page pink insert, "Sandwich", by Robin Crozier is essentially visual poetry, with a strong typographic element.

BL: P.421/162
CUL: L900.C.424
NLS: 6.2809 PER

512 Vision Broadsheet / [edited by John L. Moir?]. Glasgow: John L. Moir, No. 1 (1971)

NLS: 7.165

513 Visions and Praying Mantids / edited by Peter Hoy. Oxford: Peter Hoy, Vol. 1 no. 1 (Oct. 15 1971)–no. 7 (Nov. 26 1971)

Note: Subtitle: *The angelogical notebooks of Anthony Conran*

Unbound typed sheets on pink and yellow paper, all given over to Anthony Conran's poems and his notes on poetry. Issued free of charge.

BL: P.901/811
CUL: L727.C.492
NLS: 5.5668 PER
TCD: PER 80–398

514 Voice: a local writers' magazine / edited by G. K. Roberts. Weymouth: Voice, No. 1 [1970]–8 [1974]

BL: P.901/593

515 Voices: verse and prose. / edited by Ben Ainley, and then others. Droylsden: Manchester Unity of Arts Society, then Federation of Worker Writers & Community Publishers, [No.1, 1972?]–?. New Series, No. 1 (Sept. 1975)–?

Note: Some issues in the new series also bore a second number, which continued the sequence of the first series. Variant subtitles include: *working class poetry and prose with a socialist appeal; working class poetry and prose; working class stories and prose.*

A magazine which grew out of an English class run by Ainley at New Cross Ward Labour Club, designed "to discuss literature on the basis of a Marxist analysis, and to encourage free and original expression by the class members." Many of the earlier contributors were from this English class but the magazine encouraged new writers.

BL: [1]–6 (May 1975); New series, 1 (Sept. 1975)–8 (Summer 1977); 29 (Aug. 1983); 39 (Winter 1983/84). (P.903/549)
CUL: New series, 13–26. (L727.C.727)
NLS: New series, 7–26. (DJ.s.394 PER)
Poetry Library: [1]–5; New series, 1–[20]; [22]; [24]–[25]

516 Vole / edited by Chris M. Pickles. Hitchin, No. 1 (1972)–5 (1973)

CUL: L727.c.586
NLS: 1–3; 5. (HP1.77.1252 PER)
Poetry Library: 3

517 Vortex / edited by Derek Webb. Portsmouth: Vortex, No. 1 [1968?]

Noted in *Driftwood Quarterly* no. 1. No holdings known.

518 Wallpaper. New York and London: Wallpaper, No. 1 (Sept. 1974)–5/6 (June 1976). ISSN: 0307–5834

Related Work: *Wallpaper. Audio Arts Supplement No. 1* (1975). British Library Sound Archive shelfmark: 1CA0012461. A cassette of sound recordings by contributors to *Wallpaper.*

Experimental magazine, presenting half a dozen or so sequences of poetry and other texts and visuals in each issue. The first number was edited anonymously, after which the contributors were described as the "contributing editors" to each issue. It was an A4 stapled, mimeographed publication with a wrap-around cover consisting of a sheet of wallpaper. Despite the mimeo format, the range of visuals and other formal elements suggests a sophisticated and steady art direction to the magazine, and the poetry reflects this cerebral, avant-garde approach. An interest in the permutational suggests affinities at least with Oulipo, but, as the *Wallpaper* cassette makes explicit, there is also an interest in sound and performance. Contributors came from the world of poetry, drama, music, visual art, sculpture, and sociology, and included: Richard Quarrell, Amikam Toren, David Coxhead, Anthony Howell, John Welch, Anthony McCall, Andrew Eden, Richard Bernas, Susan Hiller, Bill Shepherd, Susan Bonvin, and others.

BL: X.0902/1003
CUL: 4–5/6. (L999.B.1.499)
NLS: 2 (Dec. 1974)–5/6 (June 1976). (DJ.m.924 PER)
TCD: 4–5/6. (PER 94–866 1975–1976)
UCL: 3–5/6

519 Wave / edited by Edwin Tarling. Hull: Sonus Press, No.1 (Autumn 1970)–8 (Spring 1974)

Related Imprint: Sonus Press published at least one collection, Joan Barton's *The mistress, and other poems* (1972), BL: X.989/15728

A very understated poetry magazine: no editorial, no reviews, no blurb, no notes on contributors. Just between thirty or forty pages of poetry per issue. Many well-known poets from a number of different traditions: Bob Cobbing, Eugen Gomringer, Elizabeth Jennings, Philip Larkin, Edwin Morgan, R. S. Thomas, Stewart Conn, Penelope Shuttle, Anne Ridler, Iain Crichton Smith, Peter Porter, Douglas Dunn, and many others. Edwin Tarling's papers connected with *Wave* are held at Hull University's Brynmor Jones Library.

BL: P.901/662
CUL: 1 (Autumn 1970)–7 (Summer 1973). (L727.C.426)
NLS: 1 (Autumn 1970)–7 (Summer 1973). (DJ.s.441 PER)
TCD: 1 (Autumn 1970)–7 (Summer 1973). (Press B SON 1970 WAV 1–7 1970–1973)
Poetry Library

520 Waysgoose / edited by Yann Lovelock and Peter Butcher. London, 1 [May 1963]–2 [Oct. 1963]. ISSN: 0509–9331

Typewritten magazine, with poems and reviews. The intention was to publish the work of only four poets per issue, namely: Barry Bowes, Bill Byrom, George MacBeth, Graham Robottom; then Taner Baybars, Fernando Garcia-Bravo, Biltin Toker, and Anselm Hollo (who also co-edited the second issue with Lovelock and Butcher).

BL: P.P.8001.oz
CUL: 1. (L999.B.1.101)
UCL: 1–2

521 WEN 3 / [edited by Peter Shingleton?].
Oxford: Lawless, then The Gemini Society, No.
1 (1968)–6 (1970)

Contributors include Peter Shingleton, Roger Garfytt, Peter
Finch, Colin Nixon, Eddie S. Linden, and others.

BL: P.901/572
CUL: L727.c.420
NLS: 1973.34 PER
UCL
Poetry Library: 6

522 Weyfarers / edited by David Colbeck,
John Emuss, Eric Harrison, and Julian Nangle;
and others. Bramley: Guildford Poets Press, 1
(Jan. 1972)– . ISSN: 0307–7276

No reviews or essays, just poems. A great number of
different contributors, making it difficult to categorise,
including J. P. Dick, e.g. in issue 20, later known as John
Burnside.

BL: P.901/3092
CUL: 21 (1978)– . (L727.C.760)
NLS: 21 (1978)– . (HJ2.54 SER)
TCD: 21 (1978)– . (PER 78–528)
UCL: 2 (1972).
Poetry Library: 13; 16–17; 20; 25; 28–30; 32–49; 51–

523 Wheels / edited by Harriet Rose.
London: Wheels, No. 1 [Jan. 1974]–4 (Nov.
1975). ISSN 0306–1663

Note: Variant subtitles: *Poetry and more poetry, A magazine of
new poetry, A vehicle for modern poetry*.

Self-consciously named after the Sitwells' magazine of the
same name. Contributors included: Gavin Ewart, Anne
Beresford, Norman Hidden, Valerie Sinason, Ivor Cutler,
Anthony Rudolf, Adrian Henri, Philip Crick, William Oxley,
Brian Patten, Judith Kazantzis, David Grubb, and others.
The third and fourth issues had a few translations of
Spanish poems, published with the editorial assistance of
Joaquina González-Marina, who an advert indicates had in
turn translated a number of English poets into Spanish for
the Málaga magazine *Caracola*, including Brian Patten, Jeni
Couzyn, Bob Cobbing, Adrian Henri, and Anthony Rudolf.

BL: P.901/1284
UCL: 2–3

524 White Lion Poets. [Birmingham]:
[White Lion Poets], No. 1 (1975)

The White Lion refers to the pub where readings took place
every fourth Tuesday in the month, in the upper room. The
first and probably only issue was essentially an anthology
of poems by Geoff Charlton, Brendan Hogan, and Peter
Buckingham. White Lion Poets events were publicised in
Muse and the Birmingham Poetry Centre's *Poetry News*.

BL: ZC.9.a.2480
CUL: L727.D.201
NLS: 1977.33 PER
TCD: PER 76–146

525 The Wivenhoe Park Review / edited
by Thomas [i..e. Tom] Clark, and Andrew
Crozier. Colchester, then London: c/o
University of Essex, then The Ferry Press, No. 1
(Winter 1965)–3 (August 1968). Then as *The
Park*, 4/5 (Summer 1969). ISSN: 0043–7107

Note: No. 3 bore two titles on its cover: *The Wivenhoe Park
Review* and *The Park*.

Contributors include: Peter Riley, Elaine Feinstein, Donald
Davie, John Temple, Tony Ward, John James, Jim Burns,
Lee Harwood, Ian McKelvie, Tom Raworth, J. H. Prynne,
John Riley, Tim Longville, Doug [i.e. Douglas] Oliver, Chris
Torrance, and others. American contributors include Robin
Blaser, Larry Eigner, Ed Dorn, Tom Clark (who edited the
first issue with Crozier, the latter editing the rest alone),
Carl Rakosi, Jack Spicer, Charles Olson, Robert Duncan,
Gilbert Sorrentino, Clayton Eshleman, Ted Berrigan, and
others. Wivenhoe Park was the Colchester location of the
University of Essex's Dept. of Literature, where the review
was first edited. Later, Crozier moved to the Dept. of
American Studies at the University of Keele, where issues
3–4/5 were edited.

BL: 1–4/5. 1 lacks pages 33 onwards. (P.901/100)
CUL: L727.C.348
NLS: 5.5924 PER
TCD: 1–3. (PER 81–972). 4/5. (PER 91–255 1969)
UCL
Poetry Library: 4/5

526 Women's Liberation Review /
[edited by Astra Blaug?]. High Wycombe, then
London: Women's Literature Collective;
[printed by the Falling Wall Press], No. 1 (Oct.
1972)–?

"This issue of the *Women's Liberation Review* grew out of a workshop on Women and Literature at the Women's Liberation Conference in Manchester (March, 1972). Most of us were women writing in the isolation of our own homes who wanted to share our experiences, communicate our ideas. All of us were women who felt the need for our movement to generate its own body of literature in response to our situation. A Women's Literature Collective which would work together to create an anthology of women's writings seemed to answer both these needs." – from the anonymous editorial in the first issue. Poems, political essays and literary criticism, illustrations, photographs, and personal testimony.

BL: 1–2 (Oct. 1973). (P.521/1616)

527 Words / edited by Dermot Marshall, Michael Boyle, and Oliver Kennedy. Belfast: Words, No. 1 (Dec. 1967)

Profiled in: Tom Clyde, *Irish Literary Magazines: an outline history and descriptive bibliography* (Dublin: Irish Academic Press, 2003), BL: 2725.g.3414

According to Tom Clyde (who owns the only known copy), this "emerged from a creative writing class attended by the editors." Non-fiction and short fiction, and poems by Seamus Heaney, Padraic Fiacc, and others.

528 Words Broadsheet. Bramley, Surrey, then Haslemere, Surrey, then London: Words Press, No. [1973]–30 [1977]

Related Imprint: Words Press

Peter Redgrove, Penelope Shuttle, Harry Guest, Ted Hughes, and others. Issues 1–10 limited to 100 numbered copies; 11–20 limited to 150 numbered copies; 21–30 limited to 200 numbered copies. Julian Nangle was a co–founder of Words Press.

BL: Cup.406.j.10
CUL: L727.C.565
NLS: Lacking 7. (P.med.1815 PER)
TCD: Lacking 7, 8 and 10. (OLS L–4–387)
UCL: 11–20

529 Wordsnare / edited by Donal A. Murphy, Mary O'Donoghue and Noel Ryan. [Nenagh, Ireland]: Wordsnare, [No. 1, Summer 1974]–3 (Summer 1977).

Profiled in: Tom Clyde, *Irish Literary Magazines: an outline history and descriptive bibliography* (Dublin: Irish Academic Press, 2003), BL: 2725.g.3414

Related Imprint: Wordsnare also published some local history publications.

Poems about Nenagh and North Tipperary, or by poets from the area (often still at school).

BL: P.901/3090
TCD: PER 81–126

530 Wordworks / Altrincham: Michael Butterworth Publications, 1 [1973?]–7 [1976?]. ISSN: 0010–9142

Note: Continues: *Corridor*

CUL: 6–7 (L999.B.1.423)
NLS: 6–7. (HP3.78.1470 PER)
TCD: 6–7 (PER 75–927)
UCL: 1–5

Workshop *See* Writers' Workshop D533

Workshop New Poetry *See* Writers' Workshop D533

531 Write First Time. Liverpool: Write First Time, Vol. 1 no. 1 (Apr. 1975)–Year 9 no. 2 (June 1984)

"Written by people who did not think they could write", a tag-line later expanded to "made by people who teach and learn in reading and writing centres." A magazine, tabloid size, largely of poetry and photography, and associated with literacy projects initially in the Liverpool area, but broadened nationally in later issues. Contributors include Ann Donovan. Edited anonymously.

BL: P.2000/726

532 Writer's Review / edited by Sydney Sheppard. Birdlip, Gloucester: United Writers, Oct. 1963–May/June 1980. ISSN: 0512–4123

Note: Continued as: *Writer*. Giles Harmon was also involved editorially.

BL: P.P.8002.bt.
CUL: L727.B.44
NLS: Lacking Feb. 1976 and Dec. 1979. (P.167 PER)
TCD: PER 93–942 1963–1980
UCL: Vol. 1 no. 4 (1964)–vol. 6 no. 2 (1972)
Poetry Library: Vol. 5 no. 3 (1968)

533 Writers' Workshop / edited by Norman Hidden. London: Writers' Workshop, [No. 1, 1967]. Then as *Workshop*. No. 2 (Winter 1967/8–no. 13 [1971]. Then as *Workshop New Poetry*, No. 14 [1972]–no. 27 [1975]. Then as *New Poetry*, No. 28 [1975]–no. 51/52 [1981]

Anthology: Dick Russell (ed.), *Hidden Talent: the Workshop poets: a celebratory anthology for Norman Hidden* (Lynwood, Wa.: Russell Hill Press, 1993), BL: YA.1994.a.7503

Contributors included Andrew Motion, Colin Bell, Jeni Couzyn, and Chris Searle. Guest editors included Jon Stallworthy, Ivor Cutler, Philip Toynbee, and Edward Lucie-Smith. Also involved editorially were Michael Johnson and John Pudney.

BL: P.901/274
CUL: *Workshop, Workshop New Poetry, New Poetry*, 2–51/52.(L727.d.150)
NLS: *Writers' Workshop*, 1. (5.3564 PER); *Workshop*, 2–13. (DJ.s.447 PER); *Workshop New Poetry*, 14–27; (DJ.s.447 PER); *New Poetry*, 28–51/52. (HJ2.9)
UCL: *Writers' Workshop, Workshop, Workshop New Poetry*, 1–27
Poetry Library: 2–3; 7–8; 11; 13–18; 20; 23–29; 47–51/52

Writing *See* Writing Published D534

534 Writing Published / edited by Sean Dorman; then Barbara Horsfall. Fowey, then Farnborough: Sean Dorman Manuscript Society, [1959]–[1971?]. Then as *Writing*, [1972?]–[Winter 1989/90]. ISSN 0308-2024

Note: Continues: *S.D's Review*. Absorbed by: *Writers News*, a magazine giving information for authors wishing to profit from their work. No issue for Spring/Summer 1986 was published.
Related Imprints: The Sean Dorman Manuscript Society published *Sounds in the Silence: the collected poems of John Lane, Sean O'Leighin* (Fowey, [1970]), BL: X.908/84497.
Concordant Press advertised *Poetry* by Ray McCarthy and *Concordant Poets 1st Anthology* in 1989, though no holdings are known.

Usually three a year, but sometimes quarterly. Poetry, fiction and articles; details of writing courses, and hints on getting writing published. Produced by duplicated typescript stencil, even into the 1980s. Helena Lane and Fred Attfield were also involved editorially.

BL: *Writing Published*, Spring 1967, Autumn 1967, Spring 1968, Spring 1969, Spring 1970, Autumn 1971. *Writing*, Autumn 1972, Spring 1974, Spring 1975, Spring 1976,

Autumn 1976–Spring/Summer 1983, Spring/Summer 1984–Spring/Summer 1985, Autumn/Winter 1986, Spring 1987, [Autumn/Winter 1987], Spring/Summer 1988, [an undesignated issue which also seems to cover Spring/Summer 1988], Winter 1988/89, [Summer 1989], [Winter 1989/90]. (P.901/293)
CUL: *Writing Published*, Autumn 1967–Autumn 1971. *Writing*. (L727.c.453)
NLS: *Writing*. Autumn/Winter 1984/85–[Winter 1989/90]. Lacking Autumn/Winter 1985. (DJ.s.545 PER).
TCD: *Writing Published*, Spring 1970–?. *Writing*. (PER 73–608)
UCL: *Writing Published*, Spring 1970–?. *Writing*,?–Autumn 1972; Spring 1974; Autum/Winter 1986–1987
Poetry Library: *Writing Published*: Spring 1969; *Writing*: Spring 1974, Autumn–Winter 1979

535 Xenia / edited by Peter and Ginny Barnfield. Bristol: Peter and Ginny Barnfield, then Xenia Press, [1, 1973]–9 (1976)

Note: The first issue was unnumbered and subtitled *Dream or reality*
Related Imprint: Xenia Press produced poetry pamphlets until at least the early 1980s, authors including Wes Magee, Nick Toczek, Alamgir Hashmir, Robin Buss, Steve Sneyd, David H. W. Grubb, Fred Beake, Alison Bielski, Susan Fearn, Vivienne Finch, and Rosemary Maxwell.

Poems, photography, and graphic art. Many of the contributors were also published by Xenia Press in pamphlet form.

BL: P.901/1105
CUL: 2–9 (L727.C.550)
NLS: 3–9. (HP3.79.655 PER)
UCL

536 Yahahbibi. Essex, c.1967

Noted in Tony Dash, *Anthology of Little Magazine Poets* (Asylum, 1968), BL: YA.1995.b.7249. No holdings known.

537 Yam / edited by Ulli McCarthy and Garrie Hutchinson. London: [Ulli McCarthy], [1, 1970?–?]

Note: The experimental presentation of text on the cover of this magazine means the title could be mistaken to be *Urge*.

A typewritten mimeographed foolscap production, with some visual work pasted in. Authors' work was divided by thin coloured card strips, some yellow, some blue. Contributors included the editors as well as Trevor James, Ross Rowan, John Rowan, Kris Hemensley, Bill Beard,

Bernard Kelly, Colin Kimwood, Charles Buckmaster, and
Jeff Nuttall. Garrie Hutchinson co-edited from Australia.

BL: [1]. (YD.2005.b.491)

538 Yorick: University of York Magazine / edited by Martin Culverwell; Tom Callaghan and others. York: University of York, March 1967–[1976?]

Note: Continued by: 'Y'

University of York, Raymond Burton Library: March 1967,
Summer 1968, Spring 1969, Festival 1969; vol. 2 (Summer
1974); vol. 3 (Autumn 1974); vol. 4 (Summer 1975); vol. 6
(Winter 1975); vol. 7 (Spring 1976). (K8.42741 YOR)
Poetry Library: vol. 8 (1976)

539 York Poetry / edited by Colin Simms. York: York Poetry Society, 1 (1971)–8 [1974?]. Then as North York Poetry 9 (1974)–2 (1975)

Note: No. 9 was entitled *North York Poetry*. The next issue
appears to have been designated no. 2, and was Bill
Cowley's *Copperty Keld*. Continued by: *Genera*.

The first volume was an anthology of poems offered to the
York Poetry Society Inaugural Poetry Competition, but later
issues were single-author collections. The first few of these
were by Simms himself, but later ones were by other poets,
e.g. no. 6 was *Scarred Temple* by Jeffrey Radley and no. 7 was
Behind Heslington Hall by Cal Clothier.

BL: 1–4; 6. (X.0908/582)
CUL: 7. (1994.8.975). *North York Poetry* 2. (1998.8.4294)
NLS: 1. (1973.260); 2. (5.5401); 3. (5.5394); 4. (5.5394)
TCD: 1. (P 28640); 2. (P 26386); 3. (P 26153); 4. (P 26017)
UCL: 1–9

Zusammen *See* Prison Clothes Press D391

Chapter E: 1976–2000

The End of the Century: Exploring Possibilities for Poetry

T HERE IS NO DOUBT that the Sixties and early Seventies saw an exceptional increase in the number of little magazines: the many hundreds of new titles certainly warrant Eric Mottram's designation of that period as the years of the British Poetry Revival. Although editors and poets of that time may feel there was a falling off in activity as the Seventies hit the halfway mark, this is not born out quantitatively. Many in the older generation of editors did close their titles: some sixty-five magazines founded in the preceding period closed between 1976 and 1979. But, while not repeating the steep mid-Sixties gradient of growth, the magazine scene continued to show an increase in the number of new titles. Most years in our survey of this period show thirty or more new titles each year, a "creativity index" as high for these twenty-five years as the years immediately before. In 1977 alone, coincidentally one of the most active years of that do-it-yourself movement, Punk, no less than forty-four new magazines were started.

As with the preceding period, however, high numbers of births of magazines were mirrored by high numbers of deaths. Across 1976-2000, there was an average annual *net* increase of just under four new titles per year. Clearly, the little magazine and the poetry it championed were in danger of appearing ephemeral, with editors sometimes relishing the transience but more often lamenting the unexpected brevity. Without a strong production, distribution, marketing, and reviewing infrastructure this was likely to remain the case. However, a combination of changes in technology, funding, mode of publication, and information networking meant that the challenge of permanence began to be answered.

Editors responded to the question of production values in a number of ways. Some continued to use cheap-to-produce stencil or mimeograph printing, gradually replacing this with photo-copying. The intervention of national and regional arts councils meant perfect binding and photo-litho printing received funding and many editors subjected themselves to the necessary public accountability procedures to secure this. Personal computers for typesetting and in some cases printing came in during the eighties and nineties and affected many magazines; finally, the Web established a way of publishing without paper and ink (and also answered a distribution need with potentially vast but non-subscription-paying audiences). The decline of the independent bookshops and of poetry's presence in bookshops in general brought distribution problems for all poetry publishers, especially for those little magazines that aspired to a general arts audience, and this remains the case for the physical object of the magazine or book. Though not solely devoted to poetry, the founding of the Association of Little Presses in 1966 meant that there was already an organisation campaigning for better representation for small presses in general. Issuing catalogues and hosting bookfairs, its importance grew as poetry's public presence declined, but it had become dormant by the end of the 1990s and in 2002 its founder and guiding light, Bob Cobbing, died. Today, an online service, Lollipop: List of Little Press Publications, founded by Bill Griffiths, Bob Trubshaw, and Peter Finch in 2000, to some degree translates the work of the ALP to the virtual medium.

Magazines that were wholly or substantially devoted to publication or events listings helped keep poetry news flowing: notably Peter Hodgkiss' *Poetry Information* and its various reincarnations (1970–1997) and *Poetry London Newsletter*, begun in 1988 (and now known as *Poetry London*), edited by Leon Cych, Pascale Petit and others. The Poetry Library also issued, and continues to issue, poetry-related information; the formation of the Scottish Poetry Library under Tessa Ransford's direction in 1984 meant there was a similar service in Scotland. Such information services became online, alongside the digital newcomers The Poetry Kit and Lollipop mentioned above. Reading and workshop series were important ways for experimental writers to find a sympathetic audience and to share their practice with other poets at the innovative end of the poetry spectrum. These included the long-established Writers Forum workshops and the SubVoicive readings in London, the Cambridge Conference of Contemporary Poetry, and Maurice Scully's The Coelacanth Press reading series in Dublin. Little magazines and other small press books would typically be sold and distributed at these events.

Finally, the creation of lasting small presses, usually originally associated with a particular magazine, began to answer the need for a sense of permanence within the little magazine world with the physical realisation of an alternative canon. While such a practice has been pursued at various times over the century, it's likely that no period has matched the last quarter of the century in the number of magazine-linked individual presses and books.

Ken Edwards' *Reality Studios* (1978–1988) is a case in point. It also shows how the little magazine and linked small press were key to the early reception of experimental American poetry in the United Kingdom: once again, this is a period where British receptivity to many different kinds of American poetry has been uneven but substantial. The roots of *Reality Studios* go back to *Alembic*, edited by Edwards, Peter Barry and Robert Hampson, which had started in 1973 and ran for six years. *Alembic* published a range of British and American exploratory or innovative poets, including Rosmarie Waldrop, Robert Lax, Allen Fisher, Eric Mottram, Tom Leonard, Barry MacSweeney, and Ulli McCarthy [Freer], and this Anglo-American editorial stance continued in Edwards' later magazine. With *Reality Studios* he became instrumental in introducing Language Poetry to the United Kingdom (a process he had already begun in *Alembic*), through reviews and discussion, and by publishing Charles Bernstein, Ray Di Palma, James Sherry, and Alan Davies. UK-based poets, including Tom Raworth, Lee Harwood, cris cheek, Carlyle Reedy, Maggie O'Sullivan, Adrian Clarke, Bill Griffiths, Alan Halsey, Gad Hollander and Robert Sheppard, appeared alongside their American counterparts, creating a sense of dialogue between experimental poets either side of the Atlantic. A major step was the creation of the Reality Studios imprint, originally based in London. This later merged with Wendy Mulford's Street Editions to become Reality Street Editions (which Edwards has run by himself in more recent years, currently from Hastings). Reality Street Editions has become a key small press, with books by many of the poets associated with the earlier magazines and their broadly modernist and postmodern poetics, notably publishing Denise Riley's *Mop Mop Georgette* (1993), Fanny Howe's *O'Clock* (1995) and the collected edition of Allen Fisher's *Place* (2005).

Paul Green's *Spectacular Diseases* (1976–1999) and *Loot* (1979–1987), based in Peterborough, also published experimental writers from England and North America, and followed through by publishing them in the Spectacular Diseases imprint. Amongst those included in the magazines were Paul Buck, Fanny Howe, Gil Ott, David Chaloner, Allen Fisher, Pierre Joris, Nigel Wheale, Peter Larkin, Alan Halsey, and Brian Marley, while the press published such writers as Bruce Andrews, Don David, Charles Cantalupo,

Ulli Freer, Dennis Barone, and Thomas Taylor, as well as the design theorist John Chris Jones. Green also acted as the distributor for the US experimental publisher Burning Deck.

Several other magazines in this earlier period with a similar interest in the experimental appeared across the country. They included Alaric Sumner, Paul Buck and others' *Words Worth* (1978–1995), published in London and Yeovil, Richard Tabor's *Lobby Press Newsletter* (1978–1982), founded in Colchester, Tony Baker's *Figs* [1980?]–(1988), founded in Durham, Tim Fletcher's *First Offence* (1986–?), published in Canterbury, and Richard Caddel's *Staple Diet* (1985–1986) with its associated Pig Press, based in Durham. *Not Poetry* (1980–84/85), published from Newcastle by Peter Hodgkiss, was a journal of prose writing, particularly by poets, including Allen Fisher, Ken Smith, Jeff Nuttall, and Alan Halsey. Hodgkiss's Galloping Dog Press published the poetry of Lee Harwood, Bob Cobbing, Tom Leonard, Geraldine Monk, Kelvin Corcoran, Alan Halsey, Guy Birchard, and Ralph Hawkins. Michael Thorp's *Cloud* (1988), also from Newcastle, had a distinctive presence due in part to its concern with poetry as a spiritual activity and "art as a means to Life", as Thorp once put it in a catalogue of his later Cloudforms project. *Cloud* might best be seen as a precursor of both Cloudforms and a related publishing venture, Markings, which together included books and pamphlets by George Oppen, Edouard Roditi, Lawrence Fixel, Werner Dürrson (in Michael Hamburger's translation), James Kirkup, and Peter Dent, amongst others. John Welch edited *Vanessa Poetry Magazine* in London from the mid-Seventies to 1981, with work by Peter Riley, Martin Thom, Tom Lowenstein, Paul Brown, and David Chaloner (whose magazine *One* eventually merged with Welch's). Welch published books and pamphlets by Lowenstein, Thom, Peter Robinson, W. G. Shepherd, James Sutherland-Smith, Alfred Celestine, and others through his The Many Press. He also edited *The Many Review* (1983–1990), dedicated to reviews and the discussion of contemporary poetry. Peter Philpott and Bill Symondson's *Great Works* (1973–1979) included work by J. H. Prynne, Jeremy Harding, John Wilkinson, Rod Mengham, and Michael Haslam. Philpott's Great Works Editions published Haslam, John Hall, Andrew Crozier, Allen Fisher, John Freeman, and John Welch. *Great Works* is another example of a magazine which has continued as an e-zine. Tom Raworth's *Infolio* (1986–1987) featured both writing and visual art, with an international list of contributors; while including a good deal of experimental work, it maintained a fairly eclectic position. cris cheek's

Language aLive (1995)–[1996?] explored the experimental end of performance-based writing, while Norman Jope's *Memes* [1989?–1994?] pursued a combined interest in experimental writing and in spirituality and magic.

And (1954–), edited by Bob Cobbing and others, may have been infrequent and irregular but in the last three decades of the century in particular its related imprint, Writers Forum, was instrumental in disseminating a vast number of publications by a wide range of experimental poets. Indeed, the list extends from Ernst Jandl and d. a. levy through Maggie O'Sullivan and Geraldine Monk to, in recent years, Jeff Hilson and Sean Bonney. Since Cobbing's death, *And* has been edited by Adrian Clarke, with Lawrence Upton being responsible for Writers Forum. While Writers Forum favours high quality photocopying as the means of production, John Kinsella and Chris Hamilton-Emery's Salt Books, at the other end of the spectrum, aspires to a much more commercial look – something which is true of other small presses in recent years – and to a more widespread presence. The press, which is a close relation of Kinsella's magazine *Salt* (1990–), publishes a long list of UK, US, and Australian poets, with an emphasis on innovative work. Anselm Hollo, Rachel Blau du Plessis, Ron Silliman, Bruce Andrews, Charles Bernstein, David Chaloner, Allen Fisher, Andrew Duncan, Chris McCabe and John Tranter are just a few of the poets involved. Robert Sheppard's *Pages* (1987–1990, with a new series from 1994 to 1998) is another example of a magazine with late modernist/postmodernist allegiances. Interestingly it has continued as an Internet publication which, unconventionally for a poetry e-zine, uses Blog technology as its means of communication. Simon Smith's *Grille* (1992–1993) and Ralph Hawkins, John Muckle and Ben Raworth's *Active in Airtime* (1992–1995) can also be seen as significant magazines in this vein. Influenced in part by both American Language and "Cambridge School" poetry, Peter Manson and Robin Purves' *Object Permanence* (1994–1997), based in Glasgow, published experimental and exploratory poetry by Scottish, English, and North American poets. Amongst the poets included were Fanny Howe, Rosmarie Waldrop, Charles Bernstein, Leslie Scalapino, Guy Birchard, Gael Turnbull, Ian Hamilton Finlay, Thomas A. Clark, Drew Milne, Allen Fisher, John Welch, Gavin Selerie, Tony Lopez, and Ken Edwards. There was also an interest in visual poetry, reflected in the decision to feature the late dom sylvester houédard's work. Once again, out of the ashes of a magazine a small press often emerges: Manson and Purves have since continued Object Permanence as a small press imprint, with publications of J. H. Prynne, Fiona Templeton, Andrea Brady, and Keston Sutherland.

A reviewing infrastructure for experimental poetry has been more fragile and discontinuous. *Angel Exhaust* [1979–], most strongly identified with the editorship of Andrew Duncan after 1991, has had a clear tendency towards critical discussion of contemporary poetry – sometimes of a combative nature – as well as presenting the poetry itself. This emphasis has also been true of Simon Jarvis and Drew Milne's *Parataxis* [1991–] and Andrew Lawson and Anthony Mellors' *Fragmente* (1990–). All these magazines have either been, irregular, infrequent or shortlived: the Australian based online journal *Jacket*, edited by John Tranter, and the Canadian magazine *The Gig*, edited by Nate Dorward, help to ameliorate the effects of this critical partial vacuum.

Perhaps less easy to categorise, a number of presses and magazines arose in the early 1980s that published poets who don't quite seem to belong to even the loose affiliations suggested by such phrases as "Cambridge School" or "Language Poetry". Tony Frazer's Shearsman Books, based in Exeter, developed alongside *Shearsman*, the magazine he founded in 1981. Frazer is especially interested in poetry which inhabits "a state of independence" (to refer to the title of an anthology he edited for Stride in 1998), and, while there is an overlap in the authors he has published, his list is arguably more catholic than Reality Street's, for example. Emmanuel Hocquard, Marcelin Pleynet, Guy Birchard, Gustaf Sobin, Christopher Middleton, David Jaffin, Peter Dent, Kelvin Corcoran, Andrew Duncan, and Martin Anderson are some of the poets published in the magazine, and many of these are published by Shearsman Books as well. Frazer also has an interest in translation and his imprint has published works by, for instance, the Peruvian modernist César Vallejo. *Shearsman* was in abeyance while Frazer collaborated with Ian Robinson and Robert Vas Dias to produce *Ninth Decade* and *Tenth Decade* (collectively, 1983–1991), a broadly exploratory poetry journal, in many ways similar to Frazer's *Shearsman* and to *Oasis*, founded in 1969 and edited principally by the late Ian Robinson. While *Shearsman* continues in hardcopy, Frazer also produces an e-zine version, using the virtual medium to offer an expanded section of reviews.

Rupert M. Loydell is another editor and publisher, also based in the South-West, who made an impact in these years, through his magazine *Stride* (1982–1995) and its related imprint, Stride Publications. Like Frazer, he is concerned with poetry that follows on, in one way or another, from modernism, and like Frazer he is an eclectic editor who has published a wide and unusual range of writers not necessarily associated with any particular movement. To mention Robert Lax, Sheila E. Murphy, Robert Sheppard, Brian Louis Pearce, Martin A. Hibbert, Peter Redgrove, Alexis Lykiard, and William Oxley gives some indication of this diversity. David Miller, co-editor of this volume, has been a contributor to *Stride* over the years and is published by Stride Publications (as well as by Shearsman Books and Reality Street Editions). Significantly, Loydell has turned *Stride* magazine into a solely e-zine production.

Another of these almost uncategorisable eclectic magazines, *The Poet's Voice* was begun by Fred Beake in 1982 and, with the added editorship of James Hogg and Wolfgang Görtschacher, continued until 2000, when it was effectively superseded by Görtschacher's *Poetry Salzburg Review*. It featured poets who, whatever their aesthetic allegiances, were thought to have been unfairly neglected: consequently, experimentalists like Bill Griffiths, Eric Mottram, and Barry MacSweeney can be found in the magazine, together with formal or conservative poets, such as Donald Ward or William Oxley. Associated presses are Beake's Mammon Press and James Hogg's and Wolfgang Görtschacher's University of Salzburg Press (later Poetry Salzburg). PQR (*Poetry Quarterly Review*) (1995–), edited by Derrick Woolf and Tilla Brading, has had a similarly open editorial stance in the poets it has published, while devoting most of its space to reviews of contemporary poetry. Tim Allen's *Terrible Work* (1993–2000) also pursued more exploratory poetry, and again saw the need for critical discourse to contextualise the poets it favoured: it gave over considerable space to reviewing. *Terrible Work*, in fact, has since become an e-zine completely devoted to poetry reviews. Steven Holt, Harry Gilonis, Richard Leigh, and Richard Barrett brought a wide-ranging concern with the arts, not just poetry, to *Eonta* (1991–1994), though poetry – of an exploratory or experimental nature – remained central to the magazine. Again, there was an emphasis on informed discussion of writing and other art forms, especially music.

Patricia Oxley's *Acumen* (1985–) and *Other Poetry* (1978–1989, 1995–), edited by Anne Stevenson, Evangeline Paterson and others, have each been very deliberately concerned with the notion of an independent approach to poetry, though at the same time tending to avoid experimentalism. Some other magazines have found a way of opening up an interesting space for poetry in the context of specialised interests: Stephen C. Middleton's *Ostinato* (1989–1993) and Peter Thomas, Anne Cluysenaar and others' *Scintilla* (1997–) come to mind, with their declared concerns with, respectively, jazz and Henry and Thomas Vaughan. *Survivors' Poetry Newsletter*, founded in 1998, later *Poetry Express*, is published by Survivors Poetry, an organisation aimed at helping survivors of mental distress through the encouragement of poetry writing and performance and other creative activity. Interestingly, it acknowledges the prevalence of mental health problems in writers, while asserting writing's therapeutic qualities.

While our survey recorded no new little magazines with an explicitly feminist stance in this period, eleven new magazines featured what the magazines identified as "Women's writing" and journals such as *Writing Women* (1981–1998) and *Mslexia*, begun in 1999, clearly emerge from a feminist tradition.

After Eric Mottram's editorship from 1971–1977, *The Poetry Review* reverted to a relatively conservative poetry platform, with a succession of editors, perhaps most notably Peter Forbes. Although Forbes was not an enthusiast for experimental poetry, he did bring a distinctive approach and look to *The Poetry Review* during his long tenure (1986–2002). His promotion of the New Generation Poets, who included the now well-known Simon Armitage and Carol Ann Duffy, was a significant media moment in the history of the wider reception of poetry in the United Kingdom, and the New Generation poets – though not likely to be categorised as experimental – varied considerably in their aesthetics. Running parallel with *Poetry Review* in the eighties and nineties was *Verse*, originally based in Oxford, but essentially a Scottish and American magazine, founded by Robert Crawford, Henry Hart, and David Kinloch in 1984. As well as publishing and interviewing many of the New Generation poets before and after their relative celebrity, it published an international range of poets from Les A. Murray to the American avant-garde (and many in translation).

PN Review, edited principally by Michael Schmidt and based in Manchester, grew out of the 1960s magazine *Carcanet* and was and is similarly catholic. Schmidt's Carcanet Press has marketing and distribution presence and a more commercial look – in fact, it could be seen as less a small press than one that occupies a middle ground between the small presses and the mainstream publishers. Schmidt's list mixes mainstream with more exploratory or innovative writing, and British poets with those from across the world. Carcanet has published Charles Olson, Tom Raworth, John Riley, R. F. Langley, Edwin Morgan, and the experimental novelist Christine Brooke-Rose, alongside Anthony Hecht, Sophie Hannah, Les A. Murray, and C. H. Sisson, as well as F. T. Prince and

Penelope Shuttle. It has also published a substantial list of Scottish poets, including Iain Crichton Smith, Hugh MacDiarmid, Frank Kuppner, Iain Bamforth, David Kinloch, and co-compiler of this volume, Richard Price. PN *Review* has been notable for, amongst other things, its features on Laura (Riding) Jackson, George Barker, John Ashbery, Donald Davie, Charles Tomlinson, and Thom Gunn.

On the other side of the Pennines, the data suggest that there was something of a Yorkshire Renaissance in these years. Yorkshire towns and cities are especially noticeable as little magazine locations, all repeating or substantially increasing their new title count compared with the performance of these towns in the Sixties and early Seventies. Six new titles are recorded from Hebden Bridge, five from Huddersfield, nine from York and no less than 12 each from Leeds and Sheffield. This fertility of titles can surely be mapped to the rise of a Yorkshire scene, from which figures such as Simon Armitage emerge. Key titles included Peter Sansom and Janet Fisher's The North (1986–) and Geoff Hattersley's The Wide Skirt (1986–1997). Both also set up associated presses, respectively, Smith/Doorstop Books and The Wide Skirt Press.

As previous chapters have reported, from at least the Fifties London ceased to be the place of publication for the majority of poetry magazines: the Yorkshire phenomenon is part of this decentralising trend. Only 24% of those recorded in our survey were produced in London in the Fifties; 23% were recorded for the period 1960–1975. There is a similar proportion for the period 1976–2000, when only about 22% of little magazines were published in the English capital. In the last decades of the century most university towns, such as Exeter (7 new titles), Newcastle (11), Birmingham (13), Glasgow (13), Dublin (19), Edinburgh (22), Cambridge (25) and Oxford (27) produced new titles at about the same rate as they did in the preceding period, though Hull and Bristol seem to have produced quite a bit more (9 new Hull titles compared to 2; and 18 new Bristol titles compared to 6). The Kent towns of Canterbury (6 new titles) and Maidstone (8) also made an impact and again, as with Yorkshire, a cultural milieu appears to be at play here: the "Outcrowd" and Stuckist writers and artists, who included Rob Earl, Sexton Ming, and Billy Childish.

Belfast fared less well than it had in previous years, our survey recording only five new titles compared to the twelve new titles in the Sixties and early Seventies; The Honest Ulsterman, founded in 1968, nevertheless maintained its steady presence throughout this period. South of the border the story was quite different. Amongst

Irish magazines, Michael Smith and Trevor Joyce's *The Lace Curtain* [1969]–(1978) and Bendict Ryan's *Broadsheet* (1968)–[1983?] have already been mentioned as keeping alive an interest in poetry in Ireland that derived its impetus from modernism. Kevin Kieley and Maurice Scully's *The Belle* (1978–1979) and Scully's *The Beau* (1979–1981) maintained this outlook (with the veteran Irish modernist poet Brian Coffey a notable contributor to *The Beau*, alongside Scully himself and English poets John Freeman and Yann Lovelock). Scully also published a collection by Randolph Healy as part of a projected Beau Booklet Series from The Beau Press, and organised poetry readings, talks, recitals and exhibitions under the umbrella of The Beau Events in the early 1980s.

Much later in the period, Billy Mills and Catherine Walsh's *The Journal* (1998–2000) pursued a fully-fledged concern with innovative or exploratory poetry. Mills and Walsh – who also ran the small press hardPressed Poetry – included Americans Charles Bernstein, Fanny Howe, Rosmarie Waldrop, Cid Corman, and Theodore Enslin, alongside such Irish poets as Scully, Coffey, and Geoffrey Squires. The poetry scene in Ireland was rich and varied, however, and there were many Irish magazines that, while steering away from the experimental or innovative, might be described as quietly modern if not modernist. These included Leland Bardwell and others' *Cyphers* (1975–), John F. Deane's *Poetry Ireland* (1978–1980), Paul Durcan and others' *The Cork Review* (1979–1981), John Jordan and others' *Poetry Ireland Review* (1981–), John F. Deane and Jack Harte's *Tracks* (1982–1996), M.G. Allen, Jessie Lendennie and others' *The Salmon* (1982–1990), Dermot Healy's *Force 10 in Mayo* (1989–1999), and Gerald Dawe's more general literary review, *Krino* (1986–1995). *The Salmon's* imprint, Salmon Publishing, founded by Jessie Lendennie, should also be noted: it survived the magazine itself to go on to publish many new Irish authors.

Very few Welsh magazines of the last few decades can be seen as exploring innovative or exploratory poetry, but *Cabaret 246* (1983–1987), edited by John Harrison, Peter Finch, Chris Broadribb and others, incorporated work by Finch, Chris Torrance, Jeremy Hilton, and B. C. Leale. The related Red Sharks Press published collections by Broadribb, Ken Cockburn, Graham Hartill, and others. Broadribb also edited *Kite* (1986/87–1987), which included Finch, Cockburn, Lee Harwood, Allen Fisher, John Seed, and Ken Edwards. Glyn Pursglove and others' *The Swansea Review* (1986–) began as a magazine of literary criticism, but later issues placed a much greater emphasis on poetry. *The Swansea*

Review has been an eclectic journal, with contributors including D. M. Black, Peter Redgrove, Brian Louis Pearce, Rupert Loydell, William Oxley, and Peter Russell. Julian Ciepluch, Chris Bendon, Kenneth Livingstone, and Sue Moules' *Spectrum* (1982–1985) included a mixture of Welsh and non-Welsh poets, such as Sheenagh Pugh, Gillian Clarke, Penelope Shuttle, and Peter Redgrove. *Spectrum* had a related imprint, of the same name, and published collections by Moules, Bendon, and Norman Jope. Other magazines active in the period included Tony Curtis and Mike Parnell's *Madog* (1977–1981) and David Fellows and Brian Phillips' *Maximum Load* [1984–1986?], while *Poetry Wales* (1965–) continued to be influential. *Poetry Wales* has in this period published English poets like Lee Harwood and Penelope Shuttle alongside such Welsh poets as John Tripp, Sheenagh Pugh, Duncan Bush, and David Greenslade. It is also related to the well-established poetry press, Seren Books. Belinda Humfrey, Peter J. Foss, Michael Parnell, and Robin Reeves' *The New Welsh Review* (1988–) should also be mentioned here, as a general literary review with a substantial emphasis on poetry.

In Scotland, *Chapman*, founded by George Hardy and Walter Perrie in 1970, but edited for most of its life by Joy Hendry, continued to represent and champion Scottish culture in a period when hopes for Scottish devolution were initially dashed, to be joined in 1979 by *Cencrastus* with a similar remit. Some Scottish magazines in this period pursued a more aesthetically-honed approach with a sharper modernist line, the most avant-garde (and the most Anglo-American) represented by *Object Permanence*, outlined above. Alec Finlay's *Morning Star Folios* (1990–1995) paid very considerable attention to design and production values, and to the interaction between text and visual image. While there was some leaning towards poets with a minimalist approach (as such, part of a trend in this period, where several haiku-related periodicals flourished), the *Folios* display a fairly catholic range, with Friederike Mayröcker and Norma Cole as well as Ian Hamilton Finlay, Frank Samperi, and Robert Lax. The same is true of the artists included in the series, though a "spareness" is prevalent. Finlay's Morning Star Publications has mainly specialised in artists' books, while also publishing various poets, such as Thomas A. Clark, Ian Stephen, Harry Gilonis, and John Burnside, and going on to produce important documentary volumes, such as *The Order of Things: An Anthology of Scottish Sound, Pattern and Concrete Poems* (2001)

Dee Rimbaud's *Dada Dance* (1984–1989) evoked a post-Punk

spirit, while including a wide range of writers, such as Alasdair Gray, Joolz, Rupert M. Loydell, and Chris Mitchell. Rimbaud later edited *Acid Angel* [1998]–(2000), with work from Gray, Edwin Morgan, Loydell, and Tim Allen. W.N. Herbert's Oxford eighties magazine *The Gairfish* was resurrected with co-editor Richard Price as simply *Gairfish* (1990–1995), and, though publishing new Scottish writing, self-consciously took its aesthetic bearings from the high Scottish modernism of the interwar years. It published what it only half-jokingly called the "McAvant-Garde", including Tom Leonard, Frank Kuppner, Tom McGrath, Peter Manson, and, in particular, "The Informationists", namely David Kinloch, Peter McCarey, Alan Riach, Robert Crawford, and the editors themselves. Vennel Press, which Price set up with Leona Medlin, published a number of the poets associated with the magazine. Price went on to edit *Southfields* (1995–2000) with Raymond Friel (and with the involvement of David Kinloch, Peter McCarey, and Donny O'Rourke). *Southfields* incorporated the work of Scottish poets such as Edwin Morgan, Gael Turnbull, D. M. Black, Fiona Templeton, Drew Milne, Don Paterson, and Kathleen Jamie, alongside poets from England, the USA and elsewhere. It, too, had a related imprint, Southfields Press.

Other notable – and varied – Scottish magazines active during the period include Carl McDougall's *Words* (1976)–[1980], Morley Jamieson's *Bruton's Miscellany* (1977–1979), Andy Scott and Andy Keighley's *AMF (Aristophanes' Middle Finger)* [1979–1980], Hamish Whyte and others' *The Glasgow Magazine* (1982/83–1985/6), Hamish Turnbull, Andrew Fox, and Brenda Shaw's *Blind Serpent* (1984–1986) and Sally Evans' *Poetry Scotland* (1997–). *The Glasgow Magazine* and *Poetry Scotland* are both associated with poetry presses, Mariscat Press and Diehard respectively. Alexander Scott and James Aitchison's *New Writing Scotland* [1983–] has been important as a more general magazine of Scottish writing, particularly for younger writers, and is published by the otherwise academic organisation the Association of Scottish Literary Studies. The general arts magazine with a strong poetry element, *Inter Arts*, was edited by Pramesh Mehta, Colin Nicholson, and Moussa Jogee, and ran from 1986 to 1991. Gerry Cambridge's *The Dark Horse*, founded in 1995, is especially interested in traditional forms in poetry and, in alliance with Dana Gioia, publishes British and American "New Formalist" poems.

Fiction, however, was arguably the overwhelmingly important literary artform in this period for Scotland, and its prominence would have repercussions throughout the United Kingdom. The

reincarnation of *The Edinburgh Review* (1985–) produced a particularly strong supporter of the Glasgow writers Alasdair Gray,
James Kelman, Agnes Owens, and Tom Leonard who saw relative
celebrity in these years and whose work has been so influential for
later Scottish writing. This influence was more than consolidated
with the Edinburgh magazine *Rebel Inc*, founded by Kevin
Williamson in 1992 (and publishing poetry as well as fiction).
Williamson championed Irvine Welsh many months before the
publication of *Trainspotting* and so contributed to a major intervention in the cultural landscape of Scottish and British fiction.

The years that close our survey see a falling off of new titles. The
only time in which new titles fall below twenty titles per year is in
the very last years of the survey (18 titles in 1999 and 14 titles in
2000). These years also record enough closures to give significant
deficits in net new titles – when "deaths" exceed "births" (–10 and
–8 respectively). Competition with fiction is not likely to be the
culprit: rather, a stronger hypothesis would be that the rise of the
Web has meant that e-zines, not recorded by this bibliography,
have begun to take over from printed magazines. It is too early to
be elegiac about the printed little magazine but if this is a trend,
then the Digital Age will surely supply a successor virtually, with
surely no less interest.

& *See* Ampersand E26

4word Magazine *See* [Four Word Magazine]
4word Magazine E297

10th Muse *See* Tenth Muse E825

1 **A.** Hackney, London: [No. 1–?, 198?]

Large-format visual work rendered like a calendar.
Contributors include Roger Ely.

King's College London, Eric Mottram Archive: 3 (1985).
(7/5/1 1985)

2 **A–3 Broadsheet** / edited by George
Roberts and Jo Lloyd. Oxford: Oxford Poetry
Society, [Vol.] 1 no. 1 (1985)–vol. 2 no. 5 (1987)

Note: Variant title: *A–3*

Poetry Library

A4 Anonymous *See* Responses E691

3 **Aabye** / edited by Gerald England. Hyde:
New Hope International, Issue A (1998)–C
(2000). ISSN: 1461–6033

Note: Continues: *New Hope International Writing* which was
part of *New Hope International Review* (NHI)
Website: www.nhi.clara.net/nhihome.htm

BL: ZK.9.a.6814
UCL
Poetry Library

4 **AbeSea: a visual paper** / edited by
Sebastian Boyle. London, Issue a [199–?]–e
(1994)

Note: Issues are given a running letter which is sometimes
also meant to be the title.

The first and second issues are called a and b respectively.

BL: C. (LB.31.c.7432); D. (LB.31.c.7433)
CUL: A–D. (L999.a.1.71)
NLS: C. (8.75); D (8.75)
TCD: C. (LB Folio Case: 2554)
Poetry Library: E

5 **Academus Poetry Magazine** / edited
by Don Hale. [Cheltenham], No. 1 (1979).
ISSN: 0143–7488

BL: P.903/606
CUL: L999.B.1.740
NLS: QP4.82.1317 PER
TCD: PER 90–389
UCL: 1

6 **Accidents & Devotions.** Cwmbran /
Bridgend: Speed Limit Press, [No. 1, 1977/8]

"The magazine of the Creative Writing Class, Cardiff
University Extra-Mural Department." Appears to continue
Madoc. The contributors were Gill Brightmore, Edwin
James, John Griffiths, Jane Verby, Ruth Verby, Edward
Sweeney, Adrianne Hawkins, Angela Roberts, Mark
Williams (tutor), and the guest writers Chris Torrance and
Jeremy Hilton.

BL: P.901/315
NLS: P.med.3770 PER
UCL
Poetry Library

7 **Acid Angel** / edited by Dee Rimbaud.
Glasgow, No. 1 [1998]–3 (May 2000)

NLS: HJ8.1850 PER
Poetry Library

8 **Active in Airtime** / edited by Ralph Hawkins, John Muckle and Ben Raworth. Colchester: [Active in Airtime], 1 (1992)–4 (1995). ISSN: 0967–8190

Related Imprint: Active Imprint published individual collections by, e.g. Ralph Hawkins and Clark Coolidge

BL: ZC.9.a.5025
UCL
Poetry Library

9 **The Activity Echo** / edited by Trish Thomas. Bognor Regis, No. 1–3 (1994)

Poetry Library

10 **Acumen** / edited by Patricia Oxley; with William Oxley, Glyn Pursglove, Danielle Hope. Brixham: Ember Press, No. 1 (1985)– . ISSN: 0964–0304

Interview: with Patricia Oxley in Görtschacher 1
Related Imprint: Acumen have also published individual poetry collections

BL: ZH.9.a.8
CUL: 1–10 (Oct. 1989); 15 (Apr. 1992)– . (L727.C.1049)
NLS: 1–10 (Oct. 1989); 15 (Apr. 1992)–16 (Oct. 1992). (DJ.s.200 PER)
TCD: 1–16 (Oct. 1992). (PER 92–746 1985–1992)
UCL
Poetry Library

11 **Admiral Connor's Hot True Steamy Confessions Quarterly.** Wissett, nr. Haleworth, [1987?]

Prose and some verse. Listed in *Zenos* 7.

No holdings known

12 **Advent** / [edited by Brian Coffey]. Southampton: Advent Books, No. I (1976)–VI (1976)

Related Imprint: Advent Books published individual collections and, beginning in 1968, had published the *Advent poems* series, devoted to a single poem each publication.

More a series of individual booklets, *Advent* was edited by the distinguished Irish poet Brian Coffey. [No.] VI was the most magazine-like issue, featuring work devoted to

another important Irish modernist poet and associate of Coffey's, Denis Devlin.

BL: II. (X.950/35568); III. (YA.1996.a.15803)
CUL: I–II; IV–VI (L727.C.976)
Poetry Library: VI

13 **The Affectionate Punch: Manchester's new literary/arts magazine** / edited by Andrew Tutty. Manchester, No 1 (1995)–15 (2000). ISSN: 1360–9556

BL: ZK.9.a.4264
Poetry Library

14 **The Agent** / edited by Georgette Munday. London: New Agency, no. 1 (July 1979)–?

Note: Succeeds: *The Transcendental Exhibitionist Review; Invisible Art; Relevant Material*
Related Imprint: News Agency also produced a largely prose broadsheet, *News Agency Sheet* [1978?–?], BL: Pressmark pending
Texts of a Dadaist and Surreal nature.

BL: 1–3 (Pressmark pending)

15 **Agog.** London: Agog Publications, No. [1, 198–?]–[4?, 1990?]

Poetry and short fiction. Agog Publications also issued *Agog Ago Go*, a little magazine on a personal computer disk.

BL: 2 [1988?]. (ZA.9.a.6964)
Poetry Library: 2 [1988?]–[4, 1990?]

16 **Aion: a review of new poetry, composition and modern art** / edited by Paul Liclés. London, No. 1–3 (1994)

Poetry Library

17 **Air.** Glasgow, No. 1 (Summer 1998)– .

BL: ZK.9.a.6229
NLS: HJ8.3150

18 **Air Space** / edited by Carol Bruggen and A. E. Horsfield. Briercliffe: Air Space, 1 (1983)–? ISSN: 0264–1836

The first issue, which may have been the only issue, includes poetry by Vernon Scannell, Eric Mottram, and others.

BL: 1. (P.903/1115)
CUL: 1. (L727.B.424)

19 Aireings: the magazine for Yorkshire writers and poets / edited by Jean Barker. Leeds: Aireings Publications, No. 1 (1980)–? ISSN: 0261–0124

Note: A supplement, *Aireloom*, edited by Jean Barker, appeared in 1990.

BL: P.901/3271
CUL: L727.d.321
NLS: 2–37. (P.la.9621 PER)
UCL
Poetry Library: 8–

20 Albab: review of Islamic & Western arts. Harlow: Arts Arabic / The Antiphon Press, Vol. 1 no. 1 (1977)–?

Contains some contemporary poetry.

UCL

ALI *See* Avon Literary Intelligencer E71

21 All The Poets / edited by Mark Schlössberg and John Tottenham. London: Spanish Magic Productions, Vol. 1 (1979)–2 (1980)

UCL
Poetry Library: 2

22 Allusions / edited by Jon Catt, Steve Lewis, Mark Di Angeli, and David Green. Lancaster, No. 1 (1979)–5/6 [1982]

BL: 1; 5/6. (ZA.9.A.2452)
CUL: L727.C.799
NLS: HP2.85.3711 PER
TCD: PER 92–855 1980–1982
UCL: 1–4
PL: 1–3; 5/6

23 Alternative Poets. Agnus Press, [No.1]–, [198?]–? ISSN: 0969–0263

Note: Related to *Preston Alternative Poets*

BL: 2 (1989) (ZC.9.a.2935)

24 AMF: Aristophanes' middle finger / edited by Andy Scott and Andy Keighley. Dundee: Dundee University Writers Workshop, No. 1 [1979]–4 [1980]

Note: Variant title: *AMF Magazine*. Continues: *Logos Magazine* but is then continued by *Logos Magazine*, i.e. it appears to have been an experimental title that reverted to the original

Short fiction and poetry, including Stewart Conn, G. F. Dutton, Carl MacDougall, A. D. Foote, Sheila Douglas, Iain Crichton Smith, John Herdman, Edwin Morgan, Jim [i.e. James] Kelman, Tom McGrath, Ian Stephen, Andrew Fox, Margaret Gillies, Ron Butlin, Val Warner, Gerald Mangan, David Annwn, and others. Andy Keighley joined Scott's editorship on the last issue.

BL: P.2000/800
CUL: 4. (L727.B.244)
NLS: 4. (P.la.7759 PER)
TCD: 4. (PER 78–459)
UCL

25 Ammonite: the all-new magazine of poetry, myth and science fiction / edited by John Howard. [Gillingham], Issue 1 (1987)–?

Contributors include Stephen C. Middleton, Maureen Macnaughton, and others.

BL: 1. (ZK.9.b.1255)
CUL: L198.B.159
NLS: 1–8 (Mar. 1997)

Amoral Svelte *See* Lateral Moves E431

26 Ampersand / edited by [G. Gunby?]. London: Firedog Mothers, Issue [1, 1991?]–2 (1993)

Note: Variant title: &.

Poetry Library

27 Ampersand (&) / edited by [Robin E. Wild]. Weston-super-Mare: Quickbeam Enterprise Designs, No. 1 [1981?]–?

Related Imprint: Quickbeam Enterprises

Poetry Library: 3 (1983)

28 **Anaconda** / edited by Dan Clayton. Salisbury, Issue 1 [198?]–?

CUL: 9. (1987). (L999.C.3.1005)
NLS: 9. (1987). (HP.med.261 PER)
TCD: 9. (1987). (PER 90–460)
Poetry Library: 2 (1985)

29 **Analect** / edited by Alison Chace, Dawn Patnode, Sharon Singleton, Lawrence Weber. London: Analect Press, Vol. 1 no. 1 (Spring 1978)

CUL: L999.C.3.643
UCL

30 **Anarchist Angel: youth poetry quarterly** / edited by Liz Berry. Lichfield, then Dudley, West Midlands: Anarchist Angel Press, then Angel Press, Issue [1] (1994)–8 (1997)

Poetry Library: [1]–8

31 **And Another Thing** / [edited by Myra Connell?]. Manchester: Amazon Press, [No. 1?, 1983?]

BL: [1?]. (YA.1999.a.4662)
Poetry Library: [1?]

32 **And What of Tomorrow?: a future world magazine** / edited by Jay Woodman. Selby: Woodman's Press, [No. 1] (Jan. 1992)–[8] (Oct. 1993). ISSN: 0965–3856

Related Imprint: Woodman's Press also published *Rustic Rub* as well as a small variety of poetry, prose, biography and local history publications

BL: ZK.9.a.1980
CUL: L996.C.394
NLS: DJ.s.597(2) PER
TCD: PER 95–698 1992–1993
Poetry Library: [1]–[3]

33 **Angel** / edited by Paula Bellot, Alan Edward, Roger Keeling and Rodney Sawers. London: The Creative Writing Group, St. Clements Hospital Social Club, Issue 7 [1998?]– .

Note: Continues: *Goalpost* (and continues its numbering)
Poetry Library: 7–

34 **Angel Arts Anthology**. London: Angel Arts, [No. 1] (1986). ISBN: 0951153706

BL: ZV.9.a.111
CUL: L727.C.922
NLS: HP2.87.1375
TCD: PR 12524 1986 (1987)

35 **Angel Exhaust** / edited by [Steven Pereira], Adrian Clarke, Scott Thurston, Andrew Duncan, Michael Gardiner, Helen Macdonald, Simon Smith, Maurice Scully, John Goodby, and Charles Bainbridge. [London]: [Islington Press]; Southend-on-Sea; Cambridge; then again London; No.1 [1979]– . ISSN: 0143–8050

Website: Information on several of the issues is given on Andrew Duncan's website www.pinko.org
Related Work: Andrew Duncan, *The Failure of Conservatism in Modern British Poetry* (Cambridge: Salt, 2003)

Beginning as a magazine of the Islington Poetry Workshop, *Angel Exhaust* developed beyond this small group by increasing the number of experimental poems from across Britain and carrying intellectual if sometimes intense reviews and essays, notably by Andrew Duncan. It became a key magazine for various British avant-gardes. The first two issues were edited by Steven Pereira with production by Jenny Pereira, joined in the third issue by Adrian Clarke as co-editor. Clarke and Steven Pereira co-edited until their last issue, no. 7 (Summer 1987), after which the characteristic A4 typescript format was dropped forever. No. 8 was a perfect-bound A5 'book', surfacing after a five year break (Autumn 1992) with Pereira replaced by Andrew Duncan, though still with Clarke as co-editor. Scott Thurston joined them for no. 9 (Summer 1993), and Macdonald and Gardiner joined the team on no. 10 (Spring 1994). By no. 12 Duncan was editing alone, but he was joined by Simon Smith for no. 16. In 1999, what looked like the last issue, no. 17, was guest edited by Maurice Scully and John Goodby, a feature on Irish modernist poetry. However, Duncan returned with co-editor Charles Bainbridge to resurrect the magazine in 2005 with the 18th issue.

BL: 1–3; 6–12; 15– . (P.903/620)
CUL: 2–3; 6– . (L727.b.334)
NLS: 2–3; 8– . (P.la.9055 PER)
TCD: 2–3; 8–15. (PER 92–861 1980–1999)

UCL: 3–4; 8–17
Poetry Library: 1–4; 8–

36 Angelaki. Oxford: Angelaki, Vol.1 no. 1 (1993)– . ISSN: 0969–725X

BL: ZC.9.a.4033
CUL: L900.C.664
NLS: HJ4.919
TCD: PER 72–234

37 Angels of Fire / edited by Penelope Hoff and Jeremy Silver. London: The Angels of Fire Collective, No.1 (1983)–2 (1984)

Anthology: Sylvia Paskin, Jay Ramsay, and Jeremy Silver, *Angels of Fire: an anthology of radical poetry in the '80s* (London: Chatto & Windus, 1986), BL: YC.1986.a.2265

BL: 2 (ZC.9.b.420)
UCL

38 [Ankle Press] / edited by Steven Wasserman and Luke Youngman. Cambridge: Ankle Press, [No. 1, 1992?]–[4] (1994)

Note: Each issue has an individual title: [1], *Bleb Residue*; [2], *Elephant Candy*; [3], *Punk at the Opera*; [4], *The Boy Detective*. Related imprint: Ankle Press

Poetry Library: [2] (1993)–[3] (1994)

39 Anomie: the magazine of the English Literature Society. Dublin: [English Literature Society, University College Dublin], [1] (1995/96)

Note: Continued by *Samizdat*

BL: ZK.9.b.11350
CUL: L727.B.370

Anonatextosaurus *See* Responses E691

40 Anthem: the Rand Society magazine / edited by Martin Tatham, Carl Hufton and Howard Roake. Nottingham: Rand Society of Poets, No. 1 [1985?]–?

UCL: 5–
Poetry Library: 1–4, 7, 10, 13

41 Anthill / edited by Astrid Wilson. London: Sarum Press, No. 1 (Jan. 1977)–3 (1977)

Index: Indexed by the UK Little Magazines Project
Profiled in: Notes attached to the index by the UK Little Magazines Project

"The policy of this magazine is to publish poetry and prose of an aesthetic that relates firstly to the tradition of English Lyrical Poetry, particularly with regard to the tone adopted by the poet, and by his choice of subject matter. In the lyric, life is approached primarily from a joyous, celebratory point of view. The stance adopted by the poet is: 'I sing about...' Herrick's introduction to 'Hesperides' is a very good example of this." – Astrid Wilson, in the first issue. Other acknowledged points of reference include Imagism, Concrete Poetry, and the writers linked with Tarasque Press, *Aggie Weston's*, and Coracle Press (Simon Cutts, Stuart Mills, and others).

BL: 1–2. (ZA.9.a.10803)
UCL
Poetry Library

42 Antwerpen 2000 / edited by Johan de Wit. London: Johan de Wit, No.1 (1991)–4 [1994]. ISSN 0964–6493

BL: ZK.9.b.4168

43 Ape. London: Ape, No. 1 (1997)–9 (2000). ISSN: 1368–2954

Note: Continued as: *The Illustrated Ape*

Short stories, poetry, illustration and graphic design.

BL: ZK.9.D.1411
Poetry Library: 1

44 Apocalipps / edited by Remi Abbas. [U.K.]: Urban Poets Society / Do Not Chew Upon This Productions, Vol. 1 (1994)

Poetry Library: 1

45 Apostrophe. Faversham: Mr. Pillows' Press, No. 1 (Spring 1991)–17 (Spring 1999). ISSN: 0967–1803

BL: ZK.9.a.2280
Poetry Library: 2–?

46 APT: Artists, Poets and Thinkers Group. Ramsgate: A.P.T. Group, [1] (Aug. 1994) ISSN: 1356–6776

BL: ZK.9.a.3828

47 Aquarius: poetry, music, anecdotes, art... / edited by H. P. Carpenter. London, [1, 198?]–2 (1988)

Poetry Library

48 Aquarius: poetry magazine / edited by John Teverson. Beckenham: Aquarius Poetry, No. 1 (1990)–27 (1993). ISSN: 0961–4486

BL: ZK.9.b.3838
Poetry Library: 2–27

49 Yr Aradr: clychgrawn Cymdeithas Dafydd ap Gwilym Rhydychen. [Oxford: Oxford Welsh Society], Vol. 1 (1991)–7 (1996)

BL: ZK.9.b.8532
CUL: 6–7. (L485.B.111)
NLS: 5–7. (HJ9.1264 PER)
TCD: 5–7. (PX–106–423)

50 The Arcadian / edited by Mike Boland. Harrow: Gothic Garden Press, No.1 (1991)–11 (2001). ISSN: 0969–2320

Note: Variant title: *The Arcadian Poetry Magazine*

BL: ZK.9.b.4513
CUL: 1–3. (L999.B.1.2437)
NLS: HP.la.2624 SER
TCD: 4–11. (PER 88–100)
Poetry Library

51 Archangel / edited by Simon Miles. Radford, Nottingham, No. 1 [1986?]–?

Poetry Library: 6 [1991?]

52 Archeus / edited by D. S. Marriott. London, No. [1]–6 (1989)

Index: Indexed by the UK Little Magazines Project
Profiled in: Notes attached to the index by the UK Little

Magazines Project

Poems, essays and reviews with a focus on avant-garde and "Cambridge school" poetry. Contributors included: Anthony Barnett, Charles Bernstein, Andrew Duncan, Paul Green, Rod Mengham, John Wilkinson and others.

UCL: [1]–6

53 Areopagus: a Christian-based arena for creative writers / edited by Julian Barritt. Winchester, No. 1 (199?)– . ISSN: 1351–5063

BL: 14 (July 1993)– . (ZC.9.b.5587)
Poetry Library: 38 (Summer 1999)–

54 Areté: the arts tri-quarterly: fiction poetry reportage reviews / edited by Craig Raine, Anne Pasternak Slater and Jeremy Noel-Tod. Oxford, No. 1 (Winter 1999)– .

BL: ZC.9.A.5915
CUL: Periodicals Dept
NLS: HJ3.2070 SER
TCD: PER 103–676
Poetry Library

55 Argo / edited by Hilary Davies and others. Oxford: c/o Evie Versieux, Wadham College, then Argo Publishing Co., Vol. 1 no. 1 (Summer 1979)–vol. 8 no. 2 (1988). ISSN: 0143–0246

Note: *Argo* merged with *Delta* in 1981 with Vol. 3 no. 2, which is also designated *Delta* [No.] 63

BL: P.901/3166
CUL: L727.c.763
NLS: DJ.s.217
TCD: PER 91–327
UCL: Vol. 1 no. 1–vol. 3 no. 3; vol. 4 no. 2–vol. 6 no. 1
Poetry Library

56 The Argotist: a deeply dilettante review / edited by Nick Watson. Liverpool, No. 1 [1996]–3 [2000?]. ISSN: 1360–3515

BL: ZK.9.a.4655
CUL: 1–2. (L999.b.1.2376)
NLS: 1–2. (HJ9.2448 PER)
Poetry Library

57 Arima / edited by Clive Fencott and Lawrence Upton. London, 1 (1976)

"A magazine devoted to all kinds of poetry by school-children."

King's College London, Eric Mottram Archive: 7/48/1 1976

58 Art-icu-lit. [Norwich]: P & P Productions, Premier issue (1995); Futurist issue (1998)

BL: Premier issue. (ZK.9.b.9087)
CUL: Premier issue. (L999.b.1.2849)
NLS: HJ9.1977 PER
TCD: PER 88–12 1995–1998

59 Artifact: painting photography poetry writing music pottery / edited by B. G. Simmonds. London: W. E. Anderton, Issue 1 (1976). ISSN: 0309–202X

BL: P.425/109
CUL: L999.B.1.409
UCL

60 Aspects of Life / by Joan Hardwick. [Peterborough]: [J. Hardwick], Vol. 1 [1992?]–5 [1996?]. ISSN 0969–1979.

Collections of the author's own poems in traditional metre.

BL: ZK.9.a.2570

61 The Asphalt Jungle. Leicester: Future Noir, No. 0 [Pilot issue, Feb. 1998]–3 [Spring 1999]. ISSN 1465–7600

Largely a short story magazine, with just one or two poems per issue. As the title suggests, an urban setting to most of the work.

BL: [Dec. 1998], 3 [Spring 1999]. (ZK.9.a.6188)

62 Asylum: arts review. Tralee: Tralee Vocational Education Committee, No. 1 (Aug. 1995)–6 (1998). ISSN 1393–256X

BL: 2 (Winter 1996). (ZC.9.b.6328)
CUL: 2 (Winter 1996). (L999.b.1.2740)
NLS: 1 (Aug. 1995)–3 (1996). (HJ9.2096 PER)
TCD: PER 92–327 1995–1998

63 At Last: a community based literary magazine from West Fife... / edited by "an editorial panel of local writers". Kincardine-on-Forth, Fife: Pen2Paper Publications, No. 1 (1995)–10 (Winter 1999)

NLS: HJ4.1401 PER
UCL: 1, 3–

64 Atlantic Review: British and American writing / [New Series] edited by Robert Vas Dias. London: Antioch International Writing Seminars; Antioch International Writing Programs, Vol. 1 no. 1 (1975/76), [New Series], No. 1 (1979)–3 (1980). ISSN: 0142–7024

Note: Merged with *Oasis* and *Shearsman* to form *Ninth Decade*

BL: [New Series], No. 1–3. (P.901/3195)
CUL: [New Series], No. 1–3. (L999.C.3.812)
NLS: [New Series], No. 1–3. (5917/C PER)
TCD: [New Series], No. 1–3. (PER 81–197)
UCL
Poetry Library

65 Atlas / edited by Jake Tilson. London: The Woolley Dale Press, No. 1 (1985)–4 [1989?]

Related Imprint: Woolley Dale Press published individual collections of experimental writing, especially by Jake Tilson, and the magazine *Cipher.*

Jake Tilson later brought together the four issues of this essentially art little magazine in a boxed set, with a video, bibliography of publications by Tilson and various other associated works including postcards and postage stamps.

BL: Boxed set (RF.2002.c.29). Video (Cup.936/1390)
CUL: 1–3. (Periodicals Dpt.)
NLS: 1–3. (DJ.m.789(1))
TCD: 1–3. (PER 91–742)
UCL

66 Atlas Anthology / edited by Alastair Brotchie, Malcolm Green, Anthony Melville and Terry Hale. London: Atlas Press, No. 1 (1983)–7 (1991)

Note: May have continued after No. 7.
Related Imprint: Atlas Press, publisher of many translations of works associated with Romanticism, Symbolism, Expressionism, Dada, early Surrealism and

various continental European post-war avant-gardes.
Website: www.atlaspress.co.uk/

The first volume was an A4 anthology with typescript pro-
duction values. Subsequent volumes were shorter in height,
had more pages, and were more attractively produced.
Some were not anthologies at all – no. 5 was *Death to the
Pigs: Selected Writings of Benjamin Perét*, no. 7 was *Raymond
Roussel: Selections from his Writings*.

BL: 1–4; 6. (P.705/311). 5. (YC.1989.a.8350). 7.
(YA.1997.a.9537)
CUL: 2 (1984)–7. (L700.c.278)
NLS: 2 (1984)–7. (HP.med.40)
TCD: 2–3. (PR 12450 1984–1985)
UCL: 1–7

67 **Aura: Manchester.** Manchester:
Modern Literature Group, University of
Manchester, No. 1 (Jan. 1993). ISSN
0968–1736

BL: 1. (ZC.9.a.3600)

68 **The Auteur: the new wave in arts
magazines.** London: The Auteur, Vol. 1,
no. 1 [Winter 1992/93]– no. 2 (Spring 1993).
ISSN 0968–7289

BL: Vol. 1 no. 1. (ZC.9.b.5201)
CUL: L999.b.1.1762
NLS: D.J.m.1912(4) PER
TCD: PER 86–856

69 **Avaganda Magazine** / edited by Albert
Benson. Liverpool: Avaganda Magazine, 1st
edition [i.e. No. 1], 1995. ISSN: 1361–3596

BL: ZK.9.b.8981
Poetry Library: I

70 **Avalon.** Merthyr Tydfil: Vampyric Press,
[No.1, 1995?–7?, 1998] . ISSN 1363–0741
Related Imprint: Vampyric Press also published *Miscellany:
a magazine of literary reviews*

BL: 3–7. (ZK.9.a.4589)

71 **Avon Literary Intelligencer: poetry,
fictions, criticism, news** / edited by
Daniel Richardson. Bristol, [1994?–1996?]

Note: Variant title: *ALI*

Poetry Library: Oct. 1994, Jan. 1995, Apr. 1995, July 1996

72 **Awen** / [edited by Kaledon Naddair].
Edinburgh: Keltia, [No. 1, 1985]–? ISSN:
0268–5736
Note: Variant title: *Search for Awen* was the title of the first
issue.

"A bardic magazine dedicated to poetry keltic, pagan or
with a reverence for nature."

BL: 1. (X.529/72694). 2. (ZC.9.a.1958)
CUL: 2 (1987). L999.c.3.1498
NLS: 1. (HP.sm.893 PER). 2. (DJ.s.713(6) PER)

73 **Awen** / edited by David-John Tyrer.
Southend-on-Sea: Atlantean Press, [1999?]– .
ISSN: 1741–9719
Index: Contents listings of some of the issues are given at
the website
Related Imprint: Atlantean Press also publishes *Garbaj*,
Monomyth and poetry booklets
Website: www.geocities.com/dj_tyrer/

BL: 6 (Oct. 2000)– . (ZK.9.b.17204)

74 **AX5: the student art magazine** /
edited by Tim Arrowsmith. London: Byam
Shaw School of Art, [No. 1, 1981?–3?, 1981?].
ISSN: 0262–7051

Listed here for its inclusion of poetry, as a student-
produced art school magazine it can be compared with
(e.g.) *Accent*, *It's: Wimbledon School of Art Magazine*, *Mute* and
The Slade Magazine. It may have continued after 1981.

BL: 2 (1981). (P.421/777)
Poetry Library: [3?], with *Poetry Pullout*

75 **Aynd** / edited by Duncan Glen. Radcliffe-
on-Trent, Nottingham: Aynd, No. 1 (1983)–17
(1986)

BL: P.903/902
CUL: L727.b.271
NLS: DJ.m.71 PER
UCL: 1–3; 5–17.
Poetry Library: 1–3; 5–17

76 Backchat: the Bury writers' magazine / edited by Alan Jowett. Bury: Bury Writers' Group, No. 1–3, 1978

UCL

B.A.D *See* Breakfast All Day E126

77 Bad Poetry Quarterly: a magazine of bloody awful writing / edited by Greg Rampley and Gordon Smith. London, No. 1 (1994)–212? (July 1999). ISSN: 0954–7827

Note: Issued weekly, despite title. Additional subtitle: *Fine writing for the 90s*. Nos. 57–60, 72–93, 112–113 appear not to have been published.

BL: 56–71;, 97; 100–212. (ZK.9.b.8612)
CUL: 56–212. (L727.b.394)
NLS: 56–212. (HJ9.1859 PER)
TCD: 55–212. (PER 92–557 1995–1999)
Poetry Library: 1–16; 18, 23; 29; 34–37; 55/56; 61–62; 94; 97; 100; 109; 111; 114; 128–129; 138; 148; 158–159; 162–164; 166–170; 172; 180; 185–186; 188; 190–192; 194–198; 200–206; 209–

78 Bad Seeds: the bad seed review / edited by Martin Myers. Newcastle upon Tyne: Bad Seed Press, Issue 1 (1987). ISSN: 0951–4929

Related Imprint: Bad Seed Press also published *The Soup Kitchen*

BL: ZC.9.a.1439
CUL: L999.c.3.1001
NLS: DJ.m.143(10) PER
TCD: PER 90–595
Poetry Library

79 Baetyl: the journal of women's literature / [edited by Sarah Francis?]. London: Baetyl Press, Issue 1 (Autumn 1993)–4 (1994). ISSN 1351–9298

BL: ZC.9.a.3671
CUL: 1–3. (L700.c.425)
NLS: 1–3. (HJ4.975 PER)
TCD: 1–3. (PER 95–381 1993–1994)

80 Bananas from the Windward Islands: a new poetry magazine / edited by Adrian Slatcher. Manchester, Issue 1 (1997)

Poetry Library

Bandito *See* Codex Bandito E183

81 Bang: Southend's art magazine / edited by John Vidler. Southend: Bang Collective, [No. 1, 1977?–6, 1979?]

CUL: 5. (L999.c.3.1387)
Poetry Library: 3; 5–6

82 Banipal: magazine of modern Arab literature / edited by Margaret Obank. London: No. 1 (1998)– . ISSN: 1461–5363.

Interview: Margaret Obank, interviewed anonymously, in *Poetry News: the Newsletter of the Poetry Society*, Autumn 2005, p.8

BL: ZC.9.b.7097
CUL: L830.b.42 [p/hole: X.104]
NLS: HJ8.1673 SER
TCD: PER 101–184
Poetry Library

83 Bare Bones: a quarterly magazine devoted to haiku and other forms of poetry in miniature / edited by Brian Tasker. Frome, Somerset, No. 1 (1991)–8 (1995). ISSN: 0966–1085

BL: ZC.9.a.3610
UCL: 5–8
Poetry Library

84 Bare Nibs / edited by Tracy Bateley, Des de Moor, John Webber and Steve Woollard. Ware: Ware Arts Centre / Bare Nibs Productions, No. 1 (1983)–13 (1986). ISSN: 0264–6137

Note: Continues: *Harteforde Poets Journal*

BL: P.901/3410
CUL: 4–13. (L718.c.376)
NLS: DJ.s.67 PER
Poetry Library: 3, 5–13

85 Bare Wires. Rotherham: Blue Rose Book Press, Spring 1990–Summer 1991. ISSN 0955–2529

Related Imprint: Blue Rose Book Press also published anthologies in the Blue Rose Pocket Poetry series.

BL: ZC.9.a.1967

86 The Bark and the Bite: a literary magazine / edited by Lalage Charlotte Phillips and Richard Grove. Bristol then Oxford, 1 (1977)–3 (1979)

CUL: 2. (L999.b.1.533)
UCL
Poetry Library: 2

87 Bark Magazine / edited by Mark Hudson, Martin Jennings and Jerry Arron. London, No. 1 (Dec. 1981)–Summer 1982

CUL: L999.b.1.739
NLS: No. 1 (HP.la.256 PER)

88 Barrow Poems. London: Barrow Publications, No. 1 (1976)

This magazine consists of poems by William Bealby-Wright, Gerard Benson, and Cicely Herbert.

Poetry Library: 1

88a Beat Scene / edited by Kevin Ring. Binley Woods, nr. Coventry: Beat Scene, No. 1 (Early Summer 1988)–

Website: www.beatscene.net

"A new independent magazine packed with all the names from the alternative and often underground world of American writing, films, music, art – you name it." – from the first issue.

BL: 1–5; 12; 15– . (ZA.9.b.2819)
UCL: 1–4; 6–31; 33– .

89 The Beau / edited by Maurice Scully. Dublin: The Beau, No. 1 (1981)–3 (1983/84)

Note: Variant title: Beau
Profiled in: Tom Clyde, Irish Literary Magazines: an outline and descriptive bibliography (Dublin: Irish Academic Press, 2003),

BL: 2725.g.3414
Related Imprint: The Beau published The Beau Booklet Series, which included Randolph Healy's 25 Poems (1983), BL: YC.1987.a.5561

Contributors include Anthony Cronin, Gavin Ewart, E. O Tuairisc, Ewart Milne, Brian Coffey, Rita Kelly, David Wright, Paul Durcan, John Jordan, Michael Mulcahy, and others. A successor to The Belle.

BL: 2. (ZD.9.a.70)
CUL: 1. (L999.c.3.902)
NLS: 1. (P.la.10,044 PER)
TCD: 1–2. (PER 90–173 1982–1983)
UCL: 1–3
Poetry Library: 1.

90 The Belle: a quarterly journal of belles-lettres / edited by Kevin Kiely and Maurice Scully. Dublin: No. 1 (Autumn 1978)–2 (1979)

Profiled in: Tom Clyde, Irish Literary Magazines: an outline and descriptive bibliography (Dublin: Irish Academic Press, 2003), BL: 2725.g.3414

Perhaps named in reaction to The Bell of the 1940s and 50s. Maurice Scully's The Beau would later succeed The Belle.

BL: P.901/3199
CUL: 1–2. (L999.c.3.791)
NLS: HP2.82.3873 PER
TCD: OLS 192.n.43
UCL

91 Benthos / edited by Christopher Woodard. London: Benthos Publications, Vol.1 no.1 (Dec. 1985)– . ISSN 0268–9456

BL: Vol. 1 no. 2 (Jan. 1986)–no. 3 (Apr.–June 1986). (ZK.9.a.3822)

92 Bentilee Voices. [Bentilee?]: [D.Thomas?], [No. 1, 1989–2, Summer 1989]. ISSN 0958–3416

BL: ZC.9.a.2771

93 Bête Noire / edited by John Osborne. Hull: c/o Department of American Studies, University of Hull, 1 (1984)–16 [1994]

As well as publishing new poetry, interviews and articles, the magazine organised a significant reading series in Hull.

BL: ZC.9.b.3525
CUL: 1–11; 16. (L718.b.188)
NLS: 5. (DJ.m.1951(6) PER)
UCL: 8/9–14/15
Poetry Library: 2/3–12/13

94 Between the Lines: poetry, prose, reviews, news / edited by Allene Tuck.
Southampton: Polygon, No. 1 [1983?]–5 [1985?]

CUL: 1; 3. (L999.c.3.1003)
NLS: 1–3. (DJ.s.17(1) PER)
Poetry Library: 1–5

95 Beyond the Boundaries. Cardiff:
Welsh Speculative Writers Foundation, No. 2 (1994)–12 (1997). ISSN 1362–6027

Note: Continues: *Mab Sêr*

BL: 2–9; 11–12. (ZK.9.b.9323)

96 Beyond the Cloister / edited by Hugh
Hellicar. Brighton, [1992?–1994?]

Poetry Library: Autumn 1992, Summer 1993, Spring 1994

97 Big Bang / edited by Bebe Zoot. St.
Albans, No. 1 (1982)–4 (1982)

Poetry Library: 2–4

98 The Big Spoon: a magazine of new writing and the arts / edited by
Martin Mooney, Mairtin Crawford, P. J. Newland and Rudi Goldsmith. Islandmagee, Co. Antrim, [1997]

Poetry Library: Summer 1997

99 Billy Liar: from the frontlines to the frontiers. Newcastle upon Tyne: Billy
Liar, 1 (15/12/97–31/3/98)–5 (Spring 2001). ISSN 1460–8529

BL: 1–3. (ZK.9.a.5744)
CUL: UL Periodicals Department
NLS: 1–2; 5. (HJ1.89 SER)
TCD: PER 96–57

100 Bizarre Angel / edited by Emanuel Z.
March. London, No. 1 [1979]–2? [Oct 1979]

From the editorial in the second issue: "poets be warned, only the best will be accepted. Bizarre Angel is not a poetry magazine and though poetry is and will be printed, only poetry of a decadent nature, or work by new and exciting poets (excite:- to rouse emotion, agitate, to stir up, to produce electric or magnetic activity.) will be featured. As far as artists are concerned, all I can say is that I am disappointed." Poetry by Steve Lockyer, Andy Robson, Ian Seed, Andrew Darlington, and others. Arthur Moyse and Vernon King contribute illustrations and other contributors include Dave Cunliffe and Michael Moorcock.

BL: 1–2. (Pressmark Pending)
Leeds University, Brotherton Library: 2. (Special Collections English Q–0.01 BIZ)
Poetry Library: 2

101 Black Sun / edited by Bob Gale. London,
No. 1 (1977)

UCL

102 The Black Writer: a reflection of the combined creative effort. London:
The Black Writers Association, Vol. 1 no. 1 (1976)

BL: YA.1989.A.18363
Poetry Library

103 Black-beetle / edited by Tristan
Ashman. Hove, No. 1 [1977]–2 (1978); Supplement [undated]. ISSN: 0140–9808

Note: The supplement (of poetry) is given a separate ISSN, 0141–3627

BL: (P.901/3097)
CUL: (L999.b.1.588)
NLS: (P.la.6947 PER)
TCD: 1–2. (PER 92–422)
UCL: 1–2
Poetry Library: 1; Supplement

104 Blackboard Review: black arts journal / edited by Lorraine Griffiths and
Marlene Smith. Birmingham: West Midlands Ethnic Minority Arts Service (WEMAS), 1 (1989)–2 (1990). ISSN: 0957–1892

Includes poems by Cindy Artiste, Annette Reis, Georgina A. Blake, Sally Neaser, Kanta Walker, Lorna Euphemia Griffiths, and C. D. Williams, as well as articles, including pieces on black art, jazz, and C. L. R. James.

BL: 1. (ZV.9.b.191)
Poetry Library

105 Blackmore Vale Writers: verse, prose. [Dorset]: Blackmore Vale Writers, Vol. 1 (1990)–2 (1991)

BL: ZC.9.a.3504

106 Blade / edited by Jane Holland and Yvonne Lally. Port Saint Mary, Isle of Man: Issue 1 (Dec. 1995 / Apr. 1996)–8 (1998). ISSN: 1361–8164

BL: ZC.9.a.4432
NLS: HJ3.1287 PER
TCD:00 PER 83–613
UCL
Poetry Library: 1–3; 5–8

107 Bleeding Cheek / [edited by Ben Graham]. Brighton, No. 1 [1999?]–?

Noted in issue 8 of the the zine ByPass as "A dynamic zine forum for the Young Blood Poets incorporating poems, prose and art collages."

No holdings known

108 Blind Serpent: a poetry broadsheet / edited by Hamish Turnbull, Andrew Fox and Brenda Shaw. Dundee, No.1 (1984)–9 (1986). ISSN: 0266–5409

BL: P.905/244
CUL: L727.b.280
NLS: HP.la.990 PER
UCL
Poetry Library

109 Blithe Spirit: journal of the British Haiku Society / edited by Richard Goring and others. Flitwick and other locations then Wingland, Sutton Bridge: British Haiku Society, Vol. 1 no. 1 (1990)– . ISSN: 1353–3320

Website: www.haikusoc.ndo.co.uk/first.html

BL: Vol. 6 no. 1–no. 4; vol. 8 no. 1– . (ZC.9.a.5226)
CUL: Vol. 6 no. 1– . (L727.c.1348)
NLS: Vol. 6 no. 1–vol. 10 no.4; vol. 13 no. 1– . (HJ4.1847 SER)
TCD: Vol. 6 no. 1– . (PER 85–420)
Poetry Library: Vol. 1 no. 1–vol. 7 no. 1; vol. 7 no. 3– .

110 The Blue Boat / edited by Thomas A. Clark. Nailsworth: Moschatel Press, No. 1–2, 1983

No. 1 consisted of work by the American poet Robert Lax ('Nine Poems'); no. 2 was a selection of poems by the French poet Jean Follain ('Twelve Poems', in "versions by Gael Turnbull in collaboration with Jean Beaupré and Jill Iles").

CUL: 1. (L999.c.3.1017)
UCL

111 Blue Cage / edited by Paul Donnelly and Barry Fogden. Southport and Lewes, [No. 1, Summer 1992]–2 (1993). ISSN: 0966–9604

Note: There seems to have been an earlier series of this magazine, beginning in 1983, and based in Adlington, Lancashire.

BL: 1. (ZC.9.a.3597)
Poetry Library

112 Boggers All / edited by Kapitan Mog [i.e. John Elsberg?]. Filey, Yorkshire: Boggers All, No. 1 (1993)–5 (1997) . ISSN 1362–2307

A magazine that tried to recapture the spirit of Bogg, notably by using a number of original Bogg contributors, including George Cairncross and Steve Sneyd. The editorial for the first issue states: "Yes, dear Readers, poetry should be fun, not locked up in the Universities and Colleges, to be dissected by the Profs and students; it should be writ large on the street hoardings, scrawled across the pavements, recited at madcap parties, given free with the cornflakes, printed on bogg rolls: in fact it should be everywhere to be enjoyed and laughed over by everyone."

BL: 2–5. (ZK.9.b.9170)
CUL: 2–5. (L727.b.346.2–)
NLS: HJ9.937 PER
TCD: 1. (PR 19159 1(1993)); 2–5. (PER 96–577)

Boite (a cockwerk whoreage) See Le Shovelle Diplomatique E739

113 **Bookmark.** [Edinburgh]: [English Department, Moray House College of Education], 1 (May 1978)–17 (199?). ISSN: 0260–0315

BL: (Spring 1980)–17 (199?). (P.2000/847)
NLS: HJ8.804 PER
TCD: 2 (Sept.1978)–16 (1988). (PER 92–540)

114 **Boox.** Winchester: Well Worth Reading, 1 [1996?]–3 (1997)

BL: ZK.9.b.9271.
CUL: UL Periodicals Dept.
NLS: HJ9.2039 PER
TCD: PER 88–59 1996–1997

115 **Borderlines** / edited by Diana Moss, then Dave Bingham and Kevin Bamford. Shrewsbury, then Welshpool, Powys: Anglo/Welsh Poetry Society, [No.1, 1981]– . ISSN: 0951–029X

Note: Includes Members' Supplements (or Sections) to no. 17 and 25, and a Review Supplement to no. 17
Website: One of the magazines featured on www.poetrymagazines.org.uk

BL: [1]; 4; 8– (P.901/3498)
CUL: [1]–5; 18–. (L727.b.376)
NLS: 4; 5; 18–. (HP.med.353)
TCD: 18– . (PER 73–824)
UCL: 2–3
Poetry Library: 11–

116 **Borderlines** / edited by Leland Bardwell. Monaghan: County Monaghan Vocational Education Committee, [1] (1989)–

Note: Subtitle for the first anthology was "Poems by South Ulster Youth". Subsequent issues had the subtitle: "Poems by young people in the border area."

A very occasional anthology, the third volume only issued in 2000.

BL: 2– . (ZK.9.a.3788)
NLS: 1. (HP2.91.1551); 2. (HP2.95.6588); 3 (HP2.201.00566)

117 **The Bound Spiral** / edited by Mario Petrucci and G. Kremer. Enfield: Open Poetry Conventicle, No. 1 (1988)–9/10 (1996/1997). ISSN: 0955–3819

BL: ZC.9.a.2371
UCL
Poetry Library

118 **Boundary: poetry + prose** / edited by Brian Jeffrey, Ray Darlington, Yvonne Taylor and Marie Hands. Runcorn: The Kings Road Writers/ Badger Press, No. 1 (198?)–10 (1988)

Note: Variant title: *Boundary Magazine*. Variant subtitles: *A Kings Road Writers Publication; The British Alternative Workshop Magazine.*

CUL: 2–10. (L718.b.179)
NLS: 3–4; 6–10. (HP.med.237 PER)
TCD: 3–10. (PER 90–785)
Poetry Library: 6; [8?]–10

119 **Box.** Northampton, [No.] 1 [1982?]–2 [1983?]

Poetry Library: 2

120 **Box of Rain** / edited by Bill Astbury and Sharon Astbury. Leeds: Rainbox Productions; (Rainbox Publications), Issue [1] (1980)–14 (1984)

BL: ZK.9.b.1189
CUL: 2–14. (L727.c.889)
NLS: 2–14. (DJ.s.148)
UCL: 2–14
Poetry Library: 12

121 **Bradford Poetry Quarterly** / edited by Clare Chapman. [Bradford]: No. 1 [1983?]–10 (1990)

BL: 10. (ZK.9.b.4473)
CUL: 6–10. (L727.b.328)
NLS: 6–10. (DJ.m.2139(3) PER)
TCD: 6–10. (PER 91–636)
UCL: 8–10
Poetry Library: 9–10

122 **Brainwaifs** / edited by Leslie Richardson... and others. York, No. 1 (1978)–6 (1985)

Note: Variant titles: *Brainwaifs Revisited*; *Brainwaifs + Other Strays*; *Brainwaifs – Not Orphan*.

BL: 5. (YC.1998.b.2980); 6.(YH.1987.b.286)
Poetry Library: 4 (*Brainwaifs Revisited*)

123 **Branch Redd Review** / edited by Bill Sherman. London, No. 1 [1977?]–?

Note: Later issues published in the U.S.. Distributed by *Spanner* in the UK.

Contributors include: Pierre Joris, Allen Fisher, Asa Benveniste, Cid Corman, Jeremy Hilton, and others.

BL: ZA.9.a.11625
UCL: 2 (1978)

124 **Brando's Hat: poetry magazine** / edited by Steven Waling, Seán Body, Emma-Jane Arkady and Angela Topping. Manchester, then Salford: 4 Eyes Press; then Tarantula Publications, No. [1] (1988)–2 (1990), [New Series], No. 1 (1998)–12 (Spring 2002). ISSN: 0954–8858

Website: The twelve issues of the new series have been digitised and appear on www.poetrymagazines.org.uk

"Brando's Hat was launched... as an occasional magazine, by Steven Waling. In 1998 it was adopted by Sean Body's Tarantula Publications in Salford and was published three times a year until issue 12 when its publication ceased." – from the note accompanying the poetrymagazines.org.uk digitised set.

BL: [1] (ZC.9.b.3780)
UCL: [1]–2
Poetry Library: [New Series], 1–12

125 **Braquemard** / edited by David Allenby. Hull, Issue 1 [199?]– . ISSN: 1354–7356

Related Imprint: Braquemard has published the collection *Triple Whammy* by Margot K. Juby (1995), BL: YK.1996.a.8146
Website: www.braquemard.fsnet.co.uk/

BL: ZK.9.a.3754

126 **Breakfast All Day** / edited by Philip Boxall. Dieppe; London: B.A.D. Press, Issue 1–[1995?]–14 (June 2000). ISSN: 1361–0465

Note: Variant title: B.A.D. Additional subtitle: *Quarterly: fiction, comment, humour, poetry, graphics*

BL: ZK.9.b.8779
CUL: 14. (L996.b.201)
NLS: HJ9.1993 (PER)
TCD: PER 96–141
Poetry Library: 6–14

127 **Breakthru Poetry** / Art Magazine. Colchester: [Breakthru], No. 1 (1979)–?

BL: No. 1 (1979). (ZK.9.c.8)

128 **Bridge** / edited by Stuart Brown. Falmouth, [1979?]

Noted by the UK Little Magazines Project.

No holdings known.

129 **The Bridge** / edited by F. J. Williams. Widnes, [1979?]

Noted by the UK Little Magazines Project.

No holdings known.

130 **The Bridge** / edited by James Mawer. Grimsby: EON Publications, [1991?–1993?]. ISSN: 0960–5762

Note: Related to *Issue One* with which it merged.

UCL: [2 unnumbered issues] (1991)
Poetry Library: [2 unnumbered issues catalogued as individual pamphlets] (1991), [1993?]

131 **Briggistanes: a broadsheet of words and images, fostering links among the communities of northern Scotland & Scandinavia** / edited by Anne Sinclair, Sean Gibson and Anne Dickie. Lerwick: Shetland Arts Trust, No. 1–2 [1989?]

Large poster format.

NLS: 1. (S.Sh.S.2.90.22); 2. (8.47)
UCL: 2
Poetry Library: 1

132 Bristol Writes: writing by local people. Bristol: Bristol Broadsides, No. 1 (1982)–3 (1983). ISSN: 0263–9211

Note: Each issue also has an ISBN

BL: P.901/3303
CUL: L999.c.3.897
NLS: HP2.86.2210 PER
Poetry Library: 1; 3

133 The Brixton Poets / edited by [Steve] Micalef. London, [Vol. 1] no. 1 [1991]–vol.2 no. 2 (1993). ISSN: 0966–0798

Related to: The Brixton Poets House Mega Zine.

BL: Vol. 1 no. 2. (ZK.9.a.2219)
Poetry Library: Vol. 1 no. 2; vol. 1 no. 4–7; vol. 2 no. 1–2.

134 The Brixton Poets House Mega Zine. London, No. [1?], 1994

Note: Variant title: The Brixton Poets House Selected Poems 14th July to 21st July 1994.

Related to The Brixton Poets. This magazine consists of work by George Lee, Steve Micalef, and Jan Noble.

Poetry Library: [1?]

Broadsheet [New Arcadians Press] See New Arcadian Broadsheet E524

135 Broadside: from the Cannon Poets. Birmingham: Century House, 1 (1990)– .

An irregular anthology from a group which meets every Sunday at the Midlands Art Centre, Birmingham.

BL: 2– . (ZK.9.a.2831)
CUL: 1. (1990.8.5549); 2. (1992.8.4537)
NLS: 1; 2; 5 (HP2.96.2821).
TCD: 1. (PL–181– 67); 2. (PL–194–679); 5. (PL–299–35)

136 Broadspeak / edited by Pete Morgan, Peter Kenny and Patricia Jackson. Edgware and Harrow: Harrow Poetry Group [No. 1, 1985–5?, 1989]

Poetry Library: [1]–[5?]

137 The Brobdingnagian Times: broadsheet / edited by Gerry Brett, Tom Curran, Giovanni Malito, Martin O'Connor and Pat Walsh. Cork, No. 1– . ISSN: 1393–3302

BL: ZK.9.a.4893
CUL: L727.c.1354
NLS: HJ4.1835 SER
TCD: PER 72–809
Poetry Library: 1; 3

138 The Brown Rice Gazette. London, [No. 1, 1982?]

Poetry Library: [1]

139 Brunton's Miscellany: a creative journal of literature and the arts / edited by Morley Jamieson. Edinburgh, Vol. 1 no. 1 (Autumn 1977)–no. 3 (1979). ISSN: 0140–8925

A literary review, with essays and articles on Scottish authors, and publishing short fiction and poems. Contributors included: George Mackay Brown, Michael Schmidt, John Herdman, George Campbell Hay, Hugh MacDiarmid, Norman MacCaig, Elspeth Davie, Giles Gordon, Gael Turnbull, Fionn MacColla, Sydney Tremayne, George Barker, Maurice Lindsay, Robin Fulton, Fred Urquhart, Ron Butlin, Iain Crichton Smith, James Aitchison, David (i.e. D. M.) Black, Stewart Conn, and others.

BL: P.901/3085
CUL: L999.c.3.744
NLS: HP3.81.493 PER
TCD: PER 92–352
UCL

140 Brushstrokes: a Chinese writers' quarterly newsletter. Liverpool: Writing Liaison Office, Toxteth Library, No.1 (Summer 1995)– . ISSN: 1360–0923

Note: Title in transliterated Chinese: Huabi.

BL: ZK.9.b.8864
NLS: HJ8.1433 SER
TCD: PER 89–293

141 Budgie Breeders Poetry Magazine: the magazine of Chace Farm Hospital / [edited by Alan Cornelius?]. [Enfield, Middlesex?, 1–?, 1995?]

Poetry Library: [two issues, both numbered issue 7 and dated Dec. 1995]

142 Bull / edited by Martin Smith and Keith Lindsay. Birmingham: Lilliput Press, Issue 1 (1985)–4 (1986)

BL: ZK.9.a.138
Poetry Library: 1–4

143 Butterfly. London: Butterfly, Summer 1998–5 [2000]. ISSN 1465–8941

144 Cabaret 246 / edited by John Harrison, Peter Finch, Norman Binding, Christopher Mills, Chris Broadribb, Dorcas Eatch, Jackie Apling, Patrick Egan and Al Campbell. Cardiff: Red Sharks Press, No. 1 (1983)–9 (1987)

Related Imprint: Red Sharks Press published collections by Ken Cockburn, Ruth McClaughry, Ifor Thomas, Christopher Mills, Graham Hartill, Chris Broadribb, Patrick Egan, and others

Peter Finch recalls that Cabaret 246 was a poetry workshop which met weekly, emerging from a creative writing class led by Chris Torrance. (see dspace.dial.pipex.com/peter.finch/cardiff.htm)

BL: P.903/954
CUL: L727.b.295
NLS: HP.1a.834 PER
UCL: 1–4
Poetry Library: 1–2; 4–9

145 The Cadmium Blue Literary Journal: journal of the Cadmium Blue Communion of Romantic Poets... / edited by Peter Geoffrey Paul Thompson. Romford: Precious Pearl Press, Issue 1 (1995)–3 (Oct. 1996). ISSN: 1358–0663

Note: Continues: The People's Poetry
Related Imprint: Precious Pearl issued several poetry collections, including Vyvian Grey's Merlin's Daughter (1994), BL: YK.1996.a.7510, and Peter Geoffrey Paul Thompson's

anthology The Lark Will Sing (1993), BL: YK.1993.a.17293

BL: ZK.9.a.8922
Poetry Library: 2–3

146 Cambrensis: Creative Writing of Wales: quarterly magazine. Bridgend: [Cambrensis], No. 1 (Dec. 1987)– .

BL: ZC.9.a.1532
CUL: L718.c.799
NLS: HJ8.1314
TCD: PER 85–551

147 Cambridge Poetry Festival [Programme]. Cambridge: Cambridge Poetry Festival Society, 1975–?.

Note: The Festival occasioned other publications by a number of different publishers, including Kettle's Yard Art Gallery.

BL: 1975 Programme. (X.909/3206); 1977 Programme. (P:901/3157); 1979 (YD.2005.a.3506).
CUL: Programme. (Cam.b.241.17.1–). 19 poem posters for the 1975 Festival (Tab.a.67.).

148 The Cambridge Poetry Magazine / edited by Rian Cooney, Ravi Mirchandani and Caroline Gonda. Cambridge: King's College, No. [1] (Autumn 1983)–2 (Spring 1984)

Note: Succeeded by: Poetry Now: incorporating The Cambridge Poetry Magazine

CUL: Periodicals Dept.
UCL
Poetry Library

149 Candle Light / edited by Laurie Linford. South Woodham Ferrers, then Clacton-on-Sea: Laurie Linford No. 16 [199?]–?

Note: Continues: Candle Light Reading

Published the work of the Lantern Light Circle of writers, poets and artists.

BL: 18 (April 1992)–41 (Autumn 1998). (ZK.9.a.2250)

150 Candle Light Reading / [edited by Laurie Linford] [South Woodham Ferrers?]: British Amateur Press Association, [No. 1, 1986?]–15 (Oct. 1991)

Note: Continued by: *Candle Light*

Published the work of the Lantern Light Circle of writers, poets and artists.

BL: 2–15 (ZC.9.a.732)

151 Cannon Fodder / edited by G. Rivka. Thames Ditton: G. Rivka, [No. 1, 1998]

BL: ZK.9.b.17700

Poetry Library

Canto *See* The Old Police Station E556

152 Caprice / edited by Keith Seddon and Jocelyn Almond. Watford Heath, No. 1 [1980?]–4 (1984). ISSN: 0144–3461

BL: P.903/691
CUL: 2–4. (L999.b.1.2079)
NLS: HP4.85.1500 PER
TCD: 2–4. (PER 92–593 1980–1981)
UCL
Poetry Library: 2

153 Cardiff Poet. Cardiff: Blue Mountain, No. 1 [1991?]–[3] (1992). ISSN 0969–2649

Note: Continued by *The Yellow Crane*

BL: ZK.9.a.2370

154 Cardiff Poetry. Cardiff: Charles Street Arts Foundation, [1986?–?]

National Library of Wales: 1986–1987. (LLP/DPB, STORFA/STACK ; YX2 CAR (4to))

155 Casablanca / [edited by Amanda Sebestyen]. London: Casablanca, Issue 0 (Aug./Sept. 1992)–18 (1997). ISSN 0967–1242

Current affairs and culture, with poems.

BL: ?–17. (ZC.9.b.5111)
CUL: 1–16. (L206.b.187)
NLS: 1–5; 7–18. (QJ9.1400 PER)
TCD: 1–6. (PER 91–949 1992–1993)
UCL: 1–6

156 Cascando: the national student literary magazine / edited by Lisa Boardman and Emily Ormond. London: Cascando Press, Issue 1 (1992)–5/6 (1996). ISSN: 0966–7628

BL: ZK.9.a.3300
CUL: 1–3. (L999.c.3.1450); 1–4. (English Faculty Library)
NLS: 1–3. (HJ8.1291 PER)
UCL
Poetry Library

157 CEJXOUQ / edited by A. Alexander. Douglas, Isle of Man: [Riakaj], 1 (June 1987)–?

A magazine produced by typewritten stencil with an unusual mixture of quotations emanating from the Baha'i and other faiths, interspersed by new and old poems and other texts.

BL: 1. (ZK.9.a.862)

158 Celtic Dawn: the International Poetry Magazine / edited by Dwina Murphy-Gibb, Terence DuQuesne and Chris Morgan. Oxford: Prebendal Press, No. 1 (1988)–6 (1990). ISSN: 0951–9068 (CD); 0951–905X (YCR)

Note: Absorbs *Yeats Club Review*, so that *Yeats Club Review* No. 2 is *Celtic Dawn* No. 1, etc.

BL: ZK.9.a.809
CUL: L727.b.316
NLS: DJ.m.702
TCD: 2–6. (PER 94–460); *Yeats Club Review* (PER 72–514)
Poetry Library

159 The Celtic Pen / edited by Diarmuid Ó Breasláin. Belfast: An Clochán,, Vol. 1 no. 1 (Autumn 1993)–vol. 2 no. 2 (Winter 1994/95). ISSN 1359–4915

"A new quarterly dealing with the literature in the Celtic languages. As you will see in this edition, both in time and in subject matter, our range is broad. [...] The Celtic Pen aims to provide a platform for information on our respective literatures and through this hopefully increase awareness of its richness, not just among Celts but in the English speaking world." – from the editorial in the first issue.

BL: Vol. 1 no. 1–no. 4; vol. 2 no. 2. (ZC.9.b.6115)
CUL: Vol. 1 no. 1– vol. 2 no. 1 (Autumn 1994)
(L999.b.1.2149)
NLS: Vol. 1 no. 1– vol. 2 no. 1 (Autumn 1994) (HJ9.472 PER)
TCD: Vol. 1 no. 1– vol. 2 no. 1 (Autumn 1994) (PER 95–109
1993–1994)

160 Cencrastus: Scottish & International Literature Arts & Affairs / edited by Sheila Hearn, Glen Murray, Cairns Craig, Raymond J. Ross, Thom Nairn, Christine Bold... and others. Edinburgh, No.1 (1979)–? ISSN: 0264–0856

Index: *Scottish Poetry Index Vol. 7*, (Edinburgh: Scottish
Poetry Library, 1997), indexes issues in period 1979–1992
inclusive, BL: ZC.9.b.6227
Profiled in: Introduction to *Scottish Poetry Library Index Vol. 7*,
(Edinburgh: Scottish Poetry Library, 1997), BL: ZC.9.b.6227

A key Scottish cultural review which also published poetry.

BL: 1–31; 33–59; 61–. (P.903/450)
CUL: P900.b.60
NLS: 1–30; 32–. (HJ9.2246 PER)
TCD: PER 79–583
UCL: 1–20; 22–32; 43–46; 49–51
Poetry Library: 7–12; 25–45; 47–

161 Centra News: the Centre for Reading Arts monthly newsletter.
Reading: Centre for Reading Arts, No. 1
(May/June 1979)–3 (1979). ISSN: 0319–0143

CUL: 1–2 (July 1979). (L999.b.1.611)
NLS: 1–2 (July 1979). HP4.81.408 PER
TCD: 1–2 (July 1979). (PER 92–525)
UCL: 3

162 Certain Gestures: Music, Fiction, Fashion, Poetry, Art / edited by David Tiffen and Andrea James. Hampton, then Aldershot, No. [1] (1982)–8 [1991]

Strong visual content, with collage, cartoon strip and, occasionally, poetry elements. Began as a zine interested in
bands such as The Birthday Party as well as William
Burroughs, but became less text-based in successive issues.

BL: 1–7. (ZC.9.b.731)
CUL: 6–8. (L999.b.1.1981)
NLS: 6–8. (HP.1a.199 PER)
UCL: 4–8

163 The Chair: Poetry Magazine / edited by Stan Wells. Billingham, [1977–1983?]

Poetry Library: 5 (1978)–8 (1979)

164 Chapter One. Coventry: Alliance of Literary Societies, 1 [1990?]–11 (April 1999). ISSN 0962–6697

Note: Continued as: *Open Book*
Website: Alliance of Literary Societies,
www.sndc.demon.co.uk

BL: 2 (April 1990)–11. (ZC.9.b.4424)
NLS: 3 (April 1991)–11. (HP.med.804 PER)

165 Chasing the Dragon: New Writing in English from Wales / edited by Niall Griffiths. Aberystwyth: Chasing the Dragon, Issue 1 (Autumn 1998). ISSN 1462–9771

BL: ZK.9.a.6127
CUL: L999.d.1.155

166 The Cheapo Review / edited by Charles Thomson. Maidstone: Cheapo Publications, No. 1 (1980)–2 [1980?]. ISSN: 0144–7432

Note: Related to *Codex Bandito, Gazunda, Uncle Nasty's* and *Ving*
Exhibition Catalogue: Frank Milner (ed.), *The Stuckists: Punk
Victorian* (National Museums Liverpool, 2004), BL:
YC.2005.a.1579
Related Imprint: Cheapo Publications also published the
anthology *The Medway Poets* [1980], BL: X.950/16649, com-
prising Bill Lewis, Rob Earl, Charles Thomson, Miriam
Carney, Billy Childish, and Sexton Ming. The Medway Poets
recorded an eponymous record on Billy Childish's label,
Hangman Records (British Library Sound Archive:
1LP0006631).

Short fiction, drawings and poems. Typewritten stencil
production. A brief account of the Outcrowd milieu, of
which the Medway Poets were a part, is given in the entry
for *Codex Bandito*.

BL: P.903/642
CUL: L999.b.1.792
NLS: HP4.81.161
TCD: PER 92–878 1980
UCL
Poetry Library

167 Chiaroscuro: a magazine for new writing / edited by Alan Hackett and Adrian Johnson. Northampton: Curious Press, Issue 1 [1989?]–4 (1990)

Note: The first two issues are called 1st and 2nd edition

Poetry Library

168 Chimera. London: King's Poetry Society, King's College, No. 1–2 [1989?]

Poetry Library

169 Chock / edited by Ian C. Durant and Graham Evans. Canterbury: Chock Publications, [1978?–1982?]. ISSN: 0140–9794

Associated with Rutherford College, University of Canterbury.

BL: 2–3. (P.901/3170)
Brotherton Library, Leeds University: 3 (197–?)–6 (1981). (Special Collections English Q–1 CHO)
Poetry Library: [1?]

170 Chocolate News / edited by John Bevis, Mark Jarman and Colin Sackett. [London], No. 1–2 (1981). ISSN: 0261–3085

BL: P.901/3283
UCL
Poetry Library

171 Choice: a magazine of literature and criticism / by M.G. Smit and M.R. Howell. Huby: M. G. Smit and M. R. Howell, [No. 1, 1977]

BL: P.901/3113
CUL: L999.c.3.719
TCD: PER 92–364

172 Christian Poetry Review / edited by Francis T. Lewis, Maria Ruth Macaraig and Val Newbrook. Lichfield: Grendon House, No. 1 (1996)–11 (1998). ISSN: 1361–5998

Note: Continues: *Grendon Grail*. Continued by: *CPR International*

BL: ZK.9.a.4393
Poetry Library

173 Chronicles of Disorder / [edited by Wayne Dean-Richards]. Warley: Wayne Dean-Richards, 1 [1995?]–5 [June 1997]. ISSN 1362–7147

Related Imprint: Chronicles of Disorder published several poetry collections, including Dean-Richards and Tony Chenery's *Poems by Two Fat Men* (1996), BL: YK.2000.b.4236, and Dean-Richards and Roshan Doug's *Thicker than Water* (1998), BL: YK.1999.a.3175

BL: ZK.9.b.9300

174 Chrysalis. Bournemouth: Helicon Press, No. 1 (1984)

BL: P.901/3525
CUL: L727.c.874
UCL

175 Cipher / edited by Jake Tilson and Stephen Whitaker. [London]: Woolley Dale Press, Vol. 1 no. 1 (1979)–no. 6 (1981). ISSN: 0260–7824

Note: Included issue called "+ (Boxed set supplement) (1981)"
Related Imprint: Woolley Dale Press published individual collections of experimental writing, especially by Jake Tilson, and the visual arts magazine *Atlas*

BL: 3. (Cup.935/386)
CUL: 1–6. (L400.c.368)
NLS: 1–6 (HP2.85.2693 PER)
TCD: 1–6 (PER 92–581 1979–1981)
UCL: 1; 3–5
Oxford University, Bodleian Library: 1–6. Boxed set supplement. (Per. 2705 e.1897 (vol. 1, no. 1–6)

176 City Dreams / edited by Jack Yates. London, [No. 1?] (1976)

Poetry Library: [1?]

177 City Writings / edited by David Wright, Megan Miranda and Paul Carey-Kent. Southampton: Caribou Press, Vol. 1 no. 1 [1993?]–8 (1996)

Related Imprint: Caribou Press published David Wright's poetry collection *Changing for Dinner* (1990), BL: YK.1993.a.6387

City Writings was the magazine of the group, The Southampton City Writers.

Poetry Library

178 Clanjamfrie / edited by Duncan McLean and Giles Sutherland. Edinburgh: Clanjamfrie, then Morning Star, No. 1 (Jan. 1984)–?

BL: P.2000/1426
NLS: P.el.396 PER
TCD: 3. (1988). (PER 90–924)

179 Clothes Bulletin / edited by Allen Fisher. London: Allen Fisher, 1 (1981)–12 (1982)

A precursor of the clothes special issue of *Spanner*. Contributors include Charles Bernstein, Opal Nations, Bill Sherman, Paul Buck, Ulli Freer, Chris Jones, Paige Mitchell, cris cheek, Ken Edwards, and Simon Pettet.

King's College London, Eric Mottram Archive: 1; 2; 4; 5; 6a; 8a; 10–12. (7/147/1–9 1981–1982)

180 Cloud / edited by Michael Thorp. Newcastle upon Tyne: Michael Thorp, No. 1–4 (1988). ISSN: 0953-2153

Related Imprint: Cloud

With the tagline "Bringing water to the seed", there was a strong spiritual element to the writing in this magazine. Contributors included R. S. Thomas, Denise Levertov, Bill Wyatt, Paul Green, David Miller, Sue Arengo, Elizabeth Smither, and others, with translations of Rilke (by Roger Thorp) and Francis Ponge (by Peter Hoy). Thorp's background in visual art was evident in his inclusion of artwork as well as in the design of the magazine. Michael Thorp's *Cloud* project arguably found its main realisation in the books and pamphlets in the *Cloudforms* and *Markings* series which succeeded the magazine itself.

BL: ZK.9.a.646
CUL: L727.c.978.1–
NLS: HJ2.178 PER
UCL
Poetry Library

181 Clunch: North London Polytechnic Literary Society magazine / edited by Alan McKurtie, Julian Bright and others. London: North London Polytechnic, No. 1 (Mar. 1977)–3 (1979)

BL: 1 (Mar. 1977). (ZA.9.a.3079)
Poetry Library: 1–2

182 Cobweb / edited by Geraldine Taylor, Timothy Gallagher and Peter Kenny. London: Cobweb Publications, No. 1 (1988)–8 [1991?]. ISSN: 0956–0165

BL: ZC.9.a.2118
Poetry Library: 3–8

183 Codex Bandito / edited by Dick Brandt and Rob Earl. Maidstone, then Mereworth: Outcrowd, No. 1 [1981]–6 [1983]

Related Imprint: Outcrowd was associated with *Cheapo Review*, *Gazunda*, *Hack Hack*, and *Ving*
Exhibition Catalogue: Frank Milner (ed.), *The Stuckists: Punk Victorian* (National Museums Liverpool, 2004), BL: YC.2005.a.1579

Writing for the stuckism.com website, the artist Charles Thomson recalls that Outcrowd was originally a reading series organised by Rob Earl and Bill Lewis in Maidstone, emerging out of a Medway scene connected to Medway College in Chatham and Maidstone College of Art. This would later lead later in the 1980s to a group known as The Medway Poets, anthologised by Thomson's Cheapo imprint and recorded on Billy Childish's label, Hangman Records (British Library Sound Archive: 1LP0006631). Tracy Emin was part of this milieu. Also part of the scene were the presses and record labels set up by Billy Childish (Hangman Press and Hangman Records), Bill Lewis (Lazerwolf Press), and Charles Thomson (Cheapo Press). The Medway scene was also later involved with the art movement Stuckism.

BL: 2 (YK.1996.a.7030); 3 (X.958/3055); 4 (YK.1989.a.3403); 5 (Cup.806.gg.14)
CUL: 2; 3; 5. (L999.d.1.36)
NLS: 1. (HP1.81.501)
TCD: 1. (PB–50–948); 2 (PB–50–949); 3 (PB–95–144); 6 (PB–50–950)
UCL: 1; 3–6
Poetry Library: 2

184 The Coffee House: a meeting place for the arts / edited by Deborah Tyler-Bennett. Loughborough: Charnwood Arts, Issue 1 (1999)– .

Website: www.charnwoodarts.com

"Charnwood Arts is an independent community arts and media organisation based in the Borough of Charnwood in the East Midlands" – from the Charnwood Arts website.

BL: ZK.9.a.6275
CUL: L727.d.267
NLS: HJ3.1795 SER
TCD: PER 101–605
Poetry Library

185 Coil: journal of the moving image
/ edited by Giles Lane. London: Coil, No.
1(1995)–9/10 (2000). ISSN: 1357–9207

Index: Indexed by the UK Little Magazines Project
Profiled in : Notes attached to the index by the UK Little
Magazines Project

Coil includes work by filmmakers, video artists, poets,
essayists, etc. Most (though not all) of the contents is
related to film and video. Poets such as Sharon Morris and
Gad Hollander contributed to the magazine, drawing on
their concerns with visual or cinematic and electronic
media. Other contributors included Pavel Büchler, Jayne
Parker, Susan Hiller, Stuart Morgan, Regina Cornwell, Sean
Cubbit, and John Stezaker.

BL: ZK.9.d.1169
CUL: L900.b.948
NLS: HJ8.1480 PER
TCD: PER 89–450
UCL

186 The Collective Seasonal.
[Abergavenny]: [Collective Writers], Vol. 1
no. 1 (Autumn 1997) . ISSN: 1460–6070

Website: www.scriveners.supanet.com/

Collective Writers later became known as Scriveners, a
writing group meeting regularly at the Hens and Chickens,
Abergavenny.

BL: ZK.9.b.12033

187 College Green: a review of arts and literature. Dublin: Graduate Students' Union of Trinity College Dublin, Vol. 1 [no. 1] (1989)– .

Note: The first issue had the full title College Green Magazine
Website: www.gsu.tcd.ie/

BL: Summer 1996– . (ZC.9.b.6687)
CUL: Vol. 1 [no. 1] (1989)–vol.3 no.1 (Nov. 1990); Summer
1996– . (L980.b.250)
NLS: Vol. 2 no. 1 (Trinity Term 1990)–vol. 3 no. 1 (Nov.
1990); Summer 1996–. Lacking Autumn 1996. (HJ10.405
SER)

TCD: Vol. 2 [no. 1] (Trinity Term 1990)–vol.3 no.1 (Nov.
1990); Summer 1996– . (PER 88–655)

College Green Magazine See College Green
E187

188 Community of Poets / edited by
Philip and Susan Benetta. Canterbury, then
Chilham: Community of Poets Press, Issue 1
(Autumn 1994)–22 (1997). ISSN: 1354–4896

BL: 1–2. (ZC.9.a.3966)
CUL: L727.d.285
NLS: HJ4.1185 SER
TCD: PER 87–463
Poetry Library

189 Comstock Lode / edited by John and
Mary Platt. Twickenham, Vol. 1 (1977)–8 (1981)

UCL: 1–6, 8

190 The Condescender / edited by A. R.
Grant and others. [U.K.: No. 1, 1985?]

Poetry Library: [1]

191 Connections / edited by Jeanne Conn.
London: [Jeanne Conn], [1, 198?–]

Note: Issues are unnumbered

Poetry Library: Summer 1987, Spring 1990–

192 Connections: the writers journal /
edited by Narissa Knights. Rochester:
Federation of Kent Writers, 1996– . ISSN
1363–4151

Note: Continues: Kent Connections

BL: Vol.3 no.5 (Spring 1996)– . (ZK.9.b.9559)
Poetry Library: Vol. 3 no. 6–no.8

193 Constant Red / Mingled Damask: obras del laboratorio ambulente de poeticas cinemategraphicas / edited by
Nigel Wheale. Cambridge: N. Wheale, [I]
(Sept. 1986)–II (April 1987)

BL: ZD.9.b.2
Poetry Library: Unnumbered and undated issue

194 Contemporary Quarterly / edited by Graham Sykes. Leeds, [c.1979]

Noted by UK Little Magazines Project.

No holdings known.

195 Contraflow / edited by Steve Davies and Richard Tabor. Yeovil: Lobby Press, No. 1 [198–?]–5 (1989)

Related Imprint: Lobby Press published various collections including Anthony Barnett's *Blues That Must Not Try to Imitate the Sky* (1978), BL: YA.1993.a.1586, and Ann Morrow's *A Kiss for My Future Queen* (1981), BL: YA.1995.b.11346

BL: ZA.9.a.6824
UCL: 5
Poetry Library: 2 [1987?]

196 Core: an international poetry magazine / edited by Mevlut Ceylan. London, No. 1 (1987)–3/4 (1990). ISSN: 0951–6190.

Note: Editorial adviser: Feyyaz Fergar

BL: ZC.9.a.1399
CUL: L727.c.1121
NLS: DJ.s.595(4) PER
Poetry Library

197 The Cork Literary Review / edited by Eugene O'Connell. Cork: Bradshaw Books, Vol. 1 (1994)– .

The literary magazine of the Cork Women's Poetry Circle, which also organises readings and published a *Newsletter* (BL: ZK.9.a.5775), later called *Tig Filí Newsletter*.

BL: ZC.9.a.4127
CUL: L727.d.243
NLS: HJ4.1263 SER
TCD: OLS L–6–113
Poetry Library: 5

198 The Cork Review / edited by Paul Durcan, then Tina Neylon, then Séan Dunne, then Thomas McCarthy. Cork: Triskel Arts Centre, [Vol. 1] no. 1 (Nov./Dec. 1979)–vol. 2 no. 3 (June 1981); 1990–1999

Profiled in: Tom Clyde, *Irish Literary Magazines: an outline and*

descriptive bibliography (Dublin: Irish Academic Press, 2003), BL: 2725.g.3414

Contributors included Derek Mahon, Francis Stuart, Seamus Heaney, John Montague, John Banville, Eiléan Ní Chuilleanáin, and others. Tina Neylon edited all issues in vol. 2 (1981) then, after what appears to have been a nine-year gap, the 1990 volume. The magazine became at that point an annual volume. Séan Dunne edited 1991, and Thomas McCarthy edited 1993.

BL: [Vol. 1] no. 3–4; Vol. 2 no. 1; vol. 2 no. 3. (DSC: 3470.836800)
CUL: 1996, 1997. (L900.b.870)
NLS: [Vol. 1] no. 1 (Nov./Dec. 1979)–vol. 2 no. 3 (June 1981). 1994/5, 1995/6, 1997. (HJ9.1418 PER)
TCD: OLS X–1–435

199 Corpus Journal: the journal of creative writing / edited by Paul Habberjam and Patricia Khan. [Leeds], No. 1 (1986)–6 [1987]

UCL
Poetry Library: 5–6

200 Counterpoint / edited by Margaret George and Irene Twite. Sheffield and Kingston upon Thames: Court Poetry Press, No. 1 (1977)–18 (1981). ISSN: 0309–3328

BL: P.901/3069
CUL: L727.c.658
NLS: DJ.s.475 PER
UCL: 2–17
Poetry Library: 6–7; 11; 13; 15; 17–18

201 Countryside Tales: tales, articles and poems about the countryside / edited by David Howarth. Cheltenham: Park Publications, No. 1 (Spring 2000)– . ISSN 1469–2244

BL: ZK.9.a.7244

Cowpat *See* The Old Police Station E556

202 CPR International. Isle of Lewis, Pilot Issue (1999)

Note: Continues *Christian Poetry Review*

BL: ZK.9.a.4393

203 The Crane Bag / edited by Mark Patrick Hederman and Richard Kearney, with various guest editors. Dublin: The Crane Bag, Vol. 1 no. 1 (Spring 1977)–vol. 9 no. 2 (Autumn 1985)

Profiled in: W. J. McCormack, "The Crane Bag (1977–1985)" in McCormack, *The Battle of the Book: two decades of Irish cultural debate* (Mullingar: Lilliput, 1986), BL: YH.1987.a.891; Tom Clyde, *Irish Literary Magazines: an outline and descriptive bibliography* (Dublin: Irish Academic Press, 2003), BL: 2725.g.3414

A key cultural review which published articles on the history and cultural politics of Ireland. No poetry or fiction was published, but essays included Edna Longley on "Poetry and Politics in Northern Ireland", interviews of Seamus Heaney, John Hewitt, John Montague, and, by Seamus Heaney and Richard Kearney, an interview of Jorge Luis Borges.

BL: P.971/405
CUL: P900.c.202
NLS: HJ4.389 PER
TCD: OLS Lo5–93–96

204 The Crystal Gate: poetry and fantasy magazine of the new renaissance. Upminster: Sharkti Laureate, No. 1 (Nov./Dec./Jan. 1994)– 3 (May 1995). ISSN 1355–4123

BL: ZK.9.a.3752
CUL: L999.d.1.124
NLS: HJ4.1394 PER
TCD: PER 95–551 1995

205 The Cúirt Journal / edited by Trish Fitzpatrick, then Charlie McBride. Galway, Ireland: Galway Arts Centre, No. 1 (1994)–5 (1995). ISSN: 1393–0516

A substantial magazine of poetry, with some short fiction. According to Fitzpatrick's opening editorial, self-consciously modelled on *The Salmon*, though taking inspiration from Galway's Cúirt literary festival. Contributors included John Montague, Sujata Bhatt, Tony Curtis, Rita Ann Higgins, Jon Silkin, Tom French, Thomas Lynch, Don Paterson, Rodney Pybus, Fred Johnston, Sinéad Morrissey, David Wheatley, Howard Wright, and others.

BL: 1–4. (ZK.9.a.3673)
NLS: HJ4.1083 PER
TCD: PER 92–326

206 The Curate's Egg: a Springboard Writing to Succeed supplement / edited by [Leo Brooks]. Prestwich, Manchester, No. 1 [199?]–

Note: Two different issues have been numbered as 5; one of them is probably no. 6. The numbering of other issues is uncertain
Website: ourworld.compuserve.com/homepages/LeoBrooks/

As the subtitle suggests, related to the magazine *Springboard* (BL: ZK.9.a.2420)

Poetry Library: 3, 5–9, [12?], 15

207 Curios Thing / [edited by Michael Leigh?] London: A–1 Waste Paper Company, [No. 1, 199?–?]

Related Imprint: A–1 Waste Paper Company
Website: www.indigogroup.co.uk/llpp/a1waste.html

Poetry Library: 14–15 (1996)

208 The Cutting Room / edited by Stephen Partridge and Wendy Richmond. Sheffield: South Yorkshire Writers, No. 1 (1991). ISSN: 0962–6212

Note: The last issue (no. 10) of *South Yorkshire Writer* was the first issue of *The Cutting Room*.

BL: ZC.9.a.2988
Poetry Library 1

209 Cutting Teeth: new writing / edited by John Ferry. Castlemilk, Glasgow: Arts and Cultural Development Office, South East Area, 1 (1994)– . ISSN 1357–132X

BL: ZK.9.b.8005
CUL: Periodicals Dept.
NLS: 1–6; 12; 14– . (HJ9.1395 SER).
TCD: PER 86–205

210 Dada Dance: the magazine for losers and boozers / [edited by Dee Rimbaud]. [Edinburgh]: Languid Lobster Press, No. 1 (1984)–4 (1989)

Poetry Library

211 **Damask Magazine** / edited by Keith
Geoghan and Terry Rooke. Birkenhead, No. 1
[1977?]–2 [1978?]

Note: Variant title: *Damask*

UCL
Poetry Library: 1

212 **Dancing Ledge Mercury** / edited by
Tim Davies. Malvern: Dancing Ledge X Press,
[c.1977–?]

Noted by the UK Little Magazines Project.

No holdings known.

213 **Dandelion Arts Magazine** / edited
by J. González-Marina. East Hunsbury then
Northampton: Fern Publications. No. 1
[198–?]–. ISSN: 0969–9430

Related Imprint: Fern Publications also publish books on
calligraphy and painting for fun, as well as *Student Magazine*
(BL: ZK.9.b.16071)

BL: ZK.9.b.4971
Poetry Library: 9 (1990)–

214 **The Dark Horse** / edited by Gerry
Cambridge. Bothwell; co-published in
Hastings-on-Hudson, New York State, No. 1
[April 1995]– . ISSN: 1357–6720

Note: Subtitles have included: "A journal of poetry and
opinion", and "The Scottish-American poetry magazine"
Website: www.star.ac.uk/darkhorse.html

Other editors who have co-edited or assisted include Aileen
McIntyre, Dana Gioia, Thomas DePietro, and Jennifer
Goodrich. Though not entirely devoted to metrical and
rhyming poetry, the magazine has a particular interest in
new poetry utilising traditional form. In this sense it is a
kindred spirit of the "New Formalists" of the American
poetry of the day.

NLS: 1; 3; 4; 6– . (HJ4.1970 PER)
UCL: 2– .
Poetry Library: 1–

215 **Dart** / edited by Bernard Simmonds.
Brentwood, [No. 1] (June 1976)–[2] (Sept 1976)

BL: YA.1989.a.16868
Poetry Library: [2] (1976)

216 **Daskhat: a journal of South Asian
literature** / edited by Seema Jena. Luton:
South Asian Literature Development Project,
No. 1 (Autumn/Winter 1992)–2
(Spring/Summer 1993). ISSN: 1351–8550

BL: 1. (ZK.9.b.6557)
CUL: L999.b.1.2870
Poetry Library

217 **Data Dump** / edited by Steve Sneyd.
Huddersfield: Hilltop Press, No.1 [199?]–?.

Note: In some cases, the same number was used for
different issues, eg. no. 25, which was used for the issue in
Jan. 1998 and in May 1998
Related Imprint: Hilltop Press publishes various science
fiction poetry, including work by Lilith Lorraine, Gavin
Salisbury, Andrew Darlington, Peter Layton, and the fantasy
poet Frances Campbell.

A magazine with a specific interest in genre poetry, e.g.
science fiction and fantasy. Special issues, with separate
ISBNS, are devoted to Steve Sneyd's various historical
surveys of the genre.

BL: 7–22; 25 (Jan. 1998); 25 (May 1998); 26, 30–32/33,
34/35; 34 (Dec. 1998); 37; 43–46; 49– . (ZK.9.a.3520)
NLS: 19/20 (HP2.98.4028); 23/24 (HP1.200.4181); 38/39
(HP2.99.4000); 47/48 (HP2.201.03820)
TCD: 15/16 (PL–334–170); 19/20 (PL–306–910); 23/24
(PL–356–732); 38/39 (PL–352–90); 47/48 (PL–350–888)

218 **Deep Earth Revue** / edited by Richard
Jones. Chessington: Deep Earth Books, No.1
[1978?]–[2] (Jan. 1979)

BL: P.903/863
CUL: L999.b.1.766
NLS: HP4.83.379 PER
TCD: PER 81–839
UCL: 1
Poetry Library: 1

219 **Déjà Vu** / edited by Rob Kelly. London,
Vol. 1 (1977)–6 (1978)

UCL

220 Delhi London Poetry Quarterly /
edited by G. Warrier. London: G. Warrier, No.
I (1986)–3 (1989). ISSN: 0950–4990

Contributors include P. Lal, Keki Daruwalla, Shiv. K.
Kumar, and others.

BL: I. (YC.1988.b.6425)
CUL: 2–3. (L999.c.3.1457)
NLS: DJ.m.2338 (3) PER
Poetry Library: 1–3

221 Delyow Derow / edited by Richard
Jenkin. Leedstown: New Cornwall, Nyver 1
(Gwaf 1988)–15 (1996)

A Cornish language magazine, edited by the Cornish poet
and activist in Mebyon Kernow, the Party of Cornwall,
Richard Jenkin (who also wrote under the pseudonym
Garfield Richardson).

BL: ZC.9.a.2077
CUL: L733.c.103
NLS: HP.sm.995 PER
TCD: PER 96–57 1988–1996

The Devil *See* The Printer's Devil E661

222 Dial 174 / edited by Terry M'ranjr
[Moran] and Joseph Hemmings. Leeds then
Fakenham, then Watlington, then King's
Lynn, Issue 1 (1989)– . ISSN: 0969–9732

Related Imprint: Dial 174 Publications

BL: 1–18; 20– (ZK.9.a.2218)
Poetry Library: 1–24; 25–

223 The Diggers Magazine. [Leeds]:
[Chapeltown Press for] Leeds Writer's
Workshop, [1985–1987?]. ISSN 0269–2783

A magazine associated with the Leeds Writer's Workshop,
namely Fred Schofield, Dominic McCarthy, Migs
Noddings, Ernest Noddings, David Stringer, and David
Hurst.

BL: [1985]. (ZC.9.a.711)
CUL: [1987]. (L999.d.1.49)
NLS: [1987]. (HP.sm.842 PER)
TCD: [1987]. (PER 90–675)

224 Distaff: a magazine for writing
women in London and the regions /
edited by Jennifer Brice, Isabel Gillard, Betty
Hand and others. [Stafford]: West Midlands
Writing Women; London: The London
Women's Centre. Vol. 1 no. 1 (Sept. 1986)– vol.
2 no. 2 (1988). ISSN: 0269–7734

This began as a magazine about West Midlands women
writers, but later acquired the subtitle, "A magazine for
writing women in London and the regions", joining forces
with the London Women's Centre.

BL: Vol. 1 no. 1. (ZC.9.b.2170)
CUL: Vol. 1 no. 2–vol. 2 no. 2 (L718.b.191)
NLS: Vol. 1 no. 2–vol. 2 no. 2 (DJ.l.43 (6) PER)
TCD: Vol. 1 no. 2–vol. 2 no. 2 (PER 94–382 [1987]–1988)
Poetry Library: Vol. 1 no. 7

225 Distant Echo / edited by Bob Lucas.
Southall, Middlesex: No Choice, [No. 1,
198?–10, 1984]

Poetry Library: 10

226 Divan /edited by Richard Hill, Colin
Morgan, and Alasdair Paterson. Liverpool:
Glasshouse Press, No. 1 (1979)–2 (1981). ISSN:
0263–1598

Related Imprint: Glasshouse Press published Peter Dent's
collection *Psalter* (1980), with illustrations by Ann Paterson,
BL: X.950/24089

Contributors included Ric Caddel, Jim Burns, Graham
Sykes, Maggie O'Sullivan, Gladys Mary Coles, Matt
Simpson, Rupert Mallin, Lee Harwood, Ian Robinson, and
others.

BL: P.901/3294
CUL: L999.c.3.883
NLS: HP.la.505 PER
TCD: PER 81–629

227 A Doctor's Dilemma: poetry, art,
fresh air / edited by Peter Godfrey and Bol
Marjoram. London: CB Press, [No. 1]–[2]
[198–?]

BL: ZK.9.b.512
Poetry Library

228 Dog / edited by Bill Lewis. [U.K.], No. 1
[197–?]–2 (1978)

Poetry Library: 2

229 Dog / edited by David Crystal. London,
No. [1] (1991)–6 [1996?]

BL: 2. (ZK.9.b.5168)
UCL: 3
Poetry Library

230 Doors Into and Out of Dorset.
Weymouth: Word and Action (Dorset), and
Wimborne: Wanda Publications. No. 1
(1979)–55 (1997). ISSN: 0142–1161

Note: Absorbed by: *South*. Editors changed with each issue,
but included Ivor Cutler, Libby Houston, and Alison
Bielski.
Related Imprint: R. G. Gregory's Wanda Publications
publish Gregory's own publications but also, for example,
Stella Davis's *Watershot* (2001), BL: YK.2002.a.20097. The
magazine was associated with *Poetry Leaf*.

BL: P.901/3128
CUL: L727.c.823
NLS: HJ4.808 PER
TCD: PER 93–48 1979–1997
UCL: 2–26
Poetry Library: 2; 17–18; 20–29; 40–42; 46; 54–55

231 Dorwey Voices. [Dorchester]: [Dorwey
Writers], No. 1 [198?]– .

"Writing by local people from the Dorchester-Weymouth
area".

BL: ZC.9.a.1601

232 Double Harness / edited by Andrew
Cozens, Jim Cozens, Paul Robinson and
Cynthia Cores. York and Oxford: Avalon
Editions, No. 1 (1978)

Related Imprint: Avalon Editions also published individual
collections by Greg Galenby and Edward Kaplan, as well as
the anthology, *Horsedealing: a farewell to Green Horses*, edited
by Andrew Cozens (1978), BL: X.909/42991

The first and probably only issue was called the "W(h)ales
Issue" and featured "extracts from Canada's best selling
whale anthology, Welsh small presses, poetry on Whales
and of Wales". Contributors included Yann Lovelock, Tony

Curtis, Frederic Vanson, Peter Finch, Nina Carroll, David
H. W. Grubb, and others.

BL: P.901/3559
CUL: L999.d.1.72
NLS: P.sm.4101 PER
UCL
Poetry Library

**233 Double Space: the East of
England's own literary and drama
magazine** / edited by Tadhg Ó Séaghdha.
Norwich: Nua Publications, No. 1 Summer
1984–3 [1985?]. ISSN: 2665417

Note: Also described as "East Anglia's own literary and
drama magazine". Poetry, short fiction, stage and
television drama. Contributors included Malcolm
Bradbury, Margaret Atwood, George MacBeth, Rupert
Mallin, and others.

BL: 1. (P.413/312)
CUL: 1; 3. (L999.b.1.2027)
Poetry Library

**234 Down to Heel: magazine of
Heeley Writers** / edited by Nick Rogers.
Heeley, Sheffield: Heeley Writers, No. 1
[198?]–?

Poetry Library: 2 [198?]

**235 Dowry: a quarterly magazine of
Catholic poetry** / edited by Leonard
Blackstone and Alex Anderson. Liverpool: The
Guild of St. George, No. 1 (1982)–12 (1985).
ISSN: 0262–8937

BL: P.903/783
CUL: L727.b.253
NLS: 1087/B PER
Poetry Library: 1–5; 8–12

236 Dragon / edited by Mike Everley, Judith
Wilson and Christiaan Van Bussel.
[Aberystwyth], [No.1] (1979)

Perhaps an anthology, but perhaps the first and only issue
of a magazine. An A5 stapled format, with short stories,
poetry (e.g. from David Annwn, Judith Wilson, Gwyn Owen
Jones, and others), and illustrations.

BL: X.909/43483
CUL: 1980.8.2262
NLS: HP2.80.1162
TCD: PL–36–732
UCL

237 Dream Catcher / edited by Paul
Sutherland and others. York, then Lincoln, No.
1 [1996?]– . ISSN: 1466–9455

Website: www.dreamcatcher-arts.co.uk. Digitised issues
are displayed at www.poetrymagazines.org.uk

BL: Edition no. 5 issue 2–. (ZK.9.a.7399)
Poetry Library: 3–

238 The Drumlin / edited by Dermot Healy.
[Cootehill, Co. Cavan, Ireland]: [The
Drumlin], [No.1] (Autumn 1978)–2 (Winter
1979)

BL: P.803/998
CUL: L488.b.58
NLS: HP4.86.424 PER
TCD: PER 91–792

239 The Dublin Review / edited by
Brendan Barrington. Dublin: Dublin Review, 1
(Winter 2000/01)– . ISSN: 1393–998X

Index: A contents listing of each issue is provided on the
website
Website: www.thedublinreview.com

From the website, June 2005: "*The Dublin Review* is a
quarterly magazine of essays, criticism, fiction and
reportage. Founded and edited by Brendan Barrington, it is
published in book format – printed on 100gsm Munken
Cream stock and thread-sewn – to a design by David Smith
(Atelier, Dublin). It is published with financial assistance
from The Arts Council of Ireland." The magazine's title
evokes the venerable *Dublin Review* which began in 1836 and
ran until 1969.

BL: ZC.9.a.6302
CUL: L900:1.c.96
NLS: HJ3.2131 SER
TCD: PER 102–714

239 Eastern Rainbow / edited by Paul
Rance. Spalding: Eastern Rainbow No. 1
[1992?]–? ISSN: 1350–2115

BL: 2 (1993)–5. (ZK.9.b.5735)

CUL: 2 (1993). (L999.b.1.1701)
Poetry Library: 3 (1994)–5. [1996?]

240 Eavesdropper / edited by Philip
Woodrow. London: Philip Woodrow, No. 1
(Apr. 1989)–22 (1991). ISSN: 0955–9450

BL: ZC.9.b.3176
CUL: L727.b.325
NLS: HP.la.2050 PER
Poetry Library: 1–11; 15; 17–21

241 The Echo Room / edited by Brendan
Cleary. Newcastle upon Tyne: Echo Room, No.
1 (1985)–19 (1994). ISSN: 0268–1366

BL: ZC.9.b.815
NLS: 1–15. (DJ.m.2131(2) PER)
UCL: 1–8
Poetry Library

242 Eclipse / edited by Elizabeth Boyd.
Neston: Everyman Press then Cherrybite Press,
Issue 1 (Aug. 1998)– . ISSN: 1464–6374

BL: ZK.9.a.5660
CUL: 1–19; 21–. (Periodicals Dept.)
NLS: 2–20; 22–. (HJ3.1763)
TCD: 2– ((PER 77–13)

243 Eco Runes. London: Front Cover, No. 1
(1988)–? . ISSN: 1462–6330

"A selection of poetry, prose, art and graphic mayhem."
The editorial to no. 4 describes a relaunch in 1992,
presumably with new numbering, but original publishing
going back to the 1988. Contributors include Sam Smith,
Steve Sneyd, Sarah J. Oswald, and others.

BL: 4. (Feb. 1996). (ZK.9.a.5934)

244 Écorché / edited by Ian Taylor.
Thornford, Nr. Sherborne, No. 1 (1997)– .
ISSN: 1460–9789

Website: www.indigogroup.co.uk/llpp/ecorche.html

Contributors include: Georges Bataille, Paul Buck, Ottó
Orbán, David Barton, Bernard Noel, David Chaloner, and
Kathy Acker (interviewed), and others.

BL: ZK.9.b.12266
Poetry Library

245 Ecuatorial: poetry: poecia / edited by William Rowe and others. London: Dept. of Spanish, King's College, No. 1 (1978)–3 (1980)

Note: Variant subtitle: *translation journal of contemporary work in Spanish, English and Portuguese.*

Includes work by Robert Creeley, Enrique Molina, Jack Spicer and others.

BL: P.903/675
CUL: 2–3. (L999.c.3.862)
NLS: HP3.85.279 PER
UCL
Poetry Library

246 Edible Society: poetry, art, fresh air / edited by Peter Godfrey. Brighton: Edible Society & Black Cat Communications, No. 1 (1994/1995)

Note: Variant subtitle: *a magazine of creative writing and art.*

BL: ZK.9.b.8093
Poetry Library

247 Edinburgh Review / edited by Peter Kravitz, Allan Massie, Robert Alan Jamieson, Gavin Wallace and others. Edinburgh: Edinburgh Review, No. 67/68 (1985)– . ISSN: 0267–6672

Note: Continues *New Edinburgh Review*, taking up its numbering. From issue 109, *Edinburgh Review* published a book alongside each issue as part of the subscription package, including Stella Rotenberg's *Shards*, translated from the German by Donal McLaughlin and Stephen Richardson (issued with 112), and Angela McSeveney's *Imprint* (issued with 111)
Anthology: Murdo Macdonald (ed.) *Nothing Is Altogether Trivial* (Edinburgh University Press, 1995), BL: HP1.95.4185
Website: www.englit.ed.ac.uk/edinburghreview/

"Scotland's leading journal of ideas, the *Edinburgh Review* publishes essays, short fiction, poetry and reviews aimed at an educated reading public with an interest in critical thought" – from the website (Oct. 2004). Referring back to the nineteenth century *Edinburgh Review* (BL: P.P. 6199.h), edited most famously by Francis Jeffrey, the new magazine attempted to make a similar cultural intervention. It was politically and philosophically internationalist in outlook from the outset, with writers as diverse as Kathy Acker, the Salvadorean Roque Dalton, Michel Foucault and Christa Wolf appearing alongside contemporary Scottish writers.

Despite the Edinburgh location, the *Review* was perhaps most significant in its first decade as a publisher of Glasgow-based writers, several of whose work emerged to transform the Scottish literary landscape, particularly in fiction. As well as Alasdair Gray, writers associated with the Glasgow renaissance included James Kelman, Janice Galloway, Agnes Owens, A. L. Kennedy, Jeff Torrington, Frank Kuppner, Tom Leonard, Peter McCarey and Alan Riach (whose collaborative piece *For What It Is* was published in no. 72), Edwin Morgan, David Kinloch, and others.

BL: P.523/237
CUL: L900.b.338
NLS: HJ10.108 PER
TCD: 67/8–105. (PER 95–965)
UCL: 67/68–70; 97
Poetry Library: 70; 85–86

248 Editor Anonymous / edited by Ju Desborough. Leeds, No. 1 [1979?]–4 (1980)

Note: May have continued after No. 4

Includes work by Jeff Nuttall, Adrian Henri, and others.

King's College London, Eric Mottram Archive: 2–4. (7/202/1–3 1980)

249 Effie / edited by Hugh Ouston. Ellon, Newburgh, Aberdeen and Edinburgh, No. 1 (1977)–7 (1981)

Contributors included Ian Stephen, Ian McDonough, Linda Chase, and others. Hugh Ouston's collection *Aline-Nadine Gossip* was published by the Edinburgh publisher Galliard in 1992 (BL: YK.1993.a.13367), and his textbook *Union issues: Scotland 1550–1750* by Hodder and Stoughton in 1998 (BL: YK.1998.b.9664).

BL: 3; 5. (Pressmark Pending)
NLS: P.sm.2499 PER
Brotherton Library, Leeds University: 2–3. (Special Collections English Q–1 EFF)
Poetry Library: 5

250 Element / edited by Mari-Aymone Djeribi. Dublin, then Cloone, Ireland: Mermaid Turbulence, No. 1 (Autumn-Winter 1993)– . ISSN: 1393–4902

Related Imprint: Mermaid Turbulence publishes artists' books and other book art
Website: www.mermaidturbulence.com/

Paperback format for this attractively produced little

magazine. Djeribi's first editorial announces that *Element* is "a literary journal with contributions from all over the world – arranged in alphabetical order – and a cooking recipe at the end." The range of work is international, with conventional, experimental, and translated texts and visuals interspersing each other. There's a light touch to the editing, as the recipe pledge suggests – and the context is as much visual arts and book arts as poetry or fiction. After the second issue each has its own theme e.g. no. 3, All Food Matters; no. 4, Exit, Escape, Exiles; no. 5, The Enemy; no. 6, Space; no. 7, What Machines?. The more literary contributors include Al Berto, Nuno Júdice, and Sophia de Mello Breyner (each translated from the Portuguese by Richard Zimler), Ciaran Carson, Tom McIntyre, and Derek Mahon (translating Philippe Jaccottet).

BL: ZC.9.a.4280
CUL: L727.c.1312
NLS: HJ4.1538 SER
TCD: PER 87–695

251 Element 5 / edited by Andy Sanderson. Swansea, [No. 1, 1981?–?]

No. 2 is noted by the UK Little Magazines Project as appearing in 1982.

Brotherton Library, Leeds University: 1. (Special Collections English Q–1 ELE)

252 Engaged / edited by Rachel Steward. London: Engaged, Issue 1 (1994)– .

"Engaged is an arts magazine that allows artists to publish their work in the way it was intended to be experienced. Each issue appears in a different medium." – from a card accompanying the fifth issue. No. 1 was a t-shirt; no. 2 a poster; no. 3 a CD-ROM; no. 4 a tinned issue; no. 5 a video; no. 6 a radio broadcast (also available in CD format); and no. 7 a comic strip. Steward worked with different editors for different issues, including David Rainbird and Martin Spinelli. The radio broadcast included work by Elizabeth James, Jane Draycott, and others

BL: 6. (Sound Archive: 1CD0121886)
CUL: 2; 3; 5. (Periodicals Dept.)
NLS: 2– . (CDROM.1350 PER); 5. (Video.363 PER)
Poetry Library: 1–

253 Entropy: archiving the futures of cultures / edited by Gareth Evans and Ben Slater. Bristol: Entropress, Vol. 1 no. 1 (1997)–no. 6 (1998). ISSN: 1368–4930

Note: Variant subtitle: *experimental culture from the margins to the edge.*

BL: ZK.9.b.12003
Poetry Library: Vol. 1 no. 1, no. 3, no. 4

254 Eonta: arts quarterly / edited by Steven Holt, Harry Gilonis, Richard Leigh and Richard Barrett. London, Vol. 1 no. 1 (1991)–vol. 2 no. 2 (1994). ISSN: 0960–3417

Index: Indexed by the UK Little Magazines Project
Profiled in: Notes attached to the index by the UK Little Magazines Project

Contemporary poetry appears alongside other art forms, including music, visual art and theatre, and an interest in writing in translation. There is also a strong interest in critical writing, in both essays and reviews. Contributors included Edouard Roditi, Frank Samperi, Ian Hamilton Finlay, Hans G. Helms, Allen Fisher, Tony Lopez, Kelvin Corcoran, Richard Leigh, Billy Mills, Geraldine Monk, Karin Lessing, Simon Smith, and David Miller. Vol. 1 no. 1 included a mini-feature on the theatrical and visual artist Tadeuz Kantor; vol. 1 no. 4 was a special Dante issue.

BL: ZK.9.a.1981
CUL: Periodicals Dept.
NLS: HJ9.2043 PER
TCD: PER 95–109 1991–1994
UCL: Vol. 1 no. 1–vol. 2 no. 1
Poetry Library

255 Eos / compiled by Louisa Lockwood, Roger Jackson, Faith Dunne and Susie Davis. [Durham?]: [Eos], June 1991

Contributors include Vernon Scannell, Geoff Hamilton, and others.

BL: ZK.9.b.5944

256 Equofinality / edited by Rod Mengham and John Wilkinson. Worcester and Birmingham, No. 1 (1982)–4 (1991)

Related Imprint: Equofinality published John Wilkinson's *Proud Flesh* (1986), BL: YH.1987.a.600

Contributors include John Wieners, Barry MacSweeney, Andrew Duncan, J. H. Prynne, Denise Riley, and others.

BL: 1; 3 (ZC.9.b.1465)
CUL: 1–3. (L718.b.170)
NLS: 1–3. (DJ.m.254(5) PER)
UCL: 1

Poetry Library

vol. 9 no. 1; vol. 10 no. 1–3; vol. 11 no. 1–

257 Eric: University of Dundee arts magazine. [Dundee]: [University of Dundee], No. (2)1 (1994)–3 (1996). ISSN: 1354–5973

Note: Continues: *Gallimaufry*, whose last number was no. 20. The first issue of *Eric* is therefore expressed as (2)1, i.e. both no. 21 of the old magazine and no. 1 of the new. The next issue is expressed as no. 2.

BL: ZK.9.a.1948
TCD: No. 2 (1). (PER 92–235 1994)

258 Excerpts: some working pages by... London, No. 1 (1989)

Note: Consists of work by Andrew Cottingham, Roger Braithwaite and Janie Reynolds, who also produced the magazine.

UCL

259 Exe-calibre / edited by Ken Taylor. Exmouth: Carmina, Vol. 1 (Samhain 1986)– vol. 4 (Equinox-solstice 1988). ISSN: 0269–5014

Note: Continued as: *X-Calibre*
Website: www.wordwrights.co.uk/pub/xcalibre/xcalibre.html#info

Had its beginnings in an Exmouth-based series of poetry workshops ran by Ken Taylor known as Wordsmiths.

BL: ZK.9.a.459
CUL: L718.c.862
NLS: DJ.s.660(2) PER

260 Exile / edited by Ann Elliott, Herbert Marr and Jane Wardle. Saltburn and other locations: Exile Publications. [Vol. 1] no. 1 (1989)– .

Note: From Jan. 2004 the numbering changed to simple succeeding numbers, i.e. no. 61 onwards

"Flying Cleveland's flag: the poetry magazine for and by the people of Cleveland and the North East."

BL: [Vol. 1] no. 3, no. 5; vol. 2 no. 2; vol. 3 no. 1; vol. 4 no. 1; vol. 10 no. 2, no. 3; vol. 11 no. 1; vol. 12 no. 1– . (ZK.9.a.2307)
UCL
Poetry Library: [Vol. 1] no. 1–4; vol. 2 no. 2–vol. 3 no. 1; vol. 3 no. 3; vol. 4 no. 1; vol. 5 no. 1–3; vol. 7 no. 2–vol. 8 no.3;

261 Extra / edited by L. [i.e. Laurie] E. Linford. Clacton-on-Sea: Lantern Light Circle, No.1 (Christmas 1996)– 2 [1997]. ISSN: 1367–4234

Note: Supplement to: *Lantern Light*. Continued by: *Star Light* (which appears to have had no poetry, so is not featured in this bibliography)

Modest poems from the local writers group Lantern Light Circle, who write, in the editor's words and emphasis "*as a hobby*".

BL: 1. (ZK.9.b.10572)

262 Extremes / edited by Shirley Cameron and Gillian Clark. Issue 1 (June/July 1976)–?

Contributors included Gay Sweatshop, Geraldine Monk, Paul Buck, Sally Potter, Jeff Nuttall, and others.

BL: 3 (Winter 1976). (ZD.9.b.76)
Nottingham Trent University, Live Art Archive: 1; 4

263 Farrago / edited by John O'Neill, Liza Nicklin and Anne Marie Johnson. West Wickham: Farrago Collective Press, No. 1 [199–?]–3 (1992)

Poetry Library: 2–3

264 Fatchance / edited by Mary Maher and Louise Hudson. Beaworthy: Fatchance, No. 1 (1993)–10 (1998). ISSN: 0966–0038

Related Imprint: The Fatchance Press published Linda Chase's collection *These Goodbyes* (1995), BL: YK.1996.a.1784

BL: ZK.9.a.2421
UCL: 3–10
Poetry Library

265 Fauxpas: alternative arts & lifestyle magazine / edited by Gwyn Lewis. Folkestone: Fauxpas Publications, No. 1–2 [1979?]. ISSN: 0142–923X

Brotherton Library, Leeds University: 1. (Special Collections English Q–1 FAU)
Poetry Library

266 Ferment: a quarterly magazine of poetry, politics and the arts / edited by Walter Perrie and Andrew Cameron-Mills. Edinburgh: Ferment Publications, [No.1] (1976)

BL: P.971/404
CUL: L999.c.3.613
NLS: HP2.78.2158 PER
TCD: PER 76–992
UCL

267 Fête / edited by Paul Buck. Maidstone, No. 1 (1979)–7 (1981)

Paul Buck recalls that *Fête* was published in an edition of 100 copies, and distributed solely by way of a mailing list: each issue consisted of a single contributor (in order of appearance, Paul Buck, Glenda George, Paul Green, Ulli McCarthy, Kathy Acker, Kris Hemensley, Sylvie Néve).

CUL: Sylvie Néve (L999.c.3.1372); Glenda George. (2003.8.5470)

268 Fife Fringe / edited by Lillian King. Kelty: Lillian King, No. 1 (Mar. 1998)–17 (2002). ISSN: 1462–5563

BL: ZK.9.a.5731

269 Fife Lines / edited by Ian Nimmo White. Leslie: Fife Lines, No. 1 (Sept. 1998)– .

BL: 1; 3– . (ZK.9.a.5731)
CUL: L727.c.1375
NLS: HJ3.1815 SER
TCD: PER 88–414

270 Figments. Belfast: Figments Publishing, No. 1 (1995)–? ISSN: 1362–3362

BL: 1–10. (ZK.9.b.9250)
Poetry Library: 9; 18

271 Figs / edited by Tony Baker. [Durham, London and Winster]: Tony Baker, No. 1 [1980?]–14 (May 1988). ISSN: 0144–4859

Related Imprint: Figlet booklets published at least pamphlets including John Levy's *Travels* [1983?], BL:YA:1993.a.24682

Note: A supplement to no. 2 was published, Chris

Mabbott's *From the Tales of Balaam and the Ass*, BL: YA.2002.a.39152

BL: P.903/613
CUL: 4; 6. (L727.b.319)
NLS: 4. (HP2.83.629 PER)
TCD: 4. (PER 90–388)
UCL
Poetry Library: 1–9; 11–13

272 Filter / edited by W. Ray, F. Harris and I. Haywood. London: Dept. of English, University College London, No. 1 (1982)

UCL

273 Fingerprint. Small Heath: Trinity Arts, No. 1 (Aug. 1983)–?

An anthology series by Small Heath Writer's Workshop, in the West Midlands. The group also produced the magazine *Hard Lines*.

BL: ZC.9.a.1233

274 Fingertips / edited by Gerald Roome and Ian Lang. Longfield: Egonibs, No. 1 (199–)–?

Poetry Library: 6–7 (1996)

275 Fire / edited by Jeremy Hilton. Malvern, then Tackley, Kidlington: Jeremy Hilton, No. 1 (1994)– . ISSN 1367–031X

Website: www.poetical.org/fire/index.htm. Many issues are digitised at www.poetrymagazines.org.uk

Fire "is radical, multicultural and international in outlook, and publishes a broad range of poetry from around the world. It tends towards the more alternative end of the poetry spectrum, and is interested in poetry with heart, spirit, imagination, innovation, risk-taking, open-endedness, and most of all poems that have something to say. Not neat, tight, closed, clever, cynical, fashionable poems." – from the Fire Manifesto mounted on the website.

BL: ZK.9.A.5046
Poetry Library

276 The Firing Squad / edited by Geoff Stevens. West Bromwich: Purple Patch, No. 1 (1989)–?

Related Imprint: Purple Patch are also the publishers of *Purple Patch* and *Purple Pastiche*
Website: purplepatchpoetry.co.uk/

Specifically political poems. About thirty issues had appeared in hardcopy, with the website publishing issues electronically from c.2004

BL: 2nd Series no. 1 (2000?). (ZK.9.b.16817)

277 First Offence / edited by Tim Fletcher. Canterbury: No. 1, 1986–? ISSN: 1462–8953

Contributors include Paul Buck, Kelvin Corcoran, Robert Hampson, Robert Sheppard, Rosmarie Waldrop, Gilbert Adair, Bruce Andrews, John Seed, John Wilkinson, Clayton Eshleman, Pierre Joris, Lawrence Upton, David Annwn, Maggie O'Sullivan, Allen Fisher, Adrian Clarke, and others.

BL: 2; 4–11. (ZA.9.b.1150).
UCL: 4– .
King's College London, Eric Mottram Archive: 1; 3; 6–8 (7/228/1–5)

278 First Time / edited by Josephine Austin. Hastings: First Time Publications, Edition 1 (1981)– . ISSN: 0266–0520

Website: www.josephineaustin.co.uk/

As the title implies, designed to encourage new authors. No. 19 (Autumn 1990) reprints a letter from a Literature Officer of the Arts Council of Great Britain, declining to fund the magazine on the grounds that the quality of material was low, that too little funding was being requested (the Arts Council tending only to fund larger projects), and that *First Time* should address the problem of its too low cover price (at the time £2). Included in the same issue, among various but formally conservative verse, were poems from Laura Hird and Toby Litt, later better known as novelists. The magazine has survived for many further issues.

BL: 1–20; 22–26; 34; 36; 37– . (P.901/3475)
CUL: 1–26; 28–. (L727.c.1318)
NLS: 1–26; 34– . (HJ4.1767)
UCL: 1–27
Poetry Library: 1–2; 7–10; 13; 15–29; 31– .

279 Five Leaves Left / edited by Richard Mason, Sharon Astbury, Jozi Darlington and Andy Darlington. Cowling and Leeds: Purple Heather Publications, No. 1 (1984)–6 (1988)

Note: No. 6 is also numbered Vol. 2 (1). Continued by *RSVP*

Related Imprint: Purple Heather published a number of single-author poetry collections, several anthologies, and another poetry magazine, *The Toll Gate Journal*

BL: P.901/3622
CUL: 1. (L999.c.3.880)
NLS: 1. (HP2.85.4693 PER)
UCL: 1–5
Poetry Library

280 Five Minute B!d. No. 1 [1986]–? ISSN: 0950–6721

Note: "No. 5 never the saw the light of day" – from the editorial, no. 9

Sci-fi and fantasy fiction and poetry.

BL: 1–4; 6–9. ZC.9.b.1804

281 Flaming Arrows. Sligo: Interaction Publications, then County Sligo Vocational Education Committee, No. 1 (1989)– .

Website: www.sligovec.ie/arts.html

BL: 2– . (ZC.9.a.2043)
CUL: Periodicals Dept.
NLS: HJ9.1905 PER
TCD: PER 73–109

282 Flesh Mouth / edited by Pete Conway. London, Issue 1 (1990)–?

UCL: 1
Brotherton Library, Leeds University: 2 (1990)–3 (Spring 1991). (Special Collections English Q–1 FLE)

283 Flint: new writing from the South of England / edited by David Orme and Brian Hinton. Colden Common, near Winchester: Writers' Club Associates, [No. 1, 1989]. ISSN: 0953–2994

Note: Continued by: *South*
Related Imprint: Writers' Club Associates published several collections, including Sharon Zink's *Rain in the Upper Floor Café* (1989; BL: YK.1993.a.593), and Conor Carson's *The Mound of the Hostages* (1990; BL: YK.1992.a.7517)

CUL: L727.c.1300
NLS: HJ4.1969 PER
TCD: PER 90–961
Poetry Library

284 The Fly Cemetery / edited by C. Heasman and L. Accola. Southsea, No. 1 (1981)

UCL: 1

285 Focus / Stockport: Society of Civil Service Authors Poetry Workshop, 1977–1997. ISSN: 0140–0878

Note: Continues: *Broadsheet*. Continued by: *Waves*

BL: P.901/3067

286 Focus / edited by Robert Holdstock, Chris Evans, Chris Bailey, Allan Sutherland and Dave Swindon. Reading, [1979?–?]

Recorded by the UK Little Magazines Project.

No holdings known.

Foldan Sceatas *See* Folded Sheets E287

287 Folded Sheets: of what new poetry is posted here / edited by Michael Haslam. Hebden Bridge: Open Township, No. 1 (Sept. 1986)–8 (Dec. 1990). ISSN: 0950–284X

Note: Variant title: *Foldan Sceatas*
Related Imprint: Open Township

Contributors included: Neil Oram, Chris Torrance, D. S. Marriott, Joseph Guglielmi (trans. Mark Callan), Rod Mengham, Paul Matthews, Catherine Byron, Peter Riley, Peter Sansom, Ken Edwards, Ian Pople, John Welch, Peter Hughes, Peter Finch, James Keery, Kelvin Corcoran, Michael Ayres, Willem Roggemann (trans. Theo Hermans), Peter Robinson, Ralph Hawkins, David Miller, David Chaloner, Billy Mills, Jay Ramsay, Anna Taylor, Jenny Chalmers, John Wilkinson, Andrew Lawson, Tom Phillips, Yann Lovelock, Nigel Wheale, Nicholas Johnson, Rupert Loydell, Keith Jebb, the editor himself, and others. Martin Thom joined Michael Haslam to co-edit issues 7 and 8.

BL: ZC.9.a.1965
CUL: 1–7. (L727.c.1070)
NLS: 1. (DJ.s.247 PER)
TCD: 1–7. (PER 91–458)
UCL
Poetry Library: 6

288 Folio / edited by Tom Bingham. Corby: Tom Bingham, No. 1 (1983)–13 (1987). ISSN: 0266–0016

Note: Variant title: *Folio International*
Related Imprint: Folio International published several collections, including Des Carroll's *Reflections from a Cell* (1986), BL: YC.1988.a.6286)

An A5 stapled format. Contributors include: Tim Love, Robert [i.e. Rob] Mackenzie, Maureen MacNaughtan, Dave Cunliffe, Steve Sneyd, Johan de Wit, Josephine Austin, Raymond Tong, David Grubb, Frederic Vanson, Gerald England, Ivor C. Treby, Rupert Loydell, and others.

BL: 1–7; 9–13. (P.901/3535)
CUL: 7–13. (L727.c.1234)
NLS: 7–13. (DJ.s.682(2) PER)
UCL: 12–13
Poetry Library: 2; 4; 11–13

Folio International *See* Folio E288

289 The Fool / edited by David Baxter. Newcastle-upon-Tyne, No. 1 (1979)–[2?, 198–?]

No. [2?] is entitled "The Apocalypse issue – a sacred civilization."

CUL: L999.b.1.760
TCD: PER 92–568
UCL: 1
Poetry Library: [2?]

290 Fool's House / edited by Allen Fisher. London: Spanner, [No. 1] (1980)

Related Imprint: Spanner also published *Spanner*

"Work from 14 London-based poets not invited to the PCL [Polytechnic of Central London] Politics & Poetry Conference June 1980." Perhaps more of an anthology than a magazine.

BL: X.955/1680
CUL: 1990.11.210
Poetry Library

291 Foolscap / edited by Judi Benson. London, No. 1 (1987)–17 (1995). ISSN: 0952–3979

Judi Benson co-edited with Ken Smith, *Klaonica: Poems for Bosnia* (Bloodaxe, 1993, BL: YK.1993.a.17288). Her own collections include *Call It Blue* (2000) and *In the Pockets of Strangers* (1993), both from Rockingham Press.

BL: ZC.9.a.1195
CUL: L727.b.361
NLS: HP.la.1801 PER
TCD: PER 95–532 1987–1995
UCL: 3–17
Poetry Library: 3–5; 7–17

292 Footnotes / edited by James Sale, Malcolm Povery and Richard Marriott. Colden Common, near Winchester: The Schools' Poetry Association. No. 1 [1986]–3 [1987]

CUL: L999.b.1.1418–
NLS: DJ.m.384(1) PER
TCD: 2. (PER 90–964)
Poetry Library: 1–2

293 Force 10 in Mayo: a journal of the northwest / edited by Dermot Healy. Co. Mayo, No. 1 (1989)–11 (1999)

Note: Known simply as *Force 10*

Contributors include: Seamus Heaney, Pat McCabe, Paul Durcan, John McGahern, John B. Keane, Maedbh McGuckian, Neil Jordan and others. Dermot Healy was a writer in residence at Mayo, and worked on *Force 10* as part of that task, with a wider-distributed but unnumbered issue appearing in 1991 after several smaller issues before (and after) that date.

BL: 1991. (YK.1993.b.8115)
CUL: 1991. (L488.b.136)
NLS: 1991. (HP4.93.124)
TCD: 1991. (PER 91–937 1991)
Queen's University Belfast, Special Collections: 1–3; 5–11. (h q PR8700 .F6)

294 Forever: poetry and prose / edited by Michael O'Neill. Didsbury, Manchester: Forever Publications, No. 1 (1976)–7/8 (1978). ISSN: 0140–3141

BL: P.901/3065
CUL: L727.c.661
NLS: DJ.s.436 PER
TCD: PER 94–307 1976–1978
UCL
Poetry Library: 2; 5

295 Forty Winks. Redcar: Nibs Publishing Association, [No.1, 1996]–? ISSN 1365–5914

Note: Continued by *Paperweight*

BL: ZK.9.b.10350

296 The Four Elements. [Cheltenham]: Friends of the Cheltenham Festival of Literature, 1989–?.

An annual fine press production, printed at the Whittington Press.

BL: 1989–1991 (HS.74/781)

297 [Four Word Magazine] 4word Magazine. Rhondda: Rhondda Community Arts, Issue 1 [1995]–7 (1996). ISSN 1360–4481

BL: ZK.9.a.4289
CUL: L727.c.1255
NLS: HJ4.1663 PER
TCD: PER 88–321 1995–1997
Poetry Library: 1; 3–6

298 Fragmente: a magazine of contemporary poetics / edited by Andrew Lawson and Anthony Mellors. Oxford, No. 1 (Spring 1990)– . ISSN: 0960–0450

Poems, reviews, and essays, with contributors including Tom Raworth, Kelvin Corcoran, Alan Halsey, Nigel Wheale, Ken Edwards, John Wilkinson, Peter Middleton, Simon Smith, Gilbert Adair, Charles Bernstein, David Bromige, Peter Finch, Lyn Hejinian, Karen Mac Cormack, Steve McCaffery, Michael Palmer, Marjorie Perloff, Rosmarie Waldrop, Peter Riley, Tony Baker, Harry Gilonis, Geraldine Monk, Bill Griffiths, John Welch, Peter Larkin, Nicholas Johnson, Richard Caddel, and others. No. 8 was guest-edited by D.S. Marriott and Vicky Lebeau.

BL: 1–3. (ZC.9.a.2606)
CUL: L727.c.1157
NLS: HJ4.1323 PER
TCD: PER 95–21
UCL: 1–6
Poetry Library: 1; 4–8

299 Frames /edited by John Edward Gimblett and Dawn Mears. Bettws: No. 1 (1984)–6 (1987). ISSN: 0265–6396

CUL: 2–4. (L718.c.823)

NLS: 2–? (DJ.s.253(2) PER)
UCL
Poetry Library

300 Free Hand / edited by Jo Wood. West
Kirby: FootPrints, [No. 1, 1998?]–? ISSN:
1463–0044

BL: Dec. 1998. (ZK.9.b.13784)

301 Freestyle Magazine / edited by Patrick
Hopewell. Bristol: Freestyle Writers' Group,
No. 1 [1994?]

Poetry Library: 1

302 The Frogmore Papers / edited by
Jeremy Page. Folkestone: The Frogmore Press,
No.1 (1983)– . ISSN: 0956–0106

Note: A supplement, *Frogmore North*, ed. Jonathan Hall, was
published in 1986
Interview: with Jeremy Page, in *Poetry News: the Newsletter of
the Poetry Society*, Spring 2004, p.8
Related Imprint: Frogmore Press has published a number
of anthologies and single-author collections, including
those by Giles Goodland, Matthew Mead, Marita Over, and
Brian Aldiss
Website: www.frogmorepress.co.uk

From the website (Nov. 2004): "Writers who have appeared
in their pages include Tobias Hill, Sophie Hannah, Linda
France, John Mole, Elizabeth Garrett, Susan Wicks, John
Whitworth, Elizabeth Bartlett, Brian Aldiss, Geoffrey
Holloway, Carole Satyamurti, James Brockway, Marita Over,
Paul Groves, Mario Petrucci, Caroline Price, Matthew
Mead, Tamar Yoseloff, Myra Schneider, Andrew
Waterhouse, John Harvey, Pauline Stainer, Ian Caws, Mike
Jenkins, Judi Benson, Jane Holland, Ian Parks, Christine
McNeil, Derek Sellen, Ros Barber, Patty Scholten, Merryn
Williams and many more ..." The magazine began as a
stapled A4 format, without a card cover, but changed to A5
with a slightly more robust cover with issue 19, production
values improving further in later issues. A poetry
competition is associated with the magazine.

BL: ZC.9.b.3573
CUL: 19– . (L727.d.312)
NLS: 19– . (HP.sm.874 SER)
TCD: 19– . (PER 85–377)
UCL: 55– .
Poetry Library: 10–45; 47– . Supplement

303 Frontal Lobe / edited by Robert T.
Miller. Huddersfield: Organism, Issue 1 [1994]
ISSN: 1357–0404

Poems, collage, short fiction, listings of magazines and
bookshops. This magazine had a music fanzine-like look
and tone, with the music editor listed as "Fulvolume".
Poets included Steve Sneyd, Dave Cunliffe, and Alistair
Paterson.

BL: ZK.9.a.3717
Poetry Library

304 Fusion: poetry, fiction / edited by
Ken Mann. London: [Fusion], 1 (1979)–? ISSN
0260–2172

Fusion "is no torch-bearer for any one genre or style of
writing. It has no literary pretensions. And all I hope for is
that one story or one piece of poetry draws a favourable
response from you, the reader." – from the editorial in the
second issue.

BL: 2. (X.0950/340)
CUL: 2 (1981). (L999.c.3.796)
NLS: 2 (1981). (HP.sm.302 PER)

**305 Fusion Magazine: the
performance journal of poetry, music
and the visual arts** / edited by James Black.
Stow-on-the-Wold: [Fusion Publishing], Vol. 1
no. 1 (1998)–?. ISSN 1464–665X

The first (and last?) issue includes work by Alison
Brackenbury, Jean 'Binta' Breeze, U. A. Fanthorpe, and
others.

BL: Vol. 1 no. 1 (ZC.9.a.5322)

306 The Gairfish / edited by W. N. Herbert.
Oxford: W. N. Herbert, Vol. 1 no. 1 (Autumn
1983)–no. 2 (Autumn 1984)

Note: Continued by: *Gairfish*

Started by W. N. Herbert when a student at Brasenose
College, Oxford. Includes early work by Robert Crawford
and David Kinloch.

CUL: L727.d.294
NLS: HP.sm.341

307 **Gairfish.** / edited by W. N. Herbert and Richard Price. Bridge of Weir then Dundee: Gairfish, [Vol. 1] (1990)–9 (1995). ISSN: 1350-4452

Note: Each volume also has an ISBN number. An A3 broadsheet of new poems was issued with several volumes, to subscribers only. Continues: The Gairfish Anthology: W. N. Herbert and Richard Price (eds.), *Contraflow on the SuperHighway*, (London: Southfields Press and Gairfish, 1994).BL: YK.1996.a.9102
Related Imprint: Vennel Press, founded by Leona Medlin and Richard Price, published several of the "Informationist" poets associated with *Gairfish*, namely W. N. Herbert, David Kinloch, Peter McCarey, Alan Riach, and Price himself. Elizabeth James and Leona Medlin, also published in *Gairfish*, each had single-author collections from Vennel Press as well.

"Gairfish is dedicated to publishing creative work in all the languages of Scotland. It is also committed to the radical reappraisal of Scottish culture without adherence to any faction, political or otherwise. However, Gairfish does not consider its rubric to be limited to Scottish writers or affairs: its aim is the greatest plurality possible stemming from a Scottish base." – the paragraph used on several issues to describe its policy. The highpoint of the magazine was probably vol. 5 (1992), "The McAvantgarde" issue, which contains contributions by a range of Scottish poets including D. M. Black (writing on the Scottish avant-garde in the 1960s), Maoilios Cambeul, Robert Crawford (an essay, "Thoughts on a Scottish Literary Avant-Garde"), Graham Fulton, Tom Hubbard, Kathleen Jamie, Robert Alan Jamieson, David Kinloch (on the use of the Scots language in his poetry), Frank Kuppner, Tom Leonard, Peter McCarey, Duncan McGibbon, Tom McGrath, John Manson, W. S. Milne, Edwin Morgan, Pseudorca (i.e. W. N. Herbert), Alan Riach (on "Tradition and the New Alliance: Scotland and the Caribbean"), Kenneth White (an essay, "The Nomadist Manifesto"), and a short essay by the artist George Wyllie on Scotland and the visual arts. Vol. 8, "Calemadonnas: Women & Scotland", guest-edited by Helen Kidd, includes a memoir of Cambridge School poet Veronica Forrest-Thomson by Wendy Mulford. W.N. Herbert solo-edited Vol. 9, "Overspill".

BL: All, but lacking the broadsheets. (ZC.9.a.3430)
CUL: All, but lacking the broadsheets. (L727.d.294)
NLS: 1–9. (HP.sm.341) Broadsheets no. 1–2. (P.el.675 PER)
Poetry Library: Nos. 1–[3], 5–9; Broadsheet no. 1.

308 **Gangway Literary Magazine.** Dublin: TCD Publications, [No. 1, 1990?]–?

BL: 2 (1990). (ZK.9.a.2325)
NLS: 2 (1990). (DJ.s.575(6) PER)
TCD: 2 (1990). (PER 91–506)

309 **Garbaj: the politically incorrect paper.** Southend-on-Sea: Atlantean, 1 [2000]– .

Related Imprint: Atlantean has also published *Awen*, *Monomyth* and poetry booklets
Website: www.geocities.com/dj_tyrer/garbaj.html

BL: 3; 4; 6–11; 13– . (ZK.9.b.17503)

310 **Gare du Nord** / edited by Alice Notley and Douglas Oliver. Paris: Alice Notley and Douglas Oliver, Vol. 1 no. 1 (1997)–vol. 2 no. 2 (1999). ISSN: 0398-7256

Published in Paris, but with substantial British content, a significant magazine of experimental prose, poetry and reviews.

BL: ZA.9.b.1970
UCL

311 **Garuda** / edited by Ulli Freer. London: Ulli Freer, 1 [198?]–2 [1987?]

Contributors include: Robert Hampson, John Wilkinson, Allen Fisher, cris cheek, Bob Cobbing, Carlyle Reedy, Maggie O'Sullivan, Robert Sheppard, and Geraldine Monk.

UCL: 2
King's College London, Eric Mottram Archive: 7/249/1–2 1992, 1993

312 **The Gay Journal: a new quarterly of culture and liberation produced by gay women and men** / produced by Anne Davison, Ian David Baker, Roger Baker, and Sheila Hillier (typesetting). London: BBD Publishing, No. 1 (Autumn 1978)–2 (Spring 1979)

Short stories, articles, debate, poetry, and visuals. Contributors include Oswell Blakeston, Ivor C. Treby, Martin Foreman, Vivien M. Bellamy, Roj Behring, and others.

BL: Cup.821.cc.17

CUL: L997.d.31
TCD: PER 80–325

313 Gazunda / edited by Uncle Nasty. Maidstone: Outcrowd, [No. 1, Sept. 1978]–3 (1980). ISSN: 0142–5439

Note: Related to *Cheapo Review*, *Codex Bandito*, *Hack Hack*, *Uncle Nasty's* and *Ving*.

Poetry, cartoons, and other visuals (notably by Bill Lewis). A4 format, issued free. A brief account of the Outcrowd milieu is given in the entry for *Codex Bandito*.

BL: 1–3. (P.973/314)
CUL: 1–2. (L999.b.1.1310)
NLS: Lacking no. 1. (P.la.7375 PER)
TCD: PER 90–621 1978–1980
UCL: 2.

314 Gentle Reader / edited by Lynne Jones. Fairwater, Cardiff: Gentle Reader, [No. 1, 1994]–26 [2003]. ISSN 1024–686X

Beginning as a magazine for South African writing, the remit was gradually extended. Mainly short stories, but poetry always included.

BL: 12 (Sept. 1998)–26. (ZK.9.a.5434)
CUL: 12 (Sept. 1998)–26. (Periodicals Dept.)
NLS: 12 (Sept. 1998)–26. (HJ3.1814)

315 Giant Steps / edited by Graham Mort and Maggie Mort. Clapham: Giant Steps, No. 1 (Spring 1983)–10 (1989). ISSN: 0265–2285

Note: The final issue is entitled *Last Steps*.

BL: 1–5; 7–8. (P.441/1058)
CUL: 1–9. (L727.c.1229)
NLS: 1–6; 8–9. (DJ.m.1633(2) PER)
UCL: 2–10
Poetry Library: 2–10

316 The Gig / edited by Nate Dorward. Willowdale, Ontario: Nate Dorward, No. 1 (Nov. 1998)– . ISSN: 1481–5133

Website: www.ndorward.com/

Despite the Canadian address, a significant publisher of experimental poetry from England, Scotland, and the Republic of Ireland (and North America). Contributors include: John Wilkinson, Alan Halsey, Trevor Joyce, Maurice Scully, Allen Fisher, Peter Manson, Clark Coolidge, Drew Milne, Tony Lopez, Gavin Selerie, R. F. Langley, Robert Sheppard, Bill Griffiths, Bruce Andrews, Randolph Healy, cris cheek, Thomas A. Clark, John Hall, Peter Riley (to whose work the double issue 4/5 was devoted), Geraldine Monk, Steve McCaffery, Helen Macdonald, Tony Baker, Lisa Robertson, Karen Mac Cormack, Keston Sutherland, Rae Armantrout, Peter Larkin, Ken Edwards, Elizabeth James, Adrian Clarke, Ralph Hawkins, Ian Patterson, David Chaloner, Tom Pickard, Leslie Scalapino, Gilbert Adair, Martin Corless-Smith, Scott Thurston, Jackson Mac Low, Rob Mackenzie, Ira Lightman, Chris Goode, Sean Bonney, Pete Smith, Tom Raworth (to whose work the double issue 13/14 was devoted), Marjorie Welish, Lisa Downe, and others.

BL: ZA.9.a.10786
CUL: P727.c.111
UCL

317 The Glasgow Magazine / [edited by Hamish Whyte, Kevin McCarra, David Neilson, Alasdair Robertson and Tom Berry]. Glasgow: Mariscat Press, No. 1 (Winter 1982/1983)–7 (Winter 1985/1986). ISSN: 0264–0422

Related Imprint: Mariscat Press have published many single author collections, including works by Edwin Morgan and Gael Turnbull. In July 2004 the Press moved from Mariscat Road, on the southside of Glasgow, to Edinburgh.

The first issue established what would continue to be a mixture of Scottish (especially Glaswegian) texts and work from further afield, a declared aim of the magazine being to be international and with contributors including Alasdair Gray, Laura (Riding) Jackson, Edwin Morgan, and Peter Porter.

BL: P.901/3478
CUL: L718.c.373
NLS: DJ.s.48 PER
UCL: 1–6
Poetry Library

318 The Glass: Literary Studies Group. Leicester: UCCF [Universities and Colleges Christian Fellowship] Associates Literary Studies Group, 1986– . ISSN 0269–770X

BL: ZC.9.a.874
CUL: 2– . (L700.d.41)
NLS: 2– . (HP.la.1735)
TCD: PER 85–147
UCL

319 Glass: poetry magazine.
Portmarnock, Co. Dublin, Oct. 1986

CUL: L999.c.3.1268
NLS: HP.la.1735
TCD: PER 91–664

320 Goalpost: friends of St. Clements
/ edited by Paula Bellot, Mike Ludlow, Alan
Edward, Jo Williams and Winston
Bartholomew. London: The Creative Writing
Club, St. Clements Hospital, [No. 1, 199?–6,
1997?]

Note: Continued by: Angel

Poetry Library: 3 (1996)

321 God's Spy: a singular magazine
showing the progression of The Life /
edited by Leszek Kobiernicki. Bristol: Ixiom
Press / Golden Circle Publications, No. 1
(1977)

Poetry Library: 1 (1977)

322 Golden Leaves. Upminster: Sharkti
Laureate, No. 1 (Mar. 1995). ISSN: 1358–1384

BL: ZK.9.a.3990
CUL: L999.d.1.151
NLS: HJ4.1535 PER
TCD: PER 92–235 1995

323 The Good Society Review: the
arts, environment and society / edited
by Masry MacGregor. Butleigh, nr.
Glastonbury: Holman's Press, Vol. 1 no. 1
(1993)–no. 9 (1995). ISSN: 0968–6665

BL: ZC.9.a.3400
CUL: L900.d.135
NLS: HJ4.1756 PER
TCD: PER 95–367
UCL

324 The Gorey Detail / edited by Paul
Funge; assistant editor, James Liddy. [Gorey,
Co. Wexford]: Funge Art Centre, [No. 1]
(Summer 1977)–7 (1983)

Paul Funge invokes the spirit of Rimbaud and Rosa
Luxembourg in the editorial of the first issue. Short fiction
and poems from John Banville, Dermot Bolger, Dermot
Healy, Francis Stuart, and many others. Perhaps
deliberately grainy photos of contributors are reproduced
in the text.

BL: [1]– 2 (Summer 1978). (P.901/3115)
CUL: 2 (Summer 1978). (L999.b.1.671)
NLS: 2 (Summer 1978). (HP3.82.625)
TCD: OLS X–2–157 no.6–12 1977–1983

325 Graffiti / edited by Kay Bourne, David
Loewe, Colin Kerr, Chris Smart, and Maureen
Sangster. Edinburgh: Graffiti, No. 1 [1980]–15
(1988)

The first two issues had the subtitle "the Stockbridge
magazine" but the reference to this locality within
Edinburgh was dropped after that, with the new phrase "a
free magazine of new poetry" adopted instead. No. 15 was
guest edited by Alan Spence.

BL: 4. (4208.020000 DSC); 15. (YA.1994.a.506)
CUL: 1–8. (L900.c.589)
NLS: DJ.s.187
TCD: 1–8. (PER 79–916)
Poetry Library

326 Grand Piano: a magazine of new
poetry / edited by John Gohorry and Roger
Burford Mason. Letchworth, No. 1 (Autumn
1981)–13 (Autumn 1989)

A simple A5 format of sixteen pages of poetry per issue,
with no editorial, essays, or reviews. Contributors include
Patricia Pogson, Peter Middleton, Maggie Gee, George
Szirtes, Hamish Whyte, Peter Forbes, William Scammell,
John Lucas, Wes Magee, John Lane, Tim Dooley, Jim C.
Wilson, Rodney Pybus, Sue Hubbard, Sue Stewart, Gillian
Fisher and others. No. 11 is an Alan Harris memorial issue.

BL: 3–5; 7; 10; 11. (P.901/3406)
CUL: 1–11; 13. (L727.c.1237)
NLS: 2–?. (HP.la.289 PER)
UCL
Poetry Library: 6; 11–12

327 Granta / edited by Bill Buford; then Ian
Jack. Cambridge; London and New York, [New
Series], No. 1 (1979)– . ISSN: 0017–3231

Related Imprint: Granta Publications
Website: www.granta.com/

Perhaps only a true little magazine in its early stages, in that, after being founded by postgraduates, it soon became a commercial journal with considerable financial backing and mainstream distribution. Nevertheless, drawing on its university association and the reputation of its predecessor *The Granta*, which ran from 1899 to 1973 (BL: PP.6058.i.), it is sometimes mentioned as a little magazine in the national press. It is included here on that basis. It has been a pioneer of fiction, non-fiction, and documentary photography, and its contributors include: Martin Amis, Julian Barnes, Saul Bellow, Peter Carey, Raymond Carver, Angela Carter, Bruce Chatwin, James Fenton, Richard Ford, Martha Gellhorn, Nadine Gordimer, Romesh Gunesekera, Milan Kundera, Doris Lessing, Ian McEwan, Blake Morrison, Gabriel Garcia Márquez, Arundhati Roy, Salman Rushdie, Zadie Smith, George Steiner, Graham Swift, Paul Theroux, Edmund White, Jeanette Winterson, Tobias Wolff, and others. Its Best of British Young Novelists campaigns have helped the reputations of many British writers.

BL: P.901/3462
CUL: Cam.b.41.16
NLS: 1–13; 15– . (HJ2.200 SER)
TCD: PER 82–209
UCL: 1–28

328 Graph: Irish Cultural Review /
edited by Michael Cronin, Barra O Seaghda, and Peter Sirr. Dublin: Graph, 1 (Oct. 1986)–1999. ISSN: 0790–8016

TCD: PER 93–911

329 Green Battle Lines: poetry, prose, cartoons / edited by Laurie Jackson, Urmilla Sinha and Neill Topley. Brighton: P.R.O.B.E., 1st Edition (1993)–2nd Edition (1993). ISSN: 0969–7934

BL: ZC.9.a.3349
Poetry Library: 1

330 The Green Book / edited by Rupert Blunt, Keith Spencer, Linda Saunders, Anna Adams and Clive Turnbull. Bath and Bristol: The Green Book Ltd. / Redcliffe Press, [Vol. 1 no. 1] (Autumn 1979)– vol. 3 no. 11 (1991). ISSN: 0265–0088

Note: Continued by *Contemporary Art*, a less wide-ranging magazine. Variant subtitles: "a celebration of the native

genius of the British & Celtic peoples"; "an illustrated journal of arts, crafts and literature, being a celebration of the native genius"; "an illustrated journal of arts, crafts and literature"; and "a quarterly review of the visual and literary arts".

Related Imprint: Redcliffe Press has published many books on the history of Bristol and the West Country

BL: P.901/3386
CUL: [Vol. 1 no. 1]–vol. 3 no. 1; vol. 3 no. 10. (L900.c.514)
NLS: [Vol. 1 no. 1]–vol. 3 no. 1. Lacking: Vol. 1 no. 4–no. 8; vol. 1 no. 10. (HP2.86.4449 SER)
TCD: [Vol. 1 no. 1]–vol. 3 no. 1. (PER 83–205 1979–1988)
UCL: Vol. 2 no. 3; vol. 3 no. 1–11.
Poetry Library: [vol. 1 no. 1]; [vol. 1 no. 8]; [vol. 1] no. 10–11; vol. 3 no. 1–11.

331 Green Lines / edited by Tim Dooley and Mark Helmore. North Weald: Exitstencil Studies, No. 1 (1976)–[2] (1978)

Related Imprint: An imprint called Exitstencil, which published the work of punk band Crass, notably *A Series of Shock Slogans and Mindless Token Tantrums* [1982?], BL: X.439/12400, seems entirely unrelated to Extistencil Studies.

UCL

332 The Greenbelt Fringe Poetry Magazine. London: Sandcastle Productions, No. 1 (1985)–?

Associated with the annual Greenbelt Festival, which presents music and other arts on a broadly Christian theme. Probably a one-off.

BL: 1. (ZC.9.B.207)
UCL: 1

333 The Greenland Magazine. [Bath, No. 1, 1976?]–? ISSN: 0142–9175

Text and collage-based conceptual art. Contributors include Johnny Havenhurst, Andrew Land, Angela Manolete, Tommy Connett, David Tidball, Andrew Barrack, and Bernard Moore.

BL: 3 (1979). (ZD.9.a.108)

334 The Grendon Grail: the magazine of Grendon House Christian Poets' Society. Lichfield: Grendon House, 1 (Spring 1995)–[Winter

1995]. ISSN: 1361–598X

Note: Continued by: *Christian Poetry Review*

BL: 3 (Autumn 1995). (ZK.9.a.4393)

335 **Grille** / edited by Simon Smith. Putney, London: Grille, Issue 1 (Spring 1992)–3 [1993]

Grille, or 'GRIllE' as Simon Smith preferred (perhaps emphasising a geometric shape in keeping with the title), was produced simply and inexpensively. It was notable for its diverse range of contributors within a broad context of what was then termed linguistically innovative poetry (experimental, avant-garde, etc.). Contributors included Lee Harwood, Peter Riley, Iain Sinclair, Denise Riley, John Welch, Tony Lopez, Peter Larkin, Maurice Scully, Kelvin Corcoran, Alan Halsey, Robert Hampson, Ken Edwards, Harry Gilonis, Andrew Duncan, Anthony Mellors, and David Rees. It also included translations of Andrea Zanzotto (by Anthony Barnett with Claire Jakens) and André du Bouchet (by George Messo). The title was derived from *Speech-Grille*, the title (in English translation) of one of German poet Paul Celan's best-known collections.

CUL: 1. (L727.b.322)
NLS: 1. (HP.la.2716 PER)
TCD: 1. (PER 94–528 1992)
UCL
Poetry Library

336 **Ground Works: literary arts review.** Ely: Fen Poetry Centre, Vol. 1 issue 1 (Jan. 1988)–? ISSN: 0953–1491

Newspaper broadsheet format. The first issue contains an interview with Martin Stannard (with a photograph of Stannard reading), poems by Steve Sneyd, Chris Bendon, Gerald England, Alex Warner, and others, as well as short fiction and a review of Rupert Mallin's *Suffer Suffolk*.

BL: 1. (ZV.9.d.39)

337 **Hack Hack.** Maidstone: Outcrowd Publications, 1987?

Note: Related to: *Cheapo Review, Codex Bandito, Gazunda, Uncle Nasty's* and *Ving*

A brief account of the Outcrowd milieu is given in the entry for *Codex Bandito*.

UCL: [unnumbered issue] [1987?]

338 **The Haiku Quarterly** / edited by Kevin Bailey. Swindon: The Day Dream Press, No. 1 (1990)– . ISSN: 0960–3638

Website: dspace.dial.pipex.com/town/park/yaw74/HQ.htm

BL: 4 (Autumn 1991). (ZC.9.a.3130)
UCL: 2– .
Poetry Library

339 **Hairst** / edited by Michael Benenson and Nielsen Dinwoodie. Dunblane: Stirling University Literary Society, 1 (1978)–3 (Autumn 1980). ISSN: 0260–826X

Contributors included Robert Garioch and Antonia Stott (translating Giuseppe Belli), Norman MacCaig, Iain Crichton Smith, Michael Alexander (translating poems from the Exeter Book), Roderick Watson, Stewart Conn, Michael Hamburger, and others.

BL: 3. (P.901/3249)
CUL: 3. (L999.c.3.838)
NLS: HP2.86.383
TCD: 3. (PER 81–336)
UCL: 3

340 **The Halifax Wednesday Morning Eye Opener** / edited by Michael Haslam. Hebden Bridge: Open Township, [No. 1] (1985)–5 (1989)

Related Imprint: Open Township. Halifax Eye Opener was also the title of a series of pamphlets published by Halslam's Open Township imprint, such as Margaret Gledhill's *Bridge Over the Calder* (1987), BL: YC.1988.a.8759, described by Haslam as "quiet traditional poems of a local, spiritual, and delicate imagination."

Presenting "some of the work done by members of a Creative Writing Class which meets at Horton House on Wednesday Mornings at 9.45 a.m., during term-time." This class was operated by Calderdale Adult Education Service, with Haslam leading the class.

BL: 1–3. (ZC.9.a.4661)
UCL: 2–5

341 **Handshake.** [Warrington]: Dunnock Press, No.1 [1994]– .

Note: "The newsletter of the British SF [i.e. Science

Fiction] Poetry Association, the Eight Hand Gang."

BL: ZK.9.b.6980

342 Handside Poets. [Welwyn]: Welwyn Quaker Concern for Mental Health. No. 1 (1989)–5 (1990)

Poetry Library: 1; 3–5

343 Hard Lines / [Small Heath]: Small Heath Writer's Workshop, 1 (1982)

Related Imrpint: The Small Heath Writer's Workshop also produced *Fingerprint*.

West Midlands Creative Literature Collection

344 Hard Lines: short stories, poetry, prose / edited by Ken Sloane, Jill Hartley and Alwyn Daley. Bradford: Inner City Press, [No. 1] [1982]–?. ISSN: 0264–1402

Produced by the Bradford Creative Writers Group, based at Bradford's Central Library. Includes poetry by Nick Toczek (who set up the group in October 1982), David Tipton, and others, short stories, and artwork. The final page of the first issue has a cartoon of Margaret Thatcher, drawn by Alex Birch, with the speech bubble: "3 million unemployed... HARDLINES! Let them eat cake or write poems in garrets."

BL: [1]. (P.901/3396)
Poetry Library: 3

345 The Hard Times: a magazine of working class culture / edited by Keith Armstrong. Sunderland: Sunderland Arts and Ceolfrith Bookshop, [No. 1] (1982). ISSN: 0260–8219

Reproduces an extract from an essay by Raymond Williams on literary magazines, taken from the *Times Literary Supplement*, as well as short fiction, poetry, and strong visual work.

BL: P.803/1200
NLS: HP4.87.246
Poetry Library

346 Harry's Hand / edited by Michael Blackburn. London, then Lincoln: Jackson's Arm, No. 1 (Spring / Summer 1987)–4/5

(1990). ISSN: 0951–6131

Related Imprint: Jackson's Arm published short collections by Kim Taplin, Brendan Cleary, Michael Blackburn (who appears to have founded the press), and others.

Contributors included Ric Caddel, Geoff Hattersley, Martin Stannard, Ian McMillan, George Charlton, Peter Middleton, Robert Sheppard, David Caddy, Judi Benson, Gilbert Adair, Janet Fisher, James Keery, Alan Dent, Johan de Wit, John Goodby, John Harvey, Michael Laskey, and others. Michael Blackburn closed *Harry's Hand* in part to concentrate on *Sunk Island Review*.

BL: ZC.9.a.1451
CUL: L999.c.3.1041
NLS: HP.med.254 PER
UCL: 1–5

347 Hartforde Poets' Journal / edited by Julian Le Saux. Hertford, then Ware: Hartforde Poets Publications, No. 5 (June 1979)–Z [i.e. 26] Part 2 (Feb.1983). ISSN: 0260–3640

Note: Variant title: HPJ. Continues: *Hartforde Poets' Newsletter*, hence numeration beginning at no. 5. Continued by: *Bare Nibs*

BL (P.901/3235)
Poetry Library: 17

348 Hartforde Poets Newsletter. [No. 1, 1977?–?]

No holdings known.

349 The Hat / edited by Ian Hogg, Phil Carradice, Karen Buckland and Alawn Tickhill. Croft: No. [1]–[2] [1986?]

Note: Related to *Hat Poetry Magazine*

Poetry Library

350 Hat Poetry Magazine / edited by Ian Hogg, Dave Garden, Dave Slater and Phil Carradice. Skegness and Alford, No. 1 [197?]–5/6 (1978)

Note: Related to *The Hat*

CUL: 3; 5/6. (L999.c.3.697)
NLS: 3–?. (HP3.80.903)
TCD: 3–5/6. (PER 94–135 1977)
UCL: 2
Poetry Library: 5/6

351 Havoc: the new literary magazine with a political edge, for the Canterbury area. Canterbury: Havoc, Issue 1 (1995)–?. ISSN: 1362–1416

BL: 1. (ZK.9.a.4531)

352 Headlock: new poetry from the South-West / edited by Tony Charles. Wellington then Somerton, Somerset: Headlock Press, No. 1 (Spring 1994)–9/10 (1999). ISSN: 1353–6567

Related Imprint: Headlock Press also published Kerry Sowerby's *Soul Kitsch / Stealth Fighter* (1996), BL: YA.2003.a.17367

BL: 3–9/10. (ZK.9.a.3995)
UCL
Poetry Library

353 Heart Throb / edited by Mike Parker. Birmingham: Heart Throb, Issue 1 (Dec. 1993)–4 (1994)

Note: Continues: *People to People*. Continued by: *Raw Edge Magazine*

"The literature magazine for the West Midlands Arts region."

BL: 1–2. (ZK.9.a.1733)
CUL: 2–3. (L999.b.1.2172)
NLS: HJ9.787 PER
TCD: 2–3. (PER 92–191 1994)

354 Helicon: poetry magazine / edited by Shelagh Nugent. Little Neston: Cherrybite Publications, Issue 1 (1995)–19 (Dec. 1999). ISSN: 1360–2721

Note: Continued by: *Reach*
Related Imprint: Cherrybite Publications
Website: www.cherrybite.co.uk/

BL: 1–14; 16–19. (ZK.9.a.4225)
CUL: 14–19. (L727.c.1369)
Poetry Library: 4–13

355 Heretic / edited by Paul Brown, Alec Gordon, Rose Law, Jenny Stannard. London: Pre-Texts, Vol. 1 no. 1–no. 2 (1981)

Note: Variant title: *Here-tic*. Referred to as "Organon of the 5th International." The publisher's name is also given as Pre-Text.

CUL: Vol. 1 no. 2. (L999.b.1.884)
NLS: Vol. 1 no. 2. (HP.la.14 PER)
UCL
King's College London, Eric Mottram Archive: 7/270/1–2 1981
Poetry Library: Vol. 1 no. 1

356 The Hermit Oberlus / edited by Tom Ruffles. London, Issue 1 (Jan. 1980). ISSN: 0143–4578

BL: P.903/614
Poetry Library

357 Highcliff. Guisborough: Highcliff, No. 1 (1997)–2 (1998) ISSN: 1460–1362

BL: ZK.9.a.5501

358 Hindman / edited by Ju Desborough. Leeds: Crow Press, [No. 1]–2 (1980)

Noted by the UK Little Magazines Project.
No holdings known.

359 Hoke / edited by Simon Coury and Cathal McCabe. York: Derwent College, University of York, [No. 1] [1985?]

Poetry Library

360 Holophrase / edited by Ian Patterson, Martin Thom and Nigel Wheale. Cambridge: [Holophrase], [1, 198?]–?

Continues: *A Vision Very Like Reality*

BL: lv. (Dec. 1983–Jan. 1984) . (ZA.9.b.1546)
UCL: 1984

361 Hooligan Heart / edited by Steve Birtles. Ashton-upon-Lyme, [No. 1, 198?]–2 (1985)

Poetry Library: 2

Hot Poetry *See* HP E364

362 Hot Tin Roof. Newcastle-upon-Tyne: Hot Tin Roof, Issue no. 1 (Spring 1992). ISSN: 0966–0046

BL: ZK.9.a.2284

363 How Do I Love Thee? the magazine for love poetry / edited by Adrian Bishop. Lymington, then Winchester: Poetry Life, Issue 1 (Spring 1997)–9 (Summer 2002)

Website: freespace.virgin.net/poetry.life/

BL: 1–7; 9. (ZK.9.b.14040)
Poetry Library: 1–2

364 HP / edited by George Mitchell, Dafydd Sheen and Frank Bangay. London: Hounslow Poetry Workshop, No. 1 (1981)–5 (1983)

Note: Variant title: Hot Poetry
Related imprint: Hounslow Poetry Workshop also published a series of broadsheets

Poetry Library: 3, 5

HPJ See Hartforde Poets Journal E347

365 Hrafnhoh / edited by Joseph Biddulph. Pontypridd: Joseph Biddulph, 1 [1987?]–33 (1998). ISSN: 0952–3294

Note: Continued by: Troglodyte. A supplement on Africa was also published, Black Eagle
Website: www.cs.vu.nl/ffidick/biddulph/hrafnhoh.html
Related Imprint: Joseph Biddulph and the Languages Information Centre publishes booklets on lesser-known languages

From the website: "HRAFNHOH, adapted from Anglo-Saxon HRÆFN, a raven, and HOH, a hill-spur, comes from the original form of RAINOW HILL near CONGLETON, at the edge of BIDDULPH parish, Staffordshire. A study of the surname and place of Biddulph and the origin of surnames and of placenames was the starting point of this fascinating compilation of bygones and origins, heraldic and hereditary bits and pieces, combined with measured poetry and reviews, social comment, philosophy, and erudite meanderings. In its own rather miscellaneous way, 'Hrafnhoh' is a magazine dedicated to the intellectual, aesthetic, and spiritual development of its readers: almost denomination-blind, it encourages an appreciation of authentic Christianity in its many manifestations: for instance, issues have alluded to Primitive Methodist history, monasticism, and Biblical study."

BL: 1; 2; 8; 13–33. (ZC.9.a.1341)
NLS: HP.la.1760 PER
TCD: PER 85–453

H.U. See The Honest Ulsterman D212

366 Hybrid. / edited by Kevin Cadwallender. Peterlee, [No. 1] (1990)–5 (1992). ISSN: 0960–3611

BL: 1. (ZC.9.a.2720)
UCL: 2
Poetry Library

367 I Want To Eat Your Stomach / edited by Ethelred Skudge Naggernunk. Burnley, [1985–?]

Noted by the UK Little Magazines Project.
No holdings known.

368 Ibid / edited by Matthew Hart, Matthew Hollis, Douglas Ramsay, Sinéad Wilson. Edinburgh: Department of English Literature, University of Edinburgh; Ibid Press. [No. 1] [1994?]–5 (Spring 1997)

Related Imprint: Ibid Press issued at least two untitled collections in the Ibid New Poets Series, the first by Kate Lowenstein and Roddy Lumsden (1996), BL: YK.1997.a.236, and the second by Matthew Hart and Sarah Osborne, with a foreword by Hugo Williams (1997), BL: YK.1998.a.1028. These appear to have been issued as supplements to Ibid

BL: 3–5. (ZK.9.a.4654)
CUL: 2; 5. (L727.c.1267)
NLS: [1]–4 .PER 88–430 1994–1997)
Poetry Library: [1]–5

369 Icarus / edited by Marc Alexander. London: Southern Cross Press, No. 1–2 (1982)

UCL

370 Iceni: tales from the East
(Anglia). Lowestoft: Lavender Publishing,
1st ed. (Summer 1997)–2nd ed. (1998). ISSN:
1368–9959

BL: ZK.9.a.5334

371 Identity Magazine: poetry,
interviews, what's on / edited by Lemm
Sissay. Manchester: Commonword;
Cultureword, Issue 1 (1990)–2 [1991]

Poetry Library

372 Illuminations: an international
magazine of contemporary writing /
edited by Simon Lewis, Tom Dobbs, Bernard
O'Keefe, and Stephen Walsh. San Francisco,
Tanzania, Ryde, then Charleston, South
Carolina: Rathasker Press, No. 1 (Autumn
1982)–14 (1998). ISSN: 0736–4725

Note: Early issues were published from San Francisco,
Tanzania, and other locations. From perhaps no. 9 to no.12
publication was from the Isle of Wight, after which the
publication moved to Charleston, South Carolina.

CUL: 3 (Spring 1984)–13 (Summer 1997). (L727.c.958)
NLS: [Unnumbered] (Spring 1987)–13 (Summer 1997).
(HJ4.902 PER)
TCD: [Unnumbered] (Spring 1987)–13 (Summer 1997).
(PER 89–447)
Poetry Library: 4 (1985); 7; [9?]–14

373 Impact: a collection of poems by
members of New Old Voices Poetry
Group. London: New Old Voices Small Press,
Anthology 1 (1996)

BL: ZK.9.a.5117

374 Imprint / edited by Terry Boyce, Tony
Frazer and Hélène Li. Hong Kong, No. 1
(1980)–4 (1982)

Contributors include Aleksis Rannit (translated from the
Estonian by Henry Lyman), Roy Fisher, Denise Levertov,
David Jaffin, Charles Simic, A. R. Ammons, Doris Lessing,
Nathaniel Tarn, Edward Jabès (trans. Keith Waldrop),
Odysseus Elytis (trans. Edmund Keeley and Philip
Sherrard), Larry Eigner, Anthony Barnett, Gael Turnbull,

Marin Sorescu (trans. from the Rumanian by Michael
Hamburger), Zhou Bang-Yan (trans. from the Chinese by
Leung Lo-you), and others.

BL: P.901/1933

375 The Incredible Spring Panda /
edited by G. A. Moore. Banbury, [No. 1?]
(1979)

Poetry Library

376 The Incurable / edited by Mark
Valentine. New Duston: Mark Valentine, Issue
1–3 (1979)

UCL
Poetry Library: 1–2

377 Infolio / edited by Tom Raworth.
Cambridge, 1 (1986)–100 (1987)

Note: Each issue consists of a single folded card, with (in
almost all instances) work by one poet/writer and one
artist.

One hundred issues of Infolio were produced in 1986 and
1987, with a wide range of writers and artists represented.
Eclectic: writers as diverse as Alan Brownjohn and Allen
Fisher, Hugo Williams and J.H. Prynne, Thom Gunn and
Julien Blaine. Other contributors included Franco
Beltrametti, Dominique Fourcade, Robert Creeley, Larry
Eigner, Ian Hamilton Finlay, Anselm Hollo, Asa
Benveniste, Lee Harwood, Norma Cole, Robert Grenier,
Anthony Barnett, Barrett Watten, Keith Waldrop, Rosmarie
Waldrop, Les Coleman, Billy Mills, and Brian Marley.

CUL: 1–40, 47, 73 (1986–87). (L900.b.725)
Poetry Library: 1–72, 74–100

378 Ink / edited by Nick Kimberley. London,
[No. 1, 198?–?]

Noted by the United Kingdom Little Magazines Project.
No holdings known.

379 Ink. [Warminster: R.D. Stevenson, 1,
1989?]

BL: ZK.9.a.1525
TCD: PB–112–648

380 Inklings / edited by David Sheen, Jeremy Syms and Margaret Lerner Wright. London: Bonaventure Studio B, [No. 1] (1977)

Poetry Library

381 Inklings: the magazine of the Barnsley Literary Society. Barnsley: Barnsley Literary Society, [No. 1, 198?–?]

Noted by the United Kingdom Little Magazines Project. No holdings known.

382 Inkshed: international poetry and fiction / edited by Anthony Smith, Leslie Markham, Sue Wilsea and Bernard Young. Hull: Inkshed, Issue 1 (1986)–26 (1994). ISSN: 0951–0427

Note: Originally with the subtitle: "Humberside poetry and fiction magazine"

BL: 2–13, 20–22. (ZK.9.a.198)
CUL: 2–13. (L718.c.766)
NLS: 2–13. (DJ.s.188 PER)
TCD: 2–13. (PER 94–382 1986–1989)
UCL: 12–26.
Poetry Library: 13; 15; 17–22

383 Innercity. London: Open Door Writers, Vol.1 no. 1 [1993?]–?

BL: Vol. 2 no. 4 (Spring 1995). (ZK.9.b.8660)

384 Insight / [edited by John Huscroft and Andrew Bruns?]. Chelmsford: J. Huscroft, [Vol. 1 no. 1] (1980)–vol. 2 no. 12 (Winter 1986). ISSN: 0260–5767

Note: Vol. 2 no. 9 appears not to have been published
BL: [Vol. 1 no. 1]; vol. 1 no. 5; vol. 1 no. 8; vol. 2 no. 6. (P.903/680)
CUL: L999.b.1.3005
NLS: [Vol. 1 no. 1] (1980); vol. 2 no. 12. (1986). (P.la.9321 PER)

385 Integument: short prose and verse. Horfield: Belston Night Works, No. 1 (1986)–?. ISSN: 0267–5633

BL: No. 1. (ZC.9.a.952)
CUL: No. 1. (L999.c.3.1467)

386 Inter Alia: international arts & literature / edited by Patrick Verdon. Cambridge: Pigment Publishing, No. 1 (Mar. 1995)–3 (Sep. 1995). ISSN: 1351–6558

BL: 1. (ZC.9.b.6101)
CUL: L727.b.352
NLS: HJ9.1856 PER
TCD: PER 95–213 1995
UCL: 1

387 Inter Arts / edited by Pramesh Mehta and Moussa Jogee. Edinburgh: Interarts, Vol. 1 no. 1 (July 1986)–no. 11 (1991). ISSN: 0951–0176

Note: Variant subtitles: "the arts of the third world"; "a journal of third world cultures"; "a quarterly journal of cultural connections"

"Interarts is a non-profit making body based in Edinburgh which aims to promote in the main the performing and visual arts of the ethnic culture." – from the first issue. Colin Nicholson later became editor (while Mehta and Jogee remained involved, Mehta becoming Arts Editor, Jogee becoming Executive Editor), and Jenny Dawe was Reviews Editor. Although this was a general cultural review, poetry was an important part of it with contributors including Nissim Ezekiel, Angus Calder, Alan Spence, David Dabydeen, David Constantine, Stephen Watts, Liz Lochhead, Jean Arasanyagan, Andrew Jackson, Eric Wishart, Janet Paisley, Tessa Ransford, Elizabeth Burns, Duncan Glen, Shamsun Rahman, Hugh McMillan, Sigmund Mjelve, and others.

BL: Vol. 1 no. 1–no. 4 (Summer 1987); no. 6 (June 1988), no. 7 (Oct. 1988); no. 9 (Sept. 1989) (ZK.9.b.472)
NLS: HP.med.217 PER
Poetry Library: Vol. 1 no. 9 (Sept. 1989)

388 Interactions / edited by Dianne M. Moore, Marcelle Mouktar, Régis Philibert, Ulrich Barth and Pedro Méndez Castillo. Exeter: University of Exeter, French Department and St. Helier, Jersey, Vol.1 pt. 1 (June 1989)–vol. 7 pt. 2 (Dec. 1995); Special Competition Publication (1996). ISSN: 0956–5396

BL: Vol. 1 pt. 1–vol. 7 pt. 2. (ZC.9.a.2212)
Poetry Library

Interarts *See* Inter Arts E387

389 Interchange / edited by Richard Marggraf Turley, Stuart Kime and Tom Hengen. Aberystwyth: Department of English, University of Wales, No. 1 (Mar. 1998)–4 [2001]. ISSN: 1462–0189

BL: ZC.9.a.5206
CUL: L727.c.1345
NLS: HJ3.1700 SER
TCD: PER 89–938
Poetry Library

390 Interference / edited by Michael Gardiner. Oxford, [No. 1, 1993]

Contributors included Edwin Morgan (translating Gennady Aygi), Richard Price (on the Informationists), W. N. Herbert, and others.

UCL
Poetry Library

International Melodic Scribble *See* Melodic Scribble E487

391 International Review / edited by J. C. R. Green. Portree, Isle of Skye, [1983?–?] ISSN: 0263–7111

Note: Related to *Prospice*, *Printer's Pie* and *The Moorlands Review*.

Noted by the United Kingdom Little Magazines Project. No holdings known.

392 The Interpreter's House: poems and short stories / edited by Merryn Williams. Wootton, No. 1 (Feb. 1996)– . ISSN: 1361–5610

Website: Issues are digitised at www.poetrymagazines.org.uk

"I believe that modern poetry has drifted dangerously far from the common reader and admire work which is technically accomplished, has powerful images, and appears to mean something." – Merryn Williams, from the statement given at www.poetrymagazines.org.uk. Contributors include: Dannie Abse, Alan Brownjohn, David Constantine, Sophie Hannah, Sheenagh Pugh, Carole Satyamurti, Vernon Scannell, R.S. Thomas, and others.

BL: 1–4; 6– . (ZC.9.a.4664)
CUL: 2; 3; 5– . (L727.c.1390)
NLS: 9– . (HJ3.1699)
Poetry Library

393 Intimacy: written being / being written / edited by Adam McKeown. Maidstone: [A. McKeown], [No. 1] (Sept. 1992)–?. ISSN: 0967–6651

Contributors include Paul Buck, Antonin Artaud (trans. Stephen Barber), Paul Green, and others.

BL: [1]. (ZD.9.a.56)
UCL: [1]
Poetry Library: [1]–[3]

394 Into Print: the magazine of Stirling Writers' Workshop. Stirling: c/o University of Stirling, [No. 1, 1985]. ISSN 0267–3738

BL: ZC.9.a.288
CUL: L999.c.3.1057
NLS: DJ.s.124(5) PER
TCD: PER 81–946

395 Intrigue: poetry, art, stories magazine. Plymouth: Pablo Publications, Preview ed. [1981]–? ISSN 0263–9238

BL: P.903/448

396 Inverse. Stowmarket: Inverse Press, 1 [198–?]–2 [1989?]

Poetry Library: 2

397 Inverse / edited by Elizabeth Eger. Cambridge, No. 1 (1993)–2 (1994)

CUL: 1. (Cam.c.41.26)
UCL

398 Invicta Literary Magazine / edited by Margaret Regan. Earls Barton: Invicta, 1 (1986)–3 (1987). ISSN: 0269–073X

BL: ZC.9.a.776
CUL: L999.c.3.965
NLS: 2–3. (HP.sm.941 PER)
TCD: 2–3. (PER 90–911)

399 **Involution: new writing** / edited by A. M. Horne, Matt Thorne, Rebecca Duffy, S.T., and Rory Drummond. Cambridge, 1 [1993?]–4 (1996)

Note: Variant subtitle: "experimental poetry"

Poetry Library: 2 (1994)–4

400 **Iota: poetry quarterly** / edited by David Holliday, then Bob Mee and Janet Murch. Chesterfield, then Stratford-upon-Avon, No. 1 (1988)– . ISSN: 0266–2922

Website: www.iotapoetry.co.uk/

BL: ZC.9.a.1303
CUL: L727.c.1187
NLS: 1–58; 60–62; 64– . (HP.sm.890 SER)
TCD: PER 85–637
UCL: 1–2; 5–

401 **Ipse: the other magazine of the International Poetry Society** / edited by Robin Gregory. Bakewell: Hub Publications, No. 1 (1976)–7 (1977)

Related Imprint: Hub Publications produced many poetry and play collections throughout the 1970s

Poetry Library: 1; 4–7

402 [Blank]

403 **Island** / edited by Robert Ford. Newark, No. 1 (1999)– .

Poetry Library

404 **Issue One** / edited by Ian Brocklebank. Grimsby: EON Publications, [Feb. 1984–1993?] ISSN: 0266–111X

Note: Related to The Bridge with which it merged

BL: [3 unnumbered issues, 1984–1992] (ZK.9.a.2350)
NLS: Lacking all between Dec. 1984 and Oct. 1985; all between Mar. and Dec. 1986; and all between May 1988 and May 1989. (HP.sm.478 PER)
UCL: [8 unnumbered issues, 1987–1993]
Poetry Library: [4 unnumbered issues, 1984–1993]

405 **Isthmus Poetry: a quarterly journal established primarily as an outlet for subscribers' own work** / edited by Maurice James. Bedford: Isthmus Poetry, [1] Spring 1990–? ISSN: 0957–3402

BL: ZC.9.a.2504

406 **Janus.** Dublin: Dublin Tutorial Centre, [1] (Summer 1992)–[2] (Summer 1993)

BL: ZK.9.b.5672
NLS: HJ9.1783 PER
TCD: PER 91–931 1992–1993

407 **Jennings Magazine** / edited by Philip Sidney Jennings, Paul Magrath and Bob Kirkpatrick. London, No. 1 (1985)–7 (1988). ISSN: 0268–5000

Stories, poems, articles, and reviews (including of other magazines). Contributors include Alan Sillitoe (poems), Derek Stanford, Martin Amis (interviewed), Gavin Ewart, Geoffrey Holloway, Iain Banks (interviewed), Tony Curtis, Nicholas Royle, Peter Daniels, Tim Love, and others.

BL: ZK.9.b.197
CUL: L718.b.173
NLS: DJ.m.273 PER
TCD: PER 90–641
UCL: 1–3
Poetry Library: 1; 5–7

408 **Joe Soap's Canoe** / edited by Martin Stannard. Clare, Felixstowe: JSC Publications, No. 1 (1978)–16 [1993]. ISSN: 0951–4864

Mark Hillringhouse, Paul Violi, Lydia Tomkiw, and Ian McMillan were also involved editorially at various stages in the magazine's history.

BL: 10. (ZC.9.a.1245)
CUL: 1–13; 14–16. (L727.b.247)
NLS: 1–11. (DJ.m.374 PER)
TCD: 1–11. (PER 92–545)
UCL: 1–15
Poetry Library: 1–3; 5; 9–10; 12–16

409 **Jonathon Magazine** / edited by Iain Pigg and Elaine Cusack. Stanley, Co. Durham: Jonathon Press, Issue 1 (Jan. 1989)–?

BL: 1. (ZA.9.a.8748)

410 The Journal / edited by Catherine Walsh and Billy Mills. Dublin; Castletroy, Co. Limerick: hardPressed Poetry, [No. 1] (1998)–2 (1999)

Website: gofree.indigo.ie/
Related Imprint: hardPressed Poetry is a significant publisher of (not exclusively) Irish poetry within the experimental / avant-garde / innovative / independent spectrum

A magazine of experimental poetry. Contributors in the first issue include: Catherine Walsh, Maurice Scully, Geoffrey Squires, Tom Raworth, and Brian Coffey (the magazine reproduces his reading notations for two sections of "Advent"). The second issue was much more North American-orientated, with poetry by Nicole Brossard, Charles Bernstein, Cid Corman, Theodore Enslin, Peter Gizzi, Fanny Howe, Keith Waldrop, Rosmarie Waldrop, and Craig Watson. It included papers delivered at the 1999 3rd Cork Conference on Experimental Irish Poetry by Alex Davis, Romana Huk, and Karen Mac Cormack.

BL: ZC.9.a.5287

411 The Journal / edited by Sam Smith. Bradford-on-Tone then Ilfracombe: Sam Smith, Issue 1 (2000)– . ISSN: 1466–5220

Note: Continues: Journal of Contemporary Anglo-Scandinavian poetry.

BL: ZK.9.b.17206
UCL

412 Journal of Contemporary Anglo-Scandinavian poetry / edited by Sam Smith. Bradford-on-Tone: Sam Smith, Issue 1 [1995]–10 [1999]. ISSN: 1357–9487

Note: Succeeded by The Journal

BL: ZC.9.a.4281
UCL
Poetry Library: 1–9

413 Kaleidoscope. London: [s.n.], [1, 1985?]–?

BL: Cup.818/30

414 Keith Wright Memorial Poetry Competition. Glasgow: University of Strathclyde, Department of English Studies, 1981–1991

Note: Continued by Keith Wright Memorial Literary Competition, with a wider remit (so not recorded here).

Contributors included Richard Price and Stephen Greenhorn (later better-known as a playwright and writer for television)

BL: X.0958/305
CUL: L727.c.841.6
NLS: HP.sm.114
TCD: PR 12083

415 Kent Connections: the Kent writers journal / edited by Narissa Knights. Rochester, Kent: Federation of Kent Writers, Vol. 1 [199?]–vol. 3 no. 4 (1995). ISSN: 1363–4143

Note: Continued by: Connections

BL: Vol. 3 no. 4. (ZK.9.b.9559)
Poetry Library: Vol. 3 no. 1; vol. 2 no. 3–no. 4

416 Kingfisher / edited by Anne K. Monaghan. Sheffield: Anne K. Monaghan, No. 1–2/3 [1978?]

CUL: L727.c.1190

417 Kissing the Sky: love and heartbreak poems / edited by Sharon Elton. Lichfield, Issue 1 [1991?]–4 (1994)

Poetry Library

418 Kite / edited by Chris Broadribb. Cardiff: Kite, No. 1 (Winter 1986/87)–2 (1987). ISSN: 0950–2998

Kite published many of those associated with the Cabaret 246 workshop (and magazine of the same name) and Red Sharks Press, but writers from further afield, too. Contributors included: Allen Fisher, Mark Williams, Paul Brown, Peter Finch, Bob Cobbing, Paula Claire, Nigel Jenkins, Gill Brightmore, Pat Egan, Ken Cockburn, Graham Hartill, Gavin Selerie, Lee Harwood, Ken Edwards, Barry MacSweeney, John Seed, Tom Raworth, Robert Sheppard, Bill Griffiths, Elaine Randell, and others.

BL: 1. (ZK.9.a.417)
UCL: 1–2
King's College London, Eric Mottram Archive: 1; 3. (7/337/1–2)
Poetry Library: 1

419 Kites / edited by Fleur Bowers. London: The Highgate Poets, 1 (1977)–

Note: Additional titles included: 1, *Kites Jubilant*; 2, *Kites Flying*; 3, *Kites Free*.

BL: 1–8; 15–. (each with a separate shelfmark)
CUL: 2–. (L727.c.1010.4)
NLS: 2 (HP2.79.630); 4 (HP2.81.21); 5 (HP2.82.662)
TCD: 16; 21– (PR 17574)
Poetry Library: 4

420 Klick: magazine of the Writing Society of the Polytechnic of Huddersfield, Communication Arts / edited by John Lancaster and Kerry Flynn. Huddersfield: The Writing Society of the Polytechnic of Huddersfield, Communication Arts, Issue 1 (1991)–2 (1992)

Poetry Library

421 Konfluence: a poetry magazine for the South-West based in the Stroud Valleys. Nailsworth: Konfluence Press, Issue 1 [Spring 1999]–6 (2003)

BL: ZK.9.a.6307
Poetry Library: 2–6

422 Krino: a literary magazine for Ireland / edited by Gerald Dawe. Corrandulla, Co. Galway; Dún Laoghaire, Co. Dublin: Krino Publications, No. 1 (1986)–18 (1995). ISSN: 0790–8172

Note: Each issue has an ISBN
Anthology: Gerald Dawe and Jonathan Williams (eds.), *Krino 1986–1996: an anthology of modern Irish writing* (Dublin: Gill and Macmillan, 1996), BL: YC.1997.b.1310

Others involved editorially included Avril Forrest; Aodán Mac Póilín; and Eve Patten. *Krino* was devoted to Irish writing, but not exclusively so. No. 14, co-edited by Dawe and Jonathan Williams, was given over to "The State of Poetry", with various poets contributing their thoughts, and their poems, e.g. Dennis O'Driscoll, Harry Clifton, Peter Fallon, Vona Groarke, Francis Harvey, Brendan Kennelly, Thomas Kinsella, Michael Longley, Medbh McGuckian, Nuala Ní Dhomhnaill, and others.

BL: 1–9; 12–18. (ZA.9.a.5824)
CUL: 1–3; 6; 12–15. (L733.c.106.1)

NLS: 1–3; 14–15. (DJ.s.113 PER)
TCD: PER 93–299 1986–1995
UCL
Poetry Library: 2–16/17

423 Kudos: poetry and art / edited by Graham Sykes. Leeds: Kudos, Issue 1 (1979)–12 (1982). ISSN: 0143–4969

From the outset wishing "to become a focal point for modern poetry and writing, not only in Britain but internationally." Although there were always visuals used in the magazine, the occasional article on art, and prose by Alan Sillitoe, Nicki Jackowska, Ian Robinson, and others, the heart of the magazine was poetry. The editorial style was eclectic, with poets including D. M. Thomas, Gerda Mayer, Peter Redgrove, John Heath-Stubbs, Steve Sneyd, Jim Burns, Clayton Eshleman, John Ash, George Bacovia (trans. Peter Jay), Adrian Mitchell, Martin Stannard, E. A. Markham, Paul Eluard, Jorge Luis Borges, and Octavio Paz (all three trans. Yann Lovelock), Takis Sinopoulos and Tassos Denegris (both trans. John Stathatos), Alan Halsey, Jeremy Reed, Ivor Cutler, D. J. Enright, Allen Fisher, Larry Eigner, Harry Guest, Tony Frazer, Peter Robinson, Antonio Cisneros (trans. Maureen Ahern and David Tipton), Robert Sheppard, Michael Hulse; and others.

BL: 1–5; 7; 8; 10; 11. (P.901/3164)
CUL: 1–11. (L727.c.838)
NLS: 1–11. (DJ.s.428)
TCD: 1–11. (PER 92–521)
UCL
Poetry Library: 1–11

424 Kunapipi: journal of post-colonial writing / edited by Anna Rutherford; and then others, including Anne Collett. Aarhus, Denmark: Dept of English, University of Aarhus; Hebden Bridge, W. Yorkshire: Dangaroo Press; Wollongong, N.S.W. (Australia): English Studies Program, University of Wollongong, Vol. 1 no. 1 (1979)–. ISSN: 0106–5734

Note: Continues: *The Commonwealth Newsletter*, but with a more literary brief. Address from vol. 22 no. 1 (2000) is Wollongong (but still copyrighted by Dangaroo Press in Hebden Bridge). Not published by Dangaroo from vol. 23 no. 1 (2001).

Index: "*Kunapipi* is an internationally refereed journal... cited in *Journal of Commonwealth Literature's* Annual Bibliography (UK), *The Year's Work in English Studies* (UK), *The*

American Journal of African Literature (USA), The Indian Assoc for Commonwealth Studies (India), The New Straits Times (Indonesia), The Australian Public Affairs Information Source (National Library of Australia), and the MLA Bibliography." – from the website.

Website: www.uow.edu.au/arts/kunapipi/

"Kunapipi is a bi-annual arts magazine of critical and creative writing with special but not exclusive emphasis on the new literatures written in English. It aims to fulfil the requirements T.S. Eliot believed a journal should have: to introduce work of little known writers of talent, to provide critical evaluation of the work of living authors, both famous and unknown, and to be truly international." – from the website (November 2004). Special issues include: vol. 19 no. 3, 'India and Pakistan, 1947–1997: A Celebration', ed. Shirley Chew; vol. 20 no. 1, 'The Windrush Commemorative Issue: West Indians in Britain, 1948–1998', ed. David Dabydeen; vol. 20 no. 3, 'Localities: Intercultural Poetics', guest edited by John Kinsella; vol. 21 no. 2, 'Post-Colonial London', guest edited by John McLeod; vol. 21 no. 3, 'South African War?: 1899–1902', guest edited by Elleke Boehmer.

BL: Vol. 1 no. 1– . (5123.450000). Second set: Vol. 1 no. 1–vol. 20 no. 3. (P.901/1743)
CUL: Vol. 1 no. 1–vol. 4 no. 2; vol. 10 no. 1–vol. 14 no. 3. (RCS.Per.1507). Vol. 15 no. 1– . (P700.c.809)
NLS: Vol. 1 no. 1–vol. 21 no. 3. (HJ4.945)
TCD: Vol. 19 no. 1– . (PER 89–153)
UCL: Vol. 10 no. 3–
Poetry Library: Vol. 19 no. 1–vol. 20 no. 1; vol. 20 no. 3–vol. 22 no. 2; vol. 23 no. 1–

425 Label / edited by Paul Beasley, Simon Carter and Ruth Harrison. London, [No. 1, Autumn 1982]–8 (Summer 1988)

BL: 3. (P.901/3547)
NLS: 3–8. (DJ.s.574(1))
UCL: 4–7
Poetry Library

426 Labrys / edited by Grahaeme Barrasford Young. Hayes, then London, then Frome, No. 1 (Feb. 1978)–11 (1985)

Related imprint: Bran's Head Books

An eclectic journal with contributors including Philip O'Connor, David Gascoyne, Kathleen Raine, Edwin Morgan, Brian Keeble, Alexis Lykiard, Douglas Barbour, Brian Ferneyhough, David Miller, and Jeremy Reed. It also included translations of Giacinto Scelsi, Tonino Guerra, Pascale Charpentier, Severo Sarduy, Marie Luise Kaschnitz,

Otfried Buthe, and others. Special issues included those on Michael Ayrton (no. 3); Lawrence Durrell (no. 5); and Alan Garner (no. 7). In no. 8 there was a George Seferis feature; and no. 9 included features on Michel Butor, George Perros and the artist John Piper. John Matthews, Robin Freeman and Douglas Barbour were also involved editorially.

BL: 1–5; 7. (P.901/3098)
CUL: 1–2; 4–5. (L718.c.250)
NLS: 1; 4–5. (HP2.82.214)
TCD: 1–5. (PER 92–461)
UCL
Poetry Library: 2; 4–6; 9; 10–11

427 LAMB: standing for literature, art, music, & baa / edited by Anthony Barnett. London: The Literary Supplement, Nothing Doing (Formally in London), Issue 1 (June 1981)–5 (March 1985). ISSN: 0261–0957

Small, A6, format, each issue only eight pages long, and each devoted to just one poet: respectively, Ralph Hawkins, Václav Pinkava, Douglas Oliver, Anthony Barnett, and Joseph Simas. There is a long gap between issue 4 (Apr. 1982) and issue 5 (Mar. 1985)

BL: P.901/3284
CUL: 1–4. (L727.e.7)
NLS: 1–4. (HP.la.197 PER)

428 Lancaster Literature Festival Poems. Lancaster: Lancaster LitFest Publications, [1, 1978?]–

BL: [17] (1994)– . (ZK.9.a.4002)
TCD: [17] (1994). (PL–267–405)

429 Language Alive / edited by cris cheek. Lowestoft: Sound & Language, No. 1 (1995)–2 [1996?]

Note: Title given as Language aLive. Issues have ISBNs rather than an ISSN
Website: www.slang.demon.co.uk/
Related Imprint: Sound & Language has published work by Caroline Bergvall, Allen Fisher, Miles Champion, Ulli Freer, Ira Lightman, and others

Language aLive, edited by the experimental poet and musician cris cheek, was concerned with performance-based writing. Number 1 had work by Fiona Templeton, Forced Entertainment, and Fiona Wright. Number 2 had Gary Stevens, Caroline Bergvall, Brian Catling, Tertia Longmire, Aaron Williamson, and Steve Benson.

UCL
Poetry Library

430 Language Issue. London, No. 1 (1992)

Language Issue was intended as a satire on Language Poetry and consisted of pseudonymous contributions (apart from a letter from J.H. Prynne, addressed to a fictitious or pseudonymous recipient).

UCL

431 Lateral Moves / edited by Alan White. Bolton: Aural Images, Issue 1 [1994?]–30 (2000). ISSN: 1360-3396

Variant titles: *Mortal Leaves* (issue 13), *Late Removals* (issue 14), *Amoral Svelte* (issue 17), *A Mole Travels* (issue 23). Insert in issue 14: *Buzzsaw (comic-strip)*

Michael Smith, Nick Britton, and Susan White were also involved editorially.

BL: 1–30. (ZK.9.a.4020)
CUL: 3–30. (L727.d.282)
NLS: 3–30. (HJ9.2369 SER)
TCD: 3–30. (PER 87–669)
Poetry Library: 7–30

432 Laughing Song / edited by William Park. High Wycombe, [c.1979–?]

Noted by the United Kingdom Little Magazines Project. No holdings known.

433 Lay Poets. Gressenhall: Gressenhall News & Views, [198–]–?

BL: 3. (P.955/1540)
CUL: 3. (L999.b.1.2938)

434 Leaf-mould / edited by Eunice Pearson. Birtley, Co. Durham: Eunice Pearson, 1 (1993)–4 (1994)

BL: 2–4. (ZK.9.a.3105)

435 Lexikon: the magazine of the Stoke-on-Trent Writers Group / edited by Francis Anderson, Roger Bradley, and Kath Bradley. Stoke-on-Trent: Stoke-on-Trent Writers Group, [Vol. 1] no. 1 (1995)–vol. 5 no.

1 [2001]. ISSN: 1362–7201

BL: [Vol. 1] no. 3 (1996)–vol. 5 no. 1 [2001] (BL: ZK.9.b.9404)
CUL: Spring 1997, Summer 1997, Dec. 1997–Jan. 1998; vol. 3 no. 2; vol. 3 no. 5. (UL Periodicals Department)
NLS: Spring-Fall 1997, Dec. 1997–Jan. 1998; vol. 3 no. 2; vol. 3 no. 5. (HJ8.1436 PER)
TCD: Winter 1996/7–? (PER 88–936)
Poetry Library: [Vol. 1 no. 2]–3, vol. 4 no. 3–?

436 Liberty: poetry and prose / [edited by Michael Paraskos]. Leeds: School of English, University of Leeds; Poetry Audience Press, Vol. 1 no. 1–no. 2 (1990)

Note: Related to *Poetry and Audience*

Poetry Library

437 The Lighthouse: poetry quarterly / edited by Esther Jones. Cardiff: Mimosa Music Publishers, Issue 1 (1996)–3 (1997)

Poetry Library

438 Linear A / edited by Johan de Wit. London, No. A [i.e. 1] (1992)–B [i.e. 2] (1996). ISSN: 0965-8556

Linear A was a magazine of criticism of contemporary poetry, but utilizing a poetic (and very individual) approach. The poet Johan de Wit was the author of the entire contents of both issues.

BL: ZC.9.a.3323
CUL: L999.d.1.100
NLS: PER
TCD: PER 87–723 1996
UCL

439 Links / edited by Bill Headdon. Tunbridge Wells: Links, [No.] 1 (Spring 1997)–. ISSN: 1366-4553

BL: 2– (ZK.9.a.5504)
UCL
Poetry Library: 6–

440 Linkway: a publication for writers and friends / edited by Fay C. Davies. Dyfed: Hayton Books, No. 1 (1995)– . ISSN: 1361–0007

BL: ZK.9.a.4270
Poetry Library: 9; 12; 14; 19–

441 Lit Up! the magazine for new writers / edited by Jeremy Rogers. Torrington: Lit Up! Publishing, Issue 1 (1994)–2 (1995)

Poetry Library

442 Literary Monthly: stories, poems, articles. Brighton: B. Hutchison, No. 1 [June 1978]–5 (Oct. 1978). ISSN: 0141–4976

BL: 1–4. (P.901/3102)
CUL: 5. (L999.c.3.631)
NLS: 1; 5. (HP2.80.1746)
TCD: 1; 5. (PER 92–417)

442a Literary Review / edited by Gillian Greenwood, then Auberon Waugh, then Nancy Sladek. Edinburgh, then London, No. 1 (5th Oct. 1979)– .

Note: Absorbed *Quarto*
Website: www.literaryreview.co.uk
Founded by Anne Smith, Department of English, University of Edinburgh.

BL: Newspaper Collections
CUL: L700.b.71
NLS: Library lacks: Sep.-Oct. 1985; May 1986; Jan., Apr., Oct. 1988; no. 255, (1999); nos. 267–269, (2000); no. 273, (2001). (HJ9.813 SER)
TCD: PER 79–451

443 Litmus / edited by Laurie Smith. London: Stukeley Press (The City Literary Institute), 1 [1982]–6 [1986?]. ISSN: 0263–4635

Note: Related to *Magma*

BL: P.901/3325
CUL: 1. (L999.c.3.951)
NLS: 1. (HP2.88.1703 PER)
Poetry Library

444 The Littack Supplement: (incorporating Littack) / edited by William Oxley. Brixham: The Ember Press, No. 1 [1976]–6 (Nov. 1980). ISSN: 0142–324X

Note: Succeeds *Littack*. Published in association with the American journal, *Lapis Lazuli*
Interview: with William Oxley in Görtschacher 1
Related Imprint: Ember Press also published *Acumen, Headland, Laissez Faire* and various single-author collections

BL: P.901/825
CUL: L727.b.173
NLS: P.la.5424 PER
TCD: PER 81–702
UCL: 2–6
Poetry Library

445 Live Writers. Newport: Stow Hill Poets, Issue 1 [1985]–?

The Stow Hill Poets were Keith Mclaren-Martin, Tim Llewellyn-Jones, Robert Sims, Pete Walsh, P. J. O'Donoghue, and David Harding.

BL: 1. (P.901/3703)

445a Liver & Lights / edited by John Bently. London: Ivory Towers Ink, No. 1 (Oct. 1984)– .

A strong visual character, with the use of calligraphy and woodcuts, mixing older texts (Byron, Emily Brontë) with contemporary poems. Later, Bently "toured the books" with musicians. The cross-arts nature (some have a very physical even sculptural aspect) and sometimes controversial content make *Liver & Lights* a particularly notable little magazine project.

BL: 1; 2; 7. (P.421/876); 23. (YK.2000.a.420); 25 (YK.2002.a.5312)
CUL: 1–4; 7; 25–. (L400.c.425)
NLS: 1–3; 6–7 (HP.med.86 PER); 23 (HP2.200.03235); 25 (HP2.200.02299); 27 (HP2.202.05079)
TCD: 1–7. (PER 90–619)

446 Living by the Sea. Chichester: Nautical Publications, Sept./Oct. 1998–Spring 1999. ISSN: 1464–0767

BL: ZK.9.b.12968

LJ *See* Lovely Jobly E457

447 Lobby Press Newsletter / edited by
Richard Tabor. Colchester then Maldon then
Cambridge: Lobby Press, 1 (1978)–18/19 (Sept.
1982)

Note: Variant titles: *Lobby Press; Lobby Newsletter*

Lobby Press Newsletter combined poems, letters, interviews
and visual work. Contributors include Paul Buck (featured
in no. 18/19), Carlyle Reedy, Bob Cobbing, cris cheek, Bill
Griffiths, Glenda George, and others. The editor used his
social security number as a pseudonym in some issues.

BL: 16–18/19. (ZA.9.a.10597)
CUL: 5; 10; 12; 18/19. (L999.b.1.747)
UCL: 1–2; 4–18/19
Poetry Library: 1; 3–5; 8–14; 18/19

448 Logos Magazine / edited by Andy
Keighley, Joanna Keighley and Andy Scott.
Dundee: Logos Magazine, No. 1 (1980)–7/8
[1982]. ISSN: 0144–2457

Note: Variant title: *Logos*. Continues: AMF: *Aristophanes'
Middle Finger*.

BL: P.903/652
CUL: 1–6. (L727.b.244)
NLS: 1–6. (P.la.7759 PER)
TCD: 1–6. (PER 92–407)
UCL
Poetry Library: 2–7/8

449 Long Pen / edited by Adrian Clarke and
Terry Jones. Brighton, [No. 1985]

UCL

450 The Long Poem Group
Newsletter / edited by Sebastian Barker and
William Oxley. Brixham: Acumen, No. 1 (May
1995)– .

Interview: With William Oxley,
www.poetrykit.org/ivoo/oxley.htm
Website: www.dgdclynx.plus.com/lpgn/lpgn1.html

Discussion and championing of the long poem as a distinct
poetic genre.

BL: ZC.9.b.6130
CUL: Periodicals Department
NLS: 1–4; 6– . (HJ9.1995 SER)
TCD: PER 77–423
UCL: 2–

451 The Longstone: poetry & art /
edited by A. J. Noctor. Ventnor: Longstone
Magazine, Issue 1 (May 1987)–? ISSN:
0951–7847

BL: 1. (ZC.9.a.1247)
CUL: 1. (L999.c.3.1451)
NLS: 1. (HP.med.255 PER)

452 Loot / edited by Paul Green.
Peterborough: Spectacular Diseases, [Vol. 1]
no. 1 (July 1979)–vol. 5 no. 4 (1987). ISSN:
0144–6436

Website: www.indigogroup.co.uk/llpp/spectac.html
Related Imprint: Spectacular Diseases has published many
poetry collections often by authors assocated with the
magazine, including works by David Miller, Tom Raworth,
Ulli Freer, Peter Larkin, Alaric Sumner, Rosmarie Waldrop,
Alan Halsey, Stephen Rodefer, Connie Fox, Paul Buck,
Elaine Randell, Gavin Selerie, Wendy Mulford, and others.
They also have acted as distributors for Burning Deck, the
American imprint.

BL: P.903/604
CUL: L727.a.17
NLS: Vol. 2 no. 1 (Mar. 1981)– . (HP.la.356)
TCD: PER 92–630 1979–1987
UCL

453 Lost Dreams. Leeds, then Norwich,
No. 1 [1989?]–3 [1990?]

Poetry Library: 2–3

454 Lot 49. Edinburgh: Exiles Press, No. 1
(Feb. 1981)–? ISSN 0261–2046

Related Imprint: Exiles Press also published Colin
MacDonald's short story collection *Under a Northern Sky*
(1980), BL: X.909/44939

BL: 1. (P.901/3261)
CUL: 1. (L999.c.3.802)
NLS: 1. (HP3.83.22)
TCD: 1. (PER 90–388)
UCL: 1

455 Love and Life: a selection of
poems, songs, and thoughts / from
Spartacus R. London: Sukisa, Vol. 1 (1988)–?

BL: Vol. 1. (ZC.9.a.2960)

456 Love Poster: writings & drawings from North London & Southern Turkey. London: E. Suleiman, [No. 1, 198–?]–?

BL: No. 9 (1991). (ZK.9.b.4260)

457 Lovely Jobly: a monthly magazine from Our Wonderful Culture / edited by Hercules Fisherman and Patricia Scanlan. London: Our Wonderful Culture, Vol. 1 no. 1 (1990)– vol. 2 no. 3 (1991). ISSN: 0959–0803

Note: Variant title: LJ
Related Imprint: Our Wonderful Culture also published a small number of books, including Scanlan and Fisherman's *Hasting Hastings* (undated), BL: YA.1996.a.19016

BL: Vol. 1 no. 1–no. 2. (ZC.9.a.2678)
Poetry Library: Vol. 1 no. 1–no. 2; vol. 2 no. 1–no.3

458 Mad Cow / [edited by Jont Whittington?]. London, [No. 1, 1994–2, 1996?]. ISSN: 1362–3346

Minimalism from both sides of the Atlantic was a strong aesthetic strand in the work of the contributors, who included Robert Lax, Thomas A. Clark, Simon Cutts, Ian Hamilton Finlay, Harry Gilonis, Spike Hawkins, Denise Levertov, Thomas Meyer, Stuart Mills, Ron Padgett, Iliassa Seguin, Jonathan Williams, Cid Corman, Colin Sackett, Stephen Duncalf, and others. The editorial, referring to the New Generation promotion of twenty younger poets, to "paraphraseable" poetry, and to other aspects of contemporary poetry, includes the lines, "For those who think anthologies make rather generous claims. / For those who aren't quite satisfied with their new generation."

BL: 1. (ZK.9.a.4482)
Poetry Library: [1–2]

459 The Mad Hatter, Exeter?, c.1980?
Known only from *The New Truth* which states that it incorporates the previous magazine.

460 Madam X / edited by M. Lollopit. London: Colophon Press, Issue 1 (1996). ISSN: 1366–3801

Related Imprint: Colophon Press

Poems and prose by Kathy Acker, Rebecca Camu, Kate Long, Alasdair Gray, Gaynor Cox, Peter Jolliffe, Duncan McLean, W.S. Milne, James Mirana, Fiona Pitt-Kethley, Rane Roberts, James Seathwaite, John Owen, Rick Plewes, Robin Robertson, Iain Sinclair, Muriel Spark, Alan Wall, and Jakob Zaaiman.

BL: ZK.9.b.10282
CUL: L999.b.1.2803
NLS: HJ9.2450 PER
TCD: PER 95–312 1996
Poetry Library

461 Madoc: the magazine of the Creative Writing Class at Cardiff University Extra-Mural Department / [Edited by Chris Torrance?] Cardiff: Cwm Nedd Press, 1 (1976/77)–2 (1978/79)

Appears to be continued by *Accidents & Devotions*

BL: 1 (P.903/566)
UCL: 1
King's College London, Eric Mottram Archive: 2. (7/367/1 1978–1979)

462 Madog: arts magazine / edited by Tony Curtis. Barry: Department of Arts & Languages, Polytechnic of Wales, Vol. 1 (Winter 1977)–vol. 3 no. 2/vol. 4 no. 1 (Spring 1981)

Eclectic mix of U.S. and U.K. writers, including Denise Levertov, Ted Hughes, Jeremy Hooker, Norman MacCaig, Gillian Clarke, Anne Stevenson, and Charles Simic. At least one *Madog* poster was also issued, no. 1 featuring the poetry of Danny Abse. The last issue was co-edited by Tony Curtis and Mike Parnell.

BL: P.421/754; Second set: 5330.960000 DSC
CUL: L985.c.169.1
NLS: HP4.84.460 PER
UCL: Vol. 1 no. 1–vol. 2 no. 1.

463 A Magazine / edited by J. Garth O'Donnell and Mike Ruddick. Bristol, 1–? [c.1984]

The third issue has a cloth (but not hardback) binding, designed and printed in yellow, black and red by Douglas White. Cut-out typewriter texts and images are used inside and there are some surrealist-influenced texts and illustrations.

BL: 3 (1984). (Pressmark Pending)

464 The Magazine / edited by Nancy Allison and Sally Russell. Coventry: Open Studies, Department of Continuing Education, University of Warwick, No. 1 (Summer 1995)–11 (Winter 2001). ISSN: 1359–1282

Note: Continued as: *Wordplay* (beyond the period of this bibliography)

BL: 1–3; 5–6. (ZK.9.a.4190)
CUL: L727.c.1339
NLS: HJ4.1793
TCD: PER 72–409
Poetry Library: 1–6

465 Magazing / edited by Chris Mitchell. Glasgow: Tape Books, [No. 1, 198?]–14 (1989)

Related Imprint: Tape Books published Steve Sneyd's *Fifty-fifty Infinity* (1986), BL: YC.1988.a.13061

UCL: No. 9–14 (1987–1989)
Leeds University, Brotherton Library: Unnumbered issue [198–]; 9 (Mar. 1987)–12 [1990?]. (Special Collections English Q–1 MAG)

466 Magma / edited by Tony Burrell. Clacton-on-Sea, No. 1 (Autumn 1979)–7 [1982?]

BL: 1–3. (ZA.9.a.2976)
CUL: 1–6. (L727.c.1139)
NLS: 1–6. (HP2.86.2207 PER)
TCD: 1–6. (PER 92–613 1979–1981)
UCL
Poetry Library

467 Magma / edited by Laurie Smith, David Boll, Helen Nicholson and others. London: The Stukeley Press (The City Literary Institute), then Magma, No. 1 (1994)– . ISSN: 1352–9269

Note: Related to *Litmus*
Website: www.magmapoetry.com/

"We look for poems which give a direct sense of what it is to live today – honest about feelings, alert about world, sometimes funny, always well crafted. When we decided on the title *Magma*, it was to suggest the molten core within the world, hidden as deep feelings are and showing itself in unpredictable movements, tremors, lava flows, eruptions." – from the website, Nov. 2004. Unusual in that each issue has a different editor, on a rotating basis. The magazine

launches each issue with a reading, often at the Troubadour Coffee House, Earls Court.

BL: ZK.9.a.3292
CUL: L727.c.1202
NLS: HJ8.2498
TCD: PER 87–163
Poetry Library

468 Maidstone Poets News, c.1984

Note: Continued by: *The Mighty Column*

No holdings known.

469 The Main Street Journal: poetry, fiction, music, essays / edited by John Moser, David Rose and Paul Lyalls. London and Ashford, Middlesex: The Main Foundation; The Main Objective, Issue 1 (1993/1994)–3 (1997), [New Series], Issue 001 (2000)– . ISSN: 0967–6104

Note: Variant title: *Main Street Journal*. Issues also have ISBNs

BL: ZK.9.a.3597
CUL: 1–3. (L999.b.1.2665). [New Series], Issue 001– . (U.L. Periodicals Dept.)
NLS: HJ9.2156
TCD: PER 95–173 1993/94–2001
UCL: 2–3
Poetry Library: 3, [New Series], Issue 001–

470 Mana: "a gathering of voices" / edited by Christopher Lewis and Richard Goldsmith. York and Hereford, No. 1 (1995). ISSN: 1359–754X

BL: ZC.9.a.4342
Poetry Library

471 Mango Season / edited by Joan Anim-Addo and Alba Ambert. London: Caribbean Women Writers Alliance, c/o The Carribean Centre, Goldsmiths College, No. 1 (Dec. 1994)– . ISSN 1369–0205

Website: www.goldsmiths.ac.uk/departments/english-comparative-literature/caribbean-centre.php

A refereed journal which features and discusses Caribbean women's writing.

BL: No.1 (Dec. 1994)–11 (Dec. 1998). (ZK.9.b.11114). Later issues on order.

472 Manifest: multi-cultural writing in English / edited by Duncan McGibbon.

London: Students Union, Institute of Education, No. 1 (1995)

BL: ZC.9.a.4165
Poetry Library

473 Manticore: surrealist communication. Leeds: Surrealist Group in Leeds, No. 1 (Spring 1997)–

Note: No. 6 was accompanied by the supplement, *Prehensile Tail No. 2*

The Surrealist Group in Leeds was founded by Kenneth Cox, Bill Howe, and Sarah Metcalf in 1994.

BL: ZK.9.a.4836

474 Manutius: the Oxford University magazine of new writing. Oxford, No. 1 (Michaelmas 1995)–3 (1996)

Note: Continued by: *Zero*

BL: 2–3. (ZK.9.a.4836)
CUL: 1; 3. (L727.c.1258.1)
NLS: 1; 3. (HJ3.1311 PER)
TCD: 1; 3. (PER 88–294 1995–1996)
Oxford University, Bodleian Library: P.F02858 (Issue 1 (1995)–issue 3 [1996])

475 The Many Review: a new magazine of criticism and commentary / edited by John Welch.

London: Many Press, Issue 1 (Spring 1983)–6 (Jan. 1990)

Related Imprint: The Many Press
Website: www.shadoof.net/many/

BL: 1–4, 6. (P.901/3412)
CUL: L718.c.787
NLS: HP.sm.350 PER

476 Mar. St Ives, Issue 1 (1989)–4 (1991)

Contributors included Jeremy Adler, Paul Buck, Herbert Burke, Robert Sheppard, and others.

Poetry Library

477 Margin: a quarterly magazine of literature, arts and ideas / edited by Robin Magowan, Walter Perrie and Richard Burns. London, then Dunning: Common Margins, No. 1 (1986)–11 (1990). ISSN: 0950–5091

Contributors include Robert Vas Dias, Tom Pickard, John Heath-Stubbs, Sorley MacLean, Clayton Eshleman, George Szirtes, and others.

BL: ZK.9.a.465
CUL: L718.c.457
NLS: DJ.m.2251
TCD: PER 92–948 1986–1990
UCL
Poetry Library: 1, 5–11

478 Markings: new writing and art from Dumfries and Galloway / general editor, John Hudson; arts editor Anne Darling; assistant editors, Elspeth Brown, Jeff White, and Donald Adamson. Kirkcudbright: Markings, No. 1 (1995)– . ISSN: 1460–7166

Related Imprint: Markings publish the Galloway Poets Series, including short collections by Elspeth Brown, Douglas Lipton, Rosemary Baker, John Manson, and others.
Website: www.btinternet.com/ffij.hudson/j.hudson/index.html

BL: ZK.9.a.5450
NLS: 8– . (HJ3.1686)
Poetry Library: 5; 6; 9–

479 Mars / edited by Kristina Dusseldorp.

London: [Kristina Dusseldorp], distributed by Paperchain, [No. 1–2, 1978?]

Contributors included Yevgeny Yevtushenko, Rabindranath Tagore, Michael Horovitz, Anthony Edkins, Yehuda Amichai, Elias Canetti, Nicanor Parra, Octavio Paz, Margaret Atwood, and others. Ted Hughes was an advisory editor.

BL: 2. (ZA.9.b.1605)
CUL: 1–2. (L999.b.1.459)

480 Martin Holroyd's Poetry Monthly / edited by Martin Holroyd. Nottingham: Martin Holroyd, Issue 1 (Apr. 1996)– 11 (Feb. 1997). ISSN: 1363–4356

Note: Continued by: *Poetry Monthly*

BL: ZK.9.a.4683
Poetry Library: 2–11

481 Matrix / edited by Stephen Hull. Katesbridge, nr. Banbridge, Co. Down: Matrix Publishing, Vol. 1 issue 1 (Apr. 1999). ISSN: 1468–621X

Associated with Queen's University, Belfast. Interview with Declan Kiberd, essay on Heaney, essay on Beckett, poetry by Alan Gillis and Frederic Legrand, short stories and reviews.

BL: ZK.9.a.6639

482 Mauvaise Graine / [edited by Walter Ruhlmann]. Ashton Keynes then South Cerney then Caen, France: Mauvaise Graine, No. 1 (1996)– . ISSN: 1365–5418

BL: 1; 3–5; 7–12. (ZK.9.a.4925)

483 Maximum Load / edited by David Fellows and Brian Phillips. Penarth and Neath: Maximum Load Press, No. 1 [1984]–2 [1986?]. ISSN: 0267–7210

Contributors include Peter Finch, Robert Minhinnick, and others.

BL: P.901/3710
CUL: L999.b.1.2191
NLS: 1. (HP.la.1448 PER)
Poetry Library

484 Meantime / edited by Paul Johnstone, David Thomas and Malcolm Williams. Cambridge: Meantime, No. 1 (Apr. 1977)

Contributors include Ian Hamilton Finlay, Roy Fisher, Tom Raworth, and (interviewed) Basil Bunting.

BL: P.901/3081
CUL: L999.c.3.700
NLS: HP3.80.1234 PER
TCD: PER 94–223 1977
UCL

485 Mediterraneans: a quarterly review: ideas new writing images / edited by Kenneth Brown and Robert Waterhouse. Manchester, then Paris: Didsbury Press, 1 (1991)– . ISSN: 0961–530X

Note: No. 5/6 was published in Paris with cover title *Méditerranéennes semestrielle*. It changed its named to *Méditerranéennes* from this point on. Each book-length issue features a theme (Marseille, Corsica, Morocco, Istanbul, Alexandria, Israel/Palestine, Beirut/Sarajevo) depicted with short stories, poetry, eyewitness accounts, interviews and photography.

BL: 1, 2/3. (ZC.9.a.3141)
CUL: 7–8/9
Poetry Library: 1–6

486 Megaphone / edited by John Ash, Paul Edwards, and Richard McCann. Manchester, No. 1 (1980)

Poetry Library

486a Melmoth / edited by Salah Faiq, with the collaboration of Michael Bullock and John W. Wilson, [No. 1–?, 1979?]

Related Imprint: Melmoth later became an imprint based in Vancouver
Surrealist texts

BL: 2. (Pressmark pending)

487 Melodic Scribble: literature magazine / [edited by Andrew Savage]. Burnley: Pleasure Publications, Issue 1 (1984)–6 [1986] + Supplement [1986]

Note: Variant Title: *International Melodic Scribble*

CUL: 5–6. (L999.b.1.1940)
NLS: 5. (HP.la.1402 PER)
Poetry Library: 1–6 + Supplement

488 Memes / edited by Norman Jope. Birmingham, then Plymouth, Issue 1 [1989?]–10 [1994?]. ISSN: 0960–4855

According to the editor's introductions in issues 1 and 3, *Memes* was concerned with a meeting between the "magical" or "spiritual" and the "artistic", and was interested in experimental writing. Contributors included Peter Redgrove, Martin A. Hibbert, Tilla Brading, Johan de Wit, Sheila E. Murphy, Jay Ramsay, Robert Sheppard, John

Mingay, Rupert M. Loydell, Stephen C. Middleton, Norman Jope, Ian Taylor, Vittoria Vaughan, Tim Allen, Sean Bonney, and others.

BL: ZC.9.a.2488
CUL: 4–10. (L727.c.1136)
NLS: HP.la.2214 PER
TCD: 4–10. (PER 86–387)
PL: 1–10
UCL: 3–10

489 Metre: a magazine of international poetry / edited by Hugh Maxton, Justin Quinn and David Wheatley. Dublin, Prague, and Hull: in association with The Lilliput Press, No. 1 (Autumn 1996)–.
ISSN: 1393–4414

BL: ZK.9.a.5166
CUL: 1–9; 12– . (L727.c.1408)
NLS: 1–9; 12– . (HJ4.1857)
TCD: PER 78–461
Poetry Library

490 Metrix / edited by David Gill and others. [London?]: Guildhall Poets, [No. 1] [1980?]
Poetry Library

491 Mica. Aberdeen: Department of English, Aberdeen University, Vol. 1 no. 1 (Winter 1992)–? ISSN: 0967–7070

BL: Vol. 1 no. 1–vol. 1 no. 3. (ZC.9.a.3291)

492 Midnight Ink / edited by Anjan Saha and Gerard Thomas. London: Sundial Arts; Sundial Press, Vol. 1 no. 1 [1996?]–no. 3 (1998)

Midnight Ink was the magazine of the Black and Asian writing collective based at the Riverside Studios, West London.

Poetry Library: Vol. 1 no. 2–no. 3

493 Midnight Oil. London: British Amateur Press Association, Vol. 1 no. 1 (1983)–? ISSN: 1354–0572

BL: Vol. 2 no. 2 (Spring 1991)–vol. 2 no. 8 (1997) . (ZK.9.a.3235)

494 The Mighty Column: poetry, art, jazz, food & fashion in Maidstone. Maidstone: Mighty Column Press, no. 4 (Feb. 1986)–no. 14 (Dec. 1986)

Note: Continues: Maidstone Poets News

BL: 11 (Sept. 1986)– BL: ZC.9.b.3763
NLS: HP.la.1403 PER
TCD: PER 90–308

495 Mind the Gap: New York / London / edited by Karin Randolph, Susan Maurer, Paul-Henri Sullivan, Andrew Neilson, Martin Mitchell and Eva Salzman. New York and London, Vol. 1 (1998)–4 (2000)

Note: Later issues are referred to as "Issue" rather than "Vol."

Poetry Library

496 Mind the Gap: a quarterly poetry magazine. London, [No. 1] (1998/1999)– .
ISSN: 1465–7155

Publishes the work of the participants of the Fulham and Chelsea Survivors' Poetry Group.

BL: ZK.9.a.6375
Poetry Library

497 Mineral Waters of the Caucasus / edited by Rod Mengham and Geoffrey Ward. Cambridge, [No. 1] (1976)

NLS: HP3.91.1152
UCL
Poetry Library

498 Miscellany: a magazine of literary reviews. Merthyr Tydfil: Vampyric Press, Issue 1 (Apr. 1994)–3 (Oct. 1996)

Related Imprint: Vampyric Press also published Avalon

BL: ZK.9.a.3436

499 Mixed-up, Shook-up / edited by Margery Hill. [London?]: [No. 1, 1979?]
Poetry Library

500 Molly Bloom / edited by Aidan Semmens and Ged Lawson. Goole, North Humberside, and Durham, [No. 1] (1980). ISSN: 0260–8413

Contributors include Tony Baker (on Paul Blackburn), Gael Turnbull, Peter Riley, Wendy Mulford, Lee Harwood, David Chaloner, and Kelvin Corcoran.

BL: P.901/3263
CUL: L999.c.3.810
NLS: P.la.9618 PER
TCD: PER 90–388
UCL
Poetry Library

501 Momentum / edited by Pat Connolly, Pamela Goodwin and Jeff Bell. Wrexham: Wrexham Writers Workshop, Vol. 1 (1985)–21 (1992)

BL: ZC.9.a.786
UCL: 1–20

502 The Mongrel Fox: a quarterly / edited by John Feeney, Ronan Sheehan and Lucile Redmond. Dublin: Irish Writers' Co-operative, No. 1 (Dec. 1976)–2 (Apr. 1977)

Profiled in: Tom Clyde, *Irish Literary Magazines: an outline history and descriptive bibliography* (Dublin: Irish Academic Press, 2003)

BL: P.901/3074
TCD: Per 90–376

503 Monkey Kettle / edited by Matthew Michael Taylor, Diane Hainsworth and Simon Edwards. Milton Keynes, 1 (1999)– .

Variant Title: M(onkey) K(ettle)

Poetry Library

504 Monomyth / [edited by D. J. Tyrer]. Southend-on-Sea: Atlantean Press, 1 [199?]– .

Related Imprint: Atlantean Press also publish *Awen, Garbaj*, and poetry booklets
Website: www.geocities.com/dj_tyrer/monomyth.html

Short stories and longer poems.

BL: 21 (Jan. 1999) – . (ZK.9.b.16955)

505 The Monster That Ate Japan / edited by Ian Joynson [and Ian Gideon?]. [London?], Vol. 1 no. 1 [1997?]–no. 3 (1999)

Note: Variant titles: *Der Monstarr Dat Eight Japaned; The Manster That Hate Chiffon*

Poetry Library

506 The Moon / edited by Robert Banks. Colne, [c.1984–?]

Noted by the United Kingdom Little Magazines Project. No holdings known.

507 Moonlight / [edited by L. Linford], South Woodham Ferrers: L. Linford, No. 1 (June 1991)–16 (1998)

BL: 1–8; 11; 13–16. (BL: ZK.9.a.1877)

508 Moonstone: poetry & prose / edited by Talitha Clarke and Robin Brooks. London: Moonstone, No. 1 (Candlemas 1981)– .

BL: 43– (ZK.9.a.2259)
CUL: 28– . (L727.c.1252)
NLS: 28– . (HJ4.1529)
Poetry Library: 17–36; 38; 40–42; 44–

509 The Moorlands Review / edited by J. C. R. Green. Leek: Anne Johnston / The Moorland Press, No. 1 (1983)–4 (1984). ISSN: 0263–712X

Note: Incorporated in *Prospice* with No. 5. Related to: *Printer's Pie* and *The International Review*

BL: P.901/3413
CUL: L999.d.1.35
NLS: 1–2. (HP1.87.2244 PER)
UCL: 2; 4
Poetry Library: 2

More Scratchings *See* Scratchings E721

510 A Morning Star Folio / edited by Alec Finlay. Dunblane, then Edinburgh: Morning Star Publications. First Series, Vol. 1 (Feb. 1990)– Sixth series, vol. 4 (1995)

Note: Also known as *Morning Star Folios*. Vol. 2 in the sixth series, planned as a collaboration between David Miller and Ian McKeever, was not published.
Index: Indexed by the UK Little Magazines Project. A catalogue raisonné of Morning Star, including the folios, is given at the press's website
Profiled in: Notes attached to the index by the UK Little Magazines Project
Related Imprint: Morning Star went on to produce the more commercial Pocket Books series of anthologies, as well as the *Under The Moon* series of folios
Website: www.platformprojects.org/htmlpages/morningstar1.htm

Morning Star Folios were distinguished by the poets and artists involved in the series, and by the often beautiful design of each issue. Alec Finlay showed a preference for a sparely worded poetry and for interactions between text and art, as well as an emphasis on poetry in translation. Most issues consisted of a single folded sheet in an envelope, often with an additional enclosure, usually also a single sheet (e.g. an essay on the featured poet). Many issues featured a single poet or writer in collaboration or conjunction with an artist, but there were also anthology issues. Poets published in the series include Robert Lax, Thomas A. Clark, Frank Samperi, Ian Hamilton Finlay, Robert Creeley, Ian Stephen, and Norma Cole. There were also translations by Cid Corman (Santoka and Masaoka Shiki), Jerome Rothenberg and Pierre Joris (Kurt Schwitters), Edwin Morgan (Attila József), Rosmarie Waldrop (Friederike Mayröcker), and others. Artists included Sol Le Witt, Jess [Collins], Hans Waanders, David Connearn, Ron Costley, and Andrew Bick.

BL: Cup.410.g.189
NLS: FB.m.484
UCL

511 Mosaic: the twice yearly magazine of stories and poetry by Nottinghamshire writers. Nottingham: Bay Window Press, 1 [1992]. ISSN: 0964–6647

BL: ZK.9.b.4419
NLS: DJ.m.1903(6) PER
TCD: PER 91–738

512 Moth / edited by Zack Samuel. London, No. 1 [1976?]–8 (1977)

BL: 3. (P.903/564)
UCL: 4–8

513 Mother Tongues / autopilot, Andrew Clay. Nottingham: Mother Tongues, Issue 1 (Autumn 1986)

Appears to have been a forerunner of *Tak Tak Tak*.

BL: ZC.9.a.1099

514 Mouthpiece: the Apples & Snakes poetry quarterly. London: Apples & Snakes, No. 1 (1995)

Poetry Library

515 Mr Tiger's Bookstop. Worthing: Somniloquence, Issue 1 (Jan. 1997)–2 (Feb. 1997). ISSN: 1366–7173

BL: ZK.9.a.5103

516 Mslexia: the magazine for women who write / [edited by Debbie Taylor]. / Newcastle-upon-Tyne: Mslexia Publications Ltd, Issue 1 (Spring 1999)– . ISSN: 1473–9399

Index: A contents listing for each issue is given at the website
Website: www.mslexia.co.uk/

From the website: "No other magazine provides *Mslexia's* unique mix of debate and analysis, advice and inspiration; news, reviews, interviews; competitions, events, courses, grants. All served up with a challenging selection of new poetry and prose." Publishes many poems and carries articles on poetry. Guest editors are often poets, too, including: Michèle Roberts, Jackie Kay, Carol Ann Duffy, Wendy Cope, Kate Clanchy, Sophie Hannah, and Liz Lochhead. Linda France contributes a twelve-part series, "First principles in contemporary poetry".

BL: ZK.9.b.14905
CUL: Periodicals Dept.
TCD: PER 102–572, ISSUES
NLS: HJ8.2144 SER
Poetry Library

517 Mugshots / edited by Mike Dobbie and Ulli McCarthy. [London?], 1 [1976?]–12 [1977?]

Apart from the Supplement on Language poetry, published in 1980, each issue consisted of the work of one poet, printed on a folded card, with a photograph of the poet on the cover. 1: Ulli McCarthy [i.e. Ulli Freer]; 2: Mike Dobbie; 3: Allen Fisher; 4: Jeff Nuttall; 5: Peter Barry; 6: Eric Mottram; 7: Glenda George; 8: Bill Griffiths; 9: Paul Buck; 10: Paul Matthews; 11: Pete Hoida; and 12: Ken Edwards.

BL: YA.1998.b.2363
CUL: 12. (1994.8.976)
UCL

518 Murid / edited by N. Coleman and others. Oxford: Pembroke College, Spring 1976

Contributors included John Wain, Wes Magee, Adiran Henri, Alex Lykiard, Frances Horovitz, Anne Stevenson, Jeff Nuttall, and others. Details taken from a catalogue by the bookseller I. D. Edrich.

BL: ZD.9.b.119

519 Mute / edited by Simon Worthington, Daniel Jackson, Stephen Faulkner and Helen Arthur; then Pauline van Mourik Broekman, Tina Spear, Daniel Jackson and Josephine Berry. London: Slade School of Art; then Skyscraper, No. 1 (1989)–4 (1990), [New Series] Pilot Issue, No. 0 (Winter 1994)–? ISSN: 1356–7748

Website: docs.metamute.com/view/Another/OmContent#OpenMute_and_Mute_History

Mute began as a student art magazine edited by Simon Worthington, Daniel Jackson, Helen Arthur and Stephen Faulkner with four issues published between 1989–1990, employing various (sometimes unusual) formats. In common with other art school magazines such as *It's: Wimbledon School of Art Magazine* and *AX5: the Student Art Magazine*, it included some poetry-related work. It was revived in 1994, as *Mute: Digital / Information / Services* (also known as *Mute: Digital Art Critique*), and later became *Mute: the Art and Technology Newspaper*.

BL: [New Series] Pilot Issue, No. 0 (Winter 1994)–6 (Autumn 1996). (ZK.9.d.1282)
CUL: [New Series], 9 (1998). (L999.b.1.3146)
NLS: [New Series], 9 (1998). (HJ8.1506 PER)
TCD: [New Series], 9 (1998). (PER 89–950)
UCL

520 Navis / edited by Robert Bush, Bill Morley and Tony O'Donovan. London, No. 1 (1993)–7 (1999)

CUL: L727.b.430
NLS: HJ8.2345
TCD: PER 102–638
Poetry Library

521 N.D.Y. / [edited by Rupert Mallin?]. Leicester: N.D.Y. Collective, Issue 1 (1985)–?

From the editorial statement: "N.D.Y. is a magazine of visual arts and writings. Our aim is to give exposure to artists and writers who for economic or social reasons do not normally have the social reasons do not normally have the facilities to realise their work in print and so reach a wider audience." Contributions include an article by John Hoffman on the crisis in South Africa with an illustration by Martin Berry, poems by Rupert Mallin and Martin Stannard, Alison Jackman on women under apartheid, and an account of the Leicester Anti-Fascist Defence Campaign. The format is photocopied and stapled, tall and narrow, with comic strips.

BL: 1. (ZA.9.c.45)

522 Nerve / edited by Ruth Black, Linda Jackson, Dave Manderson and Brian Whittingham / Glasgow: Nerve Magazine, Cardonald College, Issue 1 [1999]–? ISSN: 1466–5891

High production values for this square–shape magazine, publishing stories, poetry, screenplays, articles and reviews. Contributors include: Hamish Whyte, Des Dillon, Magi Gibson, Brian McCabe, John Maley, Kevin McNeil, S. B. Kelly, Jim Carruth, Valerie Thornton, Louise Welsh, Rachel Seiffert, Janice Galloway, Zoë Strachan, Dilys Rose, Robin Lindsay Wilson, A. M. Forster, James McGonigal, Liz Niven, Tom Bryan, Jen Hadfield, Jim Ferguson, and others.

BL: ZK.9.a.6623
NLS: HJ8.2346 PER
UCL: 2– .

523 Never Bury Poetry! / edited by Jean Tarry and Bettina Jones. Bury, No. 1 (1989)– . ISSN: 1350–4371

Website: www.nbpoetry.care4free.net/

BL: ZK.9.b.4736
Poetry Library: 1–2; 7–9; 23–41; 43–

New Arcadians *See* [New Arcadian Broadsheet]
E524

524 [New Arcadian Broadsheet] /
edited by Ian Gardner, Patrick Eyres, and
Grahame Jones. Bradford: New Arcadians
Press, 1 [1981]– .

Note: Continues: *The Blue Tunnel*
Index: A contents list is given for the first fifty-six issues in
New Arcadian Broadsheets: Index [2003?]
Website: www.leeds.ac.uk/fine_art/external/press/nap/
index.html
Related Imprint: New Arcadian Press publishes cards,
small books, print portfolios and *New Arcadians' Journal*

"The New Arcadian Broadsheets are published as serial
pages of a Book-in-Progress. These text-image prints are
overprinted onto the A4 letterheaded paper of the New
Arcadian Press. The broadsheets comprise pithy comments
upon the cultural and political environment, and are
variously commemorative, lyric, whimsical or polemic." No
actual title is given on the broadsheets; the one given here
is constructed from the prefatory information in the *Index*.

BL: 1–56. (Pressmark pending)

525 New Arcadians' Journal / edited by
Patrick Eyres; design by Ian Gardner.
Bradford: New Arcadians Press, No. 1 (Spring
1981)– . ISSN: 0262–558X

Index: Listing at www.leeds.ac.uk/fine_art/external/press/
nap/index.html
Website:
www.leeds.ac.uk/fine_art/external/press/nap/index.html
Related Imprint: New Arcadian Press publishes cards,
small books, print portfolios and *New Arcadian Broadsheet*

Founded in 1981 by Eyres, Gardner and Grahame Jones this
evolved from Eyres and Gardner's earlier *Blue Tunnel*
magazine but, unlike *New Arcadian Broadsheet*, it has a more
substantial format, publishing scholarly work on the 18th
century garden alongside new lyrical poetry and prose. The
new creative work celebrates a sense of place and the
pleasures of walking, and there are occasional polemical
pieces. Special issues include: 14, *The Atlantic Wall: Thoughts
on the Picturesque* (texts by Ian Hamilton Finlay and Patrick
Eyres); 18, *Happy Valley* (Patrick Eyres, with illustrations by
Ian Gardner); 22, *A Far Distant Landscape* (Stuart Mills, with
illustrations by Ian Gardner.); 41/42, *Landfall: Encounters with
English Landscapes* (edited by Patrick Eyres).

BL: 5–12; 17– . (P.901/3541)
CUL: 9 (Spring 1983)– . (L400.c.491)

NLS: 9 (Spring 1983)– . (HJ2.309 PER)
Poetry Library: 13–15; 18; 22; 41/42

New Hope International *See* The Hallamshire &
Osgoldcross Poetry Express D200

526 New Leaf: poetry & prose / edited
by Tony Fitzgerald, Frank Mellon, Jerry Cook,
Abbas Faiz, Edmund Hewson, Julia Pistor, Jane
Wright and Donall MacLochlainn. London:
Humanities Department, Chelsea College,
No. 1 [1979]–6 (1982)

BL: ZC.9.b.18
CUL: L727.b.210
NLS: P.la.8216 PER
TCD: PER 92–802
UCL
Poetry Library: 3 (1979)–6

527 New Poems from Portsmouth /
edited by Denise Bennett and Mike Merritt.
Portsmouth, No. 1 [1991?]–2 (1992)

Poetry Library: 2

528 New Poetry from Oxford / edited by
Amy Boesky, Keith Jebb, Helen Kidd and W. N.
Herbert. Oxford: Oxford Poetry Workshop,
No. 1 [May 1983]–6 (1988)

Oxford University, Bodleian Library: An unnumbered
issued dated 1983. (2805 e.3040)
Poetry Library: 3 (1984)–6

529 New Prospects Poetry / edited by
Tony Sims. Broadway, Worcs.: Spring
1990–Spring 1992. ISSN: 0957–8803

BL: Spring 1992. (ZK.9.a.2146)
Poetry Library: Spring 1990–Autumn 1990; Spring 1991;
Autumn 1991; Spring 1992

New Spokes *See* Spokes E773

530 The New Truth / edited by Andy
Botterill. Exeter, Issue 1 [198–?]–8 (1991)

Note: Incorporates: *The Mad Hatter*

Poetry Library: 8

531 The New Welsh Review: Wales' literary magazine in English / edited by Belinda Humfrey, Peter J. Foss, Michael Parnell and Robin Reeves. Cardiff: New Welsh Review Ltd., Vol. 1 no. 1 (1988)– . ISSN: 0954–2116

Note: Variant title: NWR. Each issue also has a running number, so that e.g. vol. 4 no. 1 is also no. 13. After vol. 14 no. 4 (issue no. 56), the simpler form was used alone, i.e. no. 57 onwards
Website: www.newwelshreview.com/

Modelled on *The Welsh Review* (1939–1948) and *Dock Leaves* and its successor *Anglo-Welsh Review* (1949–1988). "Each issue – which features a whole host of writing talent, from the literary heavy-weights to rising new stars – includes a range of critical articles, book reviews, fiction and poetry. Engagingly written, visually attractive and intellectually ambitious, *New Welsh Review* casts a challenging, exuberant eye over the literary scene in Wales. While the magazine's focus is on Welsh writing in English, its outlook is deliberately cosmopolitan, encompassing broader European and international literary contexts."– from the website, Dec. 2004. Contributors include the poets Sheenagh Pugh, Ruth Bidgood, Stephen Knight, Tiffany Atkinson, and Christopher Meredith.

BL: Vol. 1 no. 1– . Lacking vol. 3 no. 2. (ZC.9.a.1635)
CUL: Vol. 1 no. 1– . Lacking vol. 3 no. 2, vol. 3 no. 3. (L718.c.814)
NLS: Vol. 1 no. 1– . Lacking vol. 3 no. 2, vol. 3 no. 3. (HJ8.1464)
TCD: PER 77–631
UCL: Vol. 1 no. 1–vol. 2 no. 3.
Poetry Library: Vol. 1 no. 1–

532 New Writing Network / edited by Graham Stanley. London, No. 1, (1993)

Poetry Library

533 New Writing Scotland / edited by Alexander Scott and James Aitchison [and subsequent editors] . Association for Scottish Literary Studies, [No. 1, 1983]– .

Note: Often given a separate title that is individual to the volume as well as a running number
Anthology: No. 22, given the separate title, *Bringing Back Some Brightness*, edited by Valerie Thornton and Hamish Whyte, is actually an anthology selected from the preceding twenty years of the annual.

A significant annual for Scottish writers of poetry and fiction, many publishing their work here early in their writing career.

BL: ZC.9.A.788
CUL: 11–18. (L718.c.295)
NLS: HP.sm.417
TCD: [1]–7. (PER 92–203 1983–1989)
UCL: [1]–7

534 The New Yorick / edited by Peter Cockhill, Jamie Hodder-Williams and Shannon Peckham. York: Derwent College, University of York, No. 1 [198–?]–20 (1989)

Note: Continues: 'Y' (which had continued *Yorick*)

CUL: 10–11; 16–20. (L985.b.248)
NLS: 10–20. (HP.la.1499 PER)
Poetry Library: 10–12

535 New Yorkshire Writing: a quarterly review of writing / edited by Jay Jeff Jones. Hebden Bridge: Yorkshire Arts Association, No. 1 (Summer 1977)–8 (Spring 1979)

Note: Supplement to *The Month in Yorkshire*, a non-literary magazine
Related Imprint: Yorkshire Arts Association had published previous magazines, including *Yorkshire Review*, BL: ZA.9.a.2782, and had supported *Headland*, BL: P.901/539.

CUL: NPR.B.566
NLS: 7.192
TCD: PER 92–443
UCL: 1–2.
Poetry Library: 2

536 Nexus / Durham: Durham University English Society, [No. 1, 1982–4, 1984]

A poetry broadsheet.

Durham University, Palace Green Library: L 058.2129 NEX

537 Nexus: magazine of the Wandsworth Writers' Guild / edited by Julie Higgins. London: Wandsworth Writers' Guild, No. 1 [1978?]–8 [1979]. ISSN: 0142–2111

BL: 1–7. (P.903/615)
CUL: 8. (L999.c.3.701)
TCD: 8. (PER 93–65 1979)
Poetry: 7–8

538 Nineties Poetry / edited by Graham Ackroyd. Hove: Lansdowne Press, No. 1 (1994)–11 (1996/1997)

Poetry Library

539 Ninth Decade / edited by Tony Frazer, Ian Robinson, and Robert Vas Dias. London: Oasis [No.] 1 (1983)–no. 11 (1989). ISSN: 0264–6773

Note: Incorporated *Telegram* and *The Atlantic Review* as well as *Shearsman* and *Oasis*, the latter two separating out again and each beginning a new series in their own right.
Continued by: *Tenth Decade*
Related Imprint: Oasis Books published *Oasis* and many poetry collections

Ninth Decade published a wide range of significant poets, from the U.K., U.S., France and Australia. Contributors included Larry Eigner, Gael Turnbull, Roy Fisher, Lee Harwood, Paul Evans, Christopher Middleton, Philip Crick, David Jaffin, Michael Palmer, Jackson Mac Low, John Taggart, Gustaf Sobin, Michael Heller, Pierre Joris, Rosmarie Waldrop, Simon Perchik, John Yau, John Perlman, August Kleinzahler, John Tranter, George Evans, John Ash, David Chaloner, Yann Lovelock, Peter Dent, Richard Caddel, Alan Halsey, Kelvin Corcoran, Peter Middleton, Martin Anderson, Joan Retallack, Ken Edwards, Adrian Clarke, David Miller, Gig Ryan, and others. Poets in translation included Edmond Jabès (translated by Rosmarie Waldrop), Eugène Guillevic (translated by Robert Chandler), Claude Royet-Journoud (translated by Christopher Middleton), and Emmanuel Hocquard (translated by John A. Scott). Critical articles included Robert Sheppard on Paul Evans, George Evans on George Oppen, Philip Crick on Gustaf Sobin, Jane Augustine on H.D., and Eric Mottram on Paul Blackburn. There were also graphics by Ian Robinson, Ray Seaford, Thomas Wiloch, Brian Lalor, Stanley Engel, and others.

BL: 1–2. (P.901/3429)
CUL: 1–4; 6. (L727.c.943)
NLS: 1–6. (DJ.s.11 PER)
UCL
Poetry Library

540 Ninth Wave / [edited by Jeremy Silver?], [c.198?]

Note: Continued by: *Strange Mathematics*

No holdings known.

541 Nomad / edited by Julie Smith, Dominic Boyle, Alina Murze, Gerry Loose, Myra Pater, Eva Spevack and others. Glasgow: Survivors Poetry Scotland, Issue 1 [1998?]–?. ISSN: 1368–3055

A number of different editors have changed over the issues of this magazine, which publishes poetry and other texts by survivors of the mental health system, of abuse or addictions.

BL: 1–8. (ZC.9.a.4918)
NLS: HJ8.1910
Poetry Library: 1; 3; 5–

542 The North / edited by Peter Sansom and Janet Fisher. Huddersfield: Huddersfield Polytechnic, then The Poetry Business, [No. 1] (1986)–. ISSN: 0269–9885

Related Imprint: The Poetry Business's Smith/Doorstop imprint has published many collections, pamphlets and cassettes
Website: www.poetrybusiness.co.uk/

Founded by Peter Sansom as a magazine of the English Society of the Huddersfield Polytechnic, the first two issues were published by the Polytechnic itself. Contributors have included Carol Ann Duffy, Harry Guest, Jon Silkin, Michael Schmidt and Simon Armitage. *The North*, with for example *The Wide Skirt*, is associated with a Huddersfield-associated grouping of poets, notably Simon Armitage.

BL: 3–6; 8; 10– . (ZC.9.a.3557)
CUL: 5–8; 10– . (L727.b.331)
NLS: 1–8; 10–11; 13–14; 16– . (HJ9.1595 SER)
TCD: 5–. (PER 82–216)
UCL
Poetry Library: [1]; 3–

543 North Magazine / edited by John Hughes. Belfast, No. 1 (1983/1984)–7 (Winter/Spring 1987)

Profiled in: Tom Clyde, *Irish Literary Magazines: an outline and descriptive bibliography* (Dublin: Irish Academic Press, 2003), BL: 2725.g.3414

Andrew Elliott, Adrian Maddox, Patrick Ramsey, and Kevin Smith were also involved editorially.

CUL: L727.b.388
Belfast Central Library: IR
Queen's University Library: hPR8700.N8
Poetry Library: 1–5/6

544 Northern Line: a quarterly magazine of original work by children and teenagers / edited by Mark Burke. Leeds: Poetry Leeds Publications, 1 [1978]–16/17 (1983)

Note: A number of broadsheets were published in conjunction with this magazine. Broadsheet no. 3 (1980) is amongst the holdings at The Poetry Library.

CUL: 4 (1978); 13 (Summer 1981)–16/17. (L999.d.1.106)
NLS: 13 (Summer 1981)–14 (Autumn 1981). (SP.sm.24 PER)
UCL
Poetry Library: 5 (1979)–16/17

545 Northlight: poetry review / edited by Anne Thomson. Glasgow, No. 1 (1990)–5 (1992). ISSN: 0961–7558

BL: ZC.9.a.2748
NLS: 1–3. (DJ.s.676(2) PER)
UCL
Poetry Library: 1; 3–5

546 Northwords: the magazine from the North for poetry and fiction / edited by Angus Dunn, then Robert Davidson. Dingwall: Issue 1 (Autumn 1991)– . ISSN: 0964–6876

BL: ZC.9.b.4887
CUL: L727.b.421
NLS: HJ9.1592
TCD: PER 73–916
Poetry Library: 1–18; 20–

547 Not Poetry: contemporary prose writing / edited by Peter Hodgkiss. Newcastle upon Tyne: Galloping Dog Press, 1 (Spring 1980)–7/8 (Winter 1984/5) ISSN: 0144–9842

Related Imprint: Galloping Dog published collections by many contemporary poets

"The purpose of the magazine is to present a wide range of prose writing, including writing that falls in that nebulous area between poetry & prose." – editorial statement in first issue. Specifically not poetry, for example short fiction by Kathy Acker, Jeff Nuttall, Jim [i.e. James] Kelman, but the contributors are often poets, e.g. Ken Smith, Tom Pickard, Allen Fisher, Elaine Randell, Kelvin Corcoran, John

Muckle, Alan Halsey, and others.

BL: 1–4; 7/8. (P.903/679)
CUL: L718.b.110.1
NLS: HP4.83.609 PER
TCD: PER 92–705
UCL

548 Notnot: UEA writers. Norwich: Union of UEA Students, University of East Anglia, No. 1 (1990)–3 (1991)
Poetry Library

549 Numbers / edited by John Alexander, Alison Rimmer, Peter Robinson and Clive Wilmer. Cambridge, Vol. 1 no. 1 (1986)–vol. 4 no. 2 (1989/1990). ISSN: 0950–2858

Note: Each issue was also given a single running number, the set forming no. 1–6/7. The last was a double issue.

Contributors included Thom Gunn, Seamus Heaney, Elaine Feinstein, John Ashbery, John Cayley, Douglas Dunn, Christopher Middleton, Ruth Padel, Charles Tomlinson, Roy Fisher, Yves Bonnefoy, Franco Fortini, John Ash, Michael Longley, Medbh McGuckian, John Welch, U. A. Fanthorpe, August Kleinzahler, Jamie McKendrick, Gael Turnbull, Vikram Seth, Ken Smith, John Tranter, and others.

BL: ZC.9.a.2214
CUL: L727.d.237
NLS: DJ.s.619 PER
UCL: 1–4
Poetry Library: Vol. 1 no. 1– vol. 4 no. 2

550 Nutshell / edited by Jeff Phelps, Roger Pearson, Christopher Nankivell and Penny Grimley. Coventry, No. 1 [198–?]–13 (1992)

Jeff Phelps and Roger Pearson's last issue was no. 8 (Apr. 1990) after which Christopher Nankivell and Penny Grimley edited the magazine.

BL: 8–13. (ZK.9.a.2507)
UCL: 3–11
Poetry Library: 3 (1989)–9; 11–13

NWN *See* New Writing Network E532

NWR *See* New Welsh Review E531

551 O Write: written work by young people across the Midlands / edited by Peter C. Ward, Marion Chute and Billy Hanna. Birmingham: F.C.H.S. Pathways, Summer 1990–Summer 1994

Guest editors included Seamus Heaney, Iris Murdoch, P.D. James, John Mortimer, and others.

Poetry Library: Summer 1990–Autumn 1990, Spring 1991–Summer 1991, Winter 1991–Summer 1992, Summer 1993, Spring 1994–Summer 1994

552 Object Permanence / edited by Peter Manson and Robin Purves. Glasgow: Object Permanence, Issue 1 (1994)–8 (1997). ISSN: 1352–6766

Website: www.objectpermanence.co.uk
Related Imprint: Some time after the magazine closed an imprint of the same name emerged. Short individual collections have included those by J. H. Prynne and Keston Sutherland

In the 'Manditorial' to the first issue, the editors wrote: "Our idea is to try, on as regular a basis as possible, to publish the work of Scottish writers beside those experimental- and/or modern- ists (from Britain, the US or wherever) who seldom seem to reach print here." Contributors included Carl Rakosi, Cid Corman, Fanny Howe, Rosmarie Waldrop, Charles Bernstein, Clark Coolidge, Johanna Drucker, Norma Cole, Keith Waldrop, Pierre Joris, Leslie Scalapino, Gael Turnbull, Ian Hamilton Finlay, Edwin Morgan, Thomas A. Clark, Drew Milne, Frank Kuppner, Richard Price, W. N. Herbert, Allen Fisher, Barry MacSweeney, Bill Griffiths, Guy Birchard, John Welch, Peter Riley, Gavin Selerie, Maggie O'Sullivan, Johan de Wit, Geraldine Monk, Denise Riley, Tony Lopez, Peter Middleton, Harry Gilonis, Carlyle Reedy, Ken Edwards, Robert Sheppard, and Ramona Fotiade. There was also an emphasis on visual poetry and image and text, with a small feature on Dom Sylvester Houédard (dsh) and other work by Bob Cobbing, Tom Phillips, Richard Kostelanetz, John Byrum, Spencer Selby, and others.

BL: 1–7. (ZK.9.a.3092)
NLS: DJ.s.787(4) PER
UCL
Poetry Library: 1–3; 5–8

553 Obsessed With Pipework / edited by Charles Johnson. Redditch: Flarestack Publishing, Issue 1 (1997)– . ISSN: 1367–9147

Website: A selection of issues has been digitised and is available at www.poetrymagazines.org.uk
Related Imprint: Flarestack

From the editor's introduction at poetrymagazines.org.uk: "*Obsessed with Pipework* is a stapled A5 quarterly magazine of new poetry begun in Autumn 1997 as an essential complement to Flarestack Publishing's poetry pamphlet programme, to provide a platform for established or beginning writers' poems that surprise and delight."

BL: ZK.9.a.5486
Poetry Library

554 Ochre Magazine / edited by Charles Ingham and Ralph Hawkins. Ilford, then Little Clacton, Essex, No. 1 (May 1976)–6 [1980?]

A4 stapled format, with usually only five main contributors per issue, allowing each five or six pages of work. These included Ulli McCarthy, Pierre Joris, Tom Raworth, Charles Ingham, Andrei Codrescu, Anne Waldman, David Tipton, Allen Fisher, Ralph Hawkins, Rochelle Kraut, Lee Harwood, Iain Sinclair, Bill Griffiths, Anthony Barnett, Opal. L. Nations, John James, Paul Evans, Douglas Oliver, Wendy Mulford, John Welch, and others. A statement credits assistance from the University of Essex English Department.

BL: 1–4. (P.903/568)
CUL: L727.b.340
UCL: 2–5
Poetry Library: 1; 3–4; 6

555 Odyssey: a poetry and prose quarterly / edited by Derrick Woolf, Steve Davies, Mary Maher, David Rose and Tilla Brading. Pen Selwood, then Nether Stowey, Somerset: Pen Press, No. 1 (Spring 1990)–21 (1996). ISSN: 0960–8222

Related Imprint: PQR (Poetry Quarterly Review) was published under the Odyssey imprint

Special issues of *Odyssey* included: 'Poets in Their Thirties' (15), 'Poetry and Place' (18), and 'Unanchored in Ecumenopolis' (20) which was guest edited by Elisabeth Bletsoe.

BL: ZC.9.a.2554
UCL
Poetry Library

556 The Old Police Station / edited by Anthony Cooney. Liverpool: The St. Michaels & Lark Lane Community Association, No. 1 (Jan. 1979)–9 (Sept. 1979). ISSN: 0144–2848. Then, as T.O.P.S., no. 10 (Oct. 1979)–131 (Sept. 1998). ISSN: 0967–8459

Note: Two different issues are both numbered 13 and 43/44/45. No. 1–86 is Series 1. No. 87–131 is Series 2 (with the second ISSN).Variant titles: *Tops*; *Cowpat*; *The Toadbird*; *Canto*; *Witana Gemot*
Related Imprint: Lark Lane Poetry Books

Special issues included no. 104, *City Confessions* by Pauline Connor and no. 112, *Making Men of Us* by Anthony Cooney.

BL: 1–82; 88–127; 129–131. (P.903/574)
CUL: 3–4; 6–8, 10–131. (L727.b.213)
TCD: PER 92–571
UCL: 12–86
Poetry Library: 11–14; 16–46; 50–55; 57–64; 68; 71–108; 110–114; 118–129; 131

557 Omnibus: poetry / edited by Adrian Risdon and James Corbett. Bristol: Jester Press, No. 1 (1997). ISSN: 1366–2198

Poetry Library

558 Only Poetry / [edited by Geoffrey Godbert?]. London, Vol. 1 (1980)–8 [1983?]

UCL
Poetry Library: 1–[6/7]

559 Open Book. Church Stretton, Shropshire: Alliance of Literary Societies, Vol. 1 no. 1 (Apr. 2000)– . ISSN: 1474–1369

Note: Continues *Chapter One*

BL: ZC.9.b.4424

560 Open Forum / edited by Anthony Casey. Birmingham: Forum Press, Issue 1 (Mar. 1996)–4 (Sept. 1996). ISSN: 1362–6884

BL: ZK.9.a.4628

Open Press *See* Vigil E861

Open University Poetry *See* O.U.P.A Magazine E565

561 Ostinato / edited by Stephen C. Middleton. London: Completely Improvised Productions, Issue 1 (1989)–4/5 (1993). ISSN: 0955–6958

Related Imprint: Tenormen Press

Dedicated to poems about jazz, and to jazz criticism. Visually striking, with graphic design by Wendy Carlton-Dewhirst and illustrations by Owen Elias and David Smart. The first issue was stapled, while subsequent issues were perfect bound; the format was A4, with stiff, glossy covers. Contributors included: Alexis Lykiard, Douglas Barbour, Barry Wallenstein, Jim Burns, Martin A. Hibbert, Rupert M. Loydell, John Gibbens, Bill Wyatt, and Keith Jafrate.

BL: 2–3. (ZC.9.a.2227)
UCL

562 The Other Merry-Go-Round / edited by Tom Bingham. Corby, [No. 1, 197?]–?

Note: Variant title: T.O.M.

Poetry Library: 152 (1986)

563 Other Poetry / edited by Anne Stevenson, G.S. Fraser, John Campbell-Kease, P.J. Foss, Jay Parini; Evangeline Paterson, Michael Farley, Mahendra Solanki, Catherine Byron, Peter Bennett, Michael Standen, Richard Kell... and others. Oxford, then Hay-on-Wye: The Poetry Bookshop, then Leicester, then Benton, Newcastle-upon-Tyne: Other Poetry, [Vol. 1] no. 1 (1978)–27/28 (1989). Vol. 2 no. 1 (1995)– . ISSN: 0144–5847

Note: Vol. 2 is also referred to as Series 2. Publication was suspended between 1990 and 1994.
Website: www.northernpublishers.co.uk/publishers/Other_Poetry

"We are expressing our right to differ. We are a protest against monopoly and hype. We believe there are many good poems which may not conform to current trends, and we want to see these poems brought into daylight. We believe it is important to maintain outlets, however small, where work can be judged, not by whether it is commercial or fashionable, but by whether it is the authentic stuff of life – perhaps not for everybody, but for somebody; where the work of an unknown writer has as good a chance as that of the established." – From Evangeline Paterson's editorial, vol. 2 no. 1 (1995). After more than a five-year break, the magazine re-started in 1995 in Benton, Newcastle-upon-Tyne, attracting funding from Northern Arts by 1996.

BL: P.901/3153
CUL: [Vol. 1] no.1–28; vol. 2 no. 2–. (L727.c.736)
NLS: HJ4.1632 PER
TCD: PER 79–367
UCL: [Vol. 1] no. 2–28
Poetry Library: [Vol. 1] no. 1–13, 15–18, 20–25, 27/28; vol. 2 no. 1–6, 8– .

564 Otter: New Devon Poetry / edited by Richard Skinner, Mark Beeson, Christopher Southgate and Edwyna Prior. Exeter and Newton Abbot, No. 1 [1989?]–20 (1996). ISSN: 0955-9620

BL: ZC.9.a.2008
Poetry Library

565 The O.U.P.A. Magazine / edited by Sherley Bell, then Duncan Watt, then Jim Lindop and others. Bristol, No. 1 (Jan. 1981)– .

Note: Variant title: *Open University Poetry*. "Strictly for members only" – from the website, Sept. 2005
Website: www.oupoets.org.uk/index.htm

Poetry Library: 4 [Aug. 1981]

566 Out of Our Heads: art, poetry, prose. Runcorn: 'Something Else' Poetry and Writers Group, Issue 1 (1981)–5 (1983)

Note: Variant titles: *Out of Our Heads Again; Out of Our Heads (and Out of Work)*

Edited by a collective. A5 typewriter and cut-and-paste visuals, photocopied and stapled.

BL: 3–4 (P.901/3409)
CUL: 3–4. (L999.c.3.877)
NLS: 3–4. (HP2.85.3709 PER)
Poetry Library

567 Outcrop / edited by Norman Jope, Chris Bendon, K.D. Hatton, Craig Pollard, Julian Ciepluch, Steve Davie and Lynn Jope. Lampeter: New Rhymers Club, St. David's University College; and Outcrop Publications, Vol. [1] (1980)– 3 (1983). ISSN: 0260-9657

Related Imprint: Outcrop Publications published several individual collections, including Sue Moules, *Patterns* (1982), BL: X.950/12996; Chris Bendon, *In Praise of Low Music* (1981), BL: X.950/7512; and Norman Jope, *Primal Solutions* (1981), BL: X.950/6383

BL: 1. (X.955/396); 2–3. (P.901/3268)
NLS: 2–3. (P.la.9902)
UCL: 1–2
Poetry Library: 1–3

568 Outlet: Cleveland's creative output / edited by Mel McEvoy, Viv Harland, Terry Lawson, Trev Teasdel, Vera Davies, Cath McKenna, Andy Croft, Pauline Plummer, Margaret Weir, and Richard Briddon. Middlesbrough and Great Ayton, No. 1 (1986)–12 (1991)

UCL
Poetry Library: 1–12

569 Oxford Literary Journal / edited by David Winzar, Carol Gaudion, Elizabeth James and Richard McGookin. Oxford, No. 1 [1977?]–4 [1979?]

CUL: Spring 1977 (L999.b.1.462)
Poetry Library: 4

570 The Oxford Poetry Chronicle / edited by Nancy Francis. Oxford: S.A.S.A. Publishing, [Vol. 1 no. 1?–vol. 1 no. 2?] (1999)

Note: Variant title: *O.P.C.*

Poetry Library: [Vol. 1 no. 1?–vol. 1 no.2?]

571 Oxford Poetry Now / edited by James Lindesay. Oxford, 1 (1976)–4 (1978)

Poetry Library

572 Oxford Quarterly Review / edited by Ernie Hilbert, David Gowen, Kathryn James, Julian Murphy, Cynthia Saenz, William Whiteley and John R. Bradley. Oxford and New York: St. Catherine's College, Exeter College, and Christian Heller-Shoenberg, Vol. 1 no. 1 (1996)–vol. 2 no. 2/3 (1997). ISSN: 1083-978X

CUL: L999.d.1.217
TCD: PER 87–904 1996
Poetry Library: Vol. 1 no. 1–3; vol. 2 no. 2

573 Owl: new poetry and graphics /
edited by Jane Griffiths and Giles Scupham. Oxford, Vol. 1 (1989)–6 (1990)

UCL: 2–6
Poetry Library

574 Pages / edited by Robert Sheppard.
Southwick, Sussex, then Esher, then London, then Liverpool: Ship of Fools, [Series 1], 1–8 (July 1987)–217–218 (July 1990). Then, Series 2, 219–238 (Apr. 1994)–421–445 (May 1998). ISSN: 0951–7243

Note: Issues are consecutively numbered, taking into account the number of actual pages in each issue, hence the first issue is described as 1–8, with the next issue starting with 9. Some issues bore the subtitle, "linguistically innovative poetries". Continues as an e-zine at the website address below.
Website: http://robertsheppard.blogspot.com

Each issue tended to feature the work of just one poet, or, in rare cases, two. Contributors included: Adrian Clarke, Ulli Freer, Maggie O'Sullivan, Ken Edwards, Alan Halsey, Peter Middleton, cris cheek, Gilbert Adair, Hazel Smith, John Wilkinson, and others.

BL: [Series 1], 1–8–217–218. (RF.1999.b.52)
CUL: Series 2, 219–445. (L727.b.406)
UCL: Lacks: 65–72, 89–96
Poetry Library: [Series 1], 1–8; 41–64; 73–216; Series 2, 219–281; 301–445

Panda Poetry *See* Panda Quarterly Magazine E576

575 Panda Folio / edited by George A.
Moore. Banbury: Panda Press, [c.198?]

No. 34 is a single folded sheet, *Blackman Leys* by Blackie Fortuna.

Poetry Library: 34

576 Panda Quarterly Magazine / edited
by Esmond Jones. Swansea, No. 1 (2000)–4 (Oct. 2000). Then, as *Panda Poetry*, no. 5 (Jan. 2001)–. ISSN: 1469–6908

BL: ZK.9.a.6958
Poetry Library: 1; 3–

577 Panic! / edited by Jim Luchte. Brixton:
Pinko Press, 1 (1998)–7 (2000). ISSN: 1468–6201

Website: homepages.which.net/ffipanic.brixtonpoetry/index2.htm
Related Imprint: Pinko Press has published several poetry collections, some online

Began as *Panic! Brixton Poetry*

BL: ZK.9.a.6958
Poetry Library: 1; 3–

578 The Paperback / edited by second and
third years students on the Creative Writing Pathway. London: University of North London, Issue 1 (May 2000)–2 (May 2001)

BL: ZK.9.a.7744

579 Papyra / edited by Philip Woodrow.
London: Stride Publications, [No. 1] (1982)

Note: A magazine of creative work from Northwick Park Hospital. Probably a one–off, with ISBN 0950805319.

BL: X.950/36410
NLS: HP2.83.495
TCD: PL–135–347
UCL
Poetry Library

580 Paramour / Carleton Rode, Norfolk:
Paramour Press, 1 (1985)

Note: The magazine has an ISBN (0–9510373–0–7)

Contributors included Pat Bennett and Twentieth Century Boy (who together may have been the editors), Tim Holt Wilson, and others. A5 stapled, line drawings and some cut-and-paste, red-white-and-black card cover.

BL: ZC.9.a.40
Poetry Library

581 Parataxis: modernism and modern writing / edited by Simon Jarvis and Drew Milne. Brighton, then Cambridge: Parataxis Editions, No. 1 [Spring 1991]– . ISSN: 0962–9009

Index: An index to the first six issues appears in no. 7, and a listing of the contents of 1–10 appears on the website.
Website: drewmilne.tripod.com/parataxis.html
Related Imprint: Parataxis Editions has produced several collections, including John Wilkinson's *Flung Clear* (1994) and an edition of Nancy Cunard's *Parallax* (2001)

"The journal aims to develop discussion of the legacies of modernism, refusing to characterise modernism as that which is simply past while providing a forum for the discussion and debate of contemporary writing and critical theory." – from the website, Jan. 2005. Contributors include: Denise Riley, Simon Smith, Wendy Mulford, Douglas Oliver, Alice Notley, Fanny Howe, Michael Haslam, Edwin Morgan, Andrew Duncan, Charles Bernstein, Out to Lunch, Ralph Hawkins, Aaron Williamson, Peter Manson, Peter Finch, Miles Champion, Scott Thurston, Keston Sutherland, Sheila E. Murphy, Stephen Rodefer, Anthony Barnett, Peter Nicholls, Peter Larkin, J. H. Prynne, D. S. Marriott, Anthony Mellors, John Wilkinson, Alan Marshall, Tony Lopez, Richard Makin, Simon Perrill, and others. The first three issues were edited by Simon Jarvis and Drew Milne, but later ones by Milne alone. The cover of no. 5 uses a pastiche of Russian Futurist graphic design to refer to the Cambridge Conference on Contemporary Poetry (thus, CCCP). No. 6 adopts a *Blast*-like use of typography to "blast" Cambridge (Milne was then at the University of Sussex), and to Bless "All who sail in US". No. 7 (Spring 1995) was guest edited by J. H. Prynne, with translations by Jeff Twitchell and entitled 'Original: Chinese Language Poetry Group'. After 8/9 (1996) there was a long gap, with no. 10 appearing only in 2001.

BL: ZC.9.a.2952
CUL: L718.d.39
NLS: HJ4.1414 PER
TCD: PER 94–985 1991–1996
UCL
Poetry Library: 2; 4–5; 7; 10–

582 Passing Through / edited by Roger Garfitt and Noel Connor. Sunderland: Sunderland Polytechnic, No. 1 [197?]–5 [1979?]

Poetry Library: 5

583 Passion: poetry, fiction, arts, criticism, philosophy, culture / edited by Jeremy Robinson. Kidderminster: Crescent Moon Publishing & Joe's Press, Issue 1 (1994)–12 (1996). ISSN: 1352–3473

Note: Each issue also has an ISBN

BL: ZK.9.a.3301
UCL: Lacking no. 1
Poetry Library: 2–9; 11–12

584 Passport: the magazine of new international writing / edited by Mike Gerrard and Thomas McCarthy. Huntingdon: Passport Magazine, No. 1 (1990)–8 (1994). ISSN: 0960–3697

Perfect-bound, laminated colour-cover, A5 paperback format. The focus here is on prose from across the world, but several British poets contribute texts, including Ken Smith, Nicki Jackowska, Fiona Pitt-Kethley, Jim C. Wilson, Penelope Shuttle, and others. Issues included: 4: 'Children of the Revolution'; [No. 5]: 'Passport to Arabia'; 6: 'Vengeance!'; 7: 'Passport to Travel'; 8: 'Passport to Portugal'. Later issues were co-published with Serpent's Tail, London.

BL: 1–4. (ZC.9.a.2692); 5 (YK.1994.a.15346); 6 (YK.1994.a.5320); 7 (YK.1994.a.11696); 8 (YK.1995.a.478)
CUL: L996.c.349.1
UCL
Poetry Library: 1–6, 8

585 Password: Scop. Oxford: Oxford University Poetry Society, [1, 198?]–?

BL: Summer 1986. (ZC.9.a.2853)

586 Pause / edited by Johnathan Clifford and Helen Robinson. Sutton Coldfield and Fareham: Middle England Poets, then Middle England Poetry Services, then National Poetry Foundation, No. 1 [1976?]–53 (2003). ISSN: 0959–7344

Related Imprint: The National Poetry Foundation also published many single-author collections
Note: The magazine was often edited without naming the editor. The National Poetry Foundation was set up in the late 1970s, with charity status by 1980. Its logo appeared on the cover of *Pause* from issue no. 26 onwards.

BL: 14–35; 41; 43–53 (P.901/ 3135)
CUL: 14–39; 41–53. (L727.c.910)
NLS: 14–34; 37–39; 41; 43–53. (HJ4.1464)
TCD: 14–53. (PER 78–712)
Poetry Library: 24; 39

587 Peace & Freedom / edited by Andy Bruce and Paul Rance. Hartlepool and Spalding: Peace & Freedom Press, Vol. 1 no. 1 [1985]–vol. 14 no. 1 (2000). ISSN: 1351–1653

BL: Vol. 7 no. 1–vol. 11 no. 1; vol. 12 no. 1; vol. 13 no. 1. (ZK.9.b.4427)
CUL: Vol. 7 no. 1, no. 3. (L999.b.1.1955)
UCL: Vol. 1 no. 1–no. 3; vol. 7 no. 3.
Poetry Library: Vol. 2 no. 6; vol. 7 no.1–2; vol. 9 no. 1; vol. 10 no. 1; vol. 14 no. 1

588 Pebble Broadsheet. Limerick: Stony Thursday Book, 1 (1976/1977)–2 (1979)

A broadsheet produced by the magazine Stony Thursday Book

Poetry Library: 1
Western Washington University, Bellingham, U.S.A: 2 (Knute Skinner Collection)

589 Peeping Tom: the lonely man's magazine / edited by Cory Harding. Croydon, 1 (1978)–10 (1981)

A satirical magazine targeting various experimental poets, including Bob Cobbing, Eric Mottram, Allen Fisher, Lawrence Upton, David Miller, Lee Harwood, and others.
UCL

590 Peer Poetry Magazine / edited by Paul Amphlett. Bath: Peer Poetry Magazine, Oct. 1995–Apr. 1999. Then, as Peer Poetry International, 2002– . ISSN: 1460–8391

BL: Oct. 1995, Oct. 1996, Apr. 1997, Oct. 1998, Apr. 1999, 2002. (ZK.9.b.12026)
Poetry Library: Oct. 1995, Oct. 1996, April 1999

591 Pelicans New Writers / edited by Stephen Leslie, Simon Jenner, Lily Hyde... and others. Leeds: [Leeds University Union] LUU Pelicans, Vol. 1 no. 1 [1989?]–Summer 1996 issue.

Note: Sometimes bearing subtitle: The Creative Writing Society. Earlier known issues are undated while later issues are dated but unnumbered.

Poetry Library: Vol. 1 no. 2–vol. 2 no. 1; October 1991, Spring 1992, Spring 1993, Autumn 1994, Summer 1995, Summer 1996.

592 Pen and Keyboard. Windsor: SQR (Publishing) Enterprise, [Spring 1993?–Autumn 1996?]. ISSN: 0968–171X

BL: Spring 1993, Autumn 1994, Spring 1995, Autumn 1996. (ZK.9.a.2815)
Poetry Library: Autumn 1993, Spring 1994, Autumn 1994, Spring 1995, Autumn 1996

593 Pendragon Collection. [Newquay]: Pendragon Writers' Circle, 1997– . ISSN: 1460–843X

Annual collection of poems and short stories from the Pendragon Writers' Circle.

BL: 1997–2000. (ZK.9.a.5957)

594 The Penniless Press / edited by Alan Dent. Preston, Issue 1 (Autumn 1995)– . ISSN: 1361–1534

BL: 1 (Autumn 1995). (ZC.9.a.4438)
Poetry Library: 1–5; 7–

595 Pennine Ink / edited by Bob Pinder, Freda Bartram, John Calvert, Felicity Whitaker, and Laura Sheridan. Burnley: Pennine Ink Writers' Workshop, [No.] 1 [1984?]–
Website: www.openingline.co.uk/openingline/version1/magazines/pennineink/index.htm

Poetry and prose, published essentially annually. According to the National Association of Writers' Groups website, the Pennine Ink Writers' Workshop was set up in 1983, meeting weekly at the Woodman Inn, Burnley.

BL: 2–3; 5–24. (ZK.9.a.7435)
CUL: 2–23 (L727.c.1264)
NLS: 6–25. (HJ3.1347 SER)
Poetry Library: 13

596 **Penumbra: a poetry broadsheet** / edited by John Kelly. Dublin, Spring 1987

UCL

597 **Penumbra** / edited by Dave Leggett. London, No. 1 (1990)

Poetry Library

598 **People to People: new writing now in the West Midlands** / edited by Eileen Kenning and David Hart. Birmingham: West Midlands Arts, No. 1 [Apr. 1987]–19 (May 1993)

Note: Continued by: *Heart Throb*

BL: 1–18. (ZK.9.a.1733)
CUL: L727.b.400
NLS: HP.la.1675 PER
TCD: PER 92–191 1987–1993
Poetry Library: 5; 7; 9–15; 17–19

599 **The People's Poetry** / edited by Peter Geoffrey Paul Thompson. Romford: Precious Pearl Press, No. 1 (1991)–16 (1995). ISSN: 0968–1590

Related Imprint: Precious Pearl Press also published several poetry collections and the magazines *Romantic Heir* and *The Cadmium Blue Literary Journal*

The guest editor for no. 16 was Pamela Constantine.

BL: 1–6; 10–16. (ZK.9.a.2440)
CUL: 2. (L999.d.1.172)
Poetry Library: 1–13; 15–16

600 **Perceptions: women's poetry for a change** / edited by Temi Rose. Brunswick, Maine; then London; then Brookline, Massachusetts; then Austin, Texas; then Catasauqua, Pennsylvania, Issue 1 [198?]– . ISSN: 0888–9058

Note: Issues 36–39 were published in London; all other issues were published in the U.S.A.
Website: www.2cyberwhelm.org/archive/perceptions/

The guest editor for issue 36 was Lyn Westerman.

Poetry Library: 32 (1994)–

601 **Perfect Bound** / edited by Peter Robinson. Cambridge: Cambridge Poetry Society, [No. 1] (Summer 1976)–7 (Summer 1979). ISSN: 0141–268X

Note: Issues for Summer 1976 and Winter 1976/77 have no numbering but constitute nos. 1–2

Bill Bennett, Aidan Semmens, and Richard Hammersley were also involved editorially.

BL: [1]–4; 6
CUL: Cam.c.21.95
NLS: [2]–5
TCD: [2]–5
UCL
Poetry Library

602 **Periaktos: a small press magazine** / edited by John Gonzalez and Lindsay Jean Gonzalez. Ipswich: The Magic Pen Press, No. 1 (1985)–7 (1992). ISSN: 0269–4867

Note: Sometimes with the alternative subtitle: *literature magazine*

BL: ZC.9.a.204
CUL: HJ4.818 PER
NLS: L727.c.988.1
Poetry Library: 2 (1986)–4 (1987)

603 **Period Piece & Paperback: books, poetry, the arts** / edited by John Howard. Bournemouth: Helicon Books, then Gillingham: Chrysalis Books; J. Howard Books, Vol. 1 no. 1 (Autumn 1979)–no. 16 (1987). ISSN: 0260–5333

Note: Continued by: *Vigil*. The editor's name is also given as John Howard Greaves. Later issues only have issue numbers, rather than volume and issue numbers.

BL: P.903/664
CUL: L700.b.80
NLS: Vol. 1 no. 1–no. 2; nos. 4–16. (P.la.9349 PER)
TCD: PER 95–485
UCL
Poetry Library: Vol. 1 no. 4; no. 6; no. 9–16

604 Phancy / edited by Phil Dunham. Alsager: Crewe & Alsager College of Higher Education, No. 1 [1982]–4 (1984)

BL: P.901/3363
CUL: L718.c.352
NLS: HP2.87.3008 PER
Poetry Library: 4

605 Phoenix / edited by Edna Eglinton. Southsea: Portsmouth Poetry Society, [1978?]

Mentioned in *Double Harness*.
No holdings known

606 Phoenix / edited by Samin Ishtiaq. [London: Imperial College], [No. 1?] (1993)

Poetry Library

607 Phrasis / edited by Jay Basu and Luke Skrebowski. Cambridge, [No. 1, 1998?]

Note: Associated with King's College, Cambridge

Poetry Library: [1]

608 Piffle / edited by David Floyd and Jeremy Kemp. London: Piffling Publishing, Issue 1 [199?]– .

Poetry Library: 2 (1998)–

609 The Platform / edited by Fiona Short. London, Vol. 1 no. 1 (1995)

Poetry Library

610 Plinth / edited by Ed Murdwell. London, [No. 1?] (1987)

Poetry Library

611 Plume / edited by Jan Bentley and Jen Fustec. Halifax; Brighouse; Nice, Issue 1 (Autumn/Winter 1996)– . ISSN: 1364–7571

BL: 1–8. (ZK.9.a.4990)
Poetry Library: 1–6; 8–

612 PM: Poetry Merseyside / edited by Sylvia Hikins. Liverpool: Toulouse Press, [Vol. 1] no. 1 [1978?]–vol. 2 no. 1 (1981)

Note: Variant title: *Poetry Merseyside*
Related Imprint: Toulouse Press published several poetry pamphlets, including Matt Simpson's *Watercolour from an Approved School*, 1975, BL:X.909/40457

BL: P.901/3101
CUL: [Vol. 1] no.2–3. (L727.c.733)
UCL: [Vol. 1] no. 1–2
Poetry Library: [Vol. 1] no. 4; vol. 2 no. 1.

613 PN Review / edited by Michael Schmidt. Manchester: Department of English, Manchester University; then The Writing School, Manchester Metropolitan University, No. 1 [1976]– . ISSN: 0144–7076

Note: Continues: *Poetry Nation*. The first issue of *PN Review* was vol. 4 no. 1 of *Poetry Nation*. The old volume system is maintained alongside the simple number system throughout, but given less prominence. Variant title: *Poetry Nation Review*
Index: A 25–year index was issued in 1996
Website: www.pnreview.co.uk. Later issues are available digitally within Proquest's *Literature Online* database
Related Imprint: Carcanet

A poetry magazine which publishes and reviews contemporary poetry in various modernist traditions, though not exclusively so, and which is seen by the editor as a descendant of journals such as T. S. Eliot's *Criterion* and F. R. Leavis's literary criticism periodical *Scrutiny*. Feautures have appeared on Thom Gunn, Charles Tomlinson, C. H. Sisson, Donald Davie, Laura Riding, I. A. Richards, Edgell Rickword, George Barker, Sylvia Townsend Warner and John Ashbery. Contributors have included Iain Bamforth, Eavan Boland, Les Murray, Sujata Bhatt, Christopher Middleton, David Kinloch, John Peck, Sinéad Morrissey, James Tate, Mark Doty, Sophie Hannah, Adam Schwartzman, and many others.

BL: P.901/1153
CUL: P727.b.24.4–
NLS: No. 1 (1976)–9 (1979). (HJ8.171). No. 10– . Library lacks no. 116. (HJ9.2521 SER)
TCD: PER 77–705
Poetry Library: 1–22; 24–64; 67–68; 71–73; 75–99; 101–

614 PN Spark. Peterborough: Forward Press, [199?]

Website: www.forwardpress.co.uk

"PN Spark was a bi-monthly newsletter packed with poetry news and competitions, challenging workshops, and the opportunity to exchange views on poets and poetry. PN Spark was free to contributors recently accepted for a *Poetry Now* anthology" – from the Forward Press website.

No holdings known.

Poem 1 *See* Poem One E616

615 Poem Film Film Poem / edited by Nicholas Baumfield and Peter Todd. London, [No. 1] (1997)– .

Note: [No. 1] was printed in an edition of 50 copies, and is also no. 2 of the *Poem Film Society Newsletter.* No. 3 (1998) is also no. 5 of the *South London Poem Film Society Newsletter.* A special unnumbered issue, *Film Poems,* also constitutes the notes for a British Film Institute touring programme.

BL: 3– . (Pressmark pending)
Poetry Library: [1], 3– ; Film Poems

616 Poem One: London based poetry lyric, anti-poetry and artwork magazine / [edited by Page 84]. London: P.E.F. Productions, Issue 1 (1999)–?

Note: Title spelt as *Poem 1.* Related or variant title: *Poet 3*
Website: www.page84.4t.com/newpage.htm
Related Imprint: P.E.F., i.e *Page 84,* also produced *Undercurrent* and *Untouched*

Poetry Library

617 Poems by Strangers / [edited by Robert Cochrane?] Alsager: [Poems by Strangers], Edition 1 [198–?]– 2 [1983?]. ISSN: 0265–8259

Pamphlets by the Robert Cochrane were available from the same address as the magazine, perhaps indicating that he was the editor. Rupert Loydell, among others, contributes a poem to Edition 2.

BL: 2. (P.901/3693)
Poetry Library: 2

618 Poems from Portsmouth / edited by Christopher Martin. Southsea, [1978?]

Note: Mentioned in *Double Harness.*
No holdings known

Poet 3 *See* Poem One E616

619 Poetic Hours: the newsletter of the Dreamlands Poetry Group / edited by Nick Clark. Nottingham: The Dreamlands Poetry Group; Erran Publishing, No. 1 (1993)– . ISSN: 1367–8760

BL: 1– . (ZK.9.b.18319)
Poetry Library: 1–3; 5; 7–

620 The Poetry Church: a magazine of Christian poetry / edited by John Waddington-Feather. Shrewsbury: Feather Books, Vol. 1 no. 1 [199?]– .

Anthology: *The Poetry Church Anthology,* 1997– .
(BL: ZK.9.a.6655)

Related Imprint: Feather Books publishes a number of Christian poetry collections
Website: www.waddysweb.com/

This is "an ecumenical Christian poetry magazine, which features the work of international Christian poets coming from a wide variety of backgrounds in the mainline churches. The magazine has a pastoral role as well as a literary one. Some of our poets and readers suffer from terminal illness, some are handicapped or lonely. Some are seekers, wanting to know more about the Christian faith and a closer relationship with Christ and his followers. We pray for them all and for each other." – from the website.

Poetry Library: Vol. 2 no. 1 (1997), vol. 5 no. 2 (2000)–

621 Poetry Digest / edited by Alan Forrest. Leicester; Warlingham; Whitwick; Ashby de la Zouch: Bradgate Press, No. 1 (Jan. 1988)–106 (1997). ISSN: 0965–1535

Note: Variant title: *Poetry Digest Weekly, Poetry Digest News.* Later incorporated by *Poetry Monthly*
Related Imprint: Bradgate Press also published various poetry collections

BL: 1–89. (ZK.9.b.4376)
CUL: 1–86; 88–102. (L727.b.415)

NLS: 1–102. (HP.med.330 PER)
TCD: 1988–1989. (PER 94–492)
Poetry Library: 1–74; 77–106

622 Poetry Durham / edited by Michael O'Neill, Gareth Reeves and David Hartnett. Durham: Department of English, University of Durham, No. 1 (Summer 1982)–35 (1994)

BL: P.901/3516
CUL: L727.c.916
NLS: HJ4.1299 PER
UCL
Poetry Library

623 Poetry Ealing / edited by Joan Goodall and Isobel Montgomery Campbell. London: Pitshanger Poets, 1 (May 1997)–?

Website: www.pitshangerpoets.co.uk/

BL: 1 (May 1997)
Poetry Library: 4 (1998)

624 Poetry Express / edited by "Mango Chutney". Winchester: Schools Poetry Association, No. 1–2 (1985)

Poetry Library

625 Poetry Express: a quarterly newsletter from Survivors' Poetry / edited by Lisa Boardman and James Ferguson. London: Survivors' Poetry, No. 9 (Sept. 2000)– .

Note: Continues: *Survivors Poetry Newsletter*, whose numbering it takes up

The magazine is the official publication of Survivors' Poetry, an organisation aimed at helping survivors of mental distress through the encouragement of poetry writing and performance and other creative activity. Later issues – beginning with no. 16 , which focuses on spirituality – include a Poetry Broadsheet in the middle.

BL: 9–11; 13– . (ZK.9.b.20017)
Poetry Library

626 Poetry Galway / edited by Patrick F. Sherran. Galway: Galway Writers Workshop, No. 1 (1981)–2 (1981)

Profiled in: Tom Clyde, *Irish Literary Magazines: an outline and descriptive bibliography* (Dublin: Irish Academic Press, 2003), BL: 2725.g.3414

BL: 1. (Pressmark pending)

627 Poetry Ireland / edited by John F. Deane. Dublin, First Newsletter (Sept. 1978)- Sixteenth Newsletter (Mar. 1980)

Note: Related to *Poetry Ireland Poems*
Profiled in: Tom Clyde, *Irish Literary Magazines: an outline and descriptive bibliography* (Dublin: Irish Academic Press, 2003), BL: 2725.g.3414

TCD: 1–3; 5–16. (OLS X–1–361, number 1)

628 Poetry Ireland Poems / [edited by John F. Deane?]. [Dublin: Poetry Ireland?], No. 1 (Sept. 1978)–18 (Apr. 1980)

Note: Related to *Poetry Ireland* (1978–1980)

Each issue an A5 leaf with a single poem on it, signed by the poet. Contributors include Sorley Maclean, Fleur Adcock, Gerard Smyth, Robert Greacen, John Montague, Gavin Ewart, John Heath-Stubbs, Eithne Strong, and John F. Deane, among others.

BL: 1–6 (Feb. 1979); 8 (Apr. 1979)–12 (Oct. 1979); 14 (Dec. 1979)–18 (Apr. 1980). (Cup.410.g.268)
TCD: 1 (OLS X–1–361 no.2a); 7 (OLS X–1–361 no.2b); 9 (OLS X–1–361 no.2c); 10 (OLS X–1–361 no.2d); 11 (OLS X–1–361 no.2e); 12 (OLS X–1–361 no.2f)

629 Poetry Ireland Review / edited by John Jordan, then others. Mornington, Co. Meath, then Sandymount, then Dublin: Poetry Ireland, No. 1 (Spring 1981)– . ISSN: 0332–2998

Index: Hayes
Profiled in: Tom Clyde, *Irish Literary Magazines: an outline history and descriptive bibliography* (Dublin: Irish Academic Press, 2003), BL: 2725.g.3414
Interview with: Peter Sirr, in *Poetry News: the Newsletter of the Poetry Society*, Summer 2004, p.8
Website: www.poetryireland.ie/
Related Imprint: Poetry Ireland has published occasional

anthologies, translations and pamphlets, and also publishes the news and events magazine *Poetry Ireland Newsletter*, BL: ZK.9.5306

A solid literary review, tracing its lineage to previous *Poetry Irelands* and publishing most of the leading poets of Ireland as well as international figures such as Miroslav Holub, Joseph Brodsky, Edwin Morgan, Derek Walcott, and C. K. Williams. After the 1983, editors have been published on an about annual basis.

BL: 4, 7; 10–12; 18/19; 24– . (ZC.9.a.3136)
CUL: 2–3; 29–30;32– . (L727.c.1199)
NLS: 1–3; 29–30; 32– . (HJ4.289 SER)
TCD: 1–16 (OLS L–1–806 No.s 1–16); 17–30. (OLS L–1–807 No.s 17–30); 31–36. (OLS L–3–29 No.s 31–36; 37–42 (OLS L–3–30 No.s 37–42), 43–49 (OLS L–5–241 No.s 43–49), 50–55 (OLS L–5–885 No.s 50–55), 56–61 (OLS L–6–371 No.s 56–61); 62–68 (OLS L–6–855 No.s 62–68), 69–74 (OLS L–7–554 No.s 69–74); 75–79 (OLS L–8–206 No.s 75–79); 80– (OLS L–8–441 No. 80–)
Poetry Library: 1–11; 13–37; 43–44; 46–65; 67–

630 Poetry Life / edited by Adrian Bishop.
Lymington, then Winchester, Issue 1 [1994?]– . ISSN: 1354–6767

Website: freespace.virgin.net/poetry.life/

BL: ZK.9.b.8242
Poetry Library: 1–11; 13–

Poetry London *See* Poetry London Newsletter E632

631 Poetry London / Apple Magazine /
edited by Tambimuttu. London: Mather Brothers; Editions Poetry London, Vol. 1 no. 1 (1979)–1 no. 2 (1982). ISSN 0551–178X

Note: Continues the New York-based *Poetry London-New York*, BL: P.P.7615.ma, which ran for four issues from 1956 to 1960, which in turn had continued *Poetry (London)*, which began in 1939. A recording on a vinyl disc of Allen Ginsberg reading "Plutonium Ode" is included with the first issue.

BL: P.901/3258
CUL: L999.c.3.759
TCD: PER 81–710
UCL
Poetry Library

632 Poetry London Newsletter / edited
by Leon Cych, Pascale Petit, and others. London, Vol. 1 no. 1 (Autumn 1988)–no. 32 (Spring 1999). Then as *Poetry London*, no. 33 (Summer 1999)– . ISSN: 0953–766X

Note: Later issues omit volume numbers and adopt a running number for each issue
Website: www.poetrylondon.co.uk/

A magazine that, as well as carrying new poems and reviews of poetry, has a substantial listings element for poetry events in London. Katherine Gallagher, Moniza Alvi, Peter Daniels [Luczinski], Tamar Yoseloff, Greta Stoddart, Scott Verner, Anna Robinson, Maurice Riordan, and others have all been involved editorially. From no. 33 (Summer 1999) the magazine dropped "Newsletter" from its title.

BL: Vol. 3 no. 1 (Jan. 1992)– . ZK.9.b.1879
CUL: Vol. 1 no. 1, no. 2, no. 4; vol. 2 no. 1, no. 4 (May 1991)– . (L727.b.343)
NLS: Lacking: Vol. 5 no. 3 (Feb 1996). (HP.la.1931 SER)
TCD: PER 86–537
UCL
Poetry Library: Vol. 1 no. 1, no. 3–vol. 5 no. 3; no. 24–

633 Poetry Manchester. Manchester: Vol.
1 no. 1 (Feb. 1995)–vol. 2 no. 1 (Mar. 1996). ISSN: 1360–2888

Note: Continues: *Walking Naked*

BL: ZK.9.a.4169

634 Poetry Matters: journal of Harry Chambers / Peterloo Poets / edited by Harry
Chambers. Liskeard, then Calstock: Peterloo Poets, No. 1 (1983)–10 (Winter 1992)

Index: A list of each issue's contributors is provided on the website
Website: www.peterloopoets.co.uk/
Related Imprint: Peterloo Poets specialises in "poetry without frills, without fuss, and most definitely without the avant-garde" according to its website. Famously this includes the poetry of U. A. Fanthorpe as well as books by Dana Gioia, John Mole, Anne-Marie Fyfe, and others.

BL: P.441/1071
CUL: L727.c.877
NLS: HJ8.1199 PER
TCD: 10. (PER 91–666)
Poetry Library: 1–4; 5–7

Poetry Merseyside *See* PM: Poetry Merseyside
E612

635 Poetry Monthly / edited by Martin
Holroyd. Nottingham: Poetry Monthly Press,
Issue 12 (Mar. 1997)– . ISSN: 1363–4356

Note: Continues: *Martin Holroyd's Poetry Monthly*, and takes
up its numbering. Issue 13 incorporates *Poetry Digest*. Issue
41 is erroneously numbered as 42.
Website: poetry–monthly.co.uk/

Subtitles for later issues indicate the open, generalist
nature of this "magazine of poetry, articles, graphics,
comment and criticism", and from the website the editor
describes himself as "liberal about subject matter, but
[trying] to include as much variety as possible in each
issue. He looks for poetry that is imaginative, well crafted,
original and graphics of a high standard. (The graphics can
include paintings, photos, prints, embroideries, drawings
etc., and good photos of sculpture)."

BL: ZK.9.a.4683
CUL: 30–56; 58– . (L727.d.369)
NLS: 32–90; 92– . (HJ3.1828)
TCD: 32 (Nov.1998)–. (PER 101–378)
Poetry Library: 12–

Poetry Nation Review *See* PN Review E613

636 Poetry News / edited by Maxwell
MacLaren. London, No. 1 (1982)

Poetry Library

637 Poetry News: the newsletter of
the Poetry Society / edited by Andrew
Lindesay; Rachel Bourke; Martin Drewe;
Stephen Troussé; Janet Phillips. London: The
Poetry Society, Vol. 1 no. 1 (Spring 1992)– .
ISSN: 1353–7237

Note: From Spring 1994, issues are referred to solely by
date
Website: www.poetrysociety.org.uk includes selected
highlights of recent issues and an archive of selected items
from some earlier issues.

News about the activities of the Poetry Society and poetry
news generally. Includes a selection of members' poems,
profiles of poetry magazines, interviews with poets and
other features.

BL: Vol. 1 no. 1–no.3. Vol. 2 no. 1– . (ZK.9.b.6809)
CUL: Spring 1999; Spring 2000–Autumn 2001; Spring
2002–Winter 2002. (Periodicals Dept.)
NLS: Lacking: Summer 1999–Winter 1999; Winter 2001.
(HJ11.10 SER)
TCD: Spring 1999– . (PER 101–823)
Poetry Library

638 Poetry Now / edited by Ravi
Mirchandani and Rian Cooney; assistant
editor, Caroline Gonda. Sevenoaks, [3]
(Autumn 1984)–[5] (1985)

Note: Continues: *The Cambridge Poetry Magazine* and libraries
may continue its implied numbering

Contributors include Ruth Fainlight, Michael Hulse,
Donald Justice, Adrienne Rich, Denise Levertov, Thom
Gunn, Czeslaw Milosz, Charles Bukowski, Fleur Adcock,
Gary Snyder, and others.

BL: [3] (P.903/1106)
UCL
Poetry Library: [3]–[4]

639 Poetry Now: communicating
across the barriers / edited by Tracey
Walton; Pat Wilson; Kerrie Pateman; Andrew
Head; Heather Killingray; Rebecca Mee and
others. Peterborough: Forward Press, Vol. 1
no. 1 [1991]–issue. 48? (Winter 2003?). Then,
New series, No. 1 (Feb. 2004)– . ISSN:
0969–4005

Note: Includes *Young Writers' Supplement*. Later issues
numbered without reference to the volume number. It is
not clear if issue 48 (Winter 2003) was published
Website: www.forwardpress.co.uk

Regular features include "Contemporary Poetry: Modern
poems written in free verse", "A Rhyme For Our Time: Your
rhyming poetry", "Expressions: Poems written from a
Christian viewpoint", "Portraits in Verse: Send a photo with
a poem", and "Humour In Verse: Your humorous poetry".
The website states that this magazine has a circulation of
10,000.

BL: Vol. 1 issue 1 [1991]–vol. 4 issue 2 [1995]; issue 27
(1998); issue 31 (1999); issue 34 (2000); issue 35 (2000);
issue 37 (2001); issue 40 (2002)–42 (2002); issue 44
(2003)–47 (2003). New series, No. 1 (Feb. 2004)– .
CUL: Vol. 1 issue 2 (1992); vol. 2 issue 1 (Winter
1993)–issue 3 (Autumn 1994); vol. 3 issue 4 (Winter 1995);
Issue 41 (Spring 2002)– . (Periodicals Dept.)

NLS: Vol. 2 issue 2 (Summer 1993)– . Lacking Winter 2003. (HJ9.544)

TCD: Issue 41 (Spring 2002)– . (PER 78–345)

Poetry Library: Vol. 1 issue 2 (1992)–vol. 2 issue 4; vol. 3 issue 3–4; vol. 4 issue 2–vol. 5 issue 1; vol. 6 issue 1; vol. 7 issue 4– .

640 Poetry Now Newsletter / edited by Barry Tebb. Sutton, [Vol. 1] no. 1 (May 1996)– .

Note: Numbering and dating uncertain for several issues

BL: [Vol. 1] no. 1–no. 7 (Nov. 1996); no. 9 (April 1997)–12 (Nov. 1997); Vol. 2 no. 1 (Oct. 1998); vol. 3 no. 1 (Nov. 1999); Sep. 2000; Dec. 2000; June 2001. (ZK.9.b.14942)

Poetry Library: [Vol. 1] no. 1–no. 11; vol. 2 no. 5?–no.7; vol. 3 no. 1–no. 3; vol. 3 no. 5 – . Includes unnumbered Christmas 2000, May Day 2001, June 2001, October 2001, and November 2001.

641 The Poetry of Love / edited by Liila Szinai. London and Easthampton, Maine, [No. 1] (1983)–[3?] (1987)

Poetry Library: [1]–[3?]

642 Poetry On My Shoulders. London: Poetry on my Shoulders, Vol. 1 no. 1 [1993]–1 no. 3 [1994]. ISSN: 1360–5828

BL: ZC.9.a.3514
Poetry Library

643 Poetry People. Peterborough: Forward Press, [199?]

Website: www.forwardpress.co.uk

"Poetry People was a bi-monthly newsletter packed with poetry news and views, word games, mini workshops and other articles of interest to poetry enthusiasts. This newsletter was free to contributors recently accepted for an Anchor Books anthology."– from the Forward Press website. Content included news about forthcoming poetry awards, poetry competitions, poetry courses and literary festivals.

No holdings known.

Poetry Postcard Quarterly *See* PPQ: Poetry Postcard Quarterly E655

Poetry Quarterly Review *See* PQR E656

644 Poetry Round: poetry. stories. reviews / [edited by an editorial board consisting of Paul Plummer, Alfred Celestine, Colin Holcombe, and Judith Wilkinson]. London: Poetry Round, Issue [1] (Spring 1990)–2 (1990). ISSN: 0957–7467

Website: poetryround.8m.com/index.htm

Associated with the Poetry Round workshop. The editorial in the first issue implies that Poetry Round had been publishing earlier issues

BL: [1] (ZC.9.a.2537)
Poetry Library

645 [Blank]

646 Poetry Scotland / edited by Sally Evans. Edinburgh then Callander: Diehard, [No. 1] (Autumn 1997)–. ISSN: 1460–681X

Index: An author index appears on the website
Website: www.zen39641.zen.co.uk/ps/index.htm
Related Imprint: Diehard publish individual collections from Scottish-related authors, often in fine press hand-bound hardback

A4 broadsheet format with relatively small print giving a large number of poems for relatively few pages. The magazine publishes many of the contemporary poets of Scotland (and of further afield).

BL: 1–11. (ZK.9.b.12307)
NLS: HJ8.1485 PER
Poetry Library: 2–

647 Poetry South East: an anthology of new poetry / edited by Howard Sergeant; Laurence Lerner; John Rice; Patricia Beer; Barry MacSweeney; Patric Dickinson; Roger Crowley; Anthony Thwaite; Jeremy Page. Tunbridge Wells: South East Arts Association, 1 [1976]–8 (1983). Then, Folkestone: Frogmore Press, [New Series] (2000)–. ISSN: 0141–3902

BL: 1–3; 5–7. (X.0909/2037). 2000 (YK.2000.a.10247)
CUL: 1–7. (L727.c.634)
NLS: 2–8; 2000. (DJ.m.1498(2))
UCL: 1–6
Poetry Library: 1–8

648 Poetry Survey. London: Poet's Yearbook, No. 1–2 (1977). ISSN: 0142–7393

Note: "Incorporating Part One of the Poet's Yearbook" Related Imprint: The Poet's Yearbook publishes *The Poet's Yearbook*, BL: P.901/1415

An A4 pamphlet featuring each issue: one essay (Peter Redgrove on "Art for Who's Sake"; Christopher Logue on "A Proposal for the Establishment of a British Library of Recorded Sound"), forthcoming events and awards, reviews, a bibliography of newly published work, and about eight pages of poems.

BL: P.903/570
CUL: L999.b.1.2038
UCL: 1
Poetry Library

649 Poetry Voice / edited by George Robinson. Pensby: Kingstreet Publications, No. 1 [1988?]–2 [1989?]. ISSN: 0951–4805

Gladys Mary Coles, Rona Campbell, and Matt Simpson were also involved editorially. Contributors include George Szirtes, Carole Satyamurti, Fleur Adcock, Jim Burns, Gael Turnbull, Rupert Loydell, Tim Love, Henry Normal, Brian Patten, and others.

BL: 1. (YC.1988.A.9040)
CUL: L999.c.3.1171
NLS: DJ.s.162(5) PER
TCD: PER 91–608
UCL
Poetry Library: 2

650 Poetry Walk Cambridge, 1 (1979)

Broadsheet format.

King's College London, Eric Mottram Archive: 7/503/1 1979

651 The Poet's Voice / edited by Fred Beake, and then with Wolfgang Görtschacher and James Hogg. Bath: Mammon Press, [Vol. 1 no. 1] [1982]–vol. 4 no. 2/3 [1992?]; and then with Salzburg, Austria: Department of English and American Studies, University of Salzburg, New Series, No. 1 (1994)–no. 6.1 (1999/2000). ISSN: 1561–5871

Note: Vol. 2 is also referred to as Series 2. Issues in the New Series are numbered 1, 1.1, 1.2, etc.
Index: A checklist of contributors is contained in James

Hogg (ed.), *A Mingling of Streams* (University of Salzburg Press, 1989), BL: X.0909/611(78)[pt. 2]
Anthology: James Hogg (ed.), *A Mingling of Streams* (University of Salzburg Press, 1989), BL: X.0909/611(78) [pt. 2]
Profiled in: Görtschacher 1
Interview: with Fred Beake, Görtschacher 1
Related Imprint: Mammon Press; University of Salzburg Press; Poetry Salzburg

Featured poets included: Bill Griffiths (who receives a retrospective selection with bibliography in the first issue), Alison Bielski, Barry MacSweeney (a retrospective in vol. 1 no. 3), Edwin Morgan, Jenny Johnson (a retrospective in Series 2 no. 1), Brian Merrikin Hill, Wendy Mulford, William Oxley, Edward Boaden Thomas, Maggie O'Sullivan, Donald Ward, Steve Sneyd, Anthony Rudolf, Stuart Montgomery, Eric Mottram, Brian Coffey, Catherine Beeston, David Miller, Robert Rehder, and others. Features include New Zealand issue (vol. 2 no. 1), guest edited by Katrina Bachinger; South West issue (vol. 3 no. 2); Lithuanian poetry (New Series no. 6.1); and there was a marked interest in the translation of French poetry and in the long poem genre. Thomas Hartl was the guest editor for the Raymond Federman section of New Series no. 4.2. In the later years Andreas Schachermayr was also involved editorially.

BL: [Vol. 1 no. 1]–vol. 2 no. 1. (X.955/2410)
CUL: [Vol. 1 no. 1] –vol. 4 no. 2/3; New Series, no. 6.1. (L727.b.310)
NLS: [Vol. 1 no. 1, no. 3]; vol. 2 no. 1–3; Vol. 3 no. 3.–vol. 4 no. 2/3. (HP.la.1266 PER)
UCL
Poetry Library: [Vol. 1 no. 1]–vol. 2 no. 2; vol. 2 no. 2–vol. 4 no. 2/3; New Series, no.1–5.1; 6.1

652 Polygon Poets / edited by Freda Bromhead, Frances Lovell, Jean Hathaway, Lance Petit, Alana Farrell, Nadine Vokins, John Hardingham, Miranda Harris and others. [Bristol], No. 1 [198–?]–39 (2000)

Note: Some issues include a loosely inserted newsletter.

Journal of the Polygon Poets group which meets weekly, and which in the 1960s and 70s used to be known as Circle in the Square, when it published *Circle in the Square Broadsheet* and *Poetry in the Circle in the Square*

Poetry Library: 3 (1987)–13; 15–27; 29–33; 36–37; 39

653 The Pomes: the postal performance platform / edited by Adrian Spendlow. York, [No. 1, 199?–10, 1994?]

Poetry Library: [5] [1992?]–[10]

654 Port of Call / edited by David Foulds, Dennis Freeman and Kenneth Brice. [Sibford Ferris?]: Impact Press, [No. 1] (1982)

Poetry Library

655 PPQ: Poetry Postcard Quarterly / edited by Peter Taylor. London: Selected Syllables, No. 1 (1995)–3 (1996). ISSN: 1360–5828

Note: Variant Title: *Poetry Postcard Quarterly*

BL: ZK.9.a.4394
CUL: 1–2. (L727.e.10)
NLS: 1–2. (HJ1.84 PER)
TCD: 1–2. (PER 88–284 1995–1996)
Poetry Library

656 PQR: Poetry Quarterly Review / edited by Derrick Woolf and Tilla Brading. Nether Stowey: Odyssey, No. 1 (1995)– . ISSN: 1361–2255

Note: Variant title: *Poetry Quarterly Review*
Related imprint: Odyssey also published the magazine *Odyssey* and individual authors' collections, e.g. Victoria Vaughan's *The Mummery Preserver* (1996), BL: YK.1996.a.23448

PQR is mostly a magazine of reviews of contemporary poetry, but each issue also includes poems by a featured poet. Featured poets include: Mary Maher (1); Gordon Wardman (2); Elisabeth Bletsoe (3); Damian Furness (4); Sheila E. Murphy (5); Geoffrey Holloway (6); Pauline Stainer (7); Martin Stannard (8); Vittoria Vaughan (9); Steve Davies (10); Caroline Bergvall (11); Barry MacSweeney (12); Frances Presley (13); Andy Brown (14); Pascale Petit (15); Paul Violi (16); Julie Sampson and Harry Guest (17); Peter Dent (18); Helen Kidd (19); John Hall (20).

BL: ZC.9.b.6246
CUL: No. 5 (L999.b.1.2943)
UCL
Poetry Library

657 Presence: a haiku magazine / edited by Martin Lucas, David Steele and Fred Schofield. London, then Preston, [No.] 1 (1996)– . ISSN: 1366–5367

Website: freespace.virgin.net/haiku.presence/

BL: ZK.9.a.4975
UCL
Poetry Library

658 The Present Tense: a review of modern poetry / edited by Michael Abbott. Bristol: Portishead Press, No. 1 (1981)–4 (1983). ISSN: 0264–1208

Poems from Sabita Banerji, Charles Tomlinson, Derek Stanford, Bill Manhire, Anthony Rudolf, Michael Schmidt, Annemarie Austin, John Greening, Fiona Pitt-Kethley and others. There are essays, C H. Sisson on "Contemporary Influence" (no. 1), Kate Flint on "The Criticism of Contemporary Poetry" (no. 1), various authors on Seamus Heaney (in no. 1 and no. 2), Charlie Sheard on "Basil Bunting and Music" (no. 3), and the last issue has several translations of French poetry. The last three issues have a feature profiling the independent poetry presses.

BL: P.903/860
CUL: 1–2. (L999.c.3.938)
NLS: 1–2. (HP2.87.3156 PER)
UCL
Poetry Library

659 Press Pigeons / edited by Jennifer Williamson and Edward McLeod. Prestonpans, then Manchester: Pigeons Press, No. 1 (July 1977)–11 (1980). ISSN: 0142–1433

Related Imprint: Pigeons Press also published booklets in the Pigeons Real Poets series

Poems by James Peterson, Blackie Fortuna, and others.

BL: 1–3; 5. (P.901/3127)
CUL: 2–11. (L727.b.201)
NLS: 2–11. (P.la.7219 PER)
TCD: PER 92–357
UCL: 2–5
Poetry Library: 4–6; 9

660 Pretext / edited by Julia Bell and Paul Nagrs [and others]. Norwich: University of East Anglia, School of English and American Studies; then Pen & Inc Publishing, Vol. 1 (1999)– .

Related Imprint: Pen and Inc also publishes the poetry annual *Reactions* and is associated with the Creative Writing class at UEA
Website: www.inpressbooks.co.uk/penandinc/

BL: ZK.9.a.7422
CUL: L727.d.330
NLS: 1; 6– . (HJ3.2246 SER)
TCD: 7– . (PER 74–475)

Primary Sources *See* P.S. E666

661 The Printer's Devil: a magazine of new writing / edited by Sean O'Brien, Stephen Plaice, Eva Salzman, Julie Marie Charalambides, Andrew McAllister, Nigel Jones, Fiachra Gibbons, Neville Plaice. Tunbridge Wells: South East Arts; Hove; London, [No. 1, i.e. A] (1990)–? ISSN: 0959–1095

Note: Variant title: *The Devil*. From [No. 4] onwards, issues are referred to by letters of the alphabet, e.g. 'D'. Last known issue is O (2001).

BL: [1, i.e. A]–O. (ZC.9.a.2629)
CUL: [1, i.e. A]–H. (L996.c.273)
NLS: [1, i.e. A]–H. (HJ2.459 PER)
TCD: [2, i.e. B]–H. (PER 95–308)
Poetry Library

662 Product: pop, art, politics / edited by Chris Small. Edinburgh: Red Herring Arts & Media, Issue 1 (Jan. 2000)– . ISSN: 1468–9901

Website: www.product.org.uk/

An arts magazine with Scottish Arts Council support, publishing cultural debate and some poetry. It had a fitful start but relaunched in 2003.

BL: 1–5 (Winter 2001). (ZK.9.d.1946)
NLS: HJ8.2084 PER

663 Promotion / edited by Geoff Stevens. West Bromwich, No. 1 [1988]–3 [1988?]

Poetry Library

664 PROP (poems. reviews. opinion. prose) / edited by Steven Blyth and Chris Hart. Bolton, Issue 1 (Summer 1996)–10 (Winter 2001/02). ISSN: 1363–1799

Note: Jim Burns and Ra Page were also involved editorially.

BL: ZC.9.b.6538
UCL
Poetry Library: 2–10

665 Proteus: a magazine of the arts from the Open University / edited by Roger Day. Milton Keynes: The Open University Press, No. 1 (Nov. 1978)–4 (Nov. 1978)

Poems, essays, and reviews. Contributors included: Donald Davie, Patricia Beer, Charles Tomlinson, Peter Faulkner, Alexis Lykiard, Douglas Dunn, Ruth Fainlight, and others. Pauline Batchelor, Patrick Berthoud, J.B. Chambers, Chris Clark, Francis Frascina, P.N. Furbank, and A.W. Seward were also involved editorially.

BL: P.901/3093
CUL: L985.c.157
NLS: DJ.s.606 PER
TCD: PER 92–377
UCL
Poetry Library: 2–3

666 P.S.: primary sources on the international performing arts / edited by Roger Ely. London: P.S. Publications Association, No. 1 (June/July 1979)–8 (1981)

Also involved editorially: Allan V. Harrison, Ted Little, David Dawson, Jean-Claude Masson, Sue Steward, and Max Eastley.

BL: 1; 2; 5. (ZD.9.d.9)
Poetry Library

667 Psychopoetica: a magazine of psychologically-based poetry / edited by Geoff Lowe and Trevor Millum. Hull: Department of Psychology, University of Hull, Vol. 1 (1983)–47 [2001?]. ISSN: 0968–5081

Note: Vol. 42 is incorrectly numbered as 43
Anthologies: *Young Minds: Psychopoetica for Children* (1989); *Dream Pieces* (1990); *Psychopoetica in Love* (1991); *Introducing Poetry* [199–?]; *Poems about Poetry* [1994?]; *Poems of Intoxication* [1995?]; *Remembering and Forgetting* [1995?]; *Portraits* [1997?]

BL: 19–47. (ZK.9.b.4459)
CUL: 7–9. (L999.b.1.2197)
NLS: 1; 7–9. (DJ.m.2336(1) PER)
Poetry Library: 17–18; 25–47; eight anthology issues

668 P.T.O. / edited by Simon Stevens, Barry Norris, and Simon Rocker. Heslington, Manchester and Newport, Issue 1–2 [198–?]; Special Edition issue [1983?]

Poetry Library: 2; Special Edition

The Publication for Sods with Soul *See* Scribblers of Dubious Editorial Merit E723

669 Purple Pastiche / edited by Geoff Stevens. West Bromwich: Purple Patch, [No.] 1 [199–?]–4 (1994)

Related Imprint: Purple Patch is better known for its publication of *Purple Patch*.
Poetry Library: 4

670 Purple Patch / edited by Geoff Stevens. West Bromwich, No. 1 (1976)– . ISSN: 0966–5609

Note: Readers' survey, consisting of a single sheet, loosely inserted in No. 61
Related Imprint: Purple Patch also published *Purple Pastiche*
Website: www.purplepatchpoetry.co.uk/

Founded by Olive Hyett and Geoff Stevens. There have been a number of themed issues including the Max Noiprox memorial issue, a cinema issue, a dialect issue, a surreal issue, a cassette tape issue, two Dylan Thomas issues, a 50/60's Angry Young Man issue, and a poet's first draft issue.

BL: 62;64–79; 81; 82; 84–90; 92–94; 97– . (ZK.9.b.4776)

CUL: 1–8; 11; 13. (L727.c.673)
NLS: 1; 5; 7–8;11, 13. (HP3.82.624 PER)
Poetry Library: 10–12; 13–15; 35–36; 38–74; 76–94; 97–

670a Quarto. London, No. 1 (Oct 1979)–22 (Oct. 1981). ISSN: 0143–4985

Note: Absorbed by *The Literary Review*

BL: P.2000/776
CUL: L700.b.77.1–
NLS: P.el.245 PER
TCD: PER 93–53 1979–1981

671 Quartz: new writing / edited by John Davie, Clare MacDonald Shaw, Judith Kellgren Skeels, Alan Spooner, Linda Anderson, and Keith Howden. Nottingham: Department of Literature and Languages, Trent Polytechnic; then Department of English and Media Studies, Nottingham Trent University, No. 1 (Spring 1988)–6 (1992/1993). ISSN: 0954–0245

BL: ZK.9.a.1131
CUL: L718.b.275
NLS: DJ.m.1707(1) PER
TCD: PER 92–473
Poetry Library

672 Queer Words: the quarterly paperback of new lesbian and gay writing / edited by Michael Nobbs. Aberystwyth: Queer Words, No. 1 (Summer 1995)–7 (1998). ISSN: 1359–0103

BL: ZK.9.a.4312
CUL: 1–6. (Periodicals Dept.)
NLS: 1–6. (HJ4.1488 PER)
TCD: 1–6. (PER 96–779)
Poetry Library: 6

673 Rabies / edited by Bernard J. Kelly. London: London Dada Services, Vol. 1 no. 1 [1977]–no. 2 (1978). ISSN: 0140–9069

Note: The editor's name is also given as "Bernadox Kelli".

"Editorial policy is imaginary and does not exist. I exist. The next Rabies issue will be identical to the one following it. There will not be an issue 3. Nothing new will be published because it's all old hat." –from the first issue.

This is a magazine which takes its bearings from Dada and Surrealism. There are swipes at Barry MacSweeney (against his poetry and against his chairmanship of the Poetry Society), Marina Vaisey (the art critic of *The Times*), an unnamed poet ("a blubbering mess such as the Quartermass of Yorkshire [who] turns its clumsy attention to the task of crying more copiously in verse than any one else and getting away with it"), Emma Tennant and *Bananas* ("the Illiterary Newspaper"), Kingsley Amis (his imaginary answers to an Intelligence Test), and the forty poets, many of them conventionally regarded as avant-garde, attending the Cambridge Poetry Festival 1977. There are some manifestoes (including one for Dataism), and poems by Kelly and Paul Brown.

BL: Vol. 1 no. 1. (P.903/576)
CUL: Vol. 1 no. 1 (L999.b.1.466)
UCL
Poetry Library: Vol. 1 no. 2

674 Raedinga: a resurgence of visions, illustrated by poemusic / edited by Rod Webster. Reading, No. 1 [1978]–2 [1979]

Appears to be related to the Centre for Reading Art's *Centra News*.

UCL
Poetry Library: 2

675 Rain Dog / edited by Suzanne Batty and Jan Whalen. Manchester: Panshine Press, Issue 1 (Mar. 2000)– . ISSN: 1471–390X

Note: Continues: *Soup Dragon*
Index: The contents of each issue is listed on the website
Website: www.page27.co.uk/jan/ps/

BL: 2– . (ZK.9.a.7461)
Poetry Library: 2–

676 Ramp: a literary and visual magazine / edited by Alison Raftery (fiction), C. Toler (poetry) and Stephen Williams (layout). London: The Bassett Hound & Crescent Press, [No. 1] [1978?]–13 (1981). ISSN: 0143–9863

Others involved in this "co-operative magazine set up to allow publishing freedom to writers and artists and to form a forum for discussion, experiment and experience" were Chris Rice, Tam Giles, Shuna Lemoine, Kate Meynell, Nick Welch, and others. [No.] 8 was a Special Visual Issue.

BL: P.903/633
CUL: 8–13. (L900.c.538)
NLS: 8–13. (7029 PER)
TCD: 8–13. (PER 90–755)
UCL
Poetry Library: 2–13

677 Ramraid Extraordinaire / edited by Kerry Sowerby. Leeds: Damnation Publications, No. 1 (Summer 1993)–5 (1995). ISSN: 1350–6412

BL: 1–3.(ZK.9.a.2819)
CUL: 1–3. (L727.c.1172)
NLS: 1–3. (HP.med.1162 PER)
TCD: 1–3. (PER 86–667 1993–1994)
UCL
Poetry Library

678 Raw Edge Magazine / edited by Dave Reeves. Birmingham: Birmingham Writers & Readers Festival, Issue 1 (Autumn/Winter 1995)–

Note: Continues: *Heart Throb*

Free magazine devoted to publishing poetry from the West Midlands.

BL: ZK.9.b.9195

679 Rawz / edited by cris cheek. London, [No.] 1 (1977)–2 ? (1979). ISSN: 0140–3133

Note: Variant title: *Rawz Melts in the Mouth and in the Hand*. The second issue is numbered as 2 ? because it was intended as the first part of a double issue; it consists of loose sheets in a folder. Also included with the second issue is *An Edge the Poem for Croydon* by P.C. Fencott (Bluff Books, 1979)
Related Imprint: Bluff Books published several books by cris cheek, including *A Present* (1980), BL: YA.2002.b.731

Contributors included Eric Mottram (an essay in the first issue, "Declaring a Behaviour"), Dick Higgins, Allen Fisher, Ulli McCarthy, Paula Claire, Paul Buck, Lawrence Upton, Jiri Valoch, Carlyle Reedy, Jeremy Adler, Bill Bissett, bp Nichol, Shant Basmajian, Bob Cobbing, and others.

BL: 1. (P.973/333)
UCL: 1
Poetry Library

680 Re Publisch. Grantham, London and Sheffield, [No. 1?] (March 1993)–[3?] [1993?]

Poetry Library: [1?]–[3?]

681 Reach: bi-monthly poetry magazine / edited by Shelagh Nugent then Ronnie Goodyer. Little Neston, Cheshire then Predannack, Cornwall: Cherrybite Publications then Indigo Dreams Press, Issue 1 (1996)– .
ISSN: 1461–1112

Website: www.indigodreamspress.co.uk
Related Imprint: Cherrybite also published the magazine *Helicon*
BL: 7– . (ZK.9.a.5472)
CUL: 32–. (L727.d.342)
NLS: 9–48; 50– . (HJ3.1771)
Poetry Library: 10

682 Reactions / edited by Esther Morgan, then Clare Pollard. Norwich: Pen & Inc, University of East Anglia, 1 (2000)–

Website: www.inpressbooks.co.uk/penandinc/
Related Imprint: Pen and Inc also publishes the poetry annual *Pretext* and is associated with the Creative Writing class at UEA

BL: 1. (YK.2000.a.11212) 2– . (ZK.9.a.8450)
NLS: 1. (HP2.201.03643); 4. (HP2.204.2084)
TCD: 1. (PL–340–794); 4 (PL–407–263)
UCL: 1–3

683 The Reader: the termly magazine of the Oxford University Poetry Society / edited by Jessica Martell. Oxford: Oxford University Poetry Society, Issue 1 [1995?]–?

Bodleian Library, Oxford University: 2 (Hilary Term 1995)–? (P.Fo2853)
Poetry Library: 17

684 Reality Studios / edited by Ken Edwards. Orpington, and then London, Vol. 1 no. 1 (1978)–vol. 10 no. 1/4 (1988). ISSN: 0143–0122

Website: freespace.virgin.net/reality.street/
Interview: *Ken Edwards & Reality Studios: an interview taped on July 1984 and transcribed by Penelope Bailey* (London: Textures, 1985), BL: YC.1988.a.13049
Related Imprint: Reality Studios had published *Alembic* in the 1970s. In 1993 the publisher merged with Wendy Mulford's Street Editions to become Reality Street Editions, managed solely by Ken Edwards from 1998, and publishing books by Kelvin Corcoran, Allen Fisher, Maggie O'Sullivan, Denise Riley, and others.

Glenda George was guest editor for vol. 7. The last volume was a quadruple issue.

BL: Vol. 1 no. 8/10 (Jan./Mar. 1979)–vol. 3 no. 3/4 (Aug./Sept. 1981); vol. 5 no. 1/4 (1988)–vol. 10 1/4 (1988). (P.903/844)
CUL: Vol. 2 no. 1 (July/Sept. 1979)–vol.10 no. 1/4 (1988). (L727.b.235)
NLS: Vol. 2 no. 1 (July/Sept. 1979)–vol.10 no. 1/4 (1988). (P.la.7950 PER)
TCD: Vol. 2 no. 1 (July/Sept. 1979)–vol.10 no. 1/4 (1988). (PER 92–551)
UCL
Poetry Library

685 The Reater: poems and prose / edited by Shane Rhodes. Hull: Wrecking Ball Press, No. 1 (1997)– .

Note: No. 4 includes a CD. Individual issues have ISBNs
Website: www.inpressbooks.co.uk/wreckingball/default.aspx
Related Imprint: Wrecking Ball Press has published collections by Brendan Cleary, Roddy Lumsden, Tim Cumming, Dan Fante and others

Poetry Library

685a Rebel \Inc / edited by Kevin Williamson. Edinburgh: Rebel Inc, Issue 1 (1992)–5 (1995). ISSN: 0966–436X

Poetry, fiction, and artwork. The magazine that was an early champion of the fiction of Irvine Welsh.

BL: 3; 5. (ZC.9.b.5518)
NLS: HJ9.1643 PER

686 Red Herring: new poetry. Morpeth: Northumberland County Council and MidNAG, No. 1 (1995)–10 (2001). ISSN: 1357–5392

Note: Merges *Keywords* and *Intoprint*, which appear to have been library service initiatives.

A distinctive folded sheet with the image of a herring on the cover. With an aim "to widen the enjoyment of poetry" it published schoolchildren's poetry, poets from north-east England, and others from further afield. Contributors included Neil Astley, Linda France, W. N. Herbert, Andy Croft, Sean O'Brien, George Charlton, Idris Caffrey, Andrew Waterhouse, and the musician Ravi Shankar.

BL: ZK.9.b.15193
Poetry Library: 1

687 The Red Lamp: a journal of realist, socialist and humanitarian poetry / edited by Brad Evans. Islington, New South Wales; Mountain Creek, Queensland; and Cherry Hinton, 1 Mar./Aug. 1997)–9 (2001). ISSN: 1328–6013

Note: Although primarily an Australian-based magazine, The Red Lamp also had an editorial address in Cambridgeshire.

BL: 4–5; 7–9. (ZC.9.a.5579)
CUL: 1–2; 5–6. (L727.c.1378)
NLS: 1; 5–6. (HJ3.2331 SER)
TCD: PER 101–678
Poetry Library: 2–7; 9

688 The Red Wheelbarrow: a magazine of poetry and opinion / edited by Hugh Martin, Chris Jones, Lilias Fraser, Kirsti Wishart, Louisa Gairn. St. Andrews, Issue 1 (Apr. 1998)– . ISSN: 1462–2998

Website: www.st-andrews.ac.uk/ffiwww_se/redwheelbarrow/

BL: ZK.9.a.6084
CUL: 1–5; 7– . (L727.c.1363)
NLS: HJ3.1834
TCD: PER 101–138
Poetry Library

689 Reflections. Sunderland, [Issue 1, 1991?]– . ISSN: 1354–9391

BL: ZK.9.a.3467
Poetry Library: [1]–12; 14–19; 21–

690 The Reid Review / edited by Nick Reid. London: NPR Publications, Issue 1 [199–?]–2 (1991)

Poetry Library: 2

691 Responses / edited by Tony Rollinson and Steve Pereira. Totnes, 1 (1991)–19 (1993)

Note: Variant titles: A4anonymous; Anonatextosaurus.
UCL: 1–16
Poetry Library: 15; 19

692 Retort / edited by John Lemmon. Merstham near Redhill: Market Cross Publishing, Vol. 1 no. 1 (Feb 1996)–vol. 2 no. 1 (1999). ISSN: 1467–2197

BL: ZK.9.a.6416
Poetry Library: vol. 1 no. 1, no. 2, no. 4; vol. 2 no. 1.

693 Reverberations: the magazine of the Verbal Arts Association / edited by Carol Jones and Ian McMillan. Sheffield; Darfield, [No. 1] (1985)

The Verbal Arts Association campaigned for creative writing to be treated as a discipline in the same way that sculpture, painting, and music are.

Poetry Library

694 The Review: an international literary magazine / edited by Raúl Peschiera. Vancouver and London, 1 [1995]–? ISSN: 1206–9809

Note: The fifth issue is also described as vol. 3; and the sixth issue as vol. 4.
Website: www.thereviewmagazine.com/ (appears to have been last updated in 2000)

Contributors include: John Greening, Carole Satyamurti, Michael Donaghy (who is also interviewed), Anne Stevenson, Penelope Shuttle, Charles Tomlinson, Hugo Williams, and others. There is a strong translation element with a commitment to parallel texts, poets including Gabriel Zaid, Luis Miguel Auilara, Victor Manuel Mendiola (Mexico); from France, Charles d'Orléans, Louise Dupré, Pierre DesRuisseaux, Gilles Cyr, Jacques Rancourt, Max Alhau, Claire Malroux; Mauricio Novoa (Peru); Jüri Talvet (Estonia); from Hungary, Gyula Juhász, Károly Sándor; from Spain, Santiago Montobbio; from Japan Shuntarô Tanikawa; from Italy, Valerio Magrelli, from Germany, Paul Celan (translated by Michael Hamburger), and others.

BL: 3 (Summer 1997), 4 (Summer 1998), 5 ("vol. 3"), 6 ("vol 4."). (ZC.9.a.6296)
Poetry Library: 3 (1997)–?

695 Rhinoceros. Belfast, No. 1 [1989]–5 [1992]

BL: 5. (ZC.9.a.3233)
CUL: 1–4. (L727.c.1124)
NLS: 1–4. (DJ.s.274 PER)
UCL: 2–5
Poetry Library

696 The Rialto / edited by Michael Mackmin, Jenny Roberts and John Wakeman. Norwich: The Rialto, No. 1 (Autumn 1984)– . ISSN: 0268–5981

Website: www.therialto.co.uk/
Interview: with Michael Mackmin and John Wakeman in Görtschacher 2; with Michael Mackmin in *Poetry News: the Newsletter of the Poetry Society*, Summer 2001, p.8
Related Imprint: The Rialto publish poetry collections, e.g. Andrew Waterhouse's *In* (2000), BL: YK.2000.a.7920

Began with an East Anglian focus, with a link to *Samphire* via Jenny Roberts (the daughter of *Samphire's* Kemble Williams), but publishes poetry from much further afield.

BL: P.903/1068
CUL: L727.b.277
NLS: HJ9.239 SER
UCL
Poetry Library

697 The Richmond Writer: prose and poetry from the Richmond Writers' Circle. London: Richmond Writers' Circle, No. 1 [199?]–10 (1998)

Website: www.richmondwriterscircle.org.uk/
Anthology: *Circle Lines* (2004)

Poetry Library: 10

698 Riff Raff Poets / edited by Jeff Cloves, Pat van Twest and Derrick Gould. St. Albans, Bristol and London: Freedom Press, No. 1 (1982)–5 (1990)

BL: 1–3. (ZK.9.b.698)
Poetry Library: 1, 5

699 A Riot of Emotions: vagabonds on the road of life: art poetry prose reviews & more / edited by Andrew Cocker.

Wetherby: Dark Diamonds, No. 1 [1990]–6 (1996)

Related Imprint: Dark Diamonds also published several short works by Andrew Cocker

BL: ZK.9.a.2519
CUL: L900.d.126
NLS: HP.med.1008 PER
TCD: 4–6. (PER 96–47)
Poetry Library: 2

700 Rising / edited by Tim Wells. London, No. 1 [1995]– .

Note: Variant titles: *Bad Moon Rising, Suzie Q Rising, Whole Lotta Rising*, etc
Interview: With Tim Wells by Cheryl B. [i.e. Burke] at www.cherylb.com/Instigation-2.htm

A magazine with an emphasis on Performance poetry, though not exclusively so. Contributors include Clare Pollard, Salena Saliva, Yen Li, John Stammers, Roddy Lumsden, and others.

UCL: 8; 12–15; 17– .
Poetry Library: 3 [1996?]; 6–

701 The Riverside Poetry Review / edited by Gerard Thomas and Anjan Saha. London: Sundial Press, Vol. 1 no. 1–no. 2 (1998)

Associated with Riverside Studios (London).

Poetry Library

702 Rivet / edited by Eve Catchpole, Sue Cooper, Helen Marcus, Maggie Prince, Rosina Sargent, Roy Shepard, Sue Smith, Vicki Vickers, Lindsay Warden. Frieth, near High Wycombe: The Writers' Workshop, Vol. 1 no. 1 [1995]–no. 2 [1995]. ISSN: 1354–7518

In the second issue, Helen Marcus and Sue Cooper were the only editors

BL: ZC.9.b.6010
Poetry Library: Vol. 1 no. 1

703 Roads: words / edited by David Mitchell and Gordon Smith. Leeds: David Mitchell, No. 1 [1988]–4 (1990). ISSN: 0954–7827

BL: ZC.9.a.1898
CUL: L727.c.961
NLS: HP.sm.930 PER
TCD: 3–4. (PR 15225 No.1–No.2)
Poetry Library: 2; 4

704 Rock Drill / edited by Penelope Bailey and Robert Sheppard. Norwich, then Southwick, then Southsea: Supranormal Cassettes, No. 1 (1980)–5 [1985]. ISSN: 0144–7262

Profiled in: Robert Sheppard's biographical note at www.soton.ac.uk/ffibepc/poets/Sheppard.htm

Contributors include Alan Halsey, Peter Robinson, Harry Guest, Yann Lovelock, Ric Caddel, Allen Fisher, Lee Harwood, Elaine Randell, Ken Edwards, Kelvin Corcoran, Graham Sykes, John Muckle, John Ash, John Welch, Maggie O'Sullivan, Wendy Mulford, Ian Robinson, David Miller, and others.

BL: P.903/668
CUL: 1–3; 5. (L727.b.274)
NLS: 1–3; 5. (DJ.m.26(1) PER)
UCL
Poetry Library

705 Route / edited by Andy Campbell and others. Glasshoughton, then Pontefract: Route, Issue 1 [199?]–9 (2001)

Website: www.route-online.com/

Related Imprint: Route
From the website: "Route is a cultural organisation and a home for contemporary story telling and ideas. Route runs a paperback publishing programme of fiction and performance poetry and this is supported by Route-online, which presents byteback books for download, performance recordings and an online gallery, as well as news, views and features."

Poetry Library: 9 (2001)

706 R.S.V.P. / edited by Steve Davies and Paul Harrison. Keighley: Harrison Davies Press, Vol. 1 no. 1 [198?]–no. 2 (1987)

Poetry Library: Vol. 1 no. 2.

707 The Rue Bella / edited by Nigel Bird and Geoff Bird. London and Hebden Bridge, then Edinburgh, then Macclesfield, Vol. 1 [1998]–6 (2001)

Note: Later volumes have ISBNs, with individual titles, Saving the Snow, Dearth of the Cool, Blue Ruin, etc.
CUL: 1–4. (L727.c.1402)
Poetry Library: 1–6 (2001)

708 Rusk. [UK], [No. 1?] (1992)–[no. 3?, 1992?]

Poetry Library: [1?–3?]

709 Rustic Rub / edited by Jay Woodman. Selby: Woodman's Press, No. 1 [1993?]–10 (1999) ISSN: 1352–0997

Related Imprint: Woodman's Press also published And What of Tomorrow? as well as a small variety of poetry, prose, biography and local history publications

BL: ZK.9.a.3074
CUL: L727.d.315
NLS: HP.med.1165 PER
TCD: PER 85–423
UCL
Poetry Library

710 RWC / edited by Lawrence Upton. Sutton: Lawrence Upton, No. 1 (Dec. 1990)–?

Contributors include Robert Sheppard, Carlyle Reedy, Ken Edwards, Adrian Clarke, Patricia Farrell, Gavin Selerie, Ulli Freer, Virginia Firnberg, Paul Dutton, and others. Lawrence Upton also produced RWC Bulletin and RWC Extra, providing statements and context for the poetry published by RWC.

BL: 1–12; 17–21/22; 27; 28 [1995]

711 The Salmon / edited by M.G. Allen, Micheál Ó Riada, Jessie Lendennie, Luke Geoghegan, Mary Dempsey, Séamas McAndrew, and Máire Holmes. Annaghdown, Galway: Salmon Publishing, No. 3 (1982)–24/25 (Winter 1990). ISSN: 0790–1631

Note: Continues: Poetry Galway
Profiled in: Tom Clyde, Irish Literary Magazines: an outline and descriptive bibliography (Dublin: Irish Academic Press, 2003), BL: 2725.g.3414
Interview: Jessie Lendennie, in Poetry News: the Newsletter of

the *Poetry Society*, Winter 2001/02, p.4
Website: www.salmonpoetry.com/index.html
Related Imprint: Salmon Publishing, which grew out of the
magazine (later basing itself in County Clare), publishes
many poetry collections

BL: 11; 12; 14; 15; 16, 22. (P.901/3704)
CUL: 5–23. (L700.d.26)
NLS: 5–23. (DJ.s.657 PER)
TCD: 3–21. (PER 91–659)
UCL: 17–24/5
Poetry Library: 5–16; 18–24/25

712 Salopeot: the quarterly magazine of the Salopian Poetry Society / edited by Stephen Yapp, Allister Fraser and Violet Yapp. Telford: The Salopian Poetry Society, 1 (1976)– .

Note: Some issues include loosely inserted sheets of
comments ('Snippets'), edited by Violet Yapp.

Poetry Library: 41; 49–50; 52–79; 81–86; 88–95; 97–

713 Salt: an international journal of poetry and poetics / edited by John Kinsella. Applecross (Australia) and Cambridge: Salt Publishing, No. 1 (1990)– . ISSN: 1324–7131

Note: No. 1–11 published solely in Australia. Later issues
are referred to by vol. numbers, e.g. vol. 12.
Index: A contents list for each issue is given on the Salt
website
Website: www.saltpublishing.com
Related Imprint: Salt, which grew out of the magazine and
the Folio (Salt) series of chapbooks, has become a
significant publisher of collections by Australian, American
and English poets, particularly of the avant-garde,
including John James, Tony Lopez, Peter Robinson, and
John Wilkinson, Charles Bernstein, Maxine Chernoff,
Forrest Gander, Peter Gizzi, Paul Hoover, Ron Silliman,
and Susan Wheeler, and Pam Brown, Jill Jones, Kate Lilley,
Peter Rose, Tom Shapcott, and John Tranter. It also
publishes literary criticism.

BL: 12. (ZK.9.a.7832)
CUL: 10. (L727.c.1435)
TCD: 12 (PER 74–200)
UCL: 8
Poetry Library: 8–

714 Salvo: an anthology of prose and verse. Birmingham: Cannon Hill Writers' Group, [198?]–

Website: www.writers-circles.com/cannonhill.html

BL: 5– . (ZC.9.a.6496)

715 Samizdat: the UCD English Literature Society journal. [Dublin]: English Literature Society, University College Dublin, [1998?]–

Note: Continues *Anomie*
Short stories and poems.

BL: 1998; 2001/02. (ZK.9.b.11350)

716 Samizdat / edited by Joseph Piercy, with associate editors Nathaniel Mathews (Poetry) and Daniel Spicer (Short Fiction). Hassocks, West Sussex, then Brighton, Vol. 1 [1999]–4 [2002]. ISSN: 1472–8192

Note: Continued by *Lung*, a magazine publishing beyond
the period of this bibliography
Website: www.samizdatonline.com/

BL: 2; 4. (ZK.9.a.7509)

717 Saturday Morning / edited by cris cheek and Simon Pettet. London, 1 (1976)–5/6 (1978)

Contributors include Colin Simms, Andrew Crozier,
Antony [i.e. Tony] Lopez, and others. The last number was
a New York issue with work by John Cage, Ted Berrigan,
Kathy Acker, Allen Ginsberg, Alice Notley, Anne Waldman,
Peter Orlovsky, John Giorno, and Dick Higgins. George
Oppen is interviewed in no. 3.

BL: 3. (ZA.9.a.11790)
UCL

Scartch *See* Scratch E720

718 Scintilla / edited by Peter Thomas, with Anne Cluysenaar, Donald Dickson, Graham Hartill, Hilary Llewellyn-Williams, Angela Morton and Alan Rudrum. Usk: The Usk Valley Vaughan Association, 1 (1997)– . ISSN: 1368–5023

Index: A contents listing of each issue is given on the Scintilla website

Website: www.cf.ac.uk/encap/scintilla/index.html

From the website, June 2005: "Scintilla is an annual journal devoted to literature written, and inspired, by the Breconshire writers Henry and Thomas Vaughan. Each volume includes poetry, prose fiction, drama, and essays, which explore themes relevant to the Vaughans, in modern (if not necessarily fashionable) terms. Scintilla is published by the Usk Valley Vaughan Association (UVVA), founded in the tercentenary year of Henry Vaughan's death, 23 April 1695; with financial support from the Arts Council of Wales and Cardiff University. The UVVA exists to explore, celebrate, and question the works and lives of Henry Vaughan, poet and doctor, and his twin brother, the famous alchemist Thomas Vaughan, while encouraging the work of modern writers and artists."

BL: ZC.9.a.5060
CUL: L727.c.1324
NLS: HJ3.1467 SER
TCD: PER 101–825
Poetry Library

719 Scottish Poetry Library Newsletter / edited by Duncan Glen, and others. Edinburgh, No. 1 (1984)– . ISSN: 0960–0477

Note: Variant title: SPLASH

BL: ZC.9.b.4376
CUL: 1–7; 9– . (Periodicals Dept.)
NLS: HP.la.956 PER
TCD: 1–7; 9–29. (PER 95–661)
UCL: 13
Poetry Library: 1–9; 16–25; 27–

720 Scratch / edited by Mark Robinson. York, then Eaglescliffe, Issue 1 (1989)–17 (1997). ISSN: 0958–2452

Note: The cover title of issue 17 is given as Scartch. Individual issues could have their own titles, e.g. 8, Untitled Continent; 9, Exciting Poetry!; 10, Upwards and Onwards; 11, Only If Absolutely Necessary; 15, Sayings of the Lumpy Jaw; 16, Invisible Spin Doctors; 17, The Final Straw

BL: 1–15; 17. (ZC.9.a.2776)
CUL: 1–10. (L727.c.1414)
NLS: 1–10. (DJ.s.596(2) PER)
UCL
Poetry Library

721 Scratchings: poems and prose / edited by Colin Donati, Ian Morrison, Donald Paterson, Stuart R. Pryde, Sheina Rigg, Alison Smith, Alison Lumsden, David Cameron, Janice McLeod, Kate Macdonald, Iain MacDonald, Mark Willhardt, and Iain S. MacDonald. Aberdeen: Aberdeen University Creative Writing Group, English Department, University of Aberdeen, No. 1 (1981)–?

Note: Variant title: More Scratchings.

NLS: 2–?. (HP.sm.491)
Aberdeen University: 1–5; 1993. (L Per Aa P98 S)
Poetry Library: 2 –7

722 Screever / edited by Ken Singleton, with Andy Dutton and Linda Nixon. Stoke-on-Trent, No. 1 (1978)–3 [1983]. ISSN: 0264–0805

Associated with the University of Keele, from where it was produced, although the editorial address was changed with a sticker to Ken Singleton's address in Twickenham, perhaps to sell back issues after the closure of the magazine. Contributors included Fleur Adcock, Joseph Brodsky, Iain Crichton Smith, C. H. Sisson, Richard Godden, Owen Davis, Jon Silkin, Wes Magee, Tom Paulin, Anne Stevenson, Thom Gunn, and others.

BL: P.901/3390
CUL: L999.c.3.968
NLS: P.med.4313 PER
UCL
Poetry Library: 1

723 Scribblers of Dubious Editorial Merit / edited by Tom O'Brien and Arnold Moser. London, No. 1 (1992)–7 (1994)

Note: Variant titles: SODEM; SODS; The Publication for Sods with Soul

Poetry Library

724 Scrievans. Aberdeen: Robert Gordons English Department, Dec. 1979

Aberdeen University: L Per Aa N6 Rob s

725 Scrievins / edited by Peter Davidson, Alastair Wood, John Brewster, George Erskine, William Hershaw, Tom Hubbard, Margaret Wood, and Sheila Stephen. Markinch, then Glenrothes, then Dundee: Fife Writers' Group, No. 1 (1985)–9 (1992)

Note: Very occasional, several years between some issues. No. 8 includes a loosely inserted booklet, *Bass Rock Song Book*.

NLS: DJ.m.1123 PER
Poetry Library: 8–9

726 Scriptor: a collection of new short stories, poetry and essays from the South-East region / edited by John Dench and Lesley Dench. Whitstable: The Providence Press, Vol. 1 (1997)–?

BL: 1–4. (ZK.9.a.4979)
CUL: 1–2. (L727.c.1336)
NLS: 1–2. (HJ3.1476 PER)
TCD: 1–2. (PR 20289)
Poetry Library: 1–2

727 Sea Legs / edited by Paul Gogarty and Susanna Abse. London: Sea Legs, No. 1 (June 1983)

BL: YA.1989.b.2698
Poetry Library

728 Seam / edited by David Lightfoot, Robert Etty, Maggie Freeman and Frank Dullaghan. Louth, then Chelmsford, Issue 1 (1994)– . ISSN: 1345–4993

BL: ZK.9.a.3663
CUL: L727.c.1417
NLS: 11– . (HJ3.2330 SER)
TCD: PER 84–179
Poetry Library: 1–6, 8–

729 Second Light Newsletter / edited by Dilys Wood. [London]: Second Light, [No. 1, 1997?]– .

Anthology: There have been several anthologies associated with the Second Light network, including Myra Schneider and Dilys Wood (eds.), preface by U. A. Fanthorpe, *Parents:*

An Anthology of Poems by Women Writers (Enitharmon, 2000), BL: YK.2000.a.11673
Website: www.esch.dircon.co.uk/second/second.htm

From the website: "Second Light is an informal network for women poets, aged around 40 and upwards who are published/beginning to get published/serious about developing their work. It aims to promote the work of all women poets and also to develop and promote the work of its members. The network offers its members information in particular through a twice yearly newsletter which includes reviews of books by women poets including books and pamphlets by members, articles, information about workshops, courses and readings. The newsletter also includes the winning and commended poems from the Second Light competition. The editor features member poets by invitation in most issues." Lyn Moir was the guest editor for no. 6.

Poetry Library: [1]; 3–4; 6–7; 9–

730 Sepia / edited by Colin Webb. Millbrook near Torpoint, Cornwall: Kawabata Press, No. 1 (1977)–69 [Dec 2002]. ISSN: 0410–1165

Related Imprint: Kawabata Press published collections of poems and short stories and a study of the musician Captain Beefheart, *Captain Beefheart: the man and the music*, by Colin David Webb (1987), BL: YM.1987.a.396

BL: P.901/3086
CUL: L727.c.883
UCL: 1–13; 15–69
Poetry Library: [5?]–8; 10; 12; 15; 19; 21; 30–31; 33; 35–40; 43–69

731 Serendipity. Malton: Dales Publishing, 1 (1997). ISSN: 1460–8006

The magazine of the Malton and Ryedale Writers.

BL: ZK.9.a.5060

732 Seshat: cross-cultural perspectives in poetry and philosophy / edited by Terence DuQuesne and Mark Angelo de Brito. London: Seshat, No. 1 (Spring 1998)– . ISSN: 0961–7523

BL: ZC.9.a.5197
CUL: L727.b.385
NLS: HJ8.1794 PER
TCD: PER 88–424
Poetry Library: 1–2

733 Sharp Edges / edited by James Mavor, Andrew Dorward, John Fraser, Sara Worthington, Ian Robertson, Ian Deary and Andrea Joyce. Edinburgh: Sharp Edges, [1, 1983?]–?

Associated with Edinburgh University. Photocopied, stapled A5. Contributors include Peter Porter (then a writer in residence at Edinburgh), Andy [i.e. Andrew] Greig, Tom Leonard, Brian McCabe, Ron Butlin, and others. There are also poems by Ian Rankin, later celebrated as the author of the Inspector Rebus novels. James Campbell, the "J.C." of the *Times Literary Supplement*, contributes an article on "The Use of Little Magazines" in issue 2, appealing for Scots not to be sentimental when judging their own literature.

BL: [1, 1983], [2] (Oct. 1984) (P.905/235)

734 Sheaf / edited by Mavis Ainsworth, Anne Cluysenaar, and others. Sheffield: English Department, Sheffield City Polytechnic (later, Sheffield Hallam University), Vol. 1 no. 1 [1980?]–vol. 6 no. 2 (1985); unnumbered issue (1987)

Note: Continued as an e-zine edited by Trudi Taylor, *e-sheaf*, from February 2001
Profiled in: www.e-sheaf.org/index.htm
Website: www.e-sheaf.org/index.htm

The following were also involved editorially: Ruth Bush, Philip Callow, Joy Curtis, Keith Hincliffe, Simon Image, Sue Beverley, Keir Robertson, Jan Tunley, Deborah Randall, Ian McMillan, Joseph Bristow, and John Taylor.

Poetry Library: Vol. 3 no. 1 (1982), vol. 5 no. 2–vol. 6 no. 2; unnumbered issue (1987)

735 Shearsman / edited by Tony Frazer. Kuala Lumpur, then Plymouth, then Cullompton, then Exeter: Shearsman Books, No. 1 [1981]–8 (1982), New series, No. 1 (1991)– .

Note: *Shearsman* was incorporated with *Oasis*, the U.S. *Atlantic Review* and *Telegram* into *Ninth Decade* from 1983–1991. From 1991 *Shearsman* separated from *Ninth Decade* (which had become *Tenth Decade*) and began a new series.
Index: An index of contributors to the first series and a similar index to the second are given at the website
Anthology: Tony Frazer (ed.), *A State of Independence* (Stride, 1998), BL: YA.2000.a.15522

Related Imprint: Shearsman Books
Website: www.shearsman.com/index.html.

The magazine Tony Frazer set up after *Imprint*. From his editorial statement at poetrymagazines.org.uk: "If the journal has a ruling aesthetic, it is one informed by international modernism and by the more radical kinds of poetry that appeared in the USA and the UK in the 1950s and 1960s." Featured poets have included David Jaffin, Emmanuel Hocquard, Marcelin Pleynet, Harry Guest, Peter Dent, Simon Perchik, Andrew Duncan, Clive Faust, Nathaniel Tarn, and Peter Riley. Other poets who have appeared in the magazine include Gustaf Sobin, Guy Birchard, John Levy, Craig Watson, Laurie Duggan, Gael Turnbull, Christopher Middleton, Kelvin Corcoran, Trevor Joyce, Peter Larkin, Frances Presley, Tilla Brading, Ian Davidson, Andy Brown, Rupert M. Loydell, Martin Anderson, Tim Allen, and David Miller. Earlier issues have been digitized and appear on the Poetry Library's magazines site, www.poetrymagazines.org.uk/, while more recent ones appear on the Shearsman site itself.

BL: 1–3; 5–7; New series, no. 1– . (P.903/1039)
CUL: 1–3; 5–7; New series, no. 1– .(L727.b.433)
NLS: 1–7. New series, no. 47– . (DJ.m.1279)
TCD: 1–7. (PER 90–449)
UCL
Poetry Library: 3; 5–6; New Series, 1–2; 4; 7–12; 14–38; 40–

736 Sheffield Thursday: literature, art, talk / edited by E.A. Markham. Sheffield: School of Cultural Studies, Sheffield Hallam University; then PAVIC Publications; then SHU Press, No. 1 (1992)–10 (2000). ISSN: 0968–0977

Also involved editorially were Sharon Kivland, Sudeep Sen, Margaret Drabble, Mimi Khalvati, Robert Miles, Katie Wales, David Shields, Elaine Bull, Danny Broderick, Wayne Burrows, and Katy Plummer.

BL: 1–8. (ZC.9.a.3344)
Poetry Library: 1–2; 4–8; 10

737 The Shop: a magazine of poetry / edited by John Wakeman, Rhiannon Shelley and Hilary Wakeman. Goleen, Co. Cork; Schull, Co. Cork, No. 1 (Autumn/Winter 1999)– . ISSN: 1393–8681

Note: Later issues have ISBNs

John Wakeman, who was a founding editor of *The Rialto*, established this magazine with his co-editors after emigrating to the Republic of Ireland.

BL: ZK.9.a.6827
CUL: Periodicals Dept.
NLS: HJ8.2069
TCD: PER 102–176
Poetry Library

738 Shopping Music / edited by Andy Johnson. Cambridge: King's College, Cambridge, 1 (1979)

Contributors include Rod Mengham, Anthony Barnett, Andy Johnson, Dave Ward, and Ken Edwards.

King's College London, Eric Mottram Archive: 7/580/1 1979

739 Le Shovelle Diplomatique. [U.K.], Issue 1 (1994)

Note: Variant title: *Boite (a cockwerk whoreage)*
Related Imprint: Le Shovelle Diplomatique also produced a video *Riot* (1995), a copy of which is held by the Live Art Development Agency

Poetry Library: 1

740 Shrike / edited by Paul Wright and Jo Mariner. Alperton: ButcherBird, No. 1 (1995)–3 [1998] ISSN: 1360–5275

BL: ZK.9.a.4533
Poetry Library: 1–2

741 Siting Fires: a poetry journal / edited by James Sutherland Smith, Tim Dooley and Matthew Sweeney. Sittingbourne, No. 1 (1982)–2 (1983)

UCL: 2
Poetry Library: 1–2

742 Skate / edited by Chuck Connor. Halesworth: Skate Press, then Blistered Fingers Productions. [No. 1, 198?–no. 4?, 1983]

Poetry Library: [4?]

743 Skoob Review / edited by Lucien Jenkins. London: Skoob Books Publishing, Issue 1 (1989)–2 (1990)

BL: ZC.9.b.4937
Poetry Library: 1

744 Slacker. Paisley: Trinity Press, [No. 1, 1998]–2 (1999). ISSN: 1463–9289

BL: ZK.9.b.13143
Poetry Library: [1]

745 Slightly Soiled: literary review / edited by Julian Nangle, Timothy Cumming and David Crystal. London, No. 1 (June 1986)–[no. 5?, 1987?]

Contributors include the novelist Alan Sillitoe, the bookseller Bernard Stone, Gavin Ewart, Ruth Fainlight, Ivor Cutler, Roger Garfitt, Peter Redgrove, Matthew Sweeney, Brendan Cleary, Roy Fuller, Peter Porter, Jeremy Reed, and Sean O'Brien (who is interviewed in no. 3/4).

BL: 1; 3/4; (ZA.9.b.2255)
CUL: 1–3/4. (L850.b.647)
NLS: 1–3/4. (HP.la.1539 PER)
Poetry Library: 3/4 (1986)–[5?]

Slippy *See* Southfields E758

746 Slipstream: new poetry, fiction, writing / edited by Cathy Cullis and Helen Knibb. Fleet, Issue 1 (1996)–4 (1998). ISSN: 1461–1643

Poetry Library: 1–2, 4

747 Slow Dancer / edited by John Harvey. London, then Nottingham: Slow Dancer Press, No. 1 (1977)–30 (Summer 1993). ISSN: 0143–1412

Profiled in: John Harvey, "Last Chance for a Slow Dance", *Poetry London*, reproduced in full at www.mellotone.co.uk
Related Imprint: Slow Dancer Press published many poetry collections, including work by Simon Armitage, Lee Harwood, Libby Houston, and James Schuyler
Website: www.mellotone.co.uk

From "Last Chance for a Slow Dance", Harvey records: "From the first, there was a strong bias towards American poetry, either written by Americans themselves, or by those of us whose work showed, in some respects, an American influence. [...] Slow Dancer favoured poems whose language was direct and colloquial, rather than couched in 'poetic diction,' which were narrative rather than purely lyric (and certainly not epic!) and which eschewed references to Greek deities or ancient mythologies." The magazine emerged from a series of workshops held by John Harvey, Tina Fulker, Alan Brooks, and Annie Gilligan, themselves influenced by courses held by the Arvon Foundation. Some issues were given over to specific subjects, e.g. no. 15, American issue, guest-edited by Alan Brooks; 27, a Sharon Olds issue; 29, a North American issue, guest-edited by Rhona McAdam. The editor is best known as the author of the crime novels which feature the Nottingham-based detective Charlie Resnick.

BL: 1; 3–30. (P.901/3145)
CUL: 2–30. (L727.c.796)
NLS: 2–30. (DJ.m.1619 PER)
TCD: 2–30. (PER 92–442 1978–1993)
UCL
Poetry Library: 1–4; 6–30

748 Smiths Knoll / edited by Roy Blackman and Michael Laskey, then Michael Laskey and Joanna Cutts. Woodbridge: JHP Publishing Co., No. 1 (1991)– . ISSN: 0964–6310

Interview: Michael Laskey, in *Poetry News the Newsletter of the Poetry Society*, Spring 2006, p.8
Website: Many issues are digitised and available online at www.poetrymagazines.org.uk

The name is taken from a lightship moored off East Anglia. Contributors include: Colette Bryce, Amanda Dalton, Anne-Marie Fyfe, Tobias Hill, Mario Petrucci, Neil Rollinson, Jean Sprackland, Andrew Waterhouse, Glyn Wright, Cliff Yates, and others. The co-founding editor Roy Blackman died in 2002.

BL: ZC.9.a.3011
CUL: 2– . (L727.d.360)
UCL
Poetry Library

749 Snake / edited by John Avery, Nick Cook and Anne Loughlin. Sheffield: Snake Press, No. 1 (Autumn 1983)–3 (1984). ISSN: 0265–3826

BL: P.901/3505
CUL: L999.c.3.961
NLS: DJ.s.7(10) PER

UCL
Poetry Library

750 Snapshots: haiku magazine / edited by John Barlow. Liverpool: Snapshots Press, No. 1 (Jan. 1998)– . ISSN: 1461–0833

Index: Contributors to many issues are listed at the website, issue by issue
Related Imprint: Snapshots Press have also published *Tangled Hair*, individual collections and calendars
Website: www.snapshotpress.co.uk

BL: ZK.9.a.5860
Poetry Library: 1

SODEM *See* Scribblers of Dubious Editorial Merit E723

SODS *See* Scribblers of Dubious Editorial Merit E723

Sofa *See* Southfields E758

SoFi *See* Southfields E758

751 Solid Chintz: arts magazine. Guildford: Students Union, University of Surrey, No. 1 [1978?]

Poetry Library

752 Something for Nothing. Cheltenham, No. 1 [198–?]–5 [1988?]

Poetry Library: 5

753 Songs to the Westering Moon. Weston-super-Mare: Sun and Harvest Publications, [No. 1?] (Autumn 1980)

Related Imprint: Sun and Harvest Publications also produced *Sun & Harvest*

Consists of a single folded sheet.

Poetry Library: [1?]

754 Soundworks Newsletter: for poetry and health / edited by Patrick Cooper-Duffy. Southampton, [c.1994]

According to www.castleofpoetry.com, Patrick Cooper-Duffy was "born in Kingston, Jamaica of Irish Jamaican ancestry and this is reflected in his poetry. He has a professional background in nursing: psychiatry and learning disabilties."

Poetry Library: Dec. 1994

755 The Soup Kitchen / edited by Brendan Cleary and Martin Myers. Newcastle upon Tyne: Bad Seed Press, No. 1 [198?].

Related Imprint: Bad Seed also published *Bad Seeds*

Poetry Library

Soupy *See* Southfields E758

756 South: a poetry magazine from the southern counties / edited by Peter Crews, Pam Gidney, Philip Goulding, Joan Wiles, Tony Richards, Stella Davis, Jenny Deagle, John Arnold, Denise Bennett, Jenny Hamlett, R.G. Gregory, Martin Blyth... and others. Wimborne: Wanda Publications, then South, No. 1 (Apr. 1990)–26 (Oct. 2002). ISSN: 0959–1133

Note: Incorporated *Flint* from no. 1. Incorporated *Doors into and out of Dorset* from no. 15
Profiled at: www.poetrymagazines.org.uk
Related Imprint: Wanda Publications
Website: www.martinblyth.co.uk/South.htm. Some issues have been digitised and appear at www.poetrymagazines.org.uk/

Originally published by the imprint of Word & Action, a community arts organisation in Dorset, it is notable for selecting poems which are submitted without the name of the poet on them, to avoid bias. Each issue is edited by a different team from a specific regional area. Since 1997 each issue features a southern poet with an essay about him or her and a selection of their poetry. Relaunched in 2003 following the withdrawal of funding for Word & Action.

BL: ZC.9.a.2339
CUL: L727.c.1300
NLS: HJ4.1969 SER
Poetry Library: 1–8; 15–

757 South East Arts Review / edited by Jose Phillips and Richard Moore, then John Rice. Tunbridge Wells: South East Arts, Issue [1, 1977]–23 (Dec.1982). ISSN: 0141–3791

Exhibition Catalogue: Frank Milner (ed.), *The Stuckists: Punk Victorian* (National Museums Liverpool, 2004), BL: YC.2005.a.1579

A magazine that was in more wide-ranging than its title suggests, especially from Summer 1978 when John Rice briefly co-edited with Richard Moore before becoming sole editor in the Winter issue. Contributions included those from Peter France (translating Gennady Aygi), Nicki Jackowska, an article on the "British Poetry Revival, 1965–79" by Barry MacSweeney (Spring 1979), Edwin Morgan, James Berry, "A Survey of Third World Poetry" by Stewart Brown (Summer 1980), "Dada: My Heart Belongs to Dada" by Lee Harwood (Spring 1981), Fiona Pitt-Kethley, an introduction to the literary history of Zimbabwe by Colin Style, with a selection of Zimbabwean poetry (Summer 1982), and, in the final issue (Dec. 1982) an account of the Outcrowd / Medway poets by Charles Thomson and Prabhu S. Guptara on "Non Anglo-Saxon Attitudes: British Ethnic Minority Literature in English".

BL: [3]– (P.421/729)
CUL: [1]; 4–23. (L700.c.212)
NLS: [4]–23. (DJ.s.427
TCD: PER 92–384
UCL: 3–23
Poetry Library: [2]; [4]; [6]–[8]; [10]–23

758 Southfields / edited by Raymond Friel and Richard Price, with David Kinloch, Peter McCarey and Donny O'Rourke. London, then Staines, Frome, and Glasgow: Southfields Press, [Vol. 1] (1995)–vol. 6 no. 2 (2000)

Note: Earlier issues have ISBNs and may be catalogued separately by libraries. Variant titles: *SoFi*; *Soupy: a ladle magazine*; *Sofa: it's divan*; *Slippy: careful now*. The first volume was issued with *Colour Supplement*, four colour images made by Edwin Morgan
Related Imprint: Southfields Press published individual pamphlet collections by Raymond Friel and Richard Price, and, with Gairfish, the Informationist anthology edited by Price and W. N. Herbert, *Contraflow on the SuperHighway* (1994), BL: YK.1996.a.9102. The one-off broadsheet *Southfold* was also published by Southfields Press, BL: ZK.9.b.13410. In association with Au Quai, Southfields issued a supplement in 1998, *César Vallejo: Translations, Transformations, Tributes*, edited by Richard Price and Stephen Watts, BL: YK.1999.a.377

Southfields published a range of contemporary poets, often Scottish but not exclusively so. As well as poems (some in translation) there were articles, short fiction and reviews. The first volume had the subtitle *Criticism and Celebration*, the second *Exiles and Emigres*, and the third *City and Light*. The column *Renfrewshire in Old Machine Code* by "Our Special Correspondent" was later developed as part of Richard Price's short story collection *A Boy in Summer* (11:9, 2002), BL: H.2003/681. With *Verse* and *Gairfish*, *Southfields* was one of the magazines associated with the Scottish grouping of poets, the Informationists.

BL: ZC.9.a.5380
CUL: [Vol. 1]. (1997.8.1834) [Vol. 2]. (1998.8.1552); vol. 4 no. 1; vol. 6 no. 1–no.2. (L727.c.1303)
NLS: DJ.s.791 PER
TCD: Vol. 4 no.1; vol. 6 no. 1. (PER 89–186)
UCL: [Vol. 3]–vol. 6 no. 2
Poetry Library

Southfold *See* Southfields E758

759 South West Review / edited by Owen Davis then Lawrence Sail. Exeter: South West Arts, No. 1 (1977)–25 (May 1985). ISSN: 0142–9124

Anthology: Lawrence Sail (ed.), *South West Review: A Celebration* (South West Arts, 1985), BL: YC.1986.a.3156

BL: 2–25. (P.801/3182)
CUL: 8–25. (L727.c.790)
NLS: 8–25. (HJ2.220 PER)
TCD: 8–25. (PER 91–512)
UCL: 1; 5–7.
Poetry Library: 5; 20–25

760 South Yorkshire Writer / edited by Maureen Crosby, Pete DeVeaux, Nigel Green, Pete Haythorne, Wendy Richmond, Rob Payne, Fiona Peart, Scott Rayner, Alison Ross, Stan Cummings, Joe Handley, Marie Jones, Hugh Waterhouse and others. Sheffield: South Yorkshire Writer (SYW), 1 [198?]–10 (1991)

Note: Variant title: *Sywriter*. The last issue of *South Yorkshire Writer* was also the first issue of *The Cutting Room*

BL: 10. (ZC.9.a.2988)
Poetry Library: 5 (1989)–10

761 Sow's Ear / edited by R. J. Ellis. Stafford: Sow's Ear Press, 1 (1983)–12 (1992)

The first issue of *Sow's Ear*, "Accessing U.S. Little Magazines – a review of 40 current U.S. Little Magazines and their publishing context", reflects R. J. Ellis's interest as a critic and academic in the field of little magazines. Other issues featured a variety of poets, including Allen Fisher, E. A. Markham, James Berry, David Miller, John Levy, Yann Lovelock, John Lucas, and Ian McMillan. R. Brody was also involved editorially.

Poetry Library: 1; 6–7

762 Space Limited: lighthearted medium for aspiring wordsmiths / [edited by Ian Templeton?]. [Storrington?], [No. 1, 1998?]–[7?] (Sept./Oct. 1999)

Note: May/June 1999 is also numbered "2" and Sept./Oct. 1999 is also numbered "3".

BL: 2–4; [6?] May/June 1999, [7?] Sept./Oct. 1999. (ZK.9.b.12275)

763 Spark: the Cambridge arts magazine / edited by Alice Allen, Motoko Rich, Jane Menczer, Martin Hodgson, Meredith Pickford, Sophie Page, Cam Goddard, Julia Bullock, Andrea Brady... and others. Cambridge: Clare College, Cambridge, Vol. 1 no. 1 (Easter 1993)–?

Note: Numbering of issues is not consistent across the set.

CUL: 1 (Easter 1993), 1 (Lent 1994), 1 Michaelmas (1994), 1 [1995], 8 (Feb. 1997). (Cam.b.41.59)
Poetry Library: Vol. 1 no. 1; vol. 3 no. 1; vol. 4 no. 1

764 Speakeasy / edited by Martin Edwards and Ian Duckett. Norwich then Dunston, near Kings Lynn: Overdrawn Publications, Issue 1 [197?]–issue 7 (Sept. 1983)

NLS: 2–7. (HP.sm.324)
Poetry Library: 7

765 Special Twenty. London, then Watford, No. 1–8 [199–?]

Poetry Library: 1–3; 5–6; 8

766 Spectacular Diseases / edited by Paul Green. Peterborough, No. 1 (1976)-11 (1999). ISSN: 0144-9443

Note: Gaps of several years separate issues so the magazine may still be publishing.

Related Imprint: Spectacular Diseases also publish individual poetry collections and issued *Loot*. It published the annual of current French writing in English *Série d'écriture*, edited by Rosmarie Waldrop, from issue no. 1 (1986) to no. 5 (1991), before publication was taken on by the American experimental imprint Burning Deck. It has been a UK distributor for Burning Deck

Website: www.indigogroup.co.uk/llpp/spectac.html

Publishing experimental texts. No. 4 was a Latin American issue, guest edited by Paul Buck. No. 11 was a festschrift for Fanny Howe.

BL: 1-9. (Cup.818/31); 11 (YK.2000.a.4141)
CUL: 1-9; 11. (L727.c.667)
NLS: DJ.l.194 PER
TCD: 1-8. (PER 94-598 1976-1985)
UCL
Poetry Library: 4; 7

767 Spectrum / edited by Julian Ciepluch, Chris Bendon, Kenneth Livingstone and Sue Moules. Lampeter: Spectrum, Vol. 1 (Autumn 1982)-vol. 6 (1985). ISSN: 0264-1194

Related Imprint: Spectrum published a number of individual collections, e.g Norman Jope's *Spoil* (1989), BL: YC.1990.a.1887

With a particular Anglo-Welsh focus and in some issues a Children's Section.

BL: P.901/3430
CUL: L727.c.829
Poetry Library

768 Spectrum / edited by S. A. [i.e. Stuart] Paterson and G. J. [i.e. Gerry] Cambridge. Kilmarnock, Ayrshire: Kilmarnock North-West Writers' Group, Issue 1 [1990?]-3 [1992]

BL: ZK.9.b.4488

Poetry Library: 2-3

769 Sphinx: a journal for archetypal psychology and the arts / edited by Noel Cobb and Eva Loewe. London: The London Convivium for Archetypal Studies, No. 1 (1988)-5 (1993). ISSN: 0953-6582

BL: 1-3. (ZK.9.a.1009)
CUL: 1-2. (L900.c.619)
NLS: 1-2. (DJ.s.675 PER)
Poetry Library

770 The Spice-Box / edited by Malcolm Napier. Knaphill: Aramby Publishing, Issue 1 (1998)-2 (1999). ISSN: 0959-4663

Note: Continues: *Wire Poetry Magazine*

Poetry Library

771 Spindrift / edited by Paul Smith. Canterbury: Rutherford College, University of Kent at Canterbury, No. 1 [197?]-3 [1978?].

No. 3 is a special Christopher Middleton issue.

CUL: 3. (L999.b.1.516)
UCL: 1-2
Poetry Library: 1-3

772 Spindrift: poems by Scarborough Poetry Workshop / edited by Peggy Loosemore Jones. Pickering: Scarborough Poetry Workshop, [No.] 1 (1977)-[no.] 3 (1983)

BL: 2-3. (P.901/3241)
NLS: 2-3. (HP.sm.147)
UCL: 1-2
Poetry Library: 2-3

SPLASH *See* Scottish Poetry Library Newsletter E719

773 Spokes / edited by Julius Smit, Colin Blundell, A.L. Hendriks, A.J. Obrist, Donald Atkinson, John Wells-Deamer, Alistair Wisker and Gina Wisker. Flitwick: Spokes, No. 1 (Apr. 1985)-28 (1996). ISSN: 0268-294x

Note: The title on nos.18-20 is *New Spokes*

BL: 1–26. (ZC.9.a.619)
CUL: L727.c.1064
NLS: HJ8.1267 PER
UCL: 15
Poetry Library: 5–27

774 Spout: b&w poetry magazine.

Birstall: SPOUT Publications, [No. 1, 199?]–7 (1996)

Produced by the Birstall Writers, and "...the magazine of the Kirklees Writing in the Community Project."

Poetry Library: 4 (1994)–7

775 Springboard: writing to succeed /

edited by Leo Brooks, Barbara Dickinson, Ann Froggatt, Sandra Lieberman and Fiona Mallin-Robinson. Prestwich, then Great Wakering: No. 1 [1990]– ISSN: 0966–5935

Note: A supplement, The Curate's Egg, was also produced

BL: ZK.9.a.2420
Poetry Library: 10; 16–44; 46

776 Springfield Works / edited by Keiron

Brown. [UK]: Springfield Hospital, [No. 1] (1978)

Poetry Library

777 Stand and Deliver: new poetry from Newcastle / edited by Graham C.

Brown. Whitley Bay: Wordsmith and Jones Publications, No. 1 (1996)–6 (1999)

Poetry Library: 1–4; 6

778 Staple / edited by Donald Measham,

Tony Rees, Bob Windsor, David Duncombe, John Sewell, Ann Atkinson and Elizabeth Barrett. Matlock, then Sheffield: School of Humanities, Derbyshire School of Higher Education, then Staple, [No. 1, 1983]– . ISSN: 0266–4410

Profiled at: www.poetrymagazines.org.uk
Website: Some issues have been digitised and are available at www.poetrymagazines.org.uk
Related Imprint: Staple First Editions

Began as a magazine edited by Donald Measham and Tony Rees, funded by the profits of a Writers' Conference at Matlock College. No. 50 is an anthology issue, 20 Years of Twentieth Century Poetry, ed. Donald Measham and Bob Windsor.

BL: P.901/3603
NLS: Winter 1983–No. 20 (Spring 1991). Lacking: Summer 1987. (DJ.m.1568 PER)
UCL
Poetry Library: [2?] (1983/1984), [3?], 5–

779 Staple Diet / edited by Richard Caddel.

Durham: Pig Press, No. 1 (Jan. 1985)–18 (Sept. 1986); Special Issue (1992)

Interview: with Richard Caddel in Görtschacher 2
Related Imprint: Pig Press published a number of individual collections by authors associated with the magazine

Each issue consisted of work by a single poet. Featured poets included Lee Harwood, Tom Raworth, Guy Birchard, Michael Heller, Jane Augustine, Ken Edwards, Billy Mills, Elaine Randell, Robert Sheppard, Aidan Semmens, Brent MacKay, Andrew Lawson, and John Cayley. A Special Issue, a poem for Basil Bunting by Eric Mottram, was issued in 1992.

BL: 4; 6–9; 12–15; 17. (ZA.9.b.970). Special Issue. (YD.2005.b.133)
CUL: L718.b.143
NLS: DJ.m.1429
UCL: 1–8, 10–18
Poetry Library

780 Stardancer / edited by Chael Graham,

Michael S. Prochak, John D. Tatter and Warren Werner. Oxford (Ohio), then Brooklyn (New York) and Colchester: Ampersand Press, No. 1 (Spring 1976)–7 (1983). ISSN: 0363–8278

Note: The imprint is also given as "& Press".

Essentially a US magazine with what appears to be only a passing connection to England. Various publishing locations in the US over the years. No. 5/6 is a translation issue.

CUL: 7 (1983). (L999.c.3.1384)
UCL: 1
New York Public Library: JFL 93–406
Poetry Library: 5/6 (1980)

781 Start: Stoke magazine of the arts /
edited by Jeff Hartnett, Roland Bligh, Patrick
Regan, Matthew Spittles, Paul Smith, Sally
Martin and Charles Mansfield. Burslem: Start
Press, No. 1 [1978?]–19 (Jan/Feb. 1985). ISSN:
0267–2502

BL: 19. (ZC.9.a.1656)
UCL: 11
Poetry Library: 2–3; 5–6; 8–10; 18

782 Station Identification + Poetic
Injustice / edited by Ann. Norton, No. 1
[197?]–4 [1978?]

Note: No surname is given for the editor.
Poetry Library: 4

783 The Steeple: Ireland's new poetry
magazine. Cork: Three Spires Press, No. 1
[199?]–2 (1992)

Note: No. 2 has an ISBN: 1–87354–805–2
Related Imprint: Three Spires published several short col-
lections of poetry including Patrick Galvin's The Madman of
Cork (1991), BL: YA.1998.a.10396

Poetry Library: 2

784 Still: a journal of short verse /
edited by Ai Li. London: The Empty Press, Vol.
1 no. 1 (1997)–? ISSN: 1365–3334

Website: www.aili.co.uk/

BL: Vol. 1 no. 1–Vol. 5 no. 4 (2002). (ZC.9.a.4787)
Poetry Library

785 The Stinging Fly / edited by Aoife
Kavanagh and Declan Meade; poetry editor,
Eabhan Ní Shúileabháin. Dublin, Issue 1
[1998?]– . ISSN: 1393–5690

Website: www.stingingfly.org/

With a particular emphasis on the short story, but not
exclusively so. Relaunched in Summer 2005.

BL: ZK.9.b.12215
CUL: L727.b.397.1
NLS: HJ8.2020 SER
TCD: PER 89–764
UCL
Poetry Library: 1–7, 9–

786 Stomp Magazine. Hull: Mouldy
Cheese Publications, No. 1 [198?]–3 (1985)

Poetry Library: 3

787 Stone Ferry Review / edited by Sean
O'Brien and Bruce Woodcock. Hull, No. 1
(Spring 1978)–2 (1978)

Contributors include: Piotr Summer, Andrew Motion,
Pete[r] Didsbury, Douglas Dunn, and others.

BL: ZA.9.a.10609
Poetry Library: 2

788 Stone Soup: literary magazine
(casopis za knjizevnos) / edited by Igor
Klikovac, Ken Smith, Srdja Pavlovic and Vesna
Domeny-Hardy. London, No. 1 (Mar. 1995)–3
(1997). ISSN: 1357–5287

Printed bilingually, in English and the languages of the
former Yugoslavia

BL: ZC.9.a.4237
Poetry Library: 1–3

789 Stonechat / edited by Jon Flint and
Krishnan Venkatesh. [Cambridge], Issue 1
(1980)

CUL: L999.b.1.686
NLS: HP4.83.738 PER
TCD: PER 90–388
Poetry Library: 1

790 Story and Stanza / edited by Alex
Watson, George Bowie, Margaret Alexander,
Alistair Currie and Andrew Patrizio.
Dunfermline: Woodmill High School, No. 1
(Apr. 1977)–?

CUL: 16–19. (L727.c.1294)
NLS: P.la.6259 PER
Poetry Library: 10–12

791 Straight Lines / edited by Robin
Robertson, James Lasdun, Mark Hutchinson,
Steven Buckley, Giles Leaman, Jane Heather
and Kimberley Larsen. London, No. 1 (1978)–7
[198?]. ISSN: 0142–7431

Note: No. 3 appears not to have been published

BL: P.903/565
CUL: L727.b.229.1
NLS: DJ.m.75(2) PER
UCL
Poetry Library: 1–2; 4–7

792 Strange Fruit: the Humanities Dept., North Staffordshire Poly Literary Review / edited by R. J. Ellis.
Stafford: Humanities Dept., North Staffordshire Polytechnic, No. 1 [197?]–9 (1982)

Note: No. 8 was described as also *Strange Lime Fruit Stone* no. 3 and *Limestone* no. 13

Poetry Library: 9

793 Strange Lime Fruit Stone / edited by Geoffrey Adkins, Ted Burford and R. J. Ellis.
Stafford: Dept. of Humanities, North Staffordshire Polytechnic; and London: The City Literary Institute, No. 1 [197?]–3 (Winter 1981)

Note: No. 3 was described as also *Strange Fruit* no. 8 and *Limestone* no. 13. A supplement, *The British Little Magazine Scene: A Literary Mosaic*, was published in 1982, UCL: Poetry Store Quartos ELL

CUL: L727.b.262
NLS: 2–3. (HP2.84.3106 PER)
TCD: 2–3. (PER 96–217)
UCL: 2–3
Poetry Library: 3

794 Strange Mathematics / edited by Jeremy Silver, Penelope Toff and John Wright.
London: The No Such Press, No. 1 (1982)–7 (1984). ISSN: 0263–0648

Note: Continues *Ninth Wave*
Related Imprint: No Such Press published several poetry collections including Mark Williams's *The Book of Norman* (1983), BL: X.955/2452

BL: 2; 3; 5; 7. (P.973/371)
CUL: 1–3. (L999.b.1.912)
NLS: 1–3. (HP4.85.1148 PER)
UCL
Poetry Library: 1–5; 7

795 Strawberry Fare: St. Mary's College literary magazine: articles, poetry, stories, interviews / edited by John Iddon. Twickenham: English Dept., St. Mary's College, Autumn 1984–Autumn 1989

A college magazine with substantial essays, interviews and a go-getting attitude to contributors, who include Melvyn Bragg (interviewed in the first issue), John Wain, Tom Stoppard (interviewed), Peter Porter, David Lodge (interviewed), Craig Raine, Gavin Ewart, Seamus Heaney, Jonathan Miller, Richard Ellman, Dannie Abse, Bernard Bergonzi, Terry Eagleton, Philip Hobsbaum, George MacBeth, Edwin Morgan, Beryl Bainbridge, Alan Brownjohn, D. J. Enright, Michael Holroyd, Blake Morrison, Peter Redgrove, and others.

BL: Autumn 1981–Autumn 1986. (ZK.9.a.41). Autumn 1987–Autumn 1989. (8474.050100)
CUL: Autumn 1985, Autumn 1986. (L999.c.3.1134)
NLS: Autumn 1985, Autumn 1986. (DJ.m.761(7) PER)
TCD: Autumn 1985–Autumn 1989. (PER 91–528)
Poetry Library: Autumn 1984

796 Stride / edited by Rupert Loydell.
London, then Crewe, then Exeter: Stride, [No.] 1 (1982)–37 (1995). ISSN: 0262–9267

Note: Continued as an e-zine from the Stride website
Index: A contents listing of the first eighteen issues is given in no. 19.
Related Imprint: Stride has published many poetry collections as well as art, music and cultural criticism
Anthology: Rupert M. Loydell (ed.), *Ladder to the Next Floor: Stride magazine 1–33*, Salzburg: University of Salzburg Press, 1993, BL: X.0909/611(83)
Website: www.stridemagazine.co.uk/

Special issues included Alan Garner (no. 8), Brian Louis Pearce (no. 9), David H. W. Grubb (no. 29). No. 24/25, 'The Serendipity Caper', was a prose issue featuring Brian Louis Pearce, Ian Robinson, David Miller, Gary Boswell, Martin A. Hibbert, A.C. Evans, Thomas Wiloch, and others. Chris Mitchell was the guest editor for no. 33½, i.e. no. 34, (the numeration changed in reference to the speed of the Long Playing record, the issue having a particular focus on music). Graham Palmer and Gary Boswell were also involved editorially in the magazine.

BL: 1; 5; 7; 11–13; 15; 19–23. (P.901/3298)
CUL: 3–27. (L727.c.1097)
NLS: HJ4.613 PER
UCL: 3
Poetry Library: 2–33

797 Subvoicive / [edited by Bob Cobbing and Lawrence Upton?]. Sutton: Sub Voicive Poetry, No. 1 [199?]– .

Website: pages.britishlibrary.net/svp/

Issued as A4 stapled booklets to accompany the Subvoicive readings, taking place in central London. It is likely that earlier series of these exist but no holdings are known. Subvoicive organises occasional colloquia on contemporary poetry and practice and is also associated with the experimental poetry publisher Writers Forum. Form Books issued *Salute / Verse / Circumstance* (London, 1995) to commemorate Brian Coffey's Subvoicive reading on 29 March 1994, UCL: Poetry Store Boxes For: COF

BL: 4 (Kathleen Fraser and Peter Riley); 8 (Fiona Templeton and Stephen Rodefer); 12 (Anthony Rudolf, Ifigenija Simonovic). (ZA.9.a.12213); 8a (Lawrence Upton) (YA.1999.b.1877); 8b (Lawrence Upton and Bob Cobbing) (YA.1999.b.1880)

798 Sun & Harvest. Weston-super-Mare: Sun and Harvest Publications, No. 1 [197?]–12 (1980)

Related Imprint: Sun and Harvest Publications also published *Songs to the Westering Moon*

Each issue consists of a single folded sheet.

Poetry Library: 10; 12

Sunk Island New Writing *See* Sunk Island Review E799

799 Sunk Island Review / edited by Michael Blackburn. Lincoln: Sunk Island Publishing, No. 1 (1989)–10 (1995). ISSN: 0955–9647

Note: Variant title: *Sunk Island New Writing*. Later issues have ISBNs.

Sometimes with a title for the issue, e.g. no. 6, *Carnage: new writing from Europe,*; no. 8, *Schopenhauer's Blues* (which contains an interview with Thomas A. Clark); no. 9, *Outsiders*; no. 10: *Spleen*. Sylvia Blackburn, Robert Etty,- and David Lightfoot were also involved editorially.

BL: 1; 4–6. (ZC.9.a.2236)
CUL: L996.c.279
NLS: 1–9. (HJ4.1609 PER)
TCD: 2–9. (PER 95–706 1989–1995)
UCL
Poetry Library: 1; 3–6; 8–10

800 SuperReal: the British surreal journal / edited by Patricia Scanlan. London, Issue 0 (1992)–2 (1994). ISSN: 0966–7830

Note: Variant subtitles: *the British journal of surrealism; images and imagination: reflexes of the future*. Three issues were produced, numbered 0–2 (rather than 1–3). Issue 2 is referred to as vol. 2.

Issue 1 includes a feature on Edouard Roditi. Helen Cooper, Alex Sapirstein, Diane Osgood, Andrzej Borkowski, and Katrina Lindesay were also involved editorially.

BL: ZK.9.b.4716
UCL
Poetry Library

801 Survivors Poetry Newsletter [U.K.]: No. 1 (Oct. 1998)–8 (June 2000)

Continued by: *Poetry Express*

BL: ZK.9.b.20017

802 The Swansea Review: poetry – criticism – prose / edited by N. H. Reeve, then Glyn Pursglove, Judith Stevens, Caroline George, Marie-Luise Kohlke and Alex Cadogan. Swansea: Department of English, University of Wales Swansea, No. 1 (Apr. 1986)– . ISSN: 0269–8374

The Swansea Review began as a journal devoted solely to "criticism and English studies" but with issue no. 8 its focus changed to include poetry. There has been a Henry Vaughan feature (edited by Anne Cluysenaar and Glyn Pursglove), a Peter Russell issue and a Dylan Thomas issue.

BL: ZC.9.a.3837
CUL: L700.d.29
NLS: HJ4.1567
TCD: 2–. (PER 85–516)
UCL: 13
Poetry Library: 8–16; 18–

803 SYC Newsheet / edited by Simon Pitt, Gary Boswell and Jill Moore. Alsager: SYC Publications, No. 1 [198?]–10 [1984?].

Related imprint: SYC Publications published *Sydelines* and, for example, Simon Pitt's short collection *Attack of the Giant Cheese Sandwich* (1986), BL: YC.1987.a.7926

Poetry Library: 8; 10

804 Sydelines / edited by Simon Pitt, Gary Boswell and Jill Moore. Alsager: SYC Publications, [No.] 1 [198?]–6 (1983)

Note: [No.] 3 has ISBN 0–950725I–1–0.
Related Imprint: SYC Publications published SYC *Newsheet* and, for example, Gary Boswell's *Ear to a Muse* (1980), BL: X.902/5704

Birmingham University: 2 (p PR 1225)
Poetry Library: 3; 6

805 Sylva: the magazine of new poetry / edited by Catherine Roberts. Cardiff, No. 1 (1993)

Poetry Library: 1

806 Symphony: a magazine of Christian poetry / edited by Keith Barrett, Ernest W. Bacon, Philip Tait, David G. Preston and Valerie Tait. Bristol, then Reading, then Wembley: Bemerton Press, No. 1 (Spring 1976)–21. No. 1 [i.e. 22] (1986)–no. 2 [i.e. 50] (1995). ISSN: 0308–4566

Note: After no. 21, numbered as no. 1–3 (1986), no. 1–3 (1987), etc.
BL: P.901/3033
Poetry Library: 13 (1982)–21; no. 1 [i.e. 22] (1986), no. 3 [i.e. 24] (1986)–no. 2 [i.e. 50] (1995)

807 Symtex & Grimmer: poems in English, German and other notational systems / edited by Chris Jones, Alistair Noon, and Paul Cooke. Berlin and Banburgh, then St. Andrews, Oxford and Birmingham: ZZZg! Press, Issue 1 (Spring 1995)–3 (Jan. 1998). ISSN: 1368–8847

Note: Variant subtitle: *a magazine of contemporary poetry.*

Contributors include Brigitte Lange (translated by Mitch Cohen), Catherine Bowles, whose manifesto in the third issue suggests a reunion between the avant-garde and the mainstream, Peter Finch, Brendan McMahon, Giles Goodland, Paula Claire, Geoff Stevens, Johan de Wit, and others.

BL: 1 (Spring 1995); 3 (Jan. 1998). (ZK.9.b.12646)
CUL: 3. (Periodicals Dpt.)
NLS: 3. (HJ8.1823 PER)

TCD: 3. (PER 89–818)
Poetry Library: 1–3

Sywriter *See* South Yorkshire Writer E760

808 Syzygy / edited by Ray Cooke and Paul Lamprill. Reading: Centra LitGroup, then Syzygy Publications, No. 1 (1979)–3 (1980). ISSN: 0143–1064

Adrian Caesar, Bruce Thomas, and Richard Matthewman were also editorially involved after the first issue.

BL: P.901/3179
Poetry Library: 2

809 Tabla / edited by Steve Ellis and Emma Aylett. Aylesbury, then London: The Tabla Writing Collective, Issue [1, 1992]–6 (1997). ISSN: 1462–4842

Note: Continued by: *The Tabla Book of New Verse*
Website: www.bris.ac.uk/english/journals/tabla

From the website: "named after the traditional Indian drum-set which, with its ability to yield subtle variations of tone and timbre, offered the editors a metaphor for the kind of poem they hoped to hit upon. The logo represents the bowl-shaped and cylindrical drums of the tabla transformed into dancing typography." Steve Ellis's name is also given as S. J. Ellis and Stephen James Ellis. He is now known simply as Stephen James.

BL: 6. (ZK.9.a.5880)
Poetry Library

810 The Tabla Book of New Verse / edited by Stephen James. London, then Bristol: Tabla, Dept. of English, University of Bristol, 1998–2001; 2004. ISSN: 1462–5016

Note: Continues: *Tabla.* Suspended after the 2004 edition, but with the prospect of restarting at some point in the future.
Website: www.bris.ac.uk/english/journals/tabla
BL: ZK.9.b.5880
CUL: 1999. (L727.d.297)

811 Tak Tak Tak. Nottingham: Tak Tak Tak, Issue [1] (1987)–6 (1993). ISSN: 0952–9411

Note: Audio cassettes were included with issues 2 and 4.
Related Imprint: Tak Tak Tak published a novel by Roger

Wakeling, *The Dangling God* (1991), BL: YK.1992.a.2588, Jeff Nuttall's biography of Lol Coxhill, *The Bald Soprano* (1989), BL: YC.1990.a.6878, several audio cassettes, and Ted Milton's *Longes de Louanges* [1988], BL: YC.1989.a.9652. Website: There was a website at www.taktaktak.com between 2002 and 2004, which has been archived at web.archive.org and gives further details of the magazine and the press

Edited anonymously. Texts and images by perhaps more confrontational artists and writers give this magazine an edgy atmosphere. For issue 3 a larger sans-serif font was used, with a look and tone a little reminiscent of *Blast*. Contributors particularly associated with the magazine include Tim Brown, Ted Milton, Andrew Clay, Karl Blake, Tom Hopkins, and Wayne Summers. Others include Jeff Nuttall, James Keery, Rupert Loydell, Roger Wakeling, Johan de Wit, Peter Plate, Keith Jafrate, and Ann Quin.

BL: [1]; 3; 6. (ZK.9.a.1219)
Poetry Library: 1–2; 4

812 **Talus** / edited by Hanne Bramness, Shamoon Zamir, Stephen Want, Marzia Balzani and Hans Herbjornsrud. London: Dept of English, King's College London, University of London, No. 1 (1987)–9/10 (1997). ISSN: 0951–628X

BL: 1–7; 9/10. (ZK.9.a.782)
CUL: 1–8. (L700.c.401)
NLS: 1–8. (HJ8.1250 PER)
TCD: 1–8. (PER 92–35 1987–1994)
UCL
Poetry Library: 1–2; 5–7

813 **Tandem: the City University & Goldsmiths' College Writers' Workshops** / edited by Eva Tucker. London: City University & Goldsmiths' College Writers' Workshop, No. 1 (1979)–2 (1981)

Note: No. 2 was a Festival of the City of London issue.

Poetry Library

814 **Tandem** / edited by Michael J. Woods. Barbourne, No. 1 [199?]– . ISSN: 1360–5267

Website: www.cipherarts.com/tandem/index.html
Contributors include: Carol Ann Duffy, Jackie Kay, Ragnar Stromberg, Jo Shapcott, Barry Fantoni, Linda France, Pete Morgan, Matthew Sweeney, Benjamin Zephaniah, Sujata Bhatt, Stephen Knight, Judith Kazantzis, Muhammad

Yusuf, Seamus Heaney, Katie Donovan, Bernard O'Donoghue, Sheenagh Pugh, Michael Glover, Myra Schneider, David Hart, Samuel Menashe, Patrick Ryan, and others.

Poetry Library: 3 (1995)–4/5 [1997?]

815 **Tangier** / edited by John Hughes. Belfast, No. 1 [1983?]

Poetry Library

816 **Tangled Hair: an international journal of contemporary tanka** / edited by John Barlow. Liverpool: Snapshot Press, No. 1 (1999)–3 (2001). ISSN: 1465–0363

Related Imprint: Snapshots Press have also published *Snapshots*, individual collections and calendars
Website: www.snapshotpress.co.uk

BL: ZK.9.a.6615
Poetry Library

817 **Tears in the Fence** / edited by David Caddy. Stourpaine, near Blandford Forum, No. 1 (Sept. 1984)– . ISSN: 0266–5816

Note: Variant subtitles: *a literary magazine for the Green Movement; poetry prose graphics; poetry, reviews, stories, art, non-fiction, interviews, reviews*
Related Imprint: Tears in the Fence have also published individual poetry collections, e.g. Monique Caddy's *A Writers Weekend* (1994), BL: YK.1994.a.12210

Owen Davis, Paul Donnelly, Sarah Hopkins, Brian Hinton, and Jonathan Ward have also been involved editorially.

BL: P.901/3685
CUL: L718.b.206
NLS: HJ9.2287 SER
UCL: 1–3; 5; 7–
Poetry Library: 2 [1985?]–

818 **Tees Valley Writer** / edited by Derek Gregory. Middlesborough, Vol. 1 no. 1 (Summer 1990)–no. 11 (1995). ISSN: 0959–7808

Heather Bennett, Andy Croft, Carol Rumens, Peter Walker, and Fred D'Aguiar were also involved editorially.

BL: Vol. 1 no. 2 (ZC.9.a.2672)
UCL
Poetry Library: Vol. 1 no. 1–no. 10

819 Telegram: poetry fiction reviews comment / edited by Ian Robinson and John Stathatos. London: Oasis Books and Oxus Press, No. 1 (1980)–4 (1982). ISSN: 0261–1260

Related imprint: Oasis Books also published *Oasis, Ninth Decade* and many poetry collections. Oxus Press published the pamphlet collection by Nathaniel Tarn, *Weekends in Mexico* (1982), BL: X.958/17317, as well as Nassos Vayenas's *Biography and other poems*, translated from the Modern Greek by John Stathatos (1979), BL: X.909/43981, and other collections

BL: 1. (P.901/3270)
UCL
Poetry Library

820 Tell Tale: stories and poems for family reading / edited by R. E. Harvey and M. G. Harvey. Bolton, No. 1 (May 1976)–39 (Spring 1995). ISSN: 0308–4442

The official magazine of the Farnworth Writers. Typewritten A5 format.

BL: P.901/3016
Poetry Library: 12 (1978)–14; 16; 18; 20

821 Temenos: a review devoted to the arts of the imagination / edited by Kathleen Raine, Philip Sherrard, Keith Critchlow and Brian Keeble. Dulverton: Watkins, No. 1 (1981)–13 (1992). ISSN: 0262–4524

Note: Continued by: *Temenos Academy Review*
Index: A contents listing, issue by issue, is given at the website
Profiled in: Görtschacher 1
Interview: with Kathleen Raine in Görtschacher 1
Website: www.temenosacademy.org

BL: P.901/3280
CUL: P400.c.120
NLS: HJ3.754 PER
TCD: PER 91–922 1983–1992
UCL: 1–9
Poetry Library: 1–11; 13

822 Temenos Academy Review / edited by Kathleen Raine, and then Grevel Lindop. London: The Temenos Academy, [No.] 1 (1998)– . ISSN: 1461–779X

Note: Continues: *Temenos.*
Index: A contents listing, issue by issue, is given at the website
Website: www.temenosacademy.org

BL: P.901/3280
CUL: P400.c.120
NLS: HJ4.1924
TCD: PER 72–749
Poetry Library

823 The Tempest / edited by Hilary Lester, Michael Paraskos, Benedict Read, Heidi Reitmaier, Tom Steele, Rob Stone, Rebecca Stott and Urszula Szulakowska. Leeds: New Leeds Arts Club, No. 1/2 (1992/1993)–4 (1994, ISSN: 0967–5388

Note: Variant title: *The Tempest of Leeds*

BL: ZK.9.b.7880
Poetry Library: 1/2

824 Tenth Decade / edited by Tony Frazer, Ian Robinson and Robert Vas Dias. London: Shearsman Books, Oasis Books, and Permanent Press, No. 12 (1990)–14 (1991). ISSN: 0264–6773

Note: Continues *Ninth Decade* and takes up its numbering.
Related Imprint: Shearsman Books and Oasis Books published *Shearsman* and *Oasis* respectively, as well as many poetry collections. Permanent Press has been a notable publisher of American poetry, e.g. Paul Blackburn's *Against the Silences* (1980), BL: X.989/89862.

BL: 12–13. (ZC.9.a.4976)
Poetry Library

825 Tenth Muse / edited by Andrew Jordan. Southampton, [No.] 1 (1990)– . ISSN: 0959–2334

Note: Variant title: *10th Muse*. Variant subtitles: *poetry, prose, graphics; poetry and prose.*

Especially notable for Andrew Jordan's editorials, including the championing of Nonism, and his trenchant reviews of poetry collections and other magazines.

BL: ZC.9.a.2495
UCL: 2– .
Poetry Library

826 Termite Times / edited by Royston Swarbrooke and others. Shrewsbury, No. 1 [198?]–6 [1992?]

Poetry Library: 1–3; 6

827 Terrible Work / edited by Tim Allen. Plymouth: Spineless Press, then Terrible Workpress, No. 1 (Spring 1993)–10 (2000). ISSN: 1354–3091

Website: www.terriblework.co.uk

Alexis Kirke and Steve Spence were also involved editorially. Continued as a website, specialising in reviews.

BL: 4–10. (ZK.9.a.3870)
CUL: 4; 6–7. (L999.d.1.147)
NLS: 4; 6–7. (HJ3.1286 PER)
TCD: 4–7. (PER 88–130 1994–1997)
UCL: 2–7; 9
Poetry Library: 3–9

828 The Third Eye / edited by Jay Ramsay, Sylvia Paskin and Geoffrey Godbert. London, [No. 1] (1983)–[2] (1984)

The first number was described as the "Special Primitive Issue", and the second, edited by Jay Ramsay alone, as "The Psychic Issue". A4 stapled typewritten format. Contributors included John Agard, Gillian Allnutt, Harry Fainlight, Ruth Fainlight, David Gascoyne, Libby Houston, Mahmoud Jamal, Dinah Livingstone, Peter Middleton, Patricia Pogson, Jay Ramsay, Peter Redgrove, Michèle Roberts, Jeremy Silver, Valerie Sinason, and others.

BL: [2]. (P.903/987)
UCL
Poetry Library

829 The Third Half / edited by Kevin Troop. Stamford: K.T. Publications, No. 1 (Feb. 1987)–32 (2000)

Note: Variant title: The Third Half Literary Magazine. Two separate issues are numbered as issue 16.

BL: ZC.9.a.803
CUL: 9; 11–32. (L727.d.318)
NLS: 12–32. (HJ4.1080 SER)

TCD: 12–32. (PER 86–151)
Poetry Library: 4–16; 25–27

830 This Is... / edited by Carol Cornish. London: Writing Space Publications, No. 1 (Winter 1998)–2 (1998). ISSN: 1461–3824

Website: www.btinternet.com/ffiwritingspace/thisis/

Also involved editorially were Paul Seed, Gill Paul, Lindsay Fitzpatrick, Kate Cornish, Chris Lethbridge, David Boyle, and Helen Tucker. The first number was entitled "Lost Love" and the second "The Poisoned Chalice". There were plans for further issues, "Apple", "Haunting", and "Ice and Fire".

BL: ZK.9.b.12779
Poetry Library

831 Thumbscrew: an independent journal of poetry, articles and reviews / edited by Tim Kendall. Oxford, then Bristol, Vol. 1 no. 1 (1994/1995)– no. 20/21 (2002). ISSN: 1369–5371

Note: Volume numbers were dispensed with after Vol. 1 no. 4.
Related Imprint: Thumbsrew also published Jon Stallworthy's collection Skyhorse (2002), BL: YK.2002.a.15583
Website: www.bris.ac.uk/thumbscrew/jl_thumb.html

Although publishing poetry, particularly significant for its fresh critical look at sacred cows. From the website, "In a poetry world which can all too often seem insular and chummy, Thumbscrew also sets out to provoke critical debate with a series of essays re-evaluating the reputations of several 'major' contemporary poets." Reviews and review essays include Fleur Adcock and Anne Stevenson on Sylvia Plath; Fran Brearton on Michael Longley; Stephen Burt on Randall Jarrell; Neil Chilton on Peter Reading; Kate Clanchy, Terry Gifford, and Edna Longley on Ted Hughes; Philip Coleman on John Berryman; John Lyon on Geoffrey Hill; Graham Nelson on Francis Ponge; Bernard O'Donoghue on Poetry's Concern; Sheenagh Pugh on Carol Ann Duffy and David Wheatley on Les Murray. Also involved editorially were Elizabeth Lowry, Fiona Mathews, John Redmond, Ian Sansom, and Dawn Bellamy.

BL: ZC.9.a.4136
CUL: L727.d.333
NLS: HJ4.1184
TCD: PER 87–432
UCL:
Poetry Library: 1–5; 7, 10–11; 13–14; 16; 18–20/21

832 Time Haiku / edited by Erica Facey. London: The Haiku Group, No. 1 (1995)– .

BL: ZK.9.a.7380
TCD: PL-369–629
Poetry Library: 2–3; 5; 8–

The Toadbird *See* The Old Police Station E556

833 Tongue to Boot / edited by Miles Champion. London, No. 1 (1995)–3 (1996)

Tongue to Boot brought together various British and American experimental poets, including Charles Bernstein, Tom Raworth, Fanny Howe, Rae Armantrout, Caroline Bergvall, Ted Greenwald, and Ulli Freer.

UCL
Poetry Library

T.O.P.S. *See* The Old Police Station E556

834 Totentanz / edited by D. Belton. West Croydon, No. 1 [1991?]

Poetry Library

835 Tracks / edited by John F. Deane and Jack Harte. Clondalkin, Co. Dublin, then Drogheda, Co. Louth, then Dublin: Aquila (Ireland), then Daedalus Press, No. 1 (1982)–11 (1996). ISSN: 0790–021X

Note: Daedalus Press was the publisher from no. 6 onwards.
Profiled in: Profiled in: Tom Clyde, *Irish Literary Magazines: an outline history and descriptive bibliography* (Dublin: Irish Academic Press, 2003), BL: 2725.g.3414
Related Imprint: Aquila (Ireland) also published Padraig J. Daly's *A Celibate Affair* (1984), BL: YC.1987.a.2333, while Daedalus Press published collections such as *Between: Selected Poems of Agnes Nemes Nagy* , trans. Hugh Maxton (1988), BL: YK.1992.a.6145

Deane was the poetry editor, Harte the fiction. After the fifth number of this basically annual magazine Dean edited solo. Contributors included Seamus Heaney, Pat Boran, R. S. Thomas, Daniel Berrigan, Selima Hill and, fiction-wise, Pat McCabe, John Banville, and others. No. 7 was a Thomas Kinsella issue. Richard Murphy and John Montague were also featured in the magazine. There was an emphasis on translation from Eastern Europe and Scandinavia, with no. 4 a collection by the Swedish poet Tomas Tranströmer (trans. Deane).

BL: ZC.9.a.1109
CUL: 1–2; 4–5; 10. (L727.c.1205)
NLS: 1–2; 4–5. (DJ.s.56 PER)
TCD: Per 90–420
Poetry Library: 1–3; 5–8; 10–11

835a Transit / edited by Kevin Ring. Binley Woods, nr. Coventry: Beat Scene, No. 1 (Spring 1993)– .

Website: www.beatscene.net

A sister publication of *Beat Scene*, devoted to the writing of the Beats.

BL: 1–2; 4–15. (Pressmark pending)
UCL: 3, 4.

836 Trap-door / edited by Anne McGrath and Peter Overton. Bolton: [Extrance?], No. 1 [198?]–3 [1989?]

Poetry Library: 3

837 Tremblestone / edited by Kenny Knight. Plymouth, No. 1 (1999)– . ISSN: 1463–9181

Poetry Library: 1–

838 Trends: the Paisley College of Technology literary magazine / edited by Konrad Hopkins, Nigel Malin and Ronald van Roekel. Paisley: Paisley College of Technology, Vol. 1 no. 1 (1977)–vol. 5 no. 10 (1984)

Note: Parallel numbering, so that vol. 5 no. 10 is actually the tenth issue of the entire run, rather than the tenth issue of the fifth volume

Vol. 2 no. 4 included a feature on Dutch Flemish poetry, guest-edited by Theo Hermans.

BL: P.901/1828
CUL: L727.c.1231
NLS: HJ3.675 PER
UCL
Poetry Library: Vol. 1 no. 1–vol. 2 no. 2; vol. 4 no. 1

839 Trixie. London: Ampersand, No. 1 [1994?]

Poetry Library

840 Troglodyte: a cultural magazine /
[edited by Joseph Biddulph]. Pontypridd:
Joseph Biddulph, 1 (2000)– . ISSN 1470–8388

Note: Continues: *Hrafnhoh*

Related Imprint: Joseph Biddulph publishes booklets on
lesser-known languages

BL: ZK.9.b.16463
TCD: PER 103–44

841 True Thomas / edited by Gillian Bence
Jones and Derek [A.] Taylor. Nacton: Willow
Kate Book Co., No. 1 [1979?]–15 [1981?]

Note: Gillian Bence Jones' name is also given as Gillian
Bence-Jones.

CUL: 5; 7–12. (L727.b.367)
Poetry Library: 8 [1980?]–9; 11; 13; 15

842 Tuba. London: Tuba Press, No. 1
[197?]–18 (1991). ISSN: 0269–4824

Related Imprint: Tuba Press

BL: 1–16. (P.903/900)
Poetry Library: 1–3; 5–10; 13–18

843 Twisted Wrist / edited by Paul Buck.
Hebden Bridge: Paul Buck, 1 (1977)–10 (1983)

Some issues are published from Paris.

BL: 3–8; 10. (ZA.9.b.844)
CUL: 4. (L999.b.1.529)
UCL

844 Uncle Nasty's… / [edited by Rob
Earl]. Maidstone: Outcrowd, [1978–1980?]

Note: Unnumbered, each issue had a different title:
[1?, 1978], *Uncle Nasty's Trendy Friends' Free Bumper Book of
Clever Things to Do with Things People Can't Print Themselves or
Nasal Etiquette for Pigs;*
[2?, 1978], *Uncle Nasty's Original Pork Pies;*
[3?, 1978], *Uncle Nasty's Election Special;*
[4?, 1979], *Uncle Nasty's Grunty Book Featuring Smut 'n' Death
Also Called Porkers' Shuffle or Swine Song.*
[5?, 1980], *Uncle Nasty's Easter Special;*
[6?, 1980], *Uncle Nasty's Extra Special*
Related Imprint: Outcrowd were also associated with
Cheapo Review, Codex Bandito, Gazunda, Hack Hack and *Ving*

A brief account of the Outcrowd milieu is given in the entry

for *Codex Bandito*. Libraries usually catalogue each issue
individually.

BL: [1?, 1978] X.909/44786 ; [2?, 1978] X.909/42854 ; [3?,
1978] YA.1996.a.17699 ; [4?, 1979] Cup.811/64 ; [5?, 1980]
X.950/16777 ; [6?, 1980] X.950/17240
CUL: [1?, 1978] (1979.8.2579]; [2?, 1978] 1978.8.2417); [4?,
1979] (1979.8.2578); [5?, 1980] (1980.8.2423); [6?, 1980]
(1992.8.3573)
NLS: [1?, 1978] (HP2.79.701); [2?, 1978] (HP1.78.4344);
[3?, 1978] (QP1.79.218); [4?, 1979] (HP2.79.2699); [5?,
1980] (HP2.80.1226)
TCD: [1?, 1978] (PL– 47– 34); [2?, 1978] (PL– 23–145); [3?,
1978] (PB– 50–959); [4?, 1979] (PL– 47–925); [5?, 1980]
(PL–66–911); [6?, 1980] (PL–221–401)
UCL: [4?, 1979]
Poetry Library: [1?, 1978], [4?, 1979]

845 Uncompromising Positions /
editor: Cheryl Wilkinson; co-editor: David
Bateman. Liverpool and Gateshead: Jugglers
Fingers Press in conjunction with Sefton Arts,
Issue 1 (1993)–2 (1994). ISSN: 1350–9152

Contributors include Geoff Hattersley, Martin Stannard,
Mark Robinson, Levi Tafari, Bob Cobbing, and others.

BL: 1. (ZC.9.a.3719)
Poetry Library

846 Undercurrent: London: Page 84, [1,
1998?–?]

Related Imprint: P.E.F., i.e Page 84, also produced *Poem 1*
and *Untouched*
Website: www.page84.4t.com/newpage.htm

No holdings known

847 Understanding / edited by Denise
Smith; associated editor: Thom Nairn.
Edinburgh: Dionysia Press, No. 1 (1989)–.

Related Imprint: Dionysia Press has also produced
individual collections of poetry, often specialising in translations from the Greek, e.g. *The Complete Poems of George
Vafopolous* (1998), BL: YC.2003.a.7226

BL: 1; 6–8. (ZC.9.a.2513)
NLS: HJ4.973 PER
UCL
Poetry Library

848 Undertow / edited by Bryony Rogers, Ben Seymour, Saffron Walkling and Simon Brind. London: The Literary Society, Dept of English, University College London, Issue 1 [1991?]–4 (Spring 1995)

UCL: Summer 1993–Spring 1995 (College Collection Pers); 3–4. (Little Magazines)
Poetry Library: 1

849 Unknown Origins / edited by Fiona Howes, Jackie Beggs, Alison Grice, Karen Edwards, Gerry Audas, Nigel Lutt, Susan Smith and others. Leighton Buzzard: The Cedars Upper School and Community College, No. 1 (1978)–3 (1979)

Poetry Library

850 The Unruly Sun / edited by Jennifer Hoskins, Matt Westwood and Geoff Sawers. Reading: The Rising Sun Arts Centre, Issue 1 [1996?]– . ISSN: 1470–319X

BL: 4– . ZK.9.a.6974
Poetry Library: 5–

851 Untouched. London: Page 84, [1–?, c.1998–99]

Note: No. 6 is noted in issue 8 of the zine By Pass.
Related Imprint: P.E.F., i.e Page 84, also produced Poem 1 and Undercurrent
Website: www.page84.4t.com/newpage.htm
No holdings known

852 Upstart! Magazine: new writing from the new city / edited by Carol Barac, Marilyn Ricci and Alison Woodhouse. Milton Keynes: Upstart! Press, Issue 1 (Summer 1996)–4 (Autumn 1999). ISSN: 1364–3134

BL: ZK.9.a.4978
Poetry Library: 1–2; 4

853 Urthona: a magazine for rousing the imagination / edited by Ambrose Gilson. Cambridge, Issue 1 [1994?]– . ISSN: 1465–5225

Note: Associated with the Friends of the Western Buddhist Order (FWBO). Guest poetry editor for issue 3: Ananda.
Website: www.urthona.com/

BL: ZC.9.b.7200
CUL: 12– . (Periodicals Dept.)
NLS: 12– . (HJ8.2749 SER)
Poetry Library: 3

Vanessa and One See Vanessa Poetry Magazine E854

854 Vanessa Poetry Magazine / edited by John Welch. London: The Many Press, No. 1 [1976?]–7 (Spring 1981)

Note: Variant titles: Vanessa; Vanessa Magazine. No. 7 is combined with One, no. 5 (edited by David Chaloner), and is described as Vanessa and One
Related Imprint: The Many Press
Website: www.shadoof.net/many/

BL: P.903/508
CUL: L727.b.155
NLS: 7. (P.la.9433 PER)
TCD: PER 94–927
UCL
Poetry Library

855 Various Artists / edited by Tony Lewis-Jones. Bristol: Firewater Press, No. 1 [1992]–7 [1997?].

Related Imprint: Firewater Press also published Working Titles

BL: 6–7. (ZK.9.a.6847)
Poetry Library: 1–7

856 Ver Poets Voices / edited by May E. Badman. London: Colney, No. 1 [198?]–9 (1990)

Anthology: May Badman and Margaret Tims (eds.), Ver Poets' Voices: thirtieth anniversary anthology (St. Albans: Brentham, 1996), BL: YK.1996.a.19404
Related Imprint: Ver Poets also published the magazines Poetry Post, the newsletter Ver Poets Poetry World, the Vision On anthologies, c.1980–1997, and individual collections of poetry.
Website: www.hertsnews.com/arts/ver.htm

Ver Poets take their name from the River Ver, and also Verulamium, the Roman town of St. Alban's. A short history of the group is given in the anthology by Badman and Tims.

BL: 1. (X.0972/163.)
CUL: 2–5; 7. (L727.C.778)
NLS: 2–5; 7. (HP.la.476 PER)
TCD: 2–7. (PER 91–72)
UCL: 1
Poetry Library: 1; 5–7; 9

857 Verbal Underground: imaginative writing from the students of the University of North London / edited by Charlotte Cole. London: [University of North London], [No. 1] (1994)

Poetry Library

858 Verse / edited by Robert Crawford, Henry Hart and David Kinloch (founding editors), then joined by Nicholas Roe and Richard Price, and others. Various locations: Oxford and Charleston (South Carolina), then Salford, Glasgow, St. Andrews, London and Williamsburg (Virginia); then Athens (Georgia), then Richmond (Virginia), [Vol. 1] issue 1 (1984)– . ISSN: 0268–3830

Note: *Verse* was based in the U.S.A. after vol. 12 no. 2 (1995).
Index: *Scottish Poetry Index Vol. 2* (Edinburgh: Scottish Poetry Library, 1995), BL: ZC.9.b.6227
Profiled in: David Kinloch's introduction to *Scottish Poetry Index Vol. 2*
Anthology: Vol. 12 no. 2, a selection entitled *The Best Verse: Ten Years of Poetry*
Related Imprint: Verse Press publishes collections by American poets
Website: versemag.blogspot.com/

Founded by Robert Crawford, David Kinloch, and Henry Hart. After vol. 12 no. 2, Crawford, Hart, Kinloch, and Price gave up the editorship and the magazine became U.S. based, edited by Brian Henry. Amongst the poets featured in the British-based *Verse* were John Ashbery, Allen Curnow, Derek Walcott, John Montague, Miroslav Holub, Edwin Morgan, James Merrill, Frank Kuppner, Kenneth White, Amy Clampitt, Robert Pinksy, and Gennady Aygi. Frequent contributors included Simon Armitage, Iain Bamforth, Stanislaw Baranczak, Alison Brackenbury, John Burnside, Gerald Dawe, John Dixon, Raymond Friel, Dana Gioia, Chris Greenhalgh, Seamus Heaney, W. N. Herbert, Chris Hurford, Andrew Lansdown, Robert Mackenzie, Angela McSeveney, Glyn Maxwell, Les A. Murray, Alan Riach, Michael Symmons Roberts, Penelope Shuttle, Iain Crichton Smith, Elizabeth Smith, Tomas Tranströmer, John Tranter, Chris Wallace-Crabbe, and Howard Wright. Vol. 7 no. 1 was a special issue on Language poetry. Vol. 11 (3)/12(1) was a selection of interviews with poets, *Talking Verse*, edited by Robert Crawford, Henry Hart, David Kinloch, and Richard Price. Vol. 12 no. 2 was an anthology, *The Best Verse: Ten Years of Poetry*. With *Gairfish* and *Southfields*, *Verse* was one of the magazines associated with the Scottish grouping of poets, the Informationists.

BL: P.901/3712
CUL: [Vol. 1] issue. 1–vol. 11 no. 3 / vol. 12 no. 1. Vol. 16 no. 2–vol. 17 no. 1.–vol. 18 no. 1; vol. 18 no. 3– . (L727.c.1166)
NLS: [Vol. 1] issue 1–vol. 11 no. 3/ vol. 12 no. 1. (HJ2.413)
TCD: [Vol. 1] issue 1–vol. 11 no. 2. (PER 95–120 1984–1994) Vol. 11 no. 3/ vol. 12 no. 1. (PL–249–814)
UCL: [Vol. 1] issue 2– .
Poetry Library: [Vol. 1] issue. 1–6; vol. 3 no. 3–vol. 4 no. 2; vol. 5 no. 1–2; vol. 6 no. 1–vol. 13 no. 2/3

859 Versus: contemporary arts magazine. Leeds: Versus, No. 1 (Jan./Apr. 1994)–5 (1995). ISSN: 1352–4240

BL: 1. (ZC.9.d.388)
CUL: 1–3. (L999.b.1.2057)
NLS: 1–3. (HJ10.242 PER)
TCD: 1–3. (PER 95–38 1994)
UCL

860 Vertical Images / edited by Philip Woodrow, Brandon Broll, Chris Brown, Mike Diss, Brian Docherty, David Aldridge, George Squire and Peter Head. London: [Vertical Images c/o] Stroud Green Community Centre, 1 (1986)–10 (1995); Supplement [1991?]. ISSN: 0269–0063

Note: No. 8 bears the title *Constructs of Vertical Images*, ed. Russell Square
Related Imprint: Vertical Images published *New Leaves: A Celebration of Trees* (1989), BL: YC.1990.a.1189

The magazine of the work of a group meeting in North London. Issue 9 included work from further afield. Contributors include the editors, A. W. Kindness, Robert Sheppard, Alison Barry, Adrian Clarke, Bob Cobbing, David Crystal, Harry Gilonis, Norman Jope, Frances Presley, Johan de Wit, Joe Bidder, Miles Champion, Ken Edwards, Ulli Freer, Rober Hampson, Gavin Selerie, and others.

BL: 1; 6–10. (ZC.9.a.1263)

CUL: 1–4; 8– . (L727.c.1169)
NLS: 1–4; 6, 8– . (HJ4.1069 PER)
TCD: PER 84–399
UCL: 1–4; 9
Poetry Library: 1–7; 9–10; Supplement

861 Vigil / edited by John Howard. Gillingham, then Bruton: Vigil Publications, Issue 1 (1988)– . ISSN: 0954–0881

Note: Continues: *Period Piece & Paperback*. Editor's name is also given as John Howard-Greaves. A supplement of reviews, *Open Press*, was also published, of which the Poetry Library has issue 8 (1995).

BL: 3– . (ZC.9.a.1821)
CUL: 6– . (L718.c.349)
NLS: 1–4; 6– . (HP.sm.925)
TCD: 1–17. (PER 95–485)
UCL
Poetry Library: 1–7; 9–16

862 Village Voice / edited by Ian C. Durant. Canterbury: Rutherford College, University of Kent, Canterbury, [No. 1, 197?]

Poetry Library

863 A Vision Very Like Reality: radical writings / edited by Peter Ackroyd, Ian Patterson and Nick Totton. London, 1 (Dec. 1979)

Note: Continued by: *Holophrase*

BL: ZD.9.b.65
CUL: L999.b.1.1365
UCL

864 Voice & Verse / edited by Ruth Booth. London: Robooth Publications, No. 1 (1998)– . ISSN: 1466–6227

BL: 1–8; 10– . (ZK.9.b.14079)
UCL: 8–11; 15–19
Poetry Library: 1–

865 Voyage: short story & poetry magazine. Wolverhampton: Regent Publications, Issue 1 [199?]–10 [2001?]. ISSN: 1466–7541

BL: 4 [1999]. (ZK.9.a.6649)
Poetry Library: 7 [2000], 10 [2001?]

866 Walking Naked. Swinton, Manchester: Naked Publications, Spring 1994–Winter 1994

Note: Continued by: *Poetry Manchester*

BL: ZK.9.a.4256

867 Wasafiri / edited by Susheila Nasta. London: Association for the Teaching of Caribbean, African, Asian and Associated Literature (ATCAL); then Dept of English, Queen Mary and Westfield College, University of London, [Vol. 1] No. 1 (Autumn 1984)– . ISSN: 0269–0055

Note: Variant subtitles: *perspectives on African, Caribbean, Asian and Black British literature; Caribbean, African, Asian and associated literatures in English.*
Index: A contents listing of each issue is given on the website
Interview: with Susheila Nasta, in *Poetry news: the newsletter of the Poetry Society*, Summer 2006, p [8].
Website: www.wasafiri.org

A literary review for Anglophone African, Caribbean, Asian, Black British and post-colonial literature which publishes articles and reviews interspersed with poems and short stories. Contributors include Michael Ondaatje, Chinua Achebe, Caryl Phillips, Ngugi wa Thiong'o, Kamau Brathwaite, Marina Warner, Nadine Gordimer, Abdulrazak Gurnah, Merle Collins, Ferdinand Denis, Bernardine Evaristo, Maya Jaggi, Aamer Hussein, and others. Special issues include: no. 4, "Women's Issue"; no. 16, "Special Caribbean Issue"; no. 19, "Focus on South Africa"; no. 21, "India, South Africa and the Diaspora"; no. 25, "Pacific Writing Special"; no. 29, "Taking the Cake: Black Writing in Britain"; no. 31, "The Long March: Migrant Writing in Europe"; no. 32, "Transformations: Creative Writing Special Issue"; no. 36: "Writing in Britain: Shifting Geographies", and no. 44, "Frantz Fanon Special Issue".

BL: ZC.9.a.585
CUL: L700.b.152
NLS: 1–9, 11–14, 16– HJ9.1568 SER
TCD: 35– . (PER 103–409)
Poetry Library: 1–29, 31–

868 **Waves** / edited by Bill Torrie Douglas. Largs: Society of Civil Service Authors Poetry Workshop, [No. 28] (1998)– . ISSN: 0140–0878

Note: Continues: *Focus*

BL: P.901/3067
Poetry Library: 31 (2001)–

869 **Welcome to Pam's Poems** / edited by Pam Gold. Benfleet, [No. 1, 198?–3, 198?]

Poetry Library: 3

870 **West Coast Magazine** / edited by Kenny MacKenzie, Gordon Giles, Joe Murray, John Cunningham, Margaret Fulton Cook, Graham Fulton, Ronnie Smith and Brian Whittingham. Glasgow: West Coast Publications, Issue 1 (Spring 1988)–27 (1998). ISSN: 0963–732X

Anthology: Kenny McKenzie and Joe Murray (eds.), *Tales from the Coast: stories from West Coast Magazine* (Glasgow: Taranis, 1991), BL: YK.1993.a.15624)

Gordon Giles, Kenny MacKenzie, and Joe Murray were the founding editors. Short fiction, poems, articles and reviews. One of the magazines associated with the resurgence of Scottish writing in the late 1980s and 90s, initially associated with Glasgow. Contributors include the editors, Alasdair Gray, Janice Galloway, Robert Crawford, Donny O'Rourke, Hugh McMillan, J. N. Reilly, Richard Price, Agnes Owens, Gerrie Fellows, Kenneth White, Jim C. Wilson, Douglas Lipton, George Gunn, Kathleen Jamie, and others.

BL: 1–7. (ZC.9.b.4819)
NLS: 1–26. (HJ9.1587 PER)
Poetry Library: 5–8; 10–23; 25–27

871 **Westwords: quarterly magazine for the south-west: poetry prose photography** / edited by David Woolley. Plymouth, No. 1 (1986)–15 [1993?]. ISSN: 0269–9214

BL: ZK.9.a.207
CUL: L400.c.548
NLS: DJ.s.668 PER
TCD: PER 91–965 1986–1992
UCL:
Poetry Library: 1–6; 8–15

872 **The Whistle House** / edited by I. M. Wistlin. St. Helens, Vol. 1 no. 1 [1996]

UCL
Poetry Library

873 **White Paint Fumes** / edited by Albert J. Hill. Fishpond, Nr. Bridport, Issue 1 [199?]–2 [199?]

Poetry Library: 2

874 **The White Rose** / edited by Nancy Whybrow. Dartford, Issue 1 [1986]–25 [1992]. ISSN: 0268–7054

Note: Variant subtitles: *literary magazine; poetry & literary magazine*

BL: 7; 17; 22–24. (ZC.9.a.750)
CUL: L727.c.1306
NLS: 1–4; 8; 10–12; 14–18; 20–21. (HJ4.1716 PER)
TCD: PER 93–878 1986–1992
Poetry Library: 8; 20; 22

875 **'Why are you leaving, Mister Archibald?': a concoction of honest writing** / edited by Matt Davis and Jack Doyle. Croydon, [No. 1?, 1997?]

Poetry Library: [1?]

876 **The Wide Skirt** / edited by Geoff Hattersley. Sheffield, then Huddersfield, then Penistone, Issue 1 (1986)–30 (1997). ISSN: 0951–6255

Note: A biographical note for Geoff Hattersley, during his time as a Royal Literary Fund Fellow, suggests there were thirty-one issues of the magazine but this has not been confirmed by known holdings.
Related Imprint: Wide Skirt also published individual collections of poetry, including Simon Armitage's *The Distance Between Stars* (1989), BL: YC.1988.a.15093

Issue 16 was a "Huddersfield Special" issue, edited by Ian McMillan, and the magazine, with *The North*, has been associated with a Huddersfield-associated grouping of poets. The contributors to the Huddersfield issue were Janet Fisher, Steve Sneyd, Stewart Crehan, Peter Sansom, Geoff Hattersley, John Duffy, Tam Weir, Simon Armitage, Andrew Wilson, Duncan Curry, John Lancaster, John Bosley, Jeanette Hattersley, Milner Place, and Anna Taylor.

BL: ZC.9.a.1468
CUL: 3–30. (L727.c.952.3)
NLS: 3–30. (HJ8.1239 PER)
TCD: 3–30. (PER 94–502 1987–1997)
UCL: 5–30
Poetry Library: 1–30

877 Widemind: surrealist poetry /
edited by Steve Burgess. London, [No. 1?]
(Summer 1985)–[2?] (Autumn/Winter 1985)

Note: Variant subtitles: *surrealaction; surrealist poetry anthology*

Poetry Library: [1?]–[2?]

878 Wild Words: women's stories, poems, drawings and photographs /
edited by Julia Casterton, Dallas Sealy and
Diane Biondo. London, No. 1 (1984)

BL: P.903/1017
NLS: DJ.m.28(4) PER
Poetry Library: 1

879 Windows / edited by Peter Barry, Mary
Bowman, Marian Taylor, Robin Haylett and
Janet Ashley. Eastbourne: English Dept, East
Sussex College of Higher Education; then
Southampton: English Dept, La Sainte Union
College of Higher Education, No. 1 (1977)–10
(1981)

Index: In no. 10 (compiled by Peter Skerratt)

Featured poets included Lee Harwood, Bill Wyatt, Allen
Fisher, David Miller, Johnson Kirkpatrick, and Philip
Jenkins.

BL: 2. (YA.1992.a.19501)
Poetry Library: 1–6; 10

880 Wire / edited by Mal Cieslak. Woking,
then Knaphill: Aramby Publishing, No. 1
(1990)–no. 11 (1997). ISSN: 0959–4663

Note: Parallel numbering: no. 7 is also vol. 2 no. 1, etc.
Related Imprint: Publications by Aramby include those in
the Wire Poetry Booklet Series, e.g. Angela Atkin's *A Touch
of Emerald* (1996), BL: YK.1996.a.19294
Website: www.aramby.cjb.net/

Sally Roast and P. G. McCormack were also involved
editorially.

BL: 1–5. (ZC.9.a.2395)
Poetry Library: 1–5; 7–11

Witana Gemot *See* The Old Police Station E556

881 The Wolly of Swot / edited by Cory
Harding. Hove, then London: Open Mouth
Productions, No. 1 (1977)–3 (1978)

BL: 1; 3. (P.903/550)
UCL
Poetry Library

882 Wonderlust / edited by Nichola Corese.
London: Wonderlust, Issue 1 [199?]–?

Articles, fiction, poems and black and white images. The
magazine's sub-title was: *Friskily striding through
contemporary culture.*

BL: 7 (Summer 1999); 9 (2000). (ZK.9.b.14871)

883 The Word: life journal and poetry
magazine / edited by Brian Palin. Feltham:
Partners Writing Group, [Vol. 1.]
(Summer/Autumn 1998)–?

BL: [vol. 3] (Spring 1999)– [vol. 10, Autumn/Winter 2001].
(ZK.9.a.6373)
Poetry Library: [vol. 1] (Summer/Autumn 1998); [vol. 3]
(Spring 1999); [vol. 5] (Autumn/Winter 1999)

884 Wordlinks Journal / edited by Albert
Baker. [Bedford?], Vol. 1 no. 1 [198?]

Poetry Library

885 Words / edited by Carl McDougall.
Markinch: The Arts in Fife, No. 1 (Autumn
1976)–11/12 [1980]

Note: At least two unnumbered issues of a supplement,
Words Review, were issued
Index: *Scottish Poetry Index Vol. 9* (Edinburgh: Scottish Poetry
Library, 2000). BL: ZC.9.b.6227

Contributors include: Stewart Conn, Robert Garioch,
Duncan Glen, W. Price Turner, Iain Crichton Smith, D. J.
Enright, Alan Sillitoe, W. S. Graham, Blackie Fortuna, Tom
McGrath, George Mackay Brown, Michael Hamburger,
Norman MacCaig, and others.

BL: 1–3; 5–11/12. (P.903/529)

NLS: DJ.m.1169
Poetry Library: 3–11/12; Also, two unnumbered issues of *Words Review*

886 **Words: the new literary forum** / edited by Phillip Vine and Jean Shelley. Worthing: Words Publications Ltd., Vol. 1 no. 1 (June 1985)–no. 8 (1986)

Note: Continued by: *Words International: the literary monthly* Vol. 1 no. 6 included a feature on Norman MacCaig.

CUL: Vol. 1 no. 1–vol. 1 no. 6. (L700.b.98.1)
NLS: Vol. 1 no. 1–vol. 1 no. 6. (HP4.87.1622 PER)
TCD: Vol. 1 no. 1–vol. 1 no. 6. (PER 90–378)
Poetry Library: Vol. 1 no. 1–vol. 1 no. 8

887 **Words International: the literary monthly** / edited by Jean Shelley and Phillip Vine. Uckfield and Towson, Maryland: Words Publications Ltd., Vol. 1 no. 1 (1987)–vol. 1 no. 6 (1988)

Note: Succeeds *Words: the new literary forum*

BL: Vol. 1 no. 2; no. 5. (ZA.9.b.916)
Poetry Library: Vol. 1 no. 1–4; no. 6

888 **Words Worth** / edited by Alaric Sumner, Peter J. King, Rosemary Sumner, Paul Buck, and Richard Tabor. London: Zimmer Zimmer Press; Yeovil, Vol. 1 no. 1 (1978)–vol. 2 no. 1 (1995). ISSN: 0140–346X

Herbert Burke is listed as a guest editor of vol. 1 no. 1. Paul Buck edited vol. 1 no. 2.

BL: P.901/3147
CUL: Vol. 1 no. 1. (L999.c.3.705)
NLS: Vol. 1 no. 1. (3744 PER)
TCD: Vol 1 no. 1. (PER 92–443)
UCL: Vol. 1 no. 1–3
Poetry Library

889 **Words Worth: a journal from writers with vision... from the heart of Milton Keynes** / edited by Martin Brocklebank and Judy Studd. Milton Keynes: Speakeasy Press, No. 1 [1996]–6 (1998). ISSN: 1364–0542

BL: 1. (ZK.9.b.9957)
Poetry Library: 3–6

890 **Wordshare: creative writing quarterly** / edited by Keith Ashton. Lincoln: Lincolnshire County Council in collaboration with Artlink and in association with the East Midlands Arts Board, 1 (Summer 1989)– .

"WORDSHARE is written by people with disabilities and people past retirement age."

BL: 1–? (ZC.9.b.3902); 18–22 . (ZK.9.b.16854)
CUL: 11; 14–17. (L727.b.448)
Poetry Library: 5

891 **Wordsmith** / edited by David Duffin amd Shaun Roberts. London: The English Society, Goldsmiths' College (University of London), Issue 1 (1993)–5 (1995)

Note: Title given as WORDsmith.

Poetry Library: 5

892 **Working Titles** / edited by Rachel Bentham, Daniel Hershon, Tony Lewis-Jones and Tom Phillips. Bristol: Firewater Press, [Issue] 1 [1989]–9 (1999)

Related Imprint: Firewater Press also published *Various Artists*

BL: 1–5; 7–9
UCL
Poetry Library: 3–6

893 **Write Away.** Liverpool: The Windows Project, No. 1 [1987?]–5 [1988?]

Note: A magazine devoted to poetry by Merseyside children
Related Imprint: The Windows Project publishes a number of collections, including those in the Merseyside Poetry Minibooks Series and published *Smoke*
Website: www.windowsproject.demon.co.uk/index.htm

Poetry Library

894 **Write Now.** Corby: The Corby and District Writers Circle, No. 1 (June 1979)–?

BL: 1–4. (P.901/3467)

895 Write Now: the magazine for writers / edited by Dene October. Northampton: WN Publications, No. 1 (1986)–2 (1986)

Poetry Library

896 The Write Spark: a collection by Hackney Creative Group / edited by Rosetta Stone. London: Creative Arts Hackney, No. 1 (Mar. 1996)– . ISSN: 1365–9030

Also involved editorially have been Ndubuisi Anike, Shiraz Durrani, and Agatha Arnold.

BL: 1–3. (ZK.9.b.10167)
Poetry Library: 2–4; 9–

897 Write-in / edited by Glyn Hughes, David Benedictus and Peter Forbes. Farnborough, Southampton and Swindon: Farnborough Library, Southampton Libraries, and Swindon Divisional Libraries, [198?]

Poetry Library: [Three unnumbered issues, one from 1983, two from 1985]

898 Writer. St Ives: United Writers, Sept./Oct 1980–no. 112 (1986). ISSN: 0260–2776

Note: Continues: Writer's Review

BL: PP.8002.bt
NLS: HJ3.632 PER
TCD: PER 93–942 1980–1986

899 Writers' Brew: the UK TransAtlantic Critique Club's quarterly review: a collection of world wide writing from new authors. Dawley: Writers' Brew Club. [No. 1, 1998–2, 1998]. ISSN: 1461–9652

Note: Continued by: Writers' Cauldron

BL: ZK.9.a.5883

900 Writers' Cauldron. [Dawley]: Writers' Brew Club, Issue 1 (Sept. 1998)–13 (July 2001)

Note: Continues: Writers' Brew

BL: 1–8. (ZK.9.a.5670)
CUL: 9; 11; 12. (L727.d.390)
NLS: 9; 11; 12. (HJ3.2213 PER)
TCD: 11; 12. (PER 84–195)

901 Writer's Muse. Cheadle: CK Publishing, No. 1 (Summer 1999)–22 (Feb. 2003)

BL: ZC.9.b.7782

902 The Writers Rostrum / edited by Jenny Chaplin. Rothesay, Isle of Bute, No. 1 [198?]–33/34 (1992). ISSN: 0267–453X

BL: P.901/3579
CUL: L718.c.337.1
NLS: 1–32. (HJ2.388 PER)
TCD: PER 92–105 1984–1992
Poetry Library: [9?] (1986)–31

903 The Writer's Voice. Manchester: Writer's Voice, [No. 1] (Winter 1983)–10 (Summer 1986)

BL: P.903.945
CUL: 1984–1986. (L718.c.304)
NLS: NJ.526 PER
TCD: Spring 1984– . (PER 71–546)

904 Writing in Lincolnshire. Lincoln: The Word Hoard, [No. 1, 199?]–4 (1995)

Poetry Library: 2; 4

905 Writing Ulster: poems, stories, essays, art… / edited by E.A. Markham. Coleraine, Co. Londonderry: Dept of English, Media & Theatre Studies, University of Ulster, No. 1 (1990/1991)–5 (1998)

Also involved editorially were Paul Davies and Rebecca Needham.

BL: ZC.9.a.3327
CUL: L733.c.118
NLS: 1, 2; 5. (HJ8.1530 PER)
TCD: PER 88–696
Poetry Library: 1–2

906 **Writing Women** / edited by Eileen Aird, Linda Anderson, Gay Clifford, Sheila Whitaker, Rebecca Hiscock, Maggi Hurt, Cynthia Fuller, Rosalind Brackenbury, Jo Alberti, Margaret Wilkinson, Gillian Allnutt, Penny Smith, Rosemary O'Sullivan, Andrea Badenoch, Debbie Taylor, Maggie Hannan, and Pippa Little. Newcastle-upon-Tyne, Vol. 1 no. 1 (1981)–vol. 13 no. 2 (1998). ISSN: 1356–5435

Related Imprint: Writing Women and Virago collaborated on at least two anthologies of women's writing: Andrea Badenoch [et al.] (ed.), *The Nerve: The Virago Book of Writing Women* (London: Virago, 1998), BL: YK.1999.a.7176); Andrea Badenoch [et al.] (ed.), *Wild Cards*. Writing Women 2, (London Virago, 1999), BL: YK.2001.a.2259

The magazine of a women's collective based in Newcastle-upon-Tyne. Vol. 11 no. 3/vol. 12 no. 1 includes an Irish supplement, guest edited by Alibhe Smyth. Vol. 12 no. 3 includes a Fiction supplement, guest edited by Maggie Gee.

BL: P.901/3526
CUL: Vol. 1 no. 1–vol. 12 no. 2. (L718.c.286)
UCL
Poetry Library: Vol. 1 no. 1–vol. 3 no. 3; vol. 4 no. 2–4; vol. 6 no. 1, no. 3; vol. 7 no.2–vol. 8 no. 1; vol. 11 no. 3–vol. 13 no. 2.

907 **Wyrd** / edited by David Haden. Birmingham, Issue 1 (1991)

Poetry Library

908 **X-calibre** / edited by Ken Taylor and Juli Taylor. Bristol: Carmina Publishing, Vol. 5 (1988)–vol. 8 (1991). ISSN: 0269–5014

Note: Continues: *Exe-calibre*
Website: www.wordwrights.co.uk/pub/xcalibre/xcalibre.html#info

BL: 5–8. (ZK.9.a.459)
CUL: 5–8. (L718.c.862)
NLS: 5–8. (DJ.s.660(2) PER)
UCL: 5–6
Poetry Library: 6–8

909 **'Y'** / edited by Tom Callaghan, Charles Clover, Maggi Hurt, Simon Brewer, Martin Greene, Reg Wright, Melanie Friend, Fiona Roberts, P. R. Neville-Hadley and Bronia Kita. York: Derwent College, University of York; then Wentworth College, University of York, No. 1 (1977)–5 (1979)

Note: Variant title: *'Y' magazine: York University arts magazine.* Continues: *Yorick*. Continued by: *The New Yorick*.

No. 2 includes an interview with C.H. Sisson.

CUL: L985.b.194
NLS: HP4.81.406 PER
Poetry Library: 1–4

910 **The Yeats Club Review** / edited by Dwina Murphy-Gibb, Terence DuQuesne and Chris Morgan. Oxford: The Yeats Club, Vol. 1 no. 1 (1987). ISSN: 0951–905X

Note: Later issues are incorporated in *Celtic Dawn*

BL: ZC.9.a.1619
CUL: L727.b.316
NLS: HP.med.288 PER
TCD: PER 94–460 1987
Poetry Library

911 **The Yellow Crane: interesting new poems from South Wales and beyond...** / edited by Jonathan Brookes. Cardiff, No. 1 [1995]– .

Note: Continues: *The Cardiff Poet*

BL: 9 (Spring 1997)–13 (Autumn 1998). (Pressmark pending)
National Library of Wales: 1995–1998 (LLP/DPB, STORFA/STACK; YX2 YEL)
Poetry Library: 8 (1996/1997)–

912 **Young: poetry magazine** / edited by Jaya Kumar. London: University of London Union; Young Publications, [1?] (Autumn 1978)–[3?] (Winter 1979/1980)

Note: Variant subtitle: *poetry and film*

Poetry Library: [1?–3?]

913 Young Writer: the magazine for children with something to say / edited by Kate Jones. Weobley, Hereford: Just Write! Issue 1 [1996]– . ISSN: 1359–9380

Index: A table of contents for each issue is given at the website
Website: www.mystworld.com/youngwriter/

BL: CDS.9.b.61
Poetry Library: 1–4; 6–

Z See Z Magazine E914

Z2O See Zed2O E915

914 Z Magazine / edited by Victoria Hurst and Nicola Minchington. Douglas, Isle of Man, Issue 1 (1988). ISSN: 0953–6299

Note: Variant title: Z

BL: ZK.9.a.1086
Poetry Library

915 Zed2O / edited by Duncan Glen. Edinburgh, then Kirkcaldy: Duncan Glen, 1 (Mar. 1991)– . ISSN: 0962–418X

Related Imprint: Duncan Glen's Akros publish many mainly Scottish poets and other Scottish interest books and published the magazine *Akros*

A very individual mix of contemporary Scottish poetry, poetry from down the centuries, quotations and images from significant books, all rendered with Duncan Glen's professional graphic and typographical knowledge. Glen's editorials are sometimes polemical on the state of the Scottish poetry of the day and on the nature of publishing.

BL: ZC.9.b.4681
CUL: L727.b.445
NLS: HJ9.1736 SER

916 Zenos: poetry, British and international / edited by Shirley Barker, Danielle Hope, Agis Mellis and Jyoti Soar. Nottingham: Zenos Publications, No. 1 (1982)–8 (1988). ISSN: 0264–8601

Zenos included features on contemporary Greek poetry, Turkish poetry, and modern Yugoslavian and Russian poetry. Contributors include: Cory Harding, Rupert Loydell, Wes Magee, Ruper Mallin, Steve Sneyd, Martin Stannard, Nick Toczek, George Szirtes, and others.

BL: 1–5; 7. (P.901/3444)
CUL: 1–4. (L999.c.3.1342)
NLS: 2–5. (DJ.s.18(2) PER)
UCL
Poetry Library: 1–6; 8

917 Zero / edited by Jeremy Noel-Tod. Oxford: Zero, c/o New College, Issue 1 [1996?]–5 (Michaelmas 1998)

Note: Continues: *Manutius*

BL: ZK.9.a.4836

918 Zimmerframepileup / edited by Stephen Jessener. Walthamstow, London: Loose Hand Press, No. 1 (1994)–13 (1995)

BL: 12–13. (ZK.9.b.9066)
Poetry Library

919 Zip: poetry and something else from Stand and Deliver / edited by Mike Rooke, Sandy Gort, Kevin Fegan and Jane Rogers. Ashton-under-Lyne and Oldham, No. 1 [1981]–13 [1985?]. ISSN: 0260–7654

BL: 3; 7–12. (P.901/3276)
CUL: 1–12. (L727.b.256)
NLS: 1–12. (P.la.9602 PER)
TCD: 2–12. (PER 90–498)
UCL: 3–13
Poetry Library: 2–5; 7–9; 12

Chapter F

A Timeline

This section simply lists notable magazines which started in a particular year. The choice is intended to include those we regard as especially significant, but inevitably involves questions of personal choice: other chronologies could of course be made. More details, especially later locations and editors, are given in the *Compendium*'s full entry for each magazine, referenced in this list by its entry number.

1914

Blast: review of the great English vortex, edited by Wyndham Lewis, London. *Last issue* 1915. A15

The Egoist: an individualist review, edited by Dora Marsden, then Harriet Shaw Weaver, London. *Last issue* 1919. A55

Des Imagistes, edited by Ezra Pound, London. The first Imagist anthology. *Last anthology* 1930. A90

New Numbers [edited by Lascelles Abercrombie], publishing Rupert Brooke, John Drinkwater and other Georgian poets, Dymock. *Last issue* 1914. A140

1915

The Signature, edited by D. H. Lawrence, Katherine Mansfield and John Middleton Murry, London. *Last issue* 1915. A198

1917

The Hydra: journal of the Craiglockhart War Hospital, [edited by Wilfred Owen and others], Craiglockhart, near Edinburgh. *Last issue* 1918. A89

1919

The Irish Statesman, edited by G. W. Russell, Dublin. *Last issue* 1930. A97

The Monthly Chapbook, edited by Harold Monro, London. *Last issue* 1925. A128

The Owl, edited by Robert Graves and William Nicholson, London. *Last issue* 1923. A157

1920

Northern Numbers: being representative selections from certain living Scottish poets, compiled by C. M. Grieve, Edinburgh. First stirrings of the modern Scottish Renaissance before C. M. Grieve was "Hugh MacDiarmid". *Last issue* 1922. A149

1922

The Criterion, edited by T. S. Eliot, London. *Last issue* 1939. A45

The Scottish Chapbook, edited by C. M. Grieve, Montrose. Grieve publishes himself as MacDiarmid and the Scottish Renaissance is fully under way. *Last issue* 1923. A192

1923

The Bermondsey Book: a quarterly review of life and literature, London. Left-leaning quarterly publishing international modernists with editorial offices at Ethel Gutman's bookshop. *Last issue* 1930. A13

The Dublin Magazine: a quarterly review of literature, science and art, edited by Seamus O'Sullivan, Dublin. Stalwart begins its three-decades-year run. *Last issue* 1958. A53

Germinal, [edited by Sylvia Pankhurst], London. One of the political activists of the century turns her hand to publishing fiction and prose, with translations of Alexander Blok and early Anna Akmatova. *Last issue* [1924]. A78

The Klaxon, edited by Lawrence K. Emery [i.e. A. J. Leventhal], Dublin. Controversial magazine publishes its only issue: futurism, cubism and literary modernism with an Irish inflection. *Only one issue.* A103

1924

The Northern Review: a progressive monthly of life and letters, edited by Hugh MacDiarmid, Edinburgh. *Last issue 1924.* A150

To-morrow, [edited by H. [i.e. Francis] Stuart and Cecil Salkeld.], Dublin. Lennox Robinson's heretical short story loses him his job and brings this shortlived magazine to a close. *Last issue 1924.* A209

The Transatlantic Review, edited by Ford Madox Ford. Paris, London and New York. A year's worth of largely American modernism. *Last issue 1924.* A211

1927

Ray, edited by Sidney Hunt, London. Two issues of Russian and European sound and visual poetry, graphic design and experiment. *Last issue 1927.* A186

Transition, edited by Eugene Jolas, Paris. French, American and Irish modernism. *Last issue 1950.* A212

1928

Experiment, edited by William Empson, Jacob Bronowski, Hugh Sykes and Humphrey Jennings. Intellectual poetry and literary theory: grandfathers of the "Cambridge School"? *Last issue 1931.* A64

London Aphrodite, edited by Jack Lindsay and P. R. Stephensen, London. Fiercely anti-modernist magazine brings its publisher Fanfrolico Press down in six issues. *Last issue 1929.* A115

1930

The Modern Scot: the organ of the Scottish Renaissance, edited by James H. Whyte, Dundee. *Last issue 1936.* A126

1931

The Island, edited by Josef Bard, London. Voice of "The Islanders" opposed to commercialised art, including Henry Moore, Gertrude Hermes, C. R. W. Nevinson, Naomi Mitchison and Mahatma Gandhi. *Last issue 1931.* A99

The Twentieth Century, edited by Jon Randell Evans, London. The Promethean Society proposes to scrap royalty, legalise homosexuality, and bring in widespread birth control... and publish poems. *Last issue 1933.* A213

1932

The New English Weekly, edited by A. R. Orage, London. *Last issue 1949.* A137.

Scrutiny, edited by L. C. Knights, Donald Culver, F. R. Leavis and others. *Last issue 1953; commemorative volume 1963.* A195

1933

New Verse, edited by Geoffrey Grigson, London. The Auden Generation finds its advocate. *Last issue 1939.* A143

Seed, edited by Herbert Jones and Oswell Blakeston, London. Visual poetry, prose poems and other experiments. *Last issue 1933.* A196

1934

The European Quarterly, edited by Edwin Muir and Janko Lavrin, London. Kafka and European literature galore in the face of rising Fascism. *Last issue 1935.* A62

The Left Review, edited by Montagu Slater, Amabel Williams-Ellis, and T. H. Wintringham. Cultural essays, poems and socialist ideas emerging from Collett's Bookshop. *Last issue 1938.* A106

1935

International Surrealist Bulletin. (Bulletin internationale du surréalisme), Prague, then London. One of the first signs that Surrealism could have a home in England. *Last issue 1936?* A93

1936

Contemporary Poetry and Prose, edited by Roger Roughton, London. Journal particularly hospitable to Surrealism. *Last issue 1937.* A41

Ireland To-day, edited by Michael O'Donovan [i.e. Frank O'Connor], Dublin. *Last issue 1938.* A94

1937

Axis: a quarterly review of contemporary 'abstract' painting and sculpture, edited by Myfanwy Evans, London. *Last issue 1937.* A11

Twentieth Century Verse, edited by Julian Symons, London. *Last issue 1939.* A214

Wales, edited by Keidrych Rhys, Llangadog then Carmathen. The first stirrings of a modern literary revival in Wales? *Last issue 1959.* A227

1938

London Gallery Bulletin, edited by E. L. T. Mesens, London. *Last issue 1940.* A116

On the Boiler, edited by W. B. Yeats, Dublin. Yeats returns briefly to the world of little magazine. *Last issue 1938.* A153

Seven, edited by John Goodland and Nicholas Moore and others, Taunton. Poets of the New Apocalypse begin to mount their horses. *Last issue 1947.* A197

1939

Kingdom Come: the magazine of war-time Oxford, edited by John Waller and Kenneth Harris and others, Oxford. The New Apocalypse continued. *Last issue 1943.* A102

Poetry London. edited by Anthony Dickens and J. M. Tambimuttu and others, London. *Last issue 1951.* A173

The Welsh Review, edited by Gwyn Jones, Cardiff. *Last issue 1948.* A229

1940

The Bell: a survey of Irish life, edited by Sean O'Faolain, then Peader O'Donnell, Dublin. Eclectic choice in poets and serious comment and debate. *Last issue 1954.* B10

Horizon: a review of literature and art, edited by Cyril Connolly, London. *Last issue 1950.* B54

Indian Writing, edited by Iqbal Singh, Ahmed Ali, K. S. Shelvankar and A. Subramaniam. *Last issue 1942.* B56

The New Apocalypse: an anthology of criticism, poems and stories, [edited by J. F. Hendry], London. The New Apocalypse's first anthology gives them their name. *Last anthology [1945].* B77

Now, edited by George Woodcock, Maidenhead. A magazine begun by the conscientious objector. *Last issue 1947.* B91

X6, edited by Derek Stanford and John Bate, [Croydon]. Emerging from the Army Bomb Disposal Squad. *Last issue 1941.* B151

1942

Caseg Broadsheet, [edited by Brenda Chamberlain, Alun Lewis and John Petts], Llanllechid. *Last issue 1942.* B17

Citadel: literature, criticism, reportage, stories, poetry, edited by R. D. Smith, Cairo. *Last issue unknown.* B21

Personal Landscape, edited by Lawrence Durrell, Robin Fedden, and Bernard Spencer, Cairo. *Last issue 1945.* B102

Poetry Folios, edited by Alex Comfort and Peter Wells then

James Kirkup, Barnet, then London. *Last issue 1951.* B110

Salamander, edited by Keith Bullen, Cairo. *Last issue [1945?]* B123

1943

New Road: new directions in European art and letters, edited by Alex Comfort and John Bayliss, then Fred Marnau, then Wrey Gardiner, Billericay. *Last issue 1949.* B82

The Norseman: an independent literary and political review, edited by Jac. S. Worm-Müller, then H. L. Lehmkuhl, London. *Last issue 1946.* B89

Outposts, edited by Howard Sergeant, then Roland John, Blackpool. *Last issue unknown.* B99

Poetry Scotland, edited by Maurice Lindsay, Glasgow. *Last issue 1949.* B113

Review 43 [Review 45, Review 46], edited by Walter Berger and Pavel Tigrid, and then Walter Berger and E. Osers, London. *Last issue 1946.* B122

Transformation: prose, poetry, plays, edited by Stefan Schimanski and Henry Treece, London. *Last issue [1947].* B133

1944

The New Saxon Pamphlets, edited by John Atkins, Prettyman Lane, Kent. Backlash against the New Apocalypse. *Last issue (as Albion) [1947].* B84

Scottish Art and Letters, edited by R. Crombie Saunders, Glasgow. *Last issue 1950.* B125

1946

Free Unions – Unions Libres. edited by Simon Watson Taylor, London. The Surrealist Group in England resumes business after the war, with the help of E. L. T. Mesens, Alfred Jarry and Lucien Freud. *Only one issue.* B44

Jazz Forum: quarterly review of jazz and literature, edited by Arthur J. McCarthy, Fordingbridge, Hampshire. *Last issue 1947.* B61

The West Country Magazine, edited by Malcolm Elwin then J. C. Trewin, Denham, Buckinghamshire, then London. *Last issue 1952.* B144

1947

The Gate: international review of literature and art in English and German, edited by Margaret Greig, Rudolf Jung and Howard Sergeant. Post-war reconstruction in Germany via English and German literature. *Last issue 1949.* B47

The New Shetlander. Lerwick. *Continuing to publish.* B86

This Strange Adventure, edited by Fredoon Kabraji, London. *Only one issue.* B131

1948

Alba: a Scottish miscellany in Gaelic and English, edited by Malcolm MacLean and T. M. Murchison, Glasgow. *Only one issue.* B3

The Glass, edited by Antony Borrow and Madge Hales, Lowestoft. Henri Michaux, Thomas Blackburn, Anthony Thwaite, Harold Pinter and Yves Bonnefoy put Lowestoft on the literary map. *Last issue 1954.* B49

1949

The Cornish Review, edited by Denys Val Baker, Hayle. *Last issue 1952; New series, 1966-1970.* B23

Dock Leaves, edited by Raymond Garlick, Pembroke Dock. *Last issue 1957.* B33

Envoy: a review of literature and art, edited by John Ryan, with Valentin Iremonger as poetry editor, Dublin. International, modernist, open and eclectic: a high-point in the Irish literary magazine. *Last issue [1951].* B35

Forum: Stories and Poems, edited by Muriel Spark, London. Spark starts rival magazine following departure from *Poetry Review. Last issue 1950.* B42

Leeds University Poetry, edited by Robin Skelton then others, Leeds. The beginning of a strong literary presence at Leeds that would include James Kirkup, Thomas Blackburn, John Heath-Stubbs and Geoffrey Hill. *Last issue 1956.* B65

Nine, edited by Peter Russell and others, London. *Last issue 1956.* B88

1950

Icarus, edited by Cecil Jenkins, Rosalind Brett-Jones and Peter Devlin; and others, Dublin. *Continues to publish.* C46

The Window, edited by John Sankey, London. *Last issue [1956].* C122

1951

Nimbus, edited by Tristram Hull and others, London. *Last issue 1958.* C68

Ninepence, edited by Patrick Brangwyn, Charles Fox and Christopher Logue, Bournemouth. *Last issue [1952].* C69

Poetry Manchester, edited by Doreen Taylor, Brian Wright, Peter Robins and Harry Webster, Leigh. *Last issue [1953].* C88

1952

Gairm: an raitheachan Gaidhlig, edited by Ruaraidh MacThomais and Fionnlagh Domhnullach, Glaschu [Glasgow]. The key Scottish Gaelic journal. *Continues to publish.* C38

Kavanagh's Weekly: a journal of literature and politics, edited by Patrick Kavanagh, Dublin. Patrick Kavanagh speaks out. *Last issue 1952.* C50

Lines, edited by Alan Riddell; and then others, Edinburgh. *Last issue, as Lines Review, 1998.* C52

Merlin: a collection of contemporary writing, edited by Alexander Trocchi, Limerick, Me., then Paris. *Last issue 1955.* C57

New Poems, edited by Donald Hall, and others, Eynsham. *Last issue [1954].* C64

Perspectives, edited by James Laughlin, then Lionel Trilling, then Jacques Barzan, then Malcolm Cowley, then R. P. Blackmur etc., London. *Last issue 1956.* C78

The Poet, [edited by W. Price Turner], Glasgow. *Last issue 1956.* C83

Stand, edited by Jon Silkin, and others, Newcastle upon Tyne, and other locations. *Continues to publish.* C107

1953

Delta: a literary review from Cambridge, edited by Rodney Banister and Peter Redgrove, and others, Cambridge. *Last issue 1981.* C25

Encounter, edited by Irving Kristol and Stephen Spender, and others, London. The CIA gives British literature a helping hand. *Last issue 1990.* C30

1954

And, edited by Bob Cobbing, Mary Levien, John Rowan, and Adrian Clarke, London. *Continues to publish?* C4

Listen, edited by George Hartley, Hessle. *Last issue 1962.* C53

The London Magazine: a monthly review of literature, edited by John Lehmann, then Alan Ross, then Sebastian Barker, London. *Continues to publish.* C55

Ore, edited by Eric Ratcliffe, Teddington. *Last issue 1995.* C73

Poetry & Audience. Leeds. *Continues to publish.* C85

Saltire Review: of arts, letters and life, edited by Alexander Scott and others, Edinburgh. *Last issue 1961.* C102

Samovar: the magazine of the Joint Services School for Linguists, [edited by Michael Frayn, Eric Korn and others], Bodmin. *Last issue [1959].* C103

1955

The Aylesford Review, edited by Father Brocard Sewell, Aylesford. *Last issue 1968.* C10

1956

Envoi, edited by J. C. Meredith Scott and others, Cheltenham, then other locations. *Continues to publish.* C31

New Lines, edited by Robert Conquest, London. The Movement arrives. *Last issue 1963.* C63

Northern Broadsheet, edited by Dorothy Una Ratcliffe, Edinburgh. *Last issue 1960.* C71

Pawn, edited by John Blackwood and others, Cambridge. *Last issue 1972.* C76

Saint Botolph's Review, edited by David Ross, Cambridge, [No. 1], 1956. Ted Hughes was in the magazine and Sylvia Plath was at the launch party. *One issue only until commemorative issue in 2006.* C101

1957

Gambit: Edinburgh University review, edited by Peter T. Froestrup and others, Edinburgh. *Last issue, as New Gambit,* [1986]. C39

Threshold, edited by Mary O'Malley; poetry editor: John Hewitt; and others, Belfast. *Last issue 1987.* C111

1958

The Anglo-Welsh Review, edited by Raymond Garlick and others, Pembroke Dock. *Last issue 1988.* C5

1959

Agenda, edited by William Cookson and others, London. *Continues to publish.* C2

Ambit: a quarterly of poems, short stories, drawings and criticism, edited by Martin Bax, London. *Continues to publish.* C3

Critical Quarterly, edited by C. B.Cox and A. E. Dyson, and others, Bangor and Hull. *Continues to publish.* C22

Dejected Nurses,edited by Fred Leavings, Bristol. *One issue only.* C24

Jabberwock: Edinburgh University review. Burroughs, Ginsberg, Kerouac, Corso, Snyder and Creeley make an early British appearance in an unnumbered issue in 1959 of this magazine that began in 1945. *Last issue 1959?.* B60

Migrant, edited by Gael Turnbull, Ventura, Ca. and Worcester. *Last issue 1960.* C58

New Departures, edited by Michael Horovitz and David Sladen. *Continues to publish.* C61

Nonplus, edited by Patricia Murphy, Dublin. *Last issue 1960.* C70

Phoenix: a poetry magazine, edited by Harry Chambers and others, Liverpool. *Last issue 1975.* C80

Prospect, edited by Elaine Feinstein, then Tony Ward, then Jeremy Prynne, Cambridge. The first magazine of the "Cambridge School"? *Last issue [1964].* C94

The Transatlantic Review, edited by J. F. McCrindle. London and New York. *Last issue 1977.* C133

X: a quarterly review, edited by David Wright and Patrick Swift, London. *Last issue 1962.* C124

1960

Sidewalk: Scotland's quarterly review, edited by Alex Neish, Edinburgh. *Last issue [1960].* D439

1961

Gorgon, edited by Seamus Heaney [and others?], Belfast. Later Nobel Laureate, in the Hilary 1961 issue Heaney styles himself an "ex-poet". *Gorgon began in* [1959?] *Last issue* 1961. C42

Outburst, edited by Tom Raworth, London. *Last issue 1963.* D333

1962

Carcanet, edited by Farrukh Dhondy and Diane Troy, Oxford. The magazine that would inspire an imprint. *Last issue 1970.* D98

Poor. Old. Tired. Horse. Edited by J. McGuffie and P. Pond, then Ian Hamilton Finlay, Edinburgh. A quiet masterpiece of the little magazine genre. *Last issue 1967.* D385

Priapus, edited by John Cotton, Denham, then Berkhampsted. *Last issue 1972.* D389

The Review, edited by Ian Hamilton, London. *Last issue 1972.* D412

1963

Arena, edited by James Liddy, Liam O'Connor and Michael Hartnett. Coolgreany, Co. Wexford, Republic of Ireland. *Last issue 1965*. D41

My Own Mag, edited by Jeff Nuttall, Barnet. *Last issue 1966*. D293

Origins, Diversions, edited by M. J. Dyke and C. J. [i.e. Chris] Torrance, Carshalton. Poetry and jazz. *Last issue 1966*. D328

Poetmeat, edited by David Cunliffe, Tina Morris and Kirby Congdon. *Last issue 1967*. D359

Resuscitator, edited by John James, C. I. McNeill and Nick Wayte, Paulton, Somerset, then other locations. *Last issue 1969*. D411

Underdog: English poetry scene, edited by Brian Patten, Liverpool. *Last issue 1966*. D504

1964

It's: The Wimbledon School of Art Magazine, edited by Ariel Whatmore, and others, Wimbledon. *Last issue unknown*. D235

Night Train, edited by Johnny Byrne, Lee Harwood, Roger Jones and [Barry] Miles, London. *Only one issue*. D308

Sigma Portfolio, edited by Alexander Trocchi, London. *Last issue [1967]*. D440

Soho: bi-lingual review, revue bilingue, edited by Lee Harwood and Claude Royet-Journoud, London. *Only one issue*. D451

Tlaloc, edited by Cavan McCarthy, Leeds. *Last issue 1970*. D482

1965

Akros, edited by Duncan Glen, Bishopbriggs, near Glasgow then other locations. *Last issue 1983*. D12

Eleventh Finger, edited by Paul Evans and Paul Matthews, Brighton. *Last issue 1968*. D150

Exit, edited by John Hall, Ian Breakwell and Cliff Harris, Risley, Derby. *Last issue 1968*. D162

Expression, edited by Eric Ratcliffe, Brian Louis Pearce, Robert Druce and Les Surridge, Whitton. *Last issue [1973]*. D163

Long Hair: North Atlantic Turn-on, edited by Barry Miles and Ted Berrigan, London and New York. *Last issue [1966]*. D258

New Measure, edited by John Aczel and Peter Jay, Oxford,

then Northwood, Middlesex. *Last issue 1969*. D301

The Northern Review: a quarterly magazine of the arts, edited by Patrick Lynch and Michael Mitchell, Comber, Co. Down. The unofficial magazine of Hobsbaum's Belfast Group. *Last issue 1967*. D312

Once: a one-shot magazine, edited by Thomas [i.e.Tom] Clark. Brightlingsea, Essex, [1965?]. Then *Twice*, then *Thrice*, then *Thrice and a ¼*, then *Frice*, then *Vice*, then *Spice*,then *Slice*, Vol. 1 no. 1-no. 2, then *Ice*, then *Nice*, then *Dice*, then *Lice*. *Last issue [1966?]* D324

Poetry Wales: Cylchgrawn cenedlaethol o farddoniaeth newydd, edited by Meic Stephens and others, Merthyr Tydfil. *Continues to publish*. D380

Tzarad, edited by Lee Harwood, London. *Last issue 1969*. D500

The Wivenhoe Park Review, edited by Thomas [i..e. Tom] Clark, and Andrew Crozier. Colchester, then London. *Last issue 1969*. D525

1966

Arlington. Arlington Mill, Bibury, Gloucestershire. *Last issue 1968*. D44

The English Intelligencer, edited by Andrew Crozier (Series 1); Peter Riley (Series 2); and Andrew Crozier, John James, and J. H. Prynne (Series 3). *Last issue [1968]*. D153

Form, edited by Philip Steadman, Mike Weaver and Stephen Bann, Cambridge. *Last issue 1969*. D173

Modern Poetry in Translation, edited by Ted Hughes and Daniel Weissbort, London. *Continues to publish*. D285

Nothing Doing in London, edited by Anthony Barnett with Claude Royet-Journoud, London. *Last issue 1968*. D314

Platform, edited by Joan Lee, Halifax then Luddenen Foot, Yorkshire. The magazine of the Halifax and District Poetry Society, later the Pennine Poets group. *Last issue 1972*. D352

Second Aeon, edited by Peter Finch, Cardiff. *Last issue 1974*. D434

Tarasque, edited by Stuart Mills and Simon Cutts, Nottingham. *Last issue [1972]*. D473

1967

Bo Heem E Um, edited by Thomas A. Clark, [Sherborne]. *Last issue [1968]*. D78

Private Tutor. Nottingham. *Last issue 1970*. D392

Transformaction, edited by John Lyle, Harpford, nr. Sidmouth, Devon. *Last issue 1979*. D487

1968

Broadsheet, Hayden Murphy and Benedict Ryan, Dublin. *Last issue* [1984?] D89

Collection, edited by Peter Riley, Hove, then Odense, Denmark. *Last issue 1970.* D117

Grosseteste Review, edited by Tim Longville, Lincoln. *Last issue* [1983/84]. D197

The Honest Ulsterman, edited by James Simmons and then others, Castlerock then Belfast. *Continues to publish.* D212

Juillard, edited by Trevor Winkfield, Leeds, then New York. *Last issue 1972.* D238

Ronald Reagan: the magazine of poetry, edited by John Sladek. London. *Last issue 1970.* D416

Samphire, edited by Michael Butler and Kemble Williams, Ipswich. *Last issue 1981.* D421

Scottish International, edited by Robert Garioch and Edwin Morgan, Edinburgh. *Last issue 1974.* D428

1969

Aplomb Zero, edited by Charles Verey, Sherborne. *Last issue 1970.* D30

Aquarius, edited by Eddie S. Linden, London. *Continues to publish.* D34

Big Venus, edited by Nick Kimberley, London. *Last issue 1970.* D69

The Curiously Strong, edited by Fred Buck, then Ian Patterson, Cambridge. *Last issue 1975.* D127

The Journals of Pierre Menard, edited by Anthony Rudolf and Peter Hoy, Oxford. *Last issue 1969.* D237

Kontexts: an occasional review of concrete, visual, experimental poetry, edited by Michael Gibbs, Leamington Spa, then other locations 1976/77. *Last issue 1977.* D243

The Lace Curtain: a magazine of poetry and criticism, edited by Michael Smith and Trevor Joyce, Dublin. *Last issue 1978.* D246

New Edinburgh Review, edited by David Cubitt, then others, Edinburgh. *Last issue 1984.* D300

Oasis, edited by Ian Robinson, London. *Last issue 2004?* D318

Orbis, edited by Mike Shields, then Carole Baldock, [Youlgreave, Derbyshire]. *Last issue unknown.* D327

Stereo Headphones: an occasional magazine of the new poetries, edited by Nicholas Zurbrugg, Kersey, near Ipswich then Brisbane Australia. *Last issue 1982.* D460

1970

Ceolfrith. Sunderland. *Last issue unknown.* D102

Chapman, edited by George Hardie and Walter Perrie, then Joy Hendry, Hamilton, then Edinburgh. *Continues to publish.* D105

Global Tapestry and Vegan Action, edited by Dave Cunliffe and Tina Morris, Blackburn. As Global Tapestry Journal *continues to publish.* D192

Haiku Byways, edited by Gerry Loose, London. *Last issue* [1972?]. D199

ID, edited by Terri Hooley, Belfast. *Last issue* [1973]. D220

Planet: the Welsh internationalist, edited by Ned Thomas, then John Barnie, Tregaron, then Aberystwyth. *Continues to publish.* D351

Poetry Information, edited by Peter Hodgkiss and others, Newcastle-upon-Tyne, then London. So much poetry, there has to be an information service for it: this magazine tries to meet the need. *Last issue, as PALPI, 1997.* D366

Savacou: a journal of the Caribbean Artists Movement, edited by Edward Kamau Braithwaite, Kenneth Ramchand, Andrew Salkey, and others, Kingston, Jamaica and London. Key magazine of the Caribbean Artists Movement. *Last issue 1979.* D424

1971

A: a magazine of visual poetry, edited by Jeremy Adler, London. *Last issue 1977.* D1

Curtains, edited by Paul Buck, Hebden Bridge, then Maidstone. *Last issue 1978.* D129

Innti, edited by Michael Davitt, Gabriel Rosenstock and Louis De Paor. Corcaigh [Cork]. *Last issue unknown.* D228

Kroklok, edited by Dom Silvester Houédard, London. *Last issue* [1973?] D245

Ludd's Mill, edited by Steve Sneyd and Gary Wilson; then Andrew Darlington, Huddersfield. *Last issue* [1983?] D260

Okike, edited by Chinua Achebe. Enugu, Nigeria and Canterbury. *Continues to publish.* D321

Strange Faeces, edited by Opal and Ellen Nations, London, then Cambridge, Mass., then Vancouver. *Last issue unknown.* D462

Transgravity Advertiser. *Last issue, as Transgravity, in 1980.* D488

1972

Caret: a poetry magazine, edited by Robert Johnstone,

Trevor McMahon and William Peskett, Belfast and Cambridge. *Last issue 1975.* D99

The Literary Supplement, edited by Anthony Barnett, London. *Last issue 1975.* D252

Littack, edited by William Oxley, Esher. *Last issue 1976.* D253

Pair: cylchgrawn barddoniaeth, edited by Vaughan Hughes, Llandybie. *Last issue 1973.* D339

Schmuck, Cullompton, Devon. *Last issue 1976.* D425

Structure: a magazine of art and thought, edited by Michael Kane, Dublin. *Last issue 1978.* D466

1973

Aggie Weston's, edited by Stuart Mills, Belper, Derbyshire. *Last issue 1984.* D10

Alembic: a magazine of new poetry, prose and graphics, edited by Ken Edwards, Peter Barry and Robert Hampson, London, then Orpington, Kent. *Last issue 1979.* D15

The Blue Tunnel, edited by Ian Gardner, Bradford. *Last issue [1979?]* D76

Great Works, edited by Bill Symondson and Peter Philpott, Stoke-on-Trent and Bishop Stortford. *Last issue 1979 (but revived online).* D194

Iron, edited by Peter Mortimer, Cullercoats, North Shields. *Last issue 1997.* E230a

Lallans, J. K. Annand and others, Edinburgh. The key magazine for literature in Lallans / Scots / the Doric. *Continues to publish.* D248

Palantir, edited by Stuart Brown then Jim Burns, [Preston]. *Last issue [1983].* D340

Poetry Nation, edited by C.B. Cox and Michael Schmidt, Manchester. *As PN Review continues to publish.* D372

Prospice, edited by J. C. R. Green and others. Solihull, then Breakish, Isle of Skye. *Last issue 1988.* D397

1974

Spanner, edited by Allen Fisher. London, then Hereford. *Continues to publish.* D456

TR: a magazine of Arabic and English literature, London. *Last issue 1979.* D484

Wallpaper, New York and London. *Last issue 1976.* D518

1975

Bananas, edited by Emma Tennant, then Abigail Mozley,

London. *Last issue 1981.* D63

Cyphers, edited by Leland Bardwell, Eiléan Ni Chuilleanáin, Pearse Hutchinson and Macdara Woods, Dublin. *Continues to publish?* D132

Oasis, edited by Vincent Mills, Gerry McCarthy, David Neilson and others, Glasgow. Writers of the Glasgow contingent of the Scottish literary revival. *Last issue 1979.* D319

The Stony Thursday Book, edited by John Liddy and Jim Burke and others, Limerick, then Madrid. *Continues to publish?* D461

1976

Mugshots, edited by Mike Dobbie and Ulli McCarthy, [London?]. *Last issue [1977?].* E517

Ochre Magazine, edited by Charles Ingham and Ralph Hawkins. Ilford, then Little Clacton, Essex, No. 1 (May 1976)-6 [1980?]. E554

PN Review, edited by Michael Schmidt, Manchester, *Continues to publish.* E613

Poetry South East: an anthology of new poetry, edited by Howard Sergeant, Laurence Lerner, John Rice, Patricia Beer, Barry MacSweeney, Patric Dickinson, Roger Crowley, Anthony Thwaite, Jeremy Page, Tunbridge Wells, and then, Folkestone. *Continues to publish* E647

Purple Patch, edited by Geoff Stevens, West Bromwich. E670

Saturday Morning, edited by cris cheek and Simon Pettet, London. *Last issue 1978.* E717

Spectacular Diseases, edited by Paul Green. Peterborough. *Last issue 1999?* E766

Vanessa Poetry Magazine, edited by John Welch, London. *Last issue 1981?* E854

1977

Anthill, edited by Astrid Wilson, London. *Last issue 1977.* E41

The Crane Bag, edited by Mark Patrick Hederman and Richard Kearney, Dublin. *Last issue 1985.* E203

Madog: arts magazine, edited by Tony Curtis, Barry, Wales. *Last issue 1981.* E462

Rawz, edited by cris cheek, London. *Last issue 1979.* E679

Slow Dancer, edited by John Harvey, London, then Nottingham. *Last issue 1993.* E747

South East Arts Review, edited by Jose Phillips and Richard Moore, then John Rice, Tunbridge Wells. *Last issue 1982.* E757

1978

The Gay Journal: a new quarterly of culture and liberation produced by gay women and men, produced by Anne Davison, Ian David Baker, Roger Baker, and Sheila Hillier, London. *Last issue* [1979]. E312

Joe Soap's Canoe, edited by Martin Stannard, Clare, Felixstowe. *Last issue* [1993]. E408

Labrys, edited by Grahaeme Barrasford Young, Hayes, and other locations. *Last issue* 1985. E426

Lobby Press Newsletter, edited by Richard Tabor, Colchester, and other locations. *Last issue* 1982. E447

Other Poetry, edited by Anne Stevenson and others, Oxford, and other locations. *Continues to publish.* E563

Peeping Tom: the lonely man's magazine, edited by Cory Harding, Croydon. *Last issue* 1981. E589

Reality Studios, edited by Ken Edwards, Orpington and London. *Last issue* 1988. E684

Uncle Nasty's..., [edited by Rob Earl], Maidstone. *Last issue* [1980?] E844

1979

Angel Exhaust, [edited by Steven Pereira] and others, London and other locations. With Andrew Duncan's involvement, provocative assessments of modern and contemporary poetry began to appear. *Continues to publish.* E35

Cencrastus: Scottish & International Literature Arts & Affairs, edited by Sheila Hearn and others, Edinburgh. *Last issue* 2005? E160

The Cork Review, edited by Paul Durcan and others, Cork. *Last issue* 1999. E198

Doors Into and Out of Dorset, Weymouth. *Last issue* 1997. E230

Granta, edited by Bill Buford; then Ian Jack, Cambridge, then London and New York. *Continues to publish.* E327

The Green Book, edited by Rupert Blunt and others, Bath and Bristol. *Last issue* 1991. E330

Kudos: poetry and art, edited by Graham Sykes, Leeds. *Last issue* 1982. E423

Kunapipi: journal of post-colonial writing, edited by Anna Rutherford; and then others, Aarhus, Denmark, then Hebden Bridge, W. Yorkshire, then Wollongong, Australia. *Continues to publish.* E424

Loot, edited by Paul Green, Peterborough. *Last issue* 1987. E452

The Old Police Station, edited by Anthony Cooney,

Liverpool. *Last issue* 1998. E556

Poetry London / Apple Magazine, edited by Tambimuttu, London. *Last issue* 1982. E631

Rock Drill, edited by Penelope Bailey and Robert Sheppard, Norwich, and other locations. *Last issue* [1985]. E704

1981

The Beau, edited by Maurice Scully, Dublin. *Last issue* 1983/84. E89

Borderlines, edited by Diana Moss and others, Shrewsbury, then Welshpool, Powys. *Continues to publish.* E115

Codex Bandito, edited by Dick Brandt and Rob Earl, Maidstone, then Monmouth. *Last issue* [1983]. E183

LAMB: standing for literature, art, music, & baa, edited by Anthony Barnett, London. *Last issue* 1985. E427

[New Arcadian Broadsheet], edited by Ian Gardner, Patrick Eyres, and Grahame Jones, Bradford. *Continues to publish.* E524

New Arcadians' Journal, edited by Patrick Eyres, Bradford. *Continues to publish.* E525

Poetry Ireland Review, edited by John Jordan, then others, Mornington, Co. Meath, then other locations. *Continues to publish.* E629

The Present Tense: a review of modern poetry, edited by Michael Abbott, Bristol. *Last issue* 1983. E658

Shearsman, edited by Tony Frazer, Kuala Lumpur, then other locations. *Continues to publish.* E735

Temenos: a review devoted to the arts of the imagination, edited by Kathleen Raine, Philip Sherrard, Keith Critchlow and Brian Keeble, Dulverton. *Last issue* 1992. E821

Writing Women, edited by Eileen Aird and others, Newcastle-upon-Tyne. *Last issue* 1998. E906

1982

Equofinality, edited by Rod Mengham and John Wilkinson, Worcester and Birmingham. *Last issue* 1991. E256

The Glasgow Magazine, [edited by Hamish Whyte, Kevin McCarra, David Neilson, Alasdair Robertson and Tom Berry], Glasgow. *Last issue* 1985/86. E317

Poetry Durham, edited by Michael O'Neill, Gareth Reeves and David Hartnett, Durham. *Last issue* 1994. E622

The Poet's Voice, edited by Fred Beake, and then with Wolfgang Görtschacher and James Hogg. Bath, then Salzburg, Austria. *Last issue* 1999/2000. E651

The Salmon, edited by M.G. Allen, Mícheál Ó Riada, Jessie

Lendennie, Luke Geoghegan, Mary Dempsey, Séamas McAndrew, and Máire Holmes, Annaghdown, Galway. *Last issue 1990.* E711

Stride, edited by Rupert Loydell. London, then Crewe, then Exeter. *Last printed issue 1995; continued online.* E796

Tracks, edited by John F. Deane and Jack Harte, Clondalkin, Co. Dublin. *Last issue 1996.* E835

Zenos: poetry, British and international, edited by Shirley Barker, Danielle Hope, Agis Mellis and Jyoti Soar, Nottingham. *Last issue 1988.* E916

1983

Cabaret 246, edited by John Harrison and others, Cardiff. *Last issue 1987.* E144

The Frogmore Papers, edited by Jeremy Page, Folkestone. *Continues to publish.* E302

The Gairfish, edited by W. N. Herbert, Oxford. *Last issue 1984.* E306

The Many Review: a new magazine of criticism and commentary, edited by John Welch, London. *Last issue 1990.* E475

Ninth Decade, edited by Tony Frazer, Ian Robinson, and Robert Vas Dias, London. *Last issue 1989.* E539

Poetry Matters: journal of Harry Chambers, edited by Harry Chambers, Liskeard then Calstock. *Last issue 1992.* E634

Sow's Ear, edited by R.J. Ellis, Stafford. *Last issue 1992.* E761

Staple, edited by Donald Measham and others, Matlock then Sheffield. *Continues to publish.* E778

1984

Bête Noire, edited by John Osborne, Hull. *Last issue [1994].* E93

Liver & Lights, edited by John Bently, London. *Continues to publish.* E445a

The Rialto, edited by Michael Mackmin, Jenny Roberts and John Wakeman, Norwich. *Continues to publish.* E696

Strawberry Fare: St. Mary's College literary magazine, edited by John Iddon, Twickenham. *Last issue 1989.* E795

Tears in the Fence, edited by David Caddy, Stourpaine. *Continues to publish.* E817

Verse, edited by Robert Crawford, Henry Hart and David Kinloch, Oxford, and other locations. *Continues to publish.* E857

Wasafiri, edited by Susheila Nasta, London. *Continues to publish.* E867

1985

Acumen, edited by Patricia Oxley, Brixham. *Continues to publish.* E10

Atlas, edited by Jake Tilson, London. *Last issue [1989?]* E65

The Echo Room, edited by Brendan Cleary, Newcastle upon Tyne. *Last issue 1994.* E241

Jennings Magazine, edited by Philip Sidney Jennings, Paul Magrath and Bob Kirkpatrick, London. *Last issue 1988.* E407

Staple Diet, edited by Richard Caddel, Durham. *Last issue 1986; special issue 1992.* E779

1986

Exe-calibre, edited by Ken Taylor, Exmouth. *Last issue 1988.* E259

First Offence, edited by Tim Fletcher, Canterbury. *Last issue unknown.* E277

Folded Sheets: of what new writing is posted here, edited by Michael Haslam, Hebden Bridge. *Last issue 1990.* E287

Infolio, edited by Tom Raworth, Cambridge. *Last issue 1987.* E377

Inter Arts, edited by Pramesh Mehta and Moussa Jogee, Edinburgh. *Last issue 1991.* E387

Krino, edited by Gerald Dawe, Corrandulla, Co. Galway, and Dún Laoghaire, Co. Dublin. *Last issue 1995.* E422

Margin: a quarterly magazine of literature, arts and ideas, edited by Robin Magowan, Walter Perrie and Richard Burns, London. *Last issue 1990.* E477

The North, edited by Peter Sansom and Janet Fisher, Huddersfield. *Continues to publish.* E542

Numbers, edited by John Alexander, Alison Rimmer, Peter Robinson and Clive Wilmer, Cambridge. *Last issue 1989/90.* E549

Slightly Soiled: literary review, edited by Julian Nangle, Timothy Cumming and David Crystal, London. *Last issue [1987?]* E745

The Wide Skirt, edited by Geoff Hattersley, Sheffield, then other locations. *Last issue 1997.* E876

1987

Foolscap, edited by Judi Benson, London. *Last issue 1995.* E291

Harry's Hand, edited by Michael Blackburn, London, then Lincoln. *Last issue 1990.* E346

Pages, edited by Robert Sheppard, Southwick, Sussex, and other locations. *Last hardcopy issue 1998.Continues online.* E574

Tak Tak Tak. Nottingham. *Last issue 1993.* E811

1988

Brando's Hat: poetry magazine, edited by Steven Waling, Seán Body, Emma-Jane Arkady and Angela Topping, Manchester, then Salford. *Last issue 2002.* E124

Cloud, edited by Michael Thorp, Newcastle upon Tyne. *Last issue 1988.* E180

Delyow Derow, edited by Richard Jenkin, Leedstown. A Cornish language magazine. *Last issue 1996.* E221

The New Welsh Review: Wales' Literary magazine in English, edited by Belinda Humfrey, Peter J. Foss, Michael Parnell and Robin Reeves, Cardiff. *Continues to publish.* E531

Poetry London Newsletter, edited by Leon Cych, Pascale Petit, and others, London. *As Poetry London continues to publish.* E632

West Coast Magazine, edited by Kenny MacKenzie and others, Glasgow. *Last issue 1998.* E870

1989

Archeus, edited by D. S. Marriott, London. *Last issue 1989.* E52

Force 10 in Mayo: a journal of the northwest, edited by Dermot Healy, Co. Mayo, Republic of Ireland. *Last issue 1999.* E293

Memes, edited by Norman Jope. Birmingham, then Plymouth. *Last issue [1994?]* E488

Ostinato, edited by Stephen C. Middleton, London. *Last issue 1993.* E561

Sunk Island Review, edited by Michael Blackburn, Lincoln. *Last issue 1995.* E799

1990

Blithe Spirit: journal of the British Haiku Society, edited by Richard Goring and others, Flitwick, and other locations. *Continues to publish.* E109

Fragmente: a magazine of contemporary poetics, edited by Andrew Lawson and Anthony Mellors, Oxford. *Continues to publish.* E298

The Haiku Quarterly, edited by Kevin Bailey, Swindon. *Continues to publish.* E338

A Morning Star Folio, edited by Alec Finlay, Dunblane, then Edinburgh. *Last issue 1995.* E510

Northlight: poetry review, edited by Anne Thomson, Glasgow. *Last issue 1992.* E545

Odyssey: a poetry and prose quarterly, edited by Derrick Woolf and others, Pen Selwood, then Nether Stowey. *Last issue 1996.* E555

Passport, edited by Mike Gerrard and Thomas McCarthy, Huntingdon. *Last issue 1994.* E584

The Printer's Devil: a magazine of new writing, edited by Sean O'Brien and others, Tunbridge Wells. *Last issue 2001?.* E661

RWC, edited by Lawrence Upton, Sutton. *Last issue unknown.* E710

Salt: an international journal of poetry and politics, edited by John Kinsella, Applecross (Australia) and Cambridge. *Continues to publish.* E713

Tenth Muse, edited by Andrew Jordan, Southampton. *Continues to publish.* E825

1991

Eonta, edited by Steven Holt, Harry Gilonis, Richard Leigh and Richard Barrett, London. *Last issue 1994.* E254

Northwords, edited by Angus Dunn, Dingwall. *Continues to publish.* E546

Parataxis: modernism and modern writing, edited by Simon Jarvis and Drew Milne. Cambridge and Brighton. *Continues to publish.* E581

Smiths Knoll, edited by Roy Blackman and Michael Laskey,. Woodbridge. *Continues to publish.* E748

Zed$_2$O, edited by Duncan Glen. Edinburgh, then Kirkcaldy. *Continues to publish* E915

1992

Grille, edited by Simon Smith, London. *Last issue [1993].* E335

1993

Element, edited by Mari-Aymone Djeribi, Dublin, then Cloone. *Continues to publish.* E250

Ramraid Extraordinaire, edited by Kerry Sowerby, Leeds. *Last issue 1995.* E677

Terrible Work, edited by Tim Allen, Plymouth. *Last hardcopy issue 2000. Continues online.* E827

Chapter F: A Timeline

1994

The Cúirt Journal, edited by Trish Fitzpatrick then Charlie McBride, Galway, Republic of Ireland. *Last issue 1995.* E205

Fire, edited by Jeremy Hilton, Malvern, then Tackley. *Continues to publish.* E275

Mad Cow, [edited by Jont Whittington?], London. *Last issue [1996?].* E458

Magma, edited by Laurie Smith, David Boll, Helen Nicholson and others, London. *Continues to publish.* E467

Object Permanence, edited by Peter Manson and Robin Purves, Glasgow. *Last issue 1997.* E552

Thumbscrew: an independent journal of poetry, articles and reviews, edited by Tim Kendall, Oxford, then Bristol. *Last issue 2002.* E831

1995

The Affectionate Punch: Manchester's new literary arts magazine, edited by Andrew Tutty, Manchester. *Last issue 2000.* E13

The Dark Horse, edited by Gerry Cambridge, Bothwell. *Continues to publish.* E214

Journal of Contemporary Anglo-Scandinavian poetry, edited by Sam Smith, Bradford-on-Tone. *Last issue [1999].* E412

Language Alive, edited by cris cheek, Lowestoft. *Last issue [1996?]* E429

The Long Poem Group Newsletter, edited by Sebastian Barker and William Oxley, Brixham. *Continues to publish.* E450

Markings: new writing and art from Dumfries and Galloway, general editor, John Hudson, Kirkudbright. *Continues to publish.* E478

PQR: Poetry Quarterly Review, edited by Derrick Woolf and Tilla Brading, Nether Stowey. *Continues to publish.* E656

Red Herring: new poetry, Morpeth. *Last issue 2002.* E686

The Review: an international literary magazine, edited by Raúl Peschiera, Vancouver and London. *Last issue unknown.* E694

Rising, edited by Tim Wells. London. *Continues to publish.* E700

Southfields, edited by Raymond Friel and Richard Price, London, and other locations. *Last issue 2000.* E758

1996

The Interpreter's House: poems and short stories, edited by Merryn Williams, Wootton. *Continues to publish..* E392

Metre: a magazine of international poetry, edited by Hugh Maxton, Justin Quinn and David Wheatley, Dublin, Prague, and Hull. *Continues to publish.* E489

Midnight Ink, edited by Anjan Saha and Gerard Thomas, London. *Last issue 1998.* E492

1997

Gare du Nord, edited by Alice Notley and Douglas Oliver, Paris. *Last issue 1999.* E310

Manticore: surrealist communication, Leeds. *Continues to publish.* E473

Obsessed With Pipework, edited by Charles Johnson, Redditch. *Continues to publish.* E553

Poetry Scotland, edited by Sally Evans, Edinburgh then Callander. *Continues to publish.* E646

The Reater: poems and prose, edited by Shane Rhodes, Hull. *Continues to publish.* E685

1998

Banipal: magazine of modern Arab literature, edited by Margaret Obank, London. *Continues to publish.* E82

The Gig, edited by Nate Dorward, Willowdale, Ontario. *Continues to publish.* E316

The Red Wheelbarrow, edited by Hugh Martin, Chris Jones, Lilias Fraser, Kirsti Wishart, Louisa Gairn, St. Andrews. *Continues to publish.* E688

1999

Areté: the arts tri-quarterly: fiction poetry reportage reviews, edited by Craig Raine, Anne Pasternak Slater and Jeremy Noel-Tod, Oxford. *Continues to publish.* E54

Mslexia: the magazine for women who write, [edited by Debbie Taylor] Newcastle-upon-Tyne. *Continues to publish.* E516

Nerve, edited by Ruth Black, Linda Jackson, Dave Manderson and Brian Whittingham, Glasgow. *Last issue unknown.* E522

2000

The Dublin Review, edited by Brendan Barrington, Dublin. *Continues to publish.* E239

Poetry Express: a quarterly newsletter from Survivors' Poetry, edited by Lisa Boardman and James Ferguson, London. *A continuation of Survivors Poetry Newsletter. Continues to publish.* E625

Geographical Index

This list indexes place of publication. When a particular locality is the focus of a magazine this is indexed in the Subject Index.

Aarhus, Denmark E424
Aberdeen D326, E249, E491, E721, E724
Abergavenny E186
Abergele C29
Aberystwyth D135, D351, E164, E236, E389, E672
Abinger Common A1
Ackworth D330
Aldershot E162
Aldington C82
Alford E350
Alperton E740
Alsager E604, E617, E803, E804
Altrincham D530
Amersham D296
Ampthill D432
Amsterdam D243
Annaghdown E711
Applecross, Australia E713
Arbroath B4
Ardgay D385
Ashby de la Zouch E621
Ashford, Middlesex E469
Ashton Keynes E482
Ashton-under-Lyne E919
Ashton-upon-Lyme E361
Athens B50, D409
Athens, Georgia E858
Athlone D355
Austin, Texas E600
Aylesbury E809
Aylesford C10
Aylestone D64

Baile Atha Cliath B28, B29
Bakewell E401
Balerno A169
Ballachulish C31
Banbridge E481

Banburgh E807
Banbury D403, E375, E575
Bangor C22, D262, D407, D442
Barbourne E814
Barnet B110, D293
Barnsley D420, E381
Barry E462
Bath D65, D505, E330, E333, E590, E651
Beaconsfield D25
Beaworthy E264
Beckenham D494, E48
Bedford A110, E405, E884
Belfast A69, A151, A187, A216, A217, A218, B119, B134,
      B136, C42, C95, C96, C111, D81, D84, D99, D126,
      D148, D176, D212, D220, D230, D435, D455, D527,
      E159, E270, E543, E695, E815
Belper D10
Benburb D35, D160
Benfleet E869
Bentilee E92
Benton E563
Berkeley A104
Berkhamsted D338, D389
Berlin E807
Bettws E299
Bexleyheath D236
Bibury D44
Billericay B68, B82
Billingham E163
Birdlip D532
Birkenhead E211
Birmingham A183, A223, A228, B117, B118, B148, C32,
      C84, D19, D45, D47, D70, D71, D92, D156, D185,
      D241, D292, D373, D454, D464, D524, E104, E135,
      E142, E256, E353, E488, E551, E560, E598, E678, E714,
      E807, E907
Birstall E774
Birtley E434
Bishop Auckland A168
Bishop Stortford D194
Bishopbriggs D12
Blackburn D73, D192, D359

Geographical Index

Geographical Index

Geographical Index

Subject Index

Subject Index

D213, D478
Drugs C3, D271
Dub poetry D424
Durham D75
Dutch literature C84, D123, E838

East Anglia E233, E370, E696
East European literature C28, C103, C107, D40, D285,
E788, E835
Easter Rising A96, D233
Egyptian literature B123, D484, D485
Elizabethan poetry D123
Emotionism A56
England, East E233
England, Essex D363
England, Kent E166, E183, E192, E313, E337, E351, E415,
E468, E494, E844
England, Midlands B117, B148, D282, D354, E104, E184,
E224, E273, E343, E353, E551, E598, E678
England, North-East D374, E260, E568, E686, E777
England, Northern B90, C71, D165, E818
England, Nottinghamshire E511
England, South E230, E283, E756
England, South-East E647, E661, E726, E757
England, Southwest A20, A48, A52, B14, B37, B144, E132,
E230, E231, E330, E421, E564, E651, E759, E871
England, Yorkshire A87, A123, A234, C71, E19, E208,
E535, E760
Essex See England, Essex
Estonian literature D40, E374, E694
European literature A62, A64, A177, A186, A199, A211, B1,
B9, B19, B69, B80, B82, B110, B122, C28, C68, C99,
D40, D41, D63, D123, D150, D245, D252, D285, D305,
D397, D412, D434, D439, E66, E426, E485, E799, E858
Exile C77, D40
Expressionism E66

Fantasy D260, E204, E217, E280
Fascism A127
Feminism A55, A133, D526
Fife E268, E269
Film A34, E185, E615, E670, E912
Finnish literature D359
Fire Brigade B128
First World War A89, A133, A140, A230, D237
Flemish literature E838
Fluxus D425, D456
Folk music D104, D172
French literature A41, A102, A116, B5, B9, B32, B43, B44,
B49, B51, B54, B120, B123, C9, C13, C15a, C70, C122,
D63, D117, D123, D129, D153, D168, D237, D238,
D242, D256, D265, D313, D314, D322, D342, D397,
D397, D439, D451, D460, E110, E250, E374, E388,
E393, E485, E539, E651, E658, E694, E766

Front Line Generation B62, B79
Futurism A15, A50, A103, A164, D385, E58, E581

Gaelic language (Irish) See Irish language
Gaelic language (Scottish) B3, C38, D326
Gay literature E312, E672
General Strike A185
Georgian poetry A132, A140, A149, B25
German literature A150, A235, B47, B74, B110, D63, D237,
D322, D344, D398, E694, E807
Greece B50
Greek literature B21, D123, E374, E423, E426, E822, E847,
E916

Haiku D94, D197, E83, E109, E338, E657, E750, E832
Hertfordshire D436
Hospitals A89, B118, E141, E320, E579, E776
Humberside E382
Hungarian literature D385, E694

Imagism A42, A55, A90, A128, A133, E41
Indian literature B56, B131, E220, E424, E867
Informationist poets E307, E390, E758, E858
Innti poets D228, D288
Irish language A12, A19, A95, B28, B29, B59, D132, D228,
E159
Irish literature (see also Northern Irish literature) A12, A19,
A53, A91, A94, A95, A96, A97, A98, A103, A105, A134,
A187, A209, B10, B28, B29, B35, B57, B59, B63, B111,
C50, C70, D34, D41, D56, D63, D89, D132, D141, D144,
D145, D158, D228, D240, D284, D288, D298, D327,
D355, D455, D461, D466, D529, D534, E12, E35, E89,
E90, E98, E137, E197, E198, E203, E205, E238, E250,
E293, E308, E316, E319, E324, E328, E406, E422, E481,
E502, E588, E596, E626, E627, E628, E629, E711, E715,
E783, E785, E835, E906
Islam E20
The Islanders A99
Israel E485
Italian literature B9, C18, D397, E694

Jamaican literature D424
Japanese literature D94, D199, D398, E694
Jazz B61, D213, D218, E104, E561

Kent See England, Kent
Kinetic art D173

Lallans See Scots language
Language poetry D15, E410, E430, E517, E713, E833, E858
Latin American literature D9, D47, D344, E694, E766
Lebanon E485
The Left See Marxism, Socialism
Leicester C20

Liberalism A133

Lincolnshire D50, D395, E904

Lithuanian literature D40, E651

Little magazines (accounts of) B4, B51, B94, B116, C59, C125, D3, D26, D55, D173, D247, D250, D340, D366, D422, E345, E733, E764, E793

Liverpool A114, D531, E612, E893

Liverpool poets D97, D504

Long poems D19, E450, E504

Love poetry E363, E417

Majorca A71

Maltese literature D64

Marxism A8, A106, A222, D85, D515

Mass Observation A16

Medway Poets E166, E183, E757

Mental health E496, E541, E623, E754, E801

Metre C8

Mexican literature D139, D397, E423, E694

Middle Eastern literature D9

Midlands See England, Midlands

Minimalism D10, D76, D94, D385, D392, D460, D473, D488, E83, E524

Modernism A55, A59, A90, A103, A126, A128, A130, A133, A142, A177, A186, A196, A210, A211, A213, B35, B87, C2, C124, D194, D397, D466, E12, E35, E581, E613, E735

Morocco E485

The Movement B108, C25, C53, C63, C68, C94, D468

Mozambique literature D47

Music A66, B24, B61, D40, D43, D46, D47, D104, D126, D172, D213, E162, E303, E445a, E561, E796

Mysticism A223, C73, D184

Neo-paganism C73, D107, E72, E488

New Apocalypse poets A102, A151, A197, B26, B77, B84, B145

New Formalists E214

New Generation poets A177, E458

New Romanticism B68

New Year B107

New Zealand B36, E651

Nigerian literature D321

Nonism E828

North-East England See England, North-East

Northern England See England, Northern

Northern Irish literature (see also Irish literature) A151, A187, A216, A217, A218, A219, B63, B119, B135, B136, C80, C111, D34, D81, D84, D97, D99, D126, D148, D220, D230, D312, D455, D527, E116, E203, E543, E695, E815, E905

Norwegian literature B89, B122, C107

Nottinghamshire See England, Nottinghamshire

Objectivism D385

Open Field poetry D15

Orkney D427

Oulipo D518

Pacific literature E867

Pakistani literature E424

Palestine E485

Pantomime B64

Pennine Poets group D345, D352

Performance poetry E700, E705

Personal Landscape poets B102

Peruvian literature E694

Philosophy A125, B105, B115, B141, C9, C28, D300

Phonic poetry See Sound poetry

Poet Pilgrim Society poets B137

Polish literature B122, C103, C109

Political poetry E276

Polygon Poets D110, D365

Portuguese literature B44, D314, D397, E245, E250, E584

Post-colonial literature E387, E424, E757, E868

Prose poems A196, B42, B49, D15, D318, D412, E547

Quakers See Society of Friends

Radio B84

Religion B104, E157

Romanticism B6, B42, B122, E66

Royal Air Force B2

Rumanian literature E374

Russian art A186, E581

Russian literature A78, B122, C28, C32, C103, D40, D385, D469, E390, E757, E916

St Ives artists B23

Sarajevo E485

Satire A44, A51, A86, A104, A190, C40, C59, D149, E430, E589, E673

Scandinavian literature B89, E412, E835

Science fiction D260, E25, E32, E217, E280, E341

Scots language A192, B3, B20, D248, D326, D426, D427, D463, E307

Scottish literature A5, A70, A77, A106, A126, A134, A149, A150, A155, A191, A192, A193, A194, A224, B3, B5, B20, B27, B85, B113, C38, C58, C102, D89, D104, D105, D182, D190, D229, D319, D326, D327, D385, D426, D427, D428, D429, D430, D439, D463, D506, E108, E131, E160, E209, E210, E214, E247, E257, E266, E268, E307, E316, E317, E325, E339, E387, E454, E478, E510, E522, E533, E545, E546, E552, E646, E662, E688, E719, E721, E724, E725, E733, E758, E768, E858, E870, E885, E915

Scottish Renaissance A5, A77, A126, A155, A192, A224, B60, B86, B113

Subject Index

Name Index

This index contains the names of authors, artists, editors, publishers and associated organisations, including poetry workshops and publishers associated with little magazines.

A-1 Waste Paper Company E207
Abbas, Remi E44
Abbott, Michael E658
Abelard, Peter A118
Abercrombie, Lascelles A114, A123, A140, A177, A234
Aberdeen University D326, E491, E721
Abse, Dannie B79, B108, B119, B139, C67, C68, C105a, C124, D171, D341, D362, D375, E392, E462, E795
Abse, Susanna E727
Academy of Poetry A75
Accola, L. E284
Achebe, Chinua D321, E867
Acker, Kathy E244, E247, E267, E460, E547, E717
Ackerman, John D446
Ackroyd, Graham E538
Ackroyd, Peter D195, D127, D437, E863
Acumen [Press] E10
Aczel, John D301
Adair, Gilbert D456, E277, E298, E316, E346, E574
Adams, Anna E330
Adams, Derek D452
Adams, John J. A139
Adams, Richard C112
Adams, Sam B33, B53, C5, D380
Adamson, Donald E478
Adamson, Peter C105a
Adcock, Fleur D181, D348, D408, E628, E638, E649, E722, E831
Adeane, Louis B40, B61, B108, B110
Adkins, Geoffrey D250, E793
Adlard, John C26, D347
Adler, Jeremy D1, D15, D245, E476, E679
"Adrian" D335
Advent Books E12
A.E. See E., A.
Agar, Eileen A99
Agard, John E828

Agenda Editions C2
Aggie Weston's Editions D10
Agius, Christine D451
Ahern, Maureen C55, E423
Ahern, Tom D252
Aiken, Conrad A64, B81, C68
Ainley, Ben D515
Ainsworth, Mavis E734
Aird, Eileen E906
Aistrop, Jack B15
Aitchison, James D372, D430, D439, E139, E533
Akeroyd, John D70
Akmatova, Anna A78, D301, D469
Akros [Press] D12, E915
Albert-Birot, Pierre D245
Alberti, Jo E906
Alberti, Rafael D340
Albery, Peter B52
Albiach, Anne-Marie D252, D314
Alden, John C82
Aldington, Richard A9, A42, A55, A66, A90, A128, A139, A177
Aldiss, Brian C64, E302
Aldous, Monica D452
Aldridge, David E860
Alexander, A. E157
Alexander, John E549
Alexander, Marc E369
Alexander, Margaret E790
Alexander, Michael E339
Alexander, William D197
al-Haidari, Buland D484
Alhau, Max E694
Ali, Ahmed B56
Ali, Jamal D85
Allan, Edwin B32
Allen, Alice E763
Allen, M. G. E711
Allen, Mabs D113
Allen, Tim E488, E735, E827
Allenby, David E125
Alliance of Literary Societies E164, E559

Name Index

Allison, Clive D18
Allison, Nancy E464
Allmand, Michael B146
Allnutt, Gillian D63, E828, E906
Allott, Kenneth A41, A143, A181
Allwood, Brian B32, B84, B110
al-Maghut, Muhammad D484
Almond, Jocelyn E152
Aloes Books D456
al-Qasim, Smih D484
al-Shamaqmaq, Abu D484
Alston, Robin D347
al-Udhari, Abdullah D484
Alvarez, A. C64, C112, D178, D375, D478
Alvi, Moniza E632
al-Ward, Urw Ibn D484
Ambert, Alba E471
American Country Club of France A18
Ames, Bernice D423
Amichai, Yehuda E479
Amis, Kingsley A160, C53, C63, C81, D372, E673
Amis, Martin E327, E407
Ammons, A. R. E374
Ampersand Folk Club D64, D115a
Amphlett, Paul E590
Anand, Mulk Raj B5
"Ananda" E853
Anderson, Alex E235
Anderson, Andrew C64
Anderson, Francis E435
Anderson, Gwyneth C82
Anderson, Kay D454
Anderson, Linda D326, E671, E906
Anderson, Margaret A112
Anderson, Martin E539, E735
Anderson, Raymond D242
Andrews, Bruce E277, E316
Andrews, Francis A226
Andrews, Geoffrey D229
Andrews, Jean C122
Andrews, Lyman D168
Andrews, Stan A. A81
Aneurin, Ailsa B116
Anglo-Egyptian Institution B21
Anglo-Norman Literary Circle A6
Anglo/Welsh Poetry Society E115
Angus, David D463
Angus, Marion A32, A149, B20, B78
Anike, Ndubuisi E896
Anim-Addo, Joan E471
Ankle Press E38
"Ann" E782
Annand, J. K. C52, D248
Annwn, David E24, E236, E277

Antiuniversity of London D166
Antonucci, Emil D358
Ant's Forefoot [Press] D150
Anvil Press D301
ap Gwynn, Aneirin A227
Apling, Jackie E144
Apollinaire, Guillaume A226, B5, B18, B19, B54, B120,
    D117, D153, D235, D238, D242, D313
Apple & Snakes E514
Aquila [Press] D397
Aquila (Ireland) [Press] E835
Aragão, António D44
Aragon, Louis B5, B6, B13, B43, D47, D238
Aramby Publishing E880
Arasanyagan, Jean E387
Arb, Jan D150
Arc Publications D36
Archard, Cary D380
Archer, William A60
Arengo, Sue E180
Argo, Arthur D104
Aridjis, Homero D314
Arji D484
Arkady, Emma-Jane E124
Arkwright (band) B43
Armand, Émile D497
Armantrout, Rae E316, E833
Armitage, Simon E542, E747, E858, E876
Armstrong, K. D248
Armstrong, Keith D47, D85, D226, D331, D374, E345
Armstrong, Neville B140
Armstrong, Peter D485
Armstrong, Roger D126
Armstrong, T. I. F. See Gawsworth, John
Army Bomb Disposal Squad B151
Arnell, Charles John A48, A170
Arnold, Agatha E896
Arnold, Audrey M. B69
Arnold, Bruce D145
Arnold, John E756
Arnold, Jon D43
Arnold, Marian C9
Arnold, Matthew C24
Arp, Hans A186
Arron, Jerry E87
Arrowsmith, Pat D300
Arrowsmith, Tim E74
Artaud, Antonin D245, E393
Arthur (King) C73
Arthur, Helen E519
Artiste, Cindy E104
The Arts Café A41
Arts Council of Great Britain A177, E278
Arts Council of Wales E718

Arts Society, University College Galway C21
Arundel, Honor B74
Arvon Foundation E747
Ascherson, Neil D300
Ash, John E423, E486, E539, E549, E704
Ashbery, John D69, D500, E549, E613, E858
Ashcroft, Peggy A56
Ashley, Janet E879
Ashman, Tristan E103
Ashton, Keith E890
La Asociación ex Alumnas del Instituto Nacional del
    Profesorado en Lenguas Vivas "Juan R. Fernandez"
    B34
Aspden, Bryan D380
Aspenström, Werner D351
Association for Scottish Literary Studies E533
Association for the Teaching of Caribbean, African, Asian
    and Associated Literature E867
Association of Little Presses D366
Astbury, Bill E120
Astbury, Sharon E120
Astley, Neil E686
Aston, Alasdair D86
Asylum Publications D55
Atkin, Angela E880
Atkins, Frederic A. A133
Atkins, John B32, B37, B69, B84, B105, B110, B117, B121,
    B149, C83
Atkinson, Ann E778
Atkinson, Donald E773
Atkinson, Paul D300
Atkinson, Tiffany E531
Atlantean Press E73, E309, E504
Atlas, James D372
Atlas Press E66
Attfield, Fred D534
Atthil, Robert B94
Atwood, Margaret E233, E479
Audas, Gerry E849
Auden, W. H. A25, A51, A100, A106, A117, A143, A146,
    A160, A182, A213, B1, B19, C30, C41, C53, C61, C68,
    D96, D210, D301
Augustine, Jane E539, E779
Auilara, Luis Miguel E694
Auster, Paul D129, D238, D252
Austerberry, Gray D122
Austin, Annemarie E658
Austin, Dave D454
Austin, Josephine E278, E288
Austin, P. Britten B37
Author's Guild B138
Avalon Editions E232
Avery, John E749
Avril, Jean-Louis D451

Axis Experimental Poetry Theatre D59
Aygi, Gennady E390, E757, E858
Aylesford Review Poets C10
Aylett, Emma E809
Ayres, Michael E287
Ayrton, Michael B24, E426

Bachinger, Katrina E651
Bacon, Ernest W. E806
Bacovia, George E423
Bad Seed Press E78
Badenoch, Andrea E906
Badman, May D356, D376, E856
Baerlein, Henry A164
Baez, Joan D35
Bailey, Anthony C91
Bailey, Chris E286
Bailey, Kevin E338
Bailey, Penelope E684, E704
Bailey, Peter D215
Bain, Donald B152
Bainbridge, Beryl E795
Bainbridge, Charles E35
Baker, Albert E884
Baker, Denys Val B23, B26, B94, B130, B143, B150, C125
Baker, Ian David E312
Baker, Peter B67, D447
Baker, Rosemary E478
Baker, Roger E312
Baker, Tony E271, E298, E316, E500
Baldock, Carole D327
Ball, Arthur B62
Ball, David D252, D333
Ball, Hugo D117, D245
Ballard, J. G. C3, D63, D111, D416
Ballin, Malcolm C14
Baltzell, Virginia D94
Balzani, Marzia E812
Bamber, Jim D343
Bamford, Kevin E115
Bamford, Tom D479
Bamforth, Iain E613, E858
Banana, Anna D170
Bancroft, Ian A167
Banerji, Sabita E658
Bangay, Frank E364
Banister, Rodney C25, C91
Banks, Iain E407
Banks, Robert E506
Bann, Stephen D173, D392, D460, D473
Bannon, Frank D355
Banting, John B98
Banville, John D240, E198, E324, E835
Barac, Carol E852

Name Index

Beeston, Catherine E651
Beggs, Jackie E849
Begley, Caroline D241
Behan, Brendan B35
Behring, Roj E312
Belfast Writers' Club A217
Bell, Clive A127, A161
Bell, Colin D533
Bell, H. Idris See Bell, Idris
Bell, Idris B17, B119
Bell, Jeff E501
Bell, Julia E660
Bell, Julian A26
Bell, Leslie C76
Bell, Sam Hanna B63
Bell, Sherley E565
Bell, William B69
Bellamy, Dawn E831
Bellamy, Vivien M. E312
Bellerby, Frances C68, D36
Bellow, Saul E327
Belli, Gioconda D47, E339
Belloc, Hilaire A32
Bellot, Paula E33, E320
Belton, D. E834
Beltrametti, Franco D197, E377
Bence-Jones, Gillian E841
Bendon, Chris E336, E567, E767
Benedictus, David E897
Benenson, Michael E339
Benetta, Philip E188
Benetta, Susan E188
Benn, Caroline D26
Benn, Tony D26
Bennett, Alan C103, C105a
Bennett, Arnold A133
Bennett, Bill E601
Bennett, Denise E527, E756
Bennett, Heather E818
Bennet, John D4
Bennett, Pat E580
Bennett, Penelope Anne C45
Bennett, Peter E563
Bennett, T. Alan C95
Benson, Albert E69
Benson, Gerard E88
Benson, Judi E291, E302, E346
Benson, Steve E429
Bentham, Rachel E892
Bentley, Eric A195
Bentley, Jan E611
Bentley, Olive C73
Bently, John E445a
Benveniste, Asa D82, D231, D409, D443, E123, E377

Beowulf C82
Berenson, Betty D206
Beresford, Anne D523
Bergé, Carol D333
Berger, Walter B122
Bergonzi, Bernard B49, C22, C26, C81, C83, C99, C123, E795
Bergvall, Caroline E429, E656, E833
Berke, Joseph D166
Bermondsey Bookshop A13
Bernal, J. D. A25
Bernas, Richard D518
Bernhardt, Sarah B149
Bernstein, Charles E52, E179, E298, E410, E552, E581, E713, E833
Berridge, Elizabeth B83
Berrigan, Daniel E835
Berrigan, Ted D258, D324, D445, D525, E717
Berry, Felicity D182
Berry, James D250, D424, E757, E761
Berry, Josephine E519
Berry, Liz E30
Berry, Martin E521
Berry, Matilda See Mansfield, Katherine
Berry, Tom E317
Berryman, John A214, B133, C61, E831
Bert, Al E250
Berthoud, Patrick E665
Bertolla, Alan D375
Betjeman, John A117, A130, A196, A233, B51, B144, C3, C30, C95, D333
Beugger, J. D. D247
Beuys, Joseph D338
Beverley, Sue E734
Bevis, John E170
Bewick, Pauline G. C46
Bewick, Thomas D374
Bhat, K. S. A199
Bhatt, Sujata E205, E613, E814
Bianchi, Ruggero A90
Bibby, Colin D47
Bick, Andrew E510
Bidder, Joe E860
Biddulph, Joseph E365, E840
Bidgood, Ruth E531
Bieda, David D111
Biederman, Charles D385
Bielby, Nicholas D345
Bielski, Alison D397, D535, E230, E651
Billcliffe, Roger D430
Billington-Greig, Teresa A133
Billot, C. P. B70
Billson, Christine D451
Binding, Norman E144

Name Index

Bingham, Dave E115
Bingham, John C114
Bingham, Tom E288, E562
Binning, Wilfred B78
Binyon, Laurence A87, A123
Biondo, Diane E878
Birch, Alex E344
Birchard, Guy E552, E735, E779
Bird, Geoff E707
Bird, Nigel E707
Birkbeck College D283
Birmingham Peace Centre D241
Birmingham Poetry Centre D292, D373
Birmingham University D19, D70
Birstall Writers E774
The Birthday Party E162
Birtles, Steve E361
Birtwhistle, John D98, D168
Birtwistle, Iris B42, C99
Bishop, Adrian E363, E630
Bishop, Elizabeth B81, B82
Bishop, John Peale C81
Bishop, Morchard B105
Bissett, Bill D245, E679
Black, D. D31
Black, D. M. C27, C32, C39, D83, D278, D300, D385,
    D428, D477, E139, E307
Black, David D119
Black, David J. D119
Black, James E305
Black, Mark C27
Black, Nigel D333
Black, Robin A77
Black, Ruth E522
The Black Writers Association E102
Blackburn, Michael C107, E346, E799
Blackburn, Paul C94, D333, D445, E500, E539, E824
Blackburn, Sylvia E799
Blackburn, T. E. F. See Blackburn, Thomas
Blackburn, Thomas B49, B65, C54, C63, C82, C112, C122,
    D280, D469, D492
Blackman, Peter B56
Blackman, Roy E748
Blackmore, Ruthi D336, D341
Blackmore Vale Writers E105
Blackmur, R. P. C78
Blackstaff [Press] D455
Blackstone, Leonard E235
Blackwood, John C76, D469
Blaikley, Alan D61
Blaine, John W. A103
Blaine, Julien E377
Blair, Tony D85
Blake, Georgina A. E104

Blake, Karl E811
Blake, William B141
Blakeston, Oswell A18, A49, A51, A100, A181, A196, A199,
    B49, C13, C16, C44, C54, C60, E312
Bland, Pete D24
Blaser, Robin D117, D289, D324, D525
Blaug, Astra D526
Bleakley, Jeffrey S. D267
Bletsoe, Elisabeth E555, E656
Bley, Carla D314
Blok, Alexander A62, A78, B69, B133
Blond, Anthony B51
Bloodwhisker, Nathaniel C40
Bloomfield, Charles D342
Blue Dog Publications D72
Blue Rose Book Press E85
Blundell, Colin E773
Blunden, E. C. See Blunden, Edmund
Blunden, Edmund A42, A48, A102, A117, A138, A158,
    A231, B103, B105
Blunt, Anthony A220
Blunt, Marjorie C15
Blunt, Rupert E330
Bly, Robert C64, D210, D437
Bligh, Roland E781
Blyth, Martin E756
Blyth, Steven E664
Blyton, Enid B142
Boadella, David D107
Boardman, Lisa E156, E625
Bockris, Victor D236, D437
Bockris-Wylie D82
Body, Seán E123
Boehmer, Elleke E424
Boesky, Amy E528
Bogg Free-For-Postage Publications D79
Böhler, Wilfried A45
Bolan, Marc D131, D184
Boland, Eavan C46, D455, E613
Boland, Mike E50
Bold, Alan C39, D313, D415, D426
Bold, Christine E160
Bolger, Dermot E324
Boll, David E467
Bomberg, David A50
Bonaparte, Napoleon B44
Bond, Edward D167
Bone, G. D. A185
Bonheim, Helmut C58
Bonnefoy, Yves B49, D421, E549
Bonney, Sean E316, E488
Bonset, I. K. See van Doesburg, Theo
Bonvin, Susan D518
Boore, W. H. B148

Booth, Martin D171, D253, D267, D292, D318, D349,
    D397, D413, D421, D486
Booth, Ruth E864
Boran, Pat E835
Borges, Jorge Luis D237, D252, E203, E423
Borkowski, Andrzej E800
Born, Ann D469
Borrow, Antony B49, C54, C67, C99
Bosley, John E876
Bosquet, Alain D451
Bostock, C. B. D59
Boswell, Gary E796, E803, E804
Botham, Paul D309
Botterill, Andy E530
Botterill, Dennis A222, A234
Bottomley, Gordon A53
Bottrall, Ronald A26, A49, A197, B23
Boulestin, X. M. A139
Boulton, Marjorie C99
Boupacha, Djamila D488
Bourke, Rachel E637
Bourne, Kay E325
Bovill, Penny D310
Bowe, Robert D315
Bowen, John B45
Bowen, Euros D339
Bowen, Roger B102
Bowering, George C10
Bowers, Fleur E419
Bowers, Penelope A188
Bowes, Barry D520
Bowie, George E790
Bowland College, University of Lancaster D122
Bowler, Christine D450
Bowles, Catherine E807
Bowles, Patrick C61, D344
Bowman, Anna D133
Bowman, Mary E879
Bowra, C. M. B69
Boxall, Philip E126
Boyars, Arthur B69, C122
Boyce, Terry E374
Boyce, William A216
Boyd, Elizabeth E242
Boyd, John C111
Boyd, Edward B20, B124
Boyd, John B63
Boyle, David E830
Boyle, Julie E541
Boyle, Kay A49, A196, A205
Boyle, Michael D527
Boyle, Sebastian E4
Brackenbury, Alison D421, E305, E858
Brackenbury, Rosalind E906

Bradbrooke, Martin D266
Bradbury, Malcolm A24, A59, C22, C53, C118, E233
Bradbury, Ray D123
Bradford, E. E. A184
Bradford Creative Writers Group E344
Bradford Writers' Circle D399
Bradgate Press E621
Brading, Tilla E488, E555, E656, E735
Bradley, F. J. C27
Bradley, Harold F. B117
Bradley, Jerry C53, C63
Bradley, John R. E572
Brady, Andrea E763
Braga, Edgard D385
Bragg, Melvyn E795
Braithwaite, Edward Kamau see Braithwaite, Edward Kamau
Braithwaite, Roger E258
Bramness, Hanne E812
Bramley, H. R. C44, C62
Brandt, Dick E183
Brangwyn, Frank A73
Brangwyn, Patrick C40, C69
Bran's Head Books E426
Braquemard E125
Brasenose College, Oxford C7, E306
Brathwaite, Edward Kamau D424, E867
Braun, Richard Emil D197
Braun, Sarah D24
Braun, Volker D47
Braybrooke, Neville B89, B130, B134, B146, C7
Breakwell, Ian D44, D74, D162, D338, D487
Brearton, Fran E831
Brecht, Bertolt B74, C68, D41, D85, D167, D261
Breeze, Jean 'Binta' E305
Brenton, Arthur A133
Brenton, Howard C76, D453
Breton, André A41, A102, A116, B7, B82, D238, D487
Brett, Gerry E137
Brett, Sebastian D344
Brett-Jones, Rosalind C46
Brewer, Simon E909
Brewster, John E725
Bfiezina, Otokar A62
Brice, Jennifer E224
Brice, Kenneth E654
Briddon, Richard E568
Bridgwater, Patrick D155
Bridgewest Publications D222
Bridie, James A32
Briers, David D338
Bright, Julian E181
Brightmore, Gill E6, E418
Brind, Simon E848
Bristol Poets' Fellowship A20, A226

Name Index

Bristol University C24, D510a, E810
Bristol Writers Association B14
Bristow, Joseph E734
British Amateur Press Assocation D270, E493
British Association of Literary Amateurs A6
British Institute B21
British Poetry Association C48, C84
British Science Fiction Poetry Association E341
Brittain, Vera A160, B104, D40
Britton, Nick E431
Broadbent, Simon C64
Broadribb, Chris E144, E418
Brock, Edwin A177, C63, D86, D446, D478
Brocklebank, Ian E404
Brocklebank, Martin E889
Brockway, Frederick D477
Brockway, James C84, E302
Broderick, Danny E736
Brodsky, Joseph E629, E722
Brody, R. E761
Broll, Brandon E860
Bromhead, Freda E652
Bromige, David D146, E298
Bronk, William D197
Bronowski, Jacob A26, A64, A200
Brontë, Emily E445a
Brook, Peter D111
Brooke, B. J. A185
Brooke, Jocelyn C82
Brooke, Rupert A117, A140, B127
Brookes, Jonathan
Brookes, Rod D48
Brooklyn College of Technology, Birmingham D92
Brooks, Alan E747
Brooks, Cleanth A159
Brooks, Jeremy C64
Brooks, Leo E206, E775
Brooks, Robin E508
Brossard, Nicole E410
Brotchie, Alastair E66
Brotherston, Gordon D215
Brotherton, Sir Edward Allen A123
Brown, Alan D374
Brown, Andrew D332
Brown, Andy D309, E656, E735
Brown, Antony B152
Brown, Chris E860
Brown, Donovan A206
Brown, Elspeth E478
Brown, F. J. B26
Brown, George Mackay B86, C32, C39, C68, D385, D428, E139, E885
Brown, Graham C. E777
Brown, John D46, D450

Brown, Keiron E776
Brown, Kenneth E485
Brown, Margaret Gillies D182
Brown, Merle C107
Brown, Pam E713
Brown, Paul D15, D180, D277, D332, D488, D489, E355, E418, E673
Brown, Pete C58, D13, D111, D169, D213, D308, D450, D451, D504
Brown, Sam D323
Brown, Stewart E757
Brown, Stuart D340, E128
Brown, Tim E811
Brown, W. Sorley A70
Brownjohn, Alan C8, C26, C44, C53, C60, C61, C64, C81, C112, C114, C122, C123, D178, D336, D408, D465, D468, D476, E377, E392, E795
Brownlow, Timothy D144, D145
Bruce, Andy E587
Bruce, George B3, B74, B113, B125, C102, D182, D430
Bruce, Robert C60
Bruggen, Carol E18
Brunel University D291
Brunius, Jacques D487
Bruns, Andrew E384
Bryan, Pete D435
Bryan, Tom E522
Bryce, Colette E748
Bryher A108
Buchan, John A121, A149
Buchan, Tom C83, D174, D326, D428
Büchler, Pavel E185
Buchner, Georg B69
Buck, Fred D69, D117, D127, D310
Buck, Paul D69, D129, D146, D252, D437, D456, E179, E244, E262, E267, E277, E393, E447, E452, E517, E679, E766, E843, E888
Buckingham, Peter D524
Buckland, Karen E349
Buckle, Daphne D289
Buckley, Steven E791
Buckman, D. J. D472
Buckmaster, Charles D537
Buford, Bill E327
Bukowski, Charles C98, D146, E638
Bull, A. J. C82, C122
Bull, Arthur Joseph See Bull, A. J.
Bull, Elaine E736
Bull, George C7
Bullen, Keith B123
Buller, Norman C18
Bullock, Julia E763
Bullock, Michael D143, D164, D318, E486a
Bulman, Ruth C68

Name Index

Campbell, Andy E705
Campbell, Donald D248
Campbell, Frances E217
Campbell, Isobel Montgomery E623
Campbell, James D300, E733
Campbell, Joseph A209
Campbell, Roderic D288
Campbell, Rona E649
Campbell, Roy A54, B18, B24, B34, B42, B69, B105, C7, C68
Campbell, Seamus B57
Campbell-Kease, John E563
Camu, Rebecca E460
Camus, Albert B6, C70
Candappa, Leslie C60
Canetti, Elias E479
Cannell, Skipwith A90
Cannock Chase Literary Society D106
Cannon Hill Writers' Group E714
Canterbury University E169
Capek, Karel A49
Capitanchik, Maurice D333
Caravel Press A28
Carcanet [Press] D98, D372, E613
Cardenal, Ernesto D47
Cardiff University E6, E461, E718
Cardonald College, Glasgow E522
Carew, Rivers D144, D145
Carey, Peter E327
Carey-Kent, Paul E177
Caribou Press E177
Carlton, Lynn D508
Carlton-Dewhirst, Wendy E561
Carne-Ross, D. S. B88, C17
Carney, Jack B11
Carney, Miriam E166
Caroutch, Yvonne D168
Carpenter, H. P. E47
Carpenter, Maurice B80, C51
Carr, Eamonn D80, D97
Carr, Philip D329
Carradice, Phil E349, E350
Carroll, Des E288
Carroll, Donald D145
Carroll, Lewis D238, D245
Carroll, Nina D16, D226, E232
Carruth, Jim E522
Carson, Ciaran D212, D455, E250
Carson, Conor E283
Carson, Oliver B51
Carswell, Catherine A99, A126, A155
Carswell, John A137
Carter, Angela C10, C118, D63, D510a, E327
Carter, Graeme D161

Carter, Simon E425
Carver, Raymond E327
Cary, Joyce D312
Casares, Adolfo Bioy D252
Casey, Anthony E560
Cash, Peter D292
Casimir, Paul C29, C125
Casterton, Julia E878
Castillo, F. D314
Castillo, Pedro Méndez E388
Castle, Bob C31
Catchpole, Eve E702
Catholic Poetry Society A29
Catling, Brian E429
Catt, Jon E22
Catullus A185, D197
Causley, Charles B23, C69, C82
Causton, Bernard A51
Cavafy, C. P. B21
Caws, Ian D508, E302
Cayley, John E549, E779
Cedars Upper School and Community College E849
Celan, Paul C61, D252, D445, E335, E694
Celestine, Alfred E644
Cendrars, Blaise D117, D238, D332, D496
Central Intelligence Agency C30
Ceolfrith Arts Centre D102
Ceolfrith Bookshop E345
Cernuda, Luis B9, B110
Césaire, Aimé B61, B82, D424
Cevdet, Melih B32
Cevet, David D488, D489
Ceylan, Mevlut E196
Cézanne, Paul D466
Cha Tze-Chiang D333
Chace, Alison E29
Chace Farm Hospital E141
Chagall, Marc B1
Chalmers, Jenny E287
Chaloner, David D36, D55, D117, D123, D127, D143, D171, D173, D194, D197, D215, D226, D289, D325, D340, D341, D411, D437, D447, D453, D474, D496, E244, E287, E316, E500, E539, E854
Chambelland, Guy D451
Chamberlain, Brenda B17, B110, B133
Chamberlain, Michael D197
Chambers, Harry A177, C80, E634
Chambers, J. B. E665
Champion, Miles E429, E581, E833, E860
Chandler, Robert E539
Chanslor, Roy E. A104
Chant, Michael D245
Chaplin, Jenny E902
Chaplin, Sid B64

Name Index

Dobbs, Tom E372
Dobrée, Bonomy B65
Docherty, Brian E860
Dodds, E. R. A4
Dodds, Vernon C123
Dolmen Press C70, D141, D368
Domeny-Hardy, Vesna E788
Domhnullach, Fionnlagh C38
Donaghy, Michael E694
Donaldson, Alec B20, B124
Donaldson, William C41
Donati, Colin E721
Doncaster, Jill D172
Donnan, Hastings D148
Donnelly, Michael D506, E111
Donnelly, Morwenna B32
Donnelly, Paul D449, E817
Donoghue, Bernard C26
Donovan, Ann D531
Donovan, Katie E814
Dooley, Maura D63
Dooley, Tim E326, E331, E741
Doolittle, Hilda See D., H.
Dorgan, Theo D368
d'Orléans, Charles E694
Dorman, Sean C105, D534
Dorn, Ed C58, C94, D153, D171, D249, D301, D324, D333,
    D445, D453, D525
Dorward, Andrew E733
Dorward, Nate E316
Dostoyevski, Fëdor Mikhailovich A133
Doty, Mark E613
Doug, Roshan E173
Dougherty, Christopher C76
Douglas, Bill Torrie E868
Douglas, C. H. A69, A133, A137, A182, A235
Douglas, Elizabeth C115
Douglas, Keith A102, A173, B102
Douglas, Norman A59
Douglas, Sheila D104, E24
Douglas, Steven D119
Dover, Cedric B132
Dowden, George D55, D69, D150, D192, D220, D342,
    D474
Dowling, Elizabeth D155
Downe, Lisa E316
Downing, Ian C75
Downing, Richard D3, D88
Doyle, A. I. B127
Doyle, Jack E875
Doyle, Lynn A22
Drabble, Margaret E736
Drain, Richard C60
Draycott, Jane E252

Dreamlands Poetry Group E619
Drewe, Martin E637
Drinan, Adam (pen-name of Joseph Macleod) A180, B3, B5,
    B41, B74, B113, B125
Drinkwater, John A79, A140, A177, A220, A231
Druce, Robert D163
Drucker, Johanna E552
Druid Press A227
Drummond, John A39
Drummond, Rory E399
du Bouchet, André D252, E335
Dublin Gate Theatre A130
Duckett, Ian E764
Dudgeon, Patrick B34
Dudley, A. E. D106
Duffin, David E891
Duffy, Carol Ann C3, E516, E542, E814, E831
Duffy, John E876
Duffy, Maureen C15, C81, C109, C113, D111, D446
Duffy, Rebecca E399
Dufrêne, François C15a, D245
Dufy, Raoul B37
Duggan, Laurie D146, E735
Duggan, Niall D465
Duhamel, Georges B1
Duke, Jim D198
Dullaghan, Frank E728
Dulwich Poetry Group D86
Dun Emer Press A22
Duncalf, Stephen E458
Duncan, Andrew D318, E35, E52, E256, E335, E581, E735
Duncan, Bill D182
Duncan, Robert C58, C69, D301, D525
Duncan, Ronald A137, A210, B23, B37, B144, C2, C12,
    C112
Duncombe, David E778
Dundee University D182, E257
Dundee University Writers Workshop E24
Dunham, Phil E604
Dunhill, Alison D489
Dunkley, Joyce C106
Dunlop, R. O. A56
Dunn, Angus E546
Dunn, David D311
Dunn, Douglas A177, D63, D99, D174, D182, D280, D340,
    D372, D395, D468, D476, D519, E549, E665, E787
Dunn, J. Selwyn A79
Dunn, Peter B70
Dunne, Faith E255
Dunne, Séan E198
Dunsany, Lord A123
Dupin, Jacques D313
Dupré, Louise E694
DuQuesne, Terence E158, E732, E910

Name Index

Garcia-Bravo, Fernando D520
Garden, Dave E350
Gardiner, C. Wrey *See* Gardiner, Wrey
Gardiner, Michael E35, E390
Gardiner, Patrick B152
Gardiner, Rolf A235, B32
Gardiner, Wrey A176, B26, B32, B42, B47, B67, B68, B70,
    B82, B93, B94, B110, B120, B147, C48
Gardner, Alan D17
Gardner, Anne D76
Gardner, Donald D36
Gardner, Ian D76, D473, E524
Garelli, Jacques D314
Garfitt, Roger A177, D226, D395, D453, D521, E582, E745
Garioch, Robert A5, A77, A224, B113, C32, C39, C81,
    C102, D93, D300, D326, D385, D428, E339, E885
Garland, Patrick C44
Garlick, Raymond B33, C5, C60
Garman, Douglas A24
Garner, Alan E426, E796
Garrett, Elizabeth E302
Garrison, Philip D197
Garwood, Anthony C99
Gascoyne, David A41, A49, A100, A102, A137, A146, A180,
    A197, B9, B41, B69, B82, C122, C124, E426, E828
Gates, Larry D94
Gathercole, Rod D76
Gatto, Alfonso B9
Gaudion, Carol E569
Gawsworth, John A49, A54, A132, A177, A199, B46, B117,
    B123, C13
Gee, Maggie E326, E906
Gee, Peter D58
Geering, Ken D83
Gelhorn, Martha E327
Gemini Press B48, C15
Genet, Jean C57, D242, D439
Geogh, Keith E211
Geoghegan, Luke E711
George, Caroline E802
George, Glenda D15, D77, D129, E267, E447, E517, E684
George, Margaret E200
George, Michael D59, D60
George Watson's College Literary Club C79
Gerrard, Mike E584
Gervase of Tilbury D188
Gerz, Jochen C15a
Gettisburg, M. A. D383
Ghose, Zulkifar C113, C117, C118
Gibbens, John E561
Gibbon, Lewis Grassic A77, A213
Gibbon, Monk D240
Gibbons, Fiachra E661
Gibbons, Stella A69, A132

Gibbons, William F. A81
Gibbs, Michael D1, D189, D243
Gibson, M. D11
Gibson, Magi E522
Gibson, Sean E131
Gibson, Wilfrid Wilson A140, C71
Gide, André A206, B1, B54
Gideon, Ian E505
Gidney, Pam E756
Gifford, Douglas D430
Gifford, Terry E831
Gilbert, Joan D289, D474
Gilbert, John D126
Giles, Gordon E870
Giles, Tam E676
Gill, David D226, D465, E490
Gill, Eric A10, A69, A94, A118, A137
Gill, Michael D56
Gillard, Isabel E224
Gillies, Margaret E24
Gilligan, Annie E747
Gillis, Alan E481
Gilman, H. A9
Gilonis, Harry D318, E254, E298, E335, E458, E552, E860
Gilson, Ambrose E853
Gimblett, John Edward E299
Ginner, Charles A9
Ginsberg, Allen B60, C61, D189, D258, D293, D333, D409,
    D439, D445, D504, E631, E717
Gioia, Dana E214, E634, E858
Giorno, John D243, D416, E717
Giroux, Roger D256
Gizzi, Peter E410, E713
Glasgow Literary Club A32
Glasgow University D319
Glasshouse Press E226
Gledhill, Margaret E340
Gleeson, Martin D298
Gleizes, Albert A186
Glen, Duncan A126, A192, D12, D340, E75, E387, E719,
    E885, E915
Glover, Jon C107
Glover, Michael E814
Glover, T. R. D175
Glück, Louise D301, D453
Godbert, Geoffrey E558, E828
Goddard, Cam E763
Goddard, James D39
Goddard, Jules D344
Godden, Richard D133, E722
Godfrey, Peter E227, E246
Godwin, George A2
Goethe, von, Johann Wolfgang D237
Gog C27

Name Index

Gogan, L. S. A19
Gogarty, Paul D82, E727
Gohorry, John E326
Gold, Pam E869
Goldberg, Magnificent D2
Golden Eagle Pressd B85
Goldring, Maude A50
Goldsmith, Oliver D64
Goldsmith, Richard E470
Goldsmith, Rudi E98
Goldsmith Press D158
Goldsmiths' College, London E813, E891
Gomez de la Serna, Ramon B19, B103
Gomringer, Eugen D173, D235, D245, D460, D519
Gonda, Caroline E148, E638
Gonne, Maude See MacBride, Maude Gonne
Gonzalez, John E602
Gonzalez, Lindsay Jean E602
González-Marina, Joaquina D523, E213
Good Elf [Press] D193
Goodall, Joan E623
Goodby, John E35, E346
Goode, Chris D77, E316
Goodland, Giles E302, E807
Goodland, John A197
Goodman, Richard A25, A213
Goodrich, Jennifer E214
Goodwin, Christopher C81
Goodwin, Pamela E501
Gordimer, Nadine E327, E867
Gordon, Alec E355
Gordon, Giles C32, C113, E139
Gordon, Janet Z. D25
Goring, Richard E109
Gormley, Antony D329
Gorst-Williams, Jessica A. D154
Gort, Sandy E919
Görtschacher, Wolfgang B88, B99, C73, E651
Gould, Derrick E698
Gould, Jean A90
Goulding, Philip E756
Goulding, W. M. D309
Gowen, David E572
Graddon, John B142
Graham, Ben E107
Graham, Chael E780
Graham, David D133
Graham, Desmond C85
Graham, John J. B86
Graham, Marcus C56
Graham, R. B. Cunninghame A32
Graham, Rigby D64, D155, D168, D389
Graham, W. S. A173, B3, B23, B40, B61, B74, B87, B91,
    B110, B113, B125, B130, C41, C68, C93, D34, D372,

E885
Gramsci, Antonio D300
Grande, Felix D233
Gransden, K. W. C91
Grant, A. R. E190
Grant, Duncan B8
Grant, Joy A128, A135
Granta Publications E327
Grass, Günter D150
Graves, Charles B20
Graves, Ida Affleck D421
Graves, Robert A6, A60, A71, A157, A158, A159, A160,
    A225, C97, C113, D155
Graves, Sally A60
Gray, Alasdair D105, D319, E247, E317, E460, E870
Gray, John C10
Gray, Michael D125
Gray, Nigel D167
Gray, Simon C25
Greacen, Robert A151, B26, B32, B48, B57, B58, B59, B63,
    B68, B26, B82, B110, B111, B119, B136, B150, C13, C54,
    E628
Greaves, John Howard E603
Green, Adrian D452
Green, David E22
Green, Frederick Pratt C82
Green, J. C. R. D397, E391, E509
Green, Jim D292
Green, John D47
Green, Keef D43
Green, Malcolm E66
Green, Nigel E760
Green, Patricia D64
Green, Paul D88, D127, D341, D447, E52, E180, E267,
    E393, E452, E766
Green, Paul J. D159
Green, Richard D475
Green, Russell A42
Green Horse [Press] D353
Greene, Graham A117, A127, A147, B1
Greene, Martin E909
Greene, Peter C43
Greenhalgh, Chris E858
Greenham, Peter D245
Greenhorn, Stephen E414
Greening, John C73, D182, E658, E694
Greenley, Trevor D79
Greenwald, Ted E833
Greenwood, Albert C110
Greenwood, Gillian E442a
Gregory, Derek E818
Gregory, Isabella Augusta, Lady A22
Gregory, John A2
Gregory, Padraic B57

Name Index

Hamilton, Robin D174
Hamlett, Jenny E756
Hammersley, Richard E601
Hammond, Arthur C109
Hammond, M. D. D38
Hampson, Norman A167
Hampson, Robert D15, E277, E311, E335, E860
Hampton, Christopher D408
Hand, Alex D218
Hand & Flower Press C82
Handley, Joe E760
Hands, Marie E118
Handy, Betty E224
Hangman Press E183
Hangman Records E183
Hanley, James A100
Hanna, Billy E551
Hannah, Sophie E302, E392, E516, E613
Hannan, Maggie E906
Hanski, Eion D492
Hanson, Kevin D336
Hanson, Sten C15a
Harayi, Manya B19
Hard Pressed Poetry [Press] E410
Hardie, George D105
Hardiment, Melville D26
Harding, Cory E589, E881, E916
Harding, D. W. A195
Harding, David E445
Harding, Jason A2, A24, A45, A64, A143, A195
Harding, Jeremy D194, D496
Hardingham, John E652
Hardwick, Joan E60
Hardy, Henry D261
Hardy, Thomas A13, A36, A59, A117, A157, C2
Harland, Frances C27
Harland, Viv E568
Harlequin Coffee House, Fulham C54
Harlow, Jean D332
Harlow Writers D225
Harmer, J. B. A90
Harmon, Giles D532
Harmon, Maurice D141, D368
Harper, Maria D119
Harris, Alan E326
Harris, Cliff D162
Harris, F. E272
Harris, Gordon C29
Harris, Kenneth A102
Harris, Miranda E652
Harris, William A. A235
Harrison, Allan V. E666
Harrison, Austin A59
Harrison, Eric D224, D522

Harrison, G. D479
Harrison, J. D467
Harrison, John E144
Harrison, Milford D138
Harrison, Paul E706
Harrison, Roy D96
Harrison, Ruth E425
Harrison, Tony B65, C55, C58, C85, C107, C118, D51, D165, D266
Harrison, T. W. See Harrison, Tony
Harrow Poetry Group E136
Harsent, David D174
Hart, Chris E664
Hart, David E598, E814
Hart, Henry E858
Hart, Matthew E368
Harte, Jack E835
Harthill, Graham E144, E418, E718
Hartl, Thomas E651
Hartley, George C53
Hartley, Jill E344
Hartnett, Jeff E781
Hartnett, Michael D41, D89, D158, D210, D455, E622
Harvey, Adam A180
Harvey, Elizabeth D269
Harvey, Francis E422
Harvey, John D22, D178, E302, E346, E747
Harvey, M. G. E820
Harvey, Norman D505
Harvey, R. E. E820
Harwood, Lee D15, D36, D88, D95, D117, D127, D150, D153, D162, D171, D194, D198, D213, D227, D289, D307, D308, D328, D340, D377, D416, D437, D451, D500, D525, E226, E335, E377, E418, E500, E539, E554, E589, E704, E747, E757, E779, E879
Hashmir, Alamgir D535
Haslam, Michael D117, D127, D215, D252, D437, D447, D496, E287, E340, E581
Hasler, Crispin D344
Hasslacher, Henry Joseph See Blakeston, Oswell
Hathaway, Jean E652
Hatherley, Ana D44
Hattersley, Geoff E346, E845, E876
Hattersley, Jeanette E876
Hatton, K. D. E567
Haughey, Denis D160
Haughey, Edmund D160
Hausmann, Raoul C15a, D173, D245, D460
Havenhurst E333
Havering Poetry Group D375
Haward, Birkin B98
Hawkins, Adrianne E6
Hawkins, Desmond A182, A213
Hawkins, Ralph D197, D215, D456, E8, E287, E316, E427,

E554, E581

Hawkins, Spike D66, D82, D111, D169, D213, D308, D451,
D453, D504, E458

Haworth, Donald D117

Hay, Deorsa Caimbeul *See* Hay, George Campbell

Hay, E. A. A79

Hay, George Campbell B3, B20, B78, B113, C39, E139

Haycraft, Colin C12

Haylett, Robin E879

Hayman, Ronald C14

Haythorne, Pete E760

Haywood, I. E272

Haywood, Mike D311

Hazzard, Geoffrey C62, D213

H.C.M. *See* Minchin, H. Cotton

H.D. *See* D., H.

Head, Andrew E639

Head, Peter E860

Headdon, Bill E439

Headland Publications D203

Headlock Press E352

Headquarters of British Troops in Egypt B95

Healy, Denis C28

Healy, Dermot D455, E238, E293, E324

Healy, Randolph E89, E316

Heaney, Seamus C42, C79, D34, D35, D63, D89, D97,
D160, D178, D230, D240, D312, D400, D455, D476,
D527, E198, E203, E293, E481, E549, E551, E658,
E795, E814, E835, E858

Heap, Jane A112

Hearn, Sheila E160

Heasman, C. E284

Heath, Stephen D111

Heathcock, Maralyn D282

Heather, Jane E791

Heath-Miller, Mavis C115

Heath-Stubbs, John A160, B23, B24, B32, B37, B40, B65,
B67, B69, B108, B110, B139, B150, B152, C26, C67,
C68, C83, C88, C122, D34, D89, D233, D348, D398,
D423, D469, D484, E423, E477, E628

Heaton, T. C107

Hebron, C. C. D218

Hebron, Chris D150

Hederman, Mark Patrick E203

Heidegger, Martin B35, C70

Heine, Heinrich A21, A92

Heissenbuttel, Helmut D245, D252

Hejinian, Lyn E298

Heliczer, Piero D333

Hélion, Jean A11

Heller, Michael E539, E779

Hellicar, Hugh E96

Hellings, Peter A229

Hellion, Martha D425

Helm, Jeremy D32, D496

Helm, Norman C91

Helman, Cecil D170

Helman, Eduoard B44

Helmore, Mark E31

Helms, Hans G. E254

Hemans, Theo E287

Hemensley, Kris D69, D146, D147, D391, D437, D447,
D537, E267

Hemingway, Ernest A211

Hemmings, Joseph E222

Henderson, A. J. A46

Henderson, Hamish B13, B20, B21, B81, B82, B95, B113,
B123, C121, D89, D104

Henderson, Philip A56

Hendriks, A. L. E773

Hendry, J. F. A102, A148, A197, A227, B77, B82, B83, B113,
B133, B149, C83, D169, D385, D439

Hendry, Joy D105, D327

Hengen, Tom E389

Henley, W. E. C73

Henri, Adrian C39, D36, D46, D80, D97, D123, D168,
D309, D341, D504, D523, E248, E518

Henry, Brian E858

Henry, Leigh A66

Henry, Paul D380

Heppenstall, Rayner B19

Herbert, Cicely E88

Herbert, George D235

Herbert, Katherine C100

Herbert, W. N. E306, E307, E390, E528, E552, E686, E758,
E858

Herbert, Zbigniew D412

Herbjornsrud, Hans E812

Herd, David A177

Herd, Tracey D182

Herdman, E. F. A168

Herdman, John E24, E139

Here Now [Press] D205

Hermans, Theo E838

Hermes, Eric C27

Hermes, Gertrude A99

Heron Press C8

Herring, Robert A108, A196, B26, B133

Hershaw, William E725

Hershon, Daniel E892

Hervey, Charles W. A228

Heseltine, Nigel A227

Heseltine, Philip A161

Hesketh, Phoebe C71, C99, C120

Hesse, Herman B47

Hewett, Peter A180

Hewish, Roy D44

Hewitt, John A151, B35, B63, B119, C95, C111, C117, D35,

Name Index

Hooker, Jeremy D63, E462
Hooley, Ruth D212
Hooley, Terri D81, D148, D220
Hoover, Paul E713
Hope, Danielle E10, E916
Hope, Francis C63, C112, D412
Hope, Sheila D266
Hopewell, Patrick E301
Hopkins, Gerald Manley D392
Hopkins, John D500
Hopkins, Konrad E838
Hopkins, Sarah E817
Hopkins, Tom E811
Horde, John D336
Horizon [Press] B43, B54
Horn, Sebastian D119
Horne, A. M. E399
Horne, Peter D149
Hornstein, Yakov A1
Horovitz, Frances C10, C61, D22, D63, D227, D267, D341, D342, D375, D421, D437, E518
Horovitz, Michael C10, C61, C112, D13, D89, D125, D127, D143, D192, D227, D267, D289, D328, D333, D336, D341, D342, D409, D469, D478, D496, D504, E479
Horsfall, Barbara D534
Horsfield, A. E. E18
Horton, Guy D28
Horwood, Julie D430
Hoskins, Jennifer E850
Houédard, Dom Sylvester C10, D1, D30, D44, D89, D102, D162, D226, D235, D243, D245, D460, D482, D500, E552
Hounslow Poetry Workshop E364
Housman, Laurence A73, A80, A148, A236, B141, C100
Houston, David A96
Houston, Libby C32, D63, D180, D213, D291, D308, D504, E230, E747, E828
Houston, Ralph C99
Howard, Ben C65, C93
Howard, Brian A61
Howard, John E25, E603, E861
Howard, Ken D61
Howard-Greaves, John See Howard, John
Howarth, David E201
Howden, Keith E671
Howe, Bill E473
Howe, Fanny E410, E552, E581, E766, E833
Howe, Patricia C45
Howe, Peter D476
Howell, Anthony D518
Howell, David C41
Howell, M. R. E171
Howell-Jones, Gail D318
Howells, Kim D85

Howes, Fiona E849
Howorth, Margaret B120
Hoy, Peter D22, D168, D237, D256, D313, D342, D513, E180
Huang, Guiyou A90
Hub Publications D327, E401
Hubbard, Sue E326
Hubbard, Tom E307, E725
Huddersfield Polytechnic E420, E542
Hudson, John E478
Hudson, Liam C105a
Hudson, Louise E264
Hueffer, Ford Madox See Ford, Ford Madox
Hufton, Carl E40
Hughes, Cyril B117, B137
Hughes, Glenn A90
Hughes, Glyn E897
Hughes, Glynne C91
Hughes, Gwilym Rees D103
Hughes, John E543, E815
Hughes, Langston B61, B74, C61
Hughes, Leigh D496
Hughes, Peter E287
Hughes, Ted A83, C14, C22, C25, C30, C61, C63, C101, C113, D16, D63, D285, D312, D372, D528, E462, E479, E831
Hughes, Vaughan D339
Hughes-Stanton, Blair A99
Hughson, J. T. B86
Huidobro, Vincente B110
Huk, Romana E410
Hull, R. F. C. B47, C68
Hull, Stephen E481
Hull University D383a, E93, E667
Hulme, T. E. A133
Hulse, Christopher Gray D94
Hulse, Michael C107, D421, D476, E423, E638
Humfrey, Belinda E531
Humphries, Paul D282
Hunkin, Gladys B23
Hunt, Ronald D219
Hunt, Sidney A186, A196
Hunt, Violet A59
Hunter, Barbara B119
Huntly, Gordon D430
Hurford, Chris E858
Hurricane Lamp Gallery A56
Hurst, David A223
Hurst, Victoria E914
Hurt, Maggi E906, E909
Husain, Adrian D301
Huscroft, John E384
Hussein, Aamer E867
Hutchings, Reginald A100

Name Index

Hutchinson, Garrie D537
Hutchinson, Mark E791
Hutchinson, Pearse B35, D41, D132, D210, D240
Huws, Daniel C101
Huxley, Aldous A13, A59, A61, A115, A160, A161, A190,
  B43, D312
Hyatt, Mark D117, D252
Hyett, Olive E670

Ibid Press E368
Iddon, John E795
Idle, E. D. A1
Iles, Jill E110
Image, Simon E734
Imlah, Mick A160, A177
Imperial College, London E606
Inca Books D28
Incertus See Heaney, Seamus
Ingham, Charles E554
Inman, Philip C122
Inner Circle [Reading Series] D260
Inner City Publications D84
Institute for Research in Art and Technology, London D22
Institute of Contemporary Arts D255
Institute of Education, London E472
Intercultural Publications C78
International Institute of British Poetry A163
International League of Youth (British Section) A235
International Poetry Society E401
International Surrealism Exhibition 1936, A93
Ionesco, Eugene C57, D478
Iredale, Roger D389
Ireland, Denis D312
Iremonger, Valentin B32, B35
Irish Volunteers A96
Irish Writers' Co-operative E502
Iron Press D230a
Irvine, Lyn A127
Isherwood, Christopher B127
Ishikawa, Takuboku D94
Ishtiaq, Samin E606
The Islanders A99
Islington Poetry Workshop E35
Ivens, Michael C54
Ivy, Robert C91

Jabès, Edmond D146, D252, D256, D314, E374, E539
Jaccottet, Philippe C124, D233, D397, E250
Jack, Ian E327
Jackman, Alison E510
Jackowska, Nicki D15, D128, D181, D203, D222, D323,
  D379, D421, E423, E584, E757
Jackson, Alan B60, C39, D55, D309, D428
Jackson, Andrew E387

Jackson, Daniel E519
Jackson, Gordon D197
Jackson, H. J. D197
Jackson, Holbrook A133
Jackson, Laura (Riding) (See also Riding, Laura) E317
Jackson, Laurie E329
Jackson, Linda E522
Jackson, Norman D389, D395
Jackson, Patricia E136
Jackson, Roger E255
Jackson, Tony D82, D249
Jackson, Tracey Elaine A90
Jackson's Arm [Press] E346
Jacob, Max C70, D117, D500
Jacob, Violet A149
Jacobson, Dan C104, C112, D305, D412
Jaffin, David D203, D205, D250, E374, E539, E735
Jafrate, Keith D138, E561, E811
Jaggi, Maya E867
Jakens, Claire E335
Jakobiak, Bernard D451
Jamal, Mahmoud E828
James, Andrea E162
James, C. L. R. D424, E104
James, Clive C76, D98, D412, D453
James, Edwin E6
James, Elizabeth E252, E307, E316, E569
James, Eric C106
James, Erma Harvey B23
James, John D22, D24, D69, D95, D117, D127, D153, D194,
  D215, D289, D310, D411, D437, D447, D453, D474,
  D486, D525, E554, E713
James, Kathryn E572
James, M. R. A121
James, Maurice E405
James, Nick D465
James, P. D. E551
James, Stephen E809, E810
James, Trevor D537
James-Bailey, William A183
Jamie, Kathleen D182, D300, E307, E870
Jamieson, Morley E139
Jamieson, Robert Alan E247, E307
Janco, Marcel A186
Jandl, Ernst C32, D235, D245, D460
Jarman, Mark E170
Jarosy, Ivo C68
Jarrell, Randall E831
Jarry, Alfred B44, D238
Jarvis, Don D193
Jarvis, Simon E581
Jason Press B104
Jay, Peter C28, D98, D285, D301, D335a, D389, D451,
  D453, E423

Jebb, Keith E287, E528
Jeffers, Robinson C56, C83
Jeffery, Gordon B116
Jeffrey, Brian E118
Jeffrey, Francis E247
Jeffrey, William A21, A149
Jelinek, Ivan D40
Jelenski, K. A. D40
Jellett, Mainie A103, A130
Jena, Seema E216
Jenkin, Richard E221
Jenkins, Cecil C46
Jenkins, Gwyn Oliver B36
Jenkins, Heinke D389
Jenkins, Lucien E743
Jenkins, Mike D380, E302
Jenkins, Nigel D215, E418
Jenkins, Paul D36
Jenkins, Philip D126, D401, E879
Jenner, Simon E591
Jennett, Seán B26
Jennings, Elizabeth C7, C10, C26, C53, C60, C63, C64,
  C81, C97, C112, D40, D261, D313, D336, D372, D519
Jennings, Humphrey A41, A64
Jennings, Martin E87
Jennings, Philip Sidney E407
Jerrold, Douglas A59
Jervis, Simon C76
Jessener, Stephen E918
Jesus College, Cambridge D77, D328
Joe DiMaggio Press D236
Jogee, Moussa E387
John, Roland B99
Johnson, Adrian E167
Johnson, Andy E738
Johnson, Anne Marie E263
Johnson, B. S. (earlier known as Bryan Johnson) C113,
  D95, D293
Johnson, Bengt Emil C15a
Johnson, Bryan (later known as B. S. Johnson) C109, C117,
  C118, D446
Johnson, Bunk B61
Johnson, Charles E553
Johnson, Geoffrey C110
Johnson, Jenny C73, E651
Johnson, Kay C122
Johnson, Linton Kwesi D424
Johnson, Michael D533
Johnson, Nicholas E287, E298
Johnson, Patricia B105
Johnson, Ronald D385
Johnson, Willard A104
Johnston, Fred E205
Johnstone, Paul D178, E484

Johnstone, Robert D99, D212, D220
Joint Services School for Linguists C103
Jolas, Eugen A212
Jolliffe, Peter E460
Jolly, Stephen C51
Jones, Alun R. D262
Jones, Bettina E523
Jones, Brian C55, C125, D36
Jones, Carl B15
Jones, Carol E693
Jones, Chris E179, E688
Jones, David B19, C2, D380
Jones, Dewi D339
Jones, Elwyn B108
Jones, Ergo B37
Jones, Esmond E576
Jones, Esther E437
Jones, Gillian D489
Jones, Gillian Bence See Bence-Jones, Gillian
Jones, Glyn A227
Jones, Grahame E524
Jones, Gwyn A229
Jones, Gwyn Owen E236
Jones, Herbert A196
Jones, Huw C5
Jones, Islwyn D103
Jones, J. [i.e. John] Christopher D456
Jones, J. V. C33
Jones, Jay Jeff E535
Jones, Jill E713
Jones, Kate E913
Jones, Leroi D333
Jones, Lynne E314
Jones, Marie E760
Jones, Nigel E661
Jones, Peggy Loosemore E772
Jones, Peter A90, C62
Jones, Richard E218
Jones, Roger D213, D308, D451
Jones, Susan D469
Jones, T. H. C99
Jones, Terry E449
Jones, Tom Parri D339
Jope, Lynn E567
Jope, Norman E488, E567, E767, E860
Jordan, Andrew E825
Jordan, Clive C118
Jordan, John D141, D368, D461, E89, E629
Jordan, Neil E293
Joris, Pierre D127, D170, D318, D377, D445, D456, E123,
  E277, E510, E539, E552, E554
Joseph, Dermot D31
Joseph, Jenny C26, C64, C63, D478
Josephs, Laurence A99

Name Index

Josephson, Matthew A186
Jouve, Nicole Ward D63
Jouve, Pierre-Jeane B19
Jowett, Alan E76
Joyce, Andrea E733
Joyce, James A55, A57, A90, A103, A115, A212
Joyce, Trevor D246, E316, E735
Joynson, Ian E505
József, Attila D385, E510
Juby, Margot K. D452
Júdice, Nuno E250
Juhász, Gyula E694
Jung, C. J. C68
Jung, Rudolf B47
Jussawalla, Adil D98
Justice, Donald E638

Kaestlin, John A39
Kafka, Franz A62, A126, A137, B24, B40
Kahn, Joyce D206
Kandinsky, Wassily A186
Kane, David D284
Kane, Michael D466
Kantor, Tadeuz E254
Kaplan, Dylan D133
Kaplan, Edward E232
Kaplan, Nancy B22
Kaschnitz, Marie Luise E426
Kästner, Erich B80
Katrak, Adi D98
Kaul, A. N. C74
Kavan, Anna B130
Kavanagh, Aoife E785
Kavanagh, Mary A92
Kavanagh, P. J. D89
Kavanagh, Patrick A94, A97, B35, B59, C50, C68, C70, C124, D41, D158, D210, D240
Kavanagh, Peter C50
Kavanagh, Rik D507
Kavanagh, Ted D198
Kawabata Press E730
Kay, David D14
Kay, George C121
Kay, Jackie E516, E814
Kazantzis, Judith D250, D318, D421, D523, E814
Keane, Dennis C26
Keane, John B. E293
Kearney, Richard E203
Keats, John C3
Keeble, Brian E426, E821
Keeble, John C. D208
Keele University D525, E722
Keeley, Edmund E374
Keeling, Roger E33

Keen, Jeff D198
Keery, James E287, E346, E811
Keighley, Andy E24, E448
Keighley, Gladys B117
Keighley, Joanna E448
Keith, Joseph Joel C99, C110
Kell, Richard E563
Kelleher, D. L. A4
Kelli, Bernadox E673
Kelly, Bernard D15, D170, D537
Kelly, Bernard J. E673
Kelly, H. A14
Kelly, John D461, E596
Kelly, Rita E89
Kelly, Rob E219
Kelly, Robert D150
Kelly, S. B. E522
Kelly, Terence D205
Kelly, Tom D205
Kelman, James E24, E247, E547
Kelsall, Ida A32
Kemp, Jeremy E608
Kendall, Leonard C29
Kennedy, A. L. E247
Kennedy, Adam A126
Kennedy, Brian P. A94
Kennedy, John F., President D180
Kennedy, Oliver D527
Kennelly, Brendan C46, D80, D89, D97, D240, D284, D355, D455, E422
Kenning, Eileen E598
Kenny, Peter E136, E182
Kent, William D404
Kenworthy, Cicely C. A164
Keoghan, Barry B117
Keown, Anna G. A4
Kermode, Frank C53
Kernaghan, Alex D118
Kerouac, Jack B60, C61, D245
Kerr, Alan D11
Kerr, Colin E325
Kerr, Roderick Watson A149
Kerr, Sebastian C7
Kerrigan, Anthony D246
Kerrigan, Catherine A77
Kersey, Richard A203
Kettle's Yard Art Gallery, Cambridge E147
Kewell, Kevin D4
Keyes, Sidney B152, C92
Khai r-Eddine, Mohammed D451
Khalvati, Mimi E736
Khan, Patricia E199
Kiberd, Declan E481
Kidd, Helen D261, E307, E528, E656

Kiely, Kevin E90
Kierkegaard, Sören A62
Kilburn, David D196
Kilkenny Literary Society D240
Killingray, Heather E639
Killingworth, Gerald D469
Kilmarnock North-West Writers' Group E768
Kimberley, Nick D68, D69, E378
Kime, Stuart E389
Kimwood, Colin D537
Kincaid, John B20, B124
Kindness, A. W. E860
King, Elizabeth B134
King, Francis B52, B152
King, Lillian E268
King, Maude E. A43
King, Peter J. E888
King, Robert D81
King, Vernon E100
Kingham, Terry D470, D508
King's College, Cambridge C76, E148, E607, E738
King's College, London C109, D285, E168, E245, E812
Kinloch, David E247, E306, E307, E613, E758, E858
Kinsella, John C25, C107, E424
Kinsella, Thomas B59, B111, C25, C46, C53, C63, D41,
    D63, D89, D141, D158, D174, D210, D240, D246, D298,
    D455, E422, E835
Kipling, Rudyard D123
Kippon, Doug D59
Kirke, Alexis E827
Kirklees Writing in the Community Project E774
Kirkpatrick, Johnson E879
Kirkup, James B32, B46, B49, B65, B82, B90, B117, B139,
    B148, C13, C26, C44, C67, C71, C73, C88, C122, D22,
    D89, D203
Kita, Bronia E909
Kitchen, Derek D464
Kivland, Sharon E736
Klah, Myra D437
Klax-Williams, Abraham D126
Klee, Paul D333
Klein, Yves D238
Kleiner, Henry C99, C115, D162
Kleinzahler, August E539, E549
Klikovac, Igor E788
Kline, Phyllis C74
Klopper, Harry B80
Knapman, Jack B37
Kneale, Trevor D280
Knell, Marion D18
Knibb, Helen E746
Knight, Kenny E837
Knight, Stephen E531, E814
Knights, L. C. A195

Knights, Leslie D. B130
Knights, Narissa E192, E415
Kobiernicki, Leszek E321
Koestler, Arthur B83
Kohlke, Marie-Luise E802
Kohn, Jack C107
Kolakowski, Leszek C28
Koller, James D67, D150, D197
Kontexts Publications D189
Kops, Bernard C54, C61, C67, C112
Korn, Eric C103
Kostelanetz, Richard E552
Kosubei, David C47
Kraut, Rochelle E554
Kravitz, Peter E247
Krax [Press] D244
Kreitman, Norman B108
Kremer, G. E117
Kumar, Jaya E912
Kumar, Shiv. K. E220
Kundera, Milan E327
Kuo Ching Té C110
Kuppner, Frank E247, E307, E552, E858
Kusano, Shimpei D162
Kuttner, Steve D140
Kyle, Galloway A177, A223
Kypreos, Christopher D419

Labarthe, André B43
Laberc, Roy D472
Laforgue, Jules D153
Laila, Majnun D484
Laing, R. D. D440
Laird, Inge Elsa C61
Lal, P. E220
Lall, Chaman A42
Lallans Society D248
Lally, Yvone E106
Lalor, Brian E539
Lamb, Catherine C107
Lambton, Edward C118
Lamprill, Paul D161, D422, E808
Lancaster, John E420, E876
Lancaster, Osbert B50
Lancaster University D122
Land, Andrew E333
Landy, Richard D8
Lane, Brian D44
Lane, Edward B147
Lane, Giles E185
Lane, Helena D534
Lane, John A15, E326
Lane, John See O'Leighin, Sean
Lang, Ian E274

Name Index

Lange, Bertil C99
Lange, Brigitte E807
Langford, Peter D85
Langley, R. F. E316
Lansdown, Andrew E858
l'Anselme, Jean D451
Lantern Light Circle E150, E261
Laporte, Roger D256
Lark Lane Poetry Books E559
Larkin, Peter E298, E316, E335, E452, E581, E735
Larkin, Philip A167, B69, C22, C26, C53, C63, C64, C80, C81, C95, C117, D261, D383a, D468, D486, D519
Larsen, Kimberley E791
La Sainte Union College of Higher Education, Southampton E879
Lasdun, James E791
Laskey, Michael E346, E748
Latin Press A118
Lattin, Peter D242
Laughlin, James B40, C78
Laundering Room Press D82, D257
Laurila, S. E. C99
Laver, Peter D51
Lavery, Ursula A229
Lavin, Mary D41
Lavrin, Janko A62, A137
Law, Rose E355
Law, T. S. B85, B86, D205
Lawless, Emily A96
Lawrence, D. H. A2, A55, A57, A59, A90, A104, A115, A117, A139, A198, A225
Lawson, Andrew E287, E298, E779
Lawson, Sarah D15
Lawson, Terry E568
Lax, Robert D10, D15, D196, D236, D243, D385, D460, D473, E110, E458, E510
Layton, Peter E217
Lazerwolf Press E183
Leach, Bernard D199
Leahy, Maurice A29
Leaman, Giles E791
Leanse, Stephen D481
Leaper, Maurice B32
Leary, Paris C60, D168
Leary, Timothy D258
Leatham, John B130
Leavings, Fred C24
Leavis, F. R. A24, A88, A195, D123
Lebeau, Vicky E298
Ledward, Patricia B74, B121
Lee, Dada D239
Lee, George E134
Lee, Joan D352
Lee, Laurie A180, B41, D472

Leeds University B65, C85, C107, D221, E436, E591
Leeds University Poetry Society C85
Leeds Writers Workshop E223
Leeming, Owen C117
Left Book Club A171
Léger, Fernand D466
Leggett, Dave E597
Legrand, Frederic E481
Lehmann, Beatrix B98
Lehmann, John A26, A146, A180, A220, B30, B41, B87, B97, B101, C55, C125
Lehmann, Rosamond A36, B96
Lehmkuhl, H. L. B89
Leigh, Michael E207
Leigh, Richard E254
Leishman, Hugh D430
Leite, George B61
Leishmann, J. B. B69
Lekutanoy, Jocko D465
Leman, Martin D37
Lemmon, John E692
Lemoine, Shuna E676
Lendennie, Jessie E711
Lennon, John D97
Leonard, Tom D15, D89, D193, D319, D326, D428, E247, E307, E733
Lerner, Laurence C63, C100, E647
Le Saux, Julian E347
Leslie, Stephen E591
Leslie, Vera B24
Lessing, Doris C18, D96, E327, E374
Lessing, Karin E254
Lester, Hilary E823
Lester, Paul D331
Lethbridge, Chris E830
Leung Lo-you E374
Levenson, Christopher C14, C25, C41, C59, C60, C105a, C118, D472
Leventhal, A. J. A103
Levertoff, Denise *See* Levertov, Denise
Levertov, Denise B46, B139, C58, C94, D167, D197, D333, E180, E374, E458, E462, E638
Levi, Peter C2, C10, C41, C105a, D178, D233, D273, D336, D395, D468
Levien, Mary C4
Levine, Norman B23
levy, d. a. D474
Levy, John E735, E761
Levy, Mervyn C99
Levy, Michael C121
Lewis, Alun A229, B15, B17, B22, C12, D423
Lewis, Bill E166, E183, E228, E313
Lewis, C. S. B104, B120
Lewis, Cecil Day A68, A106, A107, A117, A127, A160, A206,

Name Index

Loughborough University D370
Loughlin, Anne E749
Love, Tim E288, E407, E649
Lovell, Frances E652
Lovelock, Ian *See* Lovelock, Yann
Lovelock, Yann C27, C32, C117, D28, D250, D254, D292,
    D318, D323, D340, D347, D477, D520, E232, E287,
    E423, E539, E704, E761
Lowbury, Edward A167, D347
Lowe, Geoff E667
Lowell, Amy A42, A90
Lowell, Robert B40, C2, C30
Lowenstein, Kate E368
Lowenstein, Tom D318
Lowry, Elizabeth E831
Lowy, A. E. B114
Loy, Mina A211
Loydell, Rupert M. C73, D325, E287, E288, E488, E561,
    E617, E649, E735, E796, E811, E916
Lucas, Bob E225
Lucas, John C98, E326, E761
Lucas, Martin E657
Lucas, Peter G. B9
Lucas, Tony B112
Luchte, Jim E577
Lucie-Smith, Edward C26, C53, C63, C64, D76, D174,
    D179, D226, D336, D469, D533
Lucie-Smith, J. E. M. *See* Lucie-Smith, Edward
Lucraft, Mary D451
Luczinski, Peter Daniels (see also Daniels, Peter) E632
Ludlow, Mike E320
Luke, C. J. D271
Luke, Colin D388
Luke, Peter D388
Lumsden, Alison E721
Lumsden, Roddy E368, E685, E700
Lundkvist, Artur A49
Lunt, Jane C67
Lutt, Nigel E849
Luxembourg, Rosa E324
Lyalls, Paul E469
Lykiard, Alexis C76, C118, D267, D340, D421, E426, E518,
    E561, E665
Lyle, John D74, D487
Lyle, Rob B18, C82
Lyman, Henry E374
Lynch, Jack D220
Lynch, Noreen D417
Lynch, Patrick D312
Lynch, Thomas E205
Lynd, Sylvia A1
Lyon, John E831
Lyon, Rick D122

M., H. C. *See* Minchin, H. Cotton
Mabbott, Chris E271
McAdam, Rhona E747
Mac a'Ghobhainn, Iain *See* Smith, Iain Crichton
McAllan, Olive C73
McAllister, Andrew E661
McAllister, Claire B35
McAndrew, Séamas E711
Mac Anna, Padraic D283
Macaraig, Maria Ruth E172
McArthur, Bill C39, D114
MacArthur, Donald C39
MacArthur, Ian C39
MacAulay, Ross C27
McAuley, James J. D368
MacBeth, George C7, C26, C32, C53, C63, C64, C114,
    C117, D336, D373, D408, D428, D481, D520, E233,
    E795
McBride, Charlie E205
MacBride, Maud Gonne A94
McCabe, Brian D63, D93, D300, E522, E733
McCabe, Cathal E359
McCabe, Pat E293, E835
McCaffery, Steve D383a, D460, E298, E316
MacCaig, Norman A5, A102, A197, A224, B60, B77, B82,
    B113, B145, C39, C53, C83, C102, D89, D182, D300,
    D348, D428, E139, E339, E462, E885, E886
McCall, Anthony D518
MacCallum, Neil R. D248
McCance, William A10
MacCann, George D312
McCann, Richard E486
McCarey, Peter E247, E307, E758
McCarra, Kevin E317
McCarthy, Albert J. B31, B61
McCarthy, Cavan D44, D162, D238, D482
McCarthy, Desmond A108, C94
McCarthy, Dominic E223
McCarthy, Gerry D319
M'Carthy, James A187
McCarthy, M. L. D96
McCarthy, Patricia C2, D89
McCarthy, Ray D534
McCarthy, Thomas E198, E584
McCarthy, Ulli (see also Freer, Ulli) D15, D77, D82, D170,
    D206, D236, D391, D537, E267, E517, E554, E679
McClaughry, Ruth E144
McCleery, Alistair A21
McClintock, Michael D94
McClure, Michael D114, D150, D293, D439, D456
MacColl, Dax C118
McColl, Ewan D104
MacColla, Fionn E139
McCord, Margaret D155

Name Index

McMahon, Brendan E807
McMahon, Trevor D99
McMillan, Dougald A212
Macmillan, Harold D333
McMillan, Hugh E387, E870
McMillan, Ian D395, E346, E408, E693, E734, E761, E876
MacMillan, R. G. B85
McNaughton, Adam D104
Macnaughton, Maureen E25, E288
MacNeice, Louis A117, A143, A146, A160, A220, B41, B63, D312
McNeil, Anthony D424
McNeil, Christine E302
McNeil, Kevin E522
McNeil, Neil D463
McNeill, C. I. D411
Mac Póilín, Aodán E422
McQuail, Paul C14
McQuarrie, Findlay D430
McQuoid, Jack B119
McSeveney, Angela E247, E858
MacSweeney, Barry D15, D22, D55, D69, D82, D117, D123, D127, D153, D194, D195, D198, D215, D249, D252, D267, D342, D411, D437, D447, D474, D496, E256, E418, E552, E647, E651, E656, E673, E757
MacThòmais, Ruaraidh B3, B113, C38, C102
Machado, Antonio D412
Machado, Manuel B110
Mackmin, Michael E696
Maddox, Adrian E543
Maddox, Conroy D487
Madge, Charles A25, A39, A143, A206, B108, C53, C97
Maelspine, Michel A186
Maeterlinck, Count Maurice A59
Magdalen College, Oxford A160
Magdalene College, Cambridge D32, D496
Magee, Wes D63, D80, D143, D171, D174, D267, D289, D341, D375, D389, D390, D421, D508, D535, E326, E518, E722, E916
Magee University College, Derry D6
Maggs, Derek C29, C125
Magog C27
Magowan, Robin E477
Magrelli, Valerio E694
Magritte, René A41, D117, D487
Maguire, Liam D225, D276
Maher, Mary E264, E555, E656
Mahon, Derek C46, C118, D34, D41, D56, D89, D212, D312, D455, E198, E250
Maidstone College of Art E183
Mailer, Norman D114
Mair, John A100
Mairet, Philip A137, A182
Maisels, C. K. D300

Maisongrande, Henri D451
Makepeace, Eleanor D205
Makin, Richard E581
Malanga, Gerard D69, D258, D409, D437
Malanos, Timos B21
Malcolm, Tom C27, D333, D477
Malevich, Kasimir A186
Maley, John E522
Malin, Nigel E838
Malito, Giovanni E137
Mallalieu, H. B. A180
Mallarmé, Stéphane B5, B51, D153
Mallin, Rupert D458, E226, E233, E336, E521, E916
Mallin-Robinson, Fiona E775
Malraux, André B54
Malroux, Claire E694
Malton and Ryedale Writers E731
Mammon Press E651
Manchester Metropolitan University E613
Manchester Unity of Arts Society D515
Manchester University D372, E613
Manchester University Modern Literature Group E67
Manchester University Poetry Society D140
Mandelstam, Nadezhda C107
Manderson, Dave E522
Mandeville Press D142
Manfred, Robert C82
Mangan, Gerald D89, D182, E24
"Mango Chutney" E624
Manhire, Bill D146, E658
Manifold [Press] D269
Mankowitz, Wolf B25, B117, B127
Manley, Alfred C47
Mann, Eric D413
Mann, Ken E304
Mann, Sheila D478
Mann, Thomas A126, B1
Manning, Hugo B34, B42, D253
Manning, Mary A130
Manning, Olivia B21, B83
Manolete, Angela E333
Mansell-Moullin, Peter C7
Mansfield, Charles E781
Mansfield, Katherine A2, A59, A198
Manson, John C125, D506, E307, E478
Manson, Peter D318, E316, E552, E581
The Many Press E475, E854
March, Emanuel Z. E100
March, Richard A173
March, Susan Jane D503
Marchant, Peter C12
Marcus, David B59, B111
Marcus, Helen E702
Marcus, Richard D465

[403]

Name Index

Name Index

O'Donoghue, Mary D529

O'Donoghue, P. J. E445

O'Donovan, Michael (real name of Frank O'Connor) *See* Frank O'Connor

O'Donovan, Tony E520

O'Driscoll, Dennis D63, E422

O'Duibhir, Eamon A12

Odyssey [Press] E555, E656

O'Faolain, Sean A94, A97, A126, A137, B10

O'Flaherty, Liam A94, A115, A209

Ogilvy, Stuart D375

O'Grady, Desmond D41, D89, D158, D210, D240

Ó hAodha, Séamus A19

O'Hara, Frank D117

O'Hare, John C82

O hUallachain, Peadar B29

Ó hUanacháin , Mícheál D89

O'Kane, Marianne D466

Okike [Press] D321

Olds, Sharon E747

O'Leary, C. A4

O'Leighin, Sean D534

Oliver, Douglas D22, D24, D95, D117, D127, D194, D195, D215, D310, D411, D437, D447, D525, E310, E427, E554, E581

Olson, Charles C58, C61, C94, C122, D67, D117, D411, D439, D445, D525

Olympia Press C57

O'Malley, Mary C111

Omens [Press] D323

Ó Muirthile, Liam D228

Once Books D324

Ondaatje, Michael E867

O'Neill, Eddie D504

O'Neill, John E263

O'Neill, Michael E294, E622

Ono, Yoko D314

Open Door Writers E383

Open Township [Press] E287, E340

Open University Poetry Association (later Society) E565

Oppen, George D215, D237, D314, D411, E539, E717

Opus Press B94, B142

Orage, A. R. A133, A137

Oram, Neil D308, D451, E287

Orbán, Ottó E244

Ore Publications C73

O'Reilley, SeÇn D3

Orgoglio, Giovanni A114

Ó Riada, Mícheál E711

O Riain, Liam P. A187

Origins/Diversions [Press] D328

Orla-Bardzki, Peter D119

Orlovsky, Peter E717

Orme, David E283

Ormond, Emily E156

Ormsby, Frank D212, D455

O'Rourke, Donny E758, E870

O'Rourke, P. J. D462

Orpwood, Jerry D348

Ortega, Miguel D461

Orton, I. R. *See* Orton, Iris

Orton, Iris B110, C67, C122

Orton, Joe D170

Orwell, Charles C47

Orwell, George B46, B82, B83, B84, B91, B115

Osborne, Alastair D100

Osborne, John E93

Osborne, Sarah E368

O Seaghda, Barra E328

Ó Séaghdha, Tadhg E233

Osers, E. B122

Osgood, Diane E800

O'Shaughnessy, Patrick D395

Ossian A125

O'Sullivan, Maggie D250, D323, E226, E277, E311, E552, E574, E651, E684, E704

O'Sullivan, Rosemary E906

O'Sullivan, Seamus A22, A53, A132

Oswald, Sarah J. E243

Oundle School D152

Our Wonderful Culture [Press] E457

Ouston, Hugh E249

Out To Lunch E581

Outcrop Publications E567

Outcrowd Publications D448, E166, E183, E313, E337, E757, E844

Outposts Publications B99, C15

Outsiders Forum D508

Over, Marita E302

Overton, Peter E836

Overy, Paul D61

Owen, Ian B. D334

Owen, John E460

Owen, Molly B108

Owen, Tom D507

Owen, Wilfred A9, A42, A89, A128, A230

Owens, Agnes E247, E870

Oxford English Club A181

Oxford Poetry Society E2

Oxford Poetry Workshop E528

Oxford University C26, C74, C114, D334, D335, D483, E474

Oxford University Poetry Society D335, E585, E683

Oxford University Socialist Club C74

Oxford University Socialist Group C74

Oxford Welsh Society E49

Oxley, Patricia E10

Oxley, William C73, D64, D81, D96, D148, D163, D203,

Name Index

Name Index

Name Index

Stoke-on-Trent Writers Group E435
Stokes, Kirsteen D430
Stokes, Terry D252
Stone, Bernard E745
Stone, Cyril B92
Stone, David C72
Stone, Lawrence D32
Stone, Rob E823
Stone, Rosetta E896
Stopes, Marie A190, A235, C48
Stoppard, Tom E795
Storey, Alan B130
Storey, Edward C29, C73, C125
Storn, Nigel B103
Stott, Antonia E339
Stott, Rebecca E823
Stow Hill Poets E445
Strachan, W.J. B5
Strachan, Zoë E522
Strachey, Isobel B83
Strahan, Margaret C64
Stramm, August D245
Stratford, Kevin C76
Straus, Margaret D397
Strebe, Rosemarie D143
Streetword [Press] D465
Strickland, Geoffrey A25
Stride [Press] E796
Stringer, David E223
Stromberg, Ragnar E814
Strong, Eithne D34, D35, D89, E628
Stroud Poetry Society B128
Stryk, Lucien C7, C91, D237
Stuart, A. V. B78
Stuart, Francis A4, A209, A213, D89, E198, E324
Stuart, H. See Stuart, Francis
Stuart, Iseult A209
Stuart, Muriel A99
Stubbs, John Heath See Heath-Stubbs, John
Studd, Judy E889
Style, Colin E757
Subramaniam, A. B56
Suleiman, E. E456
Sullivan, Paul-Henri E495
Summer, Piotr E787
Summers, Wayne E811
Sumner, Alaric D1, D15, D77, E452, E888
Sumner, Rosemary E888
Sun and Harvest Publications E753, E798
Sunderland Polytechnic D511, E582
Sundial Press E492, E701
Supervielle, Jules B80
Surrealist Group in England A41, A93, B44
Surrealist Group in Leeds E473

Surridge, Les D163
Survivors' Poetry E623
Survivors Poetry Scotland E541
Sussex University D444, E581
Sutherland, Allan E286
Sutherland, Giles E178
Sutherland, John D359
Sutherland, Keston E316, E552, E581
Sutherland, Paul E237
Swallow, Norman A167, B103
Swan Press A234
Swarbrooke, Royston E826
Swart, E. V. A180
Sweatshop, Gay E262
Sweeney, Edward E6
Sweeney, Matthew D34, D318, D323, E741, E745, E814
Swenson, May C98
Swift, Graham D329, D453, E327
Swindon E286
Swingler, Randall A68, A106, A197, A213, B6, B80, B98, C51
SYC Publications E803, E804
Sykes, Graham E194, E226, E423, E704
Sykes, Hugh A26, A64
Sylvester, Richard D28, D450
Symonds, Dave D449
Symonds, John B34
Symondson, Bill D194
Symons, Arthur A85, A107, A209
Symons, Julian A38, A213, A227, B91
Symons, W. T. A182
Syms, Jeremy E380
Syte, Raymond C15a
Szinai, Liila E641
Szirtes, George E326, E477, E649, E916
Szulakowska, Urszula E823

Tabor, Richard D77, E195, E447, E888
Tabori, Paul C77, D40
Tafari, Levi E845
Taggart, John E539
Tagore, Rabindranath A50, A78, A235, B5, B56, B131, D205, E479
Tait, Philip E806
Tait, Robert D428
Tait, Valerie E806
Tak Tak Tak [Press] E811
Takahashi, Shinkichi D237
Taliesin B17
Talvet, Jüri E694
Tambimuttu, J. M. A49, A173, B68, B95, C87, E631
Tamplin, Ronald C98
Tanburn, Nicholas C41
Tangent Books D471

Name Index

Thurston, Scott E35, E316, E581

Thwaite, Ann C123

Thwaite, Anthony A160, B49, C12, C26, C63, C64, C71, C74, C114, E647

Tickhill, Alawn E349

Tidball, David E333

Tidnam, Nick D308, D451

Tiffany, Daniel A90

Tiffen, David E162

Tigrid, Pavel B122

Tiller, Terence A180, B21

Tillinghurst, Anthony C118

Tilson, Jake E65, E175

Timms, David D323

Tims, Margaret D356, D376, E856

Tipton, David C27, C32, C55, D127, D171, D192, D250, D340, D446, E344, E423, E554

Titler, Doreen D413

Toczek, Nick D70, D254, D282, D292, D349, D375, D535, E344, E916

Todd, Peter E615

Todd, Ruthven A38, A41, A180, A214, B3, B34, B74, B81, B82, B110, B113, B125

Toeman, Edward B117

Toff, Penelope E794

Toibín, Colm D89

Toker, Biltin D520

Toler, C. E676

Tolkien, J. R. R. A123

Tolley, A. T. B95

Tomazos, Criton D21

Tomkiw, Lydia E408

Tomlin, Dave D13

Tomlinson, Anne C67

Tomlinson, Charles C22, C58, C82, C94, D178, D237, D411, D472, E549, E613, E658, E665, E694

Tomlinson, R. D279

Toms, Margaret C73

Tong, Raymond B48, B61, B149, C54, C73, C99, C125, E288

Tonk, Henry D126

Topley, Neill E329

Topolski, Feliks D111

Topping, Angela C73, E124

Torem, Amikam D518

Tork, Ed D507

'Torna' A19

Torrance, Chris D53, D55, D87, D112, D127, D153, D171, D199, D214, D289, D328, D380, D411, D437, D447, D500, D525, E6, E287, E461

Torrance, C. J. *See* Torrance, Chris

Torrington, Jeff E247

Tottenham, John E21

Totton, Nick D24, D95, D127, D252, D310, D314, D334, D447, D453, D494, E863

Toulouse Press E612

Toulson, Shirley D347

Townshend, Nigel B24

Townshend, Petrie A108

Toy, Geoffrey D235

Toynbee, Philip D533

Trafford, John C68

Trakl, Georg B82, B108, D150

Transformaction [Press] D74, D487

Tranströmer, Tomas D318, E835, E858

Tranter, John D146, E539, E549, E713, E858

Traversi, D. A. A8

Treby, Ivor C. E288, E312

Treece, Henry A102, A151, A197, B2, B24, B32, B42, B49, B52, B62, B68, B77, B94, B105, B110, B119, B133

Treharne, Mark D397

Tremayne, Sydney A197, B74, B108, B149, C26, C59, C83, C102, E139

Treneer, Anne B23, B144

Trent Book Shop D392

Trent Polytechnic E671

Trevor, Stan D85

Trewin, J. C. B105, B144

The Tribe D148

Trigram Press D409

Trilling, Lionel C78

Trinity College, Cambridge A64

Trinity College, Dublin C46, E187

Trinity College, Oxford D18, D344

Trinity Hall, Cambridge C14

Tripp, John D309, D380

Trocchi, Alexander C57, C68, D290, D293, D409, D449

Troop, Kevin E829

Trotman, Anthony Fiennes D42

Troubadour Coffee House, London D495, E467

Troussé, Stephen E637

Troy, Diane D98

Trumpet Books B59, B111

Tsvetayeva, Marina D40, D89, D469

Tu Fu D333

Tuarisc, E. O. E89

Tuba Press E842

Tubes, F. T. B62

Tuck, Allene E94

Tucker, Alan D175

Tucker, Eva E813

Tucker, Helen E810

Tunley, Jan E734

Tureck, Ludwig A206

Turgenev, Ivan Sergeevich A59

Turley, Richard Marggraf E389

Turnbull, Charles D297

Turnbull, Clive E330

Name Index

Title Index

The main reference is given in plain roman, e.g. A1.
Secondary references, for example a continuation of the
title, are given in italics, e.g. A7.

& *See* Ampersand (&) E27
3 Arts Quarterly *See* Three Arts Quarterly D478
4: a review of the visual arts, literature, music and drama
    C1
4word Magazine *See* [Four Word Magazine] 4word
    Magazine E297
10th Muse *See* Tenth Muse E825
365 Days of the Year *See* Three Hundred and Sixty-Five Days
    of the Year D479
2000 *See* Two Thousand D499

A (1971-77) D1
A (1980s) E1
A Magazine E463
A-3 Broadsheet E2
A4 Anonymous *See* Responses E691
Aabye D200, E3
Abandoned Notebook D2
AbeSea: a visual paper E4
The Abinger Chronicle A1
Abject D3
About This D4
Academus Poetry Magazine E5
Accent D5, E74
Accidents & Devotions E6, E461
Acid Angel E7
Acorn (1961-72) D6
Acorn (1968) D7
Active in Airtime E8
The Activity Echo E9
Acumen D203, E10, E444
Adam International Review B1, C17
The Adelphi A2
The Adelphi Magazine A3
Admiral Connor's Hot True Steamy Confessions Quarterly
    E11
Advent E12
Aegis D8

Aengus A4
The Affectionate Punch E13
Afrasian D9
Agenda C2
The Agent E14
Aggie Weston's D10, E41
Agog (1972) D11
Agog (198?-199?) E15
Agog Ago Go E15
Aion E16
Air E17
Air Force Poetry B2
Air Space E18
Aireings E19
Aireloom *See* Aireings E19
Akros D12
Alba: a Scottish miscellany in Gaelic and English B3
Alba Nuadh *See* The Free Man A77
Albab: review of Islamic & Western arts E20
Albannach A5
Albion (1968) D13
Albion (1970-74) D14
Alembic D15, E684
All In D16
All The Poets E21
Allusions E22
Almer Parkes D17
Alpha D18
Alta D19
Alternative Poets E23
Amalgam D20
Amarinth D21
Amazing Grace D22
Ambit C3
Ambivalent Propaganda *See* Collection D117
AMF: Artisophanes' Middle Finger E24, E448
Ammonite E25
Amoeba Broadsheet D23
Amoral Svelte *See* Lateral Moves E431
Ampersand E26
Ampersand (&) E27
Anaconda E28

Title Index

Axis (1970) D59, D60

Axis Bag D59, D60

Axle Quarterly D61

The Aylesford Review C10

Aynd E75

Babel: a multi-lingual critical review B9

Backchart E76

B.A.D. See Breakfast All Day E126

Bad Moon Rising See Rising E700

Bad News D62

Bad Poetry Quarterly E77

Bad Seeds E78, E755

Baetyl: the journal of women's literature E79

Bananas D63, E673

Bananas from the Windward Islands E80

Banba A12

Bandito See Codex Bandito

Bang E81

Banipal E82

Bare Bones E83

Bare Nibs E84, E347

Bare Wires E85

The Bark and the Bite E86

Bark Magazine E87

Barrow Poems E88

Barwell Broadside D115a, D64

Bath Children Write D65

Bean Train D66, D308

Beat Scene E88a, E835a

The Beau E89, E90

"Before Your Very Eyes!" D67

The Bell: a survey of Irish life B10, E90

The Belle E89, E90

Benthos E91

Bentilee Voices E92

The Bermondsey Book A13

Bête Noire E93

Between the Lines E94

Beyond the Boundaries E95

Beyond the Cloister E96

Big Bang E97

Big Big Big Venus See Big Venus D69

Big Big Venus See Big Venus D69

Big Camel D68

The Big Spoon E98

Big Venus D68, D69

Billy Liar E99

Bizarre Angel E100

Black Columbus D70

Black Country Meat Chronicle D71

Black Eggs D72

The Black Hat A14

Black Orpheus D255

Black Sun E101

The Black Writer E102

Black-beetle E103

Blackboard Review E104

Blackburn Barker D73

Blackmore Vale Writers E105

Blade E106

Blast: review of the great English vortex A15, A50, E581, E811

Blaze B11

Bleb Residue See [Ankle Press] E38

Bleeding Cheek E107

Bless 'Em All B12

Blind Serpent E108

Blithe Spirit E109

The Blue Boat E110

The Blue Cage E111

Blue Food D74

The Blue Front Door D75

The Blue Tunnel D76, D392, E524, E525

Blueprint D77

Blues D173

Bo Heem E Um D44, D78

Bogg D79, E112

Boggers All D79, E112

Boite (a cockwerk whoreage) See Le Shovelle Diplomatique E739

Bolero: a magazine of poetry A16, A102

The Book of Invasions D80, D97

A... Book of Poems by the Poet's Fellowship A17

Bookmark E113

The Booster A18, A49, A197

Boox E114

Borderlines (1981–) E115

Borderlines (1989–) E116

Both Sides Now D81, D148

The Bound Spiral E117

Boundary E118

Box E119

Box of Rain E120

The Boy Detective See [Ankle Press] E38

Bradford Poetry Quarterly E121

Brainwaifs E122

An Branar A19

Branch Redd Review E123

Brando's Hat E124

Braquemard E125

Breakfast D82, D257

Breakfast All Day E126

Breakthru International Poetry Magazine D83

Breakthru Poetry / Art Magazine E127

Breath of Fresh Air D84

Brecht Times D85

Bridge E128

Title Index

Number D317
Numbers E549
Nursing Times A45
Nutshell E550
NWN See New Writing Network E532
NWR See The New Welsh Review E531

O Write E551
On the Boiler A153
Oasis (1942–1944) B64, B93
Oasis (1951–1952) C72
Oasis (1969–) D164, D318, E64, E539, E735, E819, E824
Oasis (1975–79) D319
Oasis: the Middle East anthology of poetry from the Forces B93
Object Permanence E552
Obsessed With Pipework E553
Ochre Magazine E554
Oddments D320
Odyssey E555
Oil Slick See Ugly Duckling D503
Okike D321
The Old Police Station E556
Olive Dachsund D295, D322, D502
Omens D323
Omnibus E557
Once D324
One D325, E854
Only Poetry E558
O.P.C. See The Oxford Poetry Chronicle E569
Open Book E164, E559
Open Forum E560
Open Press See Vigil E861
Open Space D289, D326
Open Window A140
Opus B94
Orbis D327, D433
Ore C73
Orientations B95
Origins/Diversions D53, D328, D388
Origo D329
Orion: a miscellany B96
The Orpheus A154
Orpheus: a symposium of the arts B87, B97
Osgoldcross Review D200, D330
Ostinato E561
Ostrich D331
The Other Merry-Go-Round E562
Other Poetry E563
Other Times D332
Otter: New Devon Poetry E564
OU See Cinquième Saison C15a
The O.U.P.A. Magazine E565
Our Time A171, B98

Out of Our Heads E566
Outburst D333
Outcrop E567
Outlet: Cleveland's creative output E568
Outlook A126, A155
The Outpost A156
Outposts B99
Outposts Modern Poets Series B99
Outposts Poetry Quarterly See Outposts B99
The Outside Contributor A154
The Owl A157
Owl: new poetry and graphics E573
The Oxford & Cambridge Miscellany A158
Oxford and Cambridge Writing See Z: Oxford and Cambridge Writing
Oxford Left C74
Oxford Literary Journal E569
Oxford Literary Review D334
Oxford Opinion C75
The Oxford Outlook A141, A159
Oxford Poetry A160, C64
The Oxford Poetry Chronicle E570
Oxford Poetry Magazine (1973) D335
Oxford Poetry Now E571
Oxford Quarterly Review E572
Oxymoron D335a
Oyster D336, D341

P D337
Pages (1970–72) D338
Pages (1987–98) E574
Pair: cylchgrawn barddoniaeth D339
Palantir D340
Palatine Review A161
PALPI See Poetry Information D366
Panda Folio E575
Panda Poetry See Panda Quarterly Magazine E576
Panda Quarterly Magazine E576
Panic! E577
Panic! Brixton Poetry See Panic! E577
The Panton Magazine A162
The Paperback E578
Paperway D336, D341
Paperweight E295
Papyra E579
Parade B100
Paramour E580
Parataxis E581
The Park See The Wivenhoe Park Review D525
The Parnassian A163
Passing Through E582
Passion E583
Passport E584
Password: Scop E585

Title Index

Title Index

Trap-door E836
A Treasury of Modern Poets D490
Tree D308, D491
The Tree: an illustrated arts magazine D492
Tremblestone E837
Trend D493
Trends E838
The Tribune *See* The Irish Tribune A98
Trio C114
Trixie E839
Troglodyte E365, E840
Troll D494
Troubadour (1950–55) C115
Troubadour (1970?) D495
True Thomas E841
Tuba E842
Turpin D496
The Twentieth Century A213
Twentieth Century Verse A214
Twice *See* Once D324
Twice: magazine for the once bitten D497
Twice: UEA student paper D498
Twisted Wrist E843
Two Thousand D499
Tydfil: a Merthyr Tydfil miscellany C116
The Tyro A215
Tzarad D117, D307, D308, D451, D500

Ubu 8 D501
Ubullum D295, D502
Ugly Duckling D503
The Ulster Book A216
The Ulster Free Lance A217
Ulster Parade B135
The Ulster Review A218
Ulster Voices B136
Umbrella C117
Uncle Nasty's E166, E313, E337, E844
Uncompromising Positions E845
Undercurrent E616, E846, E851
Underdog D504
Understanding E847
Undertow E848
Unicorn D505
The United Scotsman D506
Universities' Poetry C118
Unknown Origins E849
Unrest A219
The Unruly Sun E850
Untouched E616, E846, E851
Upstart! Magazine E852
The Urbane Gorilla D507
Urge *See* Yam D537
Urthona E853

Vanessa and One *See* Vannessa Poetry Magazine D325
Vanessa Poetry Magazine E854
Various Artists E855, E892
Vegan Action D192
The Venture A220, A226
Ver Poets Poetry Post *See* Poetry Post D376
Ver Poets Voices D356, E856
Verbal Underground E857
The Verist B137
Verse (1945) B138
Verse (1947) B139
Verse (1984–) E307, E758, E858
Verse and Song A221
Verse Lover B140
Verse-Reel *See* Terence White's Verse-Reel A204
Versus E859
Vertical Images E860
Vice *See* Once D324
Viewpoint A106, A222
Viewpoints D508
Vigil E603, E861
The Village Review D509
Village Voice E862
Vineyard Magazine *See* The Country Heart A43
Ving E166, E183, E313, E337, E844
Vision (1919–21) A223
Vision (1961?) D510
Vision (1963) D510a
Vision & Voice D511
Vision Broadsheet D512
A Vision Very Like Reality E360, E863
Visions and Praying Mantids D513
Vistas: a literary and philosophical review B141
Voices D514
Voice & Verse E864
The Voice of Scotland A224
The Voice of Youth B142
Voices (1919–21) A225
Voices (1943–47) B94, B143
Voices (1972?–?) D515
Vole D516
Vortex D517
Voyage E865
The Voyager A226
Vril C119

Wales A227
Wales: Wartime Broadsheet *See* Wales A227
Walking Naked E633, E866
Wallpaper D518
Wasafiri E867
Wave D519
Waves D90, E285, E868
The Wayfarer A228

Title Index